The Ministers Manual for 1991

SIXTY-SIXTH ANNUAL ISSUE

THE MINISTERS MANUAL

(Doran's)

1991 EDITION

Edited by

JAMES W. COX

HarperSanFrancisco
A Division of HarperCollins*Publishers*

Editors of THE MINISTERS MANUAL

G. B. F. Hallock, D.D., 1926–1958
M. K. W. Heicher, Ph.D., 1943–1968
Charles L. Wallis, M.A., M.Div., 1969–1983
James W. Cox, M.Div., Ph.D.

Acknowledgments are on pages 331–32.

THE MINISTERS MANUAL FOR 1991.
Copyright © 1990 by James W. Cox. All rights reserved. Printed in the United States of America. For information address HarperCollins Publishers, 10 East 53rd Street, New York, NY 10022.

FIRST EDITION

Library of Congress Catalog Card Number
25–21658
ISSN 0738–5323

90 91 92 93 94 HC 10 9 8 7 6 5 4 3 2 1

This edition is printed on acid-free paper that meets the American National Standards Institute Z39.48 Standard.

CONTENTS

PREFACE

In recent years, we have heard much about preaching as story. Also narrative theology and narrative ethics have claimed considerable attention. One gets the impression that some who write and speak on the subjects believe that, if we communicate effectively with a modern audience, nothing but story or narrative of some kind will suffice.

There is no doubt about it—we have to come to terms with story as a vehicle of religious truth. Biblical precedent demands it. However, story is not the only literary or rhetorical medium in the Bible. In the Scriptures we encounter a variety of literary and rhetorical genres. In *The Ministers Manual,* the reader will find a variety of sermonic types, including narratives. William Willimon aptly argues, "Not all scripture is related directly to narrative, and not all faithful preaching need be in a narrative mode. Preachers also may use argument, exposition, logic and deductive reasoning" (*Christian Century* [February 28, 1990]). Our hearers would be poorly served if they heard only stories from us, and they would be just as poorly served if we never let the truth come to lively expression in story, whether as the vehicle of an entire sermon or as illustration of a point.

Two special features in *The Ministers Manual* for 1991 are sections with resources for preaching on the Epistle of 1 John by R. Alan Culpepper, an internationally recognized New Testament scholar and specialist in the Johannine literature, and resources for preaching on stewardship by Richard B. Cunningham, who is widely known as a scholar in the philosophy of religion and for his down-to-earth book on stewardship. These special features for the past several years have highlighted homiletical variety, as they have presented helps for preaching from the Psalms, from the parables, from the Book of Zechariah, from the miracles, from the Book of Ecclesiastes, from the Lord's Prayer, and from the Book of Jeremiah; as well as helps for monological preaching, preaching on the Apostle's Creed, on worship, on ethical issues, on Christian doctrine, and on pastoral care.

I am grateful to many individuals and publishers for permission to quote from their material. I continue to be grateful to the trustees of the Southern Baptist Theological Seminary and to President Roy Honeycutt for their practical encouragement; to Alicia Gardner, office services supervisor; to Keitha Brasler, David Akers, Donna Raley, and Henry Hinnant, who typed the manuscript; and to Clara McCartt and Dr. Lee R. McGlone for valuable editorial assistance. I am also appreciative of the careful work of the editorial staff at Harper & Row, San Francisco.

James W. Cox
The Southern Baptist Theological Seminary
2825 Lexington Road
Louisville, KY 40280

SECTION I.
General Aids and Resources
Civil Year Calendars

1991

JANUARY	FEBRUARY	MARCH	APRIL

```
        JANUARY                    FEBRUARY                    MARCH                      APRIL
 S  M  T  W  T  F  S        S  M  T  W  T  F  S        S  M  T  W  T  F  S        S  M  T  W  T  F  S
       1  2  3  4  5                    1  2                    1  2           1  2  3  4  5  6
 6  7  8  9 10 11 12        3  4  5  6  7  8  9        3  4  5  6  7  8  9        7  8  9 10 11 12 13
13 14 15 16 17 18 19       10 11 12 13 14 15 16       10 11 12 13 14 15 16       14 15 16 17 18 19 20
20 21 22 23 24 25 26       17 18 19 20 21 22 23       17 18 19 20 21 22 23       21 22 23 24 25 26 27
27 28 29 30 31             24 25 26 27 28             24 25 26 27 28 29 30       28 29 30
                                                      31

          MAY                        JUNE                       JULY                      AUGUST
 S  M  T  W  T  F  S        S  M  T  W  T  F  S        S  M  T  W  T  F  S        S  M  T  W  T  F  S
          1  2  3  4                             1        1  2  3  4  5  6                    1  2  3
 5  6  7  8  9 10 11        2  3  4  5  6  7  8        7  8  9 10 11 12 13        4  5  6  7  8  9 10
12 13 14 15 16 17 18        9 10 11 12 13 14 15       14 15 16 17 18 19 20       11 12 13 14 15 16 17
19 20 21 22 23 24 25       16 17 18 19 20 21 22       21 22 23 24 25 26 27       18 19 20 21 22 23 24
26 27 28 29 30 31          23 24 25 26 27 28 29       28 29 30 31                25 26 27 28 29 30 31
                           30

       SEPTEMBER                    OCTOBER                   NOVEMBER                   DECEMBER
 S  M  T  W  T  F  S        S  M  T  W  T  F  S        S  M  T  W  T  F  S        S  M  T  W  T  F  S
 1  2  3  4  5  6  7                 1  2  3  4  5                       1  2        1  2  3  4  5  6  7
 8  9 10 11 12 13 14        6  7  8  9 10 11 12        3  4  5  6  7  8  9        8  9 10 11 12 13 14
15 16 17 18 19 20 21       13 14 15 16 17 18 19       10 11 12 13 14 15 16       15 16 17 18 19 20 21
22 23 24 25 26 27 28       20 21 22 23 24 25 26       17 18 19 20 21 22 23       22 23 24 25 26 27 28
29 30                      27 28 29 30 31             24 25 26 27 28 29 30       29 30 31
```

1992

```
        JANUARY                    FEBRUARY                    MARCH                      APRIL
 S  M  T  W  T  F  S        S  M  T  W  T  F  S        S  M  T  W  T  F  S        S  M  T  W  T  F  S
          1  2  3  4                             1           1  2  3  4  5  6  7              1  2  3  4
 5  6  7  8  9 10 11        2  3  4  5  6  7  8        8  9 10 11 12 13 14        5  6  7  8  9 10 11
12 13 14 15 16 17 18        9 10 11 12 13 14 15       15 16 17 18 19 20 21       12 13 14 15 16 17 18
19 20 21 22 23 24 25       16 17 18 19 20 21 22       22 23 24 25 26 27 28       19 20 21 22 23 24 25
26 27 28 29 30 31          23 24 25 26 27 28 29       29 30 31                   26 27 28 29 30

          MAY                        JUNE                       JULY                      AUGUST
 S  M  T  W  T  F  S        S  M  T  W  T  F  S        S  M  T  W  T  F  S        S  M  T  W  T  F  S
                   1  2        1  2  3  4  5  6              1  2  3  4                             1
 3  4  5  6  7  8  9        7  8  9 10 11 12 13        5  6  7  8  9 10 11        2  3  4  5  6  7  8
10 11 12 13 14 15 16       14 15 16 17 18 19 20       12 13 14 15 16 17 18        9 10 11 12 13 14 15
17 18 19 20 21 22 23       21 22 23 24 25 26 27       19 20 21 22 23 24 25       16 17 18 19 20 21 22
24 25 26 27 28 29 30       28 29 30                   26 27 28 29 30 31          23 24 25 26 27 28 29
31                                                                               30 31

       SEPTEMBER                    OCTOBER                   NOVEMBER                   DECEMBER
 S  M  T  W  T  F  S        S  M  T  W  T  F  S        S  M  T  W  T  F  S        S  M  T  W  T  F  S
       1  2  3  4  5                    1  2  3        1  2  3  4  5  6  7              1  2  3  4  5
 6  7  8  9 10 11 12        4  5  6  7  8  9 10        8  9 10 11 12 13 14        6  7  8  9 10 11 12
13 14 15 16 17 18 19       11 12 13 14 15 16 17       15 16 17 18 19 20 21       13 14 15 16 17 18 19
20 21 22 23 24 25 26       18 19 20 21 22 23 24       22 23 24 25 26 27 28       20 21 22 23 24 25 26
27 28 29 30               25 26 27 28 29 30 31       29 30                      27 28 29 30 31
```

Church and Civic Calendar for 1991

JANUARY

1 New Year's Day
The Name of Jesus
5 Twelfth Night
6 Epiphany
13 Baptism of the Lord
14 Martin Luther King, Jr.'s
Birthday (Observed)
18 Confession of St. Peter
19 Robert E. Lee's Birthday
25 Conversion of St. Paul

FEBRUARY

1 National Freedom Day
2 Presentation of Jesus in the
Temple
Groundhog Day
3 Four Chaplains Memorial Day
Boy Scout Sunday
10 Race Relations Sunday
12 Lincoln's Birthday
13 Ash Wednesday
14 St. Valentine's Day
15 Susan B. Anthony Day
17 First Sunday in Lent
17–24 Brotherhood Week
18 Washington's Birthday
(Observed)
22 Washington's Birthday
24 Second Sunday in Lent
Brotherhood Day
28 Purim

MARCH

1 World Day of Prayer
3 Third Sunday in Lent
10 Fourth Sunday in Lent
17 Fifth Sunday in Lent
St. Patrick's Day
24 Palm Sunday
24–30 Holy Week
28 Maundy Thursday
29 Good Friday
30 Passover begins
31 Easter Day

APRIL

25 St. Mark, Evangelist

MAY

1 May Day
Loyalty Day
St. Philip and St. James,
Apostles
9 Ascension Day
12 Festival of the Christian Home
Mother's Day
19 Pentecost
Shavuot
20 Victoria Day (Canada)
22 National Maritime Day
26 Trinity Sunday
Memorial Sunday
27 Memorial Day (Observed)

JUNE

9 Children's Day
11 St. Barnabas, Apostle
14 Flag Day
16 Father's Day
18 Armed Forces Day
29 St. Peter and St. Paul, Apostles

JULY

1 Dominion Day (Canada)
4 Independence Day
25 St. James, Apostle

AUGUST

6 The Transfiguration
15 Mary, the Mother of Jesus
24 St. Bartholomew, Apostle
26 Woman's Equality Day

SEPTEMBER

1 Labor Sunday
2 Labor Day
8 Birth of the Virgin Mary
9 First Day of Rosh Hashanah
18 Yom Kippur (Day of
Atonement)
21 St. Matthew, Apostle and
Evangelist
23 First Day of Sukkoth
28 Frances Willard Day

29 St. Michael and All Angels
   Rally Day
30 Shemini Atzeret

OCTOBER

4 St. Francis of Assisi
6 World Communion Sunday
13 Laity Sunday
14 Columbus Day
   Thanksgiving Day (Canada)
18 St. Luke, Evangelist
24 United Nations Day
27 Reformation Sunday
28 St. Simon and St. Jude, Apostles
31 Reformation Day
   Halloween

NOVEMBER

1 All Saints' Day
2 All Souls' Day
10 Stewardship Day
11 Veterans Day
   Remembrance Day (Canada)

12 Elizabeth Cady Stanton Day
17 Bible Sunday
24 Thanksgiving Sunday
   Christ the King
28 Thanksgiving Day
30 St. Andrew, Apostle

DECEMBER

1 First Sunday of Advent
2 First Day of Hanukkah
8 Second Sunday of Advent
15 Third Sunday of Advent
   Bill of Rights Day
21 St. Thomas, Apostle
   Forefathers' Day
22 Fourth Sunday in Advent
24 Christmas Eve
25 Christmas Day
26 St. Stephen, Deacon and Martyr
   Boxing Day (Canada)
27 St. John, Apostle and Evangelist
28 The Holy Innocents, Martyrs
31 New Year's Eve
   Watch Night

Common Lectionary for 1991

The following Scripture lessons are commended for use in public worship, with some modifications, by various Protestant churches and the Roman Catholic church and include first, second, Gospel readings, and Psalms according to Cycle B from January 6 to November 24 and according to Cycle C from December 1 to December 29.

EPIPHANY SEASON

January 6 (Epiphany): Isa. 60:1–6; Ps. 72:1–4; Eph. 3:1–12; Matt. 2:1–12.
January 13 (Baptism of the Lord): Gen. 1:1–5; Psalm 29; Acts 19:1–7; Mark 1:4–11.
January 20: 1 Sam. 3:1–10 (11–20); Ps. 63:1–8; 1 Cor. 6:12–20; John 1:35–42.
January 27: Jon. 3:1–5, 10; Ps. 62:5–12; 1 Cor. 7:29–31 (32–35); Mark 1:14–20.
February 3: Deut. 18:15–20; Psalm 111; 1 Cor. 8:1–13; Mark 1:21–28.
February 10: Job 7:1–7; Ps. 147:1–11; 1 Cor. 9:16–23; Mark 1:29–39.

LENT

February 13 (Ash Wednesday): Joel 2:1–2, 12–17a; Ps. 51:1–12; 2 Cor. 5:20b–6:2 (3–10); Matt. 6:1–6, 16–21.
February 17: Gen. 9:8–17; Ps. 25:1–10; 1 Pet. 3:18–22; Mark 1:9–15.
February 24: Gen. 17:1–10, 15–19; Ps. 105:1–11; Rom. 4:16–25; Mark 8:31–38 or Mark 9:1–9.
March 3: Exod. 20:1–7; Ps. 19:7–14; 1 Cor. 1:22–25; John 2:13–22.
March 10: 2 Chron. 36:14–23; Ps. 137:1–6; Eph. 2:4–10; John 3:14–21.
March 17: Jer. 31:31–34; Ps. 51:10–17; Heb. 5:7–10; John 12:20–33.
March 24: Isa. 50:4–9a; Ps. 31:9–16; Phil. 2:5–11; Mark 11:1–11 or John 12:12–16; Mark 14:1–15, 47 or Mark 15:1–39.
March 25 (Monday): Isa. 42:1–9; Ps. 36:5–10; Heb. 9:11–15; John 12:1–11.
March 26 (Tuesday): Isa. 49:1–7; Ps. 71:1–12; 1 Cor. 1:18–31; John 12:20–36.

March 27 (Wednesday): Isa. 50:4–9a; Psalm 70; Heb. 12:1–3; John 13:21–30.

March 28 (Thursday): Exod. 24:3–8; Ps. 116:12–19; 1 Cor. 10:16–17; Mark 14: 12–26.

March 29 (Good Friday): Isa. 52:13–53:12; Ps. 22:1–8; Heb. 4:14–16, 5:7–9; John 18:1–19:42 or John 19:17–30.

March 30 (Easter Vigil): Gen. 1:1–2:2; Psalm 33; Gen. 7:1–5, 11–18; 8:6–18; 9:8–13; Psalm 46; Gen. 22:1–18; Psalm 16; Exod. 14:10–15:1; 15:1–6, 11–13, 17–18; Isa. 54:5–14; Psalm 30; Isa. 55:1–11; Isa. 12:2–6; Bar. 3:9–15, 32–4:4; Psalm 19; Ezek. 36:24–28; Psalm 42; Ezek. 37:1–14; Psalm 143; Zeph. 3:14–20; Psalm 98; Rom. 6:3–11; Psalm 114; Mark 16:1–8.

SEASON OF EASTER

March 31 (Easter): Acts 10:34–43 or Isa. 25:6–9; Ps. 118:14–24; 1 Cor. 15:1–11 or Acts 10:34–43; John 20:1–18 or Mark 16:1–8.

March 31 (Easter Evening): Acts 5:29–32 or Dan. 12:1–3; Psalm 150; 1 Cor. 5:6–8 or Acts 5:29–32; Luke 24:13–49.

April 7: Acts 4:32–35; Psalm 133; 1 John 1:1–2:2; John 20:19–31.

April 14: Acts 3:12–19; Psalm 4; 1 John 3:1–7; Luke 24:35–48.

April 21: Acts 4:8–12; Psalm 23; 1 John 3:18–24; John 10:11–18.

April 28: Acts 8:26–40; Ps. 22:25–31; 1 John 4:7–12; John 15:1–8.

May 5: Acts 10:44–48; Psalm 98; 1 John 5:1–6; John 15:9–17.

May 9 (Ascension): Acts 1:1–11; Psalm 47; Eph. 1:15–23; Luke 24:46–53 or Mark 16:9–16.

May 12: Acts 1:15–17, 21–26; Psalm 1; 1 John 5:9–13; John 17:11b–19.

SEASON OF PENTECOST

May 19 (Pentecost): Acts 2:1–21 or Ezek. 37:1–14; Ps. 104:24–34; Rom. 8:22–27 or Acts 2:1–21; John 15:26–27; 16:4b–15.

May 26 (Trinity Sunday): Isa. 6:1–8; Psalm 29; Rom. 8:12–17; John 3:1–17.

June 2: 1 Sam. 16:1–13; Psalm 20; 2 Cor. 4:5–12; Mark 2:23–3:6.

June 9: 1 Sam. 16:14–23; Psalm 57; 2 Cor. 4:13–5:1; Mark 3:20–35.

June 16: 2 Sam. 1:1, 17–27; Psalm 46; 2 Cor. 5:6–10, 14–17; Mark 4:26–34.

June 23: 2 Sam. 5:1–12; Psalm 24; 2 Cor. 5:18–6:2; Mark 4:35–41.

June 30: 2 Sam. 7:1–15; Psalm 24; 2 Cor. 8:7–15; Mark 5:21–43.

July 7: 2 Sam. 7:1–17; Ps. 89:20–37; 2 Cor. 12:1–10; Mark 6:1–6.

July 14: 2 Sam. 7:18–29; Ps. 132:11–18; Eph. 1:1–10; Mark 6:7–13.

July 21: 2 Sam. 11:1–15; Psalm 53; Eph. 2:11–22; Mark 6:30–34.

July 28: 2 Sam. 12:1–14; Psalm 32: Eph. 3:14–21; John 6:1–15.

August 4: 2 Sam. 12:15b–24; Ps. 34:11–22; Eph. 4:1–6; John 6:24–35.

August 11: 2 Sam. 18:1, 5, 9–15; Ps. 143:1–8; Eph. 4:25–42; John 6:35, 41–51.

August 18: 2 Sam. 18:24–33; Eph. 5:15–20; John 6:51–58.

August 25: 2 Sam. 23:1–7; Psalm 67; Eph. 5:21–33; John 6:55–69.

September 1: 1 Kings 2:1–4, 10–12; Psalm 121; Eph. 6:10–20; Mark 7:1–8, 14–15, 21–23.

September 8: Prov. 2:1–8 or Ecclus. 5:8–15; Ps. 119:129–136; James 1:17–27; Mark 7:31–37.

September 15: Prov. 22:1–2, 8–9; Psalm 125; James 2:1–5, 8–10, 14–17; Mark 8:27–38.

September 22: Job 28:20; Ps. 27:1–6; James 3:13–18; Mark 9:30–37.

September 29: Job 42:1–6; Ps. 27:7–14; James 4:13–17; 5:7–11; Mark 9:38–50.

October 6: Gen. 2:18–24; Psalm 128; Heb. 1:1–4; 2:9–11; Mark 10:2–16.

October 13: Gen. 3:8–19; Ps. 90:1–12; Heb. 4:1–3, 9–13; Mark 10:17–30.

October 20: Isa. 53:7–12; Ps. 35:17–28; Heb. 4:14–16; Mark 10:35–45.

October 27: Jer. 31:7–9; Psalm 126; Heb. 5:1–6; Mark 10:46–52.

November 1 (All Saints' Day): Rev. 21:1–6a; Ps. 24:1–6; Col. 1:9–14; John 11:32–44.

November 3: Deut. 6:1–9; Ps. 119:33–48; Heb. 7:23–28; Mark 12:28–34.
November 10: 1 Kings 17:8–16; Psalm 146; Heb. 9:24–28; Mark 12:38–44.
November 17: Dan. 7:9–14; Ps. 145:8–13; Heb. 10:11–18; Mark 13:24–32.
November 24: Jer. 23:1–6; Psalm 93; Rev. 1:4b–8; John 18:33–37.
November 28 (Thanksgiving Day): Joel 2:21–27; Psalm 126; 1 Tim. 2:1–7; Matt. 6:25–33.

ADVENT

December 1: Jer. 33:14–16; Ps. 25:1–10; 1 Thess. 3:9–13; Luke 21:25–36.
December 8: Bar. 5:1–9 or Mal. 3:1–4; Psalm 126; Phil. 1:3–11; Luke 3:1–6.

December 15: Zeph. 3:14–20; Isa. 12:2–6; Phil. 4:4–9; Luke 3:7–18.
December 22: Mic. 5:2–5a (5:1–4a); Ps. 80:1–7; Heb. 10:5–10; Luke 1:39–55.

CHRISTMAS SEASON

December 24, 25 (Christmas Eve/Day): Isa. 9:2–7; Psalm 96; Titus 2:11–14; Luke 2:1–20; also, Isa. 62:6–7, 10–12; Psalm 97; Titus 3:4–7; Luke 2:8–20; Isa. 52:7–10; Psalm 98; Heb. 1:1–12; John 1:1–14.
December 29: 1 Sam. 2:18–20, 26 or Ecclus. 3:3–7, 14–17; Psalm 111; Col. 3:12–17; Luke 2:41–52.
December 31 (New Year's Eve/Day): Isa. 49:1–10; Ps. 90:1–12; Eph. 3:1–10; Luke 14:16–24.

Four-Year Church Calendar

	1991	1992	1993	1994
Ash Wednesday	February 13	March 4	February 24	February 16
Palm Sunday	March 24	April 12	April 4	March 27
Good Friday	March 29	April 17	April 9	April 1
Easter	March 31	April 19	April 11	April 3
Ascension Day	May 9	May 28	May 20	May 12
Pentecost	May 19	June 7	May 30	May 22
Trinity Sunday	May 26	June 14	June 6	May 29
Thanksgiving	November 28	November 26	November 25	November 24
Advent Sunday	December 1	November 29	November 28	November 27

Forty-Year Easter Calendar

1991 March 31	2001 April 15	2011 April 24	2021 April 4
1992 April 19	2002 March 31	2012 April 8	2022 April 17
1993 April 11	2003 April 20	2013 March 31	2023 April 9
1994 April 3	2004 April 11	2014 April 20	2024 March 31
1995 April 16	2005 March 27	2015 April 5	2025 April 20
1996 April 7	2006 April 16	2016 March 27	2026 April 5
1997 March 30	2007 April 8	2017 April 16	2027 March 28
1998 April 12	2008 March 23	2018 April 1	2028 April 16
1999 April 4	2009 April 12	2019 April 21	2029 April 1
2000 April 23	2010 April 4	2020 April 12	2030 April 21

Traditional Wedding Anniversary Identifications

1 Paper	7 Wool	13 Lace	35 Coral
2 Cotton	8 Bronze	14 Ivory	40 Ruby
3 Leather	9 Pottery	15 Crystal	45 Sapphire
4 Linen	10 Tin	20 China	50 Gold
5 Wood	11 Steel	25 Silver	55 Emerald
6 Iron	12 Silk	30 Pearl	60 Diamond

Colors Appropriate for Days and Seasons

White. Symbolizes purity, perfection, and joy and identifies festivals marking events, except Good Friday, in the life of Jesus: Christmas, Epiphany, Easter, Eastertide,

Ascension Day, Trinity Sunday, All Saints' Day; weddings, funerals. Gold may also be used.

Red. Symbolizes the Holy Spirit, martyrdom, and the love of God: Good Friday, Pentecost, and Sundays following.

Violet. Symbolizes penitence: Advent, Lent.

Green. Symbolizes mission to the world, hope, regeneration, nurture, and growth: Epiphany season, Kingdomtide, Rural Life Sunday, Labor Sunday, Thanksgiving Sunday.

Blue. Advent, in some churches.

Flowers in Season Appropriate for Church Use

January. Carnation or snowdrop.

February. Violet or primrose.

March. Jonquil or daffodil.

April. Lily, sweet pea, or daisy.

May. Lily of the valley or hawthorn.

June. Rose or honeysuckle.

July. Larkspur or water lily.

August. Gladiolus or poppy.

September. Aster or morning glory.

October. Calendula or cosmos.

November. Chrysanthemum.

December. Narcissus, holly, or poinsettia.

Historical, Cultural, and Religious Anniversaries in 1991

Compiled by Kenneth M. Cox

10 Years (1981). *January 20:* Fifty-two U.S. citizens are permitted to leave Iran after being held hostage for 444 days. *March 30:* President Reagan is shot and wounded by John Hinckley, Jr., as Reagan leaves a Washington hotel. *April 12:* U.S. launches *Columbia,* the world's first space shuttle. *May 13:* Pope John Paul II is shot and wounded in Vatican City by a Turkish terrorist. *September 25:* Sandra Day O'Connor is sworn in as the first woman on the U.S. Supreme Court. *October 6:* Egyptian President Anwar Sadat is shot and killed during a military parade in Cairo.

25 Years (1966). *March 18:* Pope Paul VI relaxes conditions for mixed marriages. *June 6:* Civil rights activist James Meredith, the first black graduate of the University of Mississippi, is shot and wounded while walking in a voting-rights demonstration from Memphis to Jackson, Mississippi. *June 13:* U.S. Supreme Court rules in *Miranda* decision that the Fifth Amendment requires police officers to warn arrestees of certain rights. *November 8:* Edward Brooke of Massachusetts is elected as the first black U.S. Senator. *Debuts:* Medicare; National Organization for Women (NOW).

40 Years (1951). *February 26:* Twenty-second Amendment takes effect, forbidding election of any U.S. President to more than two terms. *April 5:* Ethel and Julius Rosenberg are convicted of selling U.S. atomic secrets to Soviet agents. *April 11:* General Douglas MacArthur is relieved of command in Korea by President Truman. *Debuts:* "Dennis the Menace"; electricity from atomic power; long-distance direct-dial telephone service.

50 Years (1941). *March 11:* Congress passes the Lend-Lease Act, giving aid to Great Britain. *September 11:* President Roosevelt orders immediate attack of German and Italian vessels found in U.S. waters. *December 7:* Japanese forces attack U.S. base at Pearl Harbor, and U.S. and Japan go to war. *December 11:* Germany and Italy declare war on U.S., and U.S. declares war on them. *Debuts:* Cheerios; *Parade.*

75 Years (1916). *November:* President Wilson wins reelection on the slogan, "He kept us out of war"; Albert Einstein announces his general theory of relativity, which revolutionizes the science of physics; Montana elects the first U.S. congresswoman, Jeannette Rankin. *Debuts:*

Mechanical windshield wipers; Mr. Peanut; the term *I.Q.*

100 Years (1891). *May 15:* Pope Leo XIII issues encyclical on labor conditions, pointing out that employers have important moral duties to improve position of workers; Jim Crow laws enacted in Alabama, Arkansas, Georgia, and Tennessee. *Debuts:* American Express traveler's checks; basketball; Carnegie Hall.

125 Years (1866). *April 9:* Congress passes a Civil Rights act over President Johnson's veto to secure for former slaves all the rights of citizenship afforded by the Thirteenth Amendment. *August 23:* Treaty of Prague ends Seven-Week War in Europe. *Debuts:* American Society for the Prevention of Cruelty to Animals; dynamite; Ku Klux Klan; the torpedo.

150 Years (1841). *April 4:* Pres. William Henry Harrison dies just one month after taking office. *Debuts:* Dallas, Texas; hypnosis; British humor magazine *Punch.*

200 Years (1791). *April 13:* Pope condemns the French civil constitution of the clergy. *December 15:* The Bill of Rights becomes law, as Virginia ratifies the first ten amendments to the U.S. Constitution of 1787. *Debut:* Thomas Paine's *The Rights of Man.*

250 Years (1741). *February 13:* British prime minister Robert Walpole uses the phrase "balance of power" in a speech, giving expression to a principle that long has guided British foreign policy; Calvinist clergyman Jonathan Edwards publishes the sermon "Sinners in the Hands of an Angry God."

Anniversaries of Hymn Writers and Hymn-Tune Composers in 1991

Compiled by Hugh T. McElrath

25 Years (1966). *Death* of Paolo Conte (b. 1891), author of "Great Redeemer, we adore thee"; George Henry Day (b. 1883), composer of GENEVA ("Holy Ghost, dispel our sadness").

50 Years (1941). *Death* of Eugene M. Bartlett, Sr. (b. 1885), author of "Victory in Jesus," composer of HARTFORD; H. Walford Davies (b. 1869), composer of CHILDHOOD ("I love to think that Jesus saw," "For all the blessings of the year"), GOD BE IN MY HEAD ("God be in my head, and in my understanding"); Sy Miller (b. 1908), coauthor of "Let there be peace on earth," cocomposer of WORLD PEACE; John Oxenham (William A. Dunkerley, b. 1852), author of "In Christ there is no east or west," and others. *Birth* of Ragan Courtney, author of "His gentle look"; William F. Smith, arranger of "Were you there," "There is a balm in Gilead," "Lord, I want to be a Christian," and numerous other Afro-American spirituals; Eugene Thomas, arranger of MAJESTY ("Majesty, worship his majesty").

75 Years (1916). *Death* of Stopford A. Brooke (b. 1832), author of "It fell upon a summer day"; George C. Martin (b. 1844), composer of HOLY FAITH ("Jesus, my Lord, my God, my All"), ST. HELENA

("Lord, enthroned in heavenly splendor"), and others; Arthur Messiter (b. 1834), composer of MARION ("Rejoice, ye pure in heart"). *Birth* of Michael Hewlett, author of "Praise the spirit in creation," "Once on a mountaintop," "Sing to him in whom creation," and others; Audrey Mieir, author of "His name is wonderful," composer of MIEIR; R. Maines Rawls, author of "Take my life, lead me Lord," composer of LANGLEY; Delma B. Reno, author of "Praise the Lord, the king of glory"; Alfred B. Smith, coauthor of "Surely goodness and mercy," cocomposer of GOODNESS; Omer Westendorf, author of "Where charity and love prevail," "You satisfy the hungry heart," "Sent forth by God's blessing," and others.

100 Years (1891). *Death* of Edward Dearle (b. 1806), composer of PENITENTIA ("Here, O my Lord, I see thee," "Weary of earth and laden with my sin," and others); John H. Hopkins (b. 1820), author of "We three kings of Orient are," composer of THREE KINGS OF ORIENT, COME HOLY GHOST ("Come, Holy Ghost, our souls inspire"); James Russell Lowell (b. 1819), author of "Once to every man and nation"; Edward H. Plumptre (b. 1821), author of "Rejoice,

ye pure in heart." *Birth* of Arthur C. Barham-Gould (d. 1953), composer of ST. LEONARDS ("May the grace of Christ our Savior," "May the mind of Christ my Savior"); Georgia Harkness (d. 1974), author of "Hope of the world," "Tell it out with gladness," and others; John Roy Harris, author of "Great Redeemer, we adore thee"; Walter K. Stanton (d. 1978), composer of CANNOCK ("All ye that fear God's holy name"); Edwin McNeely (d. 1984), author of "New life for you."

125 Years (1866). *Death* of William Jackson (b. 1815), composer of EVENING HYMN ("Father, in high heaven calling"); John Keble (b. 1792), author of "New every morning is thy love," "Sun of my soul, thou Savior dear," "God, the Lord, a king remaineth," "Blest are the pure in heart," and others; John Mason Neale (b. 1818), translator of "Of the Father's love begotten," "All glory, laud and honor," "Come, ye faithful, raise the strain," "Ye sons and daughters of the king," "Jerusalem, the golden," "The day of resurrection," "Good Christian Men (Friends) rejoice," and many others; John Pierpont (b. 1785), author of "O thou, to whom in ancient time." *Birth* of Arnold G. H. Bode (d. 1952), composer of LARAMIE ("I know not where the road"); Harry T. Burleigh (d. 1949), composer (adapter) of MCKEE ("In Christ there is no east or west"); Frederick A. Challinor (d. 1952), composer of STORIES OF JESUS ("Tell me the stories of Jesus"); Thomas O. Chisholm (d. 1960), author of "Great is thy faithfulness," "Living for Jesus"; Ozora S. Davis (d. 1931), author of "We bear the strain of earthly care"; Roby F. Davis (d. 1937), translator of "Of the Father's love begotten"; Cleland B. McAfee (d. 1944), author of "Near to the heart of God," composer of MCAFEE.

150 Years (1841). *Death* of Jonathan F. Bahnmaier (b. 1774), author of "Spread, O spread the mighty word." *Birth* of Arthur C. Ainger (d. 1919), author of "God is working his purpose out"; Frederick C. Atkinson (d. 1896), composer of MORECAMBE ("Spirit of God, descend upon my heart" and others); William Boyd Carpenter (d. 1918), author of "Before thy throne, O God, we kneel";

Mary A. Lathbury (d. 1913), author of "Break thou the bread of life," "Day is dying in the west," and others; James R. Murray (d. 1905), composer of AWAY IN A MANGER (MUELLER) ("Away in a manger"); William A. Ogden (d. 1897), author of "He is able to deliver thee," composer of DELIVERANCE; Joseph Parry (d. 1903), composer of ABERYSTWYTH ("Jesus, lover of my soul," and others); Daniel C. Roberts (d. 1907), author of "God of our fathers, whose almighty hand"; Clara H. Scott (d. 1897), author of "Open my ears that I may see," composer of SCOTT; Arthur S. Sullivan (d. 1900), composer of ST. KEVIN ("Come, ye faithful, raise the strain"), ST. GERTRUDE ("Onward Christian soldiers," and others), ST. EDMUND ("Draw thou my soul, O Christ," and others), and other tunes.

175 Years (1816). *Death* of Samuel Webbe, Sr. (b. 1740), composer of CONSOLATOR ("Come, ye disconsolate"). *Birth* of W. Sterndale Bennett (d. 1875), harmonizer of LOBE DEN HERREN ("Praise to the Lord, the Almighty"); John E. Bode (d. 1874), author of "O Jesus, I have promised"; William B. Bradbury (d. 1868), composer of ALETTA ("Holy Bible, book divine"), WOODWORTH ("Just as I am, without one plea"), BRADBURY ("Savior, like a shepherd lead us"), CHINA ("Jesus loves me"), SOLID ROCK ("My hope is built"), SWEET HOUR ("Sweet hour of prayer"), HE LEADETH ME ("He leadeth me, O blessed thought"), and many others; George J. Elvey (d. 1893), composer of DIADEMATA ("Crown him with many crowns," "Make me a captive, Lord," and others), ST. GEORGE'S WINDSOR ("Come, ye thankful people, come," and others), ST. CRISPIN ("God loved the world so that he gave," "Just as I am," and others); Edward Hopper (d. 1888), author of "Jesus, Savior, pilot me"; Daniel March (d. 1909), author of "Hark! the voice of Jesus calling"; William Pennefather (d. 1873), author of "Jesus, stand among us"; Sylvanus D. Phelps (d. 1895), author of "Savior, thy dying love," and others; Edward F. Rimbault (d. 1876), composer of HAPPY DAY ("O happy day that fixed my choice"); Wilhelm A. F. Schulthes (d. 1897), composer of LAM-

BETH ("What shall I render to the Lord," and others).

200 Years (1791). *Death* of John Wesley (b. 1703), translator of "Jesus, thy boundless love to me," "Thou hidden love of God," "Give to the winds thy fears," "Commit thou all thy griefs," and others; William Williams (b. 1717), author of "Guide me, O thou great Jehovah," and others. *Birth* of James Edmeston (d. 1867), author of "Savior, breathe an evening blessing," "Lead us, heavenly Father, lead us," and others; Henry H. Milman (d. 1868), author of "Ride on! ride on in majesty," and others.

225 Years (1766). *Birth* of Hugh Wilson (d. 1824), composer of MARTYRDOM ("Alas! and did my Savior bleed," and others).

250 Years (1741). *Birth* of Francois H. Barthelemon (d. 1808), composer of AUTUMN ("Mighty God, while angels bless thee"), MORNING HYMN ("Awake, my soul, and with the sun"), BALERMA ("O for a closer walk with God," and others).

275 Years (1716). *Death* of Christian F. Witt (b. 1660), composer of STUTTGART ("O my soul, bless God the Father," "God is love, his mercy brightens," "Grant us, Lord, the grace of giving," and others). *Birth* of Felice de Giardini (d. 1796), composer of ITALIAN HYMN ("Come, thou almighty king," "Thou, whose almighty word," "Christ, for the world we sing," and others); Anne Steele (d. 1778), author of "Father of mercies, in thy word," "The Savior calls, let every ear," and others.

300 Years (1691). *Death* of Richard Baxter (b. 1615), author of "Lord, it is in thy tender care," "Ye holy angels, bright," and others. *Birth* of Johann B. Konig (d. 1758), composer of FRANCONIA ("Blest are the pure in heart," "Lord Jesus, once a child," and others).

375 Years (1616). *Death* of Melchoir Vulpius (b. 1560), composer of GELOBT SEI GOTT ("Good Christian men rejoice and sing"), CHRISTUS, DER IST MEIN LEBEN ("Sing praise to our creator," "May choirs of angels lead you").

400 Years (1591). *Death* of William Daman (b. 1540), composer of WINDSOR ("Jesus, the very thought of thee," and others).

425 Years (1566). *Bohemian Brethren Hymnbook,* source of MIT FREUDEN ZART ("Sing praise to God who reigns above," and others), NUN SEHT UND MERKET ("The son of God goes forth to war"), and other tunes.

450 Years (1541). *Death* of Nikolaus Decius (b. 1485), author of "All glory be to God on high," composer of ALLEIN GOTT IN DER HOH.

1525 Years (466). *Death* of St. Patrick (b. 372), author of "I bind unto myself today."

Quotable Quotations

1. A painful truth is worth more than a charming temptation.—Johann Heinrich Pestalozzi

2. Most men's anger about religion is as if two men should quarrel for a lady they neither of them care for.—Halifax

3. There's no repentance in the grave.—Isaac Watts

4. The difference between perseverance and obstinacy is that one often comes from a strong will and the other from a strong won't.—Henry Ward Beecher

5. It's as much your duty to get ready to hear, as it is my duty to get ready to preach.—Sam P. Jones

6. We don't have to brag in our prayer because, finally, prayer is an act of yielding to holy God rather than justifying ourselves.—William H. Willimon

7. To shut out human need with selfish indifference is to shut out God.—Joe E. Trull

8. Where is human nature so weak as in the bookstore!—Henry Ward Beecher

9. Let us write indelibly on our minds the truth that Christianity is at its best when the world is at its worst.—A. Leonard Griffith

10. If adversity hath killed his thousand, prosperity hath killed his ten thousand.—Robert Burton

11. The decisive question for man is, Is

he related to something infinite or not? That is the telling question of life.—Carl G. Jung

12. There are eight rungs in charity. The highest is when you help a man to help himself.—Maimonides

13. Only he who keeps his eye fixed on the far horizon will find his right road.— Dag Hammarskjöld

14. Wickedness sucks in the greater part of its own venom and poisons itself therewith.—Michel de Montaigne

15. You give but little when you give of your possessions. It is when you give of yourself that you truly give.— Kahlil Gibran

16. The highest result of education is tolerance.—Helen Keller

17. The church is the only cooperative society that exists for the benefit of non-members.—William Temple

18. There is no grief which time does not lessen and soften.—Cicero

19. The Mob has many Heads but no Brains.—Thomas Fuller (1654–1734)

20. Great souls are portions of Eternity.—James Russell Lowell

21. He is a wise man who does not grieve for the things which he has not but rejoices for those which he has.— Epictetus

22. Love does not dominate; it cultivates.—Johann Wolfgang von Goethe

23. A thing is not necessarily true because a man dies for it.—Oscar Wilde

24. There is nothing so absurd but some philosopher has said it.—Cicero

25. When we stand at the foot of the cross, we look at the condemned man, and then we look inside ourselves, and we know who is truly worthy of being condemned.—Thomas G. Long

26. When Jesus Christ comes into your life, he never leaves it the same—not if he really comes.—William Powell Tuck

27. Danger is sauce for prayers.— Benjamin Franklin

28. The theme of servanthood is muffled in contemporary Christianity. In its place for many is a theology of prosperity in which the goal of life is to get the things we want with Jesus as the way to get them.—M. Vernon Davis

29. Nature has given us two ears but only one mouth.—Benjamin Disraeli

30. Fashions are induced epidemics.— George Bernard Shaw

31. The central message of Jesus of Nazareth is about heaven . . . within and around and among us, as well as in a future that is hidden from us.—Morton T. Kelsey

32. The best qualification of a prophet is to have a good memory.—Halifax

33. The only way to deal with the past is to accept the whole past and, by accepting it, to change its meaning.—Dorothy L. Sayers

34. My faith has deepened with every passing day. I wouldn't trade the worst day of the last fifteen years—and that includes seven months in prison and the time in serious surgery for cancer a year ago when I wondered if my life was slipping away—I wouldn't trade the worst day of the last fifteen years for the best day of the years that went before it.—Charles Colson (in 1988)

35. He does not believe that does not live according to his belief.—Thomas Fuller (1732)

36. The first forty years of life give us the text; the next thirty supply the commentary.—Arthur Schopenhauer

37. Understanding is the reward of faith. Therefore seek not to understand that thou mayest believe, but believe that thou mayest understand.—St. Augustine

38. Patience and fortitude conquer all things.—Ralph Waldo Emerson

39. We don't know a millionth of one percent about anything.—Thomas A. Edison

40. Trouble creates a capacity to handle it.—Oliver Wendell Holmes, Jr.

41. The church always arrives on the scene a little breathless and a little late.— Fr. Bernard Lonergan, S.J.

42. Easter is not back there, nor is it out there; it is here, now, and you and I are the proof and experience of it.—Peter J. Gomes

43. Success has always been a great liar.—Fredrich Wilhelm Nietzsche

44. Taxes are the price we pay for civilized society.—Oliver Wendell Holmes, Jr.

45. Our sex life and our soul life must both express the same values or we become a contradiction in terms, a "walking civil war," a divided self, a split personality.—William E. Hull

46. Nothing reopens the springs of love so fully as absence, and no absence so thoroughly as that which must needs be endless.—Anthony Trollope

47. Justice delayed is justice denied.—William E. Gladstone

48. Every generation laughs at the old fashions but religiously follows the new.—Henry David Thoreau

49. Providence uses choices within our control and events beyond our control.—James W. Cox

50. It is better to know some of the questions than all of the answers.—James Thurber

51. Why storm a wooden Trojan horse when you can hear the termites nibbling inside it.—Calvin Miller

52. Some people are more nice than wise.—William Cowper

53. Love is given to us to draw us toward God.—Morton T. Kelsey

54. I recommend you to take care of the minutes: for hours will take care of themselves.—Lord Chesterfield

55. But humor is also the joy which has overcome the world.—Sören Kierkegaard

56. The unexamined life is not worth living.—Socrates

57. There is at the bottom of the well of every heart, that deep, deep need to be connected, to be part of something big and special and enduring.—Roger Lovette

58. I do not believe in any creed, but I use the creeds to express, to conserve, and to deepen my belief in God.—William Temple

59. Joy is the child of faith and the father of courage.—James W. Cox

60. Here in this world He bids us come, there in the next He shall bid us welcome.—John Dunne

61. Brand any religion as false which says that it can spare its adherent the burdens and cares which are the lot and legacy, the inheritance and portion of every person born of woman.—Gardner C. Taylor

62. An invasion of armies can be resisted; an invasion of ideas cannot be resisted.—Victor Hugo

63. We first believe or consider believing because others tell us *their* story of an encounter with the living Lord.—Gordon C. Stewart

64. Everyone plays an important part; there are no secondary roles in life.—John Killinger

65. In war, whichever side may call itself the victor, there are no winners, but all are losers.—Neville Chamberlain

66. Everything's got a moral, if you can only find it.—Lewis Carroll

67. We all find time to do what we really want to do.—William Feather

68. He who hesitates is sometimes saved.—James Thurber

69. He has no hope who never had a fear.—William Cowper

70. The Devil sweetens poison with honey.—Benjamin Franklin

71. God's miracles are nowhere more difficult to see than when they occur in front of our eyes.—Martin B. Copenhaver

72. Real faith is born when Christ emerges from the dead chrysalis of formal religion to become a joyous and immediate source of power for living.—Graham W. Hardy

73. God forgives sinners but doesn't make them.—James W. Cox

74. Science without religion is lame; religion without science is blind.—Albert Einstein

75. So act as to treat humanity, whether in thine own person or in that of any other, in every case as an end withal, never as a means only.—Immanuel Kant

76. The secret cruelties that parents visit upon their children are past belief.—Karl A. Menninger

77. We have been given tents for a journey and feel cheated we did not get land for a homestead.—Daniel Aleshire

78. Wiser if not better—old eyes are less optic but more discerning.—Calvin Miller

79. Saying no and understanding *why* builds courage and character.—James W. Cox

80. To die for a religion is easier than to live it absolutely.—Jorge Luis Borges

81. Every evil to which we do not succumb is a benefactor.—Ralph Waldo Emerson

82. Wonder is the basis of worship.—Thomas Carlyle

83. If men will not understand the meaning of judgment, they will never come to understand the meaning of grace.—Dorothy L. Sayers

84. There is no sorrier spectacle than that of a church or a denomination whose fellowship is destroyed and whose credibility is undermined by internal strife and divisions.—Page H. Kelley

85. The best way to help yourself is to help someone else.—Sam P. Jones

86. The elects are the Whosoever Wills, and the nonelects are the Whosoever Won'ts.—Sam P. Jones

87. Sweet mercy is nobility's true badge.—Shakespeare

88. Better a little faith dearly won, better launched alone on the infinite bewilderment of Truth, than perish on the splendid plenty of the richest creeds.—Henry Drummond

89. The cruelest lies are often told in silence.—Robert Louis Stevenson

90. Christianity is completed Judaism, or it is nothing.—Benjamin Disraeli

91. Happiness is no laughing matter.—Bishop Richard Whately

92. Trust in the Christ of *the cross* comes only through knowing the Christ of the empty tomb—the risen Christ, who is alive forever.—Bill Kynes

93. Keep your fears to yourself, but share your courage with others.—Robert Louis Stevenson

94. What finally matters is not how long or comfortable our life has been but whether we have found the wisdom to live every day as if it were to be our last.—Joseph A. Hill

95. It matters not how long we live but how.—Philip James Bailey

96. Seize the day before the face of God.—Lifelong motto of John Calvin

97. The best is the enemy of the good.—Voltaire

98. God takes what we do and puts it in the mix, and our little efforts all together become the brick and mortar of God's tomorrow.—Joanna Adams

99. A weed is but an unloved flower!—Ella Wheeler Wilcox

100. Some healthy anger may go a long way to correct evils under which people suffer and which corrupt the word and will of a gracious God.—Paul Boecler

Questions of Life and Religion

These questions may be useful to prime homiletic pumps, as discussion starters, or for study and youth groups.

1. What will heaven be like?

2. How can wealth and poverty affect the religious life?

3. Can a lack of self-esteem cause unacceptable behavior?

4. Are "accidents" and disasters in nature "acts of God"?

5. What are the sources of marital fidelity?

6. Should age curtail our service to God?

7. Is doubt a necessary part of normal Christian experience?

8. What does the teaching about angels have to say to us today?

9. Is it wrong to get angry?

10. Is there a spiritual "prescription" for worry and anxiety?

11. Where does a backslidden Christian stand with God?

12. How does art contribute to the worship of God?

13. Can a person try too hard to be perfect?

14. How can we feel assured of God's love and acceptance of us?

15. What is the meaning of the atonement?

16. What is a hypocrite, and when is one a hypocrite?

17. In what sense does the Bible have authority over us today?

18. How can a religious revival take place in our community?

19. What is the meaning of baptism?

20. How does one begin the Christian life?

21. What makes us have faith?

22. Is it necessary as a Christian believer to belong to a church?

23. In what sense is the Bible inspired?

24. What is the new birth?

25. What causes "burnout" in church workers?

26. Do business and professional people receive proper attention and care from the various ministries of the church?

27. What should be our attitude toward government and the laws?

28. Is a "call" from God necessary for one to become a minister?

29. How does God use chastisement as a means of improving our character?

30. When do children come to know God?

31. Is being a Christian a matter of personal choice?

32. What is the significance of Jesus Christ for the spiritual life of the world?

33. How can the church achieve its God-intended unity?

34. Are the Ten Commandments relevant for our lives today?

35. How should we prepare personally to share in Holy Communion?

36. Can we compromise without loss of integrity?

37. What should we do to help oppressed people in other countries?

38. Is there value in the confession of sins?

39. What are the perils of conformity to group pressure?

40. Do we have a religious duty to protect the environment?

41. What is conversion?

42. What is the role of courage in living a useful life?

43. Are there positive steps we should take in times of personal crisis?

44. What does it mean to take up our cross as a follower of Christ?

45. What should be our attitude toward the religious cults of our day?

46. How should we think about the Second Coming of Christ?

47. Can we prepare for death in practical ways without being morbidly preoccupied with it?

48. Is it wrong to be in debt?

49. How can we make good decisions?

50. Are Christianity and democracy compatible?

51. How can one overcome destructive dependencies?

52. What constructive steps can one take to deal with depression?

53. How should we handle religious differences with other people?

54. Should every Christian practice a religious discipline?

55. Can we reconcile duty and freedom?

56. What is the meaning of Easter?

57. Why are all human beings not equal?

58. What is the simple message of the gospel of Jesus Christ?

59. Why do some people reject the good news of Christ?

60. Does God cause evil?

61. How does suffering test our faith?

62. What principles should guide our giving?

63. Is it possible to practice the Golden Rule today?

64. In what ways does the grace of God operate in our lives?

65. Why should we take the gospel into all the world?

66. Do heroes and heroines play a role in the development of character?

67. What are the marks of true greatness?

68. What factors contribute to growth toward Christian maturity?

69. Does God guide us?

70. How can one get rid of guilt?

71. What can we do about bad habits?

72. Do handicaps serve growth in character and service?

73. What is happiness?

74. Why can't we say anything good about hate?

75. How is prayer related to healing?

76. What will heaven be like?

77. What is holiness to a Christian?

78. Describe the work of the Holy Spirit.

79. Is humility a virtue to be sought?

80. How do we sometimes practice idolatry even as church members?
81. Does the gospel speak to our feelings of inferiority?
82. How can one have a lasting influence for good in the world?
83. Why do we speak of the Scriptures as inspired?
84. Is it ever right to judge others?
85. Can we be joyful even in adverse circumstances?
86. What is the doctrine of "justification by faith"?
87. Is there a good and positive place for law in Christian living?
88. What are the needed qualifications for Christian leadership?
89. What is legalism?
90. How free are we?
91. What is the meaning of life?
92. How does the Lord's Supper contribute to spiritual growth?
93. What can we do to enrich our marriage?
94. Is obedience to God difficult?
95. What are the minimum standards for parents?
96. How can one acquire the virtue of patience?
97. What hinders our prayers?
98. Do Christians have a duty to be active in politics?
99. Is the simplification of life a worthy goal?
100. How can we discover and develop our talents?

Biblical Benedictions and Blessings

The Lord watch between me and thee, when we are absent from one another.—Gen. 31:49.

The Lord bless thee, and keep thee; the Lord make his face to shine upon thee, and be gracious unto thee; the Lord lift up his countenance upon thee, and give thee peace.—Num. 6:24–26.

The Lord our God be with us, as he was with our fathers; let him not leave us, nor forsake us; that he may incline our hearts unto him, to walk in all his ways, and to keep his commandments, and his statutes, and his judgments, which he commanded our fathers.—1 Kings 8:57–58.

Let the words of my mouth, and the meditation of my heart, be acceptable in thy sight, O Lord, my strength, and my redeemer.—Ps. 19:14.

Now the God of patience and consolation grant you to be likeminded one toward another according to Christ Jesus; that ye may with one mind and one mouth glorify God, even the Father of our Lord Jesus Christ. Now the God of hope fill you with all joy and peace in believing, that ye may abound in hope, through the power of the Holy Ghost. Now the God of peace be with you all.—Rom. 15:5–6, 13, 33.

Now to him that is of power to establish you according to my gospel, and the preaching of Jesus Christ, according to the revelation of the mystery, which was kept secret since the world began, but now is manifest, and by the scriptures of the prophets, according to the commandment of the everlasting God, made known to all nations for the obedience of faith: to God only wise, be glory through Jesus Christ for ever.—Rom. 16:25–27.

Grace be unto you, and peace, from God our Father, and from the Lord Jesus Christ.—1 Cor. 1:3.

The grace of the Lord Jesus Christ and the love of God, and the communion of the Holy Ghost, be with you all.—2 Cor. 13:14.

Peace be to the brethren, and love with faith, from God the Father and the Lord Jesus Christ. Grace be with all them that love our Lord Jesus Christ in sincerity.—Eph. 6:23–24.

And the peace of God, which passeth all understanding, shall keep your hearts and minds through Christ Jesus. Finally, brethren, whatsoever things are true, whatsoever things are honest, whatsoever things are just, whatsoever things are pure, whatsoever things are lovely, what-soever things are of good report; if there be any virtue, and if there be any praise, think on these things. Those things, which ye have both learned, and received, and heard, and seen in me, do; and the God of peace shall be with you.—Phil. 4:7–9.

Wherefore also we pray always for you, that our God would count you worthy of this calling, and fulfill all the good plea-sure of his goodness, and the work of faith with power; that the name of our Lord Jesus Christ may be glorified in you, and ye in him, according to the grace of our God and the Lord Jesus Christ.—2 Thess. 1:11–12.

Now the Lord of peace himself give you peace always by all means. The Lord be with you all. The grace of our Lord Jesus Christ be with you all.—2 Thess. 3:16–18.

Grace, mercy, and peace, from God our Father and Jesus Christ our Lord.—1 Tim. 1:2.

Now the God of peace, that brought again from the dead our Lord Jesus, that great shepherd of the sheep, through the blood of the everlasting covenant, make you per-fect in every good work to do his will, working in you that which is well-pleasing in his sight, through Jesus Christ, to whom be glory for ever and ever.—Heb. 13:20–21.

The God of all grace, who hath called us unto his eternal glory by Christ Jesus, after that ye have suffered a while, make you perfect, establish, strengthen, settle you. To him be glory and dominion for ever and ever. Greet ye one another with a kiss of charity. Peace be with you all that are in Christ Jesus.—1 Pet. 5:10–11, 14.

Grace be with you, mercy, and peace, from God the Father, and from the Lord Jesus Christ, the Son of the Father, in truth and love.—2 John 3.

Now unto him that is able to keep you from falling, and to present you faultless before the presence of his glory with ex-ceeding joy, to the only wise God our Sav-ior, be glory and majesty, dominion and power, both now and ever.—Jude 24–25.

Grace be unto you, and peace, from him which was, and which is to come; and from the seven Spirits which are before his throne; and from Jesus Christ, who is the faithful witness, and the first begotten of the dead, and the prince of the kings of the earth. Unto him that loved us, and washed us from our sins in his own blood, and hath made us kings and priests unto God and his Father; to him be glory and domin-ion for ever and ever.—Rev. 1:4–6.

SECTION II.
Sermons and Homiletic and Worship Aids for Fifty-two Sundays

SUNDAY: JANUARY SIXTH

SERVICE OF WORSHIP

Sermon: The Secret of Christ
TEXT: Eph. 3:5–6, NEB

Today is known in a variety of liturgical traditions as the Feast of the Three Kings. They are called "Magi" or "wise men," and we know their story to be essential to Christmas as we know it. Tradition tells us that they were astrologers and astronomers: they knew and followed the stars. They were men of science, and they followed their instincts in the pursuit of truth. They could have spent all of their time in research and speculation on the nature of stars and the history of messianic expectation in Israel. But they did not: they, in fact, pursued the object of their curiosity until they found it. And when they found the young child beneath the star, at the end of their journey, they fell down and worshiped him: that is to say, they recognized who he was and gave to him the worth that is due; they paid him homage with themselves and their gifts.

I. Now we may admire the wise men for many things: their scientific prowess, their shrewdness in human relations, their good taste in gifts. But what commends them to the attention of the church and to us on the feast of the Epiphany is the fact that they came from a foreign place and they returned to a foreign place.

(a) They don't belong at the manger; and so, when they have finished their busi-ness there, when they concluded their worship, they returned home, to another and distant place. The wise men are for-eigners, intruders on the manger scene. They are Gentiles, non-Jews, people out-side of the ancient covenants, men with no apparent claim upon God, and men with whom God has not apparent relationship. And it is first their presence at the manger and then ultimately their return to their own country that proclaims to the world that the secret, hidden, obscure Christ is secret, hidden, and obscure no more: the manger has become God's theater for worldwide redemption, and it is not the angels nor the shepherds nor even the holy family itself but these foreigners, these Gentiles, who make that point for all of us to hear and understand.

(b) And so, the wise men serve more than an exotic purpose in the Christmas narrative. They are more than featured players in a cosmic drama. They are our representatives, far more so than ever the shepherds or angels could be. They repre-sent us because, like us, they are Gentiles, not Jews: they have no rights at the man-ger and by rights wouldn't be there were it not for the mercy of God. And neither would we. Without them, there is no room for us in Bethlehem, for the coming of the Messiah long foretold in Jewish prophecy was a Jewish thing, a secret time of re-demption to be made open in the fullness of time. We, then, my friends, we are the

Gentiles, and the Epiphany, or the manifestation of Christ to the Gentiles, is in some very particular and peculiar way our feast: without it, we are voyeurs in God's great drama of redemption. With it and because of it, we play starring roles in the greatest story every told.

II. It is this understanding that is given to Paul not only in our text this morning from Ephesians but in all of his writings in the New Testament. For Paul, a Hebrew of the Hebrews as he himself describes himself, understands that the secret of Christ, hidden in all ages up to the time of his Incarnation, Crucifixion, and glorious Resurrection, is now an open secret for the world: the promise of God made clear in Jesus Christ is that Jews and Gentiles, that is to say, all the world, are to share in God's peace, power, and love.

(a) Paul describes himself as an apostle to the Gentiles. He seeks his whole mission as a means of communicating that gospel to the Gentiles. In other words, what God began in Creation and carried forth through his prophets and witnesses in the history of Israel is now, in the person of this lowly babe of Bethlehem, made available to the whole world.

(b) And so we learn that we are part of the saving work of Christ and good intentions of God: The ancient prophecy is for us; the star guides and illumines us; the infant king is Lord not just of the Jews or of his own time and place but of us all. The star shines on God's secret plan and shared it with the world, and good for us that it did and does.

III. Now this is where it becomes dicey for many of us. It is perfectly all right to acknowledge the historical and liturgical Epiphany: to speak with favoring awe of the wise men, to acknowledge even ourselves as Gentiles and the debt we owe Paul, who proclaims the gospel to us. But what of our sharing of the gospel with others? It was hard enough to accept it for ourselves and possibly our children. But it almost seems rude in this age of tolerance and diversity to suggest that we have something that ought to be shared with others, not simply because it makes us feel good, but because it is good.

(a) We are Christians, you and I, because Christ has been made manifest to us: we have had an opportunity to see not only his star but him. None of us is a Christian out of some self-imposed act of will. We are Christians either because someone thought it important enough that we should follow Christ or we saw in someone something we wanted and by their example were led to Christ. Think of your own story: Is it not more often true than not the secret of Christ was made known to you, made real, not by some doctrine or some abstract truth, but by the power of a life in love with Christ?

(b) The Epiphany, therefore, is an invitation to the mission of the church: private, personal, public, and corporate. A Christian cannot be a Christian and not share by person and purse Christ. Ours is no secret religion, no hidden, private gospel, no special reserved stock for the chosen people alone. We are called to be manifestations of Christ in the world; we are all missionaries in the most immediate sense of that word, sharing the secret of Christ. The obligations of Christians to share their faith, to manifest Christ in their living, is still incumbent upon us. There is no substitute for it.

(c) For in us ought there be such manifestation of Christ to the Gentiles that by the light of our light, wise men and women still will seek him. Think of it: You and I have the opportunity and the obligation to share the secret of Christ with the whole world, to proclaim by what we do, who and whose we are. Be, then, an Epiphany, and let your light so shine before men that they may see your good works and give glory to your Father who is in heaven.—Peter J. Gomes

Illustrations

THE GREAT INVITATION. There are, even at home, in so-called Christian Europe, heathen without number. Missionary work has therefore become an urgent necessity among ourselves, and in this respect, too, we can already say how often it happens that just those who previously knew nothing and wished to know nothing of Christ and His Church receive the word with an impressively keen faith and how so often it is seen, just in their lives, that the man who really believes, really says yes to the invitation, is born again and becomes a new creature, since he now has a lively hope which fills him with joy unspeakable and lends to his life a seriousness of responsibility which formerly he did not know.—Emil Brunner.

MISSION ACCOMPLISHED.   Dr. George H. Lorimer, perhaps the most famous of the pastors of Tremont Temple, Boston, whose son became editor of the *Saturday Evening Post,* began his career as a theatrical man. He was won to Christ in Louisville when some women went to their pastor, Dr. Everetts, and suggested that invitations to church service be passed out at neighborhood doors. The women passed an invitation card to George H. Lorimer, but he replied, "No, you haven't any use for me. I'm a theatrical man." The women were so courteous, however, that he could not refuse their invitation and came to church. Dr. Everetts's sermon was "The summer is ended, the harvest is passed, and I am not saved." Lorimer was saved in church that Sunday, later became pastor of Tremont Temple, Boston. One of the young lawyers who attended upon his preaching was Russell H. Conwell. Lorimer led Conwell to accept Christ. Conwell went to Philadelphia and built the great Temple University and the Grace Baptist Temple there.—Benjamin P. Browne

Sermon Suggestions

THE RICHES OF THE SEA.   TEXT: Isa. 60:1–6, NEB. (1) The ancient promise to Israel. (2) The ideal fulfillment in Christ (see Matt. 2:1–12; Eph. 3:1–12).

THE SECRET OF CHRIST.   TEXT: Eph. 3:1–12, NEB. (1) What it is. (2) How it was made known. (3) Why it came.

Worship Aids

CALL TO WORSHIP.   "O Lord, our Lord, how excellent is thy name in all the earth, who has set thy glory upon the heavens!" (Ps. 8:1).

INVOCATION.   Almighty God, who before and after and every day art the same, we pause at the gate of this new year to claim thy power and proclaim thy love for all persons. As we begin our journey in worship, open us to all thou dost intend for us, gathering our past into a rich present and a hopeful future through Christ our Lord, who waits there. Amen.—E. Lee Phillips

OFFERTORY SENTENCE.   "Let each man do according as he hath purposed in his heart: not grudgingly, or of necessity: for God loveth a cheerful giver" (2 Cor. 9:7).

OFFERTORY PRAYER.   Generous Lord, we are grateful for health and food, work and shelter, friends and faith. So we give with gratitude and pray in thanksgiving through Jesus our Savior.—E. Lee Phillips

PRAYER.   Thou who has spoken from of old to the prophets at various times and in varied ways, we thank thee that thou hast spoken so clearly in the gift of thy Son, heir of all things, instrument of Creation, the blazing forth of thy glory, the image of thy substance, thy Word incarnate in human flesh.

We have responded to thy love in thy Son and commit ourselves afresh to thy will revealed in him. We thank thee for those who join us in commitment and pray for one another. Grant us the insight to understand thy truth recorded as well as incarnate, preached and taught and sung by women and men.

Grant us the dedication to shape our lives by thy truth. Forgive us every element of falsehood. May our lives reveal thy truth, spoken and written in love. In the name of thy Word who became flesh and dwelt among us, we pray.—J. Estill Jones (all unattributed prayers that follow were written by Dr. Jones)

LECTIONARY MESSAGE

Topic: A Journey of Godly Fulfillment
TEXT: Matt. 2:1–12
One of the most beautiful stories surrounding the birth of Jesus is this one de-

scribing the visit of wise men of the east. The story is found only in Matthew's Gospel. Difficulties are encountered in seeking confirmation of it either in other Gospels or in secular, Jewish, or Oriental literature. But it is quite characteristic of Matthew to include unique events. He selects material for his purpose of convincing and enlightening Israel. We cannot question this event on the grounds of its uniqueness, but we must take it together with other uniquely told events from Luke or Mark or John (each of whom has one-of-a-kind events) to form what we know about the life of Jesus. Regarding the historicity of Matthew's account, A. B. Bruce comments, "He is not inventing history, but enriching history with prophetic emblazonments for apologetic purposes, or for increase of edification" ("The Synoptic Gospels," in *The Expositor's Greek Testament*, ed. W. Robertson Nicoll [London: Hodder and Stoughton, 1897], 1:41).

I. *The eager quest of the expectant visitors.* The visitors in this passage are very meagerly described as "wise men from the east." They are called Magi, the word for representatives of the priestly caste of Media and Persia. They are uniformly believed to have been Zoroastrians, students of the stars, or astrologers, especially in relation to the stars' effect on human life. We cannot speculate with any certainty as to their exact country, but we can be satisfied that, as Bruce elsewhere says, "The homage" of the Gentile world "could not be offered by worthier representatives" (Ibid. 1:70). We may accept the embellishments of tradition that they were three in number and were "kings."

The sign that indicated the birth of a new king for the Jews was a new star whose rising in the east they had seen. Being knowledgeable of the heavens, they would know the significance of this unique sidereal event. It is a testimony to God's enlightenment of even the mystery religions of the East that these men knew of the importance of his coming Messiah and of the signs that would precede it. Whether they were students of the Hebrew prophets themselves or were informed by acquaintance with Jews of the Diaspora (those scattered abroad following the Babylonian captivity), God had alerted these scholars to the phenomenon that would lead them to a discovery having great eternal importance.

II. *God's clear guidance of earnest seekers.* God's leading came to these men from the heavens. It is not difficult to conceive of God's providing a special heavenly sign to guide men from their false theories to the embodiment of his eternal Truth. God led these men to see with their own eyes the wonder of the birth of a king for the world in the land of Judah.

God never leaves his world without evidence of his truth, and those who are alert to the need for truth, the need for God's guidance from nature or people, will surely find it.

God's leading was evident further in his supplying the help needed by the wise seekers. They naturally came to the capital of the people among whom the new king was to appear. They were reported to King Herod. Herod was the king of Judea at the time, an outsider having been installed in 40 B.C. by the Roman emperor. He had a long string of cruelties toward the Israelites when the wise men were ushered into his presence inquiring about a newborn king of the Jews. He was fearful on the counts of both his foreignness and his cruelties that his subjects would gladly replace him. The troubling word spread quickly throughout the city, causing fear among all. But Herod had the wisdom to refer Jewish questions to Jewish authorities. At his summons, the chief priests and the scribes were brought to him. These were servants of God's truth whose business it was to number and catalog all the books of Jewish literature, and they were faithful to them.

The Word of God offers leading for all who seek fulfillment. The authorities produced the prophecy of Mic. 5:2, which Matthew liberally renders (5, 6), giving Bethlehem as the place where the governor should be born. That his blessing of the nations would come as a light was foretold by Isaiah (40:6), and the first verses of Isaiah's sixtieth chapter speak of the light rising with glory, to which the Gentiles would come, led by kings. Matthew now relates that these things have happened.

God's clear guidance was evident again when these strangers set out from Jerusalem to Bethlehem, under the hypocritical command of Herod to return and tell him where the child was so that, as he said, "I may come and worship him also." Under the pretense of piety, many of Herod's kind seek constantly to betray believers. As long as we are true to God, he recognizes our sincerity with his assurance and protection, as he once again set the star in the heavens to lead the wise men step by step to the place where Jesus lay. Since Matthew reports that they found him in a house, no doubt by that time the family had found repose in the home of friends.

The ways of the wise men, however, were again directed by God. If his people are ready to listen, he offers leading into ways of safety. God came to the wise men in a dream and warned them not to return to Herod.

III. *Fulfillment—a gift of God only.* Their purpose was fulfilled in finding him whom they had come to worship. It is true that there is a desire within each of us, deeper than instinct, for a Power higher than we are, with whom we must establish a living relationship. We must, as these eastern men did, look for his signs in our world and be ready to leave "home" at whatever cost to find him. This is the central quest of every life, and it has goaded philosophers, astrologers, and pilgrims of every age, as the enlightened desire of these men guided them. God's directions are around every one of us, in his heavens, in his word, and in his people—even in the dreams he gives us—when we are in the place and state of willingness. We often pursue paths of frustration, but he has given us these ways of finding direction, of finding him who is the fulfillment of every person's life quest.

The wise men's purpose was fulfilled in their worship. Many of us know what we should do but hesitate too long to do it. These visitors came prepared to find a king and prepared to give him their possessions of utmost value. Another reason for believing them to be kings is that the gifts they brought were of such rarity and such value that only kings could have brought them. But what God wants from each of us is what each has of value to him. Our lives will be truly fulfilled only when we, like the wise men, have opened our treasures and presented them to him.

Then we, too, shall go on into our own country "another way"—I think that means "in a new condition."—John R. Rodman

SUNDAY: JANUARY THIRTEENTH

SERVICE OF WORSHIP

Sermon: Loving God Is Not Easy

Text: Matt. 22:37

Men have often broken the Ten Commandments, but they have never questioned their greatness. But great though they are, Jesus insisted that there is one commandment still greater: "Thou shalt love the Lord thy God with all thy heart and with all thy soul and with all thy mind."

I. It is not easy to love God when we consider what his world has turned out to be. It is a far cry from the Garden of Eden to the world as we know it. Some of us look upon God's handiwork as a shocking place. We see the vagaries of nature, and we are puzzled. We read of tornadoes ripping through towns and villages, leaving destruction and sorrow in their wake. We hear of famines decimating entire populations. We experience bruising winters and burning summers. We speak of floods and torrents. And as though with deliberate irony, adding insult to injury, we speak of all such things as "acts of God." And what of our own lives? What of the loss of joy or the coming of grief? What of the twisted roads and the stagnant pools? What of the moral fiascos and the spiritual disasters? What of the failures and the undeserved persecutions? What of misfortune turning our lives into tragedies or miserable comedies? No, it is not easy to love God.

But this is a dangerous subject to pursue, for in the end it strikes back at us. Job was wiser than we are when he said, "The Lord gave, and the Lord hath taken away; blessed by the name of the Lord." Why should we complain about misfortune and disaster when we do not even give him as much as a "thank you" for all the good things we have received and tasted? Life is like an alternating current—quiet and turbulent, leaving us alone and pushing us along. Life is what it is, and we must live it as it comes—with dignity and courage and understanding.

II. Our love must constantly grow. Love can never remain what it was at the beginning. When we were young, we thought that with the first experience of love we had discovered the fullness of it. That was a deception. Those young people who in the first flush of their youthful affection look upon the casual ways of their elders and say, "They do not love each other as we do," do not know the half of it. They do not know, for they cannot know, how patience and trust and understanding have ripened love into full bloom. They do not know how through trials and storms, through finding and losing, the oak of affection has stood firm.

Through the years, as life tempers our spirits and mellows our judgments, our love for God becomes deep and broad. It reaches far, and in the end it becomes irresistible. Such love is not easy.

III. Loving God is not easy because love must be continuous. There are no moments of silence in that love. It speaks when the sun stands at the zenith and laughter rings through our days like bells. It speaks when the moon is darkened and there are no words to clothe our thoughts. Now and then one hears a man or a woman, coming out of an unhappy marriage, say, "We do not love each other anymore." That cannot be. Where men and women say such things there never was love. There may have been a score of substitutes, but there was not love. There may have been feelings and emotions that went by that name, but they were counterfeits. Love is a perennial. It always lives, even when blanketed by heavy snows. It only waits for the warming touch of spring.

The closer we are to life, the more intimately we walk with men and women, the more we learn that those who have suffered most love God most. Make of that mystery what you will, but here it stands for all of us to see and read. The deeper love reaches, the firmer it grows.

IV. Loving God it not easy because love must be inclusive. Remember, there is no partial redemption. There can be no partial love. It is all or nothing. Now we understand why Jesus spoke of this as the greatest commandment: "Thou shalt love the Lord thy God with all thy heart and with all thy soul and with all thy mind." Love is all—heart and home and head and work.

V. Loving God is not easy, because love is creative. Nothing great ever happens in a man's life without love. We remember how the poet sings: "I could not love thee, dear, so much, / Lov'd I not honour more."

That is beautiful, but it is not true. That line will not bear the test of experience. We do not love man or woman or God because we are honorable or just or kind or tolerant. That would be a reversal of the spiritual order. We are just, we are kind, we are tolerant because there is something deeper and more lasting in us. We love something or we love someone. We cannot say that we make something of love; we must say that love can make something of us.

Love is constantly creative. The New Testament puts this matter with finality: "He who loves God should love his brother also" (RSV). Love cannot be forever silent; it must speak out. Love cannot be forever idle; it must reach out. Love cannot be forever unmoved; it must laugh and rejoice, it must weep and sorrow. Something always comes of love. It changes a house into a home, a relationship into a companionship, an interest into a concern, an offering into a sacrifice, a responsibility into a mission. It gives us strength in moments of weakness; it grants us courage in times of fear. All this our love of God will do.

No, loving God is not easy, but once our love takes hold upon him, it never, never lets him go.—Arnold H. Lowe

Illustrations

RESISTANCE TO GOD. Really, a young Atheist cannot guard his faith too carefully. Dangers lie in wait for him on every side. You must not do, you must not even try to do, the will of the Father unless you are prepared to "know of the doctrine." All my acts, desires, and thoughts were to be brought into harmony with universal Spirit. For the first time I examined myself with a seriously practical purpose. And there I found what appalled me; a zoo of lusts, a bedlam of ambitions, a nursery of fears, a harem of fondled hatreds. My name was legion.—C. S. Lewis

CHUCK COLSON'S CONVERSION. A lot of skeptics thought it wouldn't last, that it was just a ploy for sympathy, a foxhole conversion. I don't blame them. If the tables were turned, I'd have thought the same thing.

But not once in these ten years have I doubted that Jesus Christ lives. There is nothing of which I am more certain. And not once would I have turned the clock back. My lowest days as a Christian (and there were low ones—seven months' worth of them in prison, to be exact) have been more fulfilling and rewarding than all the days of glory in the White House.

The years before conversion were death; the years since have been life and the adventure of loving God, the purpose of that life.—Charles W. Colson

Sermon Suggestions

IN THE BEGINNING. TEXT: Gen. 1:1–5. (1) God was. (2) God acted.

BAPTISM IN THE NAME OF JESUS. TEXT: Acts 19:1–7. (1) Its purpose—incorporation into the Christian community. (2) Its result—evidence of the Spirit (see also Gal. 5:22–25).

Worship Aids

CALL TO WORSHIP. "I will sing unto the Lord because he hath dealt bountifully with me" (Ps. 13:6).

INVOCATION. It is true, our Father, that we have met to worship, but we must admit that we really don't know how to go about it. Our feeble attempts at praise seem so inadequate, our prayers so inarticulate; our gifts are so small, that it is a wonder that worship takes place at all. And yet we know that you desire our worship, so you will help us to bring it about. Today in this place help us to feel your presence in such a real way that our only possible response will be genuine worship.—James M. King

OFFERTORY SENTENCE. "The earth is the Lord's, and the fullness thereof; the world, and they that dwell therein" (Ps. 24:10).

OFFERTORY PRAYER. Jesus has taught us that discipleship means giving. Remind us today of the claim that you have in our lives. Consecrate the gifts that you have given to us and the gifts that we return to you, that as your servants we might grow in spirit and in truth.—J. Scott Hickman

PRAYER. "When we look at your heavens, the work of your fingers, the moon and the stars that you have established; what is man that you are mindful of him and the Son of man that you care for him?" But we praise you that you *are* mindful of us and that you *do* care for us. You are present in an eternal love in all the vicissitudes of our life; you draw near in the strength of the everlasting arms; in the flooding waters of some Jordan, you are the sure rock upon which we can stand.

Why, then, are we so fearful, so nervous, so anxious? Where is our faith?

Here, may we affirm our faith in you— the great God and the great King above all gods. Stretch our imagination to catch such a vision of the ineffable that we shall return to common tasks inspired to breathe into them your glory.

None of us have been at this place before in life's consciousness. It is all so new. But let us not cripple our chances for a better day by nostalgic pining for some yesterday that never was. Life is a moving stream, for you are the *living* God. Life *is*, because you *are*.

May we be sensitive to your love that is constant amidst all the changing circumstances of our lives. There are homes bereft because of the death of a loved one—families anxious because of the illness of a member. Where estrangement threatens any relationship, minister love, understanding, reconciliation. Minister a grace according to our need that we may be poised whatever the threat. Counsel us with Christ's Spirit, for it is in his name that we pray.—John M. Thompson

LECTIONARY MESSAGE

Topic: The Baptism of Jesus
Text: Mark 1:4–11

As the first coherent account of the Christian apology around the life and teachings of Jesus, this Gospel is meant to be practical in the face of the first-century persecutions of Christians, tracing the sufferings of Jesus in relation to his followers and all believers. Jesus is upheld as the first martyr to faith, whom the members of the Christian group might soon follow. It affords us practical guidance as well.

I. *The precursor and his work.* The attention of the world had been directed toward God and his coming fulfillment of Jewish prophetic expectations by the ministry of the faithful messenger, John, known as the Baptist for the special work he did.

Christians everywhere have come to accept that the gospel, as the "good news" for all mankind, was begun with John's declarations of universal need for repentance and the renunciation of sin. This message of John is the beginning of salvation for all who believe. The exact fulfillment of Isaiah's prophecy (40:3) consists in John's message that repentance is the necessary element of baptism leading to forgiveness.

(a) *The hardest part.* For us, repenting is very difficult. It means "a new mind," and the difficulty lies just in our failure to understand all that it implies. Most of us are not ready to say good-bye to the old mind with all its understandings and memories.

(b) *To whom it applies.* Many who long followed Christ as a friend still do not know him as Savior simply because they have never known what it is to repent, to realize the need for a complete changing and renewal of their minds. They have, for example, sung "The Old Rugged Cross" all their lives without ever really hearing the words "for a world of lost sinners was slain." And when these words are called to their attention, they exclude themselves: "Maybe, but I don't need that—I'm not a murderer or a thief." We must be able to see, through the preaching of a prophetic messenger and the power of God's Holy Spirit preparing his heart, that *we each need* to repent to be forgiven.

Our lives are the "wilderness" where the message of repentance must penetrate to call us on the road to Jesus Christ. No other ground for forgiveness by God is known in any of the prophets.

(c) *A further difficulty.* The difficulty of repentance is even greater for those who have always seen the word translated as "penitence." The difference in implication is all-encompassing. Not only sins, which must be confessed—and corrected—for righteousness to mean anything, but sin itself must be repented. "Penitence" implies this essential sorrow for specific misdeeds or thoughts and specific acts or recompense; but repentance is a complete submission of a sinful nature and a recognition of its negative outcomes. The idea of *merit* as a reward for penitential acts is totally foreign to both the Old and New Testaments. Repentance is not just sorrow or fear. It is recognition of hopelessness. It is an act of sincere will, but, more than that, it is an act of faith.

II. *The testimony of a surrendered life.*

(a) *The life behind the testimony.* The life of John gave testimony to his simplicity of purpose and his dedication to his message. John had stripped his "life-style" to the essentials only, so that he could be clearly the precursor of a greater One.

He was simple in his dress—camel's hair and animal skins, although among the most prized possessions of people today, were for him the near-at-hand, natural materials of a life in the desert. He was simple in his food, obtaining his necessary, healthful nutrients from the land through which he walked, its locusts and wild honey.

(b) *His testimony, an example for all.*

(1) He always pointed people away from himself to the Greater One. This was his message, his preaching content, that the Mightier One was soon to appear. It is the true message for any of us, to point people to Jesus.

(2) John compared himself to one not even worthy to be a slave to perform the most menial tasks for a master. He took no favor to himself other than to be a witness. His own true greatness lay in his signpost satisfaction, his joy derived from directing the crowds to Jesus, to let all the world see reflected in him only a way to the True Baptizer, who would be as far above him as the Holy Spirit is above river water.

(3) The lasting nature of his testimony is enough for anyone to aim for. The Apostle John (1:8) bears testimony to the Baptist's faithfulness: "He was not the light but came to bear witness to the light." He also later (5:33) quotes Jesus as saying, "You sent to John, and he has borne witness to the truth." A lasting reputation for telling truth to those who need to hear about Jesus is a reward worth trimming one's life for. It is a satisfying hope that our Lord should say the same about any of us who bear his name.

III. *Public recognition of the lordship of Jesus.*

(a) *The sign of God's Spirit.* Jesus came and was baptized by John in the Jordan. The Jordan was the river that God had used before to make his cleansing power available to Naaman, who had leprosy. Although Jesus was in this river at the time of his baptism, it was the dove, the sign of God's Holy Spirit, that was the mark of his Sonship. Mark relates simply as facts those events whose true power and glory were to be fully known only later. As Jesus had always been the Son of God, so marked by many evidences not reported by Mark, now he was entering the public phase that was to be the turning point of life not only for John and the Judeans but for everyone in any age whose faith would recognize his Sonship.

(b) *The voice from heaven.* We all are hearing the voice from heaven attesting to Jesus' Sonship. It speaks to us. It is a call of the eternal love as well as the infinite power of God, a call to receive in the commonplace elements of our lives the radiant glory of God. It assures us that, although we may not receive the baptism that Jesus received, we may receive baptism in his salvation; we may make our lives candles of the Lord, dull, ordinary materials released by his fire to give light to all around, to spend our short times glowing with his grace. We are not to deny the inner experience that changes everything, but we are to go on to the fruition of our repentance—the forgiveness of sins and the life in glory.—John R. Rodman

SUNDAY: JANUARY TWENTIETH

SERVICE OF WORSHIP

Sermon: When Trouble Comes

TEXT: Job 2:9

When Job's troubles were at their height, when he was bereft of his sons and his property and afflicted with loathsome sores from the sole of his foot to the crown of his head, his wife said to him, "Do you still hold fast your integrity? Curse God and die."

In calamity, that is how some instinctively react. Their minds turn at once to God; their feelings toward him are harsh and rebellious.

When men blaspheme, it is not God but the false god who has been presented to them whom they reject and curse.

Let me say emphatically that such a god should be blasphemed. He is a caricature of the God and Father of our Lord Jesus Christ.

When men blaspheme, it is not God but the false god who has been presented to them whom they reject and curse.

I. One of the great weaknesses of our

religious life is the inadequacy of our conception of God. We have not found with our minds a god worthy or worship, a god we can relate to the scientific age, a god who commands our intellectual respect as well as the homage of our hearts and the obedience of our lives.

(a) The weakness is most marked where the character of God is concerned. For great numbers of us, he is an exacting overlord, an inscrutable and implacable power. More than anything else, what we need to have Christianized is our thinking about God. God should not be conceived as sending evil. Calamity is not his deliberate handiwork. Disease is not of his making.

(b) Job, though bewildered and mystified by the trouble that came upon him, did not curse God. "Though he slay me, yet will I trust him" was his cry. What intrepid heroism! What selfless devotion! That cry has brought courage and resolution to many an afflicted soul. And yet, its premise has to be rejected. "Though he slay me"—will God, whose name and nature are love, whose heart is most wonderfully kind, do what no father in his senses would dream of doing, what he would rightly be sent to prison for doing?

II. It is to Jesus we should turn in such matters. He proclaimed God's fatherly rule over all his children. He taught that no sparrow falls to the ground without the Father's knowledge, that God clothes the lilies, feeds the ravens, numbers the very hairs of our heads, sends his sun and rain, his unconditioned bounty and kindness, upon good and bad, the thankful and the thankfulness. He taught us to pray, "Thy will be done," but a cloud of misconception surrounds that prayer. All sorts of lies have been told about it, and all manner of evils have been tolerated under its protection. Far too many people, when they pray, "Thy will be done," think of lonely grief, wasting sickness, premature death. Christ would have us think of the will of God in positive ways. God's will means health. He wants disease to be conquered. A great part of our Lord's time was spent in healing the sick. He cannot have thought that disease was the will of God. God's will means happy homes. Slums

cannot be the will of God. Hideous dwellings like those in lower East Harlem cannot be any part of his design. God's will means, not war, but peace. It cannot be his intention that men should manufacture deadly explosives like the nuclear weapons with which the great powers are experimenting. We should be careful how we speak of the will of God. Why should "Thy will be done" be a moan of resignation? Why should it suggest only graveyards, disease, calamity? We should associate it with health and happiness and abounding vitality.

(a) I am not suggesting that this will solve all our problems. We may not think of God as sending trouble and tragedy, but the fact remains that he permits them, that they exist in a world made by him, that they are a substantial ingredient in all our lives. It is the calamity that befalls others, not the calamity that befalls ourselves, that raises the deepest questions. It is when we see innocent children and men and women who are the soul of goodness suffer that faith is strained most, and it comes home to us that the world is not patently the creation of a loving and beneficent God.

(b) How to reconcile the griefs and graves of men with the goodness and fatherliness of God—that is the problem. And Christianity, if anything, sharpens it. The noblest soul the world has ever known, betrayed, deserted, scourged, spat upon, crucified—that is the problem. Phillips Brooks once remarked that if someone should tell him that he could explain the mystery of evil, he would close his ears to the offer. Brooks knew that when all has been said that may be said—the existence of good as well as evil; the amount of suffering due to sin and ignorance; the educative value of suffering; the world a school for character, a vale of soul-making, not a lotus-eater's paradise—there remains a dark mystery that cannot be fathomed.

III. Well, what after all is faith? It is "the assurance of things hoped for, the conviction of things not seen." In essence, faith is always a going against appearances. It is an assent to something about which you cannot prove that it is impossible that you should be mistaken. It is not belief in spite of evidence; it is belief in scorn of circumstance; it is the resolve to stand or fall by the noblest hypothesis.

(a) Besides, if there were nothing to try our faith in God, it might become shallow, flabby, feeble. But when pressed and tried by the sore problems of life it can become deep and strong. It is with faith as with virtue; it needs to be tested like steel in the fires of temptations and difficulties.

(b) How courageous men and women are made by faith in the God and Father of our Lord Jesus Christ! How strong and calm and resolute! Doubt paralyzes. It drains the energies, depletes the resources, takes the heart out of us. On the other hand, faith vitalizes. It supplies energy, increases resource, puts heart into us. This is no secondhand story I am bringing to you. This is not something you yourself can prove in your own experience. Multitudes have done so. In dark and difficult days, one thing has kept them on their feet, has saved them from the loss of nerve, has kept them free from cynicism and self-pitying complaint—their faith in God. Out of pastoral—and personal—experience I can testify that there is no misfortune, no tragedy, no burden of sorrow or sickness so great but a believing soul can come out on top of it a conqueror, more than a conqueror.

(c) Through him—it is not a case of bracing ourselves, whistling to keep our courage up, bidding ourselves play the man, rallying such interior resources as we can muster of pluck and perseverance. It is rather that morning by morning we turn to God saying, "Strong Deliverer, be thou still my strength and shield," and never turn in vain. "This is the victory that overcomes the world, our faith."—Robert J. McCracken

Illustrations

WHEN LIFE TUMBLES IN.　　When his wife died, Rossetti tells us, he passed through all that tremendous time with a mind absolutely blank, learned nothing, saw nothing, felt nothing; so that, looking back, all he could say was that, sitting in a wood with his head in his hands, somehow it was

photographed permanently on his passive mind that a certain wildflower has three petals. That was all. But by and by the gale dies down, and the moon rises and throws a lane of gold to us across the blackness and the heaving of the tumbling waters. After all, it is not in the day but in the night that star rises after star and constellation follows constellation and the immensity of this bewildering universe looms up before our staggered minds. And it is in the dark that the faith becomes biggest and bravest, that its wonder grows yet more and more. "Grace," said Samuel Rutherford, "grows best in the winter."—Arthur John Gossip

THE HUMAN FACTOR.　　A man whose three children were killed when a schoolhouse collapsed screamed curses against God because of their death. He did not know at the time that the schoolhouse had not been built properly for an earthquake area, that to save money shoddy material was used, that back of his personal tragedy was a corrupt and inefficient local government.—Robert J. McCracken

Sermon Suggestions

WHEN THE LORD SPEAKS.　　TEXT: 1 Sam. 3:1–10 (11–20). (1) His voice can be misunderstood. (2) His message may be painful to contemplate. (3) His messenger must be faithful in communication. (4) The Lord will be faithful in accomplishing his purpose.

WHO OWNS YOU?　　TEXT: 1 Cor. 6:12–20. (1) *Situation:* Many seductive arguments are made for immoral practices. (2) *Complication:* Yielding to immorality puts one in the power of forces alien to Christ. (3) *Resolution:* Realizing the cost of our salvation and our Lord's high purpose for us is the powerful motivation for responsible, moral living.

Worship Aids

CALL TO WORSHIP.　　"The Lord is my rock and my fortress and my deliverer; my God, my rock, in whom I will take refuge;

my shield, and the horn of my salvation, my high tower" (Ps. 18:2).

INVOCATION. Our Father, we come to you trusting in a love that will not let us go. Our yearning for your strength and comfort is unceasing. Help us to lean on you more fully and listen attentively to your Word to us in this hour. Amen.

OFFERTORY SENTENCE. "Woe unto you, scribes and Pharisees, hypocrites! For ye tithe mint and anise and cummin and have left undone the weightier matters of the law, justice and mercy and faith: but these ye ought to have done and not to have left the other undone" (Matt. 23:23).

OFFERTORY PRAYER. Others have given through the years, and we have heard the good news. Now we give, Lord, in response to your love that others may hear the good news of your salvation in Christ Jesus, in whose name we pray. Amen.

PRAYER. Eternal God, who art the hope of the ends of the earth, be our hope in this place of prayer. Lead us to the rock that is higher than we and be to us a high tower and a strong defense against the enemy. For our foes marshal their hosts and encompass our souls—our anxieties and fears, our sins and follies, our failures, humiliations, doubts. See how the enemies of our spiritual life beleaguer us. O God, put upon the lips of thy servants a new song this morning. "The Lord is my light and my salvation; whom shall I fear?"

Take the cloud from our vision that we may see. Give us insight to discern truth from untruth, the high from the low, the clean from the unclean, the enduring from the transient. Grant us horizon, perspective, and clarity of mind and spirit, that thy servants, bewildered and confused concerning the way they should take, may find the path made clear, thy Word a lamp unto their feet.

Strengthen our faith. Save us from credulity and all superstitious acceptance of things unsound and untrue, but all the more give us a steadfast trust in those things worth man's believing and a deep and steady faith in those truths in which a man, confiding, shall not be shaken.

As thus we pray for our own souls, our sympathies and prayers pass over all boundaries of race and creed and nation to every worshiping soul and praying assembly on the earth. Whether in church or temple, mosque or synagogue, wherever thy people lift their thoughts to thee, O thou eternal God, greater than all our names for thee, larger than all our human symbols and imagining, do thou come down to bless. We confess our partialness. We pray thee that our neighbors of other creeds may confess theirs. Bind us together in a common humility and penitence before the one God and Father of us all, and make our faith in thee no longer a cause of division but a unifying power to draw our human family together.

We lay upon the altar of our intercession this sorry, storm-tossed world. We remember the distress and catastrophe everywhere among the nations. Forgive us that we so have sinned against light and that, instead of founding a peaceful order of brotherhood under law, we have turned our backs upon the sunshine and have set our feet toward darkness and night. Ours is the sin, O God, the sin of all of us, that violence stalks broadcast across the earth. Bring the people to penitence and the rulers of the people to thy mercy seat, we beseech thee, that in the day of our opportunity we may choose light and not darkness, law and not slaughter, brotherhood and not enmity, peace and not war.

And now draw near to the stricken souls who hardly can pray for the ills of the world because their own ills oppress them so heavily. Upon bereaved spirits send thine eternal comfort; to shaken souls, thy power. Into tempted spirits send thy reinforcement for the day of their trial; into disappointed hearts, new hope; into restless and strained minds, thy peace that passeth all understanding, that the world cannot give and cannot take away.

We ask it in the Spirit of Christ.—Harry Emerson Fosdick

LECTIONARY MESSAGE

Topic: A Changed Person, a Changed Name

TEXT: John 1:35–42

In keeping with his purpose, somewhat different from that of the synoptics, John in this passage provides further evidence that Jesus is both real God and real man. He also provides evidence of the life-changing power he imparts to his followers.

I. *Jesus receives people whom others direct to him.*

(a) The Baptist revealed to his two disciples that Jesus was "the Lamb of God." But his merely saying that was not enough. They had to hear him and react. They were themselves involved in the search for the Messiah; it was their search. John (the unnamed disciple) and Andrew were beneficiaries of the shared knowledge of another. Anyone's life is a cooperative product for which the individual himself is finally responsible. All of us are links in a long chain of loving, sharing concern. But each one must act on the direction one receives.

(b) As the two disciples go and follow Jesus, they find ample opportunity for expressing their interest. The Master notices them and greets them with an invitation. He always offers opportunities to those who come to him. No one should refuse the opportunity when it is presented, since no one can predict the dangers and the loss that may follow procrastination. One can, however, be sure that time without Jesus is time lost.

(c) The question to be answered—the searching of the heart—is not so simple as appears on the surface. "What do you seek?" Can everyone give an immediate request the satisfaction of which will be good for a lifetime? One should constantly sharpen one's sense of the eternal in the desire of the moment, since they are intimately related. They call him "Rabbi," "My Greatness, My Teacher," and ask where he dwells.

II. *Jesus takes people as they are and makes them new.*

(a) Jesus answered the question of the two disciples in a way that accepted their curiosity but also challenged the depth of their interest—"Come and see." He invites them and they accept. Even if one were to come to him in idle curiosity, he would invite further acquaintance. No one needs to pass up what may be the opportunity of a lifetime to follow Jesus.

(b) Jesus changes whatever one has when he or she comes, to something more valuable. He changes interest to satisfaction and curiosity to knowledge. He changes seekers to finders. Many a person has gone to services of evangelism time after time, continually claiming to be "a seeker," seeming to be satisfied with that status. Seeking is a rewarding condition only if it ends in finding. The one who does not sooner or later say with Andrew, "I have found the Messiah," will continue to be without him.

(c) The old Simon becomes the new Peter. There is nothing wrong with changing a name. A new name usually indicates a new nature or at least a new orientation. God has given new names to many of his people. Abram ("exalted father") becomes Abraham ("father of a great nation"); Jacob ("took by the heel") becomes Israel ("a prince with God"); the sons of Zebedee become Boanerges ("sons of thunder"). Many family names have been changed in America to indicate belonging to a new country or to eliminate ties to the old that could be handicaps.

(d) Better for us today is to put new meaning into a present name. The change of a life can be reflected in such a way that a person's name becomes a watchword for the strength, dignity, service, and glory filling the new life. This is the outliving of the inward transformation.

III. *The fruit of a changed life must be related to our world.*

(a) We should ask whether the ideals and customs of our society place us who have met Jesus on a higher moral and religious plane than those of the Victorians placed them—is our materialism, our selfishness, our indifference to the sufferings of the poor any less immoral than theirs was? We may complain that the middle class has the worst of it—the very rich and the very poor can get away with anything and everything that we cannot. The rich are insulated from common morality because they can purchase a secluded and private life-style. They seem to escape the degrading legal penalties of misconduct and even the consequences and inconveniences of illness. The poor and homeless are not held to the common morality because they are deemed to have to seek solutions we think unacceptable to problems we cannot imagine.

(b) But in consequence of the change Jesus has wrought in our lives, we should faithfully communicate the power of Jesus to those in our immediate society. Not every one of us can hope to influence an entire generation or locality, but we can accept a task within our own grasp.

(c) Just as Andrew first found his brother, and Philip (in the next passage) found Nathanael, Peter was to spend his life finding others for his Lord.—John R. Rodman

SUNDAY: JANUARY TWENTY-SEVENTH

SERVICE OF WORSHIP

Sermon: Can Any Good Thing Come out of Nazareth?

TEXT: John 1:43–51

Does your life have meaning? Does it have meaning? Does it have ultimate meaning? When Philip came to Nathanael, he said, "We have found him of whom Moses and the prophets did write, Jesus of Nazareth." And Nathanael said that which you and I and all men and women have said at some time in the depths of callousness or despair or in moments of cynicism, however brief, "Can any good thing come out of Nazareth?" And Philip said to him, "Come and see."

I want to reflect with you upon the stage of your life, the place of your life, and the promise of your life.

I. It is very important for us to understand that which Jesus tried with such persistence to teach those who were attracted to him in his earthly ministry about the stage of life—the stage upon which we live.

It was the burden of Jesus' life, teaching, ministry, death, and Resurrection, the burden of his revelation of God, that you and I live upon an immortal stage. He said, "We live out our mortal lives there, our mortal efforts are set forth on that immortal stage."

How many people, you can name them, so can I, came to Jesus in the New Testament with a multiplicity of infirmities, infirmities of mind, body, and soul? They hobbled to him and said to him, "Lord, heal me." And they were healed. And they returned to Jesus and said, "You healed me." And Jesus said, "Wait a minute. I did not heal you. Thy faith hath made thee whole." When Jesus took these people and pulled away all that mortal rubbish that covers the stage of life and they could feel, could see, could be part of that immortal drama, they were made whole. It was not an act of God contradicting his own mortal realm.

Such a dichotomy grows when men and women believe that life is nothing more than mortal. In the sacred community, within such a context, on his knees, in his prayers, man waits for God's visitation. Scientists and religionists alike, we all live on this same immortal stage of God, hoping to somehow touch that immortality that brings treasure to this, our mortal existence.

II. The place, the place in life. And Nathanael said, "Can any good thing come out of Nazareth?"

In 1935 Benito Mussolini banished Carlo Levi to a small village in southern Italy called Lucania. Following the war, he wrote a book entitled *Christ Stopped at Eboli*. Eboli is the last town of any significance before one comes to Lucania. No one ever went to Lucania. The Roman soldiers never went to Lucania; the Athenian settlers never went to Lucania. Nobody ever went to Lucania except this man in his banishment and the few unhappy souls that lived there. He wrote in his book, *Christ Stopped at Eboli*, that there were no Christians in Lucania.

The last Christians were at Eboli because to be Christian one had to be human. There were no humans in Lucania. Levi wrote, "Christ went into the very depths of Hell and there tore down the door to give those wretched folks eternity, and yet, he came not to this place where there was neither sin nor redemption. There was only the pain residing forever in earthly things. Christ did not come. Christ stopped at Eboli."

Lucania is a feeling. It is a feeling we all know. It is that place in life where we fear that God has passed us by, that we are consigned forever to Lucania. It is a feeling, it is a haunt of life.

You and I have times of Lucania in our lives when human bonds are fractured, we are left alone, and we ask ourselves, "How can I go on living in this desert, in this Lucania, in this bleak world?" And Nathanael said unto him, "Can anything good come out of Nazareth?" And Philip said unto him, "Come and see."

III. Well, happily we do not spend all of our days in Lucania. We have those seasons. And it does us ill to pretend that they do not exist when they fall upon us. It would do us equally ill to stay there beyond all due course. But when we are extricated from Lucania, there is a danger, having been lifted from these great mortal trials,. that we will now invest our new spirit, our new hope, our new life, in that which is purely mortal.

We can feel the Spirit of God coursing through our veins. That is the time for us to remember that glorious lesson when the Spirit of God came to Samuel. "Samuel, Samuel." And he went to Eli and he said, "Here am I." He said, "I did not call you." "Samuel, Samuel." Again, to Eli. He said, "I did not call you." "Samuel, Samuel." Do we not, like Samuel, always go to the world, to mortal things, to mortal people when that Spirit visits us? Pray God that when we are lifted from Lucania, when we hear and feel the Spirit of God, that we do not turn to everything mortal. But that we, like Samuel, can say, "Speak, Lord, thy servant listens."—Spencer Morgan Rice

Illustrations

MEANING IN SACRIFICE.   Once, an elderly general practitioner consulted me because of his severe depression. He could not overcome the loss of his wife who had died two years before and whom he had loved above all else. Now how could I help him? What should I tell him? Well, I refrained from telling him anything but instead confronted him with the question, "What would have happened, Doctor, if you had died first and your wife would have had to survive you?" "Oh," he said, "for her this would have been terrible; how she would have suffered!" Whereupon I replied, "You see, Doctor, such a suffering has been spared her, and it was you who have spared her, and it was you who have spared her this suffering; but now, you have to pay for it by surviving and mourning her." He said no word but shook my hand and calmly left my office. Suffering ceases to be suffering in some way at the moment it finds a meaning, such as the meaning of a sacrifice.—Viktor E. Frankl

SEEING SALVATION.   He who wants a salvation which is *only* visible cannot see the divine child in the Manger as he cannot see the divinity of the Man on the Cross and the paradoxical way of all divine acting. Salvation is a child, and when it grows up it is crucified. Only he who can see power under weakness, the whole under the fragment, victory under defeat, glory under suffering, innocence under guilt, sanctity under sin, life under death can say: Mine eyes have seen thy salvation.—Paul Tillich

Sermon Suggestions

A SECOND CHANCE.   TEXT: Jon. 3:1–5, 10. (1) For Jonah. (2) For Ninevah.

FOR A TIME OF CRISIS.   TEXT: 1 Cor. 7:29–31. (1) Be realistic about the values of this world and the next, verse 31b. (2) Be prepared to make extraordinary sacrifices in view of unusual circumstances.

Worship Aids

CALL TO WORSHIP. "The heavens declare the glory of God; and the firmament showeth his handiwork" (Ps. 19:1).

INVOCATION. Eternal God, who art the hope of the ends of the earth, we worship thee. Thou art very great. The heaven of heavens cannot contain thee, much less these temples which our hand have builded. As high as the heaven is above the earth, so are thy thoughts higher than our thoughts and thy ways than our ways. May we not belittle thee by our worship, but do thou enlarge us.—Harry Emerson Fosdick

OFFERTORY SENTENCE. "But Peter said, 'Silver and gold have I none; but what I have that give I thee' " (Acts 3:6).

OFFERTORY PRAYER. We have enjoyed your good gifts to us, Father. We have wanted to use them for your glory. We remember the words of the Lord Jesus, "It is better to give than to receive." In that faith we come giving to you, knowing that you will always be giving to us. Help us to enjoy giving, for Jesus' sake.

PRAYER. Great is thy name, O God, and greatly to be praised. In thee all our discordant notes rise into perfect harmony. It is good for us to think of the wonder of thy being. Thou art most silent, yet most strong; unchangeable, yet ever changing; ever working, yet ever at rest, supporting, nourishing, maturing all things. O thou Eternal Spirit, who hast set our noisy years in the heart of thy eternity, lift us above the power and evils of the passing time, that under the shadow of thy wings we may take courage and be glad. So great art thou, beyond our utmost imagining, that we could not speak to thee didst thou not first draw near to us and say, "Seek ye my face." Unto thee our hearts would make reply, "Thy face, Lord, will we seek." And when we look up to thee, the words of our lips are words of humility and thanksgiving. Who or what are we that thou shouldst follow us with goodness and mercy all the days of life? We thank thee for our birth into a Chris-

tian community, for the church and the sacraments of thy grace, for the healing day of rest, when we enter with thy people into thy house and there make holyday; for the refreshment of soul, the joys of communion, the spiritual discipline, the inspiration of prayer and hymn and sermon. We thank thee for thy watchful care over body and soul alike. Thou hast kept our eyes from tears, or, if the tears came, thine own hand wiped them away. Thou hast kept our feet from falling, or if we fell, thou didst not forsake us but guided us back to the holy paths of Christ. We praise thee for the myriad influences of good, conscious and unconscious, that have been about us, deeply penetrating our inner life, shaping and fitting us for thy kingdom. Thou hast indeed forgiven all our iniquities and healed all our diseases and redeemed our life from destruction and crowned us with loving-kindness. Therefore would we call upon our souls and all that is within us to bless thy holy name.—Samuel McComb

LECTIONARY MESSAGE

Topic: Jesus' Power to Make Us Become
TEXT: Mark 1:14–20
The great seal of the United States bears the words *Novus Ordo Seclorum* under the pyramid, "a new order of the ages." Seventeen seventy-six marked the beginning of a new experiment in human organization. But the greatest change in the "order of the ages" occurred as Jesus preached the kingdom of God.

I. *Jesus came preaching.*

(a) In every age, the power of God is seen best and has the best effect through the agency of preaching. Yes, we must teach. Yes, we must establish doctrinal statements. Yes, we must write and publish. But as Jesus demonstrated, all his work succeeds best through preaching. Nothing else we can do can affect so many people so powerfully for so great a cause as preaching the gospel of God.

(b) The gospel Jesus preached is one of the kingdom of God. At the fullness of time, Jesus came and declared that the time was right for repentance and believing in the gospel. While the idea of a kingdom secularly interpreted might mean conquest, slavery, and subservience, the preaching of Jesus was the "good news." It was the goodness of acceptance, forgiveness, and righteousness not earned but bestowed.

(c) Preaching must have a message or it is empty words, and the message of Jesus began like that of the Baptist—"Repent"—transform your mind in its judgments and its topics. But it went beyond that of John and urged a new element in the concept of religious living—"Believe!" Truly, "the just shall live by faith." The belief we feel must be in the gospel, the good news that life begins afresh in faith.

II. *Jesus walked where men worked and saw into their hearts.*

(a) Jesus went where men were working. Later in this chapter we read that men, women, and children would seek him in great throngs, but he began by seeking people. "For the Son of man is come to seek and to save that which was lost" (Luke 19:10). Today as in Jesus' first days, one of the best places to find people is where they work. Surely places of recreation, of sport, and of eating are all good places to find people. But places where they work are very often places where hearts are open, and business makes men conscious of their places in the world and in the eyes of God. We today can seek them there.

(b) Jesus saw what he was seeking—men ready to accept the challenge of the new and unknown, ready to follow a bringer of truth and faith. Surely, we must keep our eyes open to see the magnificent beauties of God's world or to see the damage that needs to be repaired. But seeing the physical is often to be misled, to accept at face value conditions whose secret sources live much deeper.

III. *Jesus offered his followers a more valuable use for their talents.*

(a) There is no belittling of the skills, the craft, and the labor required for fishing involved in the call Jesus gave to Simon and Andrew. But he needed just such arts, skills, and labor in his work of preaching the gospel. He requires all the intelligence and skill that go into success in the world's endeavors to go out and reach all of their world, to learn his secrets, to become his disciples in order to be his witnesses. So he promised to make them become fishers of men.

(b) Can we look more closely at his ministry, at the work he calls us to do today? We can appropriate the infinite power of Christ for the benefit of all people everywhere, the power to make us all become what we can be. After all, it is Jesus, not the U.S. Army, who can make it possible to "be all you can be." The army or another service or another line of work can be the arena, the agency, the working ground of the becoming, but the capacity comes from the true Son of the Creator to put his plan into effect.

(c) The power to become is ours from him. We need it because we win our own first or we win nothing. The winning must start with us but must not stop there. Becoming is the real work of life. Growth, development, learning must be a mark of all life. He can make us do it. His very words *repent* and *believe* are the keys to unlock our self-confining cages of fear and worry, our debiliating habits of greed and materialism and—sin. He awakens our minds as our souls respond to him in faith. He removes the doubt that holds us back. He enrolls us in his class for the highest learning. He showed his perspicacity in not saying, "I will make you fishers of men." There would be no need for us if he did that. Of course, he who could have made stones into bread could "make" us anything he wanted. How glorious it was—how glorious it is—that he said to them and says to us, "I will make you become fishers of men." The strength of his power can still change our negatives into positives, our denials into great and world-conquering affirmatives.—John R. Rodman

SUNDAY: FEBRUARY THIRD

SERVICE OF WORSHIP

Sermon: From Wonder to Wrath
TEXTS: Luke 4:22–28; 1 Cor. 13:13
I. From wonder to wrath! That's the way
the mood changed on the day Jesus made
his first public appearance in his hometown. In a word: they thought he was wonderful! But then he told them that God
was working out a plan of salvation among
the Gentiles. Suddenly, all their wonder
turned to wrath! But that's how things are
with human relationships, isn't it?

(a) For instance. Consider many marriages. The first buds of romance are nurtured by the warmth of infatuation and
idolization. For a time it seems that only
these two are in existence.

Then it happens. That slow, creeping
monster we call "reality" comes crawling
into this fragile world-of-wonder. Things
begin to change, slowly, almost impercep-
tibly. The cold waters of fact quench the
fires of fantasy. It somehow seems easier
to be unkind, even ugly at times. Many
marriages go from wonder to wrath.

(b) Consider friendships. Friendship,
too, can experience the emotional swing
from wonder to wrath. Regardless of the
duration or the age, friendship is, at first,
filled with wonder. But even this wonderland of emotional bonding isn't without its
moments of wrath.

A trust is violated, a secret revealed, and
the fragile fabric of a lasting friendship
begins to unravel. The unleashing of pent-
up resentments and failed expectations
make a once flourishing friendship a fool's
paradise! Friendship, too, can swing from
wonder to wrath.

(c) And let's not forget the church! After
all, she is composed, primarily, of humans.
Like other human relationships, the one
between pastor and people sometimes
slips, haltingly, from wonder to wrath.
People come to her for all the wrong
reasons and leave her for the same. We
expect her to right our wrongs, to heal our
bad habits, to alter the consequences of
our own carelessness. We see her as the
spiritual ideal, the rock of security, the fortress of moral stability in a world of eth-
ically shifting sand. Wonder! Then she
disappoints us; she falls short of her high
calling; she fails to meet our expectations;
and we become disillusioned and discouraged. We question her depth of spiritual commitment. We criticize her
apparent collapse. We furiously denounce
her folly, failures, and seemingly ineffectual efforts at ministry! Wrath! The way of
human relationships becomes the way of
the church. From wonder to wrath.

II. And so we return to Jesus in
Nazareth, the opening day of his public
career, surrounded by those who knew
him as neighbor and friend. At first there
was wonder, and then there was wrath.
Yet, why be surprised?

(a) A young peasant woman named
Mary and a young carpenter named
Joseph receive wondrous dreams and angelic visitations. The Son of God in human
flesh. Angelic choirs fill the night sky with
the wondrous melody of promise and
praise. Lowly shepherds, locked in wondrous adoration, become the first witnesses to God's salvation. And foreign
dignitaries bear wondrous gifts to a small
child, who would be king. Each year, we
pause in silent wonder to contemplate this
event.

And yet, we know the rest of the story.
The manger is in the shadow of a cross.
The cry of a new infant life has become the
anguished lament of a crucified man. The
chorus of joy has given way to the clamor
of grief and sorrow. The witnesses to wonder have become the champions of cruelty. The very life of Jesus seems to have
flowed steadily from wonder to wrath.
And the scene in the Nazareth synagogue
is, in part, symbolic of his life. But that's
not all this story symbolizes!

(b) For the people of the small village
were not unlike the rest of this holy nation.
They'd lost a genuine sense of wonder and
a proper perspective on the place of wrath.
They were too quickly impressed and too
quickly discouraged. What they wanted
was a quick fix to the perennial problem of
human sin. Perhaps they perceived the

wrath of God as a weapon of revenge and not the wisdom of redemption. So, when Jesus challenged their pious perspectives, their shallow wonder became a sea of wrath. And why?

(c) I suppose because they were human. And like a marriage gone sour or a friendship that's spoiled, their relationship with God had become too familiar. No more surprises and even less mystery! God would act in predictable ways, through rites and rituals. Wonder was superficial and wrath deep-seated. They had forgotten the mysterious, unpredictable, and bewildering character of their God. They had become too familiar with God. And whenever humans become familiar with anything, we'll soon see movement from wonder to wrath!

III. Therein we face our greatest enemy to genuine wonder and proper praise. That enemy is familiarity! In marriage, in friendship, and before God, this common enemy threatens to rob us of a genuine joyful wonder.

(a) But it's, perhaps, in our relationship with God that familiarity becomes our greatest enemy! In our familiarity with songs and prayers and the pastor's ways, we look but rarely see; we listen but rarely hear. What wonder resides within these four walls we'll never know, as long as we're too familiar. Familiarity diminishes wonder and enlarges wrath. That's how it is with humans. But not with God!

(b) With God all is reversed, turned upside down and inside out. God is familiar with us, because God has lived and breathed and walked and talked in our flesh. God has seen with our eyes, heard with our ears, and spoken with our lips. God has felt the lift of acceptance and the drag of rejection. And God has seen and been touched by the very best and very worst of human nature. But never has God ceased to treat this human nature with anything but wonder! In fact, God has moved us from wrath to wonder in Christ our Lord. From the wrath of judgment to the wonder of redemption. From the wrath of despair to the wonder of hope. From the wrath of shame to the wonder of sainthood. From the wrath of death to the wonder of life!

IV. Perhaps we can free our marriages, friendships, and churchly relationships from the deadening process of moving from wonder to wrath. Maybe we can be freed from the bondage of familiarity. How?

(a) Well, I suppose through the wonder of love. Not just any love, mind you. But the love of God in Christ Jesus our Lord. A love that bears things others think unbearable, believes things others find questionable, hopes when others have yielded to despair, and endures when others have fallen away. Such love turns fear to faith and wrath to wonder.

(b) Don't you see? That's what sets us apart in this world where it's acceptable, even expected, that relationships move from wonder to wrath. We're called, commissioned, and inspired to turn things around, to set the world on its ear, to embody a new world order: an order established on the foundation of a divine love, moving the world from wrath to wonder each day.—Albert J. D. Walsh

Illustrations

LOVING OUR NEIGHBOR. In one of the newer apartment houses which are so flimsy that everything can be heard, there is a row going on because one of the tenants always has his radio on at top volume. In the apartment house there lived an old, wise, very philanthropically minded man who talked to one of the more exasperated tenants in the attempt to calm him down. After a long discussion, he told him as a last resort how to get along with radio-neighbors in such a situation: "Yes, you really have to love people in order to put up with them." "You mean to say," said the other, "that I should love a fellow who turns on jazz music at full volume every night at twelve o'clock?" Whereupon the old man replied, "Well, it's no trick at all to love someone who has no radio."— Helmut Thielicke

RECOGNIZING A CHRISTIAN. Not every suffering is that cross which the disciples must bear, of which he says, "Take it upon yourselves," but only the sufferings by which it becomes recognizable that we are disciples—persecution on account of our faith, mockery, estrangement from earlier friends, branding as a hypocrite and sneak. Just as one recognizes a peasant by his rough hands and his sunburned face, so one should recognize us Christians by the fact that we suffer for our Lord Christ.—Emil Brunner

Sermon Suggestions

GOD CONTINUES TO SPEAK.   TEXT: Deut. 18:15–20. (1) Through his prophets. (2) Requiring a positive response.

WHEN LOVE IS LACKING.   TEXT: 1 Cor. 8:1–13. (1) We may permit our "superior" knowledge to make us arrogant and contemptuous. (2) We may lead our "weaker" brothers and sisters to act against conscience. (3) We may withal "sin against Christ."

Worship Aids

CALL TO WORSHIP.   "The law of the Lord is perfect, restoring the soul: The testimony of the Lord is sure, making wise the simple" (Ps. 19:7).

INVOCATION.   Gracious Lord, reveal as we listen, stir as we respond, seal as we pray, lead on as we follow, through Christ, our Lord.—E. Lee Phillips

OFFERTORY SENTENCE.   "Heal the sick, raise the dead, cleanse the lepers, cast out demons: freely ye received, freely give" (Matt. 10:8).

OFFERTORY PRAYER.   Let us be the means by which you build your reign on earth, O God. Lead us that all the things for which your love hopes and dreams might come true through our service to the way of Jesus.—J. Scott Hickman

PRAYER.   Eternal Spirit, from whom our spirits come and in whom is all our peace and power, we humbly worship thee. We believe in thee with our minds; make thyself real to us in our hearts and consciences. Grant us an hour of spiritual hospitality to the Highest, and send us forth refreshed, purified, and empowered.

Grant us the grace of gratitude. Have mercy upon any here who find it difficult to be thankful. For some of us have lately been bereaved and our hearts are heavy and depressed. And some are in ill circumstance, anxious about the morrow and knowing not what will befall us there. And some are sunk in shame over iniquity, committed or planned, and are wondering why this should be a world where evil is so easy and righteousness so hard. And some of us are burdened, not for ourselves, but for others whom we love better than ourselves. How can we be thankful?

Grant that in this hour of worship we may rediscover the faith that overcomes the world, may recall the endless benedictions by which our lives have been enriched, until thanksgiving rises warmly within us. Quicken our memories concerning the homes that nourished us, the friends that have sustained us, the books that have inspired us. Refresh our recollections concerning the blessings of our civilization, bought and paid for by other toils and other tears than ours. Lead us, supremely, to the Christ through whom thou hast so radiantly shined upon us, and at the foot of his Cross we will be grateful.

Give us tranquility. Beneath the too great stress of this busy world, grant us serenity and steadfastness, that we may be like him who built his house on rock and not on sand. Give us stability, that with calmer eyes we may look on the restlessness and vicissitudes of life and possess our souls in peace.

Give us vision, Lord. Thou hast not made this earth that the children of evil should triumph here forever. Thou hast made it that thy will should be done here as in heaven. In days of industrial greed, racial strife, and threatened war, grant us insight to see that better days may come. Let us not supinely think that violence shall curse the sons of men forever or the poor forever lose their opportunity in the degrading depths of the city's slums. Give us vision.

Give us courage, Lord, courage to be honest, unafraid, straightforward, truthful. Build in us the basic virtues without which it matters nothing that we erect graceful superstructures of aspiring piety. Let there be no crooked way in us, no guile upon our tongues. Make integrity of life and character our portion now and evermore.

For all sorts and conditions of men we pray. Wherever in hospitals or in homes of sickness disease has stricken down our friends or those whose names are quite unknown to us, there let our hearts be. Wherever on the far frontiers of the world missionaries preach the Gospel or in sincerity and truth the ministers at home proclaim thy word of righteousness, there let our hearts be. Wherever lovers of children guide their early steps or servants of the aged make more peaceable the last roadway toward the sunset, there let our hearts be. Wherever soldiers of the common good fight stalwart battles for a fairer day of decency and good will on earth, for them our petitions rise.

This is our supplication before thee: that Christ, with his steadfastness, his courage, his faith, his sympathy, his victorious power, should dwell in us. Grant it, we beseech thee, for his name's sake.—Harry Emerson Fosdick

LECTIONARY MESSAGE

Topic: Jesus' Teaching and Healing Authority
TEXT: Mark 1:21–28

I. *The teaching as a prelude to healing.*

(a) The time of Jesus' teaching was the time of regular gathering of those to be taught. Jesus was ready to begin his public ministry, and the occasion presented itself at the first time when there would be a group gathered together. Mark uses his favorite expression, "straightway," to indicate Jesus' sense of urgency in reaching many people with God's kingdom message.

(b) The place of his teaching was the place of regular meeting of the ones he later said were his first responsibility, "For therefore came I forth" (v. 38). He was in the place where he as a Jew should have been in order that his teaching begun there should spread throughout the whole land. He had to have a starting point. What better place than the gathering place of those who needed his message? Per-

haps it was not ideal, but he used it for good.

(c) The message he taught is not described fully by Mark, its content is not related; but we are told of its impact. We have "teachings" of Jesus elsewhere to help us think clearly about life and its exigencies and opportunities. Here we have the great impact, the impressive response to his deep insight, his explanatory powers, his interpretative wisdom, all much more effective than the rote of those trained in the Law. Here we see the convincing divinity of, not just a holy man, but the Holy One of God.

II. *The healing outcome of Jesus' teaching.* In *The Miracle-Stories of the Gospels,* Alan Richardson says, "The relation between the teaching of the Lord and his authority over the demons is strongly displayed in this passage" (p. 70).

(a) The whole world at the time of Jesus was filled with the fear of evil demons inhabiting the physical world and controlling the realms of health, government, and economics. The Jews had practiced exorcism throughout their history (Acts 19:14), and to the new power of Jesus to control demons and cast out the fear of them from human lives, Christianity owes much of its success.

(b) During the Middle Ages the power of Christ was very important in a world still suffering from the fear of demonic activity. Insanity was considered a disabling possession by demons. Failed crops or ailing livestock were through the work of the spirits of evil. The cathedrals were designed and decorated with acknowledgment of demonic forms and power, asserting that the principal power of faith was the chaining up and the banishment of the demons. The doors of Notre Dame in Paris, for example, show the saints above ground as victorious over the multitude of evil spirits and devils entombed beneath the earth's surface.

(c) In the encounter in the synagogue at Capernaum, Jesus established the superiority over evil spirits that caused his fame to spread through the whole country immediately, as such a power has been felt in human lives ever since, immediately transforming them into messengers of the king.

As Richardson notes, "Freedom from the evil influences at work in the human personality remains as an essential offer of the Gospel."

The words of our twenty-seventh verse forcefully state the impact of his new strength among them. "What *is* this? What a *new teaching!* With authority he commands even the impure spirits, and they obey him."

The whole congregation in the synagogue immediately saw the connection between Jesus' authoritative teaching ("as one that had authority . . ," v. 22) and his authoritative exorcism of the demon. Our concept of demons today is not so all-inclusive or so active, but we cannot say that unnamed fears of all kinds do not possess us.

III. *The essential relation of a person to Christ.*

(a) One very important element in Jesus' power must not be overlooked. That is the confession, on the part of the recipient, of the identity of Jesus as the Son of God. This act of healing and exorcism could not have been performed, even by Jesus, had the man in whom the spirit dwelt not admitted, "I know you—I know who you are—the Holy One of God." This "confession of faith" is the *sine qua non* of Christian wholeness. It is the essence of victory in the conflict between God and evil in a person, between one's sin and one's salvation from it, that one know who his healer is. And victory is based on previous acknowledgment that in any such contest God will be victorious. Mark employs the congruence of teaching with exorcism to demonstrate the true source of victory over all evil, the evil of ignorance and misunderstanding as well as the evil of demon possession. That is, our confession of enlightened faith. This confession of the holiness of Jesus is in direct contrast to the uncleanness of the spirit itself.

(b) The incident here depicted as involving both teaching and healing in the same synagogue on the same day emphasizes the unity of the nature of man—mind and body, understanding and health operating together. This is the true form of the ideal of ancient Roman education, *"Mens sana in corpore sano,"* and only in Christ can a truly sound mind control a truly sound body. We can no longer let the question that all evildoers ask of Jesus, "What have you to do with us?" go unanswered. We must "have to do" with evil in vigorous and conquering acts of love.—John R. Rodman

SUNDAY: FEBRUARY TENTH

SERVICE OF WORSHIP

Sermon: Holy Humor

TEXT: John 16:33

I. Have you ever been in New Orleans for the Mardi Gras? Every spring, during the days before Ash Wednesday in the calendar of the Christian year, Mardi Gras carnivals are held, New Orleans being a popular festival location here in the United States.

The tradition is a venerable one, taking its name from two French words meaning "fat Tuesday." In medieval France on the day before Lent began, a fat ox was paraded through the town square as a symbol of fullness before the season of restraint arrived. Lent, the forty weekdays prior to Easter, signified austerity, penitence, and humility. But before accepting these disciplines, Christians indulged themselves in a time of carnival and merrymaking. They celebrated "fat Tuesday," or Mardi Gras, and then on the next day, Ash Wednesday, became serious about their souls, confessing sins and seeking forgiveness.

Mardi Gras introduced a note of celebration into an otherwise grim world when first it began, copying (as it did) an ancient Roman custom of merrymaking before a period of fasting. It provided release for pent-up emotions of the winter season and heralded the eventual arrival of spring. That it became a degenerative time, with rowdiness and drunkenness characteristic, was not the real intention. Mardi Gras was meant to be a time of joy, anticipating in Christian minds the even greater joy of Easter.

Not nearly as familiar to us as Mardi Gras is a second and complementary season that historically followed Easter. From the Monday after Easter, as Protestants and Catholics date it, to the Monday after the Eastern Orthodox observance of Easter, Christians in some places have celebrated "Holy Humor Season." Holy Humor Season also has its day of merrymaking, which is the Monday after each Easter Sunday. Traditionally, in both Western and Eastern Christianity, this was know as a "Day of Joy and Laughter." It became an occasion to celebrate the enormous practical joke that God had played on Satan by raising Jesus from the dead.

There is nothing biblical, nothing particularly theological, about that—except the genuine, joyous response of sensitive souls to the realization that God and love and goodness are greater than evil, sin, and death. Isn't it worth shouting about, isn't this something to turn our frowns into smiles, our tears to laughter? Holy Humor Season included singing, dancing, wholesome pranks, jokes, festivals, and picnics wherever it was observed. It was a way of saying that the stone truly was rolled away from Jesus' tomb—that the stones that entrap our lives also can be rolled away. Sometimes that day after Easter was known as "Bright Monday" or "White Monday," as we can understand why. Maybe the Resurrection was not exactly a joke that God played on Satan, but it clearly remains an act capable of evoking human laughter, song, and hope. The Resurrection brings light to our dark skies.

II. It makes an interesting conjunction of words: holy and humor. But why not? At its most meaningful level, humor may well have a sanctity about it, a holiness that is of powerful effect. Our capacity to see beyond the superficial, our ability to laugh at ourselves, our compliments to one another when we say he or she has a rich sense of humor—all may touch something basic and vital to our existence. We may be getting at one of those traits that identify the very image of God in us. I wonder!

It was Chesterton who speculated, "There was some one thing that was too great for God to show us when He walked upon our earth; and I have sometimes fancied that it was His mirth." Ascribing mirth to God, or humor, often gives needed perspective to a situation. From a mortal standpoint, God must possess humor in abundance, and the perspective it brings, in order to tolerate this world as it is and us as we are. Holy humor may be God's saving grace, even as humor often is a helping force for us. A time or a season set aside to think about these things still is a good idea.

There was a song on the lips of the Israelites in an ancient day when they finally were released from captivity in Babylonia and permitted to regain their Promised Land. For many of these returned exiles, their experience portended the coming of the messianic age, or the day of divine deliverance. In their song they said it was like a dream, when God brought Zion's captives home. When the reality of it came over them, "our mouths filled with laughter" (they said) "and our lips with song." They exulted over the marvels granted them by God and declared "how overjoyed we were!" Those who went sowing in tears (describing what happened at the time of their capture) now "reap with shouts of joy." All of this prepared them, if not for the messianic age, at least for a new and better future. Their earlier defeat was succeeded by a time of hope and happiness.

One can discern in this even a steady progression, going from despair to rejoicing. The Israelites suffered much, only to cherish their ultimate gain even more. They knew in their own way a "Day of Joy and Laughter" akin to what Holy Humor Season is all about. Such laughter is not sounded in silliness or scorn but in ebullience and grateful feeling. It is the overflow of blessing, the outward expression of emotions too deep to describe. It is the smile of the rainbow after the turbulence of the storm. This happiness of Israel's people when their long period of captivity was ended is summarized in the psalm verse that reads, "The Lord has done great things for us; we are glad." The psalmist knew—and teaches us—what others of a much later time taught to their people. I refer to the ruins of old Dryburgh Abbey in Scotland, where a Latin inscription still can be read above one of the doors. The words say, "Sweeten Bitter Things with Gentle Laughter."

III. Gentle laughter, or holy humor, is the way God enables us to change sobs into psalms. Several decades before Norman Cousins wrote his popular book about the healing power of laughter, a scrapbook of photographs showing men and women consumed by mirth was passed among patients at a certain hospital. One individual who had found no reason to smile for weeks because of the severity of his illness, broke free from that melancholy. He smiled broadly while looking at the pictures; many others responded the same. In one hospital room after another, doctors testified that this laugh-cure, when it really occurred, produced marked improvement. Subsequently, Norman Cousins and others have experimented and affirmed that laughter is real medicine. "It has optimistic vitamins in it," someone has said; "it revives like oxygen." Laughter may not come instantly or easily but clearly is worth cultivating.

Garrison Keillor, popular on radio as the homespun philosopher of Lake Woebegon, said it this way, "Humor is not a trick or a joke put into word. It's a presence in the world, like grace, and it's there for everyone." Humor is like grace—a serendipitous extra, a special gift for life that is available to all. And to us as Christians this insight from Kenneth Wilson, retired editor of *Christian Herald* magazine, is important. He said, "A sense of humor in religion is terribly important for the cleansing it does to one's self, but also because humor is closely related to confidence. We can't joke about things of which we are not confident, and too many people have no sense of humor about their faith. That shows a lack of confidence. I think it is important to have fun in my faith." In that vein, it was Halford Luccock who said,

"Humor is a moral banana skin dedicated to the discomfiture of all who take themselves too seriously."

A Holy Humor Season is not such an odd commemoration after all. A Mardi Gras festival that anticipates the joy of Easter deliverance need not be foolishness but a testimony of faith. A triumphant psalm articulated from the depths of crisis and sorrow may well inspire hope in others pasing through their dark vale. What I am saying is that one of God's blessings, and a vitally important one, is the ability given us to smile and laugh and to see beyond present bleakness and despair. Take this rich blessing on the authority of Christ himself. To his disciples and to us Jesus said, "In the world you have tribulation; but be of good cheer, I have overcome the world."—John H. Townsend

Illustrations

RIDICULOUS AND SUBLIME. A clown may be the first in the kingdom of heaven, if he has helped lessen the sadness of human life.—Rabbi Baroka

HEALING LAUGHTER. Many doctors are now preaching the truth of Prov. 17:22: "A merry heart doeth good like a medicine: but a broken spirit drieth the bones." They cite case after case of patients who have overcome physical ailments by learning to laugh. One doctor recently found that all of his healthy elderly patients had one thing in common—a good sense of humor.

Young medical students are being taught that helping patients to relax and laugh may do more good than some prescriptions. Psychologists are finding that those who are anxious and humorless are much more susceptible to a variety of diseases. Laughter is being dubbed "internal jogging" and "instant intellect" by many doctors. One renowned professor, recently discussing the therapeutic value of laughter at a seminar on suicide, said, "Assure your patients it's not a sin to laugh. I don't believe we know much about God if we've never heard him laugh."—Tal D. Bonham

Sermon Suggestions

A STUDY IN CONTRASTS. TEXTS: Job 7:1–7; Ps. 147:1–11. (1) The suffering that leads to prayer (Job 7:1–7). (2) The grace that leads to praise (Ps. 147:1–11).

ON MAKING SLAVES OF OURSELVES. TEXT: 1 Cor. 9:16–23, especially verse 19. (1) Our status—freedom. (2) Our constraint—voluntary servitude. (3) Our aim—effective witness.

Worship Aids

CALL TO WORSHIP. "Let the words of my mouth and the meditation of my heart be acceptable in thy sight, O Lord, my rock, and my redeemer" (Ps. 19:14).

INVOCATION. Almighty God, who hast given us grace at this time with one accord to make our common supplication unto thee and hast promised through thy well-beloved Son that when two or three are gathered together in his Name thou wilt be in the midst of them: Fulfill now, O Lord, the desires and petitions of thy servants as may be best for us; granting us, in this world, knowledge of thy truth and, in the world to come, life everlasting.—St. Chrysostom

OFFERTORY SENTENCE. "And my God shall supply every need of yours according to his riches in glory in Christ Jesus" (Phil. 4:19).

OFFERTORY PRAYER. We praise you, loving Lord, for your loving-kindness and for your wonderful works for us. We have worked for this money, and in love we bring it to you. To your glory we give it.

PRAYER. Eternal God, Source of light and life and love . . . we praise you for your gifts to us. You have not left us in darkness but have sent us the light of the world. Nor have you left us in deadness but have given us life. You have loved us in the gift of your Son. You have providentially brought us to this place. We thank you for your goodness to us.

We confess our unworthiness of your grace; we have fallen far short of your purpose; we have insisted on our way and resisted your will; we have selfishly neglected those who need us. Now help us to be good servants of Jesus Christ. Help us to use all of your gifts in your service.

We pray for the weak among us. Direct our strength to ministry. We pray for the discouraged among us. Grant that we may share our hope. We pray for the anxious among us. Help us to be calm as we minister to them. We pray for those who grieve among us. Fill us to overflowing with your love.

Now speak to us today and help us to understand. Show us your way, we pray in the name of Jesus.—J. Estill Jones

LECTIONARY MESSAGE

Topic: Strength for Living
TEXT: Mark 1:29–39

I. *Jesus was busy doing ministry.* It had been one of those days. Not a bad day, just one filled with responsibilities. Jesus spent a good portion of the day preaching and teaching in the synagogue at Capernaum. He healed a person who came to him with an unclean spirit. When Jesus arrived at Simon's house, his mother-in-law was ill. Jesus healed her. Then, no sooner had the sun gone down when a large crowd gathered outside the door. They brought their relatives who were sick and some who were possessed with demons. Jesus surely healed as many as he was able to before it got too late and he became too tired. What a day! But as quickly as his fame was spreading, the next day would be just as busy and demanding as this day.

Don't you hate it when one day ends, and you can't even relax because you know that tomorrow is going to be just as demanding, if not more so, than today? When the alarm clock goes off, we hit the floor running, hoping to get a jump on the day. That's how Jesus must have felt. Surely he was tired. We often fail to comprehend the emotional and spiritual drain on Jesus as more and more people came to him in need of healing and ministry.

II. *Jesus begins the day with prayer.* As the next day dawned, even before his feet hit the floor, Jesus was already thinking of all the demands and responsibilities he would face that day—more teaching, more healing, more ministry. And so he jumped out of bed, hit the floor running, and he "went out to a lonely place, and there he prayed" (v. 35).

What is he doing that for? Now that he's up, he can get a jump on things! Maybe even do a little teaching or healing before breakfast! He's the Son of God. If anyone could get away without daily prayer, he could! That's the point of the text. He couldn't face the day without daily prayer. That time of prayer prepared Jesus for meeting the demands of the day. It helped him understand God's will for his life. It provided him with strength as he communed with God. Considering the kind of ministry Jesus was doing—teaching, healing, giving so much of himself, caring, grieving—it would not have been long before he would have been totally powerless if he didn't begin his day with prayer.

III. *Prayer was a priority for Jesus.* Now, there were no secrets or miracles that Jesus knew in order to develop a discipline of prayer. He knew he could not continue his pace without continued renewal of God's presence and power. Therefore, prayer was a priority for Jesus. It came first before job, family, friends, responsibilities. His procedure was simple. He made time to pray. He did not try to find time to pray. If we pray when we find the time, we'll never pray! There's no time to be found! Jesus didn't find time to pray; he made time for prayer. He was intentional and disciplined in his prayer life. Jesus made time, found a quiet place, and there he prayed. Then he was ready to face the demands of the new day.

When his disciples found him praying, they said, "Everyone is looking for you!" And Jesus answered, "Let us go somewhere else—to the nearby villages—so I can preach there also. That is why I have come" (v. 38). The responsibilities of the day faced Jesus; now he was ready to go. Where will you find your strength for living?—Craig A. Loscalzo

SUNDAY: FEBRUARY SEVENTEENTH

SERVICE OF WORSHIP

Sermon: How Christ Intercedes for Us
TEXTS: Matt. 9:6; Rom. 8:34

How is it, men have asked in all the ages since Calvary, that the sight of the cross should relieve us of our burdens? Truly here is one of the supreme paradoxes of the gospel: that the death of Christ on the cross, the world's darkest sin, should remain the saving secret of forgiveness. The Greeks in their wisdom called it foolishness; the Jews in their legalism stumbled at the sight of the cross. But to men who were being saved, it has been the power of God to forgive sin.

We need to see that sin is a colossal defect deep within the souls of men, a situation incurable by tinkering on a patchwork basis. Among all the troubles, problems, needs that a congregation brings with them to church, one above all others is ever present: the need for forgiveness. Where even two or three are gathered together, there will you find this strange need for forgiveness.

Obviously, people cannot forgive themselves, for while they have sinned against themselves, they have also sinned against others, and it is not in their power to forgive their transgressions against their fellow men. Moreover, in the deepest sense they have sinned against God, and it is from God that ultimate forgiveness must come. Only an act of God could be equal to man's immemorial need.

I. In the cross, as nowhere else, we see first what sin has cost God.

(a) Until we see what sin means to God we can never know the wonder of his forgiving love, because until we see that, we have no way to measure God's love. If we imagine that God could easily discount our sins by simply signing an act of amnesty, it would mean that sin was not very serious, so easily to be dismissed. We know how difficult and painful it is to overcome separation between human hearts. Surely the far more frightful condition of separation from God we cannot expect to bridge in a less costly manner. That is why God could not deal with sin in any other way than to show us the cost that he himself has suffered.

(b) Take a long look at the cross. There you see the cosmic consequences of your sin, as the young man saw the human consequences of his when he looked into his father's heart. For to trace all our sins back through their tortuous intermediate stages is to come at last to Calvary, where we see our sins in their true light. That is what sin does! All the sins we commit against each other reach back to the same effect: the crucifixion of Christ's love. Only as God shows us that, can we ever be forgiven in the innermost closets of our separation from him.

II. Again, in the cross we see not only what sin has cost God, and thus come to know how critical a need we face; we see also the length, the breadth, and the height and depth of his love.

(a) We discover at the cross a love so great that it is willing to stand and take all the shafts of evil we drive into it and love us still. "A mighty rock within a weary land" is the way one poet phrased his faith in God. The most important single necessity that confronts people who inhabit the edges of a great desert is to keep back the drifting sand driven by pitiless winds. Sand moves like waves of the sea. Living on the edge of a desert, you may awaken any morning to find that a foot of sand has buried your garden and crept to the front door sill. Tracing our sins back to their ultimate effect, we do come to Calvary. But there we find Christ taking this enormous evil of the world's sin into himself and turning it to love. He absorbs the world's sin, reveals the love of God, which all of our transgressions cannot weaken.

(b) The Father who sacrifices himself for us is none other than God, our heavenly Father. He is willing to take the consequences of our willfulness and turn to us still with love! Then is the power of sin broken, for it has nowhere else to go. By his love our sin is taken away once and for all. Again, not the consequences; we have to pay for those, for ours is a world of moral cause and effect. But restored in love to God, accepted as his children, the consequences become the divine discipline that we bear with glad hearts as sons of God.

(c) For nearly two thousand years it has been the sight of the cross that has moved men to repentance, that has lifted the burdens of sin from off their shoulders. At the cross men have found "rest by his sorrow, life by his death." When the tenderest of all hearts stands over against the overwhelming sands of our sin and loves us still, it destroys the power of sin.

III. But on the deepest level, Christ intercedes for us by bringing us back into full fellowship with our Father.

(a) What troubles us most is the sense of rejection, being separated from God's love. It is a disturbing thing to see what sin costs God; still more moving to recognize his love in the cross. But unless we are sure that we can come home again fully restored, the whole thing might be of no effect. Here is the miracle of the prodigal son, in the radiance of which the power of sin is canceled. When the prodigal came home in the humble penitence, God threw his arms about him and brought him into the family once more. Not in disgrace, not on probation, no longer to be punished, but loved as though no separation had ever occurred! Acceptance makes the difference, loosing burdens from off our backs, burdens we need carry no longer.

(b) This great miracle of reorientation and reintegration of life Walter M. Horton once observed in what he describes as the most convincing act of forgiveness and release that ever came to his knowledge. It was performed by a nurse. In one of the great hospitals they brought in from the ambulance a young woman who had been stabbed in a drunken brawl. The case being diagnosed as beyond hope, the nurse was asked simply to sit with the girl until the end came. As she sat looking at the girl and thinking what a pity it was that such a face should have been marred by such hard lines, the girl opened her eyes.

"I want you to tell me something and tell me straight," she said. "Do you think

God cares about people like me? Do you think he could forgive anyone as bad as me?"

And the nurse says that she didn't dare to answer at first, not until she had reached out to God for help and reached out toward the poor girl until she felt one with her. Then she said, knowing it was true, "I'm telling you straight; God cares about you and he forgives you." The girl gave a little sigh and slipped back into unconsciousness, the lines of her face changing as death approached. Something tremendous happened between God and that girl in that moment; it happened through the nurse, and, as Horton reminds us, it had something to do with what happened long ago on a certain green hill far away outside a city wall. That is to say, it was through the forgiving love of Christ that peace came to that dying girl. She was brought back into the warmth and the wonder of God's love. No other gift of the gospel ever does more than that.—Robert E. Luccock

Illustrations

WHAT SIN DOES. Sin causes us to stumble. The Book of Hebrews says that it "clings so closely" (12:1). The picture is that of a Greek athlete trying to run a race in his street clothes. It would be difficult enough to undertake to do that today, but it was worse then because street clothes were more encumbering. A Greek or Roman gentleman ordinarily wore a tunic and a pallium. A tunic was a gown with a belt around it, and a pallium was a rectangular piece of cloth, five feet by twelve feet in size. The latter was folded and put over the left shoulder and around and up and over again. Encumber yourself with all of that and then endeavor to run a race! Just when you are going to sprint for the goal, you stumble and fall flat. When you are trying to make the finish, these garments cling around you until you cannot run the race triumphantly. And that, says Hebrews, is what sin is. It clings so closely that you cannot run and win the race of life.—Jack Finegan

POWER AVAILABLE. I once knew an unlettered man whose great wisdom more than compensated for his limited knowledge. One morning at the end of a service in his little church, he led the closing prayer. "Father," he said, "we don't ask for your blessings. Just help us to walk where your blessings are." What rare insight! There is little reason to pray for the sun to shine on us if we insist on living in the cellar. God's help is always given to us, but we must be willing to receive it.—Ernest A. Fitzgerald

Sermon Suggestions

THE BOW AND THE CROSS. TEXT: Gen. 9:8–17. (1) The bow in the ancient world was a sign of God's anger, by which he hurled his arrows of lightning and brought storm and flood; however, this same bow became a sign of God's promise and love (see Heb. 3:9–11). (2) The cross in the time of Jesus was a sign of human wrath and punishment; however, this same cross became a sign of God's love and his means of salvation for humankind (see 1 Pet. 3:18–22).

ON THE ONE HAND, ON THE OTHER HAND. TEXT: 1 Pet. 3:18–22. (1) The righteous One died for the unrighteous. (2) He was put to death in the flesh but made alive in the Spirit. (3) The water of the great flood in Noah's day brought destruction; the water of baptism in our day signifies salvation.

Worship Aids

CALL TO WORSHIP. "All the ends of the earth shall remember and turn unto the Lord; and all the kindreds of the nations shall worship before thee" (Ps. 22:27).

INVOCATION. Almighty and everlasting God, each of us has come here today with his or her own expectations of what will take place. Help us to forget what we expect to happen and concern ourselves only with what you expect. Surely you expect us to listen, and then you will speak. For all our sakes, Lord, speak to us so clearly and directly that we cannot deny that it is you who speaks.—James M. King

OFFERTORY SENTENCE. "[In the churches of Macedonia] in much proof of a great trial of affliction the abundance of their joy and their deep poverty abounded unto the riches of their liberality" (2 Cor. 8:2).

OFFERTORY PRAYER. Almighty God, who hath taught us, "to whom much is given much is required," grant that we will be generous with all that is ours, always remembering the poor in possessions and the poor in spirit. Let giving be our habit and sharing our joy because we would be like our Savior, who gave his life a ransom for all, rich or poor.—E. Lee Phillips

PRAYER. O you who are the meaning and mystery of all that is, was, and is to be, how can we appear before you except in awe and wonderment. In this place surrounded by the symbols of the faith, conscious of your eternal presence in the Word, heartened through Christian fellowship, we discover *ourselves* lost in wonder, love, and praise.

With what *love* you keep loving us! Even when we stray to the far country of our own willfulness, your love finds us there and calls us back home—to that life and purpose that you have ordained from our beginnings. In our every estrangement, you are there, tempting us to reconciliation. In our loneliness, we discover that we are not alone, but you are with us in the strength of the everlasting arms even as you have promised, "I will not leave you or forsake you." In our brokenness, we discover the shattered pieces in disarray strangely taking on a symmetry perfected by the *pattern* of your love. Into our winter of discontent, you breathe the new life of perennial springtime. And in our sorrows, we do find ourselves strangely surprised by joy.

O Eternal Word, keep tempting us in Christ to be and become—keep the pressure of your Spirit upon us that we may be fashioned to that eternal glory ordained from the beginning. Your call is to love you with all our heart, body, *and mind,* but

often we are so lazy intellectually, especially it seems when it comes to life and death matters, and we let others do our thinking for us even though you have warned of the fate of "the blind leading the blind."

Here we have been reminded that your thoughts are not our thoughts, for as the heavens are high above the earth, so are your thoughts higher than our thoughts. We have been challenged to think your thoughts after you as you make them known to us in Christ. How many of the hurts of this world are because we and our leaders are not thinking your thoughts! In these moments we have not only been awakened to the vision of the new heavens and the new earth but to the grace of our Lord Jesus Christ by which dreams take on the form and the substance of the real. May we not be disobedient to this heavenly vision but be the new that you are willing for our day in all the communities of which we are a part—the family, the household of faith, the civil communities, the human family.

O you who judge men and nations to save them from self-destruction, keep us from a party allegiance that would blind us to the honest, the just, the highest—deliver us from an idolatrous nationalism that would render unto Caesar what belongs to you—keep us from prejudices that blind us to our own insecurities—give us the discernment to let go of traditions that are no longer timely. With such liberation may we discover the freedom with which Christ is making us free to be your sons and daughters, brothers and sisters to one another and to all others, and is teaching us in this time and place to pray and live.—John M. Thompson

LECTIONARY MESSAGE

Topic: Preparation for Ministry
TEXT: Mark 1:9–15

Mark's Gospel quickly thrusts us into the historical context into which Jesus came. The writer does not begin with a birth narrative or genealogy but chronicles the ministry of the one known as the forerunner of the Messiah.

The first eight verses of the Gospel prepare us for Jesus' appearance; he is the one to follow John the Baptist, one who will "baptize with the Holy Spirit." In the following seven verses, three foundational events prepare Jesus for his unique vocation: baptism, the temptations, and the crisis of John's imprisonment.

I. Mark's account of the baptism of Jesus is terse; he comes from Nazareth to the Jordan where John is baptizing and submits to his baptism, which was previously described as a "baptism of repentance for the forgiveness of sins." Why, then, was Jesus baptized?

Preachers have long struggled with this text. Was Jesus in need of forgiveness like the others who gathered at the banks of the Jordan? The church has always testified that he was like us in every way, except for sin. Did he do this chiefly to identify with sinners, as an act of humility? Or, perhaps, this is a profound spiritual experience for the beloved Son, one that will inaugurate his ministry. Apparently it is a pivotal event in Jesus' life; all four Gospels record this occasion, with their own distinctive accents, of course.

II. Immediately, the Spirit drives Jesus into the wilderness to allow a time of testing and clarification as to the character of the messianic role he will play. Mark does not offer the fuller account of these temptations that is found in Matthew; he simply notes that Jesus is tried by the adversary and comforted by the messengers of God. Preparing for ministry involves perseverance through trials that will test motivation and fortitude.

III. Jesus' proclamation of the kingdom of God does not begin until John is silenced. The juxtaposition of these two events serves to clarify the relationship between John the Baptist and Jesus; John is concerned to "prepare the way of the Lord," while Jesus inaugurates the preaching of the gospel. Hence, their messages are different, although repentance is a focal theme for both.

One can minister only out of one's own experience of being claimed and formed by God for service to others. Our theology is inevitably autobiographical, and our messages will reflect God's gracious and personal investment in preparing us for ministry. We can be grateful for the distinctive role of these two servants of God; the early church was dependent upon both of them for its survival. You and I are called today to prepare the way for the Lord in proclamation and deed.—Molly Marshall-Green

SUNDAY: FEBRUARY TWENTY-FOURTH

SERVICE OF WORSHIP

Sermon: How to Handle Failure
Text: Luke 5:1–11

The most surprising fact about the great men of the Bible is that they were also men who knew the bitterest failures.

Luke 5:1–11 finds the Apostle Peter and his partners at a point of failure.

Jesus seemed determined to test his reluctant disciple by a direct command. As a disobedient disciple, Peter now stood at a crisis point in his personal relationship with Jesus. Jesus needed reliable, dependable, obedient disciples, and he wanted Peter to be among them. So he gave the command to Peter to get out into the channel where the deep waters were and to cast his nets for a catch of fish. To Peter's eternal credit, his answer, while expressing amazement at such a command in view of the previous all-night effort the fishermen had expended and yet caught nothing, was nevertheless a response of immediate obedience. "Nevertheless at thy word I will let down the net" (v. 5).

A vital connection exists between Jesus' command, the miracle which followed, and Peter's inner life. The whole story concerns Peter's need to be willing to do what the Lord wanted him to do.

I. *He was willing to change.*

(a) Jesus challenged the regular, accepted, normal, and traditional ways of fishing by his request. He asked for a fresh and unusual method of operation. One usually fished in the deep channel waters by night and at the sandbank by day. Dusk and dawn were the right times to fish, when the fish were running and feeding. But here Jesus said, "Forget the usual time, the usual place, the usual method. You have tried all through the night and caught nothing: now do it my way—a different way. Remember, this way will be in obedience to my command."

(b) Most of us are not usually that willing to change. As individuals, we resist change. We prefer the comfortable and the familiar ways of operation. If someone tells us to change our attitudes, our behaviors, or our life-styles, we normally refuse. Fear of change is quite natural and normal for men. We often are unsure about the new ways and feel apprehensive about our ability to succeed with them. Such feelings of insecurity make powerful incentives to keep us in the cozy, comfortable, satisfying, and traditional ways of doing things.

(c) Sometimes we even say "It's never been done that way before" as an argument against change. Such an attitude, if it reflects the hold that habit may have upon us, can kill a church and crush our personal discipleship.

The obedient disciple must not only be willing to change; but, like Peter, he must be prepared to show his faith in a practical manner.

II. *He was willing to risk.*

(a) All his fishermen friends were watching. A crowd of local residents filled the whole beach. Everyone knew that the fish were not running and that the night before had been fruitless. Yet Peter was bold enough to obey, when he might easily fail and when that failure could cause him vast embarrassment!

(b) Perhaps none of us can truly be obedient disciples unless we are willing to risk something in the process. We shall have successes, but we must also be prepared for some failures. Peter's persistent faith led him through all the failures to ultimate success! From a weak, unstable, impetuous person he became the "Rock-Man" which Jesus promised he would be. He strengthened his brethren, preached great gospel sermons, stood boldly before magistrates and persecutors, and wrote his lit-

tle letters full of great themes such as self-control, patience, godliness, and faith. We might have missed all that from Peter if he had never been willing to risk a little! Those who never risk will never succeed.

(c) We are all fishing too close to the shore! We need to revive a holy boldness in mission, a willingness to change and to risk, to push out into the deep, prepared to fail, if necessary, so that we may ultimately achieve.

III. *He was willing to work with others.*

(a) He went out in the boat with Andrew, and the catch of fish so swamped the boat that they had to call James and John to come over to help them handle the load. Somehow I have the feeling that, up until this point, Peter was pretty much a "loner." His failure in discipleship may well have been because he was trying to go it all alone. You can't be a disciple of Christ—alone! You are born into a family with brothers and sisters. Many of us, however, insist on trying to handle our discipleship on our own, when God's plan is that we should work with others.

(b) God gave us the church so that we could work together. We have a community of fellowship through which the Spirit can integrate all our individual efforts into a thrust filled with God's power. But too often we make the mistake of going into the world to preach the gospel alone. If you go out fishing on your own, the fish are too many for you—they will swamp you and tend to pull you under the pressures and tides of life. God has given us Christian wives, husbands, and friends so that we can work together to handle the fishing business!

(c) So we see that here Peter overcame his unwillingness to change and to risk and also his selfish independence by asking for help so that he could do with a team what he could not do on his own.

IV. *He was willing to repent.*

(a) I am sure that was the hardest thing to do. He fell at Jesus' feet and cried, "Depart from me; for I am a sinful man, O Lord" (Luke 5:8). He saw that his previous unwillingness to change, to risk, and to work with others had not only made him a disobedient disciple but had actually been a subtle way in which the forces of evil had led him into sin.

Peter had not seen himself like that before! He asked the Lord to leave him because he felt he had nothing to offer as a disciple. But Jesus said, "Fear not; from henceforth thou shalt catch men" (v. 10), and "they forsook all, and followed him" (v. 11).

(b) You see, Jesus promised to take care of the fishing if we will take care of the following! Each of the four mentioned here who followed became gospel fishermen. Peter was the public fisherman at Pentecost. Andrew was the private fisherman who brought the lad with his lunch and the Greeks who were seeking Jesus to the Master. James was the martyr in Jerusalem who by his witness won others. John wrote the Gospel of John and other Scripture and pastured the Ephesian church.

(c) Obedient discipleship, successful discipleship, is essentially a matter of the will! That is the question which Jesus poses to you if you are a disobedient disciple. You can only handle previous failure as you respond by saying, "Despite the past, despite the problems, despite the difficulties—nevertheless, at thy word, I will! I will change; I will risk; I will work with others; I will repent; and I will follow you, trusting you to do the work which you will through me."—Craig Skinner

Illustrations

FACING UP TO FAILURE. Some years ago, two students for the Christian ministry were talking over this question of failure. One was utterly miserable, for he had been guilty of certain acts and had adopted an attitude which he felt made him unworthy of the call that had come to him. He was clear in his own mind that he had, like Judas, betrayed his Lord, and he was therefore on the point of throwing it all up, resigning from his college, and going out into the wilderness. The two talked long into the night, and the one was used by God to show the other the path which Peter took long ago. The resignation was never given. For many years that man has been doing splendid work for his Master on the mission field.—John Trevor Davies

A CHALLENGE TO CHANGE. We must never forget that we may also find meaning in life even when confronted with a hopeless situation as its helpless victim, when facing a fate that cannot change. For what then counts and matters is to bear witness to the uniquely human potential at its best, which is to transform a tragedy into a personal triumph, to turn one's predicament into a human achievement. When we are no longer able to change a situation—just think of an incurable disease, say, an inoperable cancer—we are challenged to change ourselves.—Viktor Frankl

Sermon Suggestions

LIVING IN GOD'S PRESENCE. TEXT: Gen. 17:1–10, 15–19, especially verses 1 and 2. (1) *The story:* the narrative of God's covenant with Abraham. (2) *A significant truth:* those who walk obediently before God Almighty can expect amazing results to flow from their obedience. (3) *A contemporary application:* this truth holds for a church or a nation as well as for an individual.

BELIEVING "THE IMPOSSIBLE." TEXT: Rom. 4:16–25, NEB. (1) It is a matter of grace. (2) It is grounded in faith. (3) It is counted to us as righteousness. (4) Its special focus is upon the Resurrection of Jesus.

Worship Aids

CALL TO WORSHIP. "The earth is the Lord's, and the fullness thereof; the world, and they that dwell therein" (Ps. 24:1).

INVOCATION. That thou hast shined into our darkness with a *light* that goes on shining through every dark night of the world, we praise thee, O Father of all light. For the light of this first day of the week that calls us from the routine of our everyday to this appointed time and hallowed place to find our true rest in thee, we are grateful. That in Christ there has dawned into our lives the light of an *eternal* day, we worship and adore thee—Father, Son, and Holy Spirit.—John M. Thompson

OFFERTORY SENTENCE. "Whoso offereth the sacrifice of thanksgiving glorifieth me; and to him that ordereth his way aright will I show the salvation of God" (Ps. 50:23).

OFFERTORY PRAYER. Freely we have received. Freely we give—not out of necessity, for you love a cheerful giver. We are happy to share in this manner in your work. We rejoice in the opportunity to make this offering.

PRAYER. Almighty and Everlasting God, we invoke thy blessing upon all who need thee, and who are groping after thee, if happily they may find thee. Be gracious to those who bear the sins of others, who are vexed by the wrong-doing and selfishness of those near and dear to them, and reveal to them the glory of their fellowship with the sufferings of Christ. Brood in tenderness over the hearts of the anxious, the miserable, the victims of phantasmal fears and morbid imaginings. Redeem from slavery the men and women who have yielded to degrading habits. Put thy Spirit within them, that they may rise up in shame and sorrow and make confession to thee, "So brutish was I, and ignorant: I was as a beast before thee." And then let them have the glad assurance that thou art with them, the secret of all good, the promise and potency of better things. Console with thy large consolation, those who mourn for their loved dead, who count the empty places and long for the sound of a voice that is still. Inspire them with the firm conviction that the dead are safe in thy keeping, nay, that they are not dead, but live unto thee. Give to all sorrowing ones a garland for ashes, the oil of joy for mourning, and the garment of praise for the spirit of heaviness. Remember for good all who are perplexed with the mysteries of existence and who grieve because the world is so sad and unintelligible. Teach them that thy hand is on the helm of affairs, that thou does guide thine own world and canst change every dark cloud into bright sunshine. In this faith let

them rest and by this faith let them live.—Samuel McComb

LECTIONARY MESSAGE

Topic: Listen to Him!
TEXT: Mark 9:1–9

I. It was a monumental occasion for Jesus and the inner circle of disciples. At a crucial time, a moment of Divine affirmation burst upon them and gave new incentive and direction. Who wouldn't have been upset with the word that Jesus would suffer and die in Jerusalem? Such a thing clearly wasn't in the disciples' plan. It seemed all wrong. With such a heavy burden weighing on their hearts, these devoted followers needed a renewed vision of Jesus' task. Here on the mountaintop the vision became a reality, magnificently dressed in shining garments. No longer would there be any need for the disciples to question. The answer was clear: for any who would doubt, Jesus was the Messiah! They needed the reinforcement. The concept of a suffering savior was hard to accept.

We all need such high moments with Christ secure in our memory. The day will come when the dark clouds of doubt or fear will impose themselves upon us. At such moments we are one with the disciples. And then the recollection of the bright face of our Lord and our own mountaintop experiences will be cherished memories—trusted episodes in life to which we can return time and again. Authentic worship is always a shinning hour when in our need we are met face-to-face with the ultimate reality of God in Christ. A life without such moments is impoverished beyond compare.

II. And because it was so grand, who of us can blame Peter for wanting to prolong it? The three most holy men in his religious tradition were there: Moses, the lawgiver; Elijah, the prophetic voice and forerunner of the Messiah; and Jesus, the fulfillment of the Law and the Prophets. "This is good," said Peter. "Let me build three booths as permanent accommodations. We can't let this end." We can understand his feeling. Yet is it not so that any complete satisfaction has within it an inherent danger? If we follow Peter's desire we can become fixed and unmovable, unaware of future potentialities and unable to accomplish our greater tasks. The transfiguration was good. It provided needed clarity. But it was not good to prolong it.

The greater good was identified by the divine voice that spoke out of the cloud. The epiphany was once again proclaimed: "This is my beloved Son; listen to him." It is not that Moses and Elijah were not important. It is clear, though, that Jesus is the divine Son. We are to hear him and to follow his ways. Only he has the words of eternal life. In all of life, from the cradle to the grave, supreme wisdom is found in listening to him.

III. From the mountaintop, we must all move back into the real world. Awaiting the disciples and Jesus was the final rejection and Crucifixion. And yet as they went to meet it, they carried with them the theme that molds Christian faith: "Listen to him! In all things and at all times, listen to him! Proclaim his Word and live it. Love his Word and obey it. His Word is divine. Listen to him!"—Lee R. McGlone

SUNDAY: MARCH THIRD

SERVICE OF WORSHIP

Sermon: Desecrated Consecration
TEXT: Judg. 13:24–25; 16:20

The story of Samson points up this facet of evil in man's life. Evil is misdirected virtue, goodness turned sour upon itself, consecration become desecration, God's gifts misused, selflessness turned selfish. As in the life of Samson, wickedness seems inextricably mingled with holiness. The highest beginnings filled with dedicated idealism end with imprisonment and destruction of the self. At heart, Samson was a good and holy man whose saintliness was the matrix of sinfulness.

Samson was not a sinner, certainly not in his own sight. Touching the carcass of a dead lion, tasting wine upon the lips at a wedding banquet—the world does not, by and large, measure such deeds as wholly evil. Samson was derived from the fact that he was a Nazarite. Samson could not at one and the same time serve God and satisfy his own sensuous passions. Whatever the ordinary man might do, his was a consecrated life. Samson's life set him apart and made him what he was. He tried to be both priest and peasant. The duplicity of his life ultimately destroyed him.

What is true for Samson is true for all. Virtue can sow the seeds of its own destruction. What begins as integrity ends as obduracy. Many examples can be cited.

I. Take, for instance, wealth. By itself wealth is not evil. The Bible does not say that money is evil. St. Paul writes, "The love of money is the root of all evil."

(a) Wealth can be dedicated to high causes. Blessed is the child born into a home able to satisfy his needs, opening magic doors upon a splendid education, world travel, and the peace of mind of financial security. Money can relieve such a person from his own private concerns and set him free to dedicate his life to the service of others.

(b) Yet Jesus with staggering finality warns his disciples that it is easier for a camel to pass through the eye of a needle than for a rich man to enter the kingdom of heaven. The gates of heaven are closed, not by God, but by riches themselves. The temptatious preoccupation with wealth— its dangerous power, its capacity to coerce, its easy fulfillment of so many things, and most of all its fuel to the fires of egotistical unholy pride—these things can destroy the soul.

(c) The rich man has almost insuperable problems to face. His wealth sets him apart from his fellows. Wealth creates an army of lackeys and sycophants deceiving him into thinking he is worthy of their service when it is his money they seek for themselves. The rich man has few friends who are friends for friendship's sake. Only the very rich, the very poor, and the sinner know desolating loneliness.

This is the paradox of riches. Riches must be consecrated again and again before they destroy their owner.

II. Even more sincerely must innate intelligence be consecrated else it will also destroy the thinker. Far more precious than all the wealth in the banks of the world is the gift of a fine sensitive mind which has been trained and disciplined and used to build character.

(a) More of the vast resources of the country ought to be used for the encouragement of education in every section of the community. True democracy presupposes an educated, intelligent population. Only then can each citizen assume responsibility for the affairs of the nation. How far we have fallen short of this ideal may fairly be measured by the fact that television stars are paid as much in one week (for a two-hour show) as many of the teachers of our children earn in a year.

(b) Nevertheless—and this is the warning note of this section—education in and by itself will not necessarily bring peace to the human heart or the world nor necessarily make man a better person nor teach him the illusive art of how to live with his neighbor. Education too often makes rogues more effective rascals and sinners simply cleverer devils. From the vantage point of the twentieth century, we can look back and discern the fallacies of the unbounded optimism that dominated the scientific thinking of the nineteenth century. It was but a matter of time until science would conquer all life's problems. Progress was synonymous with the application of the scientific method to all walks of life. Man at heart was not really evil, only ignorant. Enlargement of the intellectual horizon was all that the dark superstitious world of mythical dogma and outmoded religious beliefs needed.

(c) Today most of the scientists are not quite so sure. From the scientist himself comes the warning that research into the nature of the physical world without a strong sense of moral integrity can lead the world to ultimate annihilation.

Like other gifts, education must be consecrated, must lead to an appreciation of the spiritual values as well as pragmatic facts and figures. Otherwise education too can become the handmaid of vice.

III. The church as an institution and Christianity as a formalized way of life have not been free from the danger of desecration of what is essentially good and holy.

(a) The church is the living spiritual Body of Christ. As the life of cells is dependent upon the health of the whole body, so the members of the church draw their strength from Christ himself. Thus speaks the theologian. Unfortunately, the analogy of the church as the Body of Christ breaks down only too easily. The Living Christ, it seems, cannot raise this body of the church from spiritual death. Again and again, too often the church has shown zeal for the nonessentials of religious faith, forgetting that Christ died for the souls of men.

(b) No one will deny the influence for good in the home and community that affiliation with the church has achieved. However similar may be the homes both of Christians and of non-Christians in the community, in the long view it is from the committed Christian families there stem the leaders and workers in the community projects.

On the other hand, too often church families acquire a familiarity with holy things that is spiritually dangerous. Grace at meals can become a type of token—unreal yet possessed of some miraculous spiritual quality. Sermons and the worship of God's house Sunday by Sunday too often provide a boring interlude for daydreaming and wishful thinking. Unlovely spiritual familiarity breeds censorious pharisaism. Bigotry and spiritual pride quarry slate-edged character.

(c) Perhaps the gift of a church inheritance is no more pathetically and irritatingly demonstrated than among those church people who apparently are certain about the nature of answered prayer and who by their continual use of the terms *guidance* and *God's plan for them* arrogate to themselves a spiritual conceit that is at times infuriating to those who know that the will of God really is the holiest and most mysterious of all God's ways with men.

Many use the authentic gift of prayer and fellowship with God to further their own unredeemed ends, taking a sacred gift and desecrating it to their own petty glory.

IV. Finally, the age in which we live demonstrates eloquently the tragic irony of how all that is noble and good can be used for the basest purposes.

(a) We have lived to see the age of miracles in the application of scientific techniques to almost every walk of life. In the areas of surgery and curative medicine, what were thought of as miraculous cures thirty years ago have become commonplace.

Life, too, has become immeasurably happier today. Reduction of working hours has enabled people to enjoy such leisure with their families and hobbies and interests unknown fifty years ago when the working day was sometimes sixteen hours.

Space and time have been annihilated, as H. G. Wells puts it, making the world a very little place and enabling greater understanding among the nations of one another's problems. Dissemination of knowledge has made the people of the world more aware of the issues involving their future destinies.

(b) Yet by the same token, never have the peoples of the world lived so near to the slumbering volcano of men's burning passions and national antagonism on a global scale. An atomic war will not wipe civilization off the face the earth. Man again shall arise. But the situation was simply pointed up by Albert Einstein himself. "I do not know," he is reported to have said, "what the implements of destruction will be in the Third World War: but for the Fourth they will be slings and stones." A blind Samson of science stands between the pillars of civilization, pleading with God for strength to avenge his enemies. At any moment, the pillars may be pushed to the ground.

V. The Samson of long ago, remembering the folly of his life, came to himself in that rock-hewn Philistine dungeon. In his dark world, he was forsaken by all save the specter of his own uneasy conscience. For

there is no pain quite like the stabbing of remorse and guilt, no darkness so Stygian as the dark midnight of the soul. There was no hope for Samson. He had broken God's holy laws; his punishment was the judgment of a righteous God.

(a) But had Samson really known the true nature of the God of the Bible, he would have realized that the judgment of God is exceeded only by His mercy and loving-kindness. As Samson had stood in his dark world amidst the clamor of the Philistines, feeling in his outstretched arms the smooth columns of the Temple, he had cried out in anguish, "Remember me, O Lord." In fact, the Lord had never forsaken him.

(b) The world is full of such sad souls who feel God has forsaken them. Men know when they have broken God's laws. Seldom is ignorance the true reason for sinning. Man, upon realization of his sin, is alone in a universe where all is persecuting guilt, imprisoned in the chattel house of his own uneasy conscience, shackled by the very chains he has slowly but too surely forged through the years. Such sinners are condemned by their own hearts. Their God is no greater than their own hearts. For their God is not the God of the Bible.

To know that God forgives is the great revelation of the Bible. Sir J. Y. Simpson, the Scottish scientist and discoverer of the anesthetic properties of chloroform, was asked on his deathbed what was the greatest discovery of his life. "That God forgives," was the reply. Thus reasons the Lord. "Though your sins be as scarlet they shall be white as snow."—George M. Docherty

Illustrations

THE STAGES OF LIFE.   The danger of middle life is just the danger of "settling down." An Old Testament prophet speaks of "the men that have settled on their lees." The sins of middle age are the sins of the mind—the desire for money, for power, and above all for security. A kind of fatty degeneration of the conscience often sets in about fifty. We are less inclined to fight about anything, least of all against our own faults. Middle-aged men are often happier than the young, but it does not follow that they ought to be.

Our middle-aged citizen has formed habits. Life has no more adventures for him. He can see the remainder of the dusty road lying straight and even before him. He has ceased to worry about himself. Too often he has come to a working compromise with the world, the flesh, and the devil. And then sometimes he unexpectedly gives way to some degrading temptation, to the surprise of his friends and perhaps of himself. This is the history of many of the moral tragedies of middle life.—W. R. Inge

PICKING UP THE PIECES.   Most of us can identify with the man who commented, "Any day that I simply get through, I count as a great victory. If I have survived, I have won."

So just picking up the pieces, trying to put them together into a package that represents some kind of totality, seems almost impossible. The paper that we use for wrapping is torn; the string that we tie things up with gets broken; insides begin to move around and fall out, and we have to lean down and pick them up and try to put them all back together again.—John B. Coburn

Sermon Suggestions

FROM INDICATIVE TO IMPERATIVE.
TEXT: Exod. 20:1–17. (1) What God has done and does is basic to the religious life. (2) What we do in response to God's deeds for us is indicative of our faith, our love, and our sense of obligation (see Rom. 12:1–2).

ON BEING SURE ABOUT THE CHRISTIAN FAITH.   TEXT: 1 Cor. 1:22–25. (1) What the world seeks: some want miracles; others want an intellectually foolproof explanation. (2) What God offers: Christ crucified—weakness and folly to some; the power and wisdom of God "to those who are called, both Jews and Greeks."

Worship Aids

CALL TO WORSHIP.   "The Lord is my light and my salvation; whom shall I fear? The Lord is the strength of my life; of whom shall I be afraid?" (Ps. 27:1).

INVOCATION.   Our Father, we may just be playing at church this morning. Our lifeless bodies are in the pews, but our hearts and minds are miles away. Draw us all and all of us together before you this morning, that we might worship you body, mind, and soul. Thank you that, while we may pretend, you are always genuine and real. Help us to worship you in the same spirit.—James M. King

OFFERTORY SENTENCE.   "He that exhorteth, to his exhorting: he that giveth, let him do it with liberality; he that ruleth, with diligence; he that showeth mercy, with cheerfulness" (Rom. 12:8).

OFFERTORY PRAYER.   We confess that whatever we might give, you are worthy of more, almighty God. So we offer these gifts asking forgiveness when we have done too little and grace to do more.—J. Scott Hickman

PRAYER.   We bless thee, our Heavenly Father, for all the help which thou hast vouchsafed in times past, and for those great and precious promises which thou has made for the future. But for the hope which we have in thee, we should be appalled at the greatness of the way before us. So mighty are those influences which draw us downward, so many are the things which tend to forgetfulness, so easy is it in prosperous circumstances to become self-indulgent, so do our very affections twine idolatrously round about earthly things, that, were we left to ourselves, we should all of us sink steadily lower and lower, until the thought of heaven would be too far away for influence—until thou thyself wouldst be hidden behind the cloud of all thy mercies. As the sun that drieth up the vapor from the earth is hidden by that which itself hath done; so thou by thy mercies art hidden, filling the air round about us with the tokens of thy goodness. We seize upon the things that are good and forget the giver. And, O Lord our God! how worse are we than little children, with their folly and frivolity and ignorance! How are we, in all things, plunging, stumbling, erring through ignorance, through untempered passions, through evils manifold! We implore thy forgiveness. But were all the forgiveness of God in the past, if we are afraid for the future. We implore even more thy presence and thine inspiring help. Go with us from step to step in all our future lives, and give us a clear understanding, a sound judgment and comprehensiveness of things right and things wrong. And grant that there may be an interpretation of duty in our very nature, that we may become so sensitive to things evil or good, that on the one hand or on the other we shall repel or draw them. And may we walk with growing strength. May habit supplement desire. May we thus fortify what we gain and hold, with growing strength, steadfastly on unto the very end of life.

Deliver us from the evil that is in the world. May we not seek to be friends of this world in all its evil aspects. May we look upon it as our field of labor. There may we delve and sow and rear the immortal harvest. And yet, may we not give ourselves to it as our chiefest good nor be seduced by its pleasures nor deceived by its deceits. Grant that we may walk in the world as not abusing it, as in it and not above it. And as our experience grows, make us to desire that rest which remaineth for the people of God.

Grant that we may so live that we shall have a vision and a foretaste of that blessed rest which belongs to the heavenly estate. And when all our temptations and dangers are past, and that work is accomplished which it is our duty to accomplish, bring us to the end of life joyfully and assuredly, that we may go out singing songs of victory, and rise to grander songs of triumph in the heavenly land.

And to thy name shall be the praise of our salvation, Father, Son, and Spirit.— Henry Ward Beecher

LECTIONARY MESSAGE

Topic: Cleansing the Temple
Text: John 2:13–25

It seems so out of character for him! Here's the one who said that if someone strikes you on the right cheek, you should turn the other cheek. He comes plowing into the Temple during one of the holiest seasons in the Jewish calendar and begins making a scene. He made a whip of cords and drove out those who were selling oxen and sheep and pigeons. And the money changers—he dumped out their coins and turned their tables over. He was angry like no one had ever seen him before. He was mad over what was taking place in the Temple.

This passage has been abused by the church over the years. We have become so legalistic at times that it's a wonder that someone didn't suggest that offerings be taken by mail or only at the door so that no money would pass hands in the "temple." Why, some churches would never allow any activities that even hinted at raising money, afraid that they might raise the ire of this table-turning Jesus. What they miss is that Jesus wasn't mad that they were selling animals in the Temple. That practice was necessary for those who came to Jerusalem to give an offering to the Lord. They would purchase a dove or a lamb to sacrifice to the Lord and then take the meat home for the passover meal. No, Jesus wasn't mad about their selling in the Temple. He was angry about how their selling practices in the Temple were taking place.

Some had lost the meaning that the sale was to enable worship to take place. Others were taking advantage of the opportunity to cheat someone. Jesus was angry about their "huckstering of piety" for profit and the "business-as-usual" atmosphere. He drove out those who were always there to take advantage of every situation. What Jesus was angry with was religion that had lost its direction, with worship that no longer had meaning, and with the behavior of those who were called God's children that was not different from anyone else's behavior.

The church did not choose this passage

of Scripture as a reading for Lent by coincidence. The season of Lent is a period of time leading up to the climax in the church's most glorious day of the year, Easter Sunday. Lent should be characterized by the church's increasing awareness of the need for devotion and worship in light of the great sacrifice that God provided on behalf of all of us. In our preparation as individuals and as a church for Easter, Jesus' cleansing of the Temple reminds us of what needs to take place when our religion has lost its direction; when our worship no longer has meaning; and when our behavior as Christians is no different than the behavior of those who do not know Christ. As we prepare for Easter, it's a time to cleanse the temple of our hearts. It's a time to prepare for the true worship that the Resurrection makes possible.—Craig A. Loscalzo

SUNDAY: MARCH TENTH

SERVICE OF WORSHIP

Sermon: Saved by Grace

Text: Eph. 2:5

We are gathered here this Sunday morning to hear this word: By grace you have been saved! Whatever else we do, praying and singing, is but an answer to this word spoken to us by God himself. The Bible alone contains this sentence. We do not read it in Kant or in Schopenhauer or in any book of natural or secular history and certainly not in any novel, but in the Bible alone. In order to hear this word we need what is called the Church—the company of Christians, of human beings called and willing to listen together to the Bible and through it to the word of God.

By grace you have been saved! No man can say this to himself. Neither can he say it to someone else. This can only be said by God to each one of us. It take Jesus Christ to make this saying true. It takes the apostles to communicate it. And our gathering here as Christians is needed to spread news, the most exciting news of all, the most helpful thing also, indeed, the only helpful thing.

I. "By grace you have been saved!" How strange to have this message addressed to us! Who are we, anyway? Let me tell you quite frankly: we are all together great sinners.

(a) Sinners are people who in the judgment of God, and perhaps of their own consciences, missed and lost their way, who are not just a little but totally guilty, hopelessly indebted and lost, not only in time but in eternity. We are such sinners. And we are prisoners. Believe me, there is a captivity much worse than the captivity in this house. There are walls much thicker and doors much heavier than those closed upon you. All of us, the people without and you within, are prisoners of our own obstinacy, of our many greeds, of our various anxieties, of our mistrust and, in the last analysis, of our unbelief.

(b) But now listen. Into the depth of our predicament the word is spoken from on high: By grace you have been saved! To be saved does not just mean to be a little encouraged, a little comforted, a little relieved. It means to be pulled out like a log from a burning fire. You have been saved! We are not told, you may be saved sometimes or a little bit. No, you have been saved, totally and for all times. You? Yes, we! Not just any other people, more pious and better than we are; no, we, each one of us.

(c) This is so because Jesus Christ is our brother and, through his life and death, has become our Savior who has wrought our salvation. He is the word of God for us. And this word is, By grace you have been saved!

Look at our Savior and at our salvation! Look at Jesus Christ on the cross, accused, sentenced, and punished instead of us! Do you know for whose sake he is hanging there? For our sake—because of our sin—sharing our captivity, burdened with our suffering! He nails our life to the cross. This is how God had to deal with us. From this darkness he has saved us. He who is not shattered after hearing this news may not yet have grasped the word of God: By grace you have been saved!

II. But more important than the fear of sudden death is the knowledge of life imparted to us: "By grace you have been saved!"

(a) By virtue of the good news, the sky truly opens and the earth is bright. What a glorious relief to be told that there I was, in that darkness, over that abyss, on the brink of death, but there I am no longer. Through this folly I lived, but I cannot and I will not do it again, never again. This happened, but I must not and it will not happen again. My sin, my captivity, my suffering are yesterday's reality, not today's. They are things of my past, not of the present nor of the future. I have been saved!

(b) Is this really so, is this the truth? Look once again to Jesus Christ in his death upon the cross. Look and try to understand that, what he did and suffered, he did and suffered for you, for me, for us all. He carried our sin, our captivity and our suffering and did not carry it in vain. He carried it away. He acted as the captain of us all. He broke through the ranks of our enemies. He has already won the battle, our battle. All we have to do is to follow him, to be victorious with him. Through him, in him, we are saved. Our sin has no longer any power over us. Our prison door is open. Our suffering has come to an end. This is a great word indeed. The word of God is indeed a great word. And we would deny him, we would deny the Lord Jesus Christ, were we to deny the greatness of this word: He sets us free. When he, the Son of God, sets us free, we are truly free.

III. Because we are saved by no other than Jesus Christ, we are saved by grace. This means that we did not deserve to be saved. What we deserved would be quite different.

(a) No one can be proud of being saved. Each one can only fold his hands in great lowliness of heart and be thankful like a child. Consequently, we shall never possess salvation as our property. We may only receive it as a gift over and over again, with hands outstretched. "By grace you have been saved!" This means constantly to look away from ourselves to God and to the man on the cross where this truth is revealed. This truth is ever anew to be believed and to be grasped by faith. To believe means to look to Jesus Christ and to God and to trust that there is the truth for us, for our lives, for the life of all men.

(b) Is it not a pity that we rebel against this very truth in the depth of our hearts? Indeed, we dislike hearing that we are saved by grace and by grace alone. We would much prefer to withdraw into our own inner circle, not unlike the snail into its shell, and to be with ourselves. To put it bluntly: we do not like to believe. And yet grace, and therefore faith as I just described it, is the beginning of the true life of freedom, of a carefree heart, of joy deep within, of love of God and neighbor, of great and assured hope! And yet grace and faith would make things so very simple in our lives!

IV. Dear brothers and sisters, where do we stand now?

(a) One thing is certain: the bright day has dawned, the sun of God does shine into our dark lives, even though we may close our eyes to its radiance. His voice does call us from heaven, even though we may obstruct our ears. The bread of life is offered to us, even though we are inclined to clench our fists instead of opening our hands to take the bread and eat it. The door of our prison is open, even though, strangely enough, we prefer to remain within. God has put the house in order, even though we like to mess it up all over again. By grace you have been saved!— this is true, even though we may not believe it, may not accept it as valid for ourselves and, unfortunately, in so doing may forego its benefits. Why should we want to forego the benefits? Why should we not want to believe? Why are we blindfolded? Honestly, why?

(b) One remark in reply must suffice. All this is so because perhaps we failed to pray fervently enough for a change within ourselves, on our part. That God is God, not only almighty, but merciful and good, that he wills and does what is best for us, that Jesus Christ died for us to set us free, that by grace, in him, we have been saved—all this need not be a concern of our prayers. All these things are true apart from our own deeds and prayers. But to believe, to accept, to let it be true for us, to begin to live with this truth, to believe it not only with our minds and with our lips but also with our hearts and with all our life, so that our fellowmen may sense it, and finally to let our total existence be immersed in the great divine truth, by grace you have been saved, this is to be the concern of our prayers. No human being has ever prayed for this in vain. Ask that you may believe this, and it will be given you; seek this, and you will find it; knock on this door, and it will be opened to you.—Karl Barth

Illustrations

THE EMERGING REVIVAL.   A number of years ago the historic People's Church in downtown St. Paul caught fire. The firemen fought furiously in sub-zero weather at two o'clock on a Good Friday morning, but their efforts were practically futile. Among the church's art treasures was an exact copy of Thorvaldsen's "The Appealing Christ." Almost miraculously, this lovely Italian marble statue was unharmed. It was taken out in front of the building, and for a while it stood in the street against a background of destruction. Flares were put around it to warn motorists. Hundreds of people who had not known it was in the church saw the statue for the first time. Many of them had not even heard of it. The crowd which passed the church did not know Christ was there!—G. Ray Jordan

A GRACIOUS INVITATION.   The foreman of a certain project, who had heard the gospel but had not accepted it, received an invitation from his boss asking him to come to his house after business hours.

The foreman came, but when he arrived his boss said to him, "Well, sir, what are you doing here? Why should you disturb me after business hours?"

The foreman, surprised, said, "Well, sir, you invited me to come, and I have come in response to your invitation."

Then his boss said to him, "I have done this to impress upon you the invitation which God's Son has given you to come to him and be saved. You respond to my invitation readily, even when I had nothing to offer you. Why do you not respond to Christ's invitation when he is offering you everlasting life?"—J. B. Lawrence

Sermon Suggestions

GOD'S LAST WORD.   TEXT: 2 Chron. 36: 14–23. (1) The story of chastisement, verses 14–21. (2) The message of hope, verses 22–23.

WHAT GRACE HAS DONE.   TEXT: Eph. 2:4–10. (1) Given us new life in Christ. (2) Given us status in Christ. (3) Given us work to do for Christ.

Worship Aids

CALL TO WORSHIP.   "Hear, O Lord, when I cry with my voice: Have mercy also upon me, and answer me" (Ps. 27:7).

INVOCATION.   Lift us, Lord, to praise and glorify thee whom alone we worship, before whom we confess our sins, in whom we find the peace that passes understanding. And let the presence of thy Spirit show us the Christ.—E. Lee Phillips

OFFERTORY SENTENCE.   "Give, and it shall be given unto you; good measure, pressed down, shaken together, running over, shall they give into your bosom. For with what measure ye met it shall be measured to you again" (Luke 6:38).

OFFERTORY PRAYER.   Great is the Lord and greatly to be praised. Out of grateful hearts and full lives we bring these offerings. We know that you can do without them, but we cannot do without making them. In praise and adoration we give our gifts to you.

PRAYER.   O Father, in these days of Lent as we seek to follow him who steadfastly set his face to go to Jerusalem—leaving the sunny skies of Galilee and braving the stormy clouds of opposition gathering in the capital—we discover ourselves lagging behind with Peter and Andrew, James and John, concerned— about our prerogatives—ambitious for our own ends—rather than disciplining ourselves after your love, as he did. In these days, call us and recall us to that commitment to which love challenges. With fresh insight to the depths of its meaning, may we hear your call in Christ: "If any person will come after me, let him forget himself and take up his cross and follow me." With your love with which you continue to love us, you keep pushing back the frontiers of our lives until we are verily your own. The claim of your love upon us has come with such clarity in the witness of this hour, we know that you are "not Lord at all until you are Lord of all."

O God, we find ourselves this morning facing new realities, some of which we would not have chosen for ourselves. Make us confident of your grace in Christ that we may not be victims but victors in the strife. Grant us the faith that can transform difficulties into opportunities. Out of the clay of which we are made, you are fashioning us to an eternal glory. In the cross we are reminded that the wholeness, which is the healing of our brokenness, does not come without pain and suffering. In the meaning of Christ's cross may we discover the strength to bear our own: "By his stripes we *are* healed." For all of life's vicissitudes, we pray for the poise of faith, knowing your love that never lets us go.

May the good work that you have begun in us as a congregation continue, that this church may be as "the light on the hill" that many may be guided in the "follow me" of Jesus.

O God, we pray for healing—for healing in the marketplace, in the halls of government, among the nations—may the strong take up the cause of the weak. May leaders entrusted with great power be sensitive to the crises of injustice from wherever they come. Hasten the day of reconciliation that Shalom may be the blessing of all peoples.—John M. Thompson

LECTIONARY MESSAGE

Topic: Who Are We and What Are We to Do?

TEXT: John 3:14–21

Who are we and what are we to do? J. A. Anders, in his article on hermeneutics in the supplementary volume of the *Interpreter's Dictionary of the Bible*, says that this is the crucial question that must be asked by the interpreter seeking to understand a biblical text. The preacher as interpreter who is attempting to communicate the meaning of a biblical text must keep this question on the cutting edge of his or her hermeneutical practice.

I. *Who are we?* Jesus had been discussing the essence of this question with Nicodemus. He explained to Nicodemus that who we really are is ultimately related to a second birth, a birth of the Spirit that comes as an act of God's intervention in the human situation. The second birth gives us a unity with the Spirit.

The lifting of the snake in the desert by Moses was an obedient act in response to God. Jesus saw in Moses' act a similarity to the lifting up of the Son of man, which has been understood metaphorically to represent the crucified Christ. Belief in the Christ becomes a crucial and essential response to the action of God. The biblical writer mentions the need for belief no less than four times in this section. Belief represents more than intellectual assent. Belief is rooted in the depth of one's being, often demonstrated in obedient response to the will of God, which is made known through God's Spirit. Faith is essential to answering the question, Who are we?

II. *What are we to do?* Belief in the Christ of God, as a response to the love that God has shown for us in not sparing his only son, is a demonstration of what we are to do. Our practice emerges out of our faith. Belief, a healthy faith, moves us from the darkness of our earthly behavior to a behavior that is characterized by those who love the light. Saying one has faith but continuing to live in the darkness is inconsistent. The writer suggests "whoever lives by the truth comes into the light, so that it may be seen plainly that what he has done has been done through God." Who we are must be manifested in what we do, how we act, how we behave toward others, how we become light in darkness. This is not a mandate that is to be understood solely in religious terms. Our lives as believers in the Christ are to reflect our beliefs in every realm of practice. Business dealings are to be controlled by the fact of who we are. Our politics and how we respond to issues such as war and peace and the environment hinge on the affirmations of our faith in Christ. What we do is controlled by who we are. The two issues cannot be separated.

The questions are haunting ones. In light of God's intervention into our world through the Christ event: Who are we? What are we going to do?—Craig A. Loscalzo

SUNDAY: MARCH SEVENTEENTH

SERVICE OF WORSHIP

Sermon: Magnificent Failure

TEXTS: Jer. 45:2–56; Luke 7:18–20

"Some men's failures," as George Macdonald has said, "are eternities beyond other men's successes." It was so with the prophet Jeremiah, who was single by the way. When he tried to arrest the course of a nation, only to be thrown down and trampled underfoot, when he cried out in bitterness of heart against the God that compelled a poet to be a prophet and a lover of men to be counted their enemy, he little knew that the record of his lonely experience of failure would inspire two millennia later. If we want to know the meaning of personal religion at its finest, we must become, like Baruch, disciples of Jeremiah.

Other prophets had their place and their measure of success. Jeremiah failed dramatically. I intend to celebrate magnificent failure, using Jeremiah as the focus.

I. The case for failure begins with surgery on the current mania for success. The successful man is the one who has scrambled to the top of the pyramid. Success has become a way of life, an endless treadmill that Americans scamper upon. There is surely an admirable quality in hard-earned success, but success has so captivated many of us that it has become a way of life, an end rather than a means.

(a) Amid our own anxious concern for success, let us learn from the life of Jeremiah that failure sometimes can be good. Failure is not bad in itself. Failure is good when success demands too much.

You may be caught in a crisis in your career when dishonesty could make the difference in getting you ahead. A builder can use second-grade materials and list them as first-grade. A doctor can recommend a costly operation when it is unnecessary. A minister can be silent on the key issues of his day. Failure is good when success demands surrender of integrity.

(b) Failure is good when the failure is for Christ's sake. David Brainerd, eighteenth-century missionary to the American Indians, failed magnificently for Christ. While Christianity for his contemporaries was a dull habit, it was for him an acute fever. He went among Indians and preached and lived. He was not put off by the task of converting them to the ways of Jesus. He was sick and often without food. He endured hardship and little success. He converted only thirty or forty Indians. He left the American forest only when he knew he was dying. David Brainerd died in the home of Jonathan Edwards, having burned himself up for Christ. His was a beautiful life, lived with a magnificent purpose. Here was a case of failure that was good.

(c) The case of failure takes added strength from the fact that failure can be creative. The exalting music of the *Messiah* was not written in the bloom of Handel's strength and health, but it was written after he had suffered a severe stroke and lived in poverty amid bleak surroundings. It came as an inspiration to him after a deep night of gloom and despair.

II. Here we need to inject a note of realism. The outcome of failure is often bitter.

Failure can destroy the person spiritually unprepared for a storm. Jeremiah was struck down by the loneliness that engulfed him when he denounced his fellowmen.

(a) Another consequence of failure is the gnawing experience of being misunderstood. Many things are easier to accept than being misunderstood. Jeremiah had the welfare of his people in mind and loved his fellowmen intensely, but they returned suspicion and misgiving. And the life of Jeremiah had no Hollywood ending. He was never warmly accepted. After his nation fell, he was taken captive into Egypt. There he continued to prophesy with courage and determination. Jeremiah never received the deserved love of his countrymen. Tradition has it that he was killed by his own people. All sight of him was lost.

(b) Still another result of failure is often doubt and disillusionment. Jeremiah was not made of steel, nor are we. When he was misunderstood, he crumbled inside. He began to cry out against God. It seemed that even God had forsaken him. He began to doubt God and to be disillusioned with men because nothing constructive seemed to be growing out of his ministry and out of his age.

III. We have said that some failure can be good and that most people have a mania for success of any kind in preference to failure of any kind. Those hardy Christians that have discovered the freedom to fail seem to possess a quiet courage.

(a) The pervasive undercurrent in our day of big institutions is, "Don't rock the boat," "Mind your own store." This subtle encouragement to conform is reflected in the standards expected of executives in big business. It is so easy to caricature the executive person in the giant corporation as "the organization man," the hollow man in the gray flannel suit, without recognizing the pressures he faces.

Jeremiah possessed courage even in his old age when some lose heart. He spoke his convictions at the risk of his life. It takes courage to fail magnificently.

(b) Another quality of magnificent failure is a solid faith in the future. Jeremiah

had a supreme faith in the future, though he predicted doom in the immediate days ahead. He had a quiet confidence in an ultimate future for Israel. This belief strengthened him. How daring was his brash act in the face of ruin. The nation was under siege, and final defeat was a matter of time. Jeremiah went out to Anathoth, the very field on which the enemy encamped, and bought a piece of land! He went through all the legal procedures to make it official. He was buying a stake in the new Israel on the promise of a new future. Jeremiah knew that finally nothing is lost in God. He invested in God's future.

IV. Courage and a solid faith in the future are qualities of the magnificent failure and are qualities that every Christian needs in our day if he or she would live unfettered and free. Truly to be capable of magnificent failure is to be free and to believe really in God.

I know that I have run counter to the assumptions of the world we face Monday morning and that what has been said may seem ludicrous. I know that we may not be called upon to be magnificent failures. I may have seemed to glorify failure too much, but I will take that risk. Failure is not good in itself, but it is good when success demands too much and when failure is for Christ's sake. Once or twice in a lifetime, every true Christian will be called upon to be a magnificent failure.—Peter Rhea Jones

Illustrations

PATHS TO POWER.   And just here is disclosed the attitude that the disciples of Christ are to assume with reference to all the sifting processes of life. It is graciously granted to every Simon to hear the voice of the Master, Christ, saying, "Simon! Satan asked to sift you—but I have prayed for thee. Before my eye your special weakness came pleadingly, and underneath the whole fearful experience, working up through it, is my prayer that your faith fail not." That is one of the great announcements that we must accredit, as I believe, to the true and perpetual mediatorship of Christ. "Simon, I have prayed for thee." It means much to any soul in distress, to any man in the throes of temptation, that anybody in, what is to him, this lonely universe, has prayed for him. It means that another life has put faith in God's good intentions; that another soul has put its shoulders under the burden that that soul reverently appreciates and feels that it is too much for one soul's weakness to bear. It means that another human reason exists on earth for God to work within his ongoing movements. But when the Christ of God, who is one with the Father and one with man, who knows the mind of heaven that works and the weakness of the humanity with which it works, pours into a man's problem his supplication unto God, his prayer for Simon, it means much more—lets the whole sweet and infinite secret out. For all this means that there is a divine purpose shining like a guiding star behind the entire affair. It means that God who is perfectly revealed in Christ— that Jesus is in active partnership with the Peter who is struggling to free himself from Simon. It means that the humanity in Christ and the divinity in him, earth and heaven are hopeful. Here we see that God's faith in the grain is expressed in Christ's prayer, that as the sifting goes on, the sifted soul's faith in the ultimate blessedness of the experience shall fail not.—Frank W. Gunsaulus

LOOKING TO GOD.   Let life be a life of faith. Do not go timorously about, enquiring what others think, what others believe, what others say. It seems the easiest; it is the most difficult thing in life to do this. Believe in God. God is near you. Throw yourself fearlessly upon him. Trembling mortal, there is an unknown might within your soul which will wake when you command it. The day may come when all that is human, man or woman, will fall off from you as they did from him. Let his strength be yours. Be independent of them all now. The Father is with you. Look to him and he will save you.—F. W. Robertson

Sermon Suggestions

TWO WAYS OF SERVING GOD.   TEXT: Jer. 31:31–34. (1) From external pressure—

the inadequacy of mere law. (2) From internal desire—the power of loving motivation.

A REAL HUMAN JESUS.   TEXT: Heb. 5:7–10. Though Jesus was the Son of God and thus divine, he was human, and as such (1) he prayed passionately, especially in Gethsemane; (2) his life of obedience to the Father unfolded through suffering, especially on the cross; (3) thus he became our great high priest, gaining for us through these intercessions eternal salvation.

Worship Aids

CALL TO WORSHIP.   "Blessed is the nation whose God is the Lord, the people whom he hath chosen for his own inheritance" (Ps. 33:12).

INVOCATION.   We are a motley group who appear before you today, O God. Some of us are afraid and others confident; some confused and others clear; some burdened and others buoyant; some depressed and others euphoric; some sad and others radiant. Help us to see today that you have a word for each of us. May we be grateful for the brighter hours and prepared for the darker hours, knowing that both sunlight and shadow belong to you and can help us to become what you want us to be.

OFFERTORY SENTENCE.   "For according to their power, I bear witness, yea and beyond their power, they gave of their own accord, beseeching us with much entreaty in regard of this grace and the fellowship in the ministering to the saints" (2 Cor. 8:3–4).

OFFERTORY PRAYER.   We bring our offerings to you, O Lord, source of every good gift. Some are small and meager. Some are large and generous. Accept them as expressions of our love and thanksgiving. They represent our best. You have given your best in Christ Jesus. Use these gifts to share your love with your world, we pray in the name of Jesus.

PRAYER. Almighty God, Source of all beauty and balm, of all peacefulness and calm. We gather in your presence, Majestic, Holy, Righteous, Gracious, Merciful. We are overwhelmed by your love and your concern for us. We thank you for noticing and helping us. We thank you for challenging us and encouraging us. We thank you for forgiving us and strengthening us. We confess our sin to you and ask your continuing forgiveness. You know all about us, and yet you love us.

Why can we not love one another? Is it because we are afraid? We remember that perfect love casts out fear. Is our love then so immature? Help us, almighty God, to love you with our whole being and to love one another as ourselves. We pray in the name of Jesus. Amen.—J. Estill Jones

LECTIONARY MESSAGE

Topic: The Cost of Discipleship
TEXT: John 12:20–33
A modern Christian disciple, Dietrich Bonhoeffer, wrote a book with this title: *The Cost of Discipleship*. Because he was faithful in his interpretation of discipleship, he paid with his life. He was executed in 1945 under the orders of Adolph Hitler. Not every disciple will pay that price, but there is a cost for every Christian disciple.

In this paragraph with its "Now is my soul troubled," John portrays the same struggle the other Gospels describe in Gethsemane. The story begins with the desire of certain Gentiles to see Jesus. Jesus recognized their approach as symbolic of God's concern for all the world and of the attraction of all people to this love—"If I be lifted up from the earth, I will draw all men unto myself." And John saw in this statement the sign of the cross.

But in between the approach of the Gentiles and the declaration of Jesus came a brief description of the cost of discipleship. There are three principles involved:

I. *Life comes through death.* It is a natural truth. Death brings life. Look at a grain of wheat. If it lives, it remains a single seed. But if it is planted in the ground, it loses its identity, its life. And out of its death springs new life. It bears much fruit.

It is this life, unbounded by national and racial ties, that is the life of the disciple. It is this life, described elsewhere as the life abundant, that the disciple lives. It is this life, cited by Paul as life incarnate ("Not I but Christ lives in me"), that characterizes the disciple. Life comes through death.

II. *Gain comes through loss.* "He that loves his life loses it" is the usual procedure, but "he that hates his life gains it." Life is a gamble, a calculated risk. Do you remember Paul's description of Epaphroditus, "risking his life" (Phil. 2:30)? He gambled and won.

This was clearly illustrated in Jesus' temptation experience. Here's an easy way to satisfy your appetite—the temptation is frightfully current. Jesus preferred to give of himself to others. Here's an easy way to win a following—the temptation is frightfully current. Jesus never dealt superficially with persons. Here's the easy way to gain a kingdom—the temptation is frightfully current. Jesus knew that one gains a kingdom only by losing one's self. Gain comes through loss.

III. *Honor comes through service.* It is the natural attitude of the disciple to his teacher. Yet it must be the "inasmuch as" service. In a parable recorded in Matt. 25: 31–46, Jesus commended those who offered unconscious, natural service. This was not offered to gain honor but to satisfy human need.

It is a life of service, not an instant, soon-to-be-forgotten decision. "If any person serve me, let him follow me," he said.

It is Martha Berty in north Georgia, serving mountain boys and girls. It is Hugh and Norma Young in Japan, teaching French and art to Japanese youth. It is Louis Smith in Hong Kong, using his medical skills. There is no other way to be his disciple—honor comes through service.

And about that time there came a voice from heaven vindicating his decision to go to the cross . . . and some said, "It thunders." The thunderous approval from God is highly desired. Discipleship costs— death, loss, and service. God offers life, gain, and honor.—J. Estill Jones

SUNDAY: MARCH TWENTY-FOURTH

SERVICE OF WORSHIP

Sermon: Hoping or Postponing?

TEXT: Matt. 16:13–17

For all of its halleluia and hosanna, Palm Sunday marks the beginning of what writers on the life of Jesus once called "the Jerusalem winter." These were the barren days, marked by the disaffection of friends, the collapse of hope, the cold and bitter taste of death. But it was not always so. Those same writers spoke also of "the Galilean spring" of Jesus, that early period in his ministry in which he enjoyed immense popularity. And I must say the Gospels yield some evidence for the truth of this. Jesus was a teacher, a healer, an exorcist. To his ministry of healing and teaching and casting out demons, great crowds of people came. He was in a house, and they came in such large numbers that desperate friends lowered a mattress through the roof to bring a cripple to the attention of Jesus. Sometimes the crowd was so large that he had to get into a boat and push away from the land in order to have room to speak. When the crowds in the villages so swelled that Jesus could not minister, he moved into the open country. The multitudes on the hillside sometimes numbered above five thousand. Jesus needed help; he chose a few, a few more, and finally twelve.

According to the records of his Galilean ministry, Jesus was extremely popular, and the text for today explains what lay at the base of that popularity. "Now when Jesus came into the district of Caesarea Philippi, he asked his disciples, 'Who do men say that the Son of man is?' And they said, 'Some say John the Baptist, others say Elijah, and others Jeremiah or one of the prophets.' He said to them, 'But who do you say that I am?' Simon Peter replied, 'You are the Christ, the Son of the living God.' And Jesus answered him, 'Blessed are you, Simon Bar-Jona! For flesh and blood has not revealed this to you, but my Father who is in heaven.' "

"What is the public opinion of me?" he asked. And the answer was, "Some say you are John the Baptist come back from the dead. Others say you are Elijah; some say Jeremiah or one of the prophets." These terms from the public opinion were not simply complimentary comparisons; these terms were titles, titles for the one who would be the forerunner of the Messiah. Before the Messiah comes, there will be one like Elijah or Jeremiah or one of the prophets. When the crowd said Jesus was John or Elijah or Jeremiah or one of the prophets, what they meant was, "We believe that Jesus is the forerunner of the Messiah." In other words, their opinion of him was the same as *our* understanding of John the Baptist.

If Jesus was regarded by the Galileans as the one announcing the coming of a messiah, then it is no wonder he was popular. He drew crowds for the same reason that John the Baptist did. "The Messiah is coming," said John. "The kingdom is at the door," said Jesus. That message would certainly bring a crowd! School was dismissed early; bread left in the oven; shops unattended; plows dropped in half-drawn furrows. Everyone came running, totally unaware of anything except the thrill of one message, "The Messiah is coming! He will be here soon! The Messiah is coming!"

And why not? Every beautiful story that they knew began, not with "Once upon a time," but with the words "When the Messiah comes . . ." To every blind beggar seated on the street, hollow eyes gazing over an empty cup: "I'm sorry, friend, but when the Messiah comes . . ." To every cripple with twisted body folded beneath him: "I'm sorry, friend, but when the Messiah comes . . ." To every beggar clutching his rags with one hand and with the other reaching up for alms: "I have no money, friend, but when the Messiah comes . . ." To every prisoner straining after that one little ray of light through the narrow window: "I'm sorry, friend, but when the Messiah comes . . ." To every couple married now over fourteen years and still rocking an empty cradle: "I'm sorry, but when the Messiah comes . . ." To every father seeking to calm a sobbing daughter assaulted by a Roman soldier: "Now, now, my child, when the Messiah comes . . ."

When I imagine these crowds drawn by messengers regarded as forerunners of the Messiah, it seems natural to envision even larger crowds when the Christians came announcing, "The Messiah is here! The Messiah has come! The Messiah has come!" You would think so. After all, if the promise brought thousands, would not fulfillment bring tens of thousands? But they did not come in larger numbers, and they do not come in larger numbers. The crowds, in fact, were smaller. Why?

If anticipation is a way of life, you do not want fulfillment. Looking forward to something can be the way you spend your whole life, and you really are disappointed if it comes to pass. Why is it that Christmas Day is the saddest day of Christmas? Because Christmas is looking forward to Christmas. In much of life, the pleasure is more in the chase than in the catch. The magnificence of life's promise is often lost in the poverty of its achievement. And as long as life remains an image in the mind, then life can be shaped to the contours of desire. While I am looking for a messiah, I can make him what I want him to be. If I am hungry, I can make him one who feeds. If I am tired, he is one who gives rest. If I am at war, he gives peace. If I am poor, he gives prosperity. If I am alone, he brings fellowship. Because I have created him out of the emptiness of my life, when I think about the Messiah coming, I know what he is going to be, and I know what he is going to do for me. And I really do not want that dream exploded by anyone, not even a messiah. I prefer the dream.

My wife and I have a cabin on a lake near our home. When I leave the office in the afternoon, we can throw a few things in the car and in less than an hour be at our cabin. It's on a small lake, clear, deep, and blue. It's peaceful there. Willows line the shore, very nice neighbors, very quiet, good fishing, a very relaxing place. We have never seen a mosquito, not a bug or fly. We have never had any vandalism. The plumbing always works perfectly. Do you know where this cabin is? It's in our minds, and you are crazy if you think we're going to trade it in on a place like yours.

Beyond this, looking forward can be a way of handling by postponement all the problems of life. Every time I see injustice, inequity, and misery in the world, I can say to myself, "But when the Messiah comes . . . all this will be changed. When he comes we'll hear the 'Battle Hymn of the Republic.' When the Messiah comes, we will hear the hammers of justice, the bells of freedom, the song of love. Upon his arrival there will be the redress of grievances, the taking up of the cause of the oppressed. But in the meantime, we must continue to look forward to his coming."

It is easier, really, to believe that a messiah will come than to believe that one has already come. You see, there is always enough misery in the world to make the announcement that a messiah *will* come believable. There is always enough misery in the world to make the announcement that a messiah *has* come unbelievable.

How then are we to account for Simon Peter's confession? If the public opinion of Jesus was, "You are the forerunner of the Messiah," how are we to account for Peter's answer to the question "And who do *you* say that I am?" "You are the Messiah." Has Simon Peter seen something that others have not seen? Has he detected in the Galilean something of the strength of Samson? Has he seen something of the shrewdness of Gideon? The leadership of Moses? The kingly qualities of Saul or David? The heroics of Jephthah? Has Simon Peter gotten something that the rest have missed? If he did, he certainly had a keen eye, because it was not obvious.

This Jesus went about his ministry without anyone ever hearing his voice aloud in the street. He incited no riots; he shouted no propaganda. This is the Messiah? "A bruised reed he would not break, a smoking wick he would not quench." He had such a tender care for the weak, for the violated, for the crushed, and even for those as obnoxious as a smoking wick. This is the Messiah?

Has Simon Peter detected that this Jesus has begun to make a move, a move that could be called messianic? If he has seen it, he certainly saw more than others saw. In fact, most of Jesus' followers grew a little bit restless with his wasting so much time on the cripples. Stop to pick up every cripple along the way and this army will never march. And the children! We stop to have a session along the road and in comes some women with small children. The children fret and begin to whimper and cry. "Get these children out of here; we're trying to get the kingdom started." And Jesus said, "Leave them alone. Bring the little children to me, for of such is the kingdom of heaven." This is the Messiah? One day Jesus attracted a large crowd, and a poor widow suffering from a hemorrhage came pushing through the group to touch the hem of his garment. She claimed that she was healed. "Who touched me?" said Jesus. "Who touched you? What do you mean, who touched you? Everybody here is pushing and shoving. We have momentum!" A blind beggar heard him coming and cried out, "Jesus, thou Son of David, have mercy on me." "Get away from here, we're busy." "Call the man here." And they bring the beggar to Jesus. More delay! This is the Messiah?

And now, contradiction of all contradictions, Jesus is saying something about going to a cross, going to be killed. Has Simon Peter picked up something that everybody else has missed? If he did, it certainly was not obvious. In fact, it was incomprehensible. And yet Simon Peter said, "You are the Messiah." How could he say it?

The answer was and is simple. Flesh and blood did not reveal this to Simon; he did not get this by observation; he did not come to this understanding by listening and watching. On the contrary, listening and watching could lead to one conclusion: Jesus is no messiah. It is absolutely impossible to say, "Jesus is the Messiah," except by the revelation of God. As Paul expressed it, "No one can say Jesus is Lord except by the Holy Spirit."

The central miracle of the Christian faith is just this, that anyone would say, "The Messiah has come, and it is Jesus." Why? Because this confession calls for a grasp of the fundamental secret of the kingdom, a reversal of one's whole perspective on life. A view that once dreamed, "Wherever the Messiah is, there is no misery," has been forged into the present conviction, "Wherever there is misery, there is the Messiah." That reversal of judgment can come about only as Jesus expressed it, "Flesh and blood has not revealed this to you, but my Father who is in heaven."

The Messiah has come, and it is Jesus of Nazareth. And the first great task of the Messiah is to get us to quit looking for one.—Fred B. Craddock

Illustrations

POSTPONEMENT.   A much-used word in the Spanish language is *mañana*, tomorrow. But what the word suggests figures into the philosophy of people everywhere. Dickens's Mr. Macawber stayed poor because he was always waiting for his ship to come in—and did nothing in the meantime. Scarlett O'Hara was always avoiding the unpleasant present by saying that she would think about a pressing matter "tomorrow."—James W. Cox

THE GODWARD LOOK.   Augustine told a wretched man who thought of nothing but his sins, "Look away from yourself and look to God." The godward look is the secret of the Christian hope.

The Christian hope is not simply a trembling, hesitant hope that perhaps the promises of God may be true. It is the confident expectation that they cannot be anything else than true.—William Barclay

Sermon Suggestions

WHAT GOD'S SERVANT DOES.   TEXT: Isa. 50:4–9a. Although this Servant Song could be primarily about true Israel, the prophet, or some other representative servant of the Lord, Christians can see how Jesus Christ reflects the servant's characteristics at their best. (1) God's servant listens alertly to God's teaching. (2) God's servant comforts with God's true Word those worn by the weight and worries of the world. (3) God's servant faces the sometimes painful consequences of commitment and obedience. (4) God's servant expects vindication by his God (see Phil. 2:5–11).

A FORMULA FOR SETTLING DISPUTES. TEXT: Phil. 2:5–11. The incarnate Christ provides the pattern. (1) He did not cling to his lofty status as one divine. (2) He went the limit of self-giving in order to serve God and bring about reconciliation, even to the extent of dying on a cross. (3) He lost nothing but rather was exalted by God in the Resurrection and demonstrated that he was worthy of the highest praise.

Worship Aids

CALL TO WORSHIP. "O magnify the Lord with me, and let us exalt his name together" (Ps. 34:3).

INVOCATION. As on that first Palm Sunday you came riding in triumph into the city, so this morning enter in majesty and ride in triumph into the innermost recesses of our hearts, Lord Jesus, we pray. We raise our hosannas and sing praises to your name and lay down before you the garments of our dedication and the palm branches of our love that with our lives we might serve you as we follow you day by day. Come, Lord Jesus, reign among us in power and love. Come this morning with salvation and healing, with strength and forgiveness. Come and call us anew unto you, we pray.—W. Henry Fields

OFFERTORY SENTENCE. "Upon the first day of the week let each one of you lay by him in store, as he may prosper, that no collections be made when I come" (1 Cor. 16:2).

OFFERTORY PRAYER. Lord, let us lay at thy feet the finest offering we can bring, just as long ago the faithful laid cloaks and palms before Jesus Christ, our Lord and Master.—E. Lee Phillips

PRAYER. O Father, as we begin this historic week so filled with the drama that has brought life and immortality to light, keep us from that casualness that would cause us to think that we can pass through these days as innocent bystanders. Make us as sensitive to the fickleness in our own lives as we are to the vacillating ways of Pilate, the betraying ways of Judas, or the denying ways of Peter.

In the events of this week, we sense that the agony of this world is your agony and that you are dying a thousand deaths that we may be reconciled to you as our Maker, Father—to our true self, as your son, your daughter—to one another, as sister, brother. Called to be your instruments of reconciliation, may we not turn from the agony of love when it comes to us in the shape of a cross. May we trust your grace in the cross of Christ that makes us ready for anything. May we be so in tune with your love purpose that we may be courageous to pray in our Gethsemane—"Not my will but yours be done."

Grant to those among us who are sick in mind, body, or spirit, the grace of your healing; to those who are lonely, bereft of loved one or friend, the consciousness of your abiding presence; to the stranger within our gates, a sense of oneness with your people.

We praise you for steps taken in the direction of peace, and we pray that the continuing efforts of these who have divided their country and exhausted its resources through years of hostility and conflict may further move from suspicion to trust, from fear to love, from retaliation to reconciliation.

We pray, too, for the peace of Jerusalem—that land we think of as holy because of your advent into history there but made so unholy today with the brokenness of hostilities and bloodshed. May those who seek its peace through justice and equanimity have the faith and courage to persevere.

May your highest aspiration for your church be confirmed in and through us, that indeed "the kingdoms of this world may become the kingdom of our Lord and his Christ" who is here as your eternal Word.—John M. Thompson

LECTIONARY MESSAGE

PALM SUNDAY

Topic: Running Against the Polls

TEXT: John 12:12–16

Every political candidate running for major office today knows the crucial importance of the pollsters and their statistical surveys. A slight flutter in the breeze of public opinion can send a candidate's approval rating in the polls tumbling several notches, endangering, in the subtle shift of whim, a long and costly campaign.

So, candidates study every poll, scrutinize every scrap of data, trying to outguess the fickle fates of political fortune, eager to exercise "spin control" over the erratic forces of public sentiment. And when the candidate senses that the wind of voter opinion has shifted, the candidate also shifts, quietly, of course, so as not to appear indecisive. But when the electorate swings in mood, the shrewd candidate must also swing, subtly altering the platform to match public desire, setting the sails for a new tack toward victory.

When Jesus came to Jerusalem that day, his image in the public mind could not have been better, his standing in the polls could not have been stronger. John tells us that word had spread of his many signs, especially the most recent and most astounding one: the raising of Lazarus from the dead. No wonder a great crowd gathered to greet Jesus. And no wonder, as well, that they chose palm branches to wave as he arrived. The palm was a symbol of militant nationalism, Jerusalem-style. To wave a palm branch in first-century Palestine would be like waving the Stars and Stripes in colonial Boston or shouting "Remember the Alamo!" in old Texas. Waving palms was a political gesture, a symbol of revolutionary fervor, a sign that the crowd considered Jesus to be the candidate of preference, the man of the hour, the one to liberate their homeland from foreign rule. "Ladies and gentlemen, wave your palm branches and give a big welcome to Jesus of Nazareth, the next king of Israel!"

But then . . . just at the moment of greatest excitement, just as it seemed that Jesus was about to mount the rolling wave of popular opinion and ride it to victory in the city, he did something no savvy candidate would ever have done. He "found a young ass and sat upon it." This is strange indeed. It is as if a presidential candidate, having just received the party's nomination, were to appear on the rostrum, in front of the screaming and applauding delegates, wearing the rags of a street person. The crowd is offering a crown; Jesus chooses a donkey. The crowd wants a nationalistic king, a military strong man to throw off gentile rule; Jesus acts out a scene from the prophet Zechariah of a humble king who cancels the military budget and declares peace to Jew and Gentile alike (Zech. 9:9–10). At the height of his popularity and with victory in his grasp, astoundingly Jesus runs against the polls and presents himself in a way that confounds every expectation of the multitude. In a classic understatement, John reports that "his disciples did not understand this at first."

But later, they did. John goes on to report that "when Jesus was glorified" (a phrase that points to Jesus' death) the truth dawned upon the disciples, and they understood what this scene meant. In other words, it was through his suffering that Jesus truly became king, not king of this or that nation, not the hero of this or that political faction, but king of all Creation. It was not in the momentary fervor of the crowd but rather in his death that Jesus was exalted. He was not glorified by being lifted up on the shoulders of an ecstatic group of nationalists; he was glorified by being lifted up on a cross, drawing all people unto himself (John 12:32). By refusing to be the king they expected, Jesus became the king they truly needed, and *our* king, too.—Thomas G. Long

SUNDAY: MARCH THIRTY-FIRST

SERVICE OF WORSHIP

Sermon: Is Resurrection a Laughing Matter?

TEXT: Acts 17:22–32

It began with the resident eleven-year-old gadfly asking, "Well, what are you going to preach on this week, Dad?" It's Easter Sunday, and he's asking me what my sermon topic is going to be? Before I can finish saying, "The Resurrection of Jesus," my wife with an unabashed grin begins singing, "Up from the grave he arose, with a mighty triumph over his foes. / He arose the victor from the dark domain and he lives forever with his saints to reign." He arose! What else is there to say or sing, preach or proclaim? There is only one Easter sermon: the Resurrection of Jesus and through him our hope of resurrection. But what is to be our response to this singular event and singularly important Easter message? I believe it is laughter.

I. First of all we discover the *laughter of ridicule.* In Athens, Paul used the language of Stoics and Epicureans along with the Greek poets, but his message was the Resurrection. "Now when they heard of the Resurrection of the dead, some *laughed.*" That word is also translated "mocked" or "sneered"; it is the laughter of ridicule. For the sophisticated Athenians, the notion of a man being "dead as a mackerel," then three days later being wondrously alive, was more than a little fishy. Here in this very court of the Aereopagus it was expressed by Aeschylus: "Once a man dies and the earth drinks up his blood, there is no resurrection." It is obvious that Paul was speaking foolishness to those who knew what was impossible.

Even in an age when the mysteries of *flora* and *fauna,* the marvels of inner and outer space, boggle the mind there is still a sophomoric pride that insists, "No Way! I have never experienced resurrection, so it can't be true." Every age has its "cultured despisers." This is worth remembering when an instantly sophisticated teenager taunts his parents, "You mean you still believe that stuff?" It is said with laughter, but it is a hollow laugh.

The laughter of the Athenians was probably a way of mocking Paul. They must have thought the "passionate earnestness" of this little homely man was funny. This is the laughter of ridicule. But then what does the servant of the Master expect? Have you forgotten already on this beautiful Easter morning, the jeering and derisive laughter of Thursday and Friday? "Who was it, omniscient king, that hit you. . . . If you are the Son of God come down. . . . Here is the king of the Jews crowned with thorns."

Of all laughter, the laughter of ridicule is the most hollow and self-condemning. For we think so little of ourselves that we must raise ourselves by inches as we stand on others. It begins not as the mockery of the cross but as the subtle put-down of racial jokes or as children poking fun at other children. Yet when we mock life, it is not because we embrace life but because we are afraid of it. This is the laughter of ridicule, and it has about it the odor of death.

II. There is yet another laughter that may greet the resurrection of Jesus. It is the *laughter of reversal.* Paul says to the Corinthians, "Death is swallowed up in victory." What a statement. What is feared more than death? What motivates us for playing the fool, even the damned fool, more than the fear of growing old and dying? Can you imagine what would happen if that enemy were defeated? It would be like teaching cancer cells to destroy themselves with no side effects. We would cry and smile, then laugh. Irwin S. Cobb has said that "humor is tragedy standing on its head with its trousers split." Laughter is the response to seeing the proud and pompous lord of death step on the banana peel. What a cause for hilarity; the mighty have been brought low. It is the laughter of reversal.

Not only that, but the lowly are exalted. Take Abraham and Sarah, for instance;

they were promised a great line of descendents. They were to be a blessing to all nations. Then Sarah, almost ninety, barren, without hope of a son, is told she is in a family way. When Abraham hears the news he falls down laughing (Gen. 17: 17). A delivery in the geriatric ward! It is all so unbelievable Sarah can't keep from laughing, and she names her son "Laughter." The barren give life, the old becomes new, the jeers turn to cheers. God is so faithful, so surprising, you have to laugh.

God is in the business of reversing "the way things are": What good can come out of Nazareth? The King of kings is born in a manger, a feed trough. Yes, Isaiah knew it: the lowly will be exalted. It is the laughter of reversal; everything is upside down. What power is greater in our lives than death? What do we run from, deny constantly . . . death? Freud knew it; he spoke of nervous gallows humor. An anxious snicker or two is understandable. No matter how high you score on achievement tests, how beautiful or powerful you are, you will die. All you own and love will be dust. Yet is there One in the grand economy of God that has defeated death? Could this be the great reversal of life over death? In a Peter DeVries novel, a character was buried alive in a landslide of tons of garbage at the city dump. When you least expect it, he rises from the garbage with a cantaloupe rind on his head, singing the doxology. What an image. Can we rise from the garbage pit of failure singing, "Praise God from whom all blessings flow," and laugh the laugh of the great reversal?

III. If we can experience the reversal of Christ's Resurrection, then the final form of laughter becomes that of rejoicing. The *laughter of rejoicing* is to cry out in victory over the worst this old world can dish out: "O death, where is your victory?" The venom does not destroy us. Dr. Conrad Hyers tells of the early Greek Orthodox tradition of clergy and laity meeting in the sanctuary the day after Easter to tell stories, jokes, and anecdotes. It seems so fitting. Satan thought he had won at Golgotha. Yet the last laugh is at the Resurrection; not a laugh of ridicule or even of reversal but a laugh of rejoicing. Sin, death, and sorrow have been swallowed up by redemption, life, and joy: "O death, where is thy sting? O grave, where is thy victory?" In Eugene O'Neill's play *Lazarus Laughed*, we hear the modern echo:

Laugh Laugh
Death is Dead
There is only laughter

Here is the great reversal, and we are caught up in it. How can we not rejoice? Can't you imagine Mary getting together with Jesus later and saying, "And I thought you were the gardener!" The couple on the road to Emmaus would also be having a good laugh with Jesus: "We were trying to tell you about the one who had died." But it wouldn't end there. Mary and the two on the Emmaus road could now laugh at the power of death. Thomas More did joke with the hangman because his conscience was clear; he was serving his God. A bishop in Hungary in the 1950s was imprisoned by the Communists because he stood up to them. In a six-by-eight solitary-confinement cell he could not be broken: "For in that room the Risen Christ was present and in communion with me I was able to prevail." Luther said it in his great hymn, "The body they may kill / his truth abideth still." Columnist Celestine Sibley was approached at a program she was giving by a nice-looking young man she did not recognize. He said, "I'm that garbage-can baby you wrote about twenty years ago." Stuffed in a garbage can after birth, he was hospitalized for a long time; now he was glowing, smiling, laughing with new life. Death where is your sting?

I came back from a hospital visit laughing and singing some silly ditty without realizing it. My wife said, "What are you doing?" Sometimes when you see the miracle of Easter it's all you can do. It is the laughter of rejoicing. May that be your soul's response to the Resurrection this morning. For when Easter invades your life, when you see the spirit of the risen Christ prevailing in hospital waiting rooms and prison chapels, you realize that Resurrection is a laughing matter.—Gary D. Stratman

Illustrations

DESTRUCTION OF DEATH. Death is terrifying. For more than two centuries we have had the English proverb "While there is life, there's hope." John Gay said that, but he was only adapting a phrase of the Roman orator Cicero, and Cicero filched it from the Greek poet Theocritus of the third century before Christ. Theocritus was more brutal than either Cicero or John Gay. He said, "For the living there is hope, but for the dead there is none." This has been the terrifying thing about death, ever since our first parents purchased their dreadful knowledge of its mystery at the cost of their sinlessness. We know our world through our senses. It is created for us by the reassuring sensations of eating, drinking, seeing, hearing, touching, smelling, tasting, feeling. This world dissolves in death, and with it the avenues of knowledge that furnish a basis for hope. Most belief in immortality, in survival after death, is less than Christian, just as mere belief in the existence of God is less than Christian. Easter is not a festival of immortality. Easter is the festival of Christ's destruction of death by his death.—Fred H. Lindemann

CHRISTIAN REALISM. The writers of the New Testament summoned their followers to look at the fact of death with Christian realism. This meant that they were to recognize death for what it is and for what it is not: an enemy, but a "reconciled" enemy; a threat, but a transformed threat; a finality, but, if you will permit a paradox, a "transitional finality." They were never asked to be chirpy and optimistic in the face of unpleasant facts; rather, they were summoned to face again the consequences of their belief! You believe that Jesus rose again? You celebrate Easter? Then if you believe "that Jesus died and rose again, even so, through Jesus, God will bring with him those who are fallen asleep" (RSV).—Elam Davies

Sermon Suggestions

GOD'S VICTORY PORTRAYED. TEXT: Isa. 25:6–9. (1) *Before:* death and reproach. (2) *After:* banquet and comfort. (3) *Caption:* "The Lord has spoken."

GOD HAS NO FAVORITES. TEXT: Acts 10:34–43, NEB. This means (1) the story of Jesus, though quite particular, is of universal significance; (2) the forgiveness of sins, though of universal application, is of individual availability.

Worship Aids

CALL TO WORSHIP. "O taste and see that the Lord is good: blessed is the man that taketh refuge in him" (Ps. 34:8).

INVOCATION. It is true, our Father, that we have met to worship, but we must admit that we really don't know how to go about it. Our feeble attempts at praise seem so inadequate, our prayers are so inarticulate, our gifts are so small that it is a wonder if worship takes place at all. And yet we know that you desire our worship, so you will help us to bring it about. Today in this place help us to feel your presence in such a real way that our only possible response will be genuine worship.—James M. King

OFFERTORY SENTENCE. "He that spared not his own Son, but delivered him up for us all, how shall he not also with him freely give us all things?" (Rom. 8:32).

OFFERTORY PRAYER. Lord of resurrection, help us to give with a sense of victory and serve with a force of tenacity because Jesus is alive and the world needs to know their Savior every day.—E. Lee Phillips

PRAYER. Eternal God, deep beyond our understanding and high above our imagining, we worship thee. We thank thee that we cannot comprehend thee, for if thou couldst be caught in our nets, if we could run the lines of our weak thought around thy being and thy ways, then wert thou too small a God. We glory in thy greatness and thy depth beyond our comprehension.

Be to us, we beseech thee, what the souls of men across the centuries have sought to find in thee. Be to us a refuge.

For the storms of life are heavy, the tempests beat upon our ships, and we need harborage and anchorage. Throw thy greatness around our littleness. Be to us the citadel of the eternal amid the anxieties of time, and let some hearts in this company rejoice that thou art our refuge and that underneath are the everlasting arms.

Be to us our judge. For when we compare ourselves with ourselves and with others, too easily self-complacency takes possession of us. Thou Spirit of all beauty, truth, and goodness, be thou our judge. Expect of us more than we expect of ourselves. Humble us with some fair vision of loveliness in character and in deed that will shame us from our self-contentment. Grant that some soul here may see thee high and lifted up and in contrition amend his life.

Be thou to us a guide. For it is not in man that walketh to direct his steps. If thou hast no purpose, then are our purposes vain. If thou hast no plan, then is our building vain. If thou hast no will, then do our steps walk waywardly and know not where they go. We beseech thee that for the reward of our worship, light may fall upon some path and some soul, confused amid the perplexities of life, may see the road that he should take.

Be to us a friend, not far off but close at hand, available for every day's most common need, so that we may but part the inward curtain of our souls and find thee there. O Eternal, so great and yet so close, make us aware of thine abiding presence and be to every one of us henceforth the inner Friend, the unseen Companion of our pilgrimage. We ask it in the Spirit of Christ.—Harry Emerson Fosdick.

LECTIONARY MESSAGE

Topic: Do Not Fear, Only Believe
TEXT: Mark 16:1–8

The women had stuck with Jesus since the heady days of success in Galilee. They had watched his Crucifixion from afar (Mark 15:40). They had watched where he was buried. And now they come to anoint his body with spices, expecting to find only a body grown cold from death's darkness. Their only concern is about managing a tomb's heavy stone. The open tomb weighs even more heavily on their hearts.

I. *The fear of the followers of Jesus.* In 4:35–41, the disciples' boat was being swamped with waves, and they feared for their lives. When Jesus awoke and calmed the storm with just a word, they were filled with a different kind of fear. It was a sense of awe at being in the presence of one with so much power. A second time they were struggling against the waves, and Jesus came to them walking on the water (6:45–52). They thought it was a ghost and turned pale with fear. But when Jesus got into their boat, the winds ceased, and their hearts were calmed.

Fear caught them again when they were on the road of Jerusalem (10:32). They knew that danger loomed ahead. Their worst fears have come to pass, Jesus has been crucified. And they think that now he lies amouldering in some grave. But brave women venture out to minister to his corpse and are let in on the greatest of news. Jesus has been raised, and they can see him again just as he had promised. But instead of being filled with joy, they are overcome by fear. They are even unable to carry out the assignment that the angels gave them. They were told to share the news with the disciples and Peter. But their lips were buttoned, for they were afraid.

II. *The Resurrection brings forgiveness.* The Resurrection of Jesus brings the glad tidings of forgiveness. Jesus was abandoned by his disciples to face his accusers alone. Peter denies him with curses. Mark reports no disciples nearby as Jesus dies. None of the eleven request the body of their Lord to give him a proper burial as the disciples of John the Baptist did when he was executed (6:29). But in the Resurrection, the word comes that he will see them in Galilee. Go tell the disciples *and Peter.* Implicit in this news is the word of forgiveness. The disciples might abandon Jesus, but he will not abandon them. They might forsake him, but he will never forsake them.

III. *The Resurrection overcomes human failure.* It is a curious way to end a Gospel—on a note of human failure. The women say nothing because they are afraid. But the readers of the Gospel and we know that the word got out. Jesus is alive. Human inadequacy, weakness, and fear are no obstacle to the power of the gospel. Despite their initial fear, the Resurrection means that Jesus will encounter them again, and he will impart strength to enable them to be witnesses to the world.

IV. *The Resurrection overcomes fear.* The angel announces that Jesus goes before them. All through the Gospel, Jesus has gone before his disciples. Now he goes before us in death so that we can learn that there is nothing to fear. We need not fear to proclaim the gospel boldly. The Resurrection makes clear that the powers that be do not have the last word. When they have done their worst, God steps in to do his best.—David E. Garland

SUNDAY: APRIL SEVENTH

SERVICE OF WORSHIP

Sermon: Our Lives, His Witnesses

TEXTS: Acts 3:12–16; 1 Cor. 15:58

God uses human lives as living testimonies of his truth. Turn with me to Acts 3:12–16. We will see that the healing of the lame man and his subsequent action bears witness to the Resurrection of Christ, which, in essence, becomes a model for similar action on our part.

I. Notice first of all in this passage what appears to be an unbelievable fact. Peter is preaching to the crowd that has gathered following the healing of a man lame from birth. They are wondering how on earth such a thing could have happened. Peter explains by saying it was done in the power of Jesus, who is the Prince, or author, of life. Then he drops the bombshell by describing Jesus as one "whom God hath raised from the dead" (v. 15).

(a) How unbelievable this would be for these people!

It was not that they had never seen amazing things. Jesus had done miracles in their minds; that wasn't the issue. The antagonism arose because, if this were true, it meant Jesus was indeed the Messiah. It meant that this lowly rabbi from despised Galilee, who had died as a criminal, was the Anointed One of God. But how could Jesus be the Messiah? This was impossible. It could not be, for he didn't fit in with their plans.

(b) There was another good reason the audience would reject the claim of Resurrection. If it were true, it meant they had put to death God's anointed! It meant that they had taken God's gift of deliverance and thrown it back into his teeth. Surely this could not be! Were they not God's chosen? Peter's claim for Jesus' Resurrection was beyond believability.

(c) Our world is not much different from this ancient one. Easter is fine as long as we speak of bunnies and eggs and flowers, making Easter just a civilized nature celebration, a great time for sentimental themes. But a resurrection? A man coming back to life after being put to death? Surely not. Isn't that really just some ancient story, some myth the disciples used to shore up their story? Surely we're not expected in the twentieth century to believe this actually happened.

II. But something extraordinary happened on that day as Peter spoke. As he talked, something incredible happened to that crowd. The Resurrection of Jesus was unbelievable, but Acts 4:4 indicates that many who heard the Word believed. How could that be? What happened to convince them?

(a) They encountered a believable witness. The healed man was bounding, leaping, praising, running all around! The witness of this man made the unbelievable real! This leaping, bounding, healed man is the living witness that Christ is truly risen from the grave!

(b) We must be leaping beggars for our unbelieving world! It is only by our witness that they can know the power and truth of the Resurrection. This great event forms the fulcrum point of history, yet it is invisible except through our lives. The world will never know the truth of Easter unless we live Easter lives!

III. First Corinthians 15:58 instructs us to witness to the reality of Christ's Resurrection by being "steadfast, unmoveable, always abounding in the work of the Lord." We should take this so very seriously.

(a) There are so many things that are common to our world that the Christian must stand firmly against. We resist the vicious revenge against our enemies and those who hurt us. We resist the "more, more, more" cry of our greedy society. And in standing uncompromisingly, we show the world that Jesus who died is now alive and lives forevermore.

(b) Paul also says that by "abounding in the work of the Lord" we witness to his Resurrection. Our involvement with God's work in this church and other places says unmistakably, "He is alive!" Every time your hand touches the handle of the church door, it is signing a message to the world. "I am not the hand I used to be. I have a new Master now. He wants me to say hello to a lonely newcomer, to take the shoulder of a wayward boy, to hold the hand of a grieving widow, to hold a Bible that shares God's plan of salvation. This hand is new by the grace of a living Lord!"

(c) But you say, "Why does only our work in the Lord give witness to his Resurrection? Aren't other organizations important?" Yes, but there is one difference; the church is God's tool for his plan. How much we appreciate the service clubs and what they do, but Jesus didn't found them. We're thankful for our school and its many activities, but Jesus didn't call the school his "bride." For the Christian, it is the church that demands his priorities! Here the good news is preached. Here men find salvation. Here is a fellowship of self-sacrificing love. Our participation in this God-ordained group is a billboard to the world that Jesus is alive and reigning!—Larry Payne

Illustrations

INITIATIVE IN WITNESS.   Every Christian ought to be exerting a deliberate and conscious influence upon others for good. The great disease of the church is the lack of that effort. Christ says to all of us, "Ye shall be my witness"—witnesses unto me. Every Christian can make some sort of a witness for Christ. Some of the least can do the most. Frequently in the Scriptures, great events are brought to pass by humble actors. The servant of Saul, when Saul wanted to turn back, brings him into the presence of Samuel and face-to-face with his destiny. The servant of Naaman, when that satrap was in a rage at Elisha, reminded him that he had come to Samaria to be cured of his leprosy and persuaded him to use the cure that Elisha had prescribed. It was a captive maid in Naaman's house who had told him of the prophet of God. Humble agents can help to work great destinies. Let none, therefore, hold back because he thinks he is not gifted or that his post is not important enough. Who can tell the effect and influence of an earnest word to another in the interests of his highest happiness and the welfare of his soul—a word of comfort, a word of hope, or a word of warning; a word spoken in season, how good it is? The author of that proverb does not say, "a word spoken in season" by a learned man or an eloquent man or a clever man or a great man, but a word spoken in season, how good it is. "In the morning sow thy seed, and in the evening withhold not thine hand." "Cast thy bread upon the waters: for thou shalt find it after many days."—Clarence E. Macartney

AND THE SPIRIT.   When, for the first time, I received the gospel to my soul's salvation, I thought that I had never really heard it before, and I began to think that the preachers to whom I had listened had not truly preached it. But, on looking back, I am inclined to believe that I had heard the gospel fully preached many hundreds of times before, and that this was the difference—that I then heard it as though I heard it not; and when I did hear it, the message may not have been any more clear in itself than it had been at former times, but the power of the Holy Spirit was present to open my ear and to guide the message to my heart.—Charles Haddon Spurgeon

Sermon Suggestions

THE ELEMENTS OF CHRISTIAN COMMUNITY.
TEXT: Acts 4:32–35. (1) Unity of spirit. (2)
Power of testimony. (3) Generosity in
stewardship.

TOWARD FELLOWSHIP WITH CHRIST AND
CHRISTIAN JOY. TEXT: 1 John 1:1–2:2.
(1) Through the forgiveness of our sins,
1:6–10. (2) Through the overcoming of
our sins, 2:1–2.

Worship Aids

CALL TO WORSHIP. "I waited patiently
for the Lord; and he inclined unto me, and
heard my cry" (Ps. 40:1).

INVOCATION. Eternal Spirit, whom we
worship with reverent lips, but too often
with insensitive hearts, grant us today a
vital experience of thy saving presence. Be
to us not alone a holy name reverently
spoken, but a living Reality within our
souls. Shine in us, like the sun returning
after the rain. Clarify our thoughts, elevate
our spirits, deepen our faith and courage,
and send us out to lay fresh hold on life
because thou hast laid strong hold on
us.—Harry Emerson Fosdick

OFFERTORY SENTENCE. "But when thou
doest alms, let not thy left hand know what
thy right hand doeth: that thine alms may
be in secret: and thy Father who seeth in
secret shall reward thee" (Matt. 6:3–4).

OFFERTORY PRAYER. God who sustains
us every day, these monetary gifts are only
part of what we offer to you in service.
Help us also to give our lives each day in
discipleship to the way of Jesus.—J. Scott
Hickman

PRAYER. God of glory, God of grace, in
the silence we are made mindful of our
desperate need for you. In the quietness,
we see the emptiness of the moment and
the fullness of your presence.
Gracious God, forgive us for filling most
of our time with shouted words and noisy
shadows, leaving no time or place for you.
In our better moments, we wonder, Why
are we so foolish?
So may our worship and praise be more
of assured silence and gentle listening, re-
treating to refresh our spirits and restoring our souls beside the still waters of
solitude. And then, we would venture to
say, "Speak, Lord, for your servants are
listening."
God of glory, speak to us in the wonder
of your Creation. Stepping into the beauty
of this day, how can we not hear thee!
Spring sings hymns of new life and spir-
ited growth. The final tug between the
cool of late winter and the warmth of early
spring tells of the rhythm and seasons of
your balanced world. We hear and are
made glad.
God of grace, speak to us in forgiveness.
We bring our sins with us, and in your
blessed presence we see clearly their
smallness, their meanness, their ugliness.
What can we say? Speak forgiveness, O
God of mercy.
God and Father of the Living Word: the
Word who became flesh . . . in the cross
and resurrection you speak mercy and
grace and salvation to us in unmistakable
and dramatic voice. May we hear and receive you in the risen Christ. What wondrous love has been spoken!
O God who speaks now, let us hear your
Word for us today. Open and embrace us
with receptivity and understanding. Abiding God, speak to us in each other.
Though we are fragile earthen vessels, we
have been chosen and we have been redeemed to share the good Word, the good
news.
As we worship and pray and listen, O
God, in that still small voice, may we hear
and truly know you.—William M. Johnson

LECTIONARY MESSAGE

Topic: The End of the Beginning
TEXT: John 20:19–31
Winston Churchill reversed the order in
his treatment of World War II. He placed
"The End of the Beginning" before "The
Beginning of the End," but he was writing
of death and destruction. I am speaking of
life and light.

Do you remember the story from John Masefield's play? The lady who witnessed the Crucifixion was overawed by it all and asked the soldier about Jesus, "Where is he now?" "Let loose in the world, Lady," he said.

I. *It is difficult to bring the beginning to an end.* Out of the haze and daze, the grief, loneliness, and disappointment, it looked more like the end to the disciples—the end of everything. One disciple was reluctant to enter the tomb. Mary Magdalene was reluctant to give up the body. Thomas was reluctant to believe. If this is all, leave them to their memories— more enjoyable, more merciful. All were hanging on to the past until Thomas's confession: "My Lord and my God."

II. *When that story is ended, our story begins.* Ours is a story of *reality.* How matter of fact is Paul's statement in 1 Cor. 15:3–5a: "For I delivered to you first of all that which also I received. . . ." He had heard stories from others—Peter and the rest. He had experienced something for himself—he appeared to me. His letters bristle with the application of Jesus' teaching to current problems . . . "Be ye kind one to another . . ." "God loved us . . ."

Ours is a story of *responsibility.* Hear the words of Jesus: "As the Father hath sent me, so send I you." It is not our privilege to live the memories of his miracles, ministry, mannerisms. As a child I felt left out when talk of the war began—then we had our own war! We cannot transport ourselves back two thousand years—four thousand miles away.

It is ours to believe. This is the word of Jesus to Thomas: "Blessed are those who have not seen and yet have believed." Ours is a faith unlimited by pseudoscience: you cannot believe in life after death . . . ridiculous (botany thrives on it). Ours is a faith unlimited by pseudosociology—the theory of a super race disappears in "All have sinned and come short . . ." Ours is a faith unlimited by pseudohistory: it never has happened. This is the best guarantee that it will.

It is ours to be like. This is the Word of Jesus: "As the Father hath sent me . . ." It is not to don the clothing of ancients and assume other roles: this is playacting. It is not to talk in ancient shibboleths and conceal the truth: this is antique collecting. The needs of salvation have not changed: there is still selfishness, greed, pride. The opportunities of Christian witness have not changed: there is yet one beggar telling another beggar where to get food.

Ours is a story of *reaction.* Much like the chain reaction of nuclear fission. This is Christian growth—this is the end of the beginning. We can grow into his likeness. Is this not the way the gospel spreads— from one collection of atoms to another? There will be occasional explosions.

The end of the beginning is experienced in the realms of reality, responsibility, and reaction. Remember Thomas's confession: "My Lord and my God!"— J. Estill Jones

SUNDAY: APRIL FOURTEENTH

SERVICE OF WORSHIP

Sermon: The Golden Bowls
TEXTS: Rev. 5:8; Matt. 5:8–13

What could be more dramatic than this little-known story in the Bible? We were reading it one morning for our family devotions when its truth burst upon me.

The prayers of the saints have evidently already been poured from the golden bowls upon the altar of God. Thereupon an angel mingles with these prayers the incense from his golden censer. "And the smoke of the incense rose with the prayers of the saints from the hand of the angel before God" (Rev. 8:4). This smoke rises well-pleasing to God; then the angel swiftly scoops up some of the fire from the altar and hurls it down on the earth; "and there were peals of thunder, loud noises, flashes of lightning, and an earthquake" (Rev. 8:5).

When saints pray, something real and important always happens. Genuine

Christian prayer is not as though a woman should take cold water and throw it in a hot frying pan; it is much more as though a man should take a burning match and cast it into a gasoline tank. The power of true prayer is explosive.

I. True prayer is, first of all, acknowledgment: "Our Father, who art in heaven, hallowed be thy name." How hard it is for modern man truly to say that!

(a) If people who know each other long and closely can't really enter into the other person's life, how much more difficult it is for modern man to feel things real outside himself! How hard it is for those stuck in the rut of their own self-interest to recognize anything as really real and important beyond their own personal ambition or interest! How intensely difficult to acknowledge God to be real!

(b) Modern man's doubts, I believe, are caused far more by his inability to acknowledge God than by a lack of intellectual grasp. Modern men—that is to say, you and I—find it easiest to begin with the self as real and hardest to acknowledge God as more real than ourselves.

That exactly is modern man's problem. Nothing is real or right for him unless he says so. He must call life's pitches. He is man-centered at the depths of his consciousness; yes, far into the formations of his unconscious, he has forgotten how to acknowledge that God is our Father. He cannot say, "Hallowed be thy name." No wonder that he cannot pray. Man's first requirement is to be brought to his knees in terms of his desperate need to acknowledge reality. May the acute crisis of mankind help us again to acknowledge God and to begin rightly to pray.

II. Prayer is also acceptance. "Thy kingdom come. Thy will be done on earth as it is in heaven." We need not only to acknowledge God by hallowing his name but also to accept his will.

(a) What can be harder for modern man? We are democratic. To accept God's will, to *obey* him, goes contrary to the very grain of our being. After all, we *are* democratic. We don't believe in lords. We don't want the will of another imposed on us.

(b) What is our answer? If this world is to be the best medium for an indefinite number of people to grow together in freedom, there must be one will for all that provides the condition for such growth in freedom and for such exercise of freedom. God's will is no foreign imposition on our wills. His will is our own deepest and best will when we understand and come to ourselves.

But acceptance of the will of God must be a total acceptance. Partial loyalty to God is ultimate loyalty to some idol, really to some other god. Most of us do sin most of the time against the First Commandment. "Thou shalt have no other gods."

(c) The difficulty with the acceptance of God's will in prayer and then in life is that to accept him we must accept all others as well. God's will is for all and entirely. To accept God is to accept all our fellowmen, generally and in particular.

There is no true Christian prayer until we are ready fully to accept God and one another. The right prescription for prayer includes "Thy kingdom come, thy will be done in earth as it is in heaven." If our prayers are really to be placed in the golden bowls of the prayers of the saints, to be consecrated on the altar of God and returned with power to help the earth, we must pray true prayers. We must learn fully and wholeheartedly to accept God's will for all.

III. Prayer is also asking. "Give us this day our daily bread, and forgive us our debts as we forgive our debtors." True Christian prayer includes petition, asking for ourselves; and intercession, asking for others.

(a) Some people are so sophisticated that they think we should never ask God for anything. God knows what we need, they claim, and our asking him is just a waste of time. Over and over again I hear sermons and discussions against petitionary prayer. I am glad that Jesus included it in his model prayer. He also affirmed, "How much more shall your Father which is in heaven give good things to them that ask him" (Matt. 7:11).

In asking, we acknowledge ourselves to be children in need of love and creatures in need of food. Our temptation is to be independent, self-sufficient, instead of ready to accept our proper place in Creation. God wants us to ask for our sake. He wants us to learn that we are not central and beyond need.

(b) In prayer, we also identify ourselves with the will of God for others. We share companionship with God himself as we offer ourselves to help others. God does not violate human freedom. He waits for willing human instruments. Asking for others lifts us up to God by his grace and lets us come down refreshed with power and insight to minister concretely to every human need.

I know no such joy and such spiritual power as when I am allowed and enabled truly to pray for others. In such prayer, I can literally feel the surge of God's power through my body. Such prayer never becomes a substitute for our doing our part. It becomes an incentive to it and gives us the power to do it the better.

(c) The text implies that our prayers are taken right into heaven to be put into the golden bowls. Then they are poured on God's altar, consecrated to him, and returned with great power into the world. Prayer is no mere matter of autosuggestion or parapsychology. God does something far beyond using our small help. The Holy Spirit is not impotent to initiate and to carry through helpful action. Only faith in God's mighty works in human history is faith in true Christian prayer.

IV. Prayer, finally, is affirmation. "For thine is the kingdom and the power and the glory, forever. Amen."

(a) True Christian prayer is positive. It begins with the acknowledgement of God and ends by the affirming of his glory. Prayer when it is right becomes participation in God. The Holy Spirit prays in and through us. The words matter less and God matters more. We believe less and less in prayer and more and more in God. Therefore, we naturally end by affirming the kingdom to be God's as well as the power and the glory. We have nothing and do nothing except in him, and in him we have all things and do all that is needed.

(b) Jesus said that he of himself could do nothing. The very works which he did, the Father worked in him. The more we become transparent to God's will, the more we, too, shall know that prayer is

participation, the more we shall know that it is God who works in us both to will and to do. The more we affirm the reality of God, the more we become partakers of that reality. We pray mostly for God to become real in and for us. He alone is fully real; our lives become realized only in him.

(c) We need prayer. Prayer aligns us at the center of our lives with the will of God and opens for us the most effective way to become of help to others. But best of all, in prayer God becomes real, and life itself finds eternal meaningfulness. With full conviction I commend to you, I urge on you, a new life of true Christian prayer.—Nels F. S. Ferré

Illustrations

DOES GOD NEED OUR PRAYER? We do not know what God "needs." Presumably he needs nothing: all things and all creatures are his, "and he made us." Perhaps the wiser question is, Does God *wish* our prayers? Creation is the act of love. God has made us to live with him in the bonds of love. Therefore, it is a fair guess that he wants our prayers. I am presently engaged in the business of collecting grandchildren and recommend it to every reader. Not long ago one of them brought a "picture" she had drawn of the lake and hills in front of our summer cottage. I would never have recognized the view from the picture, for it was a strange crisscross of lines smudged with many a small fingerprint. Did I *need* the picture? No. Did I *wish* it? Yes. Maybe our prayers are much like that picture, a crisscross of lines, many of them selfish and plentifully smudged. This appraisal is doubly true if we judge our prayers by Christ, who by our faith is the open clue to the mystery. But—dare we say it?—God wants our prayers in the longing of his love.—George A. Buttrick

THE KINGDOM FIRST. When Paul asked for the prayers of his friends, he was concerned with the progress of the kingdom and the growth in Christian character of his people: "Finally, brethren, pray for us, that the word of the Lord may have free course and be glorified." Again he wrote,

"Withal praying also for us, that God would open unto us a door of utterance to speak the mystery." He knew what it meant to be hungry and cold, but he never asked for creature comforts for himself. As we have noted, he never pleaded the cause of his own wants: "For I have learned, in whatsoever state I am, therewith to be content. I know both how to be abased, and I know how to abound: everywhere and in all things I am instructed both to be full and to be hungry, both to abound and to suffer need." Paul claimed the right to support while he preached the gospel, but he would not allow his needs to take precedence over the interests of the kingdom.—William Douglas Chamberlain

Sermon Suggestions

A POINTED WORD TO SINNERS. TEXT: Acts 3:12–19. (1) Directly or indirectly, we are responsible for the death of Christ. (2) Yet God has turned his Crucifixion to our advantage. (3) Therefore, we can repent and turn to God, assured that our sins will be forgiven.

THE WORK OF THE FATHER'S LOVE. TEXT: 1 John 3:1–7. (1) He has made us his children. (2) He will perfect us in the likeness of Jesus Christ. (3) He now motivates us to moral purity through our blessed hope.

Worship Aids

CALL TO WORSHIP. "As the hart panteth after the water brooks, so panteth my soul after thee, O God" (Ps. 42:1).

INVOCATION. O Father, for the awe and reverence for who you are that banishes all other fears, we praise you. We have not received the spirit of timidity that we should appear before you as groveling slaves, but we have received the spirit of sonship and daughtership. With what love you love us that we are your children! We praise you for the vision of your glory that this sanctuary holds for us. Praise be to you—Father, Son, and Holy Spirit.—John M. Thompson

OFFERTORY SENTENCE. "Thy vows are upon me, O God: I will render thank-offerings unto thee" (Ps. 56:12).

OFFERTORY PRAYER. The grace of giving—that's what it is. As you gave so freely to us, so we give gladly to you. Lord, help this grace of giving to abound in us. We love you, and we offer our best to you.

PRAYER. We thank thee, our heavenly Father, that we are not come upon an errand of persuasion as unto one that is reluctant or unwilling to give. Our good is already the evidence of thy willingness that we should come. It is by thy Spirit that we are drawn. Thou art granting us the sense of spiritual need. From thee is that illumination by which we see things that are right and see how far we deviate from them. The impugnings of our conscience spring from thy divine influence. Our yearnings for things better, and our reachings out toward them, are all of thee. Whatever there is of true light, whatever there is that would take hold upon nobler and nobler experiences, is the fruit of thy shining upon the soul. How waste and how barren is man, and how hopeless of culture would he be if it were not for thy divine influence! And when thou hast taken us in hand and art Husbandman to us; when thou hast begun thy royal tillage in us; how slow are we in growing, how poor is the return which we make, and how poor is the fruit that hangs upon the bough!

We thank thee, thou that art patient in over-measure, beyond our comprehension—thou that dost dwell in an infinite mercy and surround thyself with good works of kindness and of love.

O Lord our God, we confess to thee all our evil; all our unworthiness; all that is weak in us from infirmity; all our transgressions, even the most heinous. We desire to hide none of these from thine eyes nor from our own. We would look upon the face of our sins and acknowledge them and turn away from them and be cured of every desire that leads us to them. Grant that we may every day, more than for silver or for gold, more than for food or for raiment, crave those dispositions which shall make us worthy to be called the sons of God. May we count nothing so precious to us as that which makes us better. May we look upon life as but for this end. In all our gettings, may we get understanding. Whatever we lose, so that we retain thy favor, may we consider ourselves rich; and whatever we gain, if by it we fail of thy favor, may we consider ourselves poor. Grant that we may see from day to day thy work growing in more tenderness of conscience, in more gentleness of disposition, in more fruitfulness of a true beneficence. May we more and more know the sacred word of life, not for ourselves, but for others. May we follow thee, if need be, through sorrow. May we not be afraid of the cross of Christ. May we desire to bear it. May we desire to take reproach for his sake. May we become like him in rebuking evil; in seeking to heal it; in being witnesses against it.

Grant thy blessing to rest upon every one in thy presence. Give wisdom to the conscience that is burdened. Give light to all that are darkened. Give to every one that needs confirmation the word of faith. Disclose thyself to those that look for thee and cannot find thee. Grant that those who are seeking the right way may be led by the very hand of God and find the way of wisdom. May those that are tempted be able to resist temptation. May those that are fallen not be destroyed. May they be lifted up by the mercy of God and turn to better ways.

We pray that the careless may be rebuked and that none may count themselves unworthy of eternal life. Revive thy work in this church, in the hearts of all that are in it, in all our churches, and through the land.

Bless schools and colleges, bless magistrates and all laws, and grant that they may be fountains of justice and purity. And may this whole people be regenerated and become a God-fearing people. And may this nation by its prosperity be a witness for the people of Christ on earth.

Let thy kingdom come everywhere. Let thy will be done on earth as it is in heaven. And to thy name shall be the praise, Father, Son, and Spirit.—Henry Ward Beecher

LECTIONARY MESSAGE

Topic: Thus It Is Written
TEXT: Luke 24:35–48

Thus It Is Written is the name of an excellent little missions text written by Cornell Goerner. It presents the biblical background and modern motivation for the missionary enterprise.

The text in Luke 24:46 is presented as a word of Jesus at the conclusion of a long, busy day. It was Resurrection Day, beginning for Jesus early in the morning and now extending later into the evening. The New Testament records several Resurrection appearances on this first day. This Gospel records three: to the two disciples on the road to Emmaus, to Simon Peter, and to the eleven (with the two) gathered in Jerusalem.

I. *What is written?* The text deals with the fundamentals of our faith. There is a reference to the Christ, the Messiah of Israel's hope and of prophetic proclamation. The Messiah was to suffer as all Israel was to suffer, as all of God's people suffer. Serving and suffering go hand in hand. He was to rise again from the dead. It had been fulfilled on that very day. We yet bask in the rays and reality of the Resurrection. With that much all had agreement.

That the preaching of God's gracious victory should be extended to all persons was written to be sure, but this interpretation of the faith was delayed in being realized. Repentance and forgiveness were the result of God's gracious utilization of preaching. Missions, you see, is as fundamental to the faith as are the other truths. Thus it is written!

II. *We are witnesses*

(a) Witnesses to God's love for all persons. "God so loved the world." The decisive factor is God beyond history and God within history.

(b) Witnesses to God's will in world missions. . . . He who believes that the sacrifice and the Resurrection of Christ was a fulfillment of Old Testament prophecy must in all fairness believe that world missions is a fulfillment of Old Testament prophecy.

(c) Witnesses to God's leadership from this place . . . this Jerusalem of your experience: the tawdry, the boring, the commonplace, the familiar, the safe, the secure, the understood, the clean, the wholesome, the respectable, the lovable. God leads from this Jerusalem to the exciting, the dangerous, to the haunts of wretchedness and greed.

What does it mean to you? It reminds us of the significance of word—written, spoken, incarnate. It relates us to the ages—just as the Old Testament looked forward to the suffering of the servant, so the Old Testament looked forward to our mission. It relates our mission to God's purpose—open your eyes to God's working. It requires participation—by your prayer, by your enthusiasm, by your faithful stewardship. "Thus it is written!"—J. Estill Jones

SUNDAY: APRIL TWENTY-FIRST

SERVICE OF WORSHIP

Sermon: The Uniqueness of Christ

Text: Acts 4:12

To the modern man, whether he is inside the church or out of it, one of the most startling statements in the New Testament occurs in the Acts of the Apostles. "There is no salvation by anyone else." This One in whom the new life was incarnate, he alone is the source of real life. If the average American stops to think about it at all, he is likely to be puzzled by it; it seems to be an impossible claim to make for anyone.

It is an extraordinary claim under any circumstances, but even more so when you stop to think that it was made at a time when the Christian movement was hardly more than a local stir, and Jesus, in the mind of the public, hardly more than a dimly remembered criminal.

Perhaps even more extraordinary is the fact that the claim has persisted through the ages, much more carefully thought out, sometimes lacking in the spontaneity and freshness of the early days; but nevertheless it has persisted, has made its way into the formal beliefs of the Christian church, and has been the incentive of missionaries around the globe. For Christians have continued to believe, to say, and to act on the assumption that there is something about Christ both unique and ultimate and that, in the end, the world will have to come to terms with him.

I. I am going to point out only three things that are to be said about this large and fascinating subject. The first is that Christians have often been fanatical and arrogant in their claim, and the first thing for us to do is to acknowledge it with penitence.

(a) They have tried, often by force and persecution, to impose their belief on other people. The Indians on this continent did not all become Christians of their own free will, not by any means. They became Christians because they did not dare do otherwise. And every Christian should remember that there has been more than one Spanish Inquisition, many more, and not all of them have been sponsored by Catholics or taken place on foreign soil.

(b) People in the eastern part of the world have often been forced by more subtle means to accept Christianity. It was the price they often paid for Western improvements, and the Christian religion was the necessary accompaniment of Western technology. Also, Christians have often been blind and insensitive to the spiritual lives and needs of other people, to the depths of their spiritual insights, to the reality of their own religious traditions, and they have barged into foreign lands and talked to the people as though they had never seen a spark of light and never known a grain of truth. They have often tried to make people in the East accept Christianity in Western dress and, in doing so, have often confused the vessel with the thing contained in it.

(c) The Christian claim to uniqueness often seems to the non-Christian world an arrogant claim with no real facts to support it. But there was no such arrogance in Christ. He was what he was. Whatever claims he made, or were made about him by his followers, were made without violence and confirmed by what he did. They were never imposed upon anyone by force either directly or indirectly. And above everything else, he was the revelation of the unself-centered God, who loved the world so much that he gave himself to the world.

II. The second thing takes us into deeper waters and is more positive. When a person finds the key that unlocks the door of his life, he is not likely to be dispassionate about the discovery, any more than he is when he finds the love of his life. He is more likely to sing about it and to act as though this one person were the only person in the world. He is likely to go overboard in the enthusiasm of his newfound life.

(a) Moreover, if the door is one of the great doors, when he finds the key that unlocks it, he cannot help feeling that the key that unlocks it for him will unlock it for others. The door that opens from guilt into forgiveness is the same door whether it is in Boston or in Baghdad, and the same key will unlock it wherever it may be. The door that opens from self-centeredness and fear into freedom is the same door whether it is at the north or the south pole or on the equator, and the same key will unlock it wherever it is.

(b) Put it another way and try to approach this truth from a slightly different angle. When you come to something that you recognize as ultimate, you find at the same time that it is universal. To make it as simple as I can, let me say this. When you discover the ultimate truth that two and two make four, you know that it is universal as well as ultimate, and that two and two make four everywhere. You are no longer dealing with a local but a universal fact.

(c) So in life, if you discover the ultimate principle that he that loseth his life shall find it, that principle is universal, and it is just as true for a man in Africa as it is for a man in Boston. If there be any saving power in it here, there will be saving power in it there. And if life lived on any other principle is doomed here, it will be doomed there.

III. But a principle by itself does not unlock a door until it becomes a key. I know that there are many things that people may say in response to that, especially a scientist. But on the whole I think it stands. A principle—that is, an intellectual principle that you grasp only in your mind—is not likely to open one of the locked doors in your life until it becomes a key, something that you can take hold of and fit into the lock. Ideas are powerful wherever you meet them, but when they are incarnate in a person their power is infinitely greater.

(a) The Christian's experience is something like this. Principles that he may have known all his life in Christ become a key, *the* key that unlocks the door. I cannot say more than that by way of description. Those who have not experienced anything like it, I fear, will not make much sense of it, but this is what the Christian experience is at its best. This is what is behind the statement in the Acts of the Apostles, behind the claim that Christianity is unique. The experience is that the general principles, which you may often find in Greek philosophy and in the other high religions of the world, once became incarnate in a person, in Christ; and, like a key, they then had the power that the principles by themselves never had.

(b) What I should like to say to Christians everywhere and especially to missionaries—and I should have to say it very humbly because they have gone into the dangerous places where I have never gone—what I should like to say is this: the key is the thing, and the key is the cross, and the cross is none other than the love that understands, suffers, dies, and rises again, not in the abstract, but in Christ. This is the key that unlocks the door, and, if it unlocks it here, it will unlock it everywhere.

What I should like to say to all Christians is, Give them the *key,* not your theories about it and certainly not the case you carry it in. *Give* it to them; don't thrust it upon them or impose it upon them. Give it to them gladly and, if they do not want it, let it drop it. As you give it to them, look very carefully at some of their own keys and see if they are not shaped something like a cross.

(c) One of the great lessons we in America must learn, both in politics and in religion, is how to have great convictions together with great compassion and understanding. To put it even more strongly, we must learn—and it will not be easy—how to be absolutely loyal and infinitely humble. It is not a common combination; you will grant that. There is only one place under heaven where we can learn it, as far as I know, and that is in Christ. It is not so much learning it as it is living in him sufficiently to let him live in us, so that we can keep at the same time our deepest and most absolute loyalties together with our infinite humility. When we come anywhere near doing that, there is no doubt in our minds that there is no salvation by anyone else.—Theodore Parker Ferris

Illustrations

UNIQUE AND UNIVERSAL.   The Christ-image is infinitely bigger and richer—and more disturbing—than what Christians under the influence both of Catholic triumphalism and of Protestant particularism have made of it, by drawing a tight little circle around the historical Jesus (or rather, their image of him) and calling it the whole of God. *If* Jesus as the Christ is unique, it is not because he is exclusive of any other revelation or the denial of any other saving activity of God but because he is uniquely inclusive—the concentration as in a burning-glass of the light and the love that is at work everywhere, enabling one to make better sense of it than any other figure in history. As Paul puts it again from his experience, "in him all things cohere and hang together." In the title of a book on Indian Christian theology, he "is unique *and* universal."—John A. T. Robinson

PROBLEM IN CHRISTIANITY.   I shall never forget when the bishop of Ceylon was here two or three years ago, preaching at the evening service. After the service we went to the rectory and sat and talked. Naturally, I had many questions to ask him about Ceylon. I said, "What is the chief problem that you have as bishop?" He said, "It is this. The native religion of Ceylon is Buddhism, and my chief difficulty in

trying to speak to the people about Christianity is that Buddhists in that area have no record of violence!"—Theodore Parker Ferris

Sermon Suggestions

COMFORTING THOUGHT FOR THE OPPRESSED.   TEXT: Acts 4:8–12. (1) Jesus Christ, the doer of good, was rejected and persecuted. (2) Yet God raised him from the dead and made him the only means of salvation.

WHEN OUR LOVE IS REAL.   TEXT: 1 John 3:18–24, NEB. (1) It shows itself in action. (2) We can pray with confidence. (3) We give our allegiance to Christ and keep his commands, especially his command to love one another. (4) We dwell in him, and he in us. (5) The Holy Spirit is present in us.

Worship Aids

CALL TO WORSHIP.   "Why art thou cast down, O my soul? And why art thou disquieted within me? Hope thou in God; for I shall yet praise him, who is the help of my countenance and my God" (Ps. 42:11).

INVOCATION.   Grant, O God, that your holy and life-giving Spirit may so move every human heart (and especially the hearts of the people of this land), that barriers which divide us may crumble, suspicions disappear, and hatreds cease; that our divisions being healed, we may live in justice and peace; through Jesus Christ our Lord.—*The Book of Common Prayer*

OFFERTORY SENTENCE.   "And Joseph, who by the apostles was surnamed Barnabas (which is being interpreted, son of exhortation), a Levite, a man of Cyprus by race, having a field, sold it, and brought the money and laid it at the apostles' feet" (Acts 4:36–37).

OFFERTORY PRAYER.   Lord, help us to trust you more fully, live for you more completely, and serve you more willingly, because we give unsparingly and love you unreservedly.—E. Lee Phillips

PRAYER. Eternal Spirit, so high above us that we cannot comprehend thee and yet so deep within us that we cannot escape thee, make thyself real to us now. In a shaken world, we seek stability; in a noisy world, we need inner peace; in a fearful world, we want courage; and in a world of rising and falling empires, we crave a vision of thine eternal Kingdom whose sun never sets.

Seek us out, every one, in the special circumstances and needs that each soul faces. Young and old we come, the merry-hearted and the bereaved; families together here and solitary souls lonely and far from home; some of us tempted to be proud of the world's prizes and some crestfallen because of failure; some strong in body and others striving to keep the inward man renewed while the outward man perishes. O Sun of our help and strength, be to us like the sun indeed and shine this morning into every window.

While thou dost comfort us, kindle also within us sincere penitence. Let some austere world of righteousness be spoken to our consciences today. Save us from our ignoble excuses, our cheap defenses, our unworthy self-deceits. Give us grace to be honest with ourselves, that we may rightly judge our dealing with the personality thou hast entrusted to us, with the friends and family that surround us, with the opportunities thou hast put before us, and with the stewardship committed to us.

We pray for the peace of the world. Stay the evil forces that withstand good will and lay the fuse which will explode another war. For wisdom to seek peace and pursue it, for faith and character to use aright the powers man has in his unworthy hands, we pray. To that end our intercessions rise for the United Nations, for all conferences seeking disarmament and peace, of our nation, its President and all who influence its policies, and for us, the whole body of the people, that we may prove worthy of the stewardship of opportunity entrusted to us.

With thankful, yet with burdened, hearts we pray for thy Church. Across the dividing lines of mankind's bitterness today keep her fellowship real and vital. Beat down, in thy mercy, the cruel iniquities that in many lands persecute her saints, deny her liberties, destroy her sanctuaries, and even refuse to her the training of the children of her own households. And here, where we have liberty, help us to maintain her strength, rear our children in her nurture, seek afresh to understand her Gospel, and make real to the ends of the earth the salvation that is in Jesus Christ, our Lord.

Make this church, we beseech thee, a loyal servant of thy cause. To the ministers, the laymen, and laywomen of this congregation grant vision and dedication, wisdom, generosity, and devotion, that we here, a company of Christ's disciples, may exhibit his Spirit, further his work, and be faithful servants of his Kingdom.

Now may thy Spirit touch us all with some healing wisdom and strength. Kindle our faith, rebuke our infidelities, make sensitive our consciences, dedicate our strength, fortify us in our troubles, and send us out strong in the Lord and in the power of his might.—Harry Emerson Fosdick

LECTIONARY MESSAGE

Topic: The Good Shepherd

TEXT: John 10:11–18

Most of us know very little about sheep. Yet this passage of Scripture is popular. Perhaps the most popular psalm is the twenty-third, the shepherd psalm. It may be the result of a sentimental look at a baby lamb or the gentle look of the flock. It is more probable that we like the shepherd references because we know the shepherd.

I. "I am the good shepherd." *What did it mean?*

(a) Simply stated, he cares for the sheep. The shepherd feeds them, waters them, leads them. He excels the hired man who is paid to look after someone else's sheep. A wolf approaches and the hired man flees, but the shepherd will risk his life for the sheep. How easily Jesus used the symbolism to talk to his life!

(b) He knows the sheep. He knows them by name and calls them to himself. He knows them better than they know themselves. Sheep appear to wander aimlessly, belonging to no one. Historically, the Jewish people had followed many shepherds, both religious and political leaders. With what great depth Jesus compared this knowledge to that of father and son!

(c) He possesses the sheep. A shepherd loves all sheep and would grieve over a shepherdless flock. He is not comfortable so long as any are without a shepherd. He may lay claims to some his flock does not recognize. This is not rustling but revealing the shepherd's heart. With what confidence a wandering sheep realizes that a shepherd has found him!

(d) He gives his life for the sheep. No one forces him to do it. He gives his life because he is a good shepherd. His Father gave him the power to lay it down and to take it up again. And the result is life for the sheep—"that they may have life and have it abundantly."

II. "I am the good shepherd." *What does it mean?*

(a) Simply stated, Jesus cares for his own. He is shepherd and watchman of our souls (1 Pet. 2:25). He is the Great Shepherd of the sheep (Heb. 13:20). The Good Shepherd cares for his sheep.

(b) Jesus knows his own. Fellowship thrives on mutual knowledge and understanding. The perfect lover of people knows the perfect love of the Father. He knows himself to be loved and thus can love.

(c) Jesus holds his own. Here there is complete confidence for us. He holds the whole world in his hand. This does not threaten us. He is related to all Creation and seeks to be the shepherd of all people.

(d) Jesus gives his life for his own. It is a vicarious gift. It is a voluntary gift. It is a victorious gift—and his Resurrection is God's vindication of that gift. And the life he gives to his own is a part of that gift.

All of this is described as a fulfillment of the Father's will—in obedience to the Father. We are not surprised. "God is love." Should his Son be otherwise?—J. Estill Jones

SUNDAY: APRIL TWENTY-EIGHTH

SERVICE OF WORSHIP

Sermon: The Stumbling Block

TEXT: 1 Cor. 1:23

Not only does it pain us when good people neglect or reject Christianity, it also puzzles us. Why? Why do they not see and experience in Christ what is obvious and real to us? It is as puzzling as it is painful.

I. Over the years, I've heard and read many of the reasons people give for choosing to remain non-Christian.

(a) One reason people give for rejecting Christianity is that they find it unconvincing. This is rejection on the intellectual level. The claim here is that the facts of the gospel simply do not satisfy man's reason.

This is a criticism to be taken seriously, because Christianity takes man's mind seriously. And no intelligent Christian would deny that, as Christians, we must continually wrestle with tormenting doubts and difficulties. Yet I must say frankly that I think there is less genuine intellectual unbelief than we are prone to imagine. Many skeptics have never really examined the gospel records or the writings of Christian scholars. When you produce arguments demonstrating the reasonableness of faith in Christ, these skeptical people still equivocate. To those who reject our faith as unconvincing, we say—"Study it! Read about it! Let it speak for itself!" "I can only approve of those who search for truth with groaning," says Pascal in his *Pensees.* The Christian standing in the tradition of Paul, Augustine, Luther, Calvin, Temple, C. S. Lewis, and a host of others has no need to feel intellectually embarrassed!

(b) Another reason people give for rejecting Christianity is that they find it unnecessary. This is rejection on the practical level. The truth or otherwise of the gospel is not the obstacle here. Indeed, religion never bothers such people at all. They hardly ever think about it. It is neither myth nor menace: it is an irrelevance. They may be healthy and happy; they have a family, a job, holidays, hobbies, friends—and they take life as it comes. They live decent, respectable, law-abiding lives. They are warmly human. "What has Christianity to offer us?" they ask. "Honestly, it seems unnecessary. We do quite well without worship, prayer—even a Savior."

We can only proclaim to such people that Christ is as necessary in today's technological, scientific world as ever. He speaks to the eternal problems of mankind, problems which have haunted philosophers, novelists, dramatists, moralists, and ordinary people since the beginning. To those haunted by guilt, Christ speaks forgiveness; to those defeated by strong passions, Christ offers self-control; to the anxious, Christ gives peace of mind; to those who find the problems of suffering a terrible enigma, Christ brings the conviction that God's love is sovereign; to those who cringe before the prospect of death, Christ is the Resurrection and the Life. Unnecessary? Christianity is the one thing needful.

(c) A third reason people give for rejecting Christianity is that they find it unattractive. This is rejection on the institutional level. And this is perhaps the most disturbing reason of all because it is often true. The treasure is contained in, and communicated through, very earthen vessels. The institutional church can be atrociously unlike Christ: petty, divisive, timid, even blatantly hypocritical. Nevertheless, the jewel is always there! The church has survived the excesses and betrayals of its ministers and members precisely because Christ himself is there, in the midst, renewing, controlling, bringing new life out of apparent death.

II. These, then, are the stumbling blocks to faith that people commonly advance. I believe there is a deeper, more fundamental reason why people neglect or reject Christianity. It is rooted in the essential message of the gospel—the cross of Christ. So Paul wrote, "We preach Christ crucified, a stumbling block . . ." People stumble at the cross!

(a) The cross is a stumbling block to man's pride. Why was Christ crucified?

The simplest and profoundest answer the New Testament gives is that "Christ died for our sins." His death was not that of a martyr, a hero, a victim: it was the death of a Savior, the voluntary death of One who bore our sins in his own sacred body, the sinless One who was made sin for us.

Man, declares the gospel, is self-centered rather than God-centered. He has proudly rejected his destiny as God's child, usurped the throne of God, estranged himself from God. The number one enemy of civilization is first, foremost, and most undeniably—man himself! But Christ died for us!

To those who come to the cross with humble and contrite hearts, God is very kind. Miracles of healing and hope take place at Calvary. All down the centuries, multitudes of people, monuments to mercy, have allowed the cross to pour contempt on all their pride, and they have sung their grateful testimony:

> At the Cross, at the Cross,
> Where I first saw the light,
> And the burden of my heart rolled
>   away!

(b) The cross is also a stumbling block to man's moral sensitivity. "Is it right, is it just, is it morally respectable?" Earnest, thinking people wonder at the ethics of pardon and vicarious suffering. Doesn't it tend to encourage sin? Doesn't it demoralize the sinner?

How do we reply to this stumbling block, this charge of moral insensitivity? Two things need to be said at least. One is that the cross emphatically does not imply a light view of sin. Sin at the cross is exposed for what it is, judged, and condemned. Our salvation comes to us with the blood of the Lord upon it, and this refutes forever the charge that it is immoral.

The other thing to be said is that the principle of vicarious suffering is rooted deeply in life as we experience it. How indebted we all are to others, known and unknown, who have given themselves on our behalf! Every roll of honor in the land confirms this. Do we feel that such sacrifices offend our moral sensitivity? The love of God for us in Christ was a love that gave to the uttermost, a love that was willing to suffer and die to overcome our first and last enemies and break the vicious circle of egotism we in our unaided strength could never break. At the cross, the principle of vicarious suffering, which, when we encounter it in life, moves us deeply, was lifted to the highest level.

(c) Once more, the cross is a stumbling block to man's passion for freedom. Freedom is a blurred word. On the lips of some people it is little more than a cliché, a petulant cry to be raised the moment their personal desires are thwarted. On the lips of others, it is a noble sentiment, a longing for dignity, for an opportunity to fulfill their personalities, to serve, to make a significant contribution. The fact remains that the passion for freedom is one of the deepest urges in human nature.

But mark this. The cross gives us back our freedom, enriches beyond measure. It liberates us to love and serve and grow in Christ-likeness, to soar to regions where angels love to dwell. Who is really free? The slave to self or the slave to Christ? If it is true that man's only power with freedom is to give it away, to choose the form of his servitude, then if we will not enter the service of the Christ who died on the cross, we must, of necessity, enter into some other. Strange doors of service and opportunity will continually open for those who give themselves to One who loves them and gave himself up for them.—John N. Gladstone

Illustrations

IMPORTANCE OF PEOPLE.   Once I was down on Fourteenth Street trying to help a blind street singer named Virginia into a cab. This disturbed a woman nearby who was trying to feed the pigeons. "Boy!" I thought, "This is really New York. You try to help one person, and you get in trouble with somebody else." So I went over to the other woman and said, "Look, Lady, I really don't want to upset your pigeons, but I'm trying to get this woman into a cab, and right now I think people are more important than pigeons!" She looked at me and then through me

and got the point. She walked over to the street and cried, "Taxi! Taxi!" We hailed a cab and helped Virginia in.—David J. Randolph

FREEDOM IN CROSS-BEARING.   Think of Albert Schweitzer, who died in his ninety-first year, one of the outstanding men of our time. We may find his theology unacceptable, but we cannot question his life. He renounced the freedom his magnificent talents would have given him and took up his cross. Joseph, a native of Lambarene, and later Schweitzer's assistant, summed it up. "The doctor is the slave of God, and I am the slave of the doctor." The cross ceases to be a stumbling block to those who become Christ's willing slaves and find in his service perfect freedom. As Samuel Rutherford, the covenanter who loved Christ so much, once put it: "If you take that crabbed tree"—meaning the cross—"and carry it lovingly, it will become to you like wings to a bird and sails to a boat."—John N. Gladstone

Sermon Suggestions

AN OUTSIDER BROUGHT IN.   TEXT: Acts 8:26–40. (1) Through the work of providence, verses 26–27a. (2) Through the work of the Spirit, verse 29. (3) Through the work of the Word, verses 28b, 30–34. (4) Through the work of a believing witness, verses 35–40.

LOVE'S PROOF.   TEXT: 1 John 4:7–12. (1) God's love proven: he gave his Son for us, verses 7–10. (2) Our love proven: we love one another, verses 11–12.

Worship Aids

CALL TO WORSHIP.   "Thy throne, O God, is forever and ever: A scepter of equity is the scepter of thy kingdom" (Ps. 45:6).

INVOCATION.   Let this day, O God, be a festival of joy. With praise to you, with confession and pardon, with hearty and hopeful prayers, and with true thanksgiving and commitment, may our worship be acceptable in your sight.

OFFERTORY SENTENCE. "Charge them that are rich in this present world, that they be not high-minded, nor have their hope set on the uncertainty of riches, but on God, who giveth us richly all things to enjoy" (1 Tim. 6:17).

OFFERTORY PRAYER. Out of your bounty you have given, O Lord. Out of your bounty now we give to you. Grant that this might be useful to share your bounty with a world.

PRAYER. Our Father, be with us, we pray thee, not only in the great moments of experience, but also in the trivial round, the common task. Make us children of quietness and heirs of peace. Grant that we may go among our fellows with cheerful, kindly faces, ever lenient to their faults, ever glad to praise their virtues. Help us to control our tempers and to be kindly affectioned one toward another. Wherever we see need or distress, may we be ready to help, counting it our joy to bear another's burdens, and so fulfill the law of Christ. Save us from all selfish pleasure and slothful ease and idle curiosity. Keep us ever mindful of the fewness of our days and the greatness of thy work. As our day is, so let our strength be. And let thy favor be upon us; establish thou the world of our hands upon us; yea, the work of our hands, establish thou it, through Jesus Christ, our Lord.—Samuel McComb

LECTIONARY MESSAGE

Topic: The True Vine

TEXT: John 15:1–8

The vine has long been an accepted religious symbol. The prophet described Israel as the vine or the vineyard of the Lord. The Jewish nation relished the symbol in its culture. A vine appeared on Maccabean coins. A vine was used to decorate the gates of the Temple. The allegory of Jesus is simple. There are at least three spiritual principles.

I. *"I am the source of life."* It is one of his typical absolute claims introduced by "I am." It is either presumptuous—or true. Life is determined by connection with the vine. Cut a branch off the vine and the branch dies. Life is determined by connection with the vine.

Life is conditioned by dependence on the vine. "Apart from me, you can do nothing." The branch cannot bear fruit of itself. Life is justified by contribution to the vine. The story of Israel as a vineyard or Israel as a barren fig tree is always with us. Unless it bears bountifully, cut it off!

II. *The Father-God oversees life's relationships.* The Father is the vinekeeper. He is devoted to the health and productivity of the vine. He is closely related to the vine. He knows if our relationship as branches is real.

He acts responsibly . . . always for the welfare of the vine. He has seen his Son suffer. He has seen his church suffer. His is no selfish interest. He loves all. In many ways, the pruning process continues. There was an immediate contrast between Simon Peter and Judas Iscariot—the one pruned, the other withered. He offers fellowship with himself. In abiding fellowship and in effectual petitions, he offers confidence in prayer. His glory is fruit-bearing branches . . . developing Christians.

III. *Productivity is the proof of aliveness.* It is the expression of love and friendship, clearly seen in verses 12–15. It is the response of obedience to authority. Such demand for productivity is not strange: in modern business you produce or else. To "stay alive" you produce.

It is the result of the quality of life: the harvest of the Spirit is spiritual fruit: "love, joy, peace . . ." and all the rest of the list in Gal. 5:22–23. Begin with love and proceed to joy. How can a loving, joyous person keep from bearing fruit? . . . In personal spiritual qualities, in expansive friendship, in warm and joyous witness. You want to know my secret? It is my Savior. He is alive. I am alive. Why don't you come alive?

Such fruit-bearing arises out of one's own moral choice, but this is only because the Master has first chosen us. Let there be no pride or self-righteousness. The friends of Jesus are not self-appointed masters of their own destiny. They have their appointed place in a vine that gives

them life and sustains them and causes them to bear fruit.

Are you alive? In your relationship with Jesus Christ? In your responsibility in the Christian fellowship? To your opportunity of Christian witnessing?—J. Estill Jones

SUNDAY: MAY FIFTH

SERVICE OF WORSHIP

Sermon: Knowing Where to Look

TEXTS: Heb. 1:1–4, 2:5–9; Luke 24: 44–53

I. I used to have a lot of trouble with the doctrine of the Ascension, which talks about Jesus ascending into the heavens. I'll tell you why. I don't believe in a three-story universe; the underworld beneath us, the flat earth, and the dome of heaven above. That's the kind of cosmology the Ascension seems to require. I believe there is infinite space up there, at least for all practical purposes, it is. Besides, I don't think Jesus left here on a cloud. I don't think he would get very far on a cloud. But that's the image I had of the Ascension, and I had trouble with it.

(a) But more and more I came to see that what the Ascension is talking about is not a peripheral matter. It's near the core of what the gospel is all about. It is, in fact, the completion of what happened at Easter.

(b) Jesus doesn't have to ascend on a cloud, but he must be exalted. He doesn't even have to go up there someplace, but he must be over all things. He doesn't have to be sitting someplace on a throne next to an old man with a white beard, but he has to be the one who is so close to God that we, having seen Jesus, know with certainty that we know what God is like. That's what the Ascension is really about.

II. The Ascension means Jesus has completed what he came to do. The reconciliation is completed. It's over. Jesus' work is over. So like a priest at the end of the Mass, he grants us his peace. He grants us that which is the byproduct of reconciliation with God—peace. "Peace be with you." The peace that passes all understanding is now ours because of what Christ has done for us.

(a) I don't like that word *peace*. It's a dangerous word in English because it is used by so many people to mean a kind of static, benign, struggle-free existence, an escape from the pain of human existence. I don't think that's what the Bible means by peace. The Bible means something like "composure" in the midst of the struggle of human existence. It means by peace "confidence" that allows you to do the very best no matter what happens to you.

(b) When you lack confidence, you lose your composure. You are afraid of making mistakes. You're afraid of making a fool of yourself. You're afraid that you are not worthy. You're afraid that this task has been given to you is too great for you. You're afraid that the worst is going to happen to you.

(c) You know what the opposite of faith is? The opposite of faith is not doubt; the opposite of faith is fear. Faith means I can trust that God will bless me and keep me, that God will make his face to shine upon me and be gracious unto me, that God will lift his countenance upon me and give me peace. So I can do my best no matter what I do. I can concentrate on winning the battle. I don't have to worry about what will happen if I lose, I can focus on what I must do in order to win.

(d) The Ascension, even more perhaps than the Resurrection, gave Christians that kind of assurance, that composure in the midst of adversity and struggle, even in the midst of persecution and death. The Resurrection made the claim that Jesus Christ is Lord; the Ascension sealed it.

III. The Ascension at the beginning of the Acts of the Apostles says that our work now begins. Go back to that scene, those two angels standing there in white robes. They are there to tell the disciples to get to work. They appear first, as we saw, at the tomb on Easter Day to say, Don't hang around here. He's not here. Now they appear at Bethany to say, Don't hang around here either. He's not going to drop back out of the sky.

(a) So where is he? Where do you find Jesus? If he's not lying in a grave as the hero of a cult and if he's not going to fall out of the sky like a supernatural hero, then where is he?

"Where two or three are gathered together," he said, "there I will be in the midst of them." It refers to the church gathering together in fellowship, in *koinonia*. That's the word that the church used for this special being together. *Koinonia*.

(b) It's also clear that he will be there in the breaking of bread. That's the lesson from that marvelous story in the Gospel of Luke called "the supper at Emmaus." Two strangers walking along the road, Jesus joins them. They don't recognize him until they sit down and break the bread. Of course, that means Holy Communion. You will see his presence in the sacrament of Holy Communion.

(c) And finally, he said that he will be with the poorest and the lowliest and the lost. "If you do it unto the least of these, you have done it to me." If we haven't found Jesus in the world yet, maybe it's because we're hanging around with the wrong crowd. I'll give you something that's like an axiom. I think this is always going to be true. Don't expect Jesus to be now any place other than where he was then. Where was he then? Among those in need. Not with those who were helping those who are in need, not with those who served on boards of institutions that were helping those in need. He was with those who are in need.—Mark Trotter

Illustrations

COUNTERFEIT CONTENTMENT.   There are voices out there in the giants' throats. So many voices, telling us what we should want, what we should seek, what we should do. Twelve hundred advertising messages are received each week through the sensory apparatus of a single human pawn—moving us, pulling us, blurring the lines between wants and needs, and linking those carefully cultivated covetings into a kind of counterfeit contentment based on a promised happiness that doesn't happen.—Linda Eyre and Richard Eyre

ONE POWER ONLY.   Man's power is a fake. Let the reader underline the word *power* in the columns of today's newspaper; he will find that in almost every instance it is the mask of death. Then let him underline the word *power* in the Bible; he will find that in every instance, except those that describe the cankered and transitory power of evil, it is the promise of life. Carlyle contrasts the guns and guillotine of the French Revolution with the sacrament of the Lord's table. There is only one revolution—the salvation of the soul. There is only one power—the power of God's love made known in his incarnate Son.—George A. Buttrick

Sermon Suggestions

KINSHIP IN THE SPIRIT.   TEXT: Acts 10: 44–48. (1) The Spirit and the word of the gospel belong together, verse 44. (2) The Spirit crosses all human boundaries, verses 45–46a. (3) The Spirit makes possible and mandatory full incorporation of all believers into the Christian community, verses 46b–48.

ON BEING WHAT WE ARE.   TEXT: 1 John 5:1–6. (1) Our status: children of God, verse 1a. (2) Our duty: loving God and his children and keeping his commandments, verses 1b–3. (3) Our victory: faith in Jesus, the Christ and Son of God, verses 4–5.

Worship Aids

CALL TO WORSHIP.   "God is our refuge and strength, a very present help in trouble" (Ps. 46:1).

INVOCATION.   Lord, still the noise, calm the chatter, quiet the nerves too long accustomed to the sounds of this world. Fill us with the quiet of holiness, the expectation of revelation, the peace of God. Through the power of the Holy Spirit.—E. Lee Phillips

OFFERTORY SENTENCE. "For every beast of the forest is mine and the cattle upon a thousand hills" (Ps. 50:10).

OFFERTORY PRAYER. We love you because you first loved us. We give in your service because you gave to us in the form of a servant, Jesus Christ, who accepted death to give us life.—J. Scott Hickman

PRAYER. "Lord of all being, enthroned afar . . ." we acknowledge you as Creator and Lord. We know ourselves to be creatures, made in your image. We thank you for your goodness and grace. We thank you for your love and mercy.

We confess our sins to you. We are unworthy of your love. We do not deserve your gifts. But you do not deal with us as we deserve. Forgive us, merciful Father: Forgive our pride and self-righteousness. Forgive our greed and selfishness. Forgive our waste of time and energy. Forgive our neglect of those who need us. Forgive us for Jesus' sake.

Speak to us clearly today. Reveal to us your word for today. Show us your will for today. Draw us close to yourself today. We do not ask for strength beyond today, Lord, but help us serve you today.

We pray for one another. For the anxious, the troubled, we ask your peace of mind. For the physically and mentally ill, we ask your health. For the lonely and neglected, we ask your encouraging presence. And we give ourselves in ministry to those who need us in the name of and in the example of Jesus.—J. Estill Jones

LECTIONARY MESSAGE

Topic: What a Friend
TEXT: John 15:9–17

It is rare to find a member of the church who does not warm, at least secretly, to the hymn "What a Friend We Have in Jesus." Now, of course, there are many who are publicly critical of this hymn. Musicians sometimes snap that the tune is weak and overly sentimental, and the theologically sophisticated occasionally charge that the words reflect a bit too much the inward piety of its time. But

when all the criticisms have been registered, still there is something about this hymn that stirs our hearts. All of us long for a steady, enduring, loving friendship, and there is deep satisfaction in the affirmation that Jesus is such a friend—our friend. "What a Friend We Have in Jesus." That is an old hymn, a comforting hymn, a good hymn.

It is also a *dangerous* hymn—at least if we take seriously the understanding of being a friend of Jesus that is given in our passage from the Gospel of John. "You are my friends," Jesus tells his disciples, and us as well. "You are my friends *if* you do what I command you." Friendship with Jesus is not a sentiment, it is a relationship, and all good relationships involve commitment and demand.

Suppose someone tells you that he is your friend, but when you are sick, he does not visit. When you are lonely, he does not come. When you are distressed, he does not care. When you are joyful, he is concerned only about his own life. That person may *say* that he is your friend, but he is not a true friend. To be a true friend means becoming involved in the life of another; what matters to the one also matters to the other.

John tells us that in the life of Jesus what matters most is doing the will of the Father, keeping God's commandments (John 15:10). The Father's will and the Son's will are one. The Father's commandments are Jesus' commandments. Now that he is nearing the end of his ministry and his life, Jesus turns to those around him and calls them friends. By doing so, he is offering his life to them. "You are my friends if you keep my commandments" is "What has mattered most to me now matters most to you, too."

That makes sense to us, of course. We want to be Jesus' friend; we want his life to be our life. So, we are ready to keep his commandments, but what are they? Now comes the dangerous part. "This is my commandment, that you love one another as I have loved you. Greater love has no one than this, that a person lay down his life for his friends" (John 12:12–13). The secret is now revealed: To be a friend of Jesus will cost us our lives. Most of us will not die a sacrificial death as he did, but he calls us nevertheless to pour out our lives in loving and sacrificial labors for others. To have life in Christ, we must give up our lives in service.

But we are no ordinary servants. Servants are told to do this and do that, no questions asked. A servant has chores that must be done. "No longer do I call you servants," Jesus tells us; "I call you friends." We do not have toilsome chores to perform; we have a willing and joyful mission, one that comes from the very heart of God and the life of Christ. Jesus is not our slavemaster; he is our friend.

We should be careful, then, when we sing "What a Friend We Have in Jesus" because, when we do, we are choosing in love to pick up our cross and to follow where our friend is leading us.—Thomas G. Long

SUNDAY: MAY TWELFTH

SERVICE OF WORSHIP

Sermon: The Lover's Call
TEXT: Song of Sol. 2:1–13

Many have thought that the early rabbis and Christian fathers allegorized or spiritualized the Song of Solomon out of embarrassment at its vivid and explicit imagery and expression. Origen, who probably learned much from rabbis in Caesarea about interpretation during the third century, construed the words of the lover to the beloved as the whisperings of Christ either to the church or to the individual soul. In the Middle Ages, mystics such as Bernard of Clairvaux relied chiefly on the Song of Solomon for their understanding and explanation of mystical experience. Only in the post-Freudian age of the last century have interpreters felt free to treat this work exclusively as a poem about married love.

In recent years I've been wondering whether the rabbis and Christian fathers didn't have a motive deeper than embarrassment in mind when they spiritualized this poem. They lived in ages and cultures that trivialized the most intimate personal relationships known to human beings, that is, sexual relationships. Consequently, they wanted to elevate these by relating them to a still higher intimacy—the relationship between God and human beings. Instinctively, they recognized that you cannot speak about intimate relationships in literal fashion. You can do so only in poetry and art.

Recently, a friend took me to see a Hup-pah. A Huppah is a canopy under which a Jewish bride and groom stand (once they spent a week there) while they take their marriage vows. This Huppah, designed by a noted textile artist, had two tiers. The lower one depicted scenes from the Song of Solomon representationally; the upper one allegorized or spiritualized. The artist herself explained to me that she was trying to say that the most intimate of human covenants has an analogy only in the covenant each of us makes with God. Perhaps something of the same reasoning lies behind the apostle's linking of the mystery of marriage to the mystery of Christ and the church. This conjunction alone suffices to do justice to the union of two persons in the intimate bond of marriage.

I. *"Arise . . . and come away."* Marriage is, above all, a call to an intimacy beyond all earthly intimacies. "Arise . . . and come away," lovers call. Nothing must intrude on this bonding. Nothing must interfere. The union of these two into one, the forming of a new entity, requires a special solitude.

"Arise . . . and come away" speaks of the breaking of other bonds—of family and friends and job and geography. Nothing at all must hold in such a way that Dan and Rachel cannot become one.

Parents, though they have birthed and nursed and prayed and sustained them, must turn loose. That they may become "one flesh," an ancient scripture writer observed, each must *leave* father and mother and *cleave* only to one another (Gen. 2:24). Parents who cannot let go all too often wreck their children's marriages.

Friends, though they have loved and lived with and helped and encouraged, must turn loose. If they hold on, they also may impair the uniting into a new person, a uniting that transcends physical union. Well-meaning friends cannot take sides in understandings and conflicts and negotiations that accompany this union.

No, the call is "Arise . . . and come away." "Make a clean break." "Leave no dangling ropes." Nothing in human experience must interfere.

II. *"The winter is past."* To contemplate intimacy with another person of the level suggested by marriage is a fearful step, too fearful for some to take. It requires a level of self-surrender that is awesome. For two to become one necessitates a death of self. To covenant with another in this way allows neither to speak an "I will" for self alone. Each speaks also for another.

Could any concept be more difficult for us to grasp and to practice in a culture catering to individual wants and wishes as ours does? In this covenant each must decrease in order that the other may increase or, rather, that both may increase together. Each enters into a covenant of mutual servanthood out of mutual love for the purpose of mutual fulfillment. Here is not a contracting for services out of need for such and such price. No. Far from it. For Christians not *self*-serving and *other*-using but *self-using* and *other-serving* must be our pledge.

Where two persons come prepared for this kind of covenant, they discover that "winter" is past and the "rain" is over and gone. What "winter"? What "rain"?

The "winter" and the "rain" of loneliness and isolation and separation, surely. No human pain is as agonizing as the pain of loneliness, not just the loneliness of being without a companion, but that of having no one before whom you can bare your heart and soul and share your deepest secrets. No pain is as great as the pain of knowing and feeling that no one loves, honors, cares for you just as you are, faults and foibles and all.

The "winter" of loneliness is a hard one in our age and culture. You see its sufferers all around you: abandoned and abused

babies; unwanted and neglected children; drifting and runaway youth; beaten and unloved spouses; and nursing home–incarcerated older persons.

For you, the winter is past. Today you will say to each other those special words, promising to love and comfort and honor and keep one another in sickness and in health and to be faithful to one another so long as you both shall live.

III. *Spring is here!* Spring is here for the two of you and for all of us who join you in this happy celebration.

Flowers bloom.
People sing.
Turtledoves coo.
Fig trees sprout.
Vines blossom and
emit their fragrance.

Do you see and hear and smell them?

Which of us is not turned on by spring, not spring merely as a season, but rather spring as an experience? Spring lifts our hearts. Spring causes our spirits to soar. The very memory of springs past ignites our souls.

Your "spring" is here—that "spring" in which you can begin to explore the mystery of another person in ways far exceeding anything you have ever done in your life. You'll enter labyrinthine caves where together you will see

Joyous mysteries, sorrowful mysteries,
Beautiful mysteries, ugly mysteries,
Manifest mysteries, hidden mysteries,
Simple mysteries, profound
mysteries,
Wondrous mysteries, frightening
mysteries.

For life, your lives, yields all of those. Deep within those caves you may discover the mystery of Creation itself, the mystery of God.

"Spring" means you will not go alone and unaccompanied into the labyrinth. It means you will not face life's terrors, nor experience its joys, alone. It means, as you two become one, you will experience life in a new and richer and fuller way. Perhaps, and I believe God so meant it, you will become the prism through which

God's light and love will break through to the other in their glory.

Full enjoyment of this "spring" depends on transparency. The more transparent you can be to one another, the more the light of God may shine upon the other, the more the love of God may flow toward the other. "We are put on earth a little space," William Blake has reminded us, "that we may learn to bear the beams of love." In no relationship save the one we may have with God can we "learn" so well how to fulfill that statement as we can in the union of marriage.

In one ancient ritual, bride and groom prayed a prayer you may want to pray always: "May we two live our lives so happily together that God may enjoy our union of heart and spirit with each other."

"Arise and come away," then, you call to one another. "Winter is past. Spring is here."—E. Glenn Hinson

Illustrations

TRANSFIGURING MERCY. Agnes Keith, in summing up her experiences during the time she was in the Japanese internment camp, said, "I knew this, that there are just two things which can break a heart: One is the terrible harshness of man, and the other is his transfiguring mercy." What is that transfiguring mercy but the love of God?—Ernest Gordon

MAKING AND BREAKING A MARRIAGE. What we as God's church do in beginning a Christian family through the marriage service, we must continue to safeguard thereafter. All of us, as a church, share in making a marriage; all of us, as society, can share in breaking a marriage. If we are God's agents in uniting a man and a woman, we must be equally his servants in protecting that divine union. The Christian church has a responsibility to prevent any man from putting asunder what God has joined.—William Frederick Dunkle, Jr.

Sermon Suggestions

WITNESSES TO JESUS' RESURRECTION. TEXT: Acts 1:15–17, 21–26. (1) The eye-witnesses—the apostles. (2) The "faith-witnesses"—you and I.

THAT YOU MAY KNOW. TEXT: 1 John 5:9–13. (1) God obviously wants us to be assured of eternal life (see John 17:3). (2) However, we may reject all the evidence God has put forward in Jesus Christ to give us such an experience. (3) Nevertheless, the final evidence is within the heart of the believer (see Rom. 8:15–16).

Worship Aids

CALL TO WORSHIP. "O clap your hands, all ye peoples; shout unto God with the voice of triumph" (Ps. 47:1).

INVOCATION. Eternal Spirit from whom we come, to whom we belong, and in whose fellowship is our peace, we worship thee. Thou art never far from us but often we are very far from thee. From the tumult of the world and the preoccupation of its many tasks, from its noise and strife, our spirits turn again for peace, insight, power, to the quiet of thy sanctuary. Make thou our hearts a shrine. Build there thine altar. Kindle there thy fire.—Harry Emerson Fosdick

OFFERTORY SENTENCE. "Every man shall give as he is able, according to the blessing of the Lord thy God which he hath given thee" (Deut. 16:17).

OFFERTORY PRAYER. Lord, give us the faith to believe, the courage to act, the love to continue, and the willingness to sacrifice, when thou callest and where thou sendest, for the sake of Christ on earth.—E. Lee Phillips

PRAYER. Almighty God, evermore creating, we praise you for your creative genius that brought order out of chaos and fashioned this beautiful world for our home and made us in your image. Your image in us may very well be the gift of imagination and the capacity to create. What a high calling to be cocreators with you!

O heavenly Parent, who out of the imagination and creativity of your great love has ordained the family for the welfare and happiness of humankind, we give you thanks. We thank you for the nest for our incubation and for our fledgling years until we become strong enough to try our own wings. What an imaginative design for the continuing of the human race. We marvel and praise you for it!

On this day we praise you as we give special thanks to mothers and grandmothers who in so many creative and imaginative ways have made and are making your love real to us.

Whatever our role in the family, grant to us a love that is patient and kind—not judgmental, but forgiving; a love that affirms the other—believing the good rather than gloating over the evil; a love that is not easily discouraged but perseveres through sickness and health, through good times and difficult—a love that never ends.

In the relationships of the family, may children realize parents are human, too. There are times when the common denominator of parenthood can get just too common. We get fed up with thinking about children, talking about children, being used by our children. Being a parent may very well be the most challenging task in all the world. But, O Parent of us all, we would not ask for a lesser task but for a faith, a love, a hope equal to our task.

For those members and friends in this household of faith who suffer any brokenness, we pray an openness—a faith, a love, a trust—that the amazing regenerative powers of your amazing grace may make whole. For those among us passing through the valley of the shadow of death, sensing the weakness of our own finiteness, may we experience the strength of your everlasting arms.

We praise you for these persons who have come in commitment or recommitment to your love purpose interpreted in your Word becoming flesh in the person of Jesus the Messiah. Bless them with us that together we may truly be a family of faith in this time and place.

We pray for the human family—for families that today are the victims of hostility and war, displaced persons, without homeland or home, living daily with the tenuousness and uncertainties of existence as refugees. We pray for leaders of nations, who have the power to turn the tide from war to peace, that with wisdom, imagination, and courage they may persevere in seeking understanding, justice, peace among all peoples.—John M. Thompson

LECTIONARY MESSAGE

Topic: Richer than Sunshine and Roses
TEXT: John 17:11b–19

One of the most serious challenges to the Christian faith today is the "sunshine and roses" view of theology. Perhaps you have run into it. According to this view, if we believe deeply enough, trust firmly enough, and have a relationship with God that is solid enough, life's bumpy roads become smooth, and anxiety disappears like clouds burning away in the noonday sun.

So, a mother is having a round of endless conflicts with her teenage daughter, or a man is depressed because his arthritis attacks are becoming more frequent and worse each time, or a woman doubts her worth because each of her romantic relationships seems to fall apart. Inevitably there is someone around to chirp, "If your faith were strong, you would not suffer or worry so. In Christ, you can be a conqueror over all that besets and bedevils you." The faith, in other words, brings sunshine to a gloomy life and roses of happiness to brighten a dim day.

What makes this "sunshine and roses" theology so dangerous is that it is a near miss. It is a profound threat to the church precisely because it *sounds* so much like the authentic promise of the gospel. The gospel *is* a deep river of hope, giving peace and joy to the faithful. To be loved by God *is* to be set free to grow toward the security of knowing our worth in the eyes of God. There *is* a rich hope and a steadfast trust for those who rest their lives in the grace of Christ. As the familiar hymn puts it, "When other helpers fail, and comforts flee, help of the helpless, O abide with me." And yet, these strong and comforting promises of the gospel are not to be found apart from conflict and struggle but in the mist of them. There are always Gethsemanes to be faced for those who follow Christ.

The ever-present danger of the "sunshine and roses" theology was one of the reasons why the early church remembered that Jesus had prayed for them, but that he had expressly *not* prayed for them to be set free from all trials and tribulations. Indeed, quite to the contrary, he prayed, "I have given them thy word; and the world has hated them because they are not of the world, even as I am not of the world. I do not pray that thou shouldst take them out of the world . . ." (John 17:14–15b).

What Jesus' prayer acknowledges is that, even for the faithful—or maybe *especially* for the faithful—life will have jagged edges. Jesus' own life had its full share of suffering, and so will the lives of those who follow him. In John's time, the followers of Christ were under oppression, as are many Christians in the world today. The world has the potential literally to hate and to torment those who bear the gospel. Even when the forces in control in the world do not actively persecute the church, the powers in the world—anger, war, hunger, illness, and death—are present to confront us.

However tempting it may be to take up the "sunshine and roses" theology, however alluring it may be to imagine that our faith will somehow protect us from all pain and distress, this prayer of Jesus reminds us of a deeper truth: the joy of our faith comes from the Christ who walks with us in all our trials, suffers with us in our times of deepest distress, and prays for us even in the valley of the shadow. The old hymn has it right after all: "Abide with me; fast falls the eventide; the darkness deepens; Lord with me abide."—Thomas G. Long

SUNDAY: MAY NINETEENTH

SERVICE OF WORSHIP

Sermon: A Dangerous Pentecost

TEXT: Acts 2:39

There are many who are indulging the conventional longing for Pentecost, who would give scant welcome to the real thing were it suddenly to appear. It is easy, and on the whole rather a satisfying thing, emotionally, to yearn for the coming of fresh tides of Pentecostal power—with the proviso, of course, that nothing to which we have been accustomed shall be disturbed!

All of this is just another reminder that it is a terribly serious thing to pray. The real seriousness comes not in the possibility that our prayer may not be answered; the appallingly serious thing is that it *may* be answered. A real answer to prayer will usually let us in for more than we ask.

This is profoundly true of the gift of the Spirit of God, the impact and energy of God within us. If we ask for Pentecostal power, we ought to remember what the consequences and conditions will be.

I. If we study the first three chapters of the Book of Acts with some care, we will find that two things are closely allied: the new surge of power, that quickening of the being which came to the company of Christians gathered in Jerusalem, and their facing the social tasks of their time. The two things are tied up together. We will never understand what happened in the upper room in Jerusalem unless we look at it in connection with the disciples' attitude to the world outside of the room.

(a) The point most often forgotten is this: *The disciples received the Pentecostal power when they faced the Pentecostal task.* Pentecost began before they went to the upper room. It began when they ceased gazing upward into the skies on Mount Olivet and made their way back to Jerusalem. In doing that, they faced their world of need, of danger, of opportunity. Before that quickening experience, symbolized in the Book of Acts by the tongues of fire, that little company had made definite plans for a forward thrust to carry Christ into the contemporary world. The election of a disciple to take the place of Judas looked in that direction.

(b) What the experience seems to teach is a lesson of enormous significance for the church of our day and of any day, that God gives power only to men who need it. He does not waste power. He gives it to those who have tackled something so big, so overwhelming, that their own resources are quite insufficient. Such a tackling of a task too big for human power is the opening of the door through which there comes the rushing of a mighty wind of the Spirit.

II. Let us bring this a little more closely home by looking at the church of the Book of Acts. It was emphatically a church on a frontier. On many frontiers it was exploring new areas of social life and claiming them for the lordship of Jesus. For one thing, it was pioneering in thought, it was opening up for men a new and living way into the heart of the Father. In the second place, it was claiming a new moral realm, the relations of men and women, the whole perplexing field of sexual relations, for the authority of Jesus. Third, one of its first experiments was that of bringing the principle of love into economic relations. The exact form of the communistic experiment in Jerusalem is not important. What is important for all the centuries is that one of the first results of the coming of the Holy Spirit into the lives of men is that they tried to bring a better order into their economic relations one with another. Fourth, continually the church crossed racial frontiers, pioneering in the most perplexing social field in any century, be it the first or the twentieth, that of race. Fifth, the church was on a continually moving frontier as the westward horizon was sought. The church was only a few years old when the hearts of some within it were stirred with the dream of carrying the evangel of Jesus to the very limits of the world.

III. Turn from that picture of the first-century church on the moral frontiers of its time, needing power and getting it, to ourselves. What moral frontiers are we occupying?

(a) Take the old and complex one of race. Are we out on the dangerous edges of that problem, or are we dug in behind a comforting stockade of platitudes and evasive generalities? The church that has

a visitation of Pentecostal power will be the one that faces this task of making brotherhood a reality.

(b) How about another big question, essentially the same as that faced by the first-century church when it was confronting emperor worship? Our present equivalent of emperor worship is the widespread religion of prosperity of our day, that is, the ascendancy of the business philosophy and the point of view which draws from multitudes of people the attitudes of awe, reverence, devotion and loyalty, usually associated with an accepted religion. Prosperity is both a morality and a religion. It has its high sanctities—that the very ongoing of the business of the country depends on the acceptance of the profit motive as the only sufficient guarantee of the individualistic drive necessary to industry; that whatever is good for business is good for all; that the gaining of wealth is the chief end of man; that property rights precede human rights; that profit-making must never be interfered with or at least must be very tenderly dealt with both by government and by religion; that any dispute of these dogmas is a blasphemy, a heresy to be stamped out.

IV. Where is our struggle with this omnipresent Antichrist so clear-cut and sharp and definite that we need a power which comes from the measureless energy of God to assist us? That is the previous question of Pentecost.

(a) Another encumbrance which will be consumed by the Spirit of God is the habit of accommodation, of adaptation of ourselves and our gospel to the world. The church has taken over from secular education, without sufficient scrutiny, the idea that the purpose of life is successful adaptation to one's environment. In the deep sense the Christian purpose can never be adaptation to the world but the transformation of the world. What prevents a real apostolic disturbance in our lives is this diabolical skill in adapting ourselves and our message to the world. By such adaptation, of course, we mean the kind involving denaturing and compromising the message.

(b) It is easy to begin at the wrong end with this matter of Pentecostal power. The first step to get power is not to ask for it but to put ourselves into such desperate conditions that we need it. If we face Christ's task in our day, we will find that the reality of that conflict will bring the zest which we feel in the New Testament. It will be in our day the opening of the door to the rushing of a mighty wind and the coming of the Spirit of God.—Halford Luccock

Illustrations

PENTECOSTAL FIRE.   David Loth, in his *Lorenzo the Magnificent,* tells a story of the exploits of Lorenzo de' Medici as a pageant director. Lorenzo was a great showman. One of the chief interests of his life was furnishing to the citizens of Florence artistic and magnificent spectacles of many sorts. He produced many religious pageants with striking realism and effectiveness. On one occasion he surpassed himself in staging a pageant of Pentecost. The descent of the tongues of fire upon the apostles, however, was just a bit too realistic. Actual fire was used, the flimsy trimmings and stage hangings were set ablaze, and not only the stage but the whole church burned down.—Halford Luccock

WHOLENESS WANTED.   Christian spirituality means living in the mature wholeness of the gospel. It means taking all the elements of your life—children, spouse, job, weather, possessions, relationships—and experiencing them as an act of faith. God wants all the materials of our lives.—Eugene H. Peterson

Sermon Suggestions

THE QUESTION ONLY GOD CAN ANSWER. TEXT: Ezek. 37:1–14, especially verse 3. (1) The problem: spiritual "death." (2) The stubbornness of the problem: human powerlessness. (3) The solution: God's power in his Word.

WAITING FOR WHAT GOD HAS IN STORE. TEXT: Rom. 8:22–27. (1) The pain of waiting. (2) The patience for waiting. (3) The prayer while waiting.

Worship Aids

CALL TO WORSHIP.   "Have mercy upon me, O God, according to thy loving-kindness: according to the multitude of thy tender mercies blot out my transgressions" (Ps. 51:1).

INVOCATION.   Holy God, manifested in the Holy Spirit, able to go where thou wilt and move unchecked to achieve the purposes of heaven; fall upon us in power, move among us with conviction, shape us for service in Christ's name, that thy kingdom may come on earth as it is in heaven.—E. Lee Phillips

OFFERTORY SENTENCE.   "For if I do this of mine own will, I have a reward: but if not of mine own will, I have a stewardship entrusted to me" (1 Cor. 9:17).

OFFERTORY PRAYER.   Forgive us, Lord, when we have been cheap in our expressions of love. We remember David's determination not to offer to the Lord that which cost him nothing. So enlarge our spirits, widen our horizons, and deepen our affection.

PRAYER.   We thank you for a home—a place where we need no introduction and no permission to stay; a place where we know where things are; a place where we draw sustenance from the familiar; a place where the very walls are like arms around us.

We thank you for those persons with whom, wherever we are, we are at home; people with whom we need not keep our guard up, impress, or even very much explain; they know; people who know and love us anyway; people with whom we are at peace; people who are like gloves on a cold day; they make all the difference.

We pray for homes where this is not so, where this is more dream than simple truth. For people without people they can count on. For persons put upon by others who are overbearing, selfish, or rude. For families rocked by death, by immaturity, by conflict, or by betrayal. We pray for families where talk is more a knife than a spoon. We pray for all the lonely people.

We thank you that you called the disciples two by two. Not one by one, but two by two: Peter and Andrew, James and John, Philip and Bartholomew. Two by two. All twelve. Grant us our pairings, one kindred spirit; one kindred bird upon the wire; our sister or fellow disciples, and grant us the wisdom and gifts to cherish them while they are ours.—Peter Fribley

LECTIONARY MESSAGE

PENTECOST

Topic: When Leaving Is the Best Thing
TEXT: John 15:26; 16:4b–15

It is never easy to see someone we love depart, even when we know it's for the best. Often, parents who pack up their child's belongings as the child heads off to college have to fight back the tears, even though they are proud of their child and have hoped for a long time to see this day. Every sweater, each record album, every book that goes in the box has a memory attached to it, and the eyes grow moist.

A beloved minister announces to the congregation that a new call has come, a new congregation awaits, and a move must take place. The congregation has know this time would come someday, and they also truly believe and trust that this is the call of God and the right thing to do. And yet, it is so hard to let their minister go.

A friend is given a promotion, and this means locating in another town. We rejoice, of course, for our friend, but the sight of the moving van in front of our friend's house is a bitter sight. "It's for the best," we say to ourselves, "but still . . ."

Imagine, then, how the disciples must have felt when Jesus told them he was going away. "Where I am going," he told them, "you cannot follow" (John 13:36). Jesus had been their light, their life, their shepherd, and now he was departing from them. They heard his promise, perhaps even dimly believed his word, that his going away was necessary and for the best, but still. . . . It is never easy to see someone we love depart, even when we know it's for the best.

How is it that leaving someone you love, going away from someone who loves you, is ever for the best? Sometimes it is for the good of the one who leaves. The child who leaves for college or to begin working and living independently would always remain a child unless there is a separation from parents, a departure toward maturity and adulthood. A person who leaves a stifling but safe and secure job and ventures out to new work and new challenges can be strengthened and invigorated by the change. Sometimes the one who leaves is the one who receives the good.

But on the other occasions, the departure of a loved one is best for those who are left behind. A wise teacher knows when to help the students with the assignment but also knows when to leave the classroom, forcing them to struggle with the material on their own. A congregation whose minister retires after twenty-five years of ministry may discover, in the minister's absence, new understandings of what it means to be the people of God. A counselor may upset a patient by saying, "I don't need to see you anymore," knowing that only through separation will the patient find sources of inner strength.

Sometimes leaving is best for those who are left behind, and in the deepest way possible this is true of Jesus' leaving. "It is to your advantage that I go away," he tells the disciples. That must surely have been a difficult word for them to hear, a nearly incredible truth to believe. They could not imagine bearing the absence of Jesus; now he asks them to trust that his leaving is actually to their advantage. How could this be?

"If I go away," Jesus says, "I will send the Counselor, the Holy Spirit, to you." In other words, the disciples must relinquish the understanding of the Jesus they have known in order to receive the Spirit of the risen Christ who calls them into God's future. Jesus Christ will be with them, but in a new and empowering way. They will move from being followers of a man who preached in Palestine to being witnesses of the Christ whose power fills the earth. They will change from a band of disciples gathered around a rabbi to the church of

Jesus Christ, carrying on the work of God in the world.

The same is true for us, as well. Sometimes we have an understanding of Jesus Christ that is too small, too local, too inward, too much a mirror image of our own desire. When we do, God comes to give us the true Christ by taking away our little images. That is what the Spirit does. We often resist, saying, "No, I want the Jesus I have always loved, the Jesus I have always known. I can't bear to be without him." But then, we hear again the promise, "It is to your advantage. . . . I will send the Spirit of the true Christ to redeem and to confront you."—Thomas G. Long

SUNDAY: MAY TWENTY-SIXTH

SERVICE OF WORSHIP

Sermon: The Miracle of the Spirit

TEXT: Acts 2

I. Sometimes in our younger days when we stayed overnight in a youth hostel or camp, our excess energy exploded into all kinds of mischief. We descended upon innocent sleepers or dressed up as ghosts and had all kinds of fun when a small panic broke out in the dark room. We used to call this game "Here Come the Holy Ghosts." This may still be the name for it today. But why exactly should it be called by this name?

Undoubtedly, what we meant to say was, "Tonight we are playing a really silly game." And in our conception, the Holy Ghost doubtless had some connection with craziness. Anybody who had anything to do with the Holy Ghost must be crazy.

This is what the spectators at the Pentecost event meant, too, as you may read in the Book of Acts (go and read it; it's in the second chapter). They declared that the disciples, upon whom the Spirit had come, had actually been drinking too much. As far as they were concerned, that's all there was to it; one could see that without subjecting them to a blood test.

But this supposition simply did not add up. For somehow these people were willing to be put in prison for what they were supposed to have seen in delirium; they were willing to be stoned and bullied for it. This should have given the spectators pause, for alcoholic visions generally give way to a hangover. In any case, nobody is going to give up his life for such a vision. Generally one gives up one's life only for something which one has determined in a state of realistic soberness to be a matter of extreme importance, a matter, therefore, for which even in the closest calculation the price of life itself is not too high. Anybody who reads these stories of what happened at Pentecost will find that these were people who calculated and argued in utter soberness. And even the accounts themselves are as spare and matter-of-fact as police records.

II. But then what is meant by this strange term *Holy Ghost?*

(a) What the disciples were saying was, "Suddenly the scales have fallen from our eyes. We knew before that Christ was crucified and rose again. But we could do nothing with it. To us it was like Chinese music. Now, all of a sudden, we know what it means; now it speaks to us. Now it concerns us so much that we must change our lives."

(1) This can be made plain by an example. Surely you have seen an ancient cathedral with windows of stained glass. Often these windows depict stories of the Bible—Adam and Eve, the prophets, Mary beneath the cross of her Son, the women at the grave of the Savior. But if you go round the church on the outside, you will not see this at all. The windows seem to be dull and drab. But if you go inside, they shine in all the richness of their color. In a way, they preach the old stories. And anyone who takes the time can spend a whole hour listening to the pictures speaking. On the outside, however, they do not speak. They do not concern us at all.

(2) Pentecost is an event through which we are, as it were, set down within the church where the pictures and stories begin to speak. Perhaps everything you

learned in Sunday school and confirmation instruction looks dull and gray to you and says nothing to you. Then definitely that is a sign that you are seeing the windows from the wrong side and that the miracle of the Spirit has not yet led you to the inside. You and the disciples are looking at the same windows, but each is seeing them from the other side.

(b) This happens elsewhere in life, too. If you look at a mother's love from the outside as a cold, merely biological observer, then it, too, looks rather colorless—that is to say, like some kind of foolish fondness induced by glandular secretions. But when you think of your own mother, the peace of her protection, the warmth of her heart, her loving thoughts, then the picture of a mother suddenly bursts into bloom in full and warm color. Then you see mother love from the inside, as does a child that belongs to its mother.

So it is with the Holy Spirit. As he leads us into the interior of the house of God where the windows shine, suddenly we are no longer mere spectators and onlookers. Suddenly it becomes clear to us that the Father knows us, that we are his children. Once we are inside we see that it was not just anybody who once was hanged upon the cross, but that he died for me. There I am suddenly drawn into the events of the pictures; all at once I become an actor, and I, too, find myself standing with the rest beneath the cross and at the open grave. Suddenly my sins are forgiven, and I can begin life anew.

That's what the disciples meant when they said, "The scales have suddenly fallen from our eyes." Suddenly they knew: I am the one who is meant; God has looked at me and my life, and now I can no longer evade that gaze. Now I am being confronted with the question, Are you going in or are you going to go on strike and keep on in the same old rut?—Helmut Thielicke

Illustrations

NAMING AND MISNAMING GOD. Gilbert Stuart, who painted so many portraits of George Washington that one wonders how either of them ever had time for anything else, once looked at Talleyrand, the French statesman, who was visiting America, and made the remark, "If that man is not a scoundrel, God does not write a legible hand." God does write a legible hand. Sometimes he writes on a human face. Sometimes, as in our own United States at the present time, he writes on the face of the land. The succession of dust storms and floods, drought and erosion of the soil, is legible writing which tells us that whatever a man or a nation sows, that shall it also reap. When for generations men have abused and exploited the land, slaughtering the forests and skimming off the topsoil, we pay for it in disaster. Such calamities are not, as our blasphemous phrase goes, "acts of God"; they are acts of man, of man's greed.—Halford E. Luccock

POWER FOR THE FUTURE. When repentance comes, something happens for the future. We receive the gift of the Holy Spirit. Even if we repent, how are we to avoid making the same mistakes over and over again? There comes into our lives the power which is not our power, the power of the Holy Spirit, and in that power we can win the battles we never thought to win and resist the things which by ourselves we would have been powerless to resist.

In the moment of true repentance, we are liberated from the estrangement and the fear of the past, and we are equipped to face the battles of the future.—William Barclay

Sermon Suggestions

WHEN GOD CALLS TO SERVICE. TEXT: Isa. 6:1–8. (1) The confrontation. (2) The confession. (3) The cleansing. (4) The challenge.

WHAT THE SPIRIT DOES FOR US. TEXT: Rom. 8:12–17. (1) We live by the Spirit (see verse 11), verses 12–13. (2) We are led by the Spirit, verse 14. (3) We are liberated by the Spirit, verses 15–17.

Worship Aids

CALL TO WORSHIP.   "Create in me a clean heart, O God; and renew a right spirit within me" (Ps. 51:10).

INVOCATION.   O Father, that you are the Shepherd of our lives, leading us in the green pastures and beside the still waters, we praise you. That you are present in this experience of worship restoring our souls—bringing order out of chaos, wholeness out of brokenness, communion out of estrangement—we are indeed grateful. For him who is your Word of grace, the Lamb slain from the foundation of the world, we praise and adore you.—John M. Thompson

OFFERTORY SENTENCE.   "And he said, Of a truth I say unto you, this poor widow cast in more than they all: for all these did of their superfluity cast in unto the gifts; but she of her want did cast in all the living that she had" (Luke 21:3–4).

OFFERTORY PRAYER.   In gratitude for your grace, all our worship is in response to your love. As your grace knows no end, so our worship is continuing. In a spirit of thanksgiving for all your gifts, we bring your gifts now to you. Bless them and direct them to the purposes of your kingdom.

PRAYER.   We adore thee, O thou God of mercy, thou God of comfort. We adore thee when thy power is made manifest in the revelation of thyself which thou hast made, in the globe on which we dwell, in the processes and developments of history, in the whole evolution of the human race. But neither thy power nor thy love could subdue us. If we had seen only these, thou wouldst still have been afar off, and we should have gazed upon thee as upon the stars whose light comes to us, but nothing more. It is the revelation of thy love that makes thee the Sun of Righteousness, pouring light and warmth upon us and bringing life and joy to these dead hearts. We adore thee with our hearts. We have the august familiarity and sacredness and intimacy of love. To this thou dost exhort us; unto this thou dost draw us; to this thou hast brought us. Thou hast taught us by all the passages thereof. Thou hast made us to understand the inspiration and the glancing power thereof. Thou hast taught us to live by faith, and with faith to work by love. And thou art thyself supreme over us, not by the terror of thy right hand of power and not by those necessities which draw upon our self-interest and our lower life. Thou hast made us willing in the day of thy power, by all the attractions of love. Thy goodness hath led us to repentance, and thy gentleness has saved us.

And may our hearts not forget thee. If they do, may they be as the little child that, crying out in the night, hears the soothing voice of father and mother. May we hear thy voice in all distress, in all anguish. And if we say, "My God! my God! why hast thou forsaken me?" say thou to us, "Peace; be still. It is I. Be not afraid."

To thee we commend the poor and the needy. To thee we commend the interests of this land, of our fathers' land, of the lands of the hopeless in other climes. To thee, O God of the poor and needy, we commend this nation. We pray that for the sake of the needy and the weak, for the sake of those that have for so long a time been trodden down and oppressed by the rich and strong, thou wilt make the foundations of justice here immutable. Grant that there may be a love of all men established here. And may there be in the hearts of thy church, and of all true Christian men and women, that love which Jesus bore among the poor, himself poor, consorting with them, and to them preaching his Gospel.

Let thy kingdom come everywhere. It hastens. It is nearer than when we believed. The sun is coming. Already twilight is on the mountains. Thy star is in the east. Rise, O Sun of Righteousness, upon this earth, with healing in thy beams.

And to thy name shall be the praise, Father, Son, and Spirit.—Henry Ward Beecher

LECTIONARY MESSAGE

Topic: Born Again
TEXT: John 3:1–17

Now there was a person who was very religious named Nicodemus. He was even a member of the religious council. He came to Jesus, at night, hoping he wouldn't be noticed, and said, "Teacher, we know you are a teacher who has come from God. No one could perform all of the marvelous wonders you are doing if God were not with him."

"The truth is," Jesus replied, "no one can fully experience the fullness of God unless that person is born again." "How can a person be born when he or she is old?" Nicodemus asked honestly; "There's no way that a person can enter a second time into his mother's womb to be born!" Jesus answered, "I tell you quite truthfully, no one can enter the reign of God unless that one is born of water and the Spirit. That which is born from flesh is flesh. That only makes sense, but the Spirit gives birth to spirit. You shouldn't be surprised at my saying, 'You must be born again.' The wind blows wherever it pleases. You can hear the sound that it makes, and you can see its movement evidenced in the action of the trees, but you can't tell where it comes from or where it is going. That's the way it is with everyone born of the Spirit. The presence of the Spirit is sensed, but the Spirit can't be seen."

Nicodemus queried, "How does all of this make sense?"

"You are a teacher of religious matters," said Jesus, "and you don't understand these things? Truthfully, we speak of what we know, and we tell about what we have seen, but still you religious people do not accept our testimony. I have spoken to you of things that you experience every day, and you do not believe; how will you be able to believe if I speak of the things of God? No one has ever gone into heaven except the one who came from heaven—the Son of man. Just as Moses lifted up the snake in the desert as a sign of faithfulness to God, so the Son of man must be lifted up, that everyone who believes in him may have eternal life."

For God so loved the world that he gave his one and only Son, that whoever believes in him shall not perish but have everlasting life. Because, God did not send his Son into the world to condemn the world, but to save the world through him.

The familiar dialogue can be heard by religious leaders throughout the ages, trying to make logical sense out of God's infinite ways. Jesus' encounter with Nicodemus reminds us that the mysteries of God must be understood by faith. Let those who have eyes to see, see that which God is doing in the midst of us even when our minds cannot fully comprehend the wonder of it all.—Craig A. Loscalzo

SUNDAY: JUNE SECOND

SERVICE OF WORSHIP

Sermon: The Great Grace Experience
TEXT: Acts 4:32–5:11

There is a single verse in the fourth chapter of the Book of Acts that really summarizes the exciting, inspiring life of the early church. It is chapter 4, verse 33: "And with great power the apostles gave their testimony to the Resurrection of the Lord Jesus, and great grace was upon them all." Think about that, not ordinary, but great grace. The word for great is *mega*. The word for grace is *charis*, from

which we get the words *charisma* and *charismatic*. *Charis mega* was upon them *all!* This morning, I want to think with you about the great grace experience. It is a mega possibility before each of us today.

I. I want us to observe first of all that great grace is grounded in great unity. Notice verse 32, "Now the company of those who believed were of one heart and soul, and no one said that any of the things which he possessed were his own. . . ."

(a) There was a beautiful unity within the church. One of the tragedies of our day is that the church is so often divided.

Not only between denominations, but even within the local churches of the same denomination there are often tragic differences. One of the great signs of the work of the Spirit in our midst is the beautiful sense of unity he gives us.

(b) Great grace is blocked by division, jealousy, and pettiness. It is possible where believers are together with one heart and one soul that they really care about each other and about those in need.

II. Notice that the text says, "And with great power the apostles gave their testimony to the Resurrection of the Lord Jesus. . . ."

(a) Feel the power of every word: "And with great power." This is *dynamis mega.* The apostles gave their testimony. It was not somebody else's testimony that they had memorized and learned. The focus of the witness was not on the gifts of the Spirit but on the Resurrection of Jesus Christ—not upon feelings but upon the great fact.

(b) I have imagined listening to the apostles. I can imagine Thomas saying, "I know he lives because I know his presence in my heart." Certainly Peter would have been a willing and inspiring witness. I have listened in imagination to one apostle after another. With *dynamis mega* they bore their testimony to the Resurrection of the Lord Jesus.

III. As we look through the window that Luke gives us and see the life of the early church, we see not only a people with a powerful witness but also a radiant, joyous, enthusiastic people united by a great purpose—that of sharing the good news of the presence and power of the living Lord.

(a) God's power was so great that their pocketbooks were converted, and they became people of *great generosity.* Luke tells us, "For as many as were possessors of lands or houses sold them, and brought the proceeds of what was sold and laid it at the apostles' feet; and distribution was made to each as they had need" (Acts 4:34–35).

(b) That is absolutely amazing. The sale of a house or property in the Middle East is truly a life-shaking event. Property is very scarce. Houses and fields were passed from one generation to another. This is tremendous material sacrifice and commitment.

IV. The early church was not immune to difficulties. You read in chapter 5 a disturbing story of a man named Ananias and his wife Sapphira, who sold a piece of property; and with his wife's knowledge he kept back some of the proceeds and brought only a part and laid it at the apostles' feet. They had not been told they had to sell the property. God had not told them they had to bring everything. The tragedy was the tragedy of deception. Peter knew this. He said, "Ananias, why has Satan filled your heart to lie to the Holy Spirit and to keep back part of the proceeds of the land; you have not lied to men but to God" (Acts 5:3–4). The real truth is that we do not fool God or others for very long. The deception has in it the seeds of self-destruction.

V. The tragedy of Ananias and Sapphira shook the church but did not destroy the unity. The church was not diverted from its purpose by this terrible scandal.

(a) The New Testament church was a dynamically vital, growing church. Luke says, "And more than ever believers were added to the Lord, multitudes both of men and women . . ." (Acts 5:14). Then there follows this amazing statement, "So that they even carried out the sick into the streets and laid them on beds and pallets, that as Peter came by at least his shadow might fall on some of them" (Acts 5:15). Was it mere superstition? Or, is there a power that comes to a committed person's presence? In a very real sense we do cast a shadow—positive or negative, for good or evil, healing or destructive. If we are receptive to allow great grace to flow through us, then we will be blessed to be a blessing.

(b) The dynamic growth of the church was too much for the Sanhedrin. The leaders of the Sadducees were furious with jealousy and anger, and they arrested the apostles and put them in a common prison. That night something happened that no one had anticipated. Listen! "But at night an angel of the Lord opened the prison doors and brought them out and said, 'Go and stand in the Temple and speak to the people of all the words of this life.' And when they heard this, they entered the Temple at daybreak and taught . . ." (Acts 5:19–21). Isn't that amazing! Just when you think you are finished, just when you think you are trapped, God opens a door. Just when you think the chains that bind you will never release you, there is a Lord who has power greater than the things that hold you down or hold you back.

(c) Now I love to visualize the next scene. It is one of the most amusing scenes in the New Testament. The Sanhedrin gathered together for an early morning session. They gave the instructions to the officer in the prison to go and bring in the prisoners. He came back with a stunned look on his face and said to them, "They are gone! The prison doors are locked. The sentries are there, but the prisoners are gone!" At that time the word came back. They are not only out of prison, they are back in the Temple preaching again. So the apostles were arrested still one more time. Once again they were brought before the Sanhedrin. The high priest must have been shouting as he said, "We strictly charged you not to teach in this name, yet here you have filled Jerusalem with your teaching . . ." (Acts 5:28). Peter's reply was so beautiful. He and the apostles answered, "We must obey God rather than men" (Acts 5:29).

VI. There are thousands of Christians all over the world today who are in jail because they are living by this great truth. It is not easy to take that kind of risk. There is enormous pressure to say what the world wants to hear—to tone down the message so that it is popular with the people and the culture. If that happens, the church betrays the gospel! At the risk of being unpopular, "We must obey God rather than men."

(a) Peter, who never missed an opportunity to preach, went on to say, "The God of our fathers raised Jesus whom you killed by hanging him on a tree. God exalted him at his right hand as leader and Savior, to give repentance to Israel and forgiveness of sins. And we are witnesses to these things, and so is the Holy Spirit whom God has given to those who obey him" (Acts 5:30–32). When the Sanhedrin

heard this, they were so enraged they wanted to kill the apostles. They probably would have done so had it not been for the word of a very wise and wonderful old man named Gamaliel. Gamaliel was one of the teachers of Saul of Tarsus. Gamaliel said, "I tell you, keep away from these men, and let them alone; for if this plan or this undertaking is of men, it will fail; but if it is of God, you will not be able to overthrow them. You might even be found opposing God!" (Acts 5:38–39).

(b) How then did the disciples leave that experience? Did they leave broken in spirit and submissive? Did they leave with bitterness and resentment and complaint about the high cost of following Jesus? Listen with me to the concluding verses of chapter 5. This is so thrilling! "Then they left the presence of the council, rejoicing that they were counted worthy to suffer dishonor for the name" (Acts 5:41).

(c) This morning I want you to get a picture in your mind of radiant faces. This morning I want you to see faces alive with the joy of the power of the presence of the risen Lord. They are praising God that they are worthy to suffer dishonor for the name of Jesus. "And every day in the Temple and at home they did not cease teaching and preaching Jesus as the Christ" (Acts 5:42).

(d) It is thrilling and inspiring to me to know that God is doing that in our midst. There are people today who are making heroic commitments. God did not stop with the Book of Acts. The most thrilling and important opportunity of my life and yours is to join in what God is doing. To allow his Spirit to empower and quicken us so that we can be the channels of his presence in our world in our time!

The great grace experience is too thrilling to miss!—Joe A. Harding

Illustrations

UNITY. I have a story I want to share just with the children. The adults can listen if they want to. Once upon a time there was a man who could not swim; he went fishing with a sailor who was an expert fisherman. The man who couldn't swim caught an enormous fish. In his excitement in trying to get the fish into the boat with a dip net, he fell overboard. He started to cry, "Help, save me! Help, save me! Help, save me!" The sailor calmly reached out to grab the man's arm, and he gave a mighty tug; but the arm came off—because it was an artificial limb. The man was kicking and splashing around still yelling, "Help, save me!" The sailor reached out again; this time he grabbed for a leg and gave a tremendous pull, and the leg came off because it was a wooden leg. The man went under again and was still yelling for help. The sailor reached over, still maintaining his calm, grabbed the man by the hair of his head and gave a pull; but he had a toupee—and it came off. The man was still yelling when the sailor turned in disgust and said, "How can I help you if you won't stick together!"—Joe A. Harding

IN JESUS' NAME.   What does it mean to pray "in Jesus' name"? It is more than just a formula for making our prayers official, like a signature on a letter or a check. It has been said that when Jesus invited us to pray in his name, it was like one might say today, "Use my credit card!" We are on mission for him and so must never use this privilege for our selfish frivolities. And yet we must never fail to use it when our service to him is hindered by some genuine need.—W. Clyde Tilley

Sermon Suggestions

WHAT GOD SEEKS IN A LEADER.   TEXT: 1 Sam. 16:1–13. (1) *The situation:* The Lord willed that a new king replace Saul. (2) *The complications:* There was fear of Saul's reprisal; there were several fruitless attempts to find the right person among Jesse's sons. (3) *The resolution:* David was chosen, not because of his appearance or stature, but because of what the Lord saw in David's heart.

CREDIT GOD!   TEXT: 2 Cor. 4:5–12. (1) The powers of death are at work in the world and in us. (2) However, God in his transcendent power is at work in the world and in us. (3) Therefore, we can join in a "chorus of thanksgiving that rises to the glory of God," who brings life out of death.

Worship Aids

CALL TO WORSHIP.   "I will give thanks unto thee, O Lord, among the peoples: I will sing praises unto thee among the nations. For thy loving-kindness is great unto the heavens, and thy truth unto the skies" (Ps. 57:9–10).

INVOCATION.   Our Father, we know that we can't play games with you or hide truth from you. We try. But it never works, and we are only fooling ourselves with the attempt. In spite of our play-acting, our doubt, our fears, our ignorance, and our short-sightedness, we do truly believe. Through what goes on here today, strengthen the faltering faith of someone who needs hope and help and a steadying spirit in the midst of a wavering life. If that can happen, there will, indeed, be rejoicing here on earth even as there will be in heaven. So meet us now and in your way, make it happen.—Henry Fields

OFFERTORY   SENTENCE.   "He that trusteth in his riches shall fall; but the righteous shall flourish as the green leaf" (Prov. 11:28).

OFFERTORY PRAYER.   Lord, we bring with devotion and give with dedication this offering for the work of the church. Let us always be willing to do so, for Jesus' sake.—E. Lee Phillips

PRAYER.   O God, the great God and the great King above all gods, we cannot appear before you except that you call us— you call us in our creation in your image. You have not only breathed into our nostrils the breath of life, but you have given us minds with which to think your thoughts, hearts with which to receive and give your love, hands with which to shape deeds expressing your mind and heart.
  But in encountering your Word in this place, we have been confronted with the fact that we are as intent on building our own kingdoms as were the people of Capernaum and Nazareth in that first cen-

tury, who cried out: "We will not have this one to reign over us." We find ourselves not only chagrined but guilty—blood-guilty of crucifying the Christ afresh as we are more intent on serving our fear-prompted prejudices, our outdated nationalism, our racial preferences, our covert sexism than building community where your love reigns.

Forgive us, O God, that after nearly twenty centuries with all the mounting evidence of your Word present in the flesh and blood of Jesus we still cry out for the blood of the prophet rather than honoring the truth you sent him to proclaim. How often we hide out in the traditions of our fathers from the challenge to think the new thoughts that your coming invites.

May the community of your love be present in and among us as in prayer and helpfulness we reach out to one another.

That your kingdom may come to us and all peoples, deliver us from fear and the instruments of death that fear contrives; deliver us from demagogues when the peoples of the world are crying for diplomacy; lead us to brotherhood and sisterhood that celebrates the interdependence of all of life and all Creation, for you are the One God and Father of us all, present in person in your only Son, in whose name we pray.—John M. Thompson

LECTIONARY MESSAGE

Topic: Can Christians Dance?
TEXT: Mark 2:23–3:6
Question: Can Christians dance?
Answer: Some can, some can't.

That is a joke, of course, and an old one at that, but it may help us to understand something about today's passage from Mark. They say one should never explain a joke, but notice how this joke works. The question, "Can Christians dance?" can be taken in two quite different ways. On the one hand, it can be a question about whether dancing is morally allowable. In other words, will God "get ya" if you dance? On the other hand, the question can also be asking whether Christians have the gift, the physical skill, the lightness of foot to glide across the ballroom floor. In

other words, do they have the *ability* to dance? The question can be understood either way, and the confusion between these two meanings occasions the joke.

Now our text from Mark describes two dramatic actions in the ministry of Jesus that both occurred on the Sabbath, and the question that hangs in the air over these events is "Is it lawful to do *that* on the Sabbath?" The first action happened in a grain field. Jesus and his disciples were walking through the field, and the disciples began to pick the heads of the grain. The Pharisees saw it and were offended. Is it lawful to do that on the Sabbath? No, they said, and charged Jesus' disciples with breaking the Sabbath.

The second action took place on the same day, but in the synagogue instead of a grainfield. There was a sick man present in the congregation, and the Pharisees watched to see if Jesus would heal this man in violation of the sabbath? Jesus felt the heavy eyes of his accusers upon him, and so Jesus gave voice to the question that was silently on the minds of all: "Is it lawful to do this on the Sabbath?"

Now that is a question like "Can Christians dance?" You can take it two ways. On the one hand, "Is it lawful to do this on the Sabbath?" can mean, Is it allowable; is it permissible; is there a law on the books to prohibit this? If you take it that way, the Pharisees were correct, and the right answer to Jesus' question is no. It was against the rules to pick grain on the Sabbath. It was against the rules to do nonemergency healing on the Sabbath. The answer, Jesus, is *no.*

On the other hand, though, Jesus' question can be taken in another way. "Is it lawful to do this on the Sabbath?" can mean, Is doing this an expression of the will of God? That was Jesus' understanding of the law. The law, for him, was not a list of rules and regulations but the will of the loving, redeeming, and saving God. That's what the law is about, and that's what the Sabbath celebrates. God feeds the hungry and heals the sick. Is it lawful, then, for hungry people to pick grain and for sick people to be healed on the Sabbath? Yes! Feeding the hungry and healing the sick weren't violations of the

Sabbath. They weren't even emergency exceptions to the Sabbath rule. They were *expressions* of what the will of God, and thus the Sabbath, is all about. To feed and to heal were to dance to the music of the will of God, who loves and cares for humanity.

Imagine a pharmacist in a small town who closes his drugstore on Sundays because he believes in keeping the "Christian Sabbath." Every now and then, however, someone urgently needs some medicine on Sunday, and so the pharmacist will open his shop and fill the prescription. He is glad to do so whenever there is a need. Once a father whose little girl became ill on Sunday met the pharmacist at the drugstore to get the medicine his daughter required. When the pharmacist finished preparing the prescription, the father thanked him for coming out on Sunday and said, "Now you can go home and get back to keeping the Sabbath."

"Oh, no," said the pharmacist, as he handed the medicine to the father. "This is keeping the Sabbath."

Can people dance on the Sabbath? Some can, and some can't.—Thomas G. Long

SUNDAY: JUNE NINTH

SERVICE OF WORSHIP

Sermon: Persistent Faith

TEXT: 1 Kings 18 and 19

I. We find here in the Old Testament a short story as vivid and dramatic as one of Robert Louis Stevenson's. There had been a terrible drought in the land of Israel. Three long, hard years with neither rain nor dew! The drought had brought famine, and parents heard their children crying for bread. Strong men went about saying, "Where now is our God? Does the Almighty really care?"

(a) Then the stern old prophet Elijah told the people that the drought had come upon them as a penalty for their unfaithfulness. They had turned away from the God of their fathers, the God of Abraham, Isaac, and Jacob, to worship the pagan deity Baal. Then the prophet went up on the mountain to pray for rain. He went in the spirit of faith. He called out to the king, who had been present at that test. "Eat and drink, for I hear the sound of rain." High confidence to say that in the face of those three long years of unrelieved drought! He walked by faith and not by sight. All the outward signs were against him. There was not a cloud in the sky—the heavens were like brass.

(b) He went clear to the top of the mountain and cast himself upon the ground and prayed long and earnestly for rain. He said to his servant, "Go and look toward the sea." The servant went and came back saying, "There is nothing. There is nothing." The prophet prayed again and sent his servant the second time. Again the man came back with the same disappointing report.

But the prophet prayed right on, blithe, radiant, undaunted.

(c) When the servant came back the seventh time, he said, "There is something. There is a cloud rising out of the sea the size of a man's hand." Not much of a cloud, only the size of a man's hand—rather a small pint cup in which to bring a drink for that thirsty land! But it was a cloud, and to the prophet, it meant victory. He called out to his servant, "Go and say to the king, Prepare thy chariot and get thee down, for there is the sound of an abundant rain."

II. It may not be easy to draw a hard-and-fast line between the prose and the poetry in that narrative, but the spiritual content of it is clear. The principle there laid down is as valid as the multiplication table. "The fervent, effectual prayer of a righteous man availeth much."

(a) How much, and the precise form which the results of his prayer will take, must be ascertained by experience, but the principle is sound. "Lord, what a change within us one short hour spent in thy presence doth avail to make. We kneel how weak, we rise how full of power." How sorely we need that persistent faith in these difficult times! It is a day of spiritual drought and famine all over the world.

(b) All the more need then that Christian people everywhere should stand on the promises of God and "walk by faith and not by sight." There is nothing! Then go again. Keep on going—go again seven times—seventy times seven, if need be. It is so easy to pray and strive once or twice or possibly three times, and then if nothing seems to come of it, to give it up and be ready to quit. We read here that the purest and kindliest being who ever walked this earth, One whose name is above every name, "learned obedience by the things that he suffered." He learned the deeper meaning of life and the ways of the Spirit by discipline and self-sacrifice. So must we! Go again—keep on going!

III. Let me apply that principle of persistent faith in two directions which have to do with the work to which we are called as Christians.

(a) First, in learning the meaning and the value of prayer and worship! We cannot expect to ascertain the full meaning and efficacy of it by a few formal petitions or by a half a dozen hasty requests. When anyone seeks to put himself into conscious, personal relations with his Maker, when he would gather up all his best powers of mind and heart and set them flowing godward in a mighty petition, let him know that this high exercise demands intelligence, concentration, and persistent effort. He will have to go again and again, if he would know the deep things of God.

Is anything vital ever accomplished without persistent effort? Farmers plow and sow and keep on plowing and sowing, when they want good harvests. Miners dig and keep on digging, deeper and deeper, when they want silver and gold. Musicians practice and keep on practicing, month after month, year after year, when they want to play or to sing so that their audiences will hear melodies from a world unseen. And so must we—if we would know how prayer purifies, fortifies, enriches the inner life, we will have to persist. If we would know the untold benefits which may come to the lives of those for whom we pray, we will have to go again and again and keep on going.

(b) The same principle holds true in any form of Christian effort which one might name. What we have in mind as Christians cannot be done offhand or in a hurry. Here are athletes and acrobats! What long patient discipline they have undergone to be able to do certain things with such apparent ease and spontaneity! They went again and again to attain that proficiency. If we are to speak the right words, utter the more vital truths, do the significant deeds, and show the spirit which enters decisively into the building up of others in faith and hope and love, we will have to try again and again. "Every branch that beareth fruit, he disciplines, that it may bear more fruit." We will have to try again and again, even when we feel that we have failed.

(c) Here are all manner of subtle, mysterious forces which can be set to work upon the inner, higher life of the world! Here are forces which have to do with freeing men and women from the power of evil, with the renewing and transforming of human lives, with the formation of character! It is for us to know about them and to learn how to utilize them. In order to do that, we will have to go again and again to the source of power. We will have to try again and again to render that sort of august service, even though we are conscious of having failed. Go again! Keep on going! Go again seven times!—Charles R. Brown

Illustrations

THE POWER OF PRAISE. Praise is a mighty weapon against the powers of darkness! Satan is the accuser (Rev. 12: 10), and he hates it when God's people worship the Father. He would much rather we spend our time finding things to criticize and complain about.

The fact that praise lifts us up and brings encouragement is not due to some psychological trick. It is the work of the Holy Spirit, who is the very Spirit of praise (Eph. 5:18ff.). When we truly praise the Lord, we lay hold of the power of his throne of grace, and he is able to work in us and through us to accomplish his purposes. "Praise the Lord! For it is good to sing praises to our God. . . ." And praise makes a difference!—Warren W. Wiersbe and David W. Wiersbe

OUR ULTIMATE SOURCE OF STRENGTH. A dear friend of mine who was quite a lover of the chase, told me the following story: "Rising early one morning," he said, "I heard the baying of a score of deerhounds in pursuit of their quarry. Looking away to a broad, open field in front of me, I saw a young fawn making its way across, and giving signs, moreover, that its race was well-nigh run. Reaching the rails of the enclosure, it leaped over and crouched within ten feet from where I stood. A moment later two of the hounds came over, when the fawn ran in my direction and pushed its head between my legs. I lifted the little thing to my breast and, swinging round and round, fought off the dogs. I felt, just then, that all the dogs in the West could not and should not capture that fawn after its weakness had appealed to my strength." So is it, when human helplessness appeals to almighty God. Well do I remember when the hounds of sin were after my soul, until, at last, I ran into the arms of almighty God.—A. C. Dixon

Sermon Suggestions

WHY PRAISE GOD? TEXT: Psalm 57. (1) He is our refuge. (2) He fulfills his purpose for us. (3) His love is unfailing.

WE DO NOT LOSE HEART. TEXT: 2 Cor. 4:13–5:1, REB. (1) Because God renews us inwardly day by day. (2) Because our transient troubles are outweighed by things eternal.

Worship Aids

CALL TO WORSHIP. "Hear my cry, O God; attend unto my prayer. From the end of the earth will I call unto thee, when my heart is overwhelmed: lead me to the rock that is higher than I" (Ps. 61:1–2).

INVOCATION. Lift us, Lord, to praise and glorify thee whom alone we worship, before whom we confess our sins, in whom we find the peace that passes understanding. And let the presence of thy Spirit show us the Christ.—E. Lee Phillips

OFFERTORY SENTENCE. "But seek ye first his kingdom, and his righteousness; and all these things shall be added unto you" (Matt. 6:33).

OFFERTORY PRAYER. God of all, grant that our offerings may be given, not out of duty or obligation, but out of devotion and praise and worship.—J. Scott Hickman

PRAYER. Loving Father! Though thou countest the stars and bringest forth their host, yet doest thou bind up the wounds of the sick and healest the brokenhearted. If to any of us thou hast especially spoken words of comfort and of strength, we thank thee. If thou hast saved any from temptation, or answered the cry of a perplexed soul, or opened a way back to heaven and holiness for some poor prodigal child of thine, we praise thee. If thou hast touched any heart with a special joy or hast turned for any life the shadow of death into thy morning, we give thanks to thee for thy great glory. By the memory of all the outgoings of thy compassion, we would vow ourselves afresh to thee and to the work thou hast given us to do.

We pray for all. . . . We pray for those who cannot pray for themselves, who think of thee only as a vague and puzzling image of the mind. Teach them how real, how gracious, how generous thou art, the Source of life and light, without whom we were lost in death and darkness. We pray for the sick in the homes and hospitals of our land. Bless watched and watcher alike, that to the watched may come, even amid bodily pain and trial, strength of mind, calm of soul, and to the watcher, the sympathy and tenderness that bring thy message of hope. We ask for no miracle, no violation of the laws thou hast ordained, but we seek that through thy appointed channels thou wouldest send forth thy Word and heal the afflicted, so that we might praise thee for thy loving-kindness and for thy wonderful works to us. Each heart knows its own bitterness, but thou knowest the bitterness of all hearts. Thou hast a healing balm for each hurt of the soul. Bring strength to the weary, relief to the nervous and the miserable, consolation to the disconsolate, and deliverance to those who sit in the shadow of death, fast bound in misery and iron. Speak peace to the troubled conscience, strengthen the weak; confirm the strong, save the oppressed and those who have no helper. And, by thy mercy, bring us all by the paths of righteousness and the waters of comfort to thine abode of rest and glory, through Jesus Christ our Lord.—Adapted from Samuel McComb

LECTIONARY MESSAGE

Topic: Discovering the Family of God
TEXT: Mark 3:20–35

I. *Divisions—possessed by demons? (vv. 20–27).* The divisions between Jesus and his family remind us of the divisions in our own families. The divisions between Jesus and the religious leaders of his people remind us of the divisions in our own religious communities. How often we experience a "house divided" (v. 25) and a "kingdom divided" (v. 24).

Jesus' parallel parables of the divided family and the divided kingdom point to the destruction caused by such internal divisions. We see this destruction in the everyday struggles, as well as in the major tragedies, of the lives of our families and churches. Beyond this destruction, however, lies our hope for the ultimate destruction of evil. For when Mark combines these parallel parables of division (vv. 23–25) with the parable of the binding of the strong man (v. 27), they point to the ultimate defeat of Satan (v. 26). Jesus' ministry of exorcism (cf. v. 22) foreshadows our hope for the ultimate conquest of the Evil One.

Jesus' rejection by both his family and the scribes of Jerusalem recalls the rejections we have experienced. Although Jesus' family may have thought they were motivated by genuine concern for Jesus, they failed to understand him and his mission. Many of our family problems reveal similar misdirected motivations and misunderstandings. Although the scribes may have thought they were motivated by genuine concern for the kingdom, they failed to recognize what God was doing in their midst. So, they rejected Jesus by insulting him—accusing him of being demon-possessed. What irony there is in the rejection of Jesus by those whom one might suppose would have understood!

II. *Damnation—blasphemy against the Holy Spirit? (vv. 28–30).* The insulting rejection of Jesus by the scribes points beyond misunderstanding to self-chosen condemnation. By attributing God's redemption in Jesus to possession by Satan (Beelzebub—v. 22; cf. v. 30), they have decisively rejected God's redemptive offer of forgiveness and are "guilty of an eternal sin" (v. 29). As Vincent Taylor describes their grave situation, "It is a perversion of Spirit, which, in defiance of moral values, elects to call light darkness." By such intentional perversion they have rendered themselves incapable of receiving forgiveness and so are morally liable for God's judgment of their "eternal sin."

In the midst of this sad condemnation, we should not neglect the promise of forgiveness of "all sins" and "whatever blasphemies" immediately precede it (v. 28).

III. *Discovery—doing the will of God! (vv. 31–35).* Following all the bad news of rejection comes the good news of acceptance. Despite Jesus' disappointment that his family and the scribes rejected him, he proclaims the good news that all who do the will of God will be accepted into the family of God. The divisions and rejections we have experienced in our families and religious communities can be overcome by doing the will of God.

Jesus offers a redefinition of family and church—the vision of the family of God. Jesus' life models for us that discipleship may cost our old, natural family ties. If, however, we do the will of God, we shall discover ourselves as members of the new family of God.—Charles J. Scalise

SUNDAY: JUNE SIXTEENTH

SERVICE OF WORSHIP

Sermon: Forgiveness Needed in the Family

TEXT: 2 Sam. 14:14

Rape, murder, and now exile. What this must have done to David's heart! What had once been a happy family was now torn apart by crimes of the first order.

What a mess! It reads like a modern-day soap opera, doesn't it? This is a continual tale of mistake after mistake after mistake. Sin follows sin, wrong follows wrong, until it is virtually impossible to assign blame, yet that's what we most often desire to do: assign blame. Who's at fault? But that's not always easy. Let us take a few moments and look at the main characters, see how they acted, how each has a part of blame to assume, and in the process, discover principles for family relationships.

I. *The sin of David.*

(a) Let us begin with David. David's sin of adultery with Bathsheba and murder of Uriah has taken place. Was it because of his guilt that David did not condemn Amnon as he should, or because Amnon was his firstborn son? Who knows? The result is the same: David did not punish Amnon for the rape of Tamar and, in so doing, sowed the seeds of bitterness and murder in the heart of Absalom.

(b) How easy it is for us to overlook the seriousness of the sin of our family members! Far too often we make excuses for their behavior and, in so doing, aid and abet their journey down the path of disaster. How many other deeds of Amnon or his brothers had David overlooked? How many times before had David ignored their wrongdoing? We do not know, but we do know this: a life of disobedience and wrongdoing does not begin with rape. David's vacillation gave Amnon license, and he took it.

(c) Further, by not punishing Amnon as he should, David sowed a seed of resentment in the heart of Absalom. Here is a father who has lost control of his household and can do nothing but stand in the shadows and watch his children rape and murder each other.

(d) Can we learn a lesson at this point? Not only do we pay for our sins, our families do, too. Because of his own guilt, David would not punish a sinful son and thus lost not only this son but Absalom as well. As parents, our duty to discipline is not incumbent upon our own righteousness, but our ability to discipline often is directly related to our feelings of guilt.

II. *The sin of Amnon.*

(a) Amnon surely must bear his blame. Rather than asking his father if he could marry his half-sister, something that David might have allowed as Tamar suggests, he rapes her and then vilely throws her away like some used goods for which he no longer has a purpose. There is no excuse here, and surely Amnon received his due when he was killed by Absalom.

(b) Amnon is a character study in how either we will control our desires and emotions, especially what the New Testament calls "the flesh," or else we will be controlled and destroyed by them. Prior to the first murder, God warned Cain, "And if you do not well, sin is crouching at the door, and its desire is for you, but you must master it" (Gen. 4:7). Or as God's Word tells us in Romans, "Do not let sin reign in your mortal body that you should obey its lusts" (Rom. 6:12). Either you will control your desires and passions or they will control you. There is no middle of the road here!

III. *The sin of Absalom.*

(a) Then we have Absalom. Here is a lesson in bitterness and revenge. Absalom was so angry at Amnon that he did not speak to him for two years, but anger smoldered in his heart, and he waited for a chance to get even. Absalom was guilty of murder.

(b) Whenever we seek revenge on another, whether we are standing up for ourselves or for another, we are violating the will of God. " 'Vengeance is mine, I will repay,' says the Lord" (Deut. 32:35). God in his wisdom knew the difficulty that demanding vengeance would cause, for it builds a cycle of revenge that spirals higher and higher with no limit or control. Therefore, God demanded that revenge be left to him and him alone. To seek revenge is to place ourselves on the level of the one who has wronged us, something we should never do. Revenge always begets revenge.

(c) Absalom is also a study in failed forgiveness. When David allowed Absalom to return to Jerusalem from exile in Geshur, he refused to allow him to come to David's house. What a shallow form of forgiveness! How often is our forgiveness like this! With our lips we forgive, but with our hearts we never forget, and we carry resentment and antagonism toward others deep within us, refusing to let it go.

(d) True forgiveness always requires restoration, and that is why true forgiveness is so difficult. In a short while, Absalom begins to undercut his father, and before long he has fomented a full-scale rebellion that only ends with Absalom's death, an outcome that David never desired. Our refusal to fully forgive and to restore the relationship will mean only greater pain in the future.

(e) How can one forgive a deeply felt wrong? Only through the love of Jesus Christ and the power love brings. What does Paul teach us about love? "Love . . . is patient . . . keeps no record of wrongs. . . . Love never fails" (1 Cor. 13:5, 8). We cannot of our own resolve forgive and restore, but through the love of Christ we can. Here is the essence of the gospel in the middle of the Old Testament: "Yet God does not take away life but plans ways that the banished one may not be cast out from him" (2 Sam. 14:14).

(f) Where are you and your family today? Do you need forgiveness? Do you need to forgive? Do you need to stop the pain of bitterness and retaliation through a selfless act of reconciliation? Do you need the forgiveness that Jesus Christ brings in order to have the love to forgive or to ask for forgiveness? It is available right now, this very moment, through Jesus Christ, who died that all might be forgiven: even me and even you.—Robert U. Ferguson

Illustrations

NEITHER FORGIVEN NOR FORGOTTEN. This is what some people do regarding the injuries and wrongs they have sustained. They enter these injuries and wrongs in a ledger, a "grudge record," where they remain until the account has been settled with interest compounded.

Years ago my wife and I were Sunday guests in the home of an elderly couple. The man was congenial, and his wife was a good cook. The day was pleasant throughout except for one brief instance. It happened while the lady was showing us through the house that her husband had built for her early in their marriage. She came to a closet and remarked with considerable agitation, "I told him that this closet should never have been built here." The rebuke in the words spoken for her husband's benefit was in sharp contrast to the felicity that had prevailed at that moment. You would have thought that the error in judgment had been made the day before rather than many years earlier. I exchanged a sympathetic glance with the chagrined husband, now almost in his dotage, and wondered how many times in their marriage he had been verbally whipped over this misplaced closet. Strangely enough, as we moved out of the range of the closet, she regained her composure and proceeded to serve a splendid meal. She had just checked an ancient entry in her ledger of wrongs sustained and demanded another partial payment!—Jack W. MacGorman

RENDERING GOOD FOR EVIL. A veteran who had served in World War II gave his Christian testimony in a church service. He said one night he was drunk in the barracks. A Christian was reading his Bible before getting into his bunk. The veteran cursed the soldier and then threw a heavy, muddy boot at him.

The next morning when he arose, he found the boot he had thrown at the soldier on the edge of his bunk, polished. The veteran said that event made such an impression on him that he began attending worship services on the base and eventually became a Christian.—Fred Kendall

Sermon Suggestions

ONLY GOD IS GREAT.   TEXT: 2 Sam. 1:1, 17–27. (1) The mighty fall, and we lament their passing, 2 Sam. 1:17–27. (2) God remains, and he is our ultimate refuge, Psalm 46.

BEYOND WORLDLY STANDARDS.   TEXT: 2 Cor. 5:6–10, 14–17. (1) We are accountable to Christ for our lives. (2) We are now united to the risen Christ and live by his controlling love in a new order.

Worship Aids

CALL TO WORSHIP.   "Make a joyful noise unto God, all the earth; sing forth the glory of his name: make his praise glorious" (Ps. 66:1–2).

INVOCATION.   God of the ages, we ask you today to pour eternity into these brief lives of ours. Let our worship open the gates of a new and deeper fellowship, to the end that your kingdom may come and your will be done on our little spot of earth, even as it is done in heaven.

OFFERTORY SENTENCE.   "And Jesus said unto them, 'Render unto Caesar the things that are Caesar's, and unto God the things that are God's' " (Mark 12:17).

OFFERTORY PRAYER.   Now upon this first day of the week we bring what we have saved for you. Receive our offerings, we pray. Bless us as we give and bless our gifts as they are used for your glory.

PRAYER.   We thank thee, Almighty God, that thou art as a city on every side of which there are gates. Thou art accessible at all times and to all. There is no cry so feeble that the storm shall beat it down or the thunder of the world hide it. Up through all noise and opposition, the faintest wish and cry presses to thee and is heard. There is no heart so weak that it cannot make its way among hearts. There is no heart that hungers and thirsts and faints and is weary unto death but that has power with the mightiest to overcome omnipotence. By as much as we are weak, are we strong with thee. The more lowly we are, the more are we before thee evermore. With the humble and the contrite in spirit thou dost dwell; for they that need thee most are most in thy thought. And though our necessities spring from transgression, though guilt goes with want, we are nonetheless the objects of thy loving care, and of thy pardoning mercy. And though the earth has been full of crimes, though the stream of men's thoughts has rolled dark and guilty, and though the whole of creation has groaned and travailed in pain until now, vexed and tormented; yet thou hast let fly and never called back again over all this desolate world, and the floods of its iniquity, that word, "Whosoever will, let him come and take of the water of life freely." For all this hope that is set loose with thine invitation, for all the vision of thine excellent glory which we behold in this thy wonderful call, we render thee thanksgiving and praise. For thou art not the highest that thou mightest oppress, nor even that thou mightest bring to rigorous justice those that are under condemnation. Thou art the Healer of all that live. Thou art the best and yet the tenderest. Thou art the most unspotted and the most sympathetic with those that are stained, even unto death. Thou, O God, hast need of no one thyself, and yet, art the one universal Helper of those that are needy. Thou art infinitely rich, and no one can add to thy store, and yet thou art bountiful, giving forth with eternal profusion to those that are needy. Thou art the one against whom we have offended; and yet thou art the suppliant and dost stand at the door of the heart persuading and knocking, as if it were a refuge that thou doest seek against the pursuer and not as if thou were wooing and winning us to our own good.

Who shall speak thy nature; and who shall enter into all the richness of thy thoughts and their processions? Who shall be able to describe what thou art, thou glorious "God of all comfort"—thou "Father of mercies"?

We beseech of thee that thou wilt grant to all thy dear servants who are present this morning such familiarity of access, such boldness of petition, that they may ask whatever they this day may need for themselves, for their distempered hearts and dispositions, for the purposes the accomplishment of which is long delayed, or for their own households. Grant, we beseech of thee, that the thoughts of love in their wide circuits may carry with them divine benefaction; and if we think of those afar off, across the sea or in the wilderness or in circumstances of peril and of trial, may our thoughts be but the premonitions of thy fullness this day. If there be in thy presence those that are burdened and that need relief and come to thee for relief, oh! vouchsafe to them the fulfillment of thy words of mercy and do exceeding more for them than they ask or think, to the honor and glory of thy gracious name. And to thy name shall be the praise, Father, Son, and Spirit.—Henry Ward Beecher

LECTIONARY MESSAGE

Topic: The Mystery of the Seed
Text: Mark 4:26–34
This parable occurs only in Mark. The story is deceptively simple. A farmer casts seed on the ground and then does nothing. The days pass, and the farmer goes through his everyday routine of life: he sleeps, he rises, night and day. Meanwhile, the seed in the ground sprouts and grows long—he does not know how. The earth is said to produce of itself. This is a way of saying that it is God alone who gives the growth. But there is an appointed order: first the blade, then the ear of grain, and then the full corn is described. Whatever has transpired under the ground becomes visible.

But what do we focus on in the parable: the farmer, the seed, the harvest? Perhaps it is best for us to read ourselves into the parable from the perspective of the farmer.

I. *Confidence during the wait.* The parable begins with the sowing and ends with the harvest. Jesus seems to be saying that the kingdom of God follows as certainly as harvest follows the sowing of seed. Seeds buried deep in the earth germinate and find the sun. A farmer is confident that

there will be a harvest simply because he has sown the seed. In spite of what many might think, God's hour approaches as surely as the hour of harvest will come after the seed has been sown. Some may scorn. Some may waver in faith. Others may be impatient, but the harvest comes. God will bring to completion what God has begun.

But confidence requires faith. The parable portrays the kingdom as something inconspicuous and, for a while, hidden. This contrasts with the preaching of John the Baptist. John pictured it as a fiery judgment that would rumble in like a hurricane, or, to use a Mediterranean image, a sirocco. It would come, he said, with Spirit and fire. In contrast, Jesus portrays it as coming with as much noise and fanfare as seed sown in the ground; but it will produce a harvest.

The farmer does not know how the seed grows in the earth and can hardly see what transpires beneath the ground. But he trusts that God is involved and active and will bring the harvest to pass. Perhaps this strikes a chord in those who are downcast and discouraged by rejections and failures. When our eyes are clouded by disappointment and doubt, Jesus reminds us that there is a seed beneath the ground that is coming to fruition. When we despair that the will of God is being eclipsed in our world, Jesus reminds us that God will not fail.

II. *Patience during the wait.* The temptation for the people of God is to want to rush God's timetables. We cannot see off into eternity, so we want things to happen now. We may cry out, "How long, O Lord?" We may even wish to do something that will jump-start the advent of God's final kingdom.

In the parable, the farmer awaits patiently the appointed harvest. In fact, the parable draws special attention to the fact that the farmer does nothing. He continues his daily life, waiting patiently for God to do what God has promised to do. He knows that there is nothing that he can do to hurry the process. Were he to try, it would only end in disaster. He can only wait for the appointed time. The same attitude should be adopted by those who await the kingdom of God (see James 5:7–8).

The growth leading to the harvest has nothing to do with human resources, aid, or force. The earth reproduces of itself not because of the farmer's ability, knowledge, or activity. It is the same with God's kingdom. The establishment of God's kingdom depends upon God's power and not ours. Humans do not build the kingdom of God by obeying the Law or calculating its arrival, nor do they need to worry themselves about the eventual outcome. We can only wait patiently upon God and respond when it invades our lives.

III. *Getting ready for action.* The inac-tivity of the farmer while the grain was growing contrasts with the rush of activity at harvest time when the grain is ripe. Jesus announces that the harvest is ready. One should review the signs. Just as the seed produces signs that the harvest is coming, first the blade, then the ear, then the full grain in the ear, so the disciples must examine Jesus' signs before they can reach the right understanding. If they believe what Jesus says, they must be ready to bestir themselves to activity. The routine of life is broken by the urgency of the hour that will require total commitment and concentrated energy.—David E. Garland

SUNDAY: JUNE TWENTY-THIRD

SERVICE OF WORSHIP

Sermon: The Fellowship of the Unashamed

TEXTS: Rom. 1:16; Gal. 5:1

Professor Elton Trueblood, in his powerful little book *Foundations for Reconstruction,* holds that the real enemy of religion is not irreligion but what he calls a "vague religiosity." The real enemy, he says, is not the Red organizer who openly opposes the church but the reputable citizen who adopts a patronizing attitude toward the church by the gesture of joining it when he has no idea of genuine commitment to its gospel. "Our mild religiosity," Professor Trueblood continues, "will not only fail to support a sagging civilization, it cannot long retain itself. As the crisis advances we shall either become openly pagan or we shall be driven to leave this temporarily pleasant middle ground to the fourth alternative, that of commitment to the will of the living God in a radical Christianity that is not ashamed to be frankly missionary and evangelical." Professor Trueblood calls upon us for the creation of a Fellowship of the Unashamed, with the result that "ours should then become one of those glorious ages of revival." But we are a long way from that now, he concedes.

The Fellowship of the Unashamed! Unashamed of familiarity with the Bible! Unashamed of the practice of prayer! Unashamed of rugged honesty! Unashamed of the missionary passion! Unashamed of the doctrine of a free church in a free country! Unashamed of the ideals and principles and spirit of him who came to bring us life, and that more abundantly!

I. We have every reason to be unashamed of the Protestant Reformation, unashamed of what it accomplished, unashamed of its illustrious leader and of those associated with him in this stupendous task.

(a) Luther was but thirty-three when on October 31, 1517, he nailed to the door of the Castle Church at Wittenberg his Ninty-five Theses—the same age as Jefferson when he wrote the Declaration of Independence. In his study of the Bible, a flaming text in Romans profoundly affected his life. The arresting words that quite startled him when first he saw their implications were these: "The just shall live by faith." The sale of indulgences by representatives of the church touched the quick of his conscience, and he struck a blow for religious liberty that reverberated the world around. Excommunicated by the pope, he burned the papal bull at nine o'clock on the twelfth of December, 1520; and thus he broke with the most powerful organization of his day.

(b) This is not the time to enter into a detailed discussion or interpretation of the principles which became the cornerstone of Protestantism. Their implications are preached in myriad pulpits every Sunday in this and other nations. These principles have in them the heartbeat of rugged thinking. They call us to the preservation of freedoms that were purchased at so great a price—freedoms that stir our emotions like the steady beat of a drum or the strident notes of a bugle. Let it be granted that we do not always live up to these principles. Let it be confessed that we handle some of them a little gingerly, as for instance the right of private interpretation of the Scriptures. Let it be acknowledged that we have not given these fundamental principles the fullest application. Yet withal, we live and breathe the air, both religiously and politically, that was purified by the thought and deeds of the great German reformer.

(c) We are unashamed of the mighty Reformation which emerged from Martin Luther's heroic leadership, but we are sometimes ashamed of the manner and spirit in which the principles of Protestantism are presented. The poet Tennyson once said that in religion one has to choose between bigotry on the one hand and flabbiness on the other. Not many will agree with this position. For one, I repudiate it. I hold that there is a halfway house where one can stand loyally by his convictions and be neither bigoted nor flabby. I think this halfway house is where Protestantism should establish residence.

(d) Protestantism is a movement for freedom in government and in church. Protestantism is an invitation to think for oneself; and among other obligations resting on us is that of thinking no evil and always speaking what we hold to be the truth in the spirit of goodwill and love. My authority for this statement is none other than the greatest of the apostles, St. Paul!

II. We are unashamed of the heritage of freedom which has come down to us from the founding fathers of our beloved America; unashamed of the Constitution into which fifty-five men, selected because of their standing and ability, poured the plenitude of their minds and hearts; unashamed of the Bill of Rights, which is the soul of that historic document.

(a) I have said that the soul of the Constitution is the Bill of Rights, which is contained in the first ten amendments and was made law December 15, 1791. This Bill of Rights protects the citizen from his government and avers that there are some things that the government cannot do, and among these, no interference in the exercise of religion, free speech, popular assembly, and the right of petition. There are other freedoms involved in this Bill of Rights, but these four are basic. Not only is this a Bill of Rights, it is a bill of duties. We talk too much about our rights and too little about our duties. It should be noted that our American democracy, system of government, Constitution, Bill of Rights—all of these are related to the Protestant Reformation led by Martin Luther.

(b) The weaknesses of a democracy and of Protestantism are the same—namely, the abuse of liberty and inefficiency. It is not possible to have free speech, free exercise of religion, and a free press without differences of opinion, clashes, and cleavages over issues both theological and political. But it is better to have these, with sometimes their annoyances and embarrassments, than to be held together in a viselike grip by a dictator or a tyrant. There is much to be said for the privilege of making our own mistakes, and the best cure for the ills of a democracy is more democracy.

(c) The deadliest enemies of our institutions are not outside but within our borders: complacency, neglect of the ballot, indifference to the kind of men selected for public office, the lowering of standards of morality, corruption in high and low places. We are unashamed of the heritage of our founding fathers, but we are ashamed of an undiscerning and ungrateful citizenship that forgets that "eternal vigilance is the price of liberty."

(d) According to the Constitution of the United States, this is not a Protestant nation nor a Catholic nation nor a Jewish nation—but a nation where Protestants, Catholics, and Jews are given the right of the free exercise of religion, with church and state forever separate! This is basic Americanism, and woe unto us and our freedom if we tamper with the Bill of Rights, juggle its letter, or repudiate its spirit. Can you not see wisdom and justice in this position? Surely you can if you think back and recall certain horrible segments of history. Our founding fathers remembered vividly what happened in Europe and other continents when Protestants were persecuted because they were *Protestants,* Catholics were persecuted because they were *Catholics,* and Jews were persecuted because they were *Jews,* and they were determined that that should not happen here, so they gave us the Bill of Rights.

III. We are unashamed of the experiments in cooperative Christianity looking to a closer unity and a spiritual solidarity such as Protestantism has yet to achieve, so we thank God and take fresh courage.

(a) Surely we are not unaware of the progress made toward the reunion of the divided house of God in our Protestant world within the last quarter of a century. That progress is encouraging. In 1929 the union between two great Presbyterian bodies in Scotland took place, resulting in the Church of Scotland, with a membership of some 1,300,000. But before this merger occurred, there had been other important if less spectacular unions among Scottish Presbyterians. In 1932, the three Methodist bodies in Great Britain were united without a dissenting vote. In France, where Protestantism is weak, numbering about a million, and split four ways, a reunion has come about. In Canada, the union of the Methodists, Congregationalists, and about 70 percent of the Presbyterians, resulting in the United Church of Canada, was an achievement of magnitude, an expression of statesmanship of a noble spiritual quality. The union of three bodies of Methodism in America is a victory of wide significance. Eight million Methodists cannot be wrong on this issue as the souls of John Wesley, George Whitefield, and a host of others march grandly on.

(b) The glorious head of the church prayed for the oneness of all those who believe on him, and we must not forget that these believers are in every communion of Christendom, from the smallest and the humblest to the most populous and the most powerful. Perhaps we have been thinking too much of the churches and too little about *the* Church. More and more our church life must be a community of interests. I mean now the life of our congregations, which we love to think of as families of the Christ. Notice this word *community.* It means to come together bringing gifts, not necessarily money, but gifts of mind and heart, the spirit of forgiveness, the passion for justice, a genius for goodwill.

(c) I aver that as we review the history of the Protestant Reformation we are unashamed of what it was and what it did. We are unashamed of its leaders. But we are ashamed of our failure to live up to the principles and the spirit of a movement which has given us almost everything we prize. We are unashamed of the experiments and the progress looking to the reunion of the divided house of God, although we are abashed by our failure not to have done more. We are ashamed and embarrassed that we have not gotten farther along the road to unity and thus helped to answer the prayer of our Lord for the oneness of his followers. We are unashamed of the heritage left us by the founding fathers of our republic, the Constitution, and the Bill of Rights. But we acknowledge our shame where the spirit and the letter of the Bill of Rights has been flaunted and in some instances repudiated. We would repent and reconsecrate ourselves so that we could in all sincerity say with that unashamed Jew, "I am not ashamed of the gospel of Christ: for it is the power of God unto salvation to every one that believeth; to the Jew first, and also to the Greek."—Edgar DeWitt Jones

Illustrations

PEER PRESSURE.   A young United States congressman surprised his colleagues by voting against a certain bill in the House. Afterward he met a fellow member, an older man, in the washroom who asked the young man why he voted as he did. "I was under great pressure from a few important people in my constituency," came the reply. The older and widely experienced member looked him in the eye and remarked, "Young man, where are your inner braces?"—Donald Macleod

OUR FIRST LOYALTY. I had the privilege of rooming with a young man from Germany in an international hostel in Basel, Switzerland. From the time that he was fifteen he established a unique record of faithfulness to Christ and his cause. Instead of attending the Hitler youth parades on Sunday mornings, he would attend his church. Even as a teenager he saw beyond the Nazi creed to the God of Jesus Christ, who stands above all nations and stands in judgment upon them all. During World War II, he established an anti-Nazi record—even to the point of endangering his very existence. When Allied occupation forces came in, he was one of the first to be helped to take postgraduate work in Switzerland. He was "other worldly." When practically all those around him were succumbing to racial pride and national pride and power drives and lust, he felt himself under the judgment and guidance of the One who is above all particular loyalties.—John P. Newport

Sermon Suggestions

WHO OWNS THE EARTH? TEXT: Psalm 24. The tense of the verb is a main item: "is the Lord's." (1) Men have said in certain eras, "The earth is the devil's." (2) In my time in college thoughtful men were saying, "The earth is the earth's." (3) Our generation says flatly, "The earth is man's." (4) "The earth is the Lord's." As for that contention, the evidence is not far to seek. The earth proclaims its divine original, at least fitfully, even to our time-bound eyes.—Adapted from George A. Buttrick.

THE HOUR OF FAVOR . . . THE DAY OF DELIVERANCE. TEXT: 2 Cor. 5:18–6:2, REB. (1) God has made reconciliation possible through Christ. (2) God has made us agents of this good news. (3) Therefore, whoever you are, "do not let it come to nothing" in your case.

Worship Aids

CALL TO WORSHIP. "Oh, bless our God, ye peoples, and make the voice of his praise to be heard" (Ps. 66:8).

INVOCATION. We thank thee, our heavenly Father, for the light of this pleasant morning and for all the circumstances of great mercy with which thou has called us hither. We thank thee for the memories that do not fail to arise in this place, for the hopes which here brighten, for the strength which we have received, and for the hope that we have of strength yet to be imparted. Grant to us this morning the evident token of thy presence—of the Holy Spirit. Quicken our affection. Give us access to thee by the understanding, by faith, by love, and by joy in the Holy Ghost.—Henry Ward Beecher

OFFERTORY SENTENCE. "For God so loved the world, that he gave his only begotten Son, that whosoever believeth on him should not perish, but have eternal life" (John 3:16).

OFFERTORY PRAYER. In the experience of worship we express our love. You have taught us to express our love in giving. We offer ourselves even as we offer our gifts. Accept us and them, we pray in the name of Jesus.

PRAYER. Father of tender mercies and deep compassions, we gather in your presence because you love us and have helped us to love one another. We thank you for bending to reach us—for extending your loving care from eternity, from majesty, from glory beyond our comprehension. This you have done in the gift of your Son. We thank you for continuing to love us as your sons and daughters in Christ Jesus.

Now help us, we pray, to relax our pride and to extend our concern to one another—brothers and sisters in Christ Jesus. Some of us are suffering the agony of bereavement. Others are experiencing the anxiety of sickness. Yet others are feeling the frustration of time's relentless movement toward deadlines.

Minister to our needs, Father, calming our fears, healing our sickness, comforting us in our loss, teaching us the meaning of joy. Help us to be patient with one another, knowing that you have been patient with us.

We pray in the name that is above every name because he emptied himself—even in the name of Jesus Christ our Lord.—J. Estill Jones

LECTIONARY MESSAGE

Topic: What Do You Do When You Find Jesus Asleep?

TEXT: Mark 4:35–41

What do you do when you find Jesus asleep? That's the question of despair and desperation that comes during the crisis moments that all of us face in life. A patient is diagnosed as having cancer. The contract where you work is not renewed, and you are laid off, wondering how you will make ends meet, let alone pay the rent. That relationship that promised to have been made in heaven ends. It's difficult to understand! One moment everything is going great; the next moment the storm winds of crisis begin to blow, and our world is sinking around us. We cry out to God, "Don't you care if we drown?" But look, he's asleep in the boat. What do you do when you find Jesus asleep?

The crisis situations that you and I face reveal some of the same characteristics faced by the disciples in this passage from Mark's Gospel:

I. *Crisis comes suddenly.* To begin with, the storm came suddenly. Now, the disciples knew that could happen. They were keenly familiar with that waterway. They knew that a squall could quickly erupt on the horizon and spread over the entire lake. They knew that could happen, but it didn't make it any easier to deal with.

When we are confronted with crisis, no matter how prepared we may be, the sudden onset brings fear and despair.

II. *Fear of the unknown.* The disciples quickly became frightened as the storm intensified. Their boat began to fill with water. The real danger of sinking became apparent. They didn't know what was going to happen to them. They became frozen with fear.

When difficult situations impinge upon our lives, we often move from shock to fear because we don't know what is going to happen. The unknown is always frightening. Do you remember going to the dentist for the first time? Sitting in the dentist chair, even before the dentist came near your mouth, was a scary experience. Not knowing what to expect brings apprehension. Seeing all of that equipment and not knowing what it's all about is frightening. Moving to a new community is frightening. Starting in a new school is frightening. Beginning a new job is frightening. And if the unknown in everyday situations is frightening, how much more are we going to be fearful when our world is collapsing around us?

III. *Fear leads to despair.* The disciple's fear turned into despair. Their boat was sinking; that's enough to cause despair. But they were also desperate because Jesus didn't seem to care. "Don't you care if we drown?" they exclaimed.

No wonder we feel despair when financial crisis and helplessness and loneliness and illness come to us. We not only lose hope because our world is sinking around us, but at a time when we need God most, God doesn't seem to care. "Why don't you curse God and die," said Job's wife, "God doesn't care about you. You have lost everything that is dear to you. Your possessions, your family are all gone, and God doesn't care!"

IV. *Jesus was in the boat.* These characteristics, the sudden onset of crisis that brings fear and then despair, seem to be a part of the tragic situations that are so much a part of life. But don't stop there. There is another characteristic that is often missed. Jesus was in the boat with the disciples. He wasn't off at a distance as a casual observer; he was right in the middle of their crisis, as he is always a part of our crises, even though, at times, he appears to be sleeping.

What do you do when you find Jesus asleep? The text implies that we should rejoice that he's in the boat with us and claim the faith that he has the power to

help us weather any storm!—Craig A. Loscalzo

SUNDAY: JUNE THIRTIETH

SERVICE OF WORSHIP

Sermon: Liberty and Loyalty
TEXTS: Gal. 5:1; 1 Cor. 3:21

On the 4th of July, national attention is focused upon the Declaration of Independence in recognition of the anniversary of the birth of the United States. In historical perspective, however, a resolution of independence was adopted by the unanimous vote of twelve states in the Continental Congress on July 2, the New York delegation abstaining. But after further debate, the document known as the Declaration of Independence was unanimously adopted on July 4. Those who prepared this declaration, Thomas Jefferson assisted by John Adams and Benjamin Franklin, produced a document whose message and spirit were revolutionary because the claim was asserted that "these United Colonies are, and of Right ought to be Free and Independent States." The authority for this action was the doctrine of "natural rights" whereby the people should determine the form of government under which they lived. To insure the independence declared, six long years of war ensued before Great Britain acknowledged the existence of the United States by signing the Treaty of Paris in 1783.

It was, moreover, not many years after the peace treaty that Alexander Hamilton, James Madison, and John Jay recognized that unless the newly won liberty led to loyalty to the nation's central government, the freedom that had been won could be lost. At that very time, rival state governments were unwilling to cooperate, insurrection disrupted the state of Massachusetts, and local factions were unwilling to adapt their interests to the good of the whole. Anarchy was believed to be a real possibility unless a new government was formed that could command the allegiances of an independent people. This problem was resolved by the utili-

zation of certain political and religious theories and practices well known in the seventeenth and eighteenth centuries. For a long time certain Christian groups had believed that they could assemble, elect their own leaders, and jointly determine the rules and laws governing their societies. Furthermore, a leading political theorist, John Locke, had long ago argued that each man had a "natural right" to enter into contract with his fellowmen and together determine the form of government under which to live. These concepts and actions, when compared with the divine right theory for monarchy as the basis for government, were revolutionary, and they are an essential part of the American heritage—a testimony of faith in the reasonableness of man. Thus, the application of these theories under the leadership of Hamilton, Madison, and Jay (with the assistance and encouragement of many others) brought forth a new federal government. The federal Constitution of 1789 protected the rights of the states and gave added status to the rights of individuals by adopting a separate and distinct Bill of Rights. The sum of these actions was such that the people and the states gave their allegiance to the national government, and the republic was maintained. The freedom that independence conveyed to each citizen was elevated by loyalty, and that same quality of loyalty on the part of the American people has maintained our system of government.

In the spiritual arena, there is a common experience that bears a striking resemblance to the one resolved at the time of the constitutional origin of the republic. In short, individuals still declare their independence. In fact, each new generation claims freedom as a birthright. For the Christian, moreover, there is the freedom that comes through faith in Christ. The Apostle Paul wrote much about this, and in one instance he admonished the

Galatians, "Stand fast in the liberty wherewith Christ hath made us free . . ." (5:1). On still another occasion he proclaimed to the Corinthians, "All things are yours" (1 Cor. 3:21). In fact, there probably has never been a greater champion of Christian liberty than Paul. But, in each instance where he espoused freedom, he was quick to acknowledge that independence without commitment can produce anarchy. Thus, to the Corinthians he added the provision "you are Christ's." To Paul the principle was clear: liberty without loyalty is a conundrum.

Consider the relationship of liberty and loyalty in the life of a young man raised in a cramped, restrictive environment. He has been repressed by prohibitive restrictions and negative attitudes—the "do not" emphasis—from his earliest memory. In time, however, he quite naturally decides to strike out on his own; the chains of confinement and restraint are snapped. He demands his "place in the sun." But just as it is inevitable that such a person will demand his natural rights, it is equally important that he develop loyalty. Unless the person generates a positive commitment to a job, career, or develops a wholesome companionship with a young woman, his newly claimed liberty is likely to lead to listlessness, irresponsibility, and it could degenerate into a complete loss of orientation.

Many centuries ago a young man left his home in North Africa to experience the excitement of a freer life. He soon came to realize that self-indulgence was not pure pleasure, but in itself it could be the cruelest of captors. But it was Augustine's good fortune to come under the influence of Ambrose, the bishop of Milan, a man whose strong character and influence had a salubrious effect upon him. After reading Paul's Letter to the Romans, which precipitated his conversion, he was baptized and subsequently returned to Africa. There he became a prodigious writer and the center of a monastic community. Among his writings is the work entitled *Confessions,* which became one of the most widely read autobiographies and remains one of the most moving and profound self-records of a human soul and its struggles. His *De Civitate Dei* remains a landmark interpretation of history. "No other Christian after Paul was to have so wide, deep, and prolonged an influence upon the Christianity of Western Europe." It was against this experience and background that Augustine uttered his incisive dictum, "Love God and do as you please."

Into a fifteenth-century Florentine home there was born a child who was named Michelangelo. This household was very much an authority-oriented patriarchy. It was determined that the son would become a financier. When the lad dared to speak for himself and expressed a desire to pursue the study of art, he was quickly brought into line with the family's plan. But the day came when Michelangelo made his bid for freedom and the right of self-determination. After many problems and tribulations he achieved his own identity, but instead of using his newfound status as a basis for rebellion against an authoritarian home, he used it to fulfill his burning ambition to become an artist. So devoted was he to his profession that his name became synonymous with the flowering of Christian art in Renaissance Italy.

This principle of the inseparability of loyalty from liberty in the maintenance of one's freedom can also be demonstrated in the area of social relationships. In respect to the achievement and continuance of the Declaration of Independence, John Adams wrote the night before its adoption, "I am well aware of the toil and blood and treasure it will cost us to maintain this Declaration." Indeed, this bid for freedom cost several of the fifty-five cosigners of the document dearly. Richard Stockton of New Jersey was dragged from his bed by British troops, thrown into prison, and, broken in health, died prematurely at age fifty-one. Also in New Jersey, John Hart was forced to flee from the bedside of his dying wife, his thirteen children were scattered, his farm destroyed by fire, and he survived only as a fugitive for a year and a half. In Pennsylvania, John Morton was ostracized by relatives and friends for signing the Declaration, and eight months later he died. But the loyalty of these men to their fledging country provided a necessary ingredient for its survival and eventual success.

The reverse of this tenet is obviously all too true. A person who assumes that he can act as an isolated individual speaking, acting, and living in any manner he pleases is a menace to society. Eventually he injures not only himself but innocent members of the community. For example, one who learns to drive a car and procures a driver's license can be a deadly threat to all who travel the highways unless he is committed to obey the driving laws of the land. Until there is a basic respect for the proven rules of safety and the rights of other drivers, the freedom of continued motor travel is diminished for all. Each year the National Highway Safety Council composes the statistics of those whose freedom to operate a motor vehicle has been tragically terminated by the anarchists of the road who are unfaithful to the laws of the state and dictates of common sense.

Liberty itself is not the organizing center of life. It may well be disruptive and dispersive. By itself, it produces purposelessness, confusion, and eventually disillusionment. It is loyalty that organizes life, focuses one's energies, and sustains the person and the nation in the fulfillment of their goals. It is allegiance to the ideals and examples of those who produced the Declaration of Independence that will preserve the blessings of life, liberty, and the pursuit of happiness to us and our posterity.

This same principle again appears to be valid when applied in the realm of religion. Religious freedom is one of the most cherished and basic tenets of the American way of life. We do not have to be Baptist, Methodist, Presbyterian—Protestant or Roman Catholic—we are free. Many of our forefathers prayed for and dreamed about this type of liberty. In many instances, intolerance, persecution, and war over religion had been their lot. The Thirty Years War in Europe and the Civil War in England both involved deadly disagreements over religion in the seventeenth century. By contrast, today freedom from interference in the practice of one's faith is the right of millions of citizens in the Western world. But at this point a problem arises. Instead of using this freedom to exercise and develop religious conviction, it has become a freedom to exempt oneself *from* any form of religious faith. The battle for religious freedom has been won, but that is only half the issue. Now the emphasis needs to be placed on the importance of loyalty to one's religious persuasion, because positive good can not be maintained in the face of negative indifference.

The Apostle Paul was emphatic on this issue when he wrote, "For freedom did Christ set us free," then added with equal force, but "you are Christ's." We have been granted spiritual emancipation by the Master of Life, but to perpetuate requires loyalty to the Christ. Moreover, this explanation by Paul is no isolated incident in the New Testament. Jesus himself accented this truth in word and example. He elevated the right of the individual to a personal relationship with God, but he made it perfectly clear that this status was to be maintained by fealty. For example, it was he who said, "I am come that you might have life . . ."; "You shall know the truth and the truth shall make you free"; and "God so loved . . . that whosoever believeth in him should not perish but have everlasting life." But he also commanded a positive response from the beneficiaries of his grace because he added, "If you are my disciples, you will do whatsoever I command you"; "Keep my commandments"; and "Follow me." He clearly expected loyalty from the recipients of his gifts.

The American people understandably place great pride in the achievement of independence. It is well to give special recognition to this heritage. But it also need be remembered that the tradition of freedom has been maintained through loyalty. The combined elements of this tradition are equally important for the Christian and the citizen.—Frederick V. Mills, Sr.

Illustrations

TOTAL LOYALTY.   A loyal son of old Kentucky, just on the eve of the Civil War, was faced with the grave problem of which side he should support. This is the way he solved the problem: If the country should split, he would side with the South against the North. If the South should split, he would side with Kentucky against the other southern states. If Kentucky split, he would side with his county against the rest of the state. And if his county split, he would side with his town against the rest of the county.—Charles L. Wallis

EMANCIPATED?   The other day I saw a man who had lived an emancipated life—loose, irresponsible, unorganized, aimless, futile—a sorry mess of misery he had ended in. Then I went home and read again the story of Andrew Melville, one of the early Scotch reformers, threatened, one day, by the Earl of Morton with death by hanging if he did not cease his free speaking. And Melville laughed. "Tush, sir," he said, in words that every Scot remembers, "threaten your courtiers after that manner. It is the same to me whether I rot in the air or in the ground. It will not be in your power to hang or exile his truth."

Which of these two—this loose, undedicated fellow or Andrew Melville—was really free? And which of these two does the world need today? Ah, church of Christ, at any rate, keep your message clear: Liberty, all things are yours, founded on loyalty, ye are Christ's, and Christ is God's.—Harry Emerson Fosdick

Sermon Suggestions

FEAR AND FAVOR.   TEXT: 2 Sam. 6:1–15. (1) *The story:* After David's fearful experience with the *Ark* of God, he saw that God, though not to be taken for granted, blesses by his presence. (2) *The meaning:* Our experience with God, while it is often puzzling, in the end proves to be a reason for rejoicing. (3) *The application:* We sometimes prejudge the meaning of God's apparent actions; we do well to hold him in reverence; but awe must at last resolve itself into trust and rejoicing.

ACCEPTABLE GIVING.   TEXT: 2 Cor. 8:7–15. (1) It is a proof of love. (2) It is modeled after the self-giving of our Lord Jesus Christ. (3) It is according to our means. (4) It is a matter of equality and reciprocity.

Worship Aids

CALL TO WORSHIP.   "God be merciful unto us, and bless us, and cause his face to shine upon us" (Ps. 67:1).

INVOCATION.   God of liberty, give us to know in this land the meaning and purpose of our freedom: freedom with responsibility, freedom with justice, freedom to choose the righteous and do the righteous without undue governmental intervention. Grant us liberty of soul in our worship this day, that gratitude might merge with commitment to honor God in word and deed. In our strong deliverer's name we pray.—E. Lee Phillips

OFFERTORY SENTENCE.   "For whether we live, we live unto the Lord; or whether we die, we die unto the Lord: whether we live, therefore, or die, we are the Lord's" (Rom. 14:8).

OFFERTORY PRAYER.   O thou giver of every good and perfect gift, accept these offerings today and use them for thy good and perfect purpose.

PRAYER.   Eternal God, high above our imaginations, whose judgments are a great deep, we worship thee. We seek thee in the sanctuary that we may be saved from ourselves.

Save us from our weak self-pity. Our complaints rise before thee, as have the lamentations of our fathers before us. Dost thou not sit throned in light unapproachable? Canst thou understand how heavily life bears on us when the waves and the billows go over us? Yet save us from this, our self-pity. Give us deep resources of interior strength that we may face life with adequacy, may rise above the difficulties that confront us and carry off a victory in spite of them; that life may grow strong from within and be triumphant without; that we may rejoice and be glad in it, difficult though it is, and sing in thy house that we are more than conquerors through him that loved us. Save us from weak excuses. Give us the honesty to face our sins. We acknowledge that we practice subterfuge and will not be candid concerning our failures. Grant that in this place of honest prayer, where thou art from whose eyes no life is hid, we may see the evils that we do harming not only ourselves but those who trust and love us. Let there be such sincere and moving penitence among this people that lives may be redirected, that evils may be cast aside, that hands may reach out to take hold on solid good, and that thy Kingdom may come the more, in our lives and through them, because we have worshiped here.

Save us from our narrow interests and cares. Help us to live out our lives in other lives. Knowing that there is no good that comes to each that should not come to all, and no good that may come to all that should not be the care of each, knowing that we are members of one brotherhood, help us when we pray to say, as the Master said, Our—Our Father, our debts, our trespasses, our daily bread. Help us to take the common needs of every day and lift them up into the great fellowship of the human family. Cast down prejudice and across all barriers that ancient days have built of race, creed, class, and nation; grant that our generosity and friendliness may flow out to all the sons of men.

Especially we seek thy benediction upon any lives here overthrown in anxiety, fear, and sorrow. O God, in the quiet of our silent prayer may the Spirit move among this people and upon stricken hearts lay a healing, cooling hand. Let the fever subside. Let serenity, tranquility, steadiness, and peace come now into some life that sorely needs them. Throw the horizons of thy greatness around us and be our unseen Friend.

We ask it in the Spirit of the Christ.— Harry Emerson Fosdick

LECTIONARY MESSAGE

Topic: New Life for Hopeless Cases
TEXT: Mark 5:21-43
In our daily lives we struggle with prob-

lems and suffering that seem like hopeless cases. These agonizing cases force us to confront the frailty of our lives and the unanswered questions of our suffering. What can we learn from Jesus' encounter with these situations that seem beyond human hope? How can we experience the new life Jesus brings to those trapped in hopeless suffering?

This interwoven story-within-a-story illustrates Mark's "sandwich" technique. The story of the woman with the hemorrhage (vv. 24b-34) is "sandwiched" between pieces of the story of the raising of Jairus's daughter (vv. 21-24a and 35-43).

I. *Hopeless case number one: Jairus's daughter.* We witness here the suffering of a notable but desperate father and the suffering of his dying little girl. With the report of the girl's death (v. 35), desperate hope turns to hopelessness. Yet Jesus calls for Jairus's faith in the face of the fear of death (v. 36). Then hopelessness is transformed into complete "amazement" (v. 42) at the new life given by Jesus. In this case, Jesus shows us what death looks like from God's point of view—a temporary sleep from which one is soon to awake.

II. *Hopeless case number two: the woman with the hemorrhage.* We witness here the suffering of a poor, bleeding woman. She has spent all of her money on physicians (v. 26) and so now decides to try to "steal" a cure. She has been bleeding for twelve years—as long as Jairus's daughter has been alive. Bleeding makes her ritually unclean (like the corpse of Jairus's daughter). The hemorrhaging woman is cut off from the world, both socially and religiously. No one can touch her, but she touches Jesus.

After her healing, Jesus will not let her hide in the anonymity of the crowd. She confesses her healing (v. 33) and is blessed by Jesus (v. 34). Jesus addresses this woman, who through her faith has been given a new life, as "daughter," again reminding us of the child of Jairus (v. 35, also v. 23), who still needs his power.

III. *Jesus: physician for hopeless cases.* Faith in Jesus (vv. 34 and 35), as opposed to any sort of magic, is the one necessary requirement both for powerful Jairus and for the poor woman in the crowd. As Jesus deals with hopeless cases, all the distinctions of wealth, social class, and religious respectability fade into insignificance.

Jesus heals despite the confused disbelief of the disciple (v. 31) and the mocking laughter of the mourners (v. 40). Jesus heals without acclaim—a touch of his garment in the crowd and a few words in the presence of several people in a quiet room. How different are Jesus' miracles from the spectacles of many so-called faith healers in our time! Jesus' healings are signs of God's caring presence with those in suffering, which point us to the coming of the kingdom in Jesus the Messiah. The healing touch of Jesus' power (vv. 23, 27, 28, 30, 31, and 41) can offer new life to the hopeless cases with which we struggle in our world today.—Charles J. Scalise

SUNDAY: JULY SEVENTH

SERVICE OF WORSHIP

Sermon: Thorns in the Flesh

TEXT: 2 Cor. 12:1–10

While on the subject of limitations, we would probably do well to consider one more kind—"thorns in the flesh," in St. Paul's metaphor. They are small things, thorns—like blips on a large screen. But as we know, a small blip can sink you.

In this world there are things hoped for and things stuck with. The thorns are what we are stuck with. We cannot extract them. All of them cause pain, the real pain that is associated with loss: loss of health; loss of faith and hope, as when we somehow feel "unblessed"; loss of joy; loss of love; and certainly loss of power. To see how pained we are by loss of power, we have only to recall the thorn in the flesh of the nation represented by those fifty-three hostages we could not seem to extract from Iran. So humiliated were we as a people that today we feel compelled to turn almost any foreign affairs issue into a test of strength.

I. St. Paul, of course, is keenly conscious of his thorn. He tells us, "Three times I besought the Lord about this, that it should leave me. . . ."

(a) Generally, prayer is not an act of self-expression. Prayer is an act of empathy; prayer is thinking God's thoughts after him. Prayer is praying, "*Our* father who art in heaven," when everything within us longs to cry out, "*My* father," because "our" includes that horrible divorced husband, that wayward child; it includes muggers, rapists, the Iranian captors, all the people who jam thorns into our flesh.

(b) But sometimes prayer *is* an act of self-expression. It was to St. Paul: "Three times I besought the Lord about this, that it should leave me. . . ." When we do express our feelings to God, we should, like Paul, be as specific as possible. There is too much dignity in too many prayers— dignity at the expense of specificity. So never mind how crude or how trivial your prayers may sound to you. There are no unimportant tears to God.

II. "Three times I besought the Lord. . . ." What do you suppose happened the first time? What happened the second and third times?

(a) I suspect that the first time Paul probably did not receive the answer he records in the Letter to the Corinthians. It would make more sense if by way of an answer he heard nothing but rose from prayer a better person. That is no mean answer; it is, in fact, answer sufficient in many cases. In other words, the first time Paul simply unburdened himself of his anger, his grief, and his frustration. In this crazy, mixed-up world you have to "dump the mud."

(b) Now what about the second time? It would be true to life if the second time Paul received an answer that went something like this: "I hear what you're saying, Paul, but let me remind you that it takes both sunshine and rain to make one of my rainbows."

Obviously, tension is the pulse of life. Pain can bring more life than pleasure. But for this kind of life to sprout and flourish we have to stop denying and defying these thorns. We have to begin to accept them; we have to befriend the enemy.

(c) Then—a while later—comes the third time. My guess is that the third time Paul discovers the true mercy of failure. "Three times I besought the Lord about this, that it should leave me; but he said to me, 'My grace is sufficient for you, for my power is made perfect in weakness.' " That is one of the great lines of Scripture but not an easy one to understand.

III. I am sure that many of you have read "Blessed are the meek" and wondered what that meant. Does that mean you are supposed to become a doormat for people to walk over? Certainly a lot of Christians act as if that is what it meant. But the word in Greek is *praos,* and that word, as a verb, refers to the channeling of energies, as in taming horses. Before they could be useful, horses had to be "meeked." In Wycliffe's Bible we read, "Blessed are the meeked, for they shall inherit the earth."

We are meeked by the thorns in our flesh. The mercy of our failures is that they point us toward true success, which we have reluctantly to admit is with God alone. So a "messenger of Satan" can become a servant of God; the devil's subtraction can become God's addition: "When I am weak, then I am strong."

IV. So if you are up for it, take your Bible and read not only the twelfth chapter of Second Corinthians but also the fourth chapter. Read, "But we have this treasure in earthen vessels, to show that the transcendent power belongs to God and not to us." Read, "We are afflicted in every way but not crushed; perplexed but not driven to despair; struck down but not destroyed; always carrying in the body the death of Jesus, so that the life of Jesus may also be manifested in our bodies." Then go to work. Describe to God in minute detail just how you feel about that thorn in your flesh. And make it sound as full of self-pity and anger as you feel; make it sound as trivial as you want. But make it specific; get it all out. And do not ask for answers: "Lord, just listen to me; I don't want to hear anything." A week later, try it again. Maybe you will have to do it several times, if you are as angry as I am about a couple of thorns in my own flesh. But I'll tell you something: you get bored with your bitterness. After a while it gets dull dumping the mud. So the third time, you may find that you can begin the process of integration, begin to befriend the enemy.

V. Let us go back to St. Paul: "And to keep me from being too elated . . . a thorn was given me in the flesh, a messenger of Satan, to harass me, to keep me from being too elated. Three times I besought the Lord about this, that it should leave me; but he said to me, 'My grace is sufficient for you, for my power is made perfect in weakness.' " Then with a kind of nose-thumbing independence Paul says, "I will all the more gladly boast of my weaknesses, that the power of Christ may rest upon me. For the sake of Christ, then, I am content with weaknesses, insults, hardships, persecutions, calamities. . . ." And he ends triumphantly, "For when I am weak, then I am strong."—William Sloane Coffin

Illustrations

CREATIVE SUFFERING. In our personal lives as well as in those of nations, there is always suffering, tragedy, deprivation—in short, noise. Such things are always an evil that must be fought against: they have no beneficent virtue in themselves. But precisely because we must combat them, because we must react, and also because in them the mesh of old routines is broken, and our usual models of behavior no longer serve, we must turn to our innate creativity. That is what can give a new impulse to our lives, one that is more free, more thoughtful, more original, and more fruitful.—Paul Tournier

CHRIST-SUFFERING. Suffering does become Christ-suffering when it is gone through in his footsteps. It matters little whether it overtakes us directly on his account, perhaps with some kind of persecution, or with an illness or something like that. Only this makes a difference: whether the Lord Christ takes it into his hands and makes something grow out of it.—Eduard Schweizer

Sermon Suggestions

A BETTER HOUSE.   TEXT: 2 Sam. 7:1–17.
(1) David wishes to build the Lord a
house—a material one, however glorious.
(2) God wills, rather, to build David a
house—ultimately a spiritual one, fulfilled
in Jesus Christ, heir to God's promises to
David and his successors. (Cf. *Harper's
Bible Commentary* on this text.)

OF STRENGTH AND WEAKNESS.   TEXT:
2 Cor. 12:1–10. (1) *The story:* The apostle's
unusual spiritual experiences. (2) *The
meaning:* God may disclose himself to us in
special ways, not the least of which are the
apparently negative ones. (3) *The application:* God's grace can triumph in even the
most unpromising conditions of your life.

Worship Aids

CALL TO WORSHIP.   "Sing unto God, ye
kingdoms of the earth; Oh, sing praises
unto the Lord" (Ps. 68:32).

INVOCATION.   O God, the Father of our
Lord Jesus Christ, our only Savior, the
Prince of Peace: Give us grace seriously to
lay to heart the great dangers we are in by
our unhappy divisions; take away all hatred and prejudice, and whatever else may
hinder us from godly union and concord;
that, as there is but one Body and one
Spirit, one hope of our calling, one Lord,
one Faith, one Baptism, one God and Father of us all, so we may be all of one heart
and of one soul, united in one holy bond
of truth and peace, of faith and charity,
and may with one mind and one mouth
glorify thee; through Jesus Christ our
Lord.—*The Book of Common Prayer*

OFFERTORY SENTENCE.   "Offer unto
God the sacrifice of thanksgiving; and pay
thy vows unto the Most High" (Ps. 50:14).

OFFERTORY PRAYER.   Stir us, Holy God,
to generously share a portion of all that is
ours, that others who know not God may
come into contact with those who do and
thereby find the way to faith and victory.
Through him, who was raised from the
dead for us all.—E. Lee Phillips

PRAYER.   Merciful Father! Thou de-
lightest to answer our prayer. Take us at
this time into communion with thyself.
Breathe into our hearts so that our human
desires may be brought into harmony with
thy divine desire. Banish from us all pride,
arrogance, and self-conceit, all insincerity
and doubleness of mind or heart. Make us
simple with the simplicity which is in
Christ. May our desires, purged of all unworthiness, rise up before thee as the incense, and, what thou hast inspired with
us, be pleased to accept and bless.

Set us free, O Lord, from the bonds of
sense and outward things. Lift from off
us the heavy weight of custom. May we
no longer serve the traditions of men but
obey thy commandments with glad and
willing hearts. Sanctify our sorrows. Let
them not dull our minds or narrow our
hearts; but do thou work through them
thy holy ends and call us by them to a
deeper knowledge and a larger vision.
When the difficulties of the day try us,
take from us all weak lamenting and inspire us with thy strength to grapple with
them and to win from them a deeper
trust in thee. Consecrate all our work and
service. Inspire us with a spirit of devotion and patience. May we seek not our
own glory but to do thy pleasure and to
bring forth some fruit which may be to
the praise of thy grace. Grant that we
may throw aside all sloth and self-seeking
and learn the blessedness of an eager and
sacrificial life. Bless us in our intercourse
with our fellows. Quicken our hearts that
we may be swift to hear our brother's cry
from the pit of humiliation or of need.
Give us the forgiving spirit, else how
should we know ourselves forgiven by
thee? If any have wronged us, grant that
we may bring to them thy charity and win
them to a better mind. If any are in disgrace or shame, outcasts from the world,
make us thy messengers of mercy, that
we may share the pain, and by our love,
which is also thine, lead them back to thy
home and fellowship. May we be to all
men thy revealers and interpreters, bearing thy appeal to the sinning, the sorrowful and despairing. And this we would be
and do, through Jesus Christ our Lord.—
Samuel McComb

LECTIONARY MESSAGE

Topic: You Can't Go Home Again
TEXT: Mark 6:1–6

The rejection of Jesus by those in his hometown reminds us of our own experiences of rejection by those from our past who have known us. The "unbelief" (v. 6) of the people of Nazareth stands in striking contrast to the immediately preceding story of the faith of Jairus and the woman with the hemorrhage (5:21–43). The shifting attitudes of Jesus' hometown neighbors shape the process that leads to Jesus' rejection.

I. *Astonishment at his teaching (vv. 1–2).* Although the people of his hometown have politely invited Jesus to speak in their synagogue service, they are not prepared for what he has to say. They are amazed and overwhelmed by Jesus' authoritative teaching. This initial reaction of astonishment (cf. 1:22) masks an attitude of suspicion and distrust, which soon emerges in skeptical questions about the source of his wisdom and the nature of his mighty works (v. 2). Although the townspeople do not deny Jesus' wisdom and works, they raise serious questions about them. How many persons do we know who react to the authority of Jesus' teachings in a similar way today?

II. *Offense at his person (vv. 3–4).* Because they know his family personally, the people of Nazareth are deeply offended by Jesus' confident assumption of an authoritative role, as he expounds new and strange ideas. So they repudiate the idea that God is working through Jesus. They know where Jesus comes from, the limits of his social status. They think they know who Jesus "really" is. He is "the carpenter" (v. 3). Rather than naming Jesus by reference to the deceased Joseph, Jesus is labeled the "the son of Mary."

Jesus responds to the offense of the townspeople by quoting a familiar proverb, which links his own rejection by his hometown to the rejection of the prophets (v. 4). The parable is further personalized by the inclusion of the phrases 'among his own kin and in his own house.' Jesus not only experiences the rejection of his hometown, but even his own home—his own family—takes offense and rejects him (cf. 3:21).

III. *Unbelief in his mission (vv. 5–6).* Jesus did not expect such rejection from the people of his hometown. He was surprised by it and "marveled" at it (v. 6). Jesus' amazement at the "unbelief" of the people of Nazareth reveals his authentic humanity. When we experience rejection from our family and from others who have known us in the past, we are likewise often surprised and amazed.

Jesus does not proclaim his power in the face of his rejection. Except for a few healings, "he could do not mighty work there" (v. 5). Although Jesus' miracles are not caused by faith, they do not occur where there is no faith. Today, in a similar way, people who are culturally familiar with Jesus reject him by such presumptuous unbelief. As we struggle with our own experiences of rejection, we may be comforted and encouraged to know that our Lord has traveled this lonely and painful way before us.—Charles J. Scalise

SUNDAY: JULY FOURTEENTH

SERVICE OF WORSHIP

Sermon: "I'm Praying for You"—So What?
TEXTS: 1 Sam. 12:23; Luke 22:32

People who have listened to my sermons on radio often write, "Please pray for me." When I answer them, it's natural to conclude by saying, "I'm praying for you." One day not long ago I began to think about this. I felt there was a danger of using this expression too casually, as if it were something expected of a minister at any time. So I decided that in the future I would not write these words without pausing then and there to offer the prayer I was promising. Then I began to ask myself some questions about such prayers that I want to share with you.

I began with the question, "Just what am I expecting from this prayer, especially for someone I did not know and whose circumstances it was difficult to picture?" It occurred to me that many in our skeptical world would respond to the statement, "I'm praying for you," with "So what?" We have been taught to assume that it's good to have someone praying for us and that we ought to be constantly praying for others. Yet perhaps there are times when deep down there is a little whisper of "I wonder what good it really does?"

I. I began to think about what the Bible says about prayer. At first I thought about the complaints that are recorded there so bluntly by the psalmists, Job, and some of the prophets that God did not listen to their prayers. But I realized that these occasional complaints were uttered in the context of a general and often fervent belief that prayer is not only helpful but a necessity, and that it has a real effect on people's lives.

(a) The prophetic figures in the Bible, great national leaders like Abraham, Moses, Samuel, Elijah, or Isaiah and the apostolic leaders like Peter and Paul, were as varied in character and temperament as any representative group of twentieth-century statesmen or church leaders—and they were as deeply involved in the politics of their day. And they had one peculiar characteristic that is bound to strike us today; they prayed for their people. They wrestled with God on behalf of their nation, their community, and their friends and enemies—often with passion, indignation, or even anger.

(b) It may be difficult for us to understand how deeply they felt about praying for others. Moses, you remember, was often driven to distraction by the Israelites he was leading through the desert and was tempted to wash his hands of them and go his own way. Yet back he came to the Lord to plead for them. Once when he came down from Sinai with the oracles of God and found that in his absence the people had thrown an orgy around the golden idols they had made, he lost his temper, and there was bloodshed in the camp. But then he turned again to prayer: "Oh, this people have sinned a great sin and have made them gods of gold. Yet now, if thou wilt forgive their sin . . . and if not, blot me, I pray thee, out of thy book" (Exod. 32:31, 32). What a passionate, Christ-like prayer that was, and how different from our perfunctory prayers for the peace of the world or the welfare of the nation.

(c) One of the most striking words I know about intercessory prayers comes from the lips of the prophet Samuel. At the time, he was thoroughly out of tune with his people and disgusted by their desire for a king. He warned them in no uncertain terms of all the disasters that would follow if the nation forgot the sovereign Lord who had created and redeemed them. Yet he felt bound to continue his intercessions for them. "God forbid," he said, "that I should sin against the Lord in ceasing to pray for you." I can hardly imagine anyone listening to him being tempted to say, "So what?"

(d) It's often said that we live in such a different world from the people of the Bible that we can't have the same kind of belief. Many today find it almost impossible to believe that anything really happens when we ask God to do something for us, let alone for other people. It's assumed that intercession is really an outpouring of our longings for someone's welfare and is thus a kind of therapeutic exercise for our own souls. We do live in a different world than that of biblical times, and I don't want to construct an elaborate argument for prayer today. I simply want to confront the fact that the world of the Bible where prayers are made and heard is the world that Jesus accepted, and at the deepest level you and I are still in the same world today. Nothing has been discovered that rubs out of human experience the mystery of communion with God and the unfathomable ways in which our lives are linked together for good and evil within the human family. But real living begins now, as it did then, with recognition of the mystery and the acceptance of a world where God, our neighbors, you, and I are somehow linked together.

II. The trend is not necessarily away from belief in intercessory prayer. I receive more requests now for special prayers than I did many years ago. There is a great residual belief in intercession in this land of ours. This is why I am taking up the question of its real value.

(a) "I'm praying for you." "So what?" The answer, of course, depends a good deal on the spirit in which the promise of prayer is given, even the tone of voice. It can mean nothing more than an expression of sympathy, assuring someone of our goodwill. But if we don't really mean to pray we should find something else to say. Again, it can be said with a genuine mental resolve to ask God's blessing on that person when next we pray, perhaps to put the name down in some little book we use for intercessions. There is, in fact, a kind of person to whose promise of prayer few would want to reply, "So what?"

(b) The value of the words *I'm praying for you* really depends on the sincerity and saintliness of the one who makes this remark. Most of us are short on saintliness, but sincerity is within our reach. Sincerity depends a great deal on our conviction that, when we pray, something happens. Let me say right away that I believe something happens. It is inconceivable to me that prayer does no more than relieve our minds or express our sympathy.

III. I have no idea how intercession works. That's probably one of our foolish modern questions. Do we ask how love works? God doesn't always immediately give us the good things we request for someone else. Yet I find it impossible to believe that God is unwilling to act until a certain number of people have mentioned a particular person's name in their prayers.

(a) Sometimes we think of prayer as a direct line between us and God. Perhaps we should think of prayer as a kind of triangle—God, you, and the one you are praying for. That is a richer concept. Still richer is the one where we realize that our intercessions are opening the whole human drama to the inflowing of God's grace. That is what happens when, alone or in a church, we pray for such things as the moral renewal of our nation and justice and peace in the world. We are accepting our part in the human drama with its joys and sorrows, its peace and violence, its health and sickness, and making an opening through which God's healing

grace can flow, so the heavenly will be better done on earth. To pray for a special person is to open a channel for the entrance of this grace.

(b) The more we enter into the mind of Christ, the more meaning have the words *I am praying for you* and the more we begin to understand what intercession really is. For then we shall be delivered from the delusion that to pray for others means asking God to make them the kind of person we think they should be. This is one of the besetting sins of religious people. Sincere prayer for someone means asking God to do what he knows is best for them. And wouldn't you want that prayer?

(c) In the presence of Christ I know that I must keep praying for all sorts of people—those very close to me and those about whom I know little. God knows about all of them and loves to hear us pray for them. The New Testament pictures Jesus as the supreme intercessor—the one who pleaded for the whole human family and yet could say to a single wavering disciple, "I have prayed for thee, that thy faith fail not" (Luke 22:32). Jesus is still praying for us. He is praying in us. And he is praying through us for the men and women he has redeemed. It is he who gives new life and meaning to the simple words *I am praying for you.*—David H. C. Read

Illustrations

THE MYSTERY OF HIS MERCY. Tell me how you pray, and I will tell you what your faith is and who your God is. The God who in Jesus Christ makes his face shine upon us is a God who answers prayer. He is the Almighty God, the Creator and Sustainer of all things. He is the all-knowing God who is aware of all your needs even before you ask him. He is the Lord who does everything according to his will, suffering no contradiction. His reign over the world is hidden and inaccessible to human understanding. Yet at the same time he has created us for fellowship with him; he not only speaks to us, but wants us to speak with him. It is the mystery of his love that he, the Almighty, does not want to be alone, without us, his creatures; he who alone has eternal life wishes to make us partakers of his love and his life—if we are willing to pray for it. In his omnipotence he has ordered the dialogue between him and us. In his Son, he has revealed himself, he has told us his name, that of the Father to whom we may come and should come with all our troubles. It is the mystery of his omnipotence that he who knows everything and accomplishes everything nonetheless requests our prayers and, when we pray, does what he would not do otherwise. And it is the mystery of his mercy that he honors us, the unworthy, encouraging us to come before him despite our unworthiness and listening to us as though he needed us. Even better, in his omnipotence he has decreed that he really needs us, because he so wills, because he desires true fellowship with us and is not bent on carrying out his plan without participation.—Emil Brunner

HOW JESUS WON THROUGH. This divine Friend is full of sympathy for us, because he, too, fought on the battlefields of human life. He, too, tasted the bitterness of conflict; he, too, came to grips with hateful evil forces that sought his defeat and humiliation, but unfailingly he emerged a victor. Now, there are some Christian people who hesitate to believe that Christ was tempted. They forget that to rob him of his conflict is to rob him of his victory. He had to face not merely the temptation in the wilderness. Temptations assailed him throughout his life right to the foot of the cross. And let it never be forgotten that he won through by using the same spiritual resources that are open to you and to me—the strength of his own character and the spiritual power that came to him from God in answer to prayer.—John Sutherland Bonnell

Sermon Suggestions

GOD CHOOSES. TEXT: 2 Sam. 7:18–29. (1) For human greatness, 2 Sam. 7:18–29. (2) For spiritual blessing, Eph. 1:1–10. (3) For earthly service, Mark 6:7–13.

HOW GOD HAS BLESSED US. TEXT: Eph. 1:1–10. (1) In our election, verse 4a. (2) In

our character, verse 4b. (3) In our destiny, verse 5.

Worship Aids

CALL TO WORSHIP. "Blessed be the Lord God, the God of Israel, who only doeth wondrous things" (Ps. 72:18).

INVOCATION. Almighty God, let the allure of the world recede as we come to worship. Let the trivial and temporary fall away to be replaced by the holy and humble, through the Spirit of truth and the Son of righteousness.—E. Lee Phillips

OFFERTORY SENTENCE. "Let a man so account of us, as of ministers of Christ, and stewards of the mysteries of God" (1 Cor. 4:1).

OFFERTORY PRAYER. God who has created us and given us life, accept these offerings as our gifts to you. They symbolize the deeper gifts of heart, mind, and soul that we offer in your service.—J. Scott Hickman

PRAYER. Grant, we beseech thee, that all the members of this church may grow in grace and in the knowledge of the Lord and Savior Jesus Christ. We beseech of thee that thou wilt be with all that are present today, to listen to their prayers, whether of confession or of thanksgiving or of imploration. Forgive all those whose consciences plead for forgiveness. Strengthen those who in their conscious weakness look up to thee and implore help. Deliver those that are snared and cannot extricate themselves. Be near to point the way of duty to those who are perplexed and are of a doubtful mind. Cheer those that are despondent, and reencourage, as thou hast many times before, those who are almost persuaded to cast away their hope and abandon their Christian life. May none turn back. May none, having tasted the love of Christ or begun to follow in his steps, be tempted by any discouragement or by any persuasion to turn back to the beggarly elements of this world. We pray that thou wilt bless all that would return thanks to thee for mercies received, upon whom thou hast through months and years shed down thy gracious bounties, and who feel the sovereign goodness of God in this hour in his sanctuary. O Lord! behold their hearts' offerings and the consecration which they make of their preserved and restored powers for thy future service. And we beseech of thee that the memory of thy goodness to us, and of thy mercies, may soften our hearts and inspire Christian honor, that we may become better servants of Him who is never weary of doing us good.

Bless, we pray thee, the young in this congregation. Inspire them with heroic ideals of true personhood in Christ Jesus. Deliver them from the snares and temptations which beset them. Open to them all a door of honorable usefulness, and grant that they may be strengthened to go in thereat and bear the burden and heat of the day as becomes the children of the living God.

We pray that thou wilt bless the households associated here and carry the spirit of the sanctuary and the spirit of thy salvation into every dwelling.

Bless, we pray thee, all those present today who are strangers among us; and may they find such fellowship, such nearness to God, that they shall find, indeed, this to be an unexpected home and a delight to them.

May all thy people feel their kinship more and more. May all those vexing differences which have separated us pass away. May there be more and more of that forgiving spirit of love which shall unite thy people—not outwardly, but inwardly, and more blessedly.

And grant that thy kingdom may come, that thy will may be done in all the earth, that thy promises may be fulfilled, and that the whole earth may see thy salvation. We ask it for Christ's sake.—Adapted from Henry Ward Beecher.

LECTIONARY MESSAGE

Topic: Directions for Disciples

TEXT: Mark 6:7–13

Jesus' commissioning of the twelve offers guidance and empowerment for our mission in the world as his disciples. As we observe this mission experience of the twelve, we discover some of the marks of discipleship.

I. *Called (v. 7)*. The first and foundational characteristic of the twelve is that they are called by Jesus to himself. Discipleship is a response to the calling of God, not merely the result of our striving to serve God.

Jesus gives the twelve "authority" to perform exorcisms. The disciples do not go on mission under their own authority. They go out with the authority that Jesus has delegated to them as his representatives. Our mission to others is not conducted under our own authority, but we are empowered to minister to the needs of others by the authority of Christ. We are the Lord's authorized ambassadors.

Jesus does not send his disciples out alone. Following Jewish practice, they go "two by two." Disciples are to serve together in company with one another. We are not sent on mission as God's "lone rangers" to the world. Our ministry requires community with others.

II. *Charged (vv. 8–11)*. Jesus charges the twelve to maintain a life-style of simplicity in their mission. Their message is urgent. They are to travel unpretentiously and accept hospitality. The gospel they preach is not for sale. It is God's free gift, and so the bearers of the good news should not seek material gain from its proclamation. What a rebuke this teaching offers to the "health and wealth" gospel of our age! Discipleship is not for profit but for humble service. Jesus' rigorous standards for his disciples should discourage us from the temptation of relying upon our own self-sufficiency in ministry.

Jesus also instructs the twelve to handle rejection with integrity and dignity. Like their Lord (cf. 6:1–6), the disciples must develop the capacity to respond to rejection with wise perspective and divine grace. God is the final judge. As they "shake off the dust" from their feet (v. 11), the disciples are the witnesses who testify to God's judgment, not the enforcers of that judgment. As Vincent Taylor observes, "The shaking off of the dust is not an acted curse, but a testimony intended to provoke thought and to lead . . . to repentance."

III. *Obedient (vv. 12–13).* Authentic discipleship is characterized by willing obedience to the commands of Jesus. The twelve were immediately obedient to the instructions they received from Jesus. Their mission work is marked by service to the needs of the whole person: religious needs (they preached repentance, v. 12),

mental and emotional needs ("cast out many demons," v. 13), and physical needs ("anointed with oil many that were sick and healed them," v. 13). As Jesus' disciples in today's world, our mission should also exhibit such a wholistic concern for people. The Lord's directions for disciples are clear. The question is whether we will choose to obey.—Charles J. Scalise

SUNDAY: JULY TWENTY-FIRST

SERVICE OF WORSHIP

Sermon: Traveling Minus the Mountain

TEXT: Exod. 33:12–17

The Bible is very big on mountains.

Whatever the reason, biblical mountains are often the places where special and mystical encounters with God occur.

But there's an interesting thing about the mountains in the Bible . . . they never become permanent residences for God's people. Moses ascends Sinai twice to receive the Law, but he eventually returns to his people camped below. Jesus struggles with the forces of evil . . . but he returns to take up his ministry. Simon Peter wants to build three worship centers on the mount of Transfiguration, but he goes back to the Jerusalem road with his Master. Jesus dies on Golgotha, but—as far as we know—never spends any significant time there after the Resurrection. The disciples witness his ascension on a Judean mountain, but they are told, in effect, "Why do you stand here? He'll be back someday. Meanwhile . . . there's work to be done!"

I. I'm fascinated by this pattern. I believe it models spiritual pilgrimage for us all. You can have meaningful personal encounter with God—and that will be "mountaintop" in its decisiveness and its inspiration—but you can't isolate that, build a tabernacle around it, and spend the rest of your life there. You must leave the mountain and move on.

(a) Look at our text in Exodus 33; I believe there's some help for us there. This thirty-third chapter is one of those pivotal

happenings in the history of Israel. The people of God came out of Egypt, traveled three months, and stopped at the mountain called Sinai. Here the Law was given to Moses and to them. Here a community began to be forged out of a disoriented bunch of freed slaves. Here, for nearly a year, they stayed and struggled and learned, and then . . . "The Lord said to Moses, 'Depart and go up from here, you and the people whom you have brought out of the land of Egypt, to the land which I swore to Abraham, Isaac, and Jacob . . .'" (33:1).

They had finally gotten comfortable with Mount Sinai when God said . . . "Leave!"

And that provoked a crisis of faith!

(b) So Moses is told that, while God will be with him on this journey, the mountain stays behind.

And Moses wasn't too sure about that. One thing he didn't need was a chameleon God. He must have felt, "I'm not sure I want to turn loose of this mountain. At least here we've learned some things about you and your ways with us. Out there—minus the mountains where we've come to know you—your presence may not be as powerful or as meaningful. Then where will that leave us as your people?" (vv. 12–16).

(c) I can sympathize with Moses. It is important to find the mountain of God in your life and to stay there long enough to get your beginning bearings . . . especially when you've come out of spiritual slavery. We have been slaves either to that egotism that says, "I need no God but me," or to that apathy that thinks so little of self that one is at the mercy of whatever serpent speaks loudest or whatever wind blows strongest. We're all spiritual captives of one kind or another—the Bible calls us sinners—and our fragilities keep us from true wholeness.

All of which seems to say, quite clearly, that no matter what you're chained to . . . there is no realistic substitute for God!

II. It's important to find the mountain and to get your bearings there.

But it's equally important to leave the mountain—this is what Moses and Israel would learn.

Sometimes we leave it by choice: we come to college; we take a new job; we find ourselves in a new neighborhood or a different city. At other times we leave our mountains because of coincidence: we find ourselves uprooted by forces over which we have no control. Or we leave because of crisis: sickness or death or divorce force us away from a familiar life-style and living context.

But—however it happens—it's important to leave the mountain of beginnings with God . . . for at least two or three reasons.

(a) For one thing, *it allows God to grow.* I should say, it allows our understanding of God to grow. Part of spiritual growth—a major part, in fact—has to do with the emerging forms of God in our lives. And this is obvious in the biblical record. The desert God of Moses' burning bush . . . becomes the competitor God at Pharaoh's court . . . becomes the traveling God of the wilderness . . . becomes the resident God of Canaan . . . becomes the uprooted God of the Exile. The forms of God are changing, but the promise given to Moses—"My presence will go with you, and I will give you rest"—never does! And in every generation—as well as within every life's pilgrimage—that awareness and presence are sufficient to withstand the trauma of changing forms.

(b) Also, we need to leave the mountain because *it allows faith to grow.* When C. S. Lewis lost his wife of three years, he wrote of his grief—it was part of the grieving and coping process. As I read *A Grief Observed,* I was struck by his statement that he'd learned something crucial about faith. He said it's like a game of cards; unless you've got some money riding on it, it doesn't mean very much. In other words, it's only in the actual risk situations of life that we come to understand our faith! Don't read a blanket endorsement of gambling into that; the point is that faith isn't worthy of its name without some risk.

And that's a word to heed when you're away from home and your spiritual landmarks. You'll find risk aplenty here in the city: on your job, with new acquaintances, in the philosophy classes . . . in the history courses . . . in the science labs, in the agnosticism of your classmates. Your faith in God will be tested afresh during these years—and that's as it should be, for faith that never risks never grows toward maturity.

So if faith is based on a mountain from yesterday—and little more—it may be a vivid and beautiful memory, but it won't be a very vital force in our lives right now. But when we're willing to leave the mountain . . . to risk journeying into new and unfamiliar territory . . . and to be open to the leading of One who is with us, faith can grow!

(c) There is another reason for leaving the mountain—*to allow community to grow.* We do not live or die completely to ourselves, and, especially in Christian pilgrimage, we are involved with a faith community. When Moses talks with God about this proposed trip minus the mountain, he speaks of "I and thy people." This is an interesting dialogue between Moses and God; Moses stands in the gap between the people and God. God says, "These are a weak, stiff-necked, stubborn people." And Moses keeps saying, "But they're yours! They're yours!" They are weak often, sinners ever, but always God's faith community. So though they couldn't take the mountain with them, they could take each other . . . and that would often sustain them! When the forms of God and of faith are changing, the constancy of God's presence is often reinforced best by his people. When you're between mountains, thank God for a believing community who will stand beside you and journey with you!

III. So . . . there are some reasons to

travel minus the mountain. What all this means is that there are some places and times in spiritual memory that are special but that a relevant spirituality must live beyond them. My own Sinai was special—they tore the old building down and built a new one years ago—but I still have warm feelings about that old place where I made my first real commitment to Jesus Christ as Lord. Yet I have to tell you, honestly, that I've left that mountain. My relationship with God is far more vital and dynamic now because of having left it. It will forever be a warm and special memory, but my life as a Christian is a journey toward wholeness that has seen (and will continue to see) God and faith and community all having newer and deeper significance with each passing year.—William L. Turner

Illustrations

PRISONERS OF THE PAST. A certain pious young women had been admirably brought up by her aged aunts whom she loved dearly. They were women of exemplary character who returned her love wholeheartedly and who also protected her, for she was very shy. Basically, she was happy with them, without really realizing that she had remained a child, that she had abdicated. Now her aunts were dead. This was a great grief to her and also caused her some dismay. She told me of her scruples. Had she any right to depart from the austere way of life of which they had been such a fine example to her? I prepared myself to hear some quite revolutionary idea, as I asked her, "What is it in your life you would like to change?" "Oh," she answered, "I'd like to move some of the furniture round in the flat and to get rid of some of it, because there's so much of it there you can hardly move."—Paul Tournier

THE SPIRITUAL JOURNEY. Life is a journey. It is a series of changes and transitions. There is no utopia, no stationary place, because life is a process. The secret of life lies in being open to its movement, responsive to its demands. In this vision of life as a journey, peace, unity, and whole-ness come from a maturity that accepts incompleteness and ambiguity. The journey metaphor aptly describes my life because it implies that life is a process of unfolding, of discovery, of change, with change being the only constant.

The journey metaphor makes room for failure. Journeys are seldom made without incident, occurrences that redirect our lives: detours, dead-end streets, accidents, weariness, traffic jams, getting lost.

Journeys include these interruptions, and so does life.—Ben Campbell Johnson

Sermon Suggestions

ONE WRONG CALLS FOR ANOTHER. TEXT: 2 Sam. 11:1–15. (1) *The story:* David, Bathsheba, and Uriah. (2) *The timeless truth:* There is often a progression in the character of evil-doing (see Ps. 1:1; James 1:13–15). (3) *The application:* Temptation can be resisted and character strengthened through prudence and God's help (see Prov. 6:20–7:27; 1 Cor. 10:6–13).

KEEP THESE THINGS IN MIND. TEXT: Eph. 2:11–22. (1) Where you came from, verses 11–12. (2) Your present standing, verses 13–21a. (3) Your ultimate destiny, verses 21b–22. (See also 1 Pet. 2:4–5.)

Worship Aids

CALL TO WORSHIP. "How amiable are thy tabernacles, O Lord of hosts! My soul longeth, yea, even fainteth for the courts of the Lord; my heart and my flesh cry out unto the living God" (Ps. 84:1–2).

INVOCATION. Grant unto us, our heavenly Father, the inshining of the Spirit and the indwelling of thy truth, by which we shall be mightier than the accidents of life; mightier than the circumstances that surround us, mightier than our own nature; by which we shall have the power of divine grace to lift us above the weakness of the flesh, above the weakness of the affections. Teach us how to walk as the people of God. Make it real to us that we are the Lord's. Make it real to us not only that we are his, but that he is ours; that all things are for our sakes.—Henry Ward Beecher

OFFERTORY SENTENCE. "Lay up for yourselves treasures in heaven, where neither moth nor rust doth consume, and where thieves do not break through nor steal; for where thy treasure is, there will thy heart be also" (Matt. 6:20–21).

OFFERTORY PRAYER. Except the Lord abide in this place, we gather here in vain. Except the Lord accept and use our gifts, we make the offering in vain. We pray that you will accept and use our gifts.

PRAYER. O you who are true and righteous altogether, how can we appear before you except in confession of our fickleness in the presence of your faithfulness, our duplicity in the face of your authenticity, our dividedness when confronted with your wholeness? "Great is thy faithfulness!" No matter how strong the words of evil blow, the flame of truth will never go out.

How often in prayer we invoke your presence when the real need is to invoke our own. We try to saunter into your presence with our hands in our pockets, casually, halfheartedly, when you are calling us to be all here—standing at attention before you with every fiber of our being—for the first commandment is to love you with all our mind, with all our heart, with all our person.

Deliver us from any shame or pretense, for anyone who would worship you must worship in spirit and in truth. It is in our deeper self that we discover you—"Deep speaking unto deep"—and in this confrontation we are awakened to the truth that makes us free—your love so freely given that we can be honest before you, confessing all our sin, knowing that we are accepted just as we are.

Help us, O Father, to realize that to claim this grace for ourselves is to extend it to all others. May we hear your Word through the apostle: "Be kind to one another, tender-hearted, forgiving each other, even as for Christ's sake I have forgiven you." Only as we live by your grace in him can the truth be in us and between us. Only in the meaning and experience of grace are we really there for one another. Day by day may we grow in the grace and

knowledge of Christ who is among us as Lord and Savior.—John M. Thompson

LECTIONARY MESSAGE

Topic: Restful Retreat vs. Shepherdless Sheep

TEXT: Mark 6:30–34

This tender story dramatically illustrates Jesus' compassionate concern for human need. As we observe our Lord's caring, we are reminded of the "great throng" of people in our world who are "like sheep without a shepherd" (v. 34). Can we overcome our experiences of "burnout" in Christian service to minister to those in need? Can we respond with the compassion of Jesus to the cries of the lost and straying people around us?

I. *The apostles: looking for leisure.* The apostles are tired. They have just returned to Jesus after obeying his call to mission (6:7–13). As returning missionaries, they give their leader an account of "all that they have done and taught" (v. 30) as his representatives. They have preached the gospel, cast out demons, and healed the sick (6:12–13). Now they need a rest. The constant stress and hurry of their busy ministry (v. 31b) is beginning to take its toll, and the apostles need to recuperate. Jesus, their caring friend and teacher, suggests they go on a retreat to "a lonely place" (v. 31a), private and uninhabited, in the wilderness.

II. *The people: seeking a shepherd.* The plans of Jesus and his apostles for a restful retreat are interrupted as soon as they arrive at their destination. The "lonely place" has suddenly become inhabited by a "great throng" (v. 34) that has "got there ahead of them" (v. 33). It is a tribute to the power of Jesus' presence that the crowds "from all the towns" (v. 33) follow him even into the wilderness.

The people are milling about like lost "sheep without a shepherd" (v. 34). This moving and powerful image derives from the Old Testament descriptions of the scattering of Israel (Num. 27:17; 1 Kings 22:17; 2 Chron. 18:16; and Ezek. 34:5). Seeing these people as shepherdless sheep reminds us that Jesus himself is the promised good shepherd (Ezek. 34:23). There will, however, be "no rest for the weary" Jesus and his disciples.

III. *Jesus: caring with compassion.* Unlike his disciples, who are exhausted from their ministry and impatient with the crowd (vv. 35–36), Jesus is renewed as he sees the needs of the people. As the incarnate Son of God (1:1), Jesus does not shrink from suffering but embraces and bears it. The power of his "compassion" enables him to begin "to teach them many things" (or "teach them at length"—v. 34).

Jesus' caring response to the needs of the people offers a model for the ministry of all Christians. As Dietrich Bonhoeffer pointedly asserts in *Life Together,* "God will be constantly crossing our paths and canceling our plans by sending us people with claims and petitions. . . . We do not assume that our schedule is our own to manage, but allow it to be arranged by God." May we respond with the compassionate caring of Jesus, rather than the agitation of self-concern, when we encounter the shepherdless sheep on our path.—Charles J. Scalise

SUNDAY: JULY TWENTY-EIGHTH

SERVICE OF WORSHIP

Sermon: A Body for All Seasons

TEXT: 1 Corinthians 15

Letting go of the earthly body is not easy, is it? We have deep attachments to it. We cannot imagine what it will be like to transcend the body, to leave it behind.

Neither could Christians in the earliest years of the church. "How are the dead raised?" they asked when Paul preached the teaching about the resurrection to them. "With what kind of body do they come?" (1 Cor. 15:35).

I. These were Greeks who asked these questions, people who had been raised in the best traditions of Hellenistic thought. Their philosophy taught a strict dualism between the mind and body. The mind was like an ethereal bird imprisoned in the body. When the body died, the bird was free to fly away. Only, to them, this was not a joyous occasion. Because they were so wed to the life of aesthetics and the life of the flesh, they could not imagine that existence for the mind would be very pleasurable without the body. They pictured the mind as living on in a kind of gloomy underworld, devoid of interest and happiness.

(a) The idea of the resurrection must have struck them with great promise, but they could not begin to comprehend it.

"What you sow does not come to life unless it dies. And what you sow is not the body which is to be, but a bare kernel, perhaps of wheat or some other grain" (1 Cor. 15:37).

(b) There's the trick, isn't it? What we shall be when we die is somehow contained in who we are while we live, but it is more than that. Just as the apple tree comes from the apple seed and the peach tree from the peach seed and from the very seed that dies, not from some seed-in-general, so we shall come from the body-minds we are now. But as the apple tree is far more than the seed from which it grew, and the peach tree than the seed from which it sprang, so we shall be far more than anyone could tell by looking at us now.

II. It is intriguing to think what we shall be and that it is somehow related to who and what we presently are. Perhaps this is why the ethical teachings of our religion are so important; our adherence to them defines us not only in the lives we now live but in our lives to come.

(a) I knew a man who was afraid to die because, as he himself said, he had lived like Ebenezer Scrooge before Scrooge's conversion. "I know I shall go into the life to come hobbled and manacled," he said, "like some shameful criminal who has plundered the earth of its gifts and returned nothing for others." Fortunately he, like Scrooge, saw the error of his ways and began to live much differently before he died. His spirit became so sweet and generous that I am sure God was generous and gave him a good "body" after death. He proved that the seed was really there.

(b) I said that God gave the man a body. That is not my idea, you know; it is what Paul said in his Letter to the Corinthians. We sow the seed, he wrote, "and then God gives it the sort of body that he has chosen: each sort of seed gets its own sort of body" (1 Cor. 15:38, JB).

III. Receiving a heavenly body is not automatic. It is not something everybody has a right to. God gives it.

(a) This is where Christian teaching differs from other teachings about immortality. Immortality is a Greek concept; it means that life goes on automatically, at least in some form, forever. But the Christian teaching is about resurrection. Resurrection means that someone must do the raising. And that someone is God. God raises the dead in Christ. God performs an overt act by making the dead seed blossom into a heavenly plant. Without God's loving grace it would not happen.

(b) By this, the emphasis on eternal life is kept where it ought to be. It is centered on God and God's power. We have no automatic right to live forever. But God wills that those who have been saved through his Son Jesus have an eternal form beyond this life.

IV. Listen to Paul. He has been talking about the seed and the plant that springs from it—how much more remarkable the plant is than the seed.

(a) Notice the adjectives! The body that dies is perishable, contemptible, and weak. We know that, don't we? Especially if we are among the aging population. The older we become, the more perishable, contemptible, and weak we think of ourselves as being. The parts of the body, like the parts of an old machine, begin to wear out and cause dysfunction of the whole. They embarrass us by calling a disproportionate amount of attention to themselves.

(b) But this body, the physical body, is only the seed; and the body that is raised up—the spiritual body—is another story! It is imperishable, glorious, and powerful.

Think of that, if you have ever despised the body you now have: a body that is imperishable, glorious, and powerful!

It is imperishable—it will never die. No accident or illness can touch it. It will never be susceptible to termination. It will go on forever.

It is glorious. It is like the "Hallelujah Chorus" in the flesh, embodied in a person.

And it is powerful. Had you ever thought of that, that you will be powerful after you die? Perhaps this is the most incredible part of Paul's description.

(c) For the followers of Christ, such possibilities are not mere whimsy. Our faith is centered in a God who has the power to raise up our weak and perishable bodies after death and convert them into strong and everlasting bodies of a new kind, of a heavenly kind, so that we may worship and glorify him forever. Our perishable natures will put on the imperishable, as Paul says, and our mortal natures will put on immortality (1 Cor. 15:53). We shall become what it is in us now to become but what we cannot become until we have died and the seed has been raised up by God into an incredible flowering!

V. For the moment, "we see only puzzling reflections in a mirror," for our bodies are perishable, contemptible, and weak, and we are subject to great confusion. But then, when we have exchanged these earthly bodies for bodies that are imperishable, glorious, and powerful, "we shall see face to face" (1 Cor. 13:12), and everything will be cleared up. Now we have bodies for this season of life, bodies that serve us well enough for the seed time. Then we shall have bodies for all seasons, bodies for eternity, and they are beyond description!—John Killinger

Illustrations

CREATION COMPLETED.   Before the divine drama of resurrection was enacted, human beings had little sure evidence that we who were so stained with darkness could reach out to the light and be delivered from evil. Evil was in the world and had brought the great majority of humankind into its bondage. Human beings were helpless, and then in the fullness of time,

God took pity upon us and came among us to deliver us from evil. The very being of God, the Logos, the Word, became a human being and was born as a baby in Bethlehem. Creation was completed. This brings us to the second act of God's drama. The tragedy was to be redeemed and so became the great drama of salvation. Dante called his play in Italian *The Comedy.* A real comedy is a tragedy redeemed.—Morton Kelsey

LOVE AND HOPE.   Paul's faith that "love hopeth all things" is not sentimentality. It is the affirmation which Christian faith must make about what it means to trust in God. Only the man whose hope can stand the defeat of any particular project is free to hope "for all things," that is, for whatever good may really be possible under God. Such a faith is not flight from the responsibilities of this life. The God we serve is the giver of this life with its obligations and possibilities. There is no situation in which the Christian cannot find meaning and hope. There is no social wrong which need remain unattacked, unmitigated, unreformed. There is no private desperate struggle with anxiety and bitterness and failure which cannot yield new hope when we discover that God does not leave us forsaken. But those who know this, while they are released to spend themselves in doing what needs to be done, live with a certain divine carelessness concerning earthly fortunes. Their hope sees beyond the years, and they live in this demanding present under the everlasting assurance of God's love.—Daniel Day Williams

Sermon Suggestions

WHEN CONSCIENCE WAKES UP.   TEXT: 2 Sam. 12:1–14. (1) *The story:* The prophet by indirection makes David see his sin clearly and predicts the consequences. (2) *The lessons:* Conscience often lies asleep until some unusual event stabs it awake. Then the troubled conscience begins to see the consequences. The purpose of God in such painful awareness is to lead to repentance and divine forgiveness.

A PRAYER THAT FITS OUR NEEDS.   TEXT: Eph. 3:14–21. (1) For strong inner resources. (2) For a sense of the loving presence of the living Christ. (3) For a fullness of the blessings of God.

Worship Aids

CALL TO WORSHIP.   "For thou, Lord, art good and ready to forgive and abundant in loving-kindness unto all them that call upon thee" (Ps. 86:5).

INVOCATION.   How can we come before you except in awe and reverence, you who have shined into our night with a light that no darkness can ever put out. We cannot speak your name except the light that is Jesus leads us to know you as "Our Father." With what love you love us that we should be your daughters and sons. As in these days we contemplate the mystery of your coming into the history of humankind and your coming into our history, we *are* lost in *wonder, love,* and *praise.* Praise be to you—Father, Son, and Holy Spirit.—John M. Thompson

OFFERTORY SENTENCE.   "Now therefore, our God, we thank thee, and praise thy glorious name. But who am I, and what is my people, that we should be able to offer so willingly after this sort? For all things come of thee, and of thine own have we given thee" (1 Chron. 29:13–14).

OFFERTORY PRAYER.   In talent and time, in mind and spirit, in dollars and cents we serve you, almighty God. You are the source of it all. We worship you with our gifts.

PRAYER.   Loving Lord, we depend on you as the source of every good gift, as the example of every good thought, as the goal of every good life. We love you because you first loved us and gave your Son as a clear expression of that love. Out of many different experiences with your love, we have gathered today: simple satisfaction of our needs, stern guidance into your way, a challenge to sacrificial service.

We gather to praise you for your goodness and your grace, to petition you in terms of forgiveness for our sin, to plead with you for peace and reconciliation: among the rich and the poor, the well and the ill, the nations of the world. . . . Help us to be peacemakers.

Yet we are your children. Send your Spirit to interpret our needs and to phrase our prayers. We do not know how to pray as we ought. Hear our deep longings. We pray in the name of Jesus.—J. Estill Jones

LECTIONARY MESSAGE

Topic: Feeding the Multitude

TEXT: John 6:1–15

Who knows why they all came? But come they did. By the thousands they followed Jesus across the sea. Surely, out of a number so great, at least some came for noble reasons. Most, though, were enamored by the wonders that he performed. John tells us plainly, "And a multitude followed him because they saw the signs which he did on those who were diseased." Spectacular displays like that will always draw a crowd.

Yet Jesus had in mind more than attracting a crowd of halfhearted would-be followers. He came to declare the inbreaking of God's eternal kingdom. To do so, at least in John's Gospel, he would communicate his message through signs. The signs in John do the same thing signs always do: they convey a message about something greater than the sign itself. A sign points us to something, informs us, clarifies detail, and directs intentions. The account of the feeding is a sign. The multitudes followed. Jesus sat them down. He fed them miraculously. Twelve baskets of fragments remained. And when the people saw all this, they declared, "This is indeed the prophet who is come into the world!"

I. The feeding speaks appropriately of compassion. Wherever there is a multitude, there is need. Sensing the need, Jesus asked about food to feed the hungry people. While we do not live by bread alone but by every word that proceeds out of the mouth of God, we must live by some bread. In God's kingdom, such compassion is always right. A faith that calls for dependence on God, yet ignores the pleas of hurting people, is empty. Jesus made social needs a vital part of his own life. Compassion is a godlike virtue and one to be maintained in the lives of godly people.

II. The feeding speaks also of the risk of faith. Philip spoke logically: "Two hundred denarii would not buy enough for each of them to get a little." And so with Peter: "There is a lad here with five barley loaves and two fish; but what are they among so many?" Both statements are reasonable assessments of the situation. Yet both ignore the possibilities that appear when a situation is saturated in faith. How often has some small and seemingly insignificant idea, a dream, developed into something of monumental importance. The feeding seemed doomed to failure, a preposterous venture. Yet it was a success and continues to give incentive to people of faith everywhere.

III. The feeding speaks furthermore of the values that control our lives. Many came that day in order to get something for themselves. Jesus accommodated with an amazing miracle, the only one recorded in all four Gospels. At the end, the disciples gathered up twelve baskets of fragments, one for each disciple. The basket was really a little satchel in which a person could carry enough food for one day. There was to be no waste, and no stinginess. God will take care of his own. Yet notice that there was no basket for Christ. He kept back nothing for himself. He gave his all. Selfishness is to have no part in the kingdom that Jesus began.

Why did they all come that day? Who can know? But we do know what Jesus did there. Taking advantage of the opportunity, he demonstrated what the kingdom of God is like—and then for fear they would try to make him an earthly king, he fled alone into the mountain.—Lee R. McGlone

SUNDAY: AUGUST FOURTH

SERVICE OF WORSHIP

Sermon: The Love Motif Reexamined
TEXTS: Ps. 22:25–31; 1 John 4:7–12, 18;
John 15:1–8

I. I wish to God Jesus would quit tinkering with my boyhood religion. Oh, I'm quite serious. Just when I think I have my finger on it, under control and reasoned, he pulls something on me. Not that I didn't know it before; I almost always have known it. But rather that, experientially, I encounter that something at a different level of my life. I come to grips with it like never before. I seem more ready in my journey to grapple with that certain something. Today that pervasive and omnipresent love is before us for perusal, more specifically, verse 18 of 1 John 4, "perfect love casts out fear."

(a) I just glanced through the morning papers this week and noticed how many news stories there were about issues that had to do with fear of some kind: that one of our fail-safe systems would not be fail-safe; that either Palestine or Israel will lose something essential if they enter talks about their problems, so there are no talks. Officials in various capacities are undergoing trial for sundry charges from bribery to obstruction of justice by shredding evidence in national security matters. When we uncover it all, someone was afraid of something. Lawsuits are a dime a dozen because someone is afraid they will lose something that is rightfully theirs.

(b) On a more personal front, how many of us left our homes this morning after setting the security alarm, afraid that someone might help themselves to our possessions? Justified? Surely, but the point is, justified or not, a large percentage of our lives are lived in fear.

II. Then the Epistle comes along to suggest that perfect love casts out fear. "Well, that's the problem," we say. "Our love isn't perfect." Sorry. We can't hide there. Because the concept of perfect love is not "perfect as in flawless," but more the He-brew idea of "perfect as in being what it was meant to be." What this passage means is, not love that is total perfection, but love that is doing what it is meant to do. In other words, the "perfect love that casts out fear" is within the reach of all of us.

(a) That perfect love that eliminates fear starts with loving ourselves. While we may not have noticed it, Christ instructs us to love ourselves. "Love the neighbor as yourself," he says. In other words, a proper self-love is important before any other love can be given. It has been well documented in psychiatric circles that one who does not love himself cannot love another appropriately. It is no accident that those who are abusers in families today are those who were abused themselves as children. They have taken the negative imaging about themselves and put it onto their families.

(b) "Well, I've always thought that too much self-love leads to selfishness." No. Selfishness comes when we don't love ourselves properly and we need further affirmation to prove we're OK and we reach out for all manner of things or situations and pull them to us to affirm our flagging self-esteem. I don't know of any evil in the human family done by one to another that can't be traced to low self-esteem or improper self-love.

III. Now, one of the ways we can know we're afraid is in our anger. Anger is not a foundational emotion; it is believed to be a result, a spin-off from another emotion, and that emotion that gives rise to anger is, you guessed it, fear. The next time you are angry, ask yourself, "What am I afraid I'm going to lose? What's threatening me?" Almost always you and I will find that something is a threat to something else we value.

(a) Now as perfect as Jesus Christ was, I think he was threatened by—of all people—the religious leaders. He got angry with them more than with any other group. Why? Because he knew that when religion develops and begins to serve its own self-interests, it then gives up its ability to be evaluative of all of life in the name of God. And when religion does that, there is no one to call us back to God's principles, and the threat is that God's voice is lost in the land. That's why Jesus got so angry at the religion of his day. It had climbed into bed with the systems of its day. There was no one to call the people to basic repentance. And when John the Baptist did, they cut off his head. Not just Jewish religion. It happens to all religious systems.

(b) Did love cast out Jesus' fear of the religious order of his day? Yes. He took a small band of men and women, retooled their religious affection, and basically started a new religious awareness with a divested self-interest.

IV. How do we have this "perfect love that casts out fear"? Now, obviously, I don't mean the elimination of a proper fear that keeps us from putting our hands into open flames and keeps us from jumping off buildings. I mean a love that includes in rather than excludes out. The more inclusive we become in our embracing of people, the more we'll find we don't need to fear them because we've found how to love them.

(a) To me, that's what God did in Jesus. He opened his arms to the world, as brutal and violent and hate-filled as it was. That's what the passage means that says, "God so loved the world."

(b) When we find the perfect love that casts out fear and we can hold the faces of the ones we have hated in our hands, we know that theirs is really the face of God. You! You! For God is in all the world and in all the creations of the world. When we have the sight of love, the issue is clear of whose face we are touching. "How silently, how silently, the wondrous gift is given. / So God imparts to human hearts the blessings of his heaven." And part of that blessing is the perfect love that casts out fear.—Thomas H. Conley

Illustrations

LOVE AND THE HUMAN QUEST. There are only two classes of souls in the world: those who have found the Faith and those who are looking for it. It is amazing how different the world and souls look when one starts with the first principle that, as the eye needs light and the stomach food, so does the soul need God. There is not a single person in the world, regardless of the passion with which he seeks out sin, who has not in the depths of his soul a craving for the infinite. As St. Thomas says, "The whole is loved before the part, and the part is loved only because of the whole." The tumult of human love is in some way a pursuit of the Divine. As Pascal put it, "There are two kinds of reasonable people: those who love God with their whole hearts because they have found Him and those who search for God with their whole hearts because they have not found Him."—Fulton J. Sheen

THE SOLIDARITY OF LOVE. Suppose that sometime a king and a beggar and a man like yourself should come to you. In their presence, would you dare frankly to confess that in which you sought your consolation, certain that the king in his majesty would not despise you even though you were a man of inferior rank; certain that the beggar would not go away envious that he could not have the same consolation; certain that the man like yourself would be pleased by your frankness? Alas, there is something in the world called clannishness. It is a dangerous thing because all clannishness is divisive. It is divisive when clannishness shuts out the common citizen and when it shuts out the nobleborn and when it shuts out the civil servant. It is divisive when it shuts out the king and when it shuts out the beggar and when it shuts out the wise man and when it shuts out the simple soul. For all clannishness is the enemy of universal humanity. But to will only one thing, genuinely to will the Good, as an individual, to will to hold fast to God, which thinks each person without exception is capable of doing, this is what unites.—Sören Kierkegaard

Sermon Suggestions

LIFE GOES ON. TEXT: 2 Sam. 12:15b–24. (1) David's agony, verses 15b–17. (2)

David's loss, verses 18–19. (3) David's re-action, verses 20–24.

STICKING TOGETHER IN THE FAITH. TEXT: Eph. 4:1–6. (1) Because of our call-ing, verse 1. (2) Because of our hope, verse 4. (3) Because of the essential unity of our faith, verses 4–6.

Worship Aids

CALL TO WORSHIP.   "Oh, satisfy us in the morning with thy loving-kindness, that we may rejoice and be glad all our days" (Ps. 90:14).

INVOCATION.   O Lord, we would sing of your mercies; we would make known your faithfulness. Tune our hearts and open our lips, so that the world may hear the joyful sound.

OFFERTORY SENTENCE.   "Honor the Lord with thy substance and with the first-fruits of all thine increase" (Prov. 3:9).

OFFERTORY PRAYER.   Creator God, all that we know and touch belongs to you. Forgive us when we forget and hoard the fruits of the earth as if we owned them and bless that which is now returned to your service.—J. Scott Hickman

PRAYER.   Eternal Spirit, thou fountain of all that is excellent and beautiful in human life, once more we turn to thee, unreplenished, needing thy renewal; weak, needing thy strength; fatigued, needing thy rest. We have tried to content ourselves with lesser things but thou hast set eternity within our hearts. We are rest-less until we rest in thee. Into thy sanctu-ary we come with praise upon our lips. Yet save us from the ancient sin of casting palm branches before thy Christ at the week's beginning and crucifying him before the week's end. Give us sincerity, we beseech thee. From the ungenuine lead us to the genuine, from the unreal to the real.

O God of grace, who art able to strengthen us with thy Spirit in the inner man, so deal with us this day that high business may be done for thy cause in our hearts, that we may go from this place of meditation and prayer to be more worthy of our high vocation as thy sons and daughters.

Play, we beseech thee, upon all the chords of our lives. We, who so often have placed ourselves at the disposal of the world's fingers to play upon, would in this hour come before thee that thy Spirit might touch the strings of our hearts.

Play upon our gratitude. If we have held our complaints so close to our eyes that we have lost the far perspectives of thy favor, grant, we pray thee, for the reward of our worship, wide horizons in this morning hour. Remind us of the homes we came from, of the fathers and mothers who nourished us, of the better aspects of the civilization out of which we have come, of causes once defeated, now victorious, for which others shed their blood. Teach us once again that we are not our own, that we have been bought with a price, that we may go forth to make our lives part pay-ment on an unpayable debt.

Play, we beseech thee, upon our nobler fears. O thou who hast given us the power of foresight, teach us anew the lesson of the springtime, that whatsoever a man soweth, that shall he also reap. If there are lives of families here already treading the pathway of careless dalliance which, pleas-ant now, must find its end in the valley of death, awake in us, we beseech thee, a holy awe of this law-abiding universe that so inexorably moves from cause to conse-quence.

Play, we beseech thee, upon our loves. Awaken within us the spirit of friendship and kindliness. Save us from our vindic-tiveness, disillusionment, and cynicism. If some have wronged us, help us afresh to see how some have blessed us. Kindle again the fire of goodwill upon the hearth-stone of our better selves. Let benevo-lence, large-heartedness, tolerance, and friendliness share possession of our souls.

Strike, also, we beseech thee, the sterner chords. Awaken our devotions. O God, we pray thee for work to do, good work, and strength to do it with. Send us out into this great generation where no man need waste his life, to find our tasks in the home, the church, the state, and in the worldwide fraternity of mankind, that because we have lived and thought and toiled, this earth may be a more decent place for thee to raise thy children in.

So play upon us, Spirit of the living God. Let all our hearts awake to praise thy name and then may we go forth to serve thy cause.

We ask it in the name of Christ.—Harry Emerson Fosdick

LECTIONARY MESSAGE

Topic: Bread of Life
TEXT: John 6:24–35
I. *Give us bread.* The crowd's reaction to the miracle of the feeding of the five thousand falls far short of faith. They saw a miracle but did not see a sign. They only had eyes for what would improve their standard of living. So they saw nothing beyond the free fish and chips. That is why most of them chased after Jesus halfway around the lake. They only thought of him as someone who could satisfy their physical needs and desires. They must have thought to themselves that this was a neat way to get food. Just hand Jesus a few loaves and a couple of fish and you get a spread to feed hordes of hungry people. Caesar cannot do that. Let's make him king! They wanted to make him king not so that they could worship him but so that he would continue to bless them with physical benefits (6:14–15).

Give us bread, they said. What they wanted was someone who could fill their empty bellies. They failed to see that Jesus could provide them with true bread that could fill their empty lives. They want bread, but the bread they want never satisfies. It is the bread of material desires. We should all know how little this bread satisfies. We live in the most affluent society the world has known, and yet ours is a society that is afflicted by drug abuse, dissatisfaction with life, boredom, anxiety, restlessness, alienation, apathy. The trouble is that most people do not hold spiritual bread in the same estimation as

earthly bread. And because Jesus refuses to give in to the desires and demands of the crowds, the large crowds will soon begin to dissipate.

II. *Give us a sign.* When the crowds caught up to Jesus, they asked for a sign so that they might believe in him (6:30). They recall for Jesus that Moses performed signs in the wilderness and imply that if Jesus wants to make it as a prophet he needs to do something worthy of Moses. They say our father's ate manna in the wilderness (6:31), and they cite Scripture (Ps. 78:24). The irony is that they have witnessed a sign; in fact, they ate it. But apparently they saw no sign of anything.

Jesus' feeding of the crowds in the wilderness recalls several themes from the Exodus story: the giving of the Law; the feeding of the people in the wilderness; the deliverance in the sea. It also recalls the response of grumbling (6:41, 61) that so characterized the wilderness generation (Exod. 16:2, 7, 8). Moses indeed performed signs in the wilderness days; many in Jesus' day will decide to fall back. When Jesus fails to cater to their wishes and when his words become too hard, they decide to go home and wait for a messiah more to their liking. Their decision will mean that they will perish like the generation in the wilderness and that they will never experience eternal life.

III. *The true bread.* Jesus' interpretation of the bread challenges the crowds' understanding that Moses was the one who gave them the bread from heaven (6:32). Jesus says that it was God who gave them both the manna in the wilderness and the one who now gives them the true bread. This bread is Jesus, whom God has sent into the world. Unlike the manna that had to be eaten or else it would rot, this bread is eternal. Unlike the manna that merely provided physical sustenance during the desert wanderings, this bread supplies the means of eternal life.

Jesus admonishes the crowd to procure the bread that is eternal (6:27–28). But they misunderstand that they must "do" something to get this bread (6:28). This reflects their legalistic mentality. What they need to do is only believe in the one God sent (6:30). Like the manna in the wilderness and the feeding of the five thousand, the bread is free. It comes only by grace.—David E. Garland

SUNDAY: AUGUST ELEVENTH

SERVICE OF WORSHIP

Sermon: The Illusiveness of Life
TEXT: Heb. 11:8–10

God promised Canaan to Abraham, and yet Abraham never inherited Canaan: to the last he was a wanderer there. He had no possession of his own in its territory; if he wanted even a tomb to bury his dead, he could only obtain it by purchase. This difficulty is expressly admitted in the text, "In the land of promise he sojourned as in a strange country"; he dwelt there in tents—in changeful, moveable tabernacles—not permanent habitations; he had no home there. (See Acts 7:5.)

Now, the surprising point is that Abraham, deceived, as you might almost say, did not complain of it as a deception. He was even grateful for the nonfulfillment of the promise: he does not seem to have expected its fulfillment. He did not look for Canaan, but for "a city which had foundations." His faith appears to have consisted in disbelieving the letter, almost as much as in believing the spirit of the promise.

God's promises never are fulfilled in the sense in which they seem to have been given. And in the spirit of this text, we have to say that it is a wise and merciful arrangement which ordains it thus.

I. Let it be clearly understood, in the first place, the promise never was fulfilled. During one brief period, in the history of Israel, the promise may seem to have been fulfilled. It was during the later years of David and the earlier years of Solomon; but we have the warrant of Scripture itself for affirming that even then the promise was not fulfilled. In the Book of Psalms, David speaks of a hope of entering into a *future* rest. The writer of the Epistle to the Hebrews, quoting this passage, infers from it that God's promise had not been exhausted nor fulfilled by the entrance into Canaan; for he says, "If Joshua had given them rest, then would he not have spoken of another day." Again, in this very chapter, after a long list of Hebrew saints—"These *all* died in faith, not having received the promises." To none, therefore, had the promise been fulfilled. Accordingly, writers on prophecy, in order to get over this difficulty, take for granted that there must be a future fulfillment because the first was inadequate.

(a) Our senses deceive us; we begin life with delusion. Our senses deceive us with respect to distance, shape, and color. To the earlier ages, the stars presented the delusion of small lamps hung in space. All experience is a correction of life's delusions—a modification, a reversal of the judgment of the senses.

(b) Our natural anticipations deceive us—I say *natural* in contradistinction to extravagant expectations. Every human life is a fresh one, bright with hopes that will never be realized. There may be differences of character in these hopes; finer spirits may look on life as the arena of successful deeds, the more selfish as a place of personal enjoyment.

With man, the turning point of life may be a profession—with woman, marriage; the one gilding the future with the triumphs of intellect, the other with the dreams of affection. But in every case, life is not what any of them expects but something else. Where is the land flowing with milk and honey?

(c) Our expectations, resting on revelation, deceive us. The world's history has turned round two points of hope: one, the *first*—the other, the *second* coming of the Messiah. The magnificent imagery of Hebrew prophecy had described the advent of the conqueror; he came—"a root out of a dry ground, with no form or comeliness: and when they saw him there was no beauty in him that they should desire him." The promise in the letter was unfulfilled. For ages the world's hope has been the second advent. The early church expected it in their own day. "We, which are alive and remain until the coming of our Lord."

The promise has not been fulfilled, or it has been fulfilled, but in either case anticipation has been foiled and disappointed. The ancient saints felt as keenly as any moralist could feel the brokenness of its promises. They confessed that they were strangers and pilgrims here; they said that they had here no continuing city. But they did not mournfully moralize on this. They felt that all was right; they knew that the promise itself had a deeper meaning: they looked undauntedly for "a city which hath foundations."

II. The second inquiry, therefore, is the meaning of this delusiveness.

(a) It serves to allure us on. We are led through life as we are allured upon a journey. The uncertainty of what may be seen beyond the next turn keeps expectation alive. The view that may be seen from yonder summit—the glimpse that may be caught, perhaps as the road winds round yonder knoll—hopes like these, not far distant, beguile the traveler on from mile to mile and from league to league.

So does God lead on, through life's unsatisfying and false reward, ever educating: Canaan first; then the hope of a redeemer; then the millennial glory.

It is thus that God has led on his world. He has conducted it as a father leads his child when the path homeward lies over many a dreary league. He suffers him to beguile the thought of time by turning aside to pluck, now and then, a flower, to chase now a butterfly. The butterfly is crushed, the flower fades, but the child is so much nearer home, invigorated and full of health and scarcely wearied yet.

(b) This nonfulfillment of promise fulfills it in a *deeper* way.

To some, doubtless, it was delusion. They expected to find their reward in a land of milk and honey. They were bitterly disappointed and expressed their disappointment loudly enough in their murmurs against Moses and their rebellion against his successors. But to others, as to Abraham, Canaan was the bright illusion which never deceived but forever shone before as the type of something more real. The kingdom of God was forming in their souls, forever disappointing them by the unreal and teaching them that, what is spiritual and belongs to mind and character, alone can be eternal.

We do not preach that all is disappointment—the dreary creed of sentimentalism; but we preach that *nothing* here is disappointment, if rightly understood. We do not comfort the poor man by saying that the riches that he has not now he will have hereafter. God has no Canaan for his own; no milk and honey for the luxury of the senses: for the city which hath foundations is built in the soul of man. He in whom godlike character dwells has all the universe for his own—"All things," saith the apostle, "are yours; whether life or death or things present or things to come; if ye be Christ's, then are ye Abraham's seed and heirs according to the *promise.*"—Frederick W. Robertson

Illustrations

LOOKING BEYOND. How could the prophets speak as they did? How could they paint these most terrible pictures of doom and destruction without cynicism or despair? It was because, beyond the sphere of destruction, they saw the sphere of salvation; because, in the doom of the temporal, they saw the manifestation of the Eternal. It was because they were certain that they belonged within the two spheres, the changeable *and* the unchangeable. For only he who is also beyond the changeable, not bound within it alone, can face the end. All others are compelled to escape, to turn away.—Paul Tillich

A CENTER FOR LIFE. A mother has a child. She belongs to the child. She is not free. Day and night that child rules her with a thralldom stronger than a rod of iron. Then the child dies. Now she is free; she can come and go as she will; no voice calling her now makes her run at its bidding. But see this strange woman heartbroken at her newfound freedom! This liberty of hers is the heaviest burden ever laid upon her. If we could give her back her child, if the old sense of belonging could return again, then she would feel free and be herself once more. We human beings are much more complex than we take ourselves for. We think we want liberty, but the only liberty worth having is founded on loyalty.

Here is the strange paradox of all rich and fulfilled living. We do want to be free from external restraints, from moral and political dictators and tyrants, but when we ask why we want to be free, we run straight into a paradoxical answer: We crave liberty so that we may find loyalty, may freely give ourselves to something that masters us, saying to it, I belong to you; you shall organize my life, shall save me from aimlessness and give direction and meaning to my days.—Harry Emerson Fosdick

Sermon Suggestions

PRAYER FOR A TIME OF DISTRESS.   TEXT: Ps. 143:1–8. (1) The distress, verses 1–7 (see, e.g., 2 Sam. 18:1, 5, 9–15). (2) The desire, verse 8a. (3) The direction, verse 8b.

ON BEING LIKE CHRIST.   TEXT: Eph. 4:25–5:2. (1) Your behavior. (2) Your talk. (3) Your spirit.

Worship Aids

CALL TO WORSHIP.   "It is a good thing to give thanks unto the Lord and to sing praises unto thy name, O Most High" (Ps. 92:1).

INVOCATION.   O Father, with your gracious calling in love, our fears subside, and we know that our lives are set in a friendly universe. In Christ, you are turned toward us in the eternity of your love. Therefore, we need not come in timidity but can come in boldness claiming your presence in the Word made flesh and dwelling among us.

What a joy to be among your people in this place: to unite in songs of praise, to hear your Word read and preached, to know sins forgiven, to experience the promise of spring in the renewing of your Spirit.

Praise be to you: Father, Son, and Holy Spirit.—John M. Thompson

OFFERTORY SENTENCE.   "Here, moreover, it is required in stewards that a man be found faithful" (1 Cor. 4:2).

OFFERTORY PRAYER.   For all the beauties of your Creation, for all the beauty of holiness, for all the beauty of love, we thank you, Lord. Accept our gifts as expressions of thanksgiving and use them to love your world.

PRAYER.   There are times, O Father, when we seem not so much a human being as a civil war. We are torn between the inertia of the *past* and the call to a *new* day. We are torn between a religion that lulls us to sleep and the gospel that shakes us awake—between the safety of the rear echelon and the challenge of the front lines— torn between our desire for comfort and ease and the needs and demands of others—torn between the desire to crawl back into the womb of infantile ways rather than to grow into the maturity to which Christ calls—torn between the cowardice to live by our fears and the courage to live by faith.

How we need to hear your Word, which from the beginning brings order out of chaos! How we need a fresh vision of who you are—the great God above all gods. In our more insightful moments we know that the war within—our confusion—our division—is the proliferation of the gods we serve. We are not loving you with *all* our heart, mind, and strength. Only the pure in heart shall see you—only those who concentrate—only those who are committed—only those who give themselves completely in a loving trust.

May your Word, bringing order out of chaos, come to us in Jesus' "Follow me." In discipleship may we discover the meaning and fulfillment that you will for us. In him we discover what it means to be your person—a person for others—to go out not knowing where we are going but assured of the light of your presence—nothing else really matters!

You have called us to be your church in this time and place. We thank you for those who have heard your call, "Whom shall I send and who will go for us?" and have responded, "Here am I, send me!" to be leaders in the life of our congregation. May their commitment inspire a recommitment in us to do with all our heart what our hands find to do.

As comrades of the Way, we pray for each other. Where there is loneliness, we pray that we may give ourselves in loving companionship. Where there is bereavement, we pray the comfort—the courage, the strength—that leads one *through* the valley of the shadow. When there is brokenness in health, we pray for the healing of the body according to your will. But, more than that, we pray for the wholeness of the person in mind and spirit that transcends the physical.

We pray, too, for the human family in its brokenness. With so many of the resources of this planet poised as instruments of destruction, with over a third of our brothers and sisters going to bed hungry every night and millions with no home to go to, we know there is something very wrong. We pray for those who persevere in ways of peace, and may that powerful image of the prophet find fulfillment in our time, of swords beaten into plowshares and spears into pruning hooks.

We pray through him who teaches, "Blessed are the *peacemakers* for they are the children of the Father," and is here as our Elder Brother teaching brothers and sisters here and everywhere to pray and live.—John M. Thompson

LECTIONARY MESSAGE

Topic: Feeding on Christ

Text: John 6:35, 41–51

To experience the real meaning of life, we must ask the right questions. In this text, the story of the desert feeding (which is probably John's version of the institution of the eucharistic meal), Jesus moves the questions the people ask from the superficial to the true. People are often afraid to ask the real questions of life; in this story the question the crowd avoided was "Who is this one—can he satisfy our deep yearning, or is he one more messianic imposter?" Popular belief looked for a recurrence of manna in the messianic age, according to 2 Baruch. It appears that the crowds wanted little more than this. Yet, Jesus wanted their inquiry to focus on "the food that lasts."

We, like the clamoring crowd from Capernaum, often see no further than the immediacy of consuming for temporary satisfaction; thus, we ignore our deeper hunger.

Jesus wanted the people who sought him to identify their true hunger and that which alone will satisfy, the True Bread. In this narrative, we hear Jesus' definition of what will supply true life; it is Christ himself, and they are to learn to "feed on him." Manna will assuage hunger pangs only temporarily—such perishable bread could not grant eternal life, he reminds them. The Bread Christ offers to spiritually hungry people is himself—living, broken, and dying for them.

"Less than All cannot satisfy . . ." wrote William Blake. Do we realize that *all* we need is to be found in Christ, who beckons us to commune with him? But we, too, pursue him at times for the wrong reason. Many of us are like those who followed Christ into the wilderness; they wanted a bread-giver like Moses. They did not know they needed a savior. Moreover, they wanted to press a particular political agenda with Jesus. They wanted to make him king, that he might galvanize their populist bid for national power. The manic excitement of the crowd was not satisfied with the self-giving leadership he was offering. Knowing their desperation, Jesus fled. He knew the futility of having it their way.

The early Christians were accused of bizarre, cannibalistic behavior as they celebrated the Lord's Supper. It was said that behind closed doors they ate the flesh and drank the blood of their master. Perhaps some today think that the church attaches too much meaning to eucharistic symbols. Perhaps we do not attach enough! "Feeding on Christ" is a way of saying that we confess that, in Christ, God provides nourishment for the real hunger of our lives.

In the sacramental moment of receiving Christ's life, symbolized in the bread and cup, we see how all of life is to be lived—literally as Eucharist, in grateful solidarity with Christ. Receiving the Bread of Life is more than "the medicine of immortality,"

as Ignatius put it; it is more than a memory of Christ's sacrifice; it serves to remind us that only Christ satisfies, nourishing our deepest hunger.

As with living water, so it is with the Bread from heaven. It provides enduring nourishment for those who turn away from laboring for perishable bread.—Molly Marshall-Green

SUNDAY: AUGUST EIGHTEENTH

SERVICE OF WORSHIP

Sermon: Life's Forced Decisions
TEXT: James 4:14
I. Religious confusion and uncertainty are nothing new. Multitudes of people do not know what they think. In this congregation there must be many of us who even when faced with basic matters of religious faith—God, Christ, the Bible, prayer, or immortality—often ask ourselves in our own secret thinking what our opinion is.

(a) James, the Lord's brother—in a different setting, to be sure—asked that question in the fourth chapter of his letter and the fourteenth verse: "What is your life?" Not now, What is your opinion about this religious matter or that? but, What is your life?

(b) A clear contrast confronts us between the question that so commonly bewilders us in matters of religion, What is our opinion? and this question that James asks, What is our life? We can postpone answering the question about our opinion. What is our opinion about God? We may not be able to answer that.

While, however, we can thus avoid answering the question, What is our opinion? we cannot avoid answering the question, What is our life? For here is a fact so momentous that no single sermon can sum up its significance, that, while we can avoid making up our minds, we cannot avoid making up our lives. We can hold our opinions in suspense, but we cannot hold our living in suspense. We live one way or the other.

(c) To be sure, there are areas of life where our opinions do not affect our living

and hence where our living does not force decision about our opinions. As to which of the various theories concerning the atmosphere on Mars is true, I do not know. One does not have to guess. One does not have to make up his mind about that because one does not have to make up his life about that. That is not a forced decision.

But most of the troublesome questions that seriously perplex us are forced decisions. You have to make up your life one way or the other. They remind one of being in a rowboat, going down a powerful river and debating whether or not to stop at a given point. There may be opposing considerations that an open and unprejudiced mind ought to face. Continue, then, your debate as to whether or not you will stop. But in the meantime the river has not waited the conclusion of your argument, and sooner or later, if your debate has not decided the question, the river conclusively will have settled it. You will not have stopped. How much like life that is you know well.

(d) This morning our proposition is that religion is a forced decision. Whether or not this universe is aimless or whether there is purpose at the heart of it; whether it all came from the fortuitous self-arrangement of atoms or whether our lives and labors are sustained by a Being, most like intelligence and goodwill when at their best they rise in us; whether Christ is a revelation of something deep at the heart of Reality or a psychological spark struck off from physical collisions; and whether the end of it all is a coffin and an ash heap or an open sepulcher and a hope—you have to live one way or the other.

II. For one thing, what is your life with reference to your faith in God?

(a) Our proposition today is that we cannot be altogether neutral on that point. If I ask you what your opinion is you may say you have not made up your mind, but what is your life? You are living one way or the other. You young people here this morning may not believe that at first. You may suppose that on a matter like faith in God you can be quite neutral in your living. But you cannot.

(b) Love comes into your life radiant and beautiful, and you do inevitably tend to take one attitude or the other, either that it is a revelation of something deep at the heart of reality or else a fortuitous by-product of a physical process. Work comes into your life, sometimes very hard, disappointing, onerous, costing sacrifice, and you do inevitably tend to take one attitude or the other, either that it is small use trying to do anything for these blundering, animal automata that we call men or else that our Father works hitherto and we work and that all faithful labor begun, continued, and ended in him will not fail of its final fruits. Trouble comes into your life, devastating, crushing, and you do inevitably tend to take one attitude or the other. Your life does get made up one way or the other.

(c) I would agree on intellectual grounds alone with one of our leading American philosophers that, of all systems of magic ever offered to the credulity of man, there never was a system of magic so incredible as the proposition that a number of physical particles fortuitously moving in an empty void could arrange themselves into planets, sunsets, mothers, music, art, science, poetry, Christ. Materialism is not thinking through philosophy. Materialism is running away from philosophy to believe in magic.

This morning, however, we are getting at the question from another approach. The decision between God and no-God, between an aimless and a purposeful universe, is not forced by your opinion but by your life. Do you say this morning that you are an agnostic, that you are neutral?

What is your life? It is being made up one way or the other.

III. Again, what is your life with reference to faith in man?

(a) To be sure, that idea presents serious difficulties. We human beings are not only driven from behind but are lured by ideals ahead of us, enticed by chosen goals and purposes. Imagine a machine doing that! And we human beings repent—sometimes with heartbreaking remorse—for wrongs done and penitently seek pardon and make restitution. No machine ever did that.

(b) When, then, our materialistic friends insist that we human beings are mere machines, while we grant that it is quite obvious that there is a mechanistic aspect to us all, one wonders what simpletons they think us to be that we should be so frightened and hoodwinked by a word. At least they must acknowledge that we are machines that think, love, distinguish between right and wrong, repent, follow ideals, sacrifice for one another, believe in God, hope for immortality, and construct philosophies to explain the universe. Queer machines! Nevertheless, we might be, I suppose, some kind of physicochemical product. Or it might be, on the other hand, that the deeper truth lies in the ancient faith that "we are children of God and, if children, then heirs; heirs of God and joint-heirs with Christ."

(c) This morning we are saying that we cannot be neutral on that question. If I should ask you what your opinion is, you might say you have no opinion, but we are asking a deeper question today: What is your life? For, soon or late, assumptions do appear in your life, with reference to human value and destiny, on which you habitually act.

Is there someone here today who has thought himself neutral on this question? You are fooling yourself about your neutrality. What is your life?

IV. Once more, this same truth holds about faith in the future, about hope and hopelessness.

(a) It may be that death ends all, that this generation is a bonfire to warm the hands of the next generation and that that generation will be another bonfire to warm the hands of the next and that in the end this whole human conflagration on the planet will burn itself out and end in an ash heap. That might be. Or it might be that, the Creative Power at the heart of all things being spiritual, the creative process cannot end in an ash heap, that every Calvary will have its Easter Day and every winter its spring, that this corruptible must put on incorruption and this moral put on immortality, and what eye hath not seen nor ear heard is laid up as a consummation for the spiritual life that upon this earth has had so promising a start. That might be true.

(b) And so, because it is so difficult to get an assured answer, people think that they will reserve their opinions and not make up their minds. But what is your life? For, my friends, hope and hopelessness are not simply theories. They are ways of living.

It may be that there are some here this morning whose life is better than their creed. If we should ask them whether they believe in God, the soul, and immortality, they would say, No, we do not. But they live as though they did. We all know people whose life is better than their creed.

(c) There probably are folk here whose life is worse than their creed. How many of us in a resounding declaration would say that, of course, we believe in God, in man as God's child, and in immortality as man's goal. Do we really? What is our life?

And there surely would be some here who would say that they do not know, that they have tried to make up their mind and could not. They might even say emphatically that they have stopped trying to answer such unanswerable questions. Have you really? What is your life? It is being made up one way or the other. Neutrality is a figment of the imagination on any basic issue of life. To live as though this were a godless, purposeless universe, as though human life were a combat between jackals and jackasses, a combat whose end is to be a coffin and an ash heap, that is hell on earth. And to live as though God were the kind of being whom Christ revealed, as though man, God's child, had boundless possibilities worth working for, that is heaven and earth. What is your life?—Harry Emerson Fosdick

Illustrations

A GENUINE OPTION. If I say to you, "Choose between going out with your umbrella or without it," I do not offer you a genuine option, for it is not forced. You can easily avoid it by not going out at all. Similarly, if I say, "Either love me or hate me"; "Either call my theory true or call it false," your option is avoidable. You may remain indifferent to me, neither loving nor hating, and you may decline to offer any judgment as to my theory. But if I say, "Either accept this truth or go without it," I put on you a forced option, for there is no standing place outside of the alternative. Every dilemma based on a complete logical disjunction, with no possibility of not choosing, is an option of this forced kind.—William James

HOW LIFE GETS MADE UP. Anatole France, the French litterateur, ought to have been happy. What did he lack to make a man happy? Creative gifts, large achievement, the adulation of countless friends, plenty of material resources—why should he not have been happy? Listen to him. "There is not in all the universe a creature more unhappy than I. People think me happy. I have never been happy for one day, not for a single hour." He was an utter skeptic about any spiritual significance in life, and life does get made up one way or the other.

Or William Wilberforce—should he not have been unhappy? After a long life fighting for the abolition of the British slave trade, at seventy-one years of age he lost his fortune. Accustomed to wealth and comfort, he had to leave his favorite residence at threescore years and ten and seek a home with his married sons. Should he not, too, have been unhappy? Yet two days after he learned the full extent of his losses we read this in his diary: "A solitary walk with the psalmist—evening quiet." You see, life gets made up one way or the other.—Harry Emerson Fosdick

Sermon Suggestions

WHY WE RETURN TO GOD. TEXT: Ps. 102:1–12. (1) Not because of an untroubled life, verses 1–11. (2) Rather, because God is always there, always in final control, verse 12.

GOOD ADVICE FOR EVIL DAYS. TEXT: Eph. 5:15–20, REB. (1) Avoid whatever will harm you. (2) Discover the will of God for your behavior. (3) Let the Holy Spirit overflow from you for blessing others.

Worship Aids

CALL TO WORSHIP. "O come, let us sing unto the Lord; let us make a joyful noise to the rock of our salvation" (Ps. 95:1).

INVOCATION. As we inquire in your temple, O Father, we are reminded of your mercies that have been ever of old: "You have been our dwelling place in all generations. Before the mountains were brought forth or ever you had formed the earth and the sea, from everlasting to everlasting you are God."
As we inquire, we are reminded of your mighty acts through your people Israel and your mighty Word proclaimed in Jesus the Messiah.
As we inquire, we are told of an amazing grace by which we live and move and have our being.
For all your goodness to us and to all peoples, we praise you: Father, Son, and Holy Spirit.—John M. Thompson

OFFERTORY SENTENCE. "Nay; but I will verily buy it of thee at a price; neither will I offer unto the Lord my God that which cost me nothing" (2 Sam. 24:24).

OFFERTORY PRAYER. We do not give to get, Lord. We give because we have got. In thanksgiving and praise, we bring our offerings. In thanksgiving and praise, we offer ourselves through Jesus Christ.

PRAYER. Almighty God . . . holy, powerful, loving, good. We thank you for yourself whom we have come to know in love, love expressed in generous gifts, love revealed in your Son, Jesus, who called you "Father."
Father of tender mercies, some of us are bruised and battered . . . we plead for the healing balm of your Spirit. Some of us are anxious and overly ambitious . . . we ask for peaceful satisfaction in doing your will. Some of us are concerned about family and friends . . . we seek comfort in a sense of your presence.
Father of forgiving grace, we have sinned against you—your goodness and self-giving love. We have sought to go our own way, refusing to follow your will. We have self-righteously exalted ourselves, ignoring your conflicting righteousness. We ask you to forgive us our sin.
Father of this fellowship, where there is discord, let there be peace. Where there is loneliness, let there be love. Where there is sadness, let there be joy. Where there is sickness, let there be health. Where there is poverty, let there be true wealth.
We are your children, daughters and sons through Christ Jesus. Minister to our needs, we pray, in the name of Jesus.—J. Estill Jones

LECTIONARY MESSAGE

Topic: The Bread of Life
TEXT: John 6:51–58
Sometimes it is difficult to make sense out of life. Life can be a rat race. We feel like a squirrel in a cage, running with all of our might but getting nowhere. We get so busy in the routine of life that we don't even stop to consider how chaotic our lives are. We want to ask, Is this all that life is about? Is life only getting up and going to work to make money so that I can buy food to eat so that I have enough strength to get up and go to work tomorrow?
Life can be frustrating. We can only take so much of the squirrel-in-the-cage syndrome. Yet, that leads to an interesting observation. Most of us, because of the life-styles we have, don't really know how to rest and relax. The statistics are alarmingly high concerning those who retire and within one or two years are struck with a massive heart attack and die. Experts state that those people led such high-stress

lives that when they retired it was like putting a brick wall in front of a moving train and watching the train collapse in on itself. The built-up stress finally took its toll. Listen to the haunting words of their widowed spouses: "We worked so very hard to make a good life for ourselves so we could really enjoy our retirement." Sometimes it is difficult to make sense out of life—going, going, going, and getting nowhere.

This is just what Jesus was talking about. Those people had been there when he miraculously fed five thousand people with a couple of fish and a few loaves of bread. After that feast, Jesus and his disciples crossed the Sea of Galilee. Well, lo and behold, the next day the crowds came again. Jesus said, "You came to find me so that I could feed you again. Do not labor for the food that perishes but for the food that lasts forever." They reminded him of the manna that was given to their ancestors in the wilderness. And Jesus pointed out that that perishable food for their bodies lasted for only a day. Then he said to them, "I am the Bread of Life." Here is a marvelous metaphor as to the meaning of real life. Real life is not life in pursuit of bread that will mold. Real life is life spent consuming Christ—bringing him totally into ourselves—making him a part of us in the same way that food becomes part of us: consuming him spiritually for nourishment and strength.

Hence, the purpose of the communion meal celebration is to be a reminder to us, to bring us back to the center of our faith, to be a stopping place for us to examine our lives, to see where we are going. It is a place for us to ask, What kind of bread have I been working for? Do I spend my days and my weeks working for the bread that money can buy? Am I trying to satisfy my appetite with the tangible bread of things that rust, break apart, need paint, and burn oil? Is my life centered in the bread of compliments, how others think about me? Is it centered in the bread of power?

The text reminds us that chasing the bread provided for us in the world is the rat race of life, getting us nowhere. When we consume Christ, absorbed in his teachings, his ways, his character, his mind, he becomes a part of us. He is the bread of life, and the life that he gives is not characterized by chaos and frustration. The life that he offers is eternal.—Craig A. Loscalzo

SUNDAY: AUGUST TWENTY-FIFTH

SERVICE OF WORSHIP

Sermon: How Fares Your Faith?
TEXT: Heb. 1:1–4; 2:9–11
I. How fares your faith? Does it sustain you through tough and tragic times? Has it got a hold on you that won't let go? I hope so. But if not, you stand in very good company. That Christian community that received what we call the Letter to the Hebrews began to give up on the Christian faith. We really don't know very much about them. We don't know who wrote the letter. We think those who received it lived somewhere in Italy. We suspect the recipients knew a great deal about the rituals and institutions of Jewish tradition. Elusive as these facts may be, one additional fact stands out. The community's faith is exhausted. They suffer, as one commentator suggests, from "tired blood."

"Is goodness really at the heart of the universe?" they ask. They can't see or experience goodness through the persecution they encounter. "Is the way of Christ the wave of the future?" they wonder. The wave of the future seems to be the same old tyrannies, deceptions, and dog-eat-dog. Amid the routine, the change, the tragedy of human life, their firm convictions about life's meaning and how to live it are cooling off. As Christians, they're a burnt-out case.

Do you know what the author of the Letter to the Hebrews—whoever it is—do you know what the author does? He sends a letter of encouragement. "I know you're weary," he says. "I know you're ready to drift away from the faith. I know you're isolated and times are tough. But let me insist in the face of all this: regardless of what happens to you, through everything threatening your faith and driving you to discouragement, we know that through the life, death, and victory over death of Jesus, the things that dishearten you and get you down do not have the last word."

II. As we confront and muddle through life with all its frustration, pain, and failure; with all its bizarre accidents, untimely deaths, and twisted relationships; we confess through all of this a love at the heart of Creation never letting us go. We bet on a promise for a cosmic community of grace and peace finally brought to fruition, against all evidence to the contrary, by the God revealed through Jesus of Nazareth, the Christ. "Take heart!" our author exclaims. "The love of God remains in charge through the worst life can do to us." Our author stands with Paul in asserting that "nothing in all Creation can separate us from the love of God in Christ Jesus our Lord."

Do you believe that? I suppose some of us do; and some of us don't but wish we could. Like that ancient community whose faith wore thin, our faith, too, can tire out; we can rummage through the religious attics or spiritual junkyards, grasping for this or that. Surely there's plenty out there: gurus, shamans, therapists, New Age mystics—each of them recommending diets, mind control, physical disciplines, worldviews, seances, you name it. The quest for hope and meaning touches us all.

Some of you are no doubt familiar with a story told by Stephen Hawking, that Einstein of our day, introducing his reflection on the meaning and purpose of Creation. In his *Brief History of Time*, Hawking says he's trying to "read the mind of God." He begins with a chapter on our "picture of the universe." What's it look like? he wonders. How shall we see it? What's at its center and periphery? He writes as follows:

A well-known scientist (some say it was Bertrand Russell) once gave a public lecture on astronomy. He described how the earth orbits around the sun, and how the sun in turn orbits around the center of a vast collection of stars called our galaxy. At the end of the lecture, a little old lady at the back of the room got up and said, "What you have told us is rubbish. The world is really a flat plate supported on the back of a tortoise." The scientist gave a superior smile before replying, "And what is the tortoise standing on?" "You're very clever, young man, very clever," said the old lady. "But it's turtles all the way down."

Turtles all the way down? For some of us, it might as well be. Our faith grows cold; it burns out. In a world of suffering children, rampant greed, simmering and explosive hatreds; in a world where so much seems to be mucked up by our own stupidity and self-deception; affirming some moral core at the heart of Creation seems almost absurd. Arthur Koestler looked out on what he deemed to be an unfeeling, tragic, and random existence and observed, "God seems to have left the receiver off the hook and time is running out."

III. How fares your faith? In the face of all that may threaten it, can you buy into the deep conviction of our author to the Hebrews? He tells us that we discover the indefatigable love undergirding Creation and reaching out for each of us at the very moment it appears most distant and through the very person who appears least likely: Jesus Christ on the cross. If God ever left the phone "off the hook" with time running out, it was at Calvary. Our author takes the very moment when faith might fare the worst, when goodness gets strung up, when hope for human life drains away—our author takes that moment and says, "Look, there at the cross we see through the very things that subvert our faith and erode our hope: not, finally, the absence of God; but the presence of One who sustains us through the worst life can do to us."

The author points to the suffering of Jesus as the primary illustration of love's sovereignty over suffering. He doesn't deny suffering in this world; he doesn't curse it or avoid it or call it unreal. He says to those of us whose faith wavers because of suffering, "Don't get discouraged or cynical; don't despair; don't drift off. Take heart! The power of God lies not in protecting you from failure, frustration, tragedy, death; the power of God lies in taking the worst life can do to us and transforming it into a new, deeper, and more profound reality. In faith we see the love of God working through the suffering of the tragic—and yes, the triumphant—cross of Jesus confirming the steadfast, life-transforming, loving power of God."

IV. I have a feeling I can say that to you till I'm blue in the face but that somehow you must see it. Look, then, at this holy table. Here lies the ground on which to rest a tired faith. Here we see flesh and blood broken in suffering and tragedy. At this table, in cynical terms, we see the clearest absence of anything even close to a loving God. Really? Does this table represent the absence of God? Hardly. For as we eat this bread and drink this cup together—each of us, perhaps, a man or woman of wavering or tender faith—we surely recognize the cruel threats to faith in our world. Yet, in the same act, we rejoice in the tenacious, irrevocable love bearing with us, seeing us through all the challenge and crisis of this life, into the promised life within the everlasting arms of almighty God. That's what our breaking, our pouring, our sharing represent.

V. So, how fares your faith in the care, concern, and presence of the living God in this troubled world? Is your faith wavering, burning out? Is it going through tough times? Come to this holy table and witness, on the one hand, in the bread broken and wine poured, a death posing the darkest threat to faith. But be assured at this very same table—in faith, in hope—that we witness, share, and are undergirded by "love divine, all loves excelling": steadfast, radiant, abiding.—James W. Crawford

Illustrations

FAITH AND A CROSS.   What is it that can draw men together? In the end it is some form of suffering. Now, it is easy to talk pious nonsense and cant about suffering. There is a suffering that brutalizes and repels for which we can find no reason and which seems feeble. But there is also a suffering that unites and that seems necessary to human existence. There is no family that can persist without voluntary suffering of some kind among its members, and no nation can exist except on the same basis. The same principle applies to all great expressions of the human spirit. The Shakespeares and Miltons of this world draw us to them because time and time again we discover in them an openness to suffering; they have sat where we sit. As Goethe puts it: "Who never spent his nights in tears / He knows you not ye Heavenly Powers." And the mystery of the Jews! What makes the figure of the wandering Jew, despite the hate that it has evoked, an irresistible one is the fact that he is one who has taken upon himself a suffering mission. The history of the Jews has taken the shape of the cross and draws us to them as a strange enigma still.—W. D. Davies

THE PRESENCE OF GOD.   I remember one friend telling me that sometimes in the acutest dangers of the war an almost physical sense of the reality and power of God came to him and drove away all fear. The brother of another, traveling alone by night to London on the way to the front, experienced, as the hours went by, an ever-deepening sense of the presence of God, which changed the whole course of his life. Yet another once described to me how, in rock climbing in a remote and sterile region in the northwest of Scotland, his companion was suddenly killed beside him and how in the vast and wonderful mountain solitude around him, as he stood beside the shattered body far from human aid, the whole scene became suddenly full of the Divine Presence. If such experiences are truthful, their only possible explanation is that something that blinds us has been taken away.—D. S. Cairns

Sermon Suggestions

GOD'S SHINING FACE. TEXT: Psalm 67.
(1) *What?* A prayer for God's gracious blessing. (2) *Why?* So that God's purpose may be known and experienced everywhere.
(3) *How?* Through God's unbiased justice and universal blessing.

MODELS FOR MARRIAGE. TEXT: Eph. 5:21–33. (1) The basic principle, verse 21. (2) The attitude of the wife, verses 22–24. (3) The attitude of the husband, verses 25–31. (4) The on-going mystery, verses 32–33.

Worship Aids

CALL TO WORSHIP. "Oh, come, let us worship and bow down; let us kneel before the Lord our Maker" (Ps. 95:6).

INVOCATION. O thou, so near yet so very far away, from whom we can run but never escape, in whom is judgment and testing, yet mercy and forgiveness; deal with us not after our sins, but pour out on us a blessing because we pause to worship and adore the Lord our God.—E. Lee Phillips

OFFERTORY SENTENCE. "And this, not as we had hoped, but first they gave their own selves to the Lord and to us through the will of God" (2 Cor. 8:5).

OFFERTORY PRAYER. We are overwhelmed by your generous grace, loving God. We respond in faith, and these gifts are tokens of our faith. Use them as you will.

PRAYER. Thou, O Lord! art the searcher of the spirit. Thou knowest the heart altogether. We do not know thee, but thou knowest us. Naked and open are we before him with whom we have to do. And yet we are commanded to come boldly before thee. Thy knowledge is not for our condemnation. Thy thoughts are thoughts of mercy, and thy knowledge is for salvation. And we beseech of thee that we may from day to day draw near with boldness and simplicity, with sincere penitence, with earnest desires, that we may be godly, living above this present world while living in it, with purer motives, with nobler aims, with a better endeavor than other men. Because we are called by thy name, may we have thy spirit, walk in thy footsteps, bear about thy precious example, and be, according to the measure of our knowledge and our strength, to others what thou art to us. Forgive the deficiency of our past lives. Forgive the outright sins which we have committed. Our forgetfulness, our heedlessness, our infirmities—we beseech of thee, not only that thou wilt pass them by, but that thou wilt give us strength in time to come. For we desire, not so much to remove pain and penalty, as to remove impurity and selfishness and pride. It is not so much joy that we seek, as that we may have a better manhood, nobler thoughts, truer purposes, and purer hearts, and be more gracious and generous and beneficent, as thou art. And we beseech of thee that thou wilt grant us that we may grow in grace and in the knowledge of our Lord and Savior Jesus Christ and to thy name shall be the praise, Father, Son, and Spirit.—Henry Ward Beecher

LECTIONARY MESSAGE

Topic: Bread for Eternal Life

TEXT: John 6:55–69

In Matt. 15:17ff., Jesus speaks of the inconsequential meaning of what one eats; what comes out of the mouth is what is important, he insisted, for it is capable of defiling the speaker. Here, in the sixth chapter of John, another perspective is recorded. Jesus is speaking about the surpassing significance of what one turns to for sustenance.

Teaching in the synagogue at Capernaum, Jesus declares that his very being must be ingested by those who would desire eternal life. In this passage, the Evangelist anticipates the teaching of John 15, which stresses the relationship of the vine to the branches. The same accent on a mutual abiding—Christ in the believer and the believer in Christ—is offered here.

The graphic language, with clear eucharistic overtones, delineates for the reader (and hearer) that receiving eternal life is inseparable from receiving Christ. Like the earlier part of chapter 6, there is a contrast between Moses the bread-giver and Jesus the giver of eternal life. This "new Moses" does not pretend to be the source of a new form of existence apart from the power and approval of God. Conscious that he lived because of the One who sent him, he offered a similar opportunity for these to live in a relationship of dependence and security.

Like the recalcitrant children of Israel in the wilderness, the disciples murmured at his teaching. Jesus responds by probing the source of offense, realizing that if they could not comprehend this, further disclosures might prove even more unsettling! The haunting words of the prologue are being played out: "He came unto his own, and his own did not receive him . . ."

"What if you were to see the Son of man ascending where he was before?" he asked them. Students of the Gospel of John are familiar with the distinct spatial and temporal language employed by the fourth evangelist. Here on the lips of Jesus is the metaphor of above (Jesus' true origin) and below (where he had been sent as the "revealer of life from above.") He alone evidences the full expression of spirit and flesh and seeks to inform his hearers of their need to seek "bread for eternal life"—the very Word of God.

Jesus has no illusions about the difficulty of belief; his testimony of "being sent" troubles these Jewish followers, and, thus, many "disciples drew back and no longer went about with him." He asks those who remain, the Twelve, if they, too, plan to desert him. Simon Peter (whom the Fourth Gospel presents as usually *misunderstanding* the focus of Jesus' teaching) offers a compelling confession to God's unique presence in the one he calls Master. With uncharacteristic understanding, he interprets the metaphor that Jesus has been using throughout this narrative on the true bread that comes from God. Peter realizes that to forsake Jesus would be to forsake eternal life—that quality of life made possible by receiving him who was sent. Will we also turn only to the Christ who alone has the words of eternal life?— Molly Marshall-Green

SUNDAY: SEPTEMBER FIRST

SERVICE OF WORSHIP

Sermon: Courage to Work
TEXT: Acts 28:14b–16

The Apostle Paul was at last in Rome, but not as he had originally planned. He was in custody, exercising his rights as a citizen to have the emperor's court settle the matter of his innocence in the face of false charges made by some Jewish foes. Now, after much turmoil on land and many terrors at sea, Paul had reached the city.

Paul was eager to be done with it all but apprehensive, no doubt, not knowing just how much time would pass before his case could be tried. With so much pending, with so much that was uncertain, and with so much still remaining to be done in the ministry, Paul needed a word of cheer. He needed encouragement. He found it in the graciousness some Roman Christians showed him. A world of expressiveness opens up to us in Luke's comment about Paul facing his godly friends: "On seeing them, Paul thanked God and took courage."

I. More often than not, courage is generated in company. Paul, facing a hard period in his life, is readied for his ordeal by the assisting presence of caring friends.

(a) Paul had known times of direct encouragement from the Lord. There was that time when he was praying in the Temple and heard Jesus speak directly to him in words of wisdom and encouragement, as Acts 22:17–18 and 21 tells us. There was another time when he was in jail overnight and heard the reassuring voice of the Lord, as Acts 23:11 informs us. But now God was using another method to renew his courage—the caring presence of fellow believers.

(b) Paul had been encouraged by fellow believers before. In fact, many of his letters to churches contain open requests for prayers that God help him remain courageous in his work. It has never been easy to witness without cost to oneself. Paul was accustomed to opposition, but he knew that bearing up under it all was partly the result of community prayers on his behalf.

(c) Paul needed courage to keep on witnessing and working for Jesus. He had to endure constant disputes, stubborn unbelievers, hostile opposers, and would-be assassins. It took courage for him to be outspoken, frank, and bold under such circumstances. This time, God deepened Paul's courage through the caring presence of Christian friends. By their ministry of love, the apostle was renewed for the next stage of his journey.

II. The text tells us that Paul "took courage" when he was greeted by those caring believers. They had come out to meet him, indeed to escort him, as it were, into Rome. Although he was a prisoner in chains, they came. He was a despised man in some quarters, but these persons knew his worth to God and the church, so they came.

(a) The fact of their presence there on the Appian Way inspired courage; a part of the group from Rome had come out forty-three miles to meet him. As they all walked on together, Paul found another delegation waiting for him ten miles nearer the city. Such travel witnessed well that these believers cared enough to put themselves to some trouble to reach Paul. His being a prisoner made them all the more eager to be his escorts, so that his entrance into Rome would be an honorable one nevertheless.

(b) The faces in the group deepened courage. Phoebe must have been in the group; she was one among twenty-six persons Paul knew and mentioned by name when he wrote to the Roman congregation. Prisca and Aquila were probably in the group; they had shown love and loyalty to Paul time without number. I would

like to believe that Epaenetus, Paul's first convert in Asia, and Urbanus, whom he had met and known while there in Asia, were in that group, for both were now living in Rome. John Mark might have been part of that greeting group, chastened and matured now after the rash independence he showed while assisting Paul and Barnabas during his younger years.

(c) We do not know for certain who was in that caring group of greeters, but whoever they were, they were there. They were there in love, with interest, eagerness, caring, and the will to help their brother.

The future Paul faced would demand courage on his part. The presence of these believers helped him to have that courage.

III. The Greeks considered courage as one of the four ultimate virtues of human conduct. The other three virtues were wisdom, temperance, and justice. Courage was rightly lauded because it is the power of mind and spirit to overcome fear and act with concern to effect an end. Courage is not the absence of fear, nor is it the dismissal of anxiety. Courage is rather that conspicuous and unrelenting will to venture, to risk oneself to achieve a necessary result.

(a) The early church considered courage as one of the by-products of faith, and the members knew that it is deepened by caring and sharing in fellowship. They, therefore, prayed for each other, and they linked hands with each other to face their troubles in the loyalty of love.

(b) The need for courage to do our work continues. There are places in our world where conditions threaten a full witness of the gospel, places where intent witnesses need courage to do their work. In some places, the church is being unreasonably caricatured and criticized by unbelieving opponents. Serious servants for Christ in many lands are under attack for their conscience-smiting witness. Our prayers, reassurances, and active presence where possible can help to strengthen their courage.

(c) Depression is a possible foe against any person, believers included. Unrelenting pressure can do damage to our minds and spirits, and uncontrolled conditions can break down our bodies. Paul often needed a lift for his faith. In 2 Cor. 4:8–10, Paul confesses that he, too, experienced those times of inward turmoil and depression. Luke wrote tellingly about Paul's humanness along this line in those brief but illuminating words of our text: "On seeing [the believers from Rome], Paul thanked God and took courage," renewed for the next stage of his journey in the will of God. He had received increased courage to work.

IV. It is no small matter to be regarded and loved. There is a world of meaning in being part of a fellowship, part of the family of faith, and in knowing that we belong in a special kind of way.

(a) No person moves through life without having times of loneliness, and very few escape the deadening weights of depression. Paul did not escape these. But the Christian community did its part to help Paul with the pressure he knew and felt in being obedient to God.

(b) Acts of love toward each other deepen our sense of belonging and security. They also generate the courage we need to do our work. Sharing ourselves, not to be served but to serve, is to live our Lord and keep our relations with each other meaningful and steady despite the cost.

(c) Paul was stirred by what that Christian group from Rome did in his interest. Those believers gave themselves, and because they did, Paul gained courage to continue giving himself. Once located in Rome, he courageously used the time spent waiting to be tried as a time of witnessing about Christian truths. The cause of the gospel thus continued to advance. Christian friends had done their part to help make it so.

(d) When did you last encourage someone? What service did you render in their interest? Remember this: someone's life and work will depend upon the courage you help to generate and inspire within them. Resolve to be a caring person and ask God to help you to be supportive and encouraging in all of your relationships with others.—James Earl Massey

Illustrations

THE PRACTICALITY OF LOVE.   Too often we have spoken of love and interpreted it negatively. We have measured it by the scope of our willingness to deny ourselves, how much we are willing to give up for others. And this can be pretty depressing. We don't come off too well.

But Paul puts love within reach. It is something we can do today, this very day in this year of our Lord. He says, "Bear one another's burdens, and so fulfill the law of Christ."

Perhaps the need to do this sort of thing is greater than most of us are aware of. Some fellow student may be about to lose his spiritual and moral capital by gambling with his private interpretation of situation ethics. He needs caring for. A student wife and mother may be crushed or bruised by a series of events that she could not prevent. She needs caring for. A professor may be overextending himself as he goes beyond the call of duty in trying to be of help to his students. He needs caring for.

These needs indicate some of the kinds of things we can do for one another. At the same time they represent opportunities to experience what it means to be truly human, to be a part of a community that cares.—James W. Cox

WHAT TURNS THE SCALES.   As soon as I heare God testifie of Christ at his Baptisme, This is my beloved Sonne in whom I am well pleased, I finde that Sonne of his led up by the Spirit, to be tempted of the Devill. And after I heare God ratifie the same testimony againe, at his Transfiguration, (This is my beloved Sonne, in whom I am well pleased) I finde that beloved Sonne of his, deserted, abandoned, and given over to Scribes, and Pharisees, and Publicans, and Herodians, and Priests, and Souldiers, and people, and Judges, and witnesses, and executioners, and he that was called the beloved Sonne of God, and made partaker of the glory of heaven, in this world, in his Transfiguration, is made now the Sewer of all the corruption, of all the sinnes of this world, as no Sonne of God, but a meere man, as no man, but a contemptible worme. As though the greatest weaknesse in this world, were man, and the greatest fault in man were to be good man is more miserable then other creatures, and good men more miserable then any other men.

But then there is Pondus Gloriae, An exceeding waight of eternall glory, and that turns the scale; for as it makes all worldly prosperity as dung, so it makes all worldly adversity as feathers.—John Donne (1572–1631)

Sermon Suggestions

WHERE SHALL I FIND HELP?   TEXT: Psalm 121, REB. (1) Because God is Creator, he can help us. (2) Because God is our Guardian, he will protect us.

HOW TO BE A SURVIVOR.   TEXT: Eph. 6:10–20. (1) Find your strong defense in God, verses 10–17a. (2) Make your strong offense with the Word of God in the power of the Spirit, verses 17b–18. (3) Remember the purpose for which we live, verses 19–20.

Worship Aids

CALL TO WORSHIP.   "Oh, sing unto the Lord a new song: Sing unto the Lord, all the earth" (Ps. 96:1).

INVOCATION.   Grant, we pray thee, this morning, such an illumination to thy people, such a joy and liberty of heaven, that they may rise up round about thee. Yea, may there be found many a singing heart, this morning, clasping thy feet, and with all tokens of gladness owning thee, appropriating thee, and rejoicing to be honored of thee, and to be strengthened by thee.—Henry Ward Beecher

OFFERTORY SENTENCE.   "Offer unto God the sacrifice of thanksgiving and pay thy vows unto the Most High" (Ps. 50:14).

OFFERTORY PRAYER.   Neither large nor small need be the gift God leads your heart to share; bring only that which is God's will dedicated in God's clear care.—E. Lee Phillips

PRAYER.   Eternal Spirit, whom we worship with reverent lips, but too often with insensitive hearts, grant us today a vital experience of thy saving presence. Be to us not alone a holy name reverently spoken but a living Reality within our souls. Shine in us like the sun returning after the rain. Clarify our thoughts, elevate our spirits, deepen our faith and courage, and send us out to lay fresh hold on life because thou has laid strong hold on us.

For all that makes life rich and beautiful, we thank thee. With gratitude we remember our homes and the affection and loyalty of our families. Gratefully we think of our friends and of their comforting and sustaining fidelity. For great books, great music, great art, we thank thee, and for all noble souls—Christ over all—who, despite man's evil, have sustained our faith in man's dignity and possibility. Especially today we are grateful for thy Church. Despite her failures she has been to us the guardian of the great tradition, the trustee of our spiritual heritage, the preserver of faiths and principles which man forgets at his salvation's peril. Thanks be to thee for the truths which she kept for us across the centuries, which have been our hope and our redemption.

As thus with gratitude we bring our best into thy presence, so too with penitence we bring our worst. Thou seest us with our self-centeredness and ill temper, our jealousy and animosity, tempted by worldly pride and lust. Thou seest us surrendering to our fears, losing our faith, compromising with evil, letting the world's chaos and our private troubles make us victims instead of victors in the battle of life. Spirit of the living God, come to some distressed and beaten souls here and repeat again the miracle of thy grace that, being transformed by the renewing of our minds, we may go out to be more than conquerors.

Upon the altar of our intercession we lay our anxious concern for this storm-tossed world. We are burdened by the tumult and bloodthirstiness of the nations. Ours is the sin, O God, the sin of all of us, that violence stalks the earth. Before it is too late, we beseech thee, bring the people to penitence and the rulers of the people to wisdom, that in the day of our opportunity we may choose light not darkness, law not slaughter, brotherhood not enmity, peace and not war.

Especially we pray for our children. God forgive us that we of elder years hand on to the world's youth burdens so heavy and unsolved problems so difficult. For the intelligence and character of the oncoming generation, we pray. Make them wiser and better than we have been. As science opens the doors on unimaginable vistas of adventure, let not mankind commit suicide for lack of wisdom, integrity, and goodwill. Raise up leaders among our young men and women who will show us the way. If it be thy will, lay thy hand on some youth here today, who may be the pioneer of a new era.

For this congregation of thy people, we lift our heartfelt prayer. May we not fail thee! May we match our opportunity with our devotion and rise to the occasion that invites our service to the community, the nation, and the world. So enlarge our vision, our generosity, and our dedication that we may deserve thine approval as good and faithful servants.

In the name and Spirit of Christ we make our prayer.—Harry Emerson Fosdick

LECTIONARY MESSAGE

Topic: The Heart of a Man
Text: Mark 7:1–8, 14–15, 21–23

I. Jesus was never more plain about the intent of his mission than here. Already he had declared in his inaugural sermon the call to repentance as central. In the Sermon on the Mount, he made it clear that the intentions and motivations from within were more important than overt actions. But here his claims were made personal—and specific.

The disciples were guilty. There was little doubt of that. They ate with unwashed hands and in doing so were flying in the face of religious tradition. Minute legal requirements had overtaken the glory of Jewish faith. High ethical standards had given way to concerns about clean pots and pans and hands. A great faith had degenerated into a list of ceremonial mo-

tions. Jesus made no defense of his disciples' behavior. Instead, he issues a judgment against superficial religion: "This people honors me with their lips, but their heart is far from me." Yes, the disciples were guilty of breaking with tradition, but the Pharisees were guilty of deceit. Our own complacency, selfish ambitions, and trivial pursuits make us guilty of the same.

II. No one ought to miss what Jesus intended here.

(a) Religion that is real is internal, not external. What matters is the heart, the seat of the human spirit and will. Externals, like those that so held the attention of the Pharisees, are not evil in and of themselves. Yet they cannot, by themselves, provide the fullness of life we seek. Here is the unique contribution of the gospel—and Jesus showed us the way. His emphasis was on the inward life, the contemplative exercise of faith. Out of one's inward experience with God comes fullness of life.

(b) Likewise, it is the inward experience that can defile us. Jesus was right—nothing that goes into us from the outside can defile us. It may kill us, but it can't control us. It is that which resides in the inner sanctum that controls us. We are controlled by the heart. A long list of such vices that proceed from the heart is given: evil thoughts, fornication, theft, murder, adultery, coveting, wickedness, deceit, licentiousness, envy, slander, pride, foolishness. These are the deeds Jesus was concerned with, not with whether or not someone had kept the ceremonial rules.

(c) Religious life that centers on a logical system of external rules and behaviors will rob the church of its vitality. Sure enough, it can provide ready accommodation for the many who seem to need such strictures. Yet to place the free and moving wind of God, that force which is continually renewing life, into old archaic forms is to destroy its potential. Jesus came preaching about a kingdom in which there is life abundant and free, where relationships are redeemed, where our only law is to love God supremely and to love our neighbors as ourselves. It is the heart that matters. From within the heart comes all that creates turmoil in the world. And from within the heart comes all that cre- ates our finest and most noble joy.—Lee R. McGlone

SUNDAY: SEPTEMBER EIGHTH

SERVICE OF WORSHIP

Sermon: The Hidden and Revealed God

TEXT: Isa. 45:15

"Between God and us there stands the hiddenness of God." This quotation, taken from the *Dogmatics* of Karl Barth, is, I think, the truth. And when pondering this meditation for today, it occurred to me that I ought to read in the *Dogmatics* and learn what Barth meant by that statement. But then I decided I did not want to know that much about it!

"Between God and us there stands the hiddenness of God." Let the theologians—and I use this term generously and in a pedestrian sense, to refer to you and to me—ponder this word of Barth. The theologian would much more likely say, "Between God and us there stands the revelation of God." And to say this would be to tell the truth. It would make the theologian happy. But there is another true word that may not put the theologian so much at ease, namely, "Between God and us there stands the hiddenness of God."

The ancient prophet of Israel once declared, "Verily thou art a God that hidest thyself, O God of Israel, the Savior." The prophet proclaims that God not only reveals himself, he hides himself. The context of the prophetic word leaves us free to ponder in the light of our faith what the prophet meant to convey to us. How is it that devout men can declare that God hides himself, and yet call that affirmation "faith"? Does the prophet say that because he doubts? No! The context of the word suggests that he simply tells the truth. God does hide himself. And it is not faith to deny it. It is faith to declare it— "Verily thou art a God that hidest thyself."

I. What does the word of Isaiah mean to us today? It means, first of all, that the hidden God is the revealed God.

(a) God is not discovered but revealed. The prophetic word means that men may undertake to look for God in an effort to assure themselves of their genius. Well, in a case like that, God is not beyond a little holy "hide and seek." Man simply is never able to say, "I have found him! In my native genius, at the end of my brilliant search, I have found him!" Isaiah was saying you do not find God at the end of a long trail. In the most unexpected ways and times, *he* finds *you.*

(b) Isn't this something we have learned in our most holy faith? He is hidden and revealed to faith in a man crucified between malefactors. He is hidden and revealed to faith in a man raised from the dead. Revelation is there—a revelation of God himself. But it is hidden where human wisdom would never find it and where faith, the gift of God, *always does!* God's greatest revelations are hidden away from all human wisdom and revealed only to humble trust. Paul wrote to the church at Corinth, "What no one ever saw or heard, / What no one ever thought could happen, / Is the very thing God prepared for those who love him."

(c) The hidden God is revealed only to faith. And where there is no faith, the revealed God is hidden. Jesus said, "I thank thee, Father, Lord of heaven and earth, that thou hast hidden these things from the wise and understanding and revealed them to babes."

II. What does the word of Isaiah mean to us today? It means, in the second place, that the revealed God remains the hidden God. And this fact is not one the theologian easily accepts. After all, is it not the duty of the expert to reveal his subject? What expert is prepared to glory, not in what he knows, but in what he does not know? The theologian is prepared to accept the observation that the hidden God is revealed, but is he prepared to accept the observation that the revealed God is hidden?

(a) It is one of our great temptations

that we want to live by faith *and* sight. How good to bolster faith with knowledge that makes faith less demanding and less all-encompassing. One of the cleverest ways to do this (and it seems exceptionally pious) is to bolster faith by ferreting out holy secrets through the wizardry of esoteric excavations of biblical texts. If we can remove more and more veils from God, if we can point to proof that proves faith, how in heaven's name could we otherwise have it so good? One of the cleverest sins of the theologian is to try to take the wraps off God in the name of faith.

(b) But the revealed God remains the hidden God. God does not deliver himself into human hands not even into the holy hands of theologians. Karl Barth has reminded us that God is not an object we can subjugate to our spiritual supervision and control. It is not our business to bolster faltering faith by mastering God. It is not our business to take faith out of faith. It is our business to live by faith and not by sight. Whenever we require God to submit to us, he hides from us and waits until we submit ourselves to him. I am deeply troubled by the kind of Christianity that assures man that if he gets the right key, he will be able to take the mystery out of God. I am wary of a Christianity that takes the faith out of faith.

Does this mean that faith will not express itself through theology? No, indeed! But it does mean that theology will always be the servant of faith, not its master. Martin Luther once said that God is held not in the hand but in the heart.

We who officiate at the altar must be content with the revelation that is granted. Nothing of God remains hidden from us which faith cannot trust to God. Faith can trust the hiddenness of God because of the revelation of God in his Son, our Lord. Faith can live without answers because it lives with assurance that is the gift of the Holy Spirit.

(c) John once wrote, "Beloved, we are God's children now; it does not yet appear what we shall be, but we know that when he appears we shall be like him, for we shall see him as he is." That is faith. The God who is hidden has been revealed. And the God who has been revealed remains hidden. And faith, which accepts what has been revealed, trusts God with what is hidden. That is faith. And faith is the life of the theologian. Faith remembers with Isaiah the prophet that the God who is hidden is the Savior of Israel.—Raymond Bryan Brown

Illustrations

THE ELUSIVE PRESENCE. The reality of the presence of God stands at the center of biblical faith. This presence, however, is always elusive. "Verily, verily, thou art a God that hidest thyself!" The deity of the Hebrew-Christian Scriptures escapes man's grasp and manipulation, but man is aware of the presence of that Deity in such a powerful way that he finds through it a purpose in the universe; he confers upon his own existence a historical meaning; and he attunes his selfhood to an ultimate destiny. . . .

Alone in their cultural milieu, the Hebrews developed a unique theology of presence. They worshiped a God whose disclosure or proximity always had a certain quality of elusiveness. Indeed, for most generations of the biblical age, Israel prayed to a *Deus Absconditus.*—Samuel Terrien

PRESENT IN THE WORD. The voice of the Old Testament prevents us from thinking of the presence of God in the world as being evident and demonstrable. Creation, no less than redemption, is a work of eternal love; but as such it is also no less hidden than the redemption. Only in the Word is it perceivably present to faith through the working of the Holy Spirit. Therefore, preaching is concerned to bear witness to the Word, which, as Guido Gezelle said, "plunged so deep" and is "so sweet"—sweet, because it radiates God's good pleasure (Pss. 145:9, 15f.; 147:7ff.; 148:3ff.).—Kornelis H. Miskotte

Sermon Suggestions

LIVING SMART. TEXT: Prov. 2:1–8. (1) The price of wisdom, verses 1–5. (2) The source of wisdom, verses 6–7a. (3) The rewards of wisdom, verses 7b–8.

THE WAY OF THE WORD. TEXT: James 1:17–27, REB. (1) The Word brings us to birth, verse 18. (2) The Word has power to save, verse 21. (3) The Word requires action as well as hearing, verses 22–25.

Worship Aids

CALL TO WORSHIP. "O sing unto the Lord a new song, for he hath done marvellous things; his right hand, and his holy arm, hath wrought salvation for him" (Ps. 98:1).

INVOCATION. Creator God, alert our senses to your world. Let sight and sound, taste and touch remind us that you have made us and have given us the good earth as our home. May all that is within us and all that surrounds us glorify your name.

OFFERTORY SENTENCE. "But as ye abound in everything, in faith and utterance and knowledge and in all earnestness and in your love to us, see that ye abound in this grace also" (2 Cor. 8:7).

OFFERTORY PRAYER. You, O God, are worthy of our praise, for you are the One who held back no good thing from your children. Give us grace not to hold back any part of our beings as we follow the way of Jesus Christ.—J. Scott Hickman

PRAYER. O God, we confess that we have been slow to hear your voice in the cry of human need and in its silence; too often we have been unmoved by human misery, even our own; our understanding has been self-serving, and we have kept busy, a condition we clearly prefer; we have been cozy with the pharoahs of this world, endlessly patient with their empty promises, and too loathe to work and pray for their destruction; and the strange, bright world of your peace and justice frightens us.

We have not trusted in your promises; we have not disciplined our bodies and spirits to serve you, and we have not eaten and drunk the goodness you provide. Dabbling in many things, we have not willed one thing with all our heart; risking little, we have succeeded; and at the end of

the day, things ranged against you loom too large and you too small.

Have mercy upon us, O God, and turn our hearts from evil and resignation and from that good which is less than you purpose; drive away our demons and to our guardian angels open our eyes; cause us to see what you see and to hear what you hear; and, like Moses, to receive your commission for your people in bondage by name and by fire.—Peter Fribley

LECTIONARY MESSAGE

Topic: A Life Changed
TEXT: Mark 7:31–37

The miracle was true to form. Jesus was traveling about the countryside. The crowds, knowing of his reputation as a miracle worker, brought to him a man plagued with deafness and an impediment of speech. Laying on of his hands was understood as the vehicle through which the healing would occur. After touching his ears and tongue, Jesus commanded that the man's ears "be opened." The healing was immediate. The people were ordered not to tell what they had seen, but "the more he charged them, the more zealously they proclaimed it." The episode ends with the people's astonishment and admiring words about Jesus.

I. One way of reading this account is to spiritualize it at all aspects. The man can represent a brazen humanity that cannot, or will not, listen to God. It is indeed true that spiritual deafness lies at the heart of the world's ills. Unable to discern the "still small voice of God," myriad voices from a secular world capture our hearing. Insensitivity to the ways of God naturally gives way to a brutal disregard for the rest of humanity. Because we can't hear God, our ears are closed to the cries of others around us. A healing of our hearing that would result in greater understanding, compassion, and love is truly a needed miracle in our day. In addition to the miracle of healing there is the miracle of speaking. As hearing and speaking are related psychically, so they are related physically, so they are related spiritually. How noble are the simple words, "his tongue was released, and he spoke plainly." Is there a greater need in the church today than for a clear proclamation of God's Word? At every turn in twentieth-century life there has remained the need for the church to speak with prophetic assurance. This healing episode may well be an example of the kind of spiritual reformation that new life in Christ can offer to the faithful.

II. Yet this narrative speaks at an even deeper lever. A healing? Yes! And why? And why this man? Indeed, why did Jesus heal anyone? Obviously not all the sick, lame, deaf, and dumb received this gift of grace. And even though some were healed of their particular physical malady, the day would come when they, too, would face the last and greatest physical enemy, death, and would be defeated by it. Why was this man, and others like him in subsequent episodes, made the recipients of such kindness? It may be that in healing there is an example of the kind of life that can be anticipated when the fullness of God's kingdom comes on earth. In the eternal realm the physical maladies that so plague us now will be entirely removed. In that glad day, God's people will be able to hear perfectly. They will be sensitive to God and to all his people. In that day, God's people will speak plainly. Our words will echo eternal truth. The healing may then be a glimpse into the future, a dramatic display of God's compassion and affection. It can say to us, "Here is what God will do for everyone. Here is our hope for a better day. Life in the fullest sense is lived out only in God's way. You will want to be a part of it."

Human life can be changed when it is touched by the life of Christ. When Jesus is received to be one's Lord and Savior, a transformation is in the making.—Lee R. McGlone

SUNDAY: SEPTEMBER FIFTEENTH

SERVICE OF WORSHIP

Sermon: A Call to Prayer

TEXT: James 5:16

The verse that is our text for today is not simply a beautiful verse of Scripture. Instead, it is a timeless testimony to the power of prayer that has been proved throughout the ages. King James translates the verse like this: "The effectual fervent prayer of a righteous man availeth much."

In this verse there are two words that imply power. One is the Greek word from which our word *energy* comes. The other is a Greek word that means "strength." What the verse means is that there is a dynamic, energetic force that is set loose through the prayer of God's people.

Because I want us to realize anew the great power that is available through prayer, I stand before you to call you again to the ministry of prayer.

I. I want us this morning to recommit ourselves as a church and as individuals to prayer, because prayer is a power that marks us as children of God.

(a) Remember the experience of Daniel. Daniel was highly esteemed by Darius, king of praise. Jealousy ran rampant among the older rulers of Persia, so they devised a plan to discredit Daniel. They persuaded Darius to sign a decree that stated that any person who gave allegiance to any God or man beside Darius would be thrown into the lion's den. Listen to what the Bible says: "Now when Daniel knew that the document was signed, he entered his house: . . . and he continued kneeling on his knees three times a day, praying and giving thanks before his God, as he had been doing previously" (Dan. 6:10).

(b) Daniel's prayer was the activity that marked him as a child of God. So it has been in every generation. God's people have always been praying people. Noah prayed for protection. Abraham prayed for direction. Jocob prayed for a blessing. Moses prayed for deliverance. Joshua prayed for victory. John the Baptist prayed for a responsive people. God's people have always been a praying people.

(c) In today's world when the prevalent mood is "I'll do it my way" and when the preeminent concern is for self-actualization, when you and I get down on our knees and say to the world, "We are determined to do it God's way," when we give ourselves to prayer, then we will be marking ourselves as children of God.

II. I want us this morning to recommit ourselves as a church and as individuals to prayer, because prayer is a power that matures us as believers.

(a) Remember the experience of Paul. Have you ever wondered why Paul was so strong in his faith? Why he had such keen spiritual insights? The secret of Paul's spiritual power is found in Galatians 1 where he explains his conversion experience. He says, beginning in verse 15, "But when he who had set me apart was pleased to reveal his Son in me, that I might preach him among the Gentiles, I did not immediately consult with flesh and blood, nor did I go up to Jerusalem to those who were apostles before me, but I went away to Arabia."

(b) Paul begins the next chapter with this statement: "Then after three years."

Those three years in the Arabian desert alone with God are the key to Paul's powerful Christian life, for in those three years Paul developed a habit of prayer that was to go with him through all the years of his ministry.

That is always the ultimate outcome of prayer, not to get something from God but to grow us into the kind of Christian God can use. This is why Jesus told his disciples in Luke 18:1 that "they should always pray and not give up" (NIV). The only way we can develop a faith strong enough to enable us to persevere in our service for God is through the habit of daily prayer.

III. I want us this morning to recommit ourselves as a church and as individuals to prayer, because prayer is the power that maximizes our fellowship with our heavenly Father.

Remember the experience of Abraham.

(a) In the Old Testament, the principal term for worship is *shachah,* which means "to bow down" or "to prostrate oneself." It conveys the idea of reverence and adoration.

In the New Testament, the principal term for worship is *proskuneo,* which means "to kiss the hand toward one" or "to prostrate oneself." Again the idea is of reverence and adoration.

(b) To worship God is to express our adoration and love for him, to seek constantly to encounter him in a new and fresh way, to spend time with him. That was the key to Abraham's life. He was a giant for God because he was God's friend. And as God's friend, he lived in ultimate fellowship with God, because of his life of prayer.

(c) So it will be for us. As James put in in his Epistle, "Draw near to God, and he will draw near to you" (4:8). That is the greatest word in the Bible about prayer—that through prayer we are able to draw near to God and experience a rich fellowship with him.

IV. I want us this morning to recommit ourselves as a church and as individuals to prayer because prayer is a power that mobilizes God's people.

(a) Remember the experience of the early church. This little band of disciples with nothing going for them, humanly speaking, went out into the city of Jerusalem, then into the surrounding countryside of Palestine, then out into the Roman world, and finally to Rome itself and brought men to their knees in allegiance to Christ. How did it happen? The answer is found in Acts 1:14 where the Bible says, "These all with one mind were continually devoting themselves to prayer."

(b) Trace Christian history and you will find the same key. Whenever there has been a great spiritual awakening, whenever there has been a mighty movement of the people of God, that awakening and that movement can be traced back to Christians on their knees before God in prayer.

(c) As we spend time with God daily in prayer, as we see his face and feel his hand clasp our own—then we can go from his presence into the world where we are called to do battle in his name, "strong in the Lord of hosts and in his mighty power." We can face life with this proclamation on our lips, "I can do all things through Christ who strengthens me" because we have stood in the presence of our great Leader and have looked deeply into his eyes.

V. There is one more thing that must be said about prayer. I want us this morning to recommit ourselves as a church and as individuals to prayer because prayer is a power that magnifies the Lord our God.

(a) Remember the experience of Elijah on Mount Carmel. Elijah confronted the prophets of Baal and Asherah that day on Mount Carmel in a spiritual battle par excellence. The biblical writer tells us, "And when all the people saw it, they fell on their faces; and they said, 'The Lord, he is God; the Lord, he is God!' " (v. 39).

(b) That is the ultimate end of prayer. When we as a church commit ourselves to the ministry of prayer and are marked as God's children and are matured as believers and maximize our fellowship with God and are mobilized as witnesses, then the people around us will recognize who we are and will realize whose we are, and they will cry out as did the people in Elijah's day, "The Lord, he is God. The Lord, he is God."

(c) That's why James said, "The prayer of a righteous man is powerful and effective" (James 5:16, NIV)—because there is no power on earth like the power released through the prayer of God's people.—Brian Harbour

Illustrations

GOD AWAITS OUR PRAYERS. God is our Father—that means precisely that He hears. He stands in a reciprocal relationship with us; there is communication between us and Him. God awaits our prayer, and because He longs to extend His Kingdom not only over men but through men and with men, God accomplishes some things only when they are asked for; God earnestly awaits our prayer. We dare believe that our prayers make possible for us some action of God not otherwise possible. To believe this, and actually to pray in such trust, is surely the most daring thing a man can do.—Emil Brunner

OPEN CHANNELS. What happens in intercessory prayer cannot be fully explained and scientifically demonstrated. Its validity is, and probably always will be, a matter of faith and experience rather than proof. However, if one accepts the basic assumption that God is real and that there are spiritual forces in the universe that transcend though they do not violate natural law, the way is open to its possibility.

This does not mean that God will override the will of the person who is prayed for. In this, as in every other relation between God and man, God respects the freedom he has given us. The person for whom we pray may refuse to be helped by God or man, and we may need to try to win him to a more receptive mood. Or perhaps the change may need to take place within ourselves, lest our intercession unconsciously take the form of an attempt to dominate the will of another by our desires. In any case, if the spirit of the person prayed for is open to God, so are the channels of God's power.—Georgia Harkness

Sermon Suggestions

IS IT WORTH IT? TEXT: Prov. 22:1–2, 8–9. (1) Greed and the injustices that feed it come to calamity. (2) The lordship of God recognized in kindly concern for others is its own reward and yet earns a good name.

SEARCHING QUESTIONS FOR PRIVILEGED CHRISTIANS. TEXT: James 2:1–5, 8–10, 14–17, REB. (1) Are you impartial in your treatment of fellow Christians? (2) Are you breaking the "sovereign law laid down in Scripture"? (3) Do your actions match your professed faith?

Worship Aids

CALL TO WORSHIP. "Make a joyful noise unto the Lord, all the earth: Break forth and sing for joy, yea, sing praises" (Ps. 98:4).

INVOCATION. Eternal God, give light to minds caught in the dark and peace to hearts in need of rest. Strengthen pilgrims with tasks more difficult than they have ever known before. Empower the meek with the strength of lions, as together we seek thy face and pray.—E. Lee Phillips

OFFERTORY SENTENCE. "In all things I gave you an example, that so laboring ye ought to help the weak and to remember the words of the Lord Jesus that he himself said, It is more blessed to give than to receive" (Act 20:35).

OFFERTORY PRAYER. Your love in Christ, your mercy in forgiveness, your care in providential guidance—these and countless other gifts you have given. We offer only ourselves—represented by these expressions of our devotion.

PRAYER. O God, who in all ages calls men and women, youth, boys and girls to serve you through the life of your church, we thank you for these moments of worship through which your call is renewed. May we not miss it in the hymns sung, the prayer made, the Word read and spoken, the fellowship felt.

Your call has become incarnated in one Jesus, as he simply says, "Follow me." Why have we let so many things get in the way of our obedience to this simple command? We have done everything but follow him! We have formulated rigid creeds that have divided our ranks; we have written "high-sounding" liturgies that have become ends in themselves; we have built expensive buildings that have become fortresses in which we hide. How often we wait for special days and other places to live out the gospel, when you are calling us in the here and now of our every day.

Grant to us, O Father, the faith and courage to accept more fully the challenge of Christ's "follow me" in the opportunities of this new week. May we love even as he loved—to the uttermost. May we seek to comprehend the height, the breadth, the depth, the length of your great love for all of our relationships. For the intimate life of our families, grant love that listens to the other with insight and understanding that we may be your instrument in calling the other out to his or her unique potential. As your church, may we affirm the power of your love to bring reconciliation wherever there is estrangement. May

we know your peace that we may give ourselves to bring peace to the world. Where physical infirmities cannot be removed because of age or other disability, grant that strength of mind and of spirit that celebrates your wholeness even in the face of them. May those of us who find the loneliness of our bereavement most difficult experience more deeply the companionship of thy eternal Spirit. Bless the president of these United States and the leaders of all nations and of the United Nations, that they may have that disposition of mind to seek your will that all peoples may know life—not death.—John M. Thompson

LECTIONARY MESSAGE

Topic: Silence and Sound
TEXT: Mark 8:27–38
"And he charged them that they should tell no one about him." That's strange talk coming at the high point of Jesus' ministry. This charge to silence came immediately after the confession of Jesus as the Messiah. It is as if Jesus had said, "You be quiet about this."

A short time later, as the story goes, Jesus began to speak of suffering, rejection, death, and resurrection. He was speaking so clearly and so forcefully that Simon Peter, who had confessed him as Messiah, rebuked him. It is as if Peter had said, "You be quiet about this."

I. There are times when a disciple should be silent. Ask any teacher. When the student does not understand the lesson, he ought to be silent. Peter thought only in terms of the glory of the messiahship. Jesus knew better. When the student's word would do more harm than good, he ought to be silent. Imagine the trouble Peter could have stirred up: "Here's the Messiah."

When his own selfish ambition shows clearly, the student ought to be silent. When the teacher's message is drowned out by the student's own life, he ought to be silent. We have a way of saying, "What you do speaks so loudly I cannot hear what you say." Of course, there is a remedy for each of these problems. Until the remedy effects healing and understanding, the disciple should be silent.

II. There are times when the Lord should be heard. Jesus' interpretation of his messiahship was quite different from that of Peter. He saw the outcome of faithfulness. He knew what he must do. It was only fair that he should prepare his students for the worst. He knows more about the will and the presence of God. He had experienced both. Hear him when he speaks of rejection and suffering and death and resurrection.

He understands the nature of discipleship. He's the Lord. He's the master teacher. He avoided the popular position. His students may not yet be popular. He did not try to make discipleship easy. We do prospective disciples an injustice if we try to make it easy. He did not promise comfort and safety. There are perils in discipleship. Hear him!

III. There are times when a disciple should sound forth. It is yet true. When he sees the cross clearly, he has something to say. The message is one. Sound it forth: (1) He is the Christ; (2) he was crucified and raised from the dead; (3) the cross is for every disciple.

When a disciple can distinguish between the glory and the gory, he should sound forth. Little is said about the gory nature of the cross in the New Testament. But then little is said about the purely "honor" aspects of Christian service. The glory of Christian leadership is a modern concept. Much needs to be said about the response of Christian discipleship.

Many will be challenged with specific opportunities. Many will offer themselves for difficult tasks. All of us need to sound forth: Jesus Messiah is Lord . . . because we understand the nature of his messiahship and the nature of the cross . . . on this side of the Resurrection.

Break the silence of misunderstanding. Sound forth . . . "but if you mouth it as many of our players do I had as lief the town-crier spoke the lines!"—J. Estill Jones

SUNDAY: SEPTEMBER TWENTY-SECOND

SERVICE OF WORSHIP

Sermon: Zacchaeus: The Man Who Found Himself up a Tree

TEXT: Luke 19:1–10

If Zacchaeus would give a testimony of his conversion experience, it would be somewhat strange, yet perhaps not without being similar to most stories of salvation. His testimony was like two sides of the same coin.

I. *The sinner seeking God.* The heart longs after God, whether we realize it or not. When Christ came through Jericho, Zacchaeus "sought to see who Jesus was" (v. 3a). The curious little man was anxious to see Jesus, yet several obstacles stood in his way.

One barrier was the crowd, as they pressed in upon him (v. 3b). The crowd stood between him and Jesus.

Zacchaeus endangered himself by going among the large crowd. Many people nudged and hit the tiny fellow. He could have been trampled to death.

Besides, the people called Zacchaeus a sinner, and that he was. Yet, they never offered him forgiveness. As Grady Nutt, the Christian humorist, commented, "The critics of sinners are never the redeemers of sinners."

A second obstacle to seeking God was his physical limitation of small stature (v. 3c). As hard as he shoved for position, Zacchaeus was too short to see Jesus over the crowd, and the Jews would not move over for such a hated enemy. His shortcoming in height could have caused Zacchaeus to give up, but it didn't.

A fellow minister was preaching behind a lectern that was shaped like a cross. Because he was below average in height, the congregation could barely see him behind the lectern. He said with a touch of humor, "I was told by an elderly pastor once that a preacher ought to hide himself behind the cross, so that's what I'm doing today." His small size did not prevent him from preaching a fine sermon.

A third obstacle in seeking God was Zacchaeus's hated position in society. He was the superintendent of tax collectors in Jericho for the hated Roman government. At one time, Zacchaeus was one of the Jews. Somewhere along the way he betrayed his own people to accept this despicable office.

A tax collector paid for his own office. Zacchaeus had bid to earn his position. He knew the complicated Roman tax law, and the average Jew did not. A tax collector had enormous power, since he could stop passersby, unpack their baggage, and assess whatever amount he wanted. After paying the Romans the legal amount required, he kept the amount he had overassessed. Then, too, if they did not have the money available, he gave them a loan at an inflated interest rate. Dishonest business practices had made him a rich man. No wonder Zacchaeus had a hard time finding God.

II. *God seeking the sinner.* Jesus said, "For the Son of man is come to seek and to save that which was lost." The imagery of a shepherd seeking his lost sheep is used here. The biblical view of "lost" is to get off the track, not to know where you are going. God wants to put the lost person on the right road leading to salvation. Let's look at the ways God seeks after lost people.

(a) First of all, God is no respecter of persons. Forgetting the damage to his popularity, Jesus stepped aside from the shouts of acclamation to speak to Zacchaeus, the despised one. Of all the well-to-do's in the crowd, Jesus chose a publican with whom to dine.

Jesus went against the prejudice of the crowd when he proclaimed, "This day has salvation come to this house, forasmuch as he is also a son of Abraham." Nobody is so off the beaten track that Christ cannot put him or her back on the right road. Christ seeks to save every lost person, irregardless of background or social status.

(b) Furthermore, as God seeks the lost, the spiritual world can overcome physical obstacles in anyone's life. Now Zacchaeus

was not one to go around climbing trees at his age, but curiosity overcame his fear.

Jesus walked straightway to the sycamore tree and looked Zacchaeus directly in the eyes and called the little man's name, commanding him to come down. Zacchaeus nearly fell out of the tree, he was sliding down so fast. No amount of money he ever swindled made him feel this good. His whole outlook on life changed.

Zacchaeus had found God, and God had found him. No greater evidence of his repentance could be given than vowing to give half his money to the poor and to restore fourfold everything he had stolen. Walter Rauschenbush said, "Here a camel passed through a needle's eye."

III. *The aftereffects of seeking God.* There is a story about Zacchaeus after his conversion in the tree. Every day Zacchaeus would begin his day by taking a walk while carrying a spade and a water jar. His wife became curious and followed one day. She watched him go to that old sycamore tree. Scraping away the dirt, he poured water over its roots and stroked its trunk. Then he said, "I found him here. Here is where I found him."

If it takes climbing a tree to find Jesus, so be it. Now please pardon me, for I think I will go and water that old sycamore tree near my house.—Ron Blankenship

Illustrations

EMPTY LIFE. Zacchaeus had a great emptiness in his life. He could hardly enjoy his money, living every day under the frowns and disapproving eyes of his fellow citizens. What could a million dollars or ten cents mean to him if he had to lie awake at night worrying about how he got it? Lush formal gardens, sparkling fountains, and marbled walls could scarcely beguile his dreams of children crying from hunger.

Every sacred feast, every family gathering reminded Zacchaeus of his great spiritual distance from his childhood neighbors, his old friends, and his own relatives. Yet he may have made a great pretense of indifference. People often do. What they cannot enjoy, they scorn. What they cannot have in themselves, they laugh at in others. What their money cannot buy, they say they do not want anyway. But rare moments of insight dawn even in the most callous. The sound of carefree laughter, the haunting refrain of a song heard in childhood, the sight of an unexpected tragedy—any one of these was enough to shatter the walls of Zacchaeus's pride and send a chill of despair to his heart.—James W. Cox

KNOWING JESUS CHRIST. I must start by walking this road of natural, human togetherness with him. I can do that with the excitement of an experimenter, realizing that the road I dare to travel in association with Jesus may be the road that leads me into life. It may be that I will experience the reality of the promise, "him who comes to me I will not cast out." It may be that Christ holds me more than I hold him. Everything that we know about Christ or experience with him is built up from below in this way. It begins with the most human level. If we try to gulp down dogmas prematurely, we may choke on them. The God who became man at Christmas and who has come to us on the front lines wants us to receive him as a man. He wants us to say to him, "Good evening. Who are you? May I walk along a little way with you? I don't know you, but something about you draws me."—Helmut Thielicke

CURIOSITY AND SIMPLICITY. There was a soft spot still left in Zacchaeus's heart, and that soft spot was this: Zacchaeus was as eager as any schoolboy in all Jericho to see Jesus who he was. And like any schoolboy, he ran before and climbed up into a sycamore tree to see Jesus, for he was to pass that way. And simple things like that, childlike and schoolboylike things like that, always touched our Lord's heart. Of such is the kingdom of heaven, he was wont to say when he saw simplicity like that and self-forgetfulness and naturalness and impulsiveness or anything else that was truly childlike. We would not have done what Zacchaeus did. We are too stiff. We are too formal. We have too much starch in our souls. Our souls are made of starch, just as Bishop Andrewes's soul was made of sin. But starch is more deadly than sin. Your soul may be saved from sin but scarcely from starch. "Curiosity and simplicity," says Calvin, "are a sort of preparation for faith."—Alexander Whyte

Sermon Suggestions

WISDOM? TEXT: Job 28:20–28. (1) Wisdom does not belong to this earth and earth's creatures, verses 20–22. (2) Wisdom properly belongs to God alone, verses 23–27. (3) Yet, somehow it is a mark of wisdom in us when we have proper regard for the Lord and "depart from evil," verse 28.

WHEN WISDOM IS REAL. TEXT: James 3:13–18, REB. (1) When it comes from God and is pure. (2) When it is peace-loving. (3) When it is considerate. (4) When it is open-minded. (5) When it is impartial. (6) When it is sincere. (7) When it is compassionate and does good to others.

Worship Aids

CALL TO WORSHIP. "O give thanks unto the Lord, call upon his name; make known among the peoples his doings" (Ps. 105:1).

INVOCATION. Lord, help us this day so to capture a vision of the holy that everything else we do hereafter will be done differently because we have met our maker and cannot live as before.—E. Lee Phillips

OFFERTORY SENTENCE. "The children of Israel brought a freewill offering unto the Lord, every man and woman, whose heart made them willing to bring for all the work which the Lord had commanded to be made by Moses" (Exod. 35:29).

OFFERTORY PRAYER. We cannot match your gifts, Father. We can but respond in love and gratitude with these of our own. Receive them, we pray, and make them clear expressions of our devotion.

PRAYER. Heavenly Father, Creator of heaven and earth, whom all of us claim as Parent through Jesus Christ your Son;

Source of all spiritual gifts; providential guide on whose leadership we depend; we praise you for your many-colored ministries to us. We acknowledge you as our God.

We confess our sins to you: not only human weaknesses but acts of rebelliousness; not only neglect of others, but attitudes of cruelty; not only pride, but all of the sin that grows from it. . . . We ask your forgiveness for Jesus' sake.

We love you because you first loved us. We love one another because you taught us to love. We pray for one another. Some are grieving over the death of a loved one . . . send your comforting Spirit we pray. Some are anxious because of sickness among family and friends . . . grant your healing Spirit. Some are confused and worried about your will . . . share with us your wisdom that we may know your will. You know our needs better than we, and so we commit ourselves to your care.

For world peace we pray and for national peace we pray and for family peace we pray. Grant us the insight and love to be peacemakers, we pray in the name of Jesus.—J. Estill Jones

LECTIONARY MESSAGE

Topic: Life in the Kingdom
TEXT: Mark 9:20–37

I. Confusion once again sets the scene for another of the Lord's teaching moments about the kingdom. The disciples still did not understand, though Jesus had told them already, at Peter's confession, of his coming suffering and death. Their confusion is understandable. Hearing Jesus' words about being delivered into the hands of sinful men and being killed was foreign to their conception of the kingdom. Their reluctance to believe in a crucified God and the way of suffering and humility that leads to redemption is understandable, especially since it is the same reluctance we carry about with us today. The cross and all that it symbolizes, while revered in the mind of many as a holy symbol, has never been fully accepted in the church as a way of life for us. We are much more at ease with the gospel as a model for successful living. The cross may well adorn our architecture, but desire for upward mobility has claimed our hearts. The disciples were confused at his relatively clear saying. It was more than they could bear.

II. The story continues to unfold. Upon arriving at their destination in Capernaum, Jesus took issue with the topic of their conversation along the way. When confronted, the disciples remained silent, for they knew well what had been said. Even among the closest followers of Jesus a brazen competition had surfaced. "Who among us is greatest?" they had asked. The quest for greatness, in the first century or the twentieth, is a clear indication of one's misunderstanding about the Lord's intentions for us. A place of preeminence, a cherished position of authority, an upward ascent toward the top, the ability to control the lives of others— all these are common thoughts of our humanity. Yet they are not the models of godly living that Jesus taught and practiced. The fact that the disciples remained silent at the interrogation of Jesus implies that they already knew their competition would not meet with his approval. Their personal ambitions were not appropriate for kingdom behavior.

III. Like a loving parent who needs to make clear a message to the children, Jesus drew the disciples to his side, sat down with them, and clarified the teaching: "If anyone would be first, he must be last of all and servant of all." Here is the central word of Jesus' teaching about life in the kingdom of God. It turns the thought processes of every generation upside down. The ordinary barometers of greatness are cast aside as obsolete. Pomp and circumstance, power, glory, and adulation are irrelevant. True greatness would now be measured by one's willingness to pour out his or her life for others— to be a servant of all. And is that not what the cross of Christ is all about? The disciples did not understand and were not comfortable with the prediction of his passion, and neither are we. Yet it is the cross that represents the values of life we are to cherish most. Jesus poured out his own life for others. He became servant of all.

Because we are his followers we are called to follow his example.

IV. In the end, and to make the matter even more plain, Jesus brought before the disciples a little child. With the child, Jesus dramatized what he meant by the teaching on greatness. "See the child," Jesus said. "If you can willingly give yourself to this little one, this one who has nothing to offer you in return, and do it in my name, you also give yourself to me and my Father who sent me." In giving ourselves to someone who has no obvious benefit for us personally, we are practicing life in the kingdom.—Lee R. McGlone

SUNDAY: SEPTEMBER TWENTY-NINTH

SERVICE OF WORSHIP

Sermon: Dives and Lazarus

TEXT: Luke 16:19–31

I. Sophisticated sleaze—that is the label Donald Hanrahan, Pulitzer Prize–winning music critic of the *New York Times*, applies to an age when fancy department stores advertise at $190 a town jacket, careful copy of those worn by the poor, "street couture" featuring tattered, wrinkled, and apparently dirty clothes.

Sophisticated smugness—that could be the label with which a biblical scholar like Eugene Laverdier would head a commentary on the wrathful warning from Amos and the clear parable of Jesus.

II. Either label alerts us that today's proclamations are not meant to comfort, such as would be the case at a memorial mass, nor to heal, as in a liturgy emphasizing the sacrament for the sick. Amos's sadness that these ensconced sprawlers cared nothing about the destruction of Israel and Jesus' tragic account of Dives's not noticing Lazarus's hunger call for a liturgy that urges us to the Sacrament of Penance, to examination, to admission, to repentance. For, concentrating on our own pleasure, our own friends, our own advancement, our own problems, we may have cared nothing about our roommate who is so homesick he may not return some Sunday evening; our classmate who is so discouraged by language, text, technology she may not last until midterm; our family who wonders when their college student will begin again to keep in touch.

These local, personal instances are minor compared to the national and global failures of revelers who simply do not let themselves know the sufferings of the uninvited. Jewish prophets like Amos twenty-eight hundred years ago tried to shake hearers from their indifference, but the assembly did not listen. Eight hundred years ago, Christians like Bernard of Clairvaux warned the people of God, "Your stones you dress with gold; your children you abandon all nude." Those heedless hedonists soon underwent the decline of their civilization and the scourge of plague.

Buddhist lore includes the question of Lord Buddha, "Who will feed the hungry?" A banker reacts that his wealth is not sufficient. A commissioned general insists he would give his life for his country but needs more food for his own family than the PX provides. An estate holder rejoins that he needs all the income from his crops to pay the government taxes. Then a beggar interjects, "I'll feed the hungry." To the incredulous chorus of "How?" she responds, "from your resources and supplies: financial houses, military might, utopia of agribusiness."

Twentieth-century historians are still attempting to deal with the phenomenon that so few of the Turkish and German people, so few humanitarian organizations, so few national and religious leaders noticed the slaughter of millions of the Armenian people after World War I, the attempted genocide of the Jewish race in the holocaust of World War II.

III. In this decade American colleges, like those of the 1960s, do respond to the message of Amos, of Jesus, of Buddha in that we are making sure financiers, investors, politicians, producers, and consumers pay attention to the evils of racism, especially in South Africa. Yet one of our professors recalls that in the sixties her generation of Northerners responded more vigorously to the need for human rights in the South than to discrimination in their own neighborhoods of study, play, and work. Now she is "fascinated" by our preoccupation with injustice in the Third World, what "they" are imposing or what "they" are suffering there. In the face of our preoccupation with personal success she asks, "What are we noticing in our locale, our own suburbia, our inner cities?"

Over twenty years ago, John Galbraith, whose writings we study in courses of economics, contemporary history, and college composition, warned that America was becoming the affluent society, one oblivious of people still on the poverty level. This Harvard scholar and American ambassador is still concerned at America's lack of concern for the hidden poor. The *New York Times*, dean of the secular not religious press, reiterates the human condition that Amos, Jesus, Buddha, Galbraith deplore, "The affluent do what they can to avoid contact with the desperate and downwardly mobile." For, if we open ourselves to come closer to sufferers, it is harder to refuse them help.

Tithing, a contribution of a percentage of one's income to the needs of our local religious congregation, is widely accepted in Jewish, Protestant, and an increasing number of Roman Catholic assemblies. By their request for voluntary donations each weekend, our friends in justice and peace programs do help us avoid the sin of not noticing the needs of others. The collection does remind us of the needs of those for whom tattered, worn, unpressed clothing and slimming diets are not sophisticated sleaze but depressing deprivation.

Tithing one's income is not asked of students. What we can do is challenge, first ourselves, then one another to tithe our time—one hour a week? one day a month? two of our vacation weeks?—also, that we notice, use our energy, our creativity to comfort, to heal the Joseph, the Lazarus, the poor, the abused, the oppressed of Brockton, of our hometown, of Appalachia, of the Third World. We can tithe our study time so as to take an hour, a day to be informed, become analytical, be involved in education for justice. As symbolized in today's welcome to liturgy, Jesus Christ invites all of us to shed our sleaze and smugness so as to be included in the banquet of lasting love and sharing.

IV. As our representatives move forward with gifts at the offertory, let us individually offer our contrition for not noticing the needs of others. At communion let us accept the forgiveness and encouragement of Jesus Christ as we receive the Eucharist through bread and cup.—Grace Donovan, S.U.S.C.

Illustrations

WORLD HUNGER.   Concern for world hunger, a cause whose time has come, is also addressed by the parable. Lazarus was hungering to the point of desperation. The rich man was feasting to the point of dissipation. The mental picture of a glutton of rotund proportions, a merchant with a Santa Claus figure emerges. Even so, there are enclaves of poverty in our midst, continents of hunger around us. Helmut Gollwitzer opens his volatile volume, a book that bears the provocative title *The Rich Christians and Poor Lazarus*, with a question whose answer stings:

Who are we? Answer: We are the rich man. That is, uncontestably, the most exact description of us. "We belong to that third of humanity which is concerned with slimming cures, while the other two-thirds are concerned with hunger." And this third consists for the most part of baptized Christians, the other two-thirds of unbaptized persons.—Peter Rhea Jones

SELLING OUT.   Everything that makes our life spacious and fascinating—our money, our vitality, our happy temperament, the fact that we are loved—can come between us and God. All this we can enjoy selfishly. Even the friends we make and the help we give can be enjoyed selfishly. Even the greatest of all gifts, "goods, fame, child, and wife," can be the price for which we sell our eternal life. And this process of selling out can begin quite simply and very hiddenly with our ignoring of the Lazarus at our door.—Helmut Thielicke

Sermon Suggestions

OWNING UP. TEXT: Job 42:1–6. (1) A tardy acknowledgment, verses 1–2. (2) An honest confession, verses 3–5. (3) A fitting surrender, verse 6.

TWO VIEWS OF LIFE. TEXT: James 4:13–17; 5:7–11. (1) The short view, 4:13–17. (2) The long view, 5:7–11.

Worship Aids

CALL TO WORSHIP. "Bless the Lord, O my soul; and all that is within me, bless his holy name" (Ps. 103:1).

INVOCATION. O Lord, our Lord, give us to know again today, the reality of thy near presence in this hour of worship. Let us seek thee, desire thee, think of thee, and be obedient to thy revelations, for our good and thy glory.—E. Lee Phillips

OFFERTORY SENTENCE. "And if I bestow all my goods to feed the poor, and if I give my body to be burned, but have not love, it profiteth me nothing" (1 Cor. 13:3).

OFFERTORY PRAYER. With music in our souls and love in our hearts we bring these gifts to you. Grant that this process of receiving and giving may draw us close to you.

PRAYER. Lord and Father of us all, we praise you and we honor you. We love you and we thank you.

You have not dealt with us as we deserve. You have been gracious and generous with your gifts: life and light, friends and family, church and challenge.

You have been loving and merciful with your forgiveness, and we confess our sins to you once more: our rebellious pride and independence, our selfish neglect or manipulation of others, our waste of time

and energy. We ask your forgiveness for Jesus' sake.

We pray for one another. For the recently bereft, we pray your comfort. For the ill, both physically and emotionally, we ask your healing. For those of us who are anxious and troubled, at loose ends or homesick, we seek your calming presence.

Now hear us Lord, as we pray, and accept the worship we offer through Jesus Christ our Savior.—J. Estill Jones

LECTIONARY MESSAGE

Topic: Accentuate the Positive
TEXT: Mark 9:38–50

In 1893, Henry Drummond, the distinguished Scottish scientist and evangelical Christian, delivered the Lowell lectures in Boston under the title "The Ascent of Man." Dwight L. Moody invited him to include the Northfield Conference in his itinerary, and Drummond agreed to come. However, a group of antievolutionists, aware of Drummond's views as expressed in his Lowell lectures, made representations to Moody to cancel Drummond's appearance on the Northfield program. Moody heard them out and then asked for a day to reflect upon their protest. When they returned for his decision, Moody told them he had laid the whole issue before the Lord and the Lord showed him that Drummond was a better man than Moody himself and, therefore, he must be allowed to speak.

Our Scripture text from Mark, chapter 9, has been identified by biblical scholars as a discrete collection of Jesus' sayings in a somewhat fragmentary pattern. Upon careful reading, however, one discovers a common thread that gives a measure of coherence to the three seemingly unconnected remarks. There are here three negatives that Jesus offsets by implying and emphasizing vigorous positives.

I. *The problem exposed (vv. 38–41).* The disciples saw a man doing in his own way the very things Jesus was carrying out in God's name, and they remonstrated with him because "he was not following us." His works could not possibly be authentic, they thought, because he was not in some sort of "apostolic succession." But the problem here was not this man's ecclesiastical status; it was the disciples' intolerance, a first cousin of a negative attitude that Jesus punctured with a firm rebuke: "He that is not against us is for us." Jesus knew that a negation leaves a matter at a dead end. A positive attitude, on the other hand, sets human helpfulness into motion. Jesus' position, then, was that whosoever does what is akin to his way and ethic has his sanction and blessing. Social services, outreach to the poor and homeless, tearing out of slums, etc.—all these can be reflections today of his Spirit at work and may fulfill his claims for all humankind.

Some will ask, however, why then be Christian? Because only in the Christian community is a good deed more likely to generate other good deeds, and with these the action is multiplied and kept alive. No one can be a Christian in isolation. The contagion of good works initiated by the Spirit and example of Christ has been the key, for example, to the world mission of the church and its evangelical outreach through the centuries. Moreover, the presence of the intention of Christ in any purpose for good provides something extra: the vision in the end of the redemption of all human society. And anyone who contributes even in a small way to that end should not be excluded from the camaraderie of Christ.

II. *The problem engaged (vv. 42-48).* There follows this difficult segment in which Jesus seems to join with the negative. Not so, however, because in every high endeavor one must sometimes take a step backward in order to go forward. Note what he says: "cut it off," "pluck it out." What is this? Sheer hyperbole? Jesus meant that whatever hinders you from living positively must be extracted. Jesus' goal for all of us was and is to "enter into life" (v. 43). Everything that prohibits this end must be cut out in the name of spiritual progress. Development sometimes demands limitation. (Cite here John the Baptist and Jesus in the "wilderness" and Paul in Arabia). The challenge of the vision and the dimensions of the task demand that the called—to use John Milton's phrase—"scorn delights and live laborious days." Moreover, the early followers of Jesus had to endure the loss of friends and the loss of many other personal advantages because they knew, as Paul put it, ". . . I count everything as loss because of the surpassing worth of knowing Christ Jesus my Lord" (Phil. 3:8). The Christian life is not one of ease. It costs. It involves self-surrender. You and I cannot enter this new life in partnership with Christ with all the barnacles of materialism still clinging to us or the constricting attitudes of intolerance and negativism haunting our souls. The writer of the Letter of the Hebrews calls us "to lay aside every weight and the sin which clings so closely" (12:1) in order to be free to grow into Christ-like stature.

III. *The problem resolved (vv. 49, 50).* Jesus' call to the whole world of failing and troubled folk is "Come unto me . . . and I will give you . . ." Give what? A solution to our problem—pride, greed, intolerance, social status, exclusiveness, racism—the whole ball of wax. We must heed his command—cut, pluck out, etc. Life must be cleaned up, but it must not remain empty or inert or neutral. This would be "the kiss of death" to spiritual growth. A stimulus is needed in order to rethink one's direction, reorder one's values, and reshape one's purpose. None of us can do this alone. An auxiliary power is needed. Only a dynamo can make a machine run and work. We have to get something into ourselves.

Jesus said, "Have salt *in* yourselves" (v. 50). What did this metaphor mean? The fisher folk who heard him knew all too well. They knew what salt does. It counteracts impurities, preserves vital substance, and brings out latent flavor. These characteristics of salt spell action. And this action symbolizes the working of the human will. The disciples were being called out from idle, dull, and purposeless living into a future with a cutting spiritual edge. Life would have now a new and vital interest sufficient to the woman of Samaria who was filling the water jar at Jacob's well: "Whoever drinks of the water that I shall give him will never thirst; the water that I shall give him will become in him a spring of water welling up to eternal life" (John 4:14). This is the key to living in the positive lane, accompanied by him who fills our life with everything high and broad and deep.—Donald Macleod

SUNDAY: OCTOBER SIXTH

SERVICE OF WORSHIP

Sermon: Learning to Eat at the Lord's Table

TEXTS: Exod. 16:14–21; Mark 14:22–25

Many of us come to the Lord's table oblivious to the presence of the One with whom we are coming to commune. We are simply not aware of the sacredness of this occasion, and so we sit through it and miss the beauty, mystery, and wonder of the event. This morning I would like for us to think about ways of approaching the Lord's table that may enable us to commune more effectively.

I. The first reminder that I would offer you today is this: Remember that Jesus Christ himself is the host of this table. The Lord's table is not your table nor my table. It is not this church's table. It is the Lord's table. Jesus Christ is the host. He is the one who took bread and broke it. He is the one who took the cup and shared it with his disciples. It was he who blessed the bread and the cup. Today we celebrate the One who is host because he was victor over sin and death. We come to this table at his invitation. He extends his hands to all Christians, all sinners who will trust him, to come and commune with him at his table. "Come unto me all ye who are weak and are heavy laden." "Wherever two or three are gathered together in my name, there I am in the midst of them." Remember Jesus Christ is the host at this table.

II. Remember that we come to this table to receive. We are receivers—receivers of what he has given for us. As we come to this table, we acknowledge that we are sinners saved by grace. We are recipients of God's love, grace, and forgiveness.

(a) "This is my body for you," Jesus said. "For you, Peter. For you, James and Andrew. For all you twelve who are gathered here. It is for you that I lay down my life." But it is also for you and for me. Martin Luther said that authentic religion is always best expressed in personal pronouns. God didn't love us abstractly. In Jesus Christ we have seen his love for us, and each of us is able to receive it now.

(b) The Old Testament lesson today focuses on the manna that was given to the children of Israel in the wilderness. They were told that they could not hoard it. They had to gather it fresh each day. What a powerful lesson for all about our relationship to God. May persons think they can "feed" on God and then "store" up that experience without seeking a fresh experience. They worship God occasionally and then wonder why their life goes stale and flat. They do not understand why their religion seems worthless and doesn't sustain them during difficult times. Our experience with God must always be fresh. We have to come again and again to his table to be fed. We come again and again to worship, to confess our sins, renew our spirit, and go forth to serve. Having received his forgiveness, love, and grace, his presence is made real in our lives, and then we can live more effectively for him.

III. We gather at this table to express thanksgiving. He blessed and so must we. We bless God this day for what he has done for us through Jesus Christ. We gather at this table as a sign of our thanksgiving to God, who cared enough for each of us that his Son laid down his life that we might have life. One of the biblical words for the Lord's Supper is *Eucharist.* Eucharist means thanksgiving. We come to this table in thanksgiving for what God has done for us. As we take this bread and cup, it is a sign of our gratitude to God for what he has done for us through his love.

IV. But we also come to this table as a

sign of covenant. Jesus said that this cup is the new covenant. That night in the upper room was the end of the old covenant and the beginning of the new covenant.

Jeremiah prophesied that the day would come when the covenant that had been written in stone would be written on the human heart. In that upper room where Jesus took bread and broke it and took a cup and shared it, that was the beginning of the new covenant. At that moment the covenant was written on the human heart as a new community emerged. You and I are a part of that covenant community when we commit our lives to Christ and pledge our loyalty to him. As the new community, we covenant with one another to bear each other's burdens and support each other in times of need. We draw strength from each other and the Lord of the new covenant. Each time we eat at the Lord's table is a sign of the covenant. It is a sign of our covenant with Christ and his covenant with us and our covenant with one another as his people. So, let us come to his table this morning and pause to reflect on how we eat this meal.—William Powell Tuck

Illustrations

MOCKED FOR US.   At the Lord's table, he always reminds you of that hour when he spoke of pouring out his blood and of the breaking of his body. He is reminding you of that hour when he was nothing but a Savior who was mocked and derided. This is your God, to whom you are coming, and you must never forget this: a Savior who is mocked and derided. There he hangs in utter loneliness—and if the solitude of his suffering can be intensified, it is by this mockery. It has come to this, that he is surrounded only by curious spectators. All who are most closely involved in this scene have no compassion at all but are full of mockery and hatred. This is our God, a God at whom people laugh.

And you who have come here to confess your sins and to receive communion, you must see the gospel which is contained in this part of the Passion story. He who hangs here has indeed, of his own accord, exposed himself to the fact that he is on the cross. He has indeed given himself, of his own accord, to this miserable situation. The almighty Christ willed it so that he would be mocked. Part of the work of redemption is taking place here. The evangelists have no desire to spare us at this point. Again and again they underline the fact: He is a Savior at whom people laugh. They emphasize this because it is the gospel.—Helmut Gollwitzer

PRAYER OF FORGIVENESS.   The prayer goes on down the centuries because the followers of Christ, strengthened by his Spirit, have prayed it. Here is proof in the life of an English soldier who wrote a German mother, "As a member of a party of Commandos raiding a village in France, it became my duty to kill your son. . . . I earnestly ask your forgiveness, for I am a Christian. . . . I hope I may, someday after the war is over, talk with you face-to-face." The German mother received the note several months later, and she wrote the English soldier in turn: "I find it in my heart to forgive you, even you who killed my son; for I too am a Christian. . . . If we are living after the war is over, I hope you will come to Germany to visit me, that you may take the place in my home, if only for a time, of my son whom you killed."— James T. Cleland

Sermon Suggestions

THE ARITHMETIC OF MARRIAGE.   TEXT: Gen. 2:18–24. (1) There is one, verses 18–20. (2) There are two, verses 21–22. (3) The two are one, verses 23–24.

THE SUPERIOR CHRIST.   TEXT: Heb. 1:1–4; 2:9–11. (1) He is prophet, and we listen to him, 1:1–3a. (2) He is priest, and he forgives our sins, 1:3b; 2:9–10. (3) He is king, and we bow to him and obey him, 1:3b–4; 2:9. (Cf. *Oxford Annotated Bible.*)

Worship Aids

CALL TO WORSHIP.   "O give thanks unto the Lord; for his is good; for his lovingkindness endureth for ever" (Ps. 107:1).

INVOCATION.   Grant to us, from thine high and holy place, O Lord our God, those quickening influences by which we shall know thee and rise up into communion with thee. Deliver us from the thrall of our senses. Deliver us from the course and current of habits that sweep us away from God and from heaven. Drive away the doubts that cloud our minds, that the light may shine clearly and strongly upon us. Quicken our spiritual apprehension and the joy of love and its humble boldness by which we may draw near to the very Holy of holies and partake of all that thou hast there, being heirs with Christ to the inheritance of eternal glory. These mercies we ask in the name of the Beloved.—Henry Ward Beecher

OFFERTORY SENTENCE.   "And he said unto them, Take heed, and keep yourselves from all covetousness: for a man's life consisteth not in the abundance of the things which he possesseth" (Luke 12:15).

OFFERTORY PRAYER.   Aid us, loving God, as we give ourselves over to your presence in worship. And remind us that our worship is in both our receiving and our giving, for in each you enter our lives in new and powerful ways.—J. Scott Hickman

PRAYER.   Eternal, God, lead us into the blessedness of the mystery of communion with thee. Bow our spirits in deepest reverence before thee, yet uplift us into a sense of kinship. Send the Spirit of thy Son into our hearts, crying "Abba, Father," that all unworthy fear may be banished by the gladness of thy perfect love. Thy love is like the luminous heaven, receiving only to purify the foulest breath of earth. Thy gentleness is like the sun, seeking to cheer and warm the chilled hearts of men. Touch us, O our Father, with a feeling of thy great realities, for though our thought about thee is better than our words, our experience of thee is better than our thought.

Bestow upon us, we beseech thee, the grace for which we severally crave. Troubles overwhelm the heart: lead us to the rock that is higher than we. Doubts assail us. Give us a supreme trust that will not let thee go, until the day break and the shadows flee away. We are unstable, easily moved by external circumstance. Strengthen us that we may play the man and in thy might play the man and in thy might grant us to gain dominion over the world. Our hearts are sad, thinking, as we do, of dear ones, so tenderly loved, but now taken from us, or of living griefs that will not heal. Wipe thou our tears away. O God of hope! save us from despair. Thou bringest the dead out of the living and the living out of the dead. Come and work thy wonders in the hearts of those who grieve and wound us and cause us to drink of bitter tears, that sorrow may flee away and our mouth be filled with laughter and our tongue with singing.

We entreat thee, O Lord, to remember us in our daily work. Let us do it heartily as unto thee and not as unto men. Grant that our tasks may be congenial to us; that we may give ourselves wholly to them. Consecrate all our powers of body and mind to thy service. Give us enthusiasm, a fervent spirit, a cheerful, hopeful temper, so that we may do our work with ease and self-control, not with idle worry or fruitless fear. Let us not think too much of our rights but always of our duties, and when we have done all, then let us say, "We are unprofitable servants." And when thou drawest the curtain of night upon our labor, give us the sweet gift of sleep. All this we ask for Jesus' sake.—Samuel McComb

LECTIONARY MESSAGE

Topic: Jesus' Hard Sayings: Divorce
TEXT: Mark 10:2–16

Marriages may well be made in heaven, but they must be lived out here on earth where fallen humans tend to destroy their relationships. Divorce has been around as long as marriage. In Jesus' day it was a time-honored way of disposing of an unwanted wife. Divorce was so accepted as a regular part of life that it is used as an image to describe the broken relationship between Israel and God (Isa. 50:1; see Jer.

3:8). So Jesus startled his audience and also us with his words that forbid divorce. But for some, his words have served only to compound the pain of a broken relationship.

I. *God's intention for marriage?* Jesus' opponents attempted to ensnare him in some way with a test question on divorce. Jesus ignored the human controversy, however, and raised the question to the level of the unconditional will of God.

The question of the opponents was based on a false premise. They began with Deut. 24:1–4 and assumed, as nearly everyone did, that God endorses divorce. They only thought in terms of the commands concerning the dissolution of a marriage and ignored the fact that God originated and purposed the couple's union. From Jesus' perspective, the law in Deut. 24:1–4 did not make divorce acceptable. He began instead with God's commands at the beginning. What God intends for marriage is not to be found in Deut. 24:1–4 but in Genesis 1–2. God's intention for marriage was that it was to be a lifelong commitment. It was to take precedence over all other relationships, including the relationship to parents. It was designed by God to be indissoluble. Jesus punctuated this with the familiar saying: "What God has joined together let not a man put asunder" (Mark 10:9; Matt. 19:6).

II. *The invasion of the kingdom of God.* Even though it seems to have a biblical warrant because of the legal provisions found in Deut. 24:1–4, Jesus rejected divorce as contrary to the will of God. Since God had joined the couple together, God is the lord of the marriage. Consequently, the husband may not dispose of his wife as if he were the lord of the marriage. With the breaking in of the kingdom of God in Jesus' ministry, one can no longer deal with God on the basis of what Moses may have "permitted" and where the pettifoggers might find loopholes. God's will, revealed by Jesus, invades all areas of life, including what is culturally accepted and legally permitted.

III. *Is remarriage adultery?* Jesus' teaching has been used to compound the woes of those who have experienced a broken marriage. No action a man might take and no court decision can ever truly sunder the marriage relationship in the eyes of God. Therefore, he shocks his hearers by saying that divorce and remarriage is equivalent to adultery. This word has been used to beat divorced persons over the head and causes them to feel stygmatized. But Jesus was not concerned about denouncing those who should ever remarry. He was concerned with making clear the will of God concerning marriage and divorce. His statements about adultery serve only to underline the permanence and sanctity of marriage.

IV. *What about a second chance?* Divorce is clearly a breach of God's will for marriage. It is a sin that springs from a hardness of heart, and the church needs to take a stand against the rising tide of easy divorce in our society. Many enter marriage today without any sense of it being a lifelong commitment. To have and to hold as long as we both shall live has been changed to as long as my spouse meets my needs and I am fulfilled. For Jesus, marriage is not a temporary, romantic alliance that can be terminated whenever one or both wish. On the other hand, the church needs to communicate the grace of God and forgiveness of sin, including divorce. God hates divorce because, like all sin, it destroys. Like an atomic bomb, it leaves deep emotional craters and strikes all kinds of innocent bystanders with the fallout. It is another contribution to chaos in the world.

But God does not hate the divorced person. Therefore, the church must balance on a tightrope by proclaiming the sanctity of marriage while proclaiming God's forgiveness to sinners who violate that sanctity. We must remember that when Jesus spoke these words, he *was not* addressing those who were experiencing the brokenness of a marriage failure. He was dealing with opponents who were trying to trap him. What he might have said to those who had failed in their marriage commitments we can only surmise from what he said to the woman caught in adultery (John 7:53–8:11) and to the Samaritan woman who had five husbands and was now living with a man who was not her husband (John 4:4–29). To them he of- fered forgiveness and love.—David E. Garland

SUNDAY: OCTOBER THIRTEENTH

SERVICE OF WORSHIP

Sermon: The Energy of Love

TEXT: 1 John 4:7–11; 3:16–18

Paul wrote in that famous chapter 13 of 1 Corinthians, "Though I bestow all my goods to feed the poor, and though I give up my body to be burned, and have not charity [love], it profiteth me nothing." Good works without love are empty. But there is another side of the coin: Love without good works is both impotent and unreal.

I. *Love is often confused with pity.* The two are similar—both see a need; both feel concern. But pity, seeing a need, wrings its hands, shakes its head sadly, and feels so bad. Love, however, is characterized by an energetic concern. It rolls up its sleeves to help; it has a strong back; it is muscular as it sees a need and responds to it. Authentic love always moves us to loving action.

Recall that time when Jesus wept over the city of Jerusalem. His lament was, "O Jerusalem, Jerusalem. . . . How often would I have gathered your children together as a hen gathers her brood under her wings, and you would not!" (Matt. 23: 37). And so he wept because he saw the great city on a dead-end street. But now suppose that picture of Jesus weeping were all that we had. Surely we would remark, "What a sensitive soul was this man to see the distress of Jerusalem and to be moved to tears." But, significantly, we have more than this picture of Jesus weeping over Jerusalem. And as our text expresses it, "By this we know love, that he laid down his life for us" (1 John 3:16). Jesus showed his love for Jerusalem in positive action that is symbolized by a cross. That cross gives concretion to his love.

II. *Christian love is plagued with counterfeits.*

(a) There are many counterfeits to this kind of love. There is the counterfeit called "love-talk." Thus, love becomes a doctrine, something we talk about; it becomes an accepted concept, an exalted virtue. How easy it is for people close to a church to talk with words of love.

Our text reminds us of the danger of reducing *agape* to love-talk: "Little children, let us not love in word or speech but in deed and in truth" (1 John 3:18). Mere words of love are counterfeits to genuine love.

(b) A second counterfeit substitute for Christian love is the feeling of love. Often we desire to revel in an emotional sensation of love. It is true that when we sing about God's love, when we in a worship experience find ourselves caught up in an exalted state, when we truly sense the love of God for us, this leaves us with what C. S. Lewis called "a tingling in the gizzard." And this emotion is proper if it is not cultivated for its own sake alone. And yet, surely churches must beware of seeking after the feelings of love apart from genuine acts of love, lest they fall victims to sentimentalizing love.

(c) Talking about love and searching for the feeling of love leads us to a third counterfeit, and that is conceiving love as a beautiful abstraction. We can permit ourselves to talk about love, to use all the right words, and to discover the feeling of love to such a degree that we are lulled into a state of spiritual euphoria; and we can leave the walls of the church and be blind to the needs of people. We see needs, but our eyes go right through them. They are invisible to us. There is a constant danger of divorcing our piety and our worship from muscular, practical goodness.

III. *Christian love is unconditional.*

(a) What then is true Christian *agape?* First, it is the full and unstinting recognition of my neighbor's worth. God's love is unconditional. He did not love me under certain conditions; he did not wait until I merited love. Rather, his love came to me while I was yet a sinner. Yet, how often our love is conditional, as though we had not learned the unconditional love that comes from God.

(b) Our love is chained and riveted to a need for reinforcement from the one toward whom we direct our love. Those persons who respond to my ministry, who attend services, who express appreciation, who give, who serve, who respond to love—those are easy to love. We need to learn something about God's love that accepts all people where they are and as they are.

IV. *Christian love makes unlimited claims.*

(a) Not only is true Christian love unconditional; it makes an unlimited claim upon us. Our text describes God's love shown in the ultimate picture of the cross. "By this we know love, that he laid down his life for us." And then it goes on to say that we, too, are called on to be ready to make the ultimate sacrifice for love: "We ought to lay down our lives for the brethren."

(b) Seldom are we confronted with this call to risk our lives out of love for another. I was moved as I read in *Time* (Dec. 7, 1970) about a woman who had cancer of the colon. Only six intestinal transplants had been made previous to this; all of them had proved fatal. Her sister knew the odds, yet she had also heard on good medical authority that a person can live on one-half of his own small intestine. And so the woman's sister, a mother of three, donated half of her small intestine. At Manhattan Memorial Hospital the transplant was made. The sister was responding to the boundless claims of love.

V. *Christian love responds to need.* The very next verse of the text is an abrupt descent from the sublime tone of verse 16 to very practical matters. Not only must we be willing to lay down our lives for our brother, but in practical ways our love must be responsive to needs. "But if any one has the world's goods and sees his brother in need, yet closes his heart against him, how does God's love abide in him?" Here John took love out of the realm of the unlikely—risking one's life—

and drew it into the probable situations. In John's day those persons who were in such need—lacking food and clothing—were plainly visible; they were on street corners; they knocked at your door. Today they are more likely than not to be invisible. le. We can leave centrally heated and air-conditioned homes and travel in comfortable cars to a comfortable job or to a comfortable church and never see the world's need. We need to sensitize ourselves to see the practical demands that love makes on us.

VI. *Christian love is hindered by apathy.* If then this is what true Christian *agape* is, what are the stumbling blocks to such energetic love? The chief stumbling block is apathy, doing nothing, not caring enough to act.

We have the vocabulary of love. We know the right words. We have the correct doctrine. All our concepts are in place. But do we have the energizing power to set love in motion? The lights that illumine this building are backed up by wires and transformers and generators. But until some power turns the turbine, no light is forthcoming. In a similar sense, we have all we need to know about loving—whom to love, in what ways, all the vocabulary—but do we have the energy to love?—Daniel C. Whitaker

Illustrations

GOD'S YES AND NO. God, in his divine determination and his divine perfection, will say yes to us. But God's yes is a holy and wholesome yes, comprising always a no. It is the no to everything in us and about us which he must reject for his sake and our own. He treats us like a doctor who prescribes pills and medication we utterly dislike. I shall never forget how as a little boy I had to drink a glass of cod-liver oil every morning for many years. It tasted terrible, but it obviously did me some good. The doctor may even send us to the hospital, certainly not a very cheerful place. He may perform a minor or major operation, a most disagreeable undertaking indeed, yet how important for recovery! This is how God's yes, with the loathsome no in it, works.—Karl Barth

PRACTICING CHARITY. If, then, you bear a hatred toward anyone, overcome it by doing that person a favor. You can begin to like classical music only by listening to it, and you can make friends out of your enemies only by practising charity. "If anyone strike you on the right cheek, turn your left"—for that kills hate! Hate dies in the germ.

Your knowledge will get out of date; your statistics will be old next month; the theories you learned in college are already antiquated. But love never gets out of date. Love, therefore, all things and all persons in God.

So long as there are poor, I am poor;
So long as there are prisons, I am a
    prisoner;
So long as there are sick, I am weak;
So long as there is ignorance, I must
    learn the truth;
So long as there is hate, I must love;
So long as there is hunger, I am
    famished.
—Fulton J. Sheen

Sermon Suggestions

THE CONSEQUENCES OF DISOBEDIENCE. TEXT: Gen. 3:8–19. (1) Guilt, verses 8–11. (2) Shifting of blame, verses 12–13. (3) Many afflictions, 14–19.

WHAT WE MUST FEAR. TEXT: Heb. 4:1–3, 9–13, REB. (1) The promise: rest, in a blessed future with God, verses 1a, 3–4, 9–10. (2) The obstacle: knowledge without faith, verse 2. (3) The requirement: diligence, verse 11. (4) The motivation: God's piercing knowledge, verses 12–13.

Worship Aids

CALL TO WORSHIP. "O that men would praise the Lord for his loving-kindness and for his wonderful works to the children of men!" (Ps. 107:21).

INVOCATION. Lord, we are incomplete without thee. Fill our thirst for knowledge of holy things. Stir our desire for the ways of God. Conform our wills to thy will, even now as we begin our worship, even now as

prayers of invocation flood our souls.— E. Lee Phillips

OFFERTORY SENTENCE. "And the multitude of them that believed were of one heart and soul: and not one of them said that aught of the things which he possessed was his own; but they had all things common" (Acts 4:32).

OFFERTORY PRAYER. You loved us so much that you gave, Father. We love you so much that we give. Neither our love nor our gifts compare with yours. We ask only that you will make our gifts effective in telling the story of your love.

PRAYER. O Living God, we thank thee that thou hast not left us to ourselves. Thou has been our Teacher. All through the past we can trace thy self-unveiling. Through law and sacrifice and prophecy thou hast sought to keep alive within the minds of men the knowledge of thyself. And in the fullness of time thou didst send thy Son, that in him thou mightest declare thine inmost heart, thy love, which triumphs over sin and pain and death. By the glory of thy manifested life, let us rejoice in the sense of sins forgiven, in the assurance that one day the tangled skein of our lives shall be unraveled and their mystery made plain. In times past, we have not been willing to take all thy love nor enter into all thy joy. We have often wandered from thee into wastes wherein is no refreshment for our thirst, no rest for our weariness. But now we would be led by the green pastures and the still waters. Now we would lay aside our self-will and freely surrender ourselves to the guiding of thy hand. Allay our fears; quicken our better hopes; and so work in us that we may will what thou willest and because thou willest it.

We cannot come into thy presence without bringing with us all our brothers. Are we not all thy children, and hast thou not a purpose of good for us all? Give us a large and a nobler outlook. Give us more interest in each other, more zeal for each other's happiness, more willingness to share each other's pain. Take from us all miserable aims that end in self. May we, in the power of Christ's Spirit, help the weak and neglected; comfort the afflicted and sorrow-laden; and bring a sense of fellowship to those who are friendless and lonely. We pray for the advancement of Christ's cause and kingdom. We believe that it is the cause of goodness and truth, of all that makes life worth living. Awake, O Most Mighty, and scatter the banded powers of evil that delay the coming of thy kingdom, the victory of the crucified. May all the ills that work ruin in our social and civic life be banished from our midst. Cleanse our hearts and lips, that we may be made meet for thy service, mighty to the pulling down of strongholds and to the building up of the city of God, wherein dwelleth righteousness. And this we ask for thy name's same.—Samuel McComb

LECTIONARY MESSAGE

Topic: The Secret to Life
TEXT: Mark 10:17–30
A smartly dressed young man runs up to Jesus, bows reverently before him and asks, "Good Teacher, tell me the secret to life." Jesus' deflects the ideal flattery of a man who wants the key to eternal life. The man wants to know the path to salvation, but Jesus says he already knows the way. It centers on God and God's commandments, not on the schemes or wisdom of humans.

I. *Know the commandments.* How disappointing it must have been to the man for Jesus to tell him the same thing he had been taught all his life, the Ten Commandments. There was nothing new here. As Jesus rattles them off one by one, the rich man impatiently interrupts—interestingly enough, before Jesus gets to the one about covetousness. He says that he not only knows all this but that he has kept them all from his youth.

Obviously, the man was not present at the Sermon on the Mount where Jesus located murder in the angry heart and adultery in the lustful leer. But with the anticipation of one who thinks that he is on the verge of winning a long sought victory, he asks if there might be something that he lacks, something minor that he might have overlooked, just in case.

II. *Sell all.* Perhaps the man expected congratulations from Jesus. Perhaps he expected Jesus to give him a list of a few expensive, good works to fund. Instead, Jesus gives him a jolt by inviting him to sell *all* that he has and to give it to the poor. He wants him to surrender all, not just 10 percent. Jesus does not discount obedience to the commandments, but his platform in the Sermon on the Mount was that one's righteousness must exceed that of even the most righteous to enter the kingdom of God. It is clear that Jesus' word surpasses the old in the rigor of its demands. To no one's surprise, the man walks away to get a second opinion, for, Marks says, he had great possessions. He lacked for nothing in this world, but for the world to come he apparently lacked charity.

III. *The needle's eye.* Had we been there, we might have been tempted to run after the man and work out some kind of compromise. A man of his means could help to bolster a lackluster budget. Jesus, however, let him walk away. He turns to his disciples and uses a striking cartoon image to point out that the wealthy will have the hardest time entering the kingdom. He says that it is easier for a camel to slip through the eye of needle than for a rich man to enter into heaven. The camel was the largest animal (see Matt. 23:24), and the eye of the needle was the smallest opening imaginable. This portrays the chances of the fat cats for salvation as pretty slim.

But over the years, the wealthy and the not so wealthy have watered down the force of this saying. Many, who may know nothing about the Bible, have heard and remembered some line about the needle's eye as the name of a low gate in Jerusalem, which a camel, if it got down low, could squeeze through. The rich can then comfort themselves that they have nothing to worry about as long as they get down low and be humble. They can say to themselves, All these things I have done from my youth. Others have said that this particular rich man was a special case. Jesus knew him to be guilty of greed, and he chose a difficult test just for him. We can say to ourselves that we are quite different, and Jesus would hardly need to ask this of us. It is so tempting to turn the needle's eye into a large loophole. But one cannot escape the radical force of Jesus' words so easily. The astonished reaction of the disciples to this word, "Who then can be saved?" discredits any interpretation that allows one to feel too comfortable. The disciples understood Jesus to be saying that salvation for the rich is next to impossible.

IV. *Asking the wrong question?* The rich man wants to know what he must do to inherit life. That question is, first of all, entirely self-centered and probably reflects a life that is entirely self-centered. The man is concerned only about his own personal salvation. He wants to know what he can do to ensure eternal life for himself. The question also misunderstands what eternal life is. It perceives it to be a reward for good deeds rather than a relationship with God. For him, it was like a good investment plan. He wants to set up a game plan to achieve an eternal reward. He is not really interested in serving God for the sake of serving God. He is not interested at all in ministering to the poor. Let them fend for themselves.

The question also indicates that the man expects to attain salvation on the basis of his own resources. Perhaps that is why it is so difficult for the rich because they are so used to pulling strings and pulling things off with their influence and power.

Jesus makes clear that no one enters the kingdom on his or her own resources. Salvation comes only as a gift from God. That gift cannot be received when one's fist is tightly closed around one's possessions. It is received by those who open up their hands to God and to others.—David E. Garland

SUNDAY: OCTOBER TWENTIETH

SERVICE OF WORSHIP

Sermon: Fret Not! Fear Not! Faint Not!

There is much talk today about taking the right positive attitude. We all know that the Bible teaches the necessity of such positive attitudes as faith, hope, love, forgiveness, patience, and self-control.

But just as surely as we should hold right positive attitudes, the Bible teaches that we are to avoid certain negative attitudes. These negative attitudes will hinder us from having right positive attitudes. So the Bible forbids these negative attitudes. The Bible says, "Fret not . . . fear not . . . faint not," when you face the problems of life.

I. *The Bible warns against fretting.* "Fret not . . ." (Ps. 37:1).

(a) *Fret* is kin to the word, *friction.* Friction causes destructive heat; it wears away and irritates and annoys. The heat of such friction does not generate power, instead it wears one down.

That's the verb side of the definition. The noun side is that fretting is a poisonous mixture of worry, anger, and envy. Fretting is self-talk; it is telling ourselves how bad things are, how hopeless they are, how unfair they are.

(b) The causes of fretting are legion. But two common stimulants to fretting are perspective and pride.

We fret because we have the wrong perspective on our experiences. We fret because of how we perceive things, how we see them as being good or bad for us. Too often we view an incident from the wrong perspective.

We fret over things that for the moment seem good but are denied us or look bad and are imposed upon us. Don't fret; wait on God to sharpen vision and clear the shadows.

Pride also causes us to fret. We feel we do not get enough appreciation, not enough recognition, not enough compensation, not enough elevation. We fret because our name is not being hallowed. We're not too concerned about God's name being hallowed, but our name—

that's different. We fret over it if our name is not on the right lists and spoken with proper respect.

(c) Fretting over things that happen to us has a destructive effect. It becomes habitual, an unconscious response to life. It speckles our personality like rust. Then, little by little, it mars the beauty of our person and erodes the strength of our spirit.

Fretting has a progressive effect. Notice in Psalm 37 where the Scripture warns against fretting over the evil person. Soon we fret over the successful person; then we are so poisoned by fretting that we become like the evil ones we fret about. "Fret not thyself in any way to do evil" (v. 8).

II. *The Bible pleads against fearing.* "Fear not . . ."

(a) The very first human emotion mentioned in the Bible is that of fear. When God found Adam and Eve hiding in the garden and inquired, "Why?" Adam replied, "We were afraid." Ever since then, God has been trying to get his people not to be afraid. All through the Bible is the plea for us not to fear.

(b) Fear does not need to be defined for us. We have all cringed before an adversary. We have all cried in the flames of conflict. We have all curled from the visceral pain of a threat. We have all been cold from the clammy sweat of fear. We know what fear is.

(c) The reasons for fear are multitude. We fear we'll lose things we have, and we fear we'll be denied things we want. Fear comes in many forms. One common source of fear is that of comparison. Concerning comparison, Paul says we are not to compare ourselves among ourselves (2 Cor. 10:12). But instead of obeying that Scripture, we turn comparison into an exquisitely painful experience.

(d) It is true that fear intensifies activity rather than paralyzes. But fear often paralyzes a good response to the problem and instead perverts to destructive action. It takes a great deal of control, while in the grip of fear, to function creatively and reasonably.

III. *The Bible encourages us against fainting.* "Faint not . . ."

(a) Deut. 20:2 says, "And it shall be, when ye are come nigh unto the battle, that the priest shall approach and speak unto the people and shall say unto them, . . . ye approach this day unto battle against your enemies; let not your heart faint . . . for the Lord your God is the one who goes with you to fight against your enemies to give you victory."

(b) In the Christian life, fainting is first an attitude before it becomes an act. It is the mind and the spirit that faint first. For our brief consideration, fainting has three facets.

(1) My grandfather used to say when he was physically exhausted, "I'm just plain give-out." Brooks Faulkner calls it "burn-out" in his book by that name. But Brooks points also to our emotional and spiritual exhaustion. We've all heard someone say, "I'd rather burn out for God than rust out." But God says we are not to do either. We are to carefully shepherd our physical strength.

(2) Fainting also means giving in. Sometimes spiritual fainting permits compromising convictions and standards that we know we should keep. Compromise is not always a bad word. It's often the wisest thing we should do. But we faint when we compromise where we should not. We occasionally weary of holding to God's standards and just faint and give in.

(3) Fainting means giving up, quitting. We know there comes a time and place in life when we need to change, when we know we should quit pursuing a certain goal. That's not fainting; that takes wisdom and strength.

But the kind of quitting I'm talking about is the giving up that comes from despair.

(c) There are two causes of fainting that have plagued me over the years. They are inactivity and emptiness. By inactivity I do not mean idleness. This inactivity comes from circumstances that hinder us from doing those things that seem significant, meaningful, and exciting. This inactivity confines living into a monotonous routine instead of propelling us ahead into new experiences.

Fainting in the Christian life is also caused by emptiness, the emptiness of the spirit. There are many ways that strength seeps from our souls and leaves us barren. One that has troubled me often has been the absence of a challenge.

With this emptiness, we hear no clarion call to a new task. We see no unique opportunity in our community. We get no encouragement in our labor. We've tried it all with these people; they're not going to change. There is no challenge where we live!

Have you ever heard that kind of talk about where you live and work?

My experience has led me to believe that often our greatest challenge is to have no obvious challenge. In the Nazareths of life, in the common place, amid the tedious tasks of ministry, there find a challenge hidden, awaiting God's servant who will not faint.

Inactivity and emptiness make it easy to faint when we face our problems. But God encourages us: "Faint not!"

(d) *Fret not! Fear not! Faint not!* when you face your problems. Despite all our difficulties, the victory will be ours through Jesus Christ our Lord. Amen.—John T. Wallace

Illustrations

LIFE'S RAW MATERIAL. Watching people, one sometimes thinks that most of them expect to find life ready-made and hope to find it fortunate and happy. But we never find life; all we find is raw material, sometimes rough stuff and at first sight unpromising, but still, raw material out of which we have to make life. Existence is what we find; life is what we make, and in these days that requires the deep, interior resources of spiritual power that spring from inward fellowship with God.—Harry Emerson Fosdick

FEAR AND SUCCESS. The fear of not succeeding is, for many people, the biggest obstacle in their way. It holds them back from trying anything at all. And for lack of trying, they never give themselves a chance of succeeding—the very thing that would cure them of their doubts. It is not, after all, such a terrible thing not to succeed straightaway in some new undertaking. What is serious is to give up, to become stuck in a life that just gets emptier.—Paul Tournier

Sermon Suggestions

GOD'S STRANGE PLAN. TEXT: Isa. 53:7–12. (1) It includes suffering. (2) It transforms suffering. (3) It rewards suffering. (4) It is the model for the suffering of the Christ and Christians (see 1 Pet. 2:21–25).

BECAUSE OF JESUS, THE SON OF GOD. TEXT: Heb. 4:14–16. (1) Our goal: to be faithful believers. (2) Our privilege: to have an understanding Savior. (3) Our encouragement: to seek with confidence forgiveness for past sins and grace to live victoriously now and in the future.

Worship Aids

CALL TO WORSHIP. "From the rising of the sun unto the going down of the same, the Lord's name is to be praised" (Ps. 113:3).

INVOCATION. Lord, make us to rejoice in this special day that you have made for rest and gladness. Open our hearts to your love, our minds to your truth, and our wills to your service.

OFFERTORY SENTENCE. "And the Lord spake unto Moses, saying, Speak unto the children of Israel, that they take for me an offering: of every man whose heart maketh him willing ye shall take my offering" (Exod. 25:1).

OFFERTORY PRAYER. We do not offer the bodies of slain animals as a sacrifice to you, Father. We offer our broken and contrite spirit—and these gifts as representing our commitment.

PRAYER. "O Lord, our Lord, how excellent is thy name in all the earth."

The hymn of the ancient singer becomes our psalm of praise. We thank you for your mercy even as we praise you for majesty. Your gracious provision in your Creation overwhelms us with gratitude and makes us conscious of our unworthiness. Your mercy in forgiveness overshadows our sin and challenges us to be stronger in temptation. Your presence with this group gathered in your name today assures us of your loving leadership in this place.

And so in this fellowship of praise, we commit one another to your care. We pray for those who are physically ill and ask your healing. We pray for those who are anxious and lonely and ask your calming presence. We pray for those whose joy is threatened by discord and ask your peace.

We pray for your world, loving it after your fashion. For the hungry, teach us to share. For the warlike, show us how to be peacemakers. For the angry, the greedy, the envious, the cruel, we pray. Help us to help them.

We thank you for the good folks, generous, kind, forgiving, loving, and ask that you will include us today in that group. For Jesus' sake.—J. Estill Jones

LECTIONARY MESSAGE

Topic: Are You Able?

TEXT: Mark 10:35–45

When one reads the Gospels, it becomes clear that Jesus did not choose his disciples because they were brighter or nicer than other folk. Apparently, they weren't. In the Gospel of Mark, they always seem to be missing the point and once again demonstrate their inability to understand what Jesus was talking about. This is the third time in Mark's Gospel that Jesus privately announces to his disciples that he will die. For the third time they fail to grasp the significance of his words. They were conditioned to think of the Messiah in terms of victory and glorious rule, so whenever Jesus talked of giving his life, it went in one ear and out the other.

I. *Get behind me, Satan.* In chapter 8, Simon moved quickly to the head of the class when Jesus asked him, "Whom do you say that I am?" Simon grandly replied, "You are the Christ!" But when Jesus informed him that the Son of man is to be rejected and put to death, Simon quickly interrupted him with a resounding "No!" "The Messiah is not going to die, the Messiah is supposed to win. And we will march with you proud and pretty in the victory celebration. We will kick out the Romans on their ears and begin our great and glorious rule." But Jesus rebuked Simon and said, "Get behind me Satan!" Simon the Rock suddenly turned into Simon the rockhead. And Jesus continued: "If you want to be my disciple, you must deny yourself and pick up your cross and join me in the procession to Golgotha."

II. *Who's the greatest?* In chapter 9, Jesus told his disciples once again that the Son of man would be handed over to be killed. This time the disciples kept quiet. But they understood no better than before, because the very next thing they did was squabble about who was the greatest. Jesus broke that up with the pronouncement that the greatest is the one who puts himself last and who becomes the servant of all.

III. *Make us great!* In our passage in chapter 10, Jesus has poured out his heart to his disciples for the third time: "I am going to die." What happens next leaves us incredulous. James and John come sidling up to him to make a special request. When Jesus is talking about how much he is about to give, like so many of us, James and John come to him with a shopping list of all the things they want to get. They want a piece of the action in Jesus' glorious kingdom. They want to sit, one on his right hand and one on his left hand. They want to apply for the positions of secretary of state and secretary of defense.

They are not unlike us. We, too, would like to rule the roost. Not many of us are interested in following Jesus down the path where the sign says to Golgotha. Not many of us are enamored with the idea of taking up a cross and joining Jesus on that godforsaken hill of the skull on his right and on his left. The problem is, as one preacher has said, the cross is often worn but seldom borne.

And those other disciples standing on the sidelines are biting their lips in anger not because James and John were so callously indifferent to Jesus' grief but because James and John jumped the gun on them. They wanted to be the superstars of the kingdom, and James and John beat them to the punch. They were not so bold as to ask, but they had the same visions of grandeur. So, like so many of us, they would rather bear a grudge than a cross.

IV. *The call of discipleship.* When we look at these disciples, it is almost as if we are looking in a mirror. We can see ourselves jockeying for position. We, too, would just as soon skip Suffering 101 and move on to Advanced Glory 999. The Son of man humbled himself for us, and we, like James and John, would seek honors. The Son of man took the form of a servant, and we seek to rule. The Son of man became poor for our sakes, and we run after riches. But the Son of man came to give his life as a ransom and expects his disciples to give their lives in service. He does not promise glory or comfort or ease in this life. For some, it will cost everything they have. For some, it may cost even their lives. And Jesus asks us, "Are you able to drink that cup?" The real question is, Are we willing to drink that cup?—David E. Garland

SUNDAY: OCTOBER TWENTY-SEVENTH

SERVICE OF WORSHIP

Sermon: If You Go with Us

TEXT: Num. 10:32

The Hebrews were encamped at Mount Sinai, where they had received the commandments and other directions for organizing their life. Now it was time for them to set out on their long journey through the wilderness, and they needed a guide. Moses spoke to his father-in-law, Hobab, about going with him. He told him that if he would join the company, "we will do you good." But Hobab was not moved by this appeal, and he said that he would not go with them because he wanted to go home. Then Moses tried another approach. He asked Hobab to go with him because he was needed and he could do something for Israel. Said Moses, "Do not leave us, I pray you, for you know how we are to encamp in the wilderness, and you will serve as eyes for us." And then he came to the real clincher, "And if you go with us, whatever good the Lord will do to us, the same will we do to you."

I. Moses began by saying, *I will do something for you.* This sounds like the best way to many people, and indeed we are told quite often that men are fundamentally selfish. If we are to persuade others to do something we want them to do, we will have to make them believe it is to their advantage. Moses began on this level.

(a) What is the nature of man finally? Is it true that he is only a selfish animal and never makes any decision unless he can see a personal profit? It has become a rather popular assumption in our time that an unselfish appeal belongs in the same category with fairy stories and Sunday school teaching. Which is to say that realism demands that we come face-to-face with the futility of all idealism. Man, we are told, will do only what seems to him to be to his own advantage.

(b) This is the interpretation of those who believe that society is made up of conflicting classes and that the class struggle is inevitable. It is the Communist doctrine which declares that it is naive to expect cooperation between capital and labor, between the poor and the rich, between those who have and those who have not. One class must rule, according to this theory, and the dictatorship of the proletariat must be established before justice is possible.

(c) This is the spirit which rules most of our commercialism and especially our advertising. When we turn to that lowest and most vulgar of all public appeals—TV commercials—we discover this teaching in all its unlovely aspects. Whether we are worse off in my part of the country than in others, I do not know, but it is both amusing and disillusioning to listen to the TV hucksters selling cars. Always for some reason or other, profit is a secondary motive. The impression is given that if you will simply call the number or better still, visit the agency, they will practically pay you a bonus for just driving one of their cars off the lot. The trouble is that the listeners get hardened to this nonsense and after a little while they simply do not believe it.

(d) There is a modern tendency to turn our Christianity into a self-help religion. This has been an American emphasis, and the "peace of mind" brethren have appealed mainly to those who want Christianity to do something for them. Preaching has become a selling device to convince customers and clients that being a Christian is a very profitable matter. No one can deny that Christianity brings great joy to people, but when you divorce it from the cross, you turn it into something it was never meant to be. It is no longer Christianity.

II. In the second place, Moses made his appeal on the basis which seems to say that *you can do something for us.* He turns to another side of human nature which is often ignored. He assumes that men have a desire to be used for the service of their brethren and that men need to be needed. This is such a radical departure from the first appeal that we should look at it rather closely.

(a) Consider, for example, the great civil rights movement of our day. It is not only our black brethren who are involved in it but thousands of white Americans who stand shoulder to shoulder beside them. When Martin Luther King, Jr., sent out a call for help, preachers from all over the nation responded and went to Selma, Alabama, to march. Young men who could not afford the trip financially found the money or took it from their savings and joined the march. One might have thought they would say that, since they already have their civil rights, of what concern was it to them? But on the contrary, they felt that those who were denied these rights ought to have them, and they joined the struggle. To have asked these men to travel to Alabama for some personal gain would have left them unmoved. When, however, their witness was needed for the benefit of their brethren, they sacrificed to be with them.

(b) Whenever a man gets involved in a reform movement, he is always disturbed at the connections entrenched evil has established with money and power. But he is also impressed with the number of people, who have nothing to gain personally from the reform, who will join his efforts because it is right. There seems to be in the heart of most of us a desire to stand by a man who is waging a brave battle for a good cause. There is much more of this in all of us than we realize.

III. Now the third thing which Moses suggested to Hobab was that they should *do something together.* Moses' word was "And if you go with us, whatever good the Lord will do to us, the same will we do to you."

We need one another, and we need to be associated in a common cause. Men who have gone through difficult times together find values that are to be discovered in no other place.

(a) There seems to be an unwritten law of human nature that men become their best only when they are working together for something that is bigger than individual ambition. It is the big cause that fulfills man's needs and dreams. Let this be remembered in marriage, for two people who have nothing beyond themselves to hold them together and carry them onward will not go very far nor rise very high. A very wise Frenchman once said that being in love is not a matter of standing and gazing forever into each other's eyes, but of turning and looking together at the world.

(b) It has troubled me that men who have no time for church work, or at least so they say, will join a service club and put many hours of time on some community project. I have come to the conclusion that the fault is not theirs but ours. We have failed to make clear that the church is a company of men and women dedicated to the service of Christ and his kingdom. It is for us to present to our people the big purpose and to hold before them the big demand, for only as we understand this shall we experience the big joy. The Christian church should be Moses telling every man that we are to go together and find our fulfillment in his service.

IV. Finally, we ought to note that *this is the way God deals with us.* His call is for participation in the common cause and for membership in his kingdom. He comes to us as Moses came to Hobab with an invitation to go with him and share with him.

(a) Here we run directly into the mystery of the love of God. It certainly is not an easygoing affection which always gives us what we want. It does not resemble some sentimental elder who wants to be sure that the young people have a good time. It is a strong, austere, and severe love which will lead us through suffering and pain. There is nothing sentimental about God's relationship with people.

(b) The final sign of what we are saying is the cross. In spite of all appearances to the contrary, the cross is God's Word to men that he goes with them to the very end to redeem them and take them home. But it is a final word of hope and confidence that in our going with him we shall never get beyond his care. It is here that we find the meaning of our life. It is here that we find ourselves a part of a mighty purpose that draws us close to one another and takes us into the presence of the Almighty. It is not an easy way, and it has difficulties. But finally it is the joy we have of participating with God in the redemption of the world. And without this experience, life is never satisfactory or complete. He knows us better than we know ourselves.

(c) Surely it is wonderful to think that our God does not seek to win our love by promising to do something for our advantage. He goes deeper than that and calls us by making us aware of the world's need and the world's pain. But best of all, we become a part of his process of healing.

Perhaps the most wonderful part of it all is the assurance that, from that moment on, Christ will go with us wherever he wants us to go. It is this assurance that fills us with power and peace. We become partners with God in the tasks which he has to fulfill for our time.—Gerald Kennedy

Illustration

PERSONAL CONCERN. If there is any posture that disturbs a suffering man or woman, it is aloofness. The tragedy of Christian ministry is that many who are in great need, many who seek an attentive ear, a word of support, a forgiving embrace, a firm hand, a tender smile, or even a stuttering confession of inability to do more, often find their ministers distant men who do not want to burn their fingers. They are unable or unwilling to express their feelings of affection, anger, hostility, or sympathy. The paradox, indeed, is that those who want to be for "everyone" find themselves often unable to be close to anyone. When everybody becomes my "neighbor," it is worth wondering whether anybody can really become my *proximus,* that is, the one who is most close to me.—Henri J. M. Nouwen

Sermon Suggestions

WHEN PRAISE IS FITTING. TEXT: Jer. 31:7–9. (1) When God saves his people from suffering of any sort, as he saved Israel from exile. (2) When in all circumstances of his deliverance, he lends his very presence, his guidance, and his support.

A DIFFERENT KIND OF PRIEST. TEXT: Heb. 5:1–6, RSV. (1) Like other high priests, Jesus (a) offered sacrifice for sin, (b) dealt "gently with the ignorant and wayward," (c) acted on the basis of a call of God. (2) Different from other high priests, Jesus (a) did not offer sacrifice for his own sin, (b) had an eternal priesthood "after the order of Melchizedek."

Worship Aids

CALL TO WORSHIP. "O give thanks unto the Lord; for he is good; for his lovingkindness endureth forever" (Ps. 118:1).

INVOCATION. We swing wide the gate, Lord, as with minds set on the things of God, we enter the challenges set before us. Gather every day of our life, unto meaning, that our moments and hours may be God honoring, beginning with this act of corporate worship.—E. Lee Phillips

OFFERTORY SENTENCE. "If a brother or sister be naked and in lack of daily food, and one of you say unto them, Go in peace, be ye warmed and filled; and yet ye give them not the things needful to the body; what doth it profit?" (James 2:15–16).

OFFERTORY PRAYER. Receive these offerings, Lord, as a part of our worship. In spirit and in truth we seek to worship you. Cleanse our spirits and accept our gifts, we pray, in the name of Jesus.

PRAYER. Eternal Spirit, far above us and yet deep within us, we worship thee. The world is too much with us. We are distracted by its varying claims and tossed by its many winds. We would escape for a while from its clamorous noises into another and higher world where there are unity and purpose, sense and meaning, faith and hope. Clarify our minds, we beseech thee. Give us great ideas that we may strike our roots into them and be strong when the heavy winds descend. Clarify our hearts. Save us from the folly of vindictiveness to the wisdom of magnanimity, and let goodwill have its way in our lives. Clarify our wills, we beseech thee. Save us from our cross-purposes and contradictory ambitions, and let some soul cry today, This one thing I do!

As we pray for ourselves, we know ourselves at one with all the souls of men. It is when we stand before the Eternal that we see of how little moment are the divisions of race and color, nation and speech, that separate man from man. Our souls are one; our deep needs are alike; our highest aspirations are the same. Thou hast made of one blood all mankind to dwell upon the face of the earth. Grant us not only to believe this but to live it. Make every one of us a faithful servant of human brotherhood.

We lift our prayer today for those who forget to pray for themselves. If there are boys and girls offering no petition for themselves, happy with the passing days, making no earnest supplication for their lives, we pray for them. Our hope is in them. Couldest thou, O Lord, lay thine hand on one of them, he might swing the gate of a new era for mankind. We lift up in our solicitous petition the youth of the world.

If there are churches that forget to pray for themselves, complacent and content, we pray for them. Thou didst give unto us so great a Founder, forgive us that we are so little worthy of him. Shame us in his presence. Impress his portrait on our imaginations that we may not forget him, that he may rebuke us constantly and then guide us toward that day when Christianity shall possess the quality of Christ.

We pray for all governors of nations, for all who hold significant office and position among the sons of men, if they are not praying for themselves. Forgive them for the ineptitude and selfishness with which the world is governed, and forgive us, the people, that we support them in it. Grant unto the leaders of the nations wisdom and insight, unselfishness and courage, lest they bring down the temple of mankind about our ears.

Especially we pray for those so harassed by difficulty and so lost to all high and vivid faith that they cannot pray for themselves. Grant to someone such today a vision of blue sky through the gathering clouds that they may be sure again that the sun is shining. Give us radiance instead of darkness; give us stability instead of bewilderment; and set some sore-stricken and shaken soul today upon such deep foundations that his house shall not fall.

Now send us all out to make goodness attractive. Give us grace and radiance. May we make righteousness lovable because of what we are. Forgive us that we should ever misrepresent Christ, that the world should not see him in us. Lift us up until our religion shall sing in our lives. We ask it in the Spirit of the Master.— Harry Emerson Fosdick

LECTIONARY MESSAGE

Topic: Come and *See*
TEXT: Mark 10:46–52
Jesus' healing of blind Bartimaeus is a miracle that also speaks as a parable of our blindness and the way to light and life. Jesus' encounter with him occurs immediately before the Lord's triumphal entry

into Jerusalem—and immediately following encounters with people who fail to see what Jesus' ministry is all about. In treating Bartimaeus's story as an enacted parable, we must not look for a full allegory of Jesus' ministry. Still, this text presents a powerful illustration of the call of Christ that bids us come from blindness and begging to faith and light through faith in him.

I. Everyone Jesus meets is essentially like Bartimaeus. Bartimaeus was blind, a beggar, a social outcast. He was powerless to effect change in his own life. Were the other people Jesus met really any different? Two of the apostles had just asked Jesus for the places of honor in his kingdom. They, along with the other disciples, were blind to the true self-sacrificial ministry of Jesus. The religious leaders with whom Jesus clashed were blinded by their traditions and self-righteousness from seeing the grace of God in Jesus' life-giving acts. The rich young ruler had all the benefits of social status, material prosperity, and religious training, yet he begged for truly meaningful life.

Are we any different today? Masses of people remain blind to Jesus' invitation to life because of preconceptions about religion. The social norm calls for single-minded dedication to the accumulation of personal possessions. Still, a spiritual yearning impels people to search through cults and New Age religion for truly satisfying life. We are like Bartimaeus!

II. Jesus' great desire is to give people meaningful life. Without doubt, Baritmaeus had heard the stories about Jesus and his compassionate healings and gifts of grace. Bartimaeus knew the sting of rebuke, the cruelty of pranks, and the emptiness of rejection. His life was devoid of hope. He was hopeless, that is, until he heard the good news that Jesus was coming his way.

Jesus' words to Bartimaeus are life and health to us, as they were to him. "What do you want me to do for you?" (v. 51). Jesus had asked James and John the same question when they came seeking places in his kingdom (Mark 10:36). Even when we are off the mark with the specific request we make, Jesus wants to usher us on to the full life that comes by faith in him. Bartimaeus responds rightly—in both literal and figurative senses—when he asks for his sight. Jesus answers Bartimaeus's confession with the gift of life and light. His words, "Your faith has healed you" (v. 52), can be translated as accurately, "Your faith has saved you."

III. Jesus offers light and life to all who respond to him in faith. Perhaps a slogan for all of the gospel could be "Come and see." That is Jesus' perennial call. By faith in Jesus, Bartimaeus received physical and spiritual sight and began from that day to follow Jesus. That good news continues to us, today. To all who come and see in faith, Jesus offers God's gift of light and life.—J. Edward Culpepper

SUNDAY: NOVEMBER THIRD

SERVICE OF WORSHIP

Sermon: We Are All in This Together!
TEXT: Eccles. 4:9–12
The sermon text contains some very important principles regarding teamwork.

I. The first is this: two or more people have the potential to accomplish more than twice as much as one working alone. It is a fundamental fact of the human personality: most of us can function best when we are teamed up with at least one other person.

(a) One person against a problem—or goal—is seldom a match. But two people! That is a different story. If you can find one other person who is willing to join you in your quest, you have not merely doubled your capabilities, you have increased them exponentially.

(b) Unfortunately, in our highly sports-oriented society, the notion of teamwork too often serves as a synonym for competition. In fact, in developing "team spirit," "school spirit," "community pride," it always helps to have some common "enemy" in mind or, at least, some powerful competitor in view. Americans just seem to work more enthusiastically in a competitive environment.

(c) This understanding of teamwork, school spirit, and community pride is profoundly misleading and dreadfully shallow, however. It simply does not work for the Christian community.

Competitiveness is always exclusive. It sets up a win-lose situation. In fact, in a competitive environment, competitors not only work against each other, teammates often do also. Where there is recognition, influence, or power at stake, if one gets into trouble, the others may be actually glad to see that person's misfortune.

(d) Using the analogy of the human body, the Apostle Paul warned the Corinthian Christians about the dangers of competitiveness within the Christian fellowship. Where that kind of atmosphere prevails, some will inevitably suffer from a sense of inferiority.

(e) Few have that kind of self-confidence. But the person who feels that he or she is indispensable to the cause of Christ is the most dangerous person within the Body of Christ. He will soon discover that others have little or no desire to be around him. He cares only for himself. He finds it impossible to be a team player.

II. The second principle regarding teamwork is this: results are better when work is done as a team. A team not only accomplishes more work, but the work accomplished is also of a better quality.

(a) People tend to be more conscientious when they know their peers are watching them. Someone once said that work inspected is always of a higher quality than work merely expected.

Perhaps that helps to explain why churches tend to periodically plateau. With the exception of professional staff and paid employees of a church, there is little—if any—accountability from church leadership.

There is no excuse for low performance standards among Christians. We have the greatest cause and purpose in the world. We have the power of God backing our mission and work. We are commanded to do our jobs as though we are working directly for the Lord. What else do we need to motivate us to high standards of performance?

Apparently, we are people who need "the stretch" created from working in partnership with others who are willing to give their best.

(b) That leads to a second consideration regarding the improved quality of work resulting from a team effort. When people have a common goal, they tend to work harder individually. They know that their failure can also cause the failure of their peers.

Consequently, there is a "one for all and all for one" spirit in a genuine team. That's why we will sometimes hear an exhausted athlete say, "I don't care who gets the credit. I was playing as hard as I could so we could win." It's the spirit that grows out of the knowledge that "if my end of the boat sinks, so does yours."

Such an attitude requires consistency in cooperation and effort. In other words, successful team play requires more than average effort today and outstanding effort tomorrow. It also requires more than a periodic major effort. Sustained success demands steady, sustained effort.

III. The third principle regarding teamwork is this: team members are quick to help each other out of difficult situations. When a group is working as a team, every individual on that team supports the others. The reason: if one person fails or has difficulty, it affects the entire team.

(a) The Apostle Paul clearly understood this concept. He enunciated it clearly in his letter to the Roman Christians. He wrote, "Rejoice with those who rejoice, weep with those who weep. Live in harmony with one another; do not be haughty . . . never be conceited. If possible, so far as it depends upon you, live peaceably with all. . . . Never avenge yourselves, but leave it to the wrath of God" (12:15–19).

(b) Christians only grow and thrive in the company of other Christians—groves of them, known as churches. We get reinforcement, strength, and encouragement from others. W. H. Auden was certainly right when he said that "we must love one another or die." Helping fellow team members is simply not an option.

(c) The point is we are all in this together. And if we are ever going to make it, each one of us must be willing to carry our share of the load!—Gary C. Redding

Illustrations

A TRACKAGE FOR FELLOWSHIP.   There are definite laws of association and corporate living.

1. You must not try to dominate the group.

2. You must not try to use the group.

3. Acquire and cultivate the power to put yourself in the other person's place.

4. Determine to hold no secret criticism of one another.

5. Don't look for perfection in people.

6. Look on others, not as they are, but as they can be.

7. Determine to settle differences as they arise—don't let them get cold.

8. Refuse to look for slights.

9. Don't allow yourself to become petty—keep big.

10. Look for privileges of service rather than for your rights.

11. Don't try to do people good—love them.

12. Often decide with the group against yourself.

13. If there is any basic injustice in the relationships in the group, don't counsel patience only—right the injustice.

14. Don't try to have fellowship—work together for great ends and fellowship will follow.

15. Remember, we are "organs for one another."

16. Expect the best from others.

17. Help others to help themselves—don't smother them by being overanxious to help.

18. Keep your power of laughter.

19. Keep the thought ever before your group that the group is disciplined by something beyond itself—the Kingdom.—E. Stanley Jones

EACH FOR ALL.   Here are words written by Goethe long ago in his *Poetry and Truth*, in which I have found great comfort. They rebuke both my envy and my vanity and help me to rejoice in good work done.

"If, in the course of our life," he said, "we see others achieve a work we once dreamed of doing but had to give up, along with many another dream, then we feel the blessed truth that only all mankind taken together makes the true man, and that the individual can only be happy and at rest when he finds himself as a part of the whole."

How wise those words are! How many things we have dreamed of doing and saw our dream broken and defeated! Then, alas! we saw someone else do what we had dreamed, and we felt hurt of soul.

Instead, we ought to be big enough to rejoice that it has been done, better than we could have done it perhaps. At any rate it has been achieved and has been added to the common treasure.

Long ago St. Bonaventure pictured heaven as a place where each will be "adorned with his distinguishing trophies and grace, in which everyone will possess in others every gift he has not, and all other gifts which himself has, doubled so many times as he has partners in joy."

All envy, vanity, and pettiness are lost. What belongs to all mankind is ours, too, in interest and appreciation, if not by execution—if we are large enough of soul to appropriate it and use it.

"All things are yours," said St. Paul, "whether Paul or Apollos or Cephas or the world or life; things present or things to come; all are yours." It is ownership by appreciation, and it is valid.

The great poems, paintings, symphonies, the lives of the saints, the trophies of genius and culture—all are ours to enjoy. They are the common property and possession of all mankind.

Of none of these things can we say "mine," save in so far as we develop the capacity to understand and, therefore, possess them in the truest sense. This attitude exalts us, humbles us, enriches us.—Joseph Fort Newton

Sermon Suggestions

NOW HEAR THIS!   TEXT: Deut. 6:1–4. (1) The kind of God we have, verse 4. (2) The kind of devotion he requires and deserves, verse 5. (3) The kind of reminders we need, verses 6–9. (4) The kinds of reward God promises, verses 2–3.

THE ENTIRE STORY. TEXT: Heb. 7:23–28, NEB. (1) *Who?* Jesus Christ, the Son of God. (2) *What?* Absolute salvation for those who approach God through him. (3) *When?* Perpetually, for "he is always living to plead on their behalf." (4) *Where?* He has been "raised high above the heavens for his intercessory work." (5) *Why?* He was appointed by God "by the words of the oath" (Ps. 110:4). (6) *How?* He offered himself as a once-for-all sacrifice.

Worship Aids

CALL TO WORSHIP. "O give thanks unto the Lord; for he is good; for his loving-kindness endureth forever" (Ps. 118:29).

INVOCATION. O Lord, our Lord, give us to know again today the reality of thy near presence in this hour of worship. Let us seek thee, desire thee, think of thee, and be obedient to thy revelations, for our good and thy glory.—E. Lee Phillips.

OFFERTORY SENTENCE. "And to whomsoever much is given, of him shall much be required; and to whom they commit much, of him will they ask the more" (Luke 12:48).

OFFERTORY PRAYER. You have given much to us, Father, not because you love us more than others, but because you have entrusted us with a stewardship. We remember that it is required of a steward that he be found faithful. Help us to be faithful stewards of your good gifts. Amen.

PRAYER. This is the day that you have made. Thank you, God. May we receive it in all its uniqueness. It is unlike any other day that we have ever lived. May we appreciate its freshness. No matter what yesterday may have been, the creative power of your Spirit is with us making all things new. May we have the discernment to see what *new* thing you are doing in our day and the willingness to be an instrument in the coming of your kingdom.

O the *wonder* of this day: your glory manifest in the mystery of your presence in all the world about us and in us: "Earth's crammed with heaven / And every common bush afire with God." May we approach all the opportunities of today with reverence and rejoicing.

Thank you, Father, for one another. May we be understanding of each other in our foibles and encourage one another to strength. Help us to comprehend more sincerely what it means to be members of the Body of Christ. We all have not the same office, but your Spirit equips us for ministry according to our gifts. How great that we can complement one another and that the fullness of your love can be manifest in and through our life together!

We would pray for each other; may your love reach out through us to touch the life of each member of our church family. May we seek out those closest to us and minister according to their need. May those who are shaken because life has been so difficult, gain poise to handle creatively whatever life holds for them. Where the ache of loneliness persists, minister the balm of Gilead—the sense of your presence. May those walking through the valley have the faith to say, I will not fear, for thou art with me. Free those who are ill, from fear and anxiety, that they may be open and trusting to receive the health of your healing grace.

Grant to us who are citizens of this community, state, nation a sense of responsibility for our share in the democratic processes. May we earnestly seek for good government, exercising our influence responsibly. May we pray and work for the coming of your kingdom, that all peoples may be one family, as you ordain. In the name of him in whom word and deed are one and who teaches us to pray and live.—John M. Thompson

LECTIONARY MESSAGE

Topic: Not Far to True Faith
TEXT: Mark 12:28–34
You have seen that kind of student: scrupulously prepared for class; current with all of the readings; meticulous notes from previous classes typed and filed. This

is the student who asks the questions no one else thinks of—but always with a motive. "What can I ask to get the teacher to notice me?"

A budding rabbi noticed how Jesus handled the questions others had asked. Here was his chance to be recognized! He asked the great question: "Of all the commandments, which is the most important?" (v. 28). When Jesus answered, the cocky student concurred; "You are right. To love God with all your heart . . . and to love your neighbor as yourself are greater than burnt offerings and sacrifice." Jesus smiled and replied, "You are not far from the kingdom of God."

What a judgment, "not far"! "Not far" means you are close but not there yet either. What did the sharp student lack that kept him from attaining the kingdom of God? The two commands to which he agreed may bring inquiring persons to the outskirts of the kingdom but do not of themselves usher us in.

I. *There is a subtle danger in misdirected assent to the first commandment.* Certainly, one of the cornerstones of faith is the recognition of the supreme uniqueness and solitary majesty of God. Our right response to God is wholehearted love and commitment of our lives. However, centuries of Judeo-Christian religion have demonstrated the human propensity for faith going awry. Sometimes our private understanding of God rather than the fullness of the nature of God, himself, becomes the object of our devotion. In the name of heaven, prejudice has been nourished and wars have raged. Perhaps truer to the worship of God, but still afar from the kingdom, some people become "so heavenly minded that they are no earthly good." When people become so enraptured in contemplation of God that they fail to hear his call to service and ministry, the reality of Jesus' kind of kingdom has not yet gripped their lives.

II. *The second commandment also is insufficient of itself for reaching the kingdom of God.* God's love and grace set the example for all acts of human kindness and fraternity. Great admiration is lavished upon humanitarians, public servants, citizens of the year, and good friends. Still, the life of faith in Christ demands more.—J. Edward Culpepper

SUNDAY: NOVEMBER TENTH

SERVICE OF WORSHIP

Sermon: In His Place—Ezekiel

TEXT: Ezek. 3:15

I. God has called Ezekiel to be a prophet. He is to hear God's message and warn men from him. His congregation is made up of a company of exiles. They are people who have suffered. Many have lost their loved ones. Some have lost their God. Ezekiel was sent, therefore, to a congregation acquainted with grief, to a people whose eyes were blinded with tears.

For this difficult task the prophet needed a special preparation. To what school did God send him? To what seminary did he go to obtain his education for this high and trying task? He went and sat down among the people to whom he was to minister. "I sat where they sat." He looked out upon the world through their eyes. He bled through their wounds. He wept in their tears.

II. A like preparation is needed by ourselves.

(a) We need it in our international relationships. How different our history would have been if we had learned this long ago! Had we done so, the supreme tragedies of human history would have been averted. Had we done so, our rivers would not have so often run red with blood. What a difference it would make in tomorrow if each nation should learn to put itself in the other nation's place! Then truly we would beat our swords into plowshares and our spears into pruning hooks and learn war no more.

(b) What a revolution this would work in our industrial relationships! Suppose capital should put itself in the place of labor and labor put itself in the place of capital.

Then there would be a rivalry in serving and not in being served. Then there would be a struggle in the high task of giving and not simply in the mean task of getting.

(c) Then how helpful this would be in our relationships one with another. How looks the world from the windows of the sick room? How does it look to him whose every breath is a breath of pain? We who are strong and well need sometime to put ourselves in the place of the sick.

We who are older need to sit in the seat of the youth. How seems it to be young? Then youth, if possible, need to sit in the seat of the aged. How seems it to be old? How looks it to him who has wept over many a grief and many a grave? Oh, we do not know, many of us. If we did, we might be kinder to these aged bodies that are about us.

The man of opportunity needs to sit in the seat of the unprivileged. The intellectually trained needs to look through the cobwebbed, smoke-begrimed, dirt-darkened windows of the ignorant. You sit quite comfortably among the cultured and refined. How fares it with you when you are called to sit among the crude and the unschooled?

(d) If we in the home should learn to put ourselves in each other's place, what a benediction this would bring to our domestic life! If the husband, for instance, would sometimes sit where his wife sits. If he would get her viewpoint, if he could realize the thousand petty worries and annoyances of home-keeping and child nurture! If he could only realize how she misses the little nameless acts of courtesy and of love by which he won her! How the husband needs to sit where his wife sits!

Then the wife needs to sit where the husband sits. She needs to see the world through his eyes. If she might sit sometimes through the irritating grind of a day at the office! If she might realize his business worries, his constant battle to keep the wolf from the door! If these two, the husband and wife, could only put themselves each in the other's place, how many heartaches would be avoided! How many abodes of domestic tragedy would be changed into homes of happiness and peace!

Then we who are parents need to sit where our children sit. We cannot be as patient and understanding as we should be without this. We need as fathers to realize that we were not always staid and settled and perfect, as no doubt we are today. And mothers need to remember that they sometimes giggled and flirted, even as do their daughters.

Then, what is far harder, we sons and daughters need, if possible, to put ourselves in the place of father and mother. It is not easy for us to do this. But many a broken heart and many a bitter tear would be saved if we only would. If we could only realize how we hold the happiness of father and mother in our keeping! How we might gladden them if we only would!

III. What would be the good of our thus putting ourselves in another's place?

(a) Such sympathy would lead to a larger knowledge. We never really know people until we are able so to enter into sympathy with them as to sit where they sit and to look on the world through their eyes. It is only by thus entering into sympathy with another that we can come to know him as he really is.

(b) Not only would such sympathy lead to a larger knowledge, but the knowledge thus acquired would lead to a larger love. To know folks is to love them. Now, I know on the spur of the moment that you are ready to differ from me. In your mind you are saying, "The reason I do not like John Smith is because I know him so well." No, you are mistaken. The reason you do not like him is because you know him so little. If you knew him well, knew the real heart of him, you would doubtless love him well.

(c) Then the outcome of this fuller love born of a deeper knowledge is a larger helpfulness. Love is always eager to help. It will do the big thing if it can. If it cannot, it will do the little thing. It will give a fortune if it has it within its power. If not, it will dare cast in two mites. But serve it will, and help it will somehow, in some way. For the passion of love is not getting but giving. It is not leaning; it is lifting.

IV. Now this big question: How was Ezekiel able to sit in the other man's seat? That is no easy matter. It is not easy for us.

Answer: He did it through the power of God. We have the secret from his own lips: "The hand of the Lord was upon me." He did not succeed in the energy of the flesh. He did not succeed by taking his selfishness in his own hard hands and strangling it. He succeeded through the help of God.

And that same help is available for you and me. If we are partakers of the divine nature, if Jesus Christ is in us the hope of glory, then he will do through us what he has been doing all through the centuries. He is always sitting where we sit. That is what he was doing when, though rich, for our sakes he became poor. That was the vision that Isaiah had of him. "He was wounded for our transgressions; he was bruised for our iniquities. The chastisement of our peace was upon him, and with his stripes we are healed. All we like sheep have gone astray. We have turned everyone to his own way. But the Lord hath made to light on him the iniquity of us all." If he took our place, we ought to take the place of each other. "If he laid down his life for us, we ought to lay down our lives for the brethren."—Clovis G. Chappell

Illustrations

OVERCOMING DIVISIONS.   How broad are we? The divisions in the Christian church have nearly always come about because devout people could not differ and still pull together in one fellowship. There must be room in the church for diverse types of worship, differing interpretations of the gospel, many varieties of missionary activity, a vast range of forms of social helpfulness. We have to be large enough to allow others to express their loyalty to Christ in ways which are not congenial to ourselves and rejoice in them as fellow-workers unto the kingdom of God.

How bighearted are we? The church must embody the friendliness of Jesus. Metals fuse only at high temperatures, and folk of various stations in life merge as comrades only where love is warm.—Henry Sloane Coffin

WHY WE HATE.   "I hate him," said Charles Lamb of a certain individual.

"Why," was the reply, "I did not think you even knew him." "I don't," was the answer. "That is the reason I hate him."—Clovis G. Chappell

Sermon Suggestions

GOD WILL TAKE CARE OF YOU.   TEXT: 1 Kings 17:8–16. (1) *The story:* The widow's believing and faithful participation in the prophet's ministry. (2) *The meaning:* God will provide for the real needs of those who serve and trust him (see Matt. 6:19–21, 24–34). (3) *The application:* (a) Do not be misled by false prophets who seek to enrich themselves. (b) Live with discerning generosity. (c) Live with trusting confidence.

THE SACRIFICE OF CHRIST.   TEXT: Heb. 4:24–28. (1) It was a better sacrifice. (2) It was a once-for-all sacrifice.

Worship Aids

CALL TO WORSHIP.   "I will lift up mine eyes unto the mountains: From whence shall my help come? My help cometh from the Lord, who made heaven and earth" (Ps. 121:1–2).

INVOCATION.   Almighty God, we come to you in weakness and seek your strength. Our temptations are too much for us without your presence. Our burdens are too heavy without your help. Our lives are too empty without your joy. Come to us and stay with us. Amen.

OFFERTORY SENTENCE.   "For whosoever would save his life shall lose it; and whosoever shall lose his life for my sake shall find it" (Matt. 16:25).

OFFERTORY PRAYER.   Bless us, dear God, as Jesus blessed the widow who gave the mite, not because we give much, but because we gladly give with a pure and thankful heart.—J. Scott Hickman

PRAYER.   "The heavens declare the glory of God and the firmament showeth forth his handiwork." And we mortals look lovingly upward. We thank you for the beauties of your Creation. We thank you for the blessings of your providential care. We love you because you first loved us and taught us the meaning of love in the gift of your Son.

We are not worthy of your grace. We have sinned, and we ask your merciful forgiveness.

We thank you for one another, and we pray for one another. Some in our family are ill—we ask your healing. Some are rejoicing—we thank you for that joy. Some are discouraged—we offer our friendship. Some are in turmoil—we pray for your calm. Some are grieving—grant them your comfort.

And outside our family, there's a world out there . . . fractured and bleeding, hungry and hurting. Grant us the ability and the willingness to help, Lord, and make our help effective.

Today—ah, today, Father—make us good followers of Jesus Christ. . . . We pray in his name.—J. Estill Jones

LECTIONARY MESSAGE

Topic: All for Thee?
TEXT: Mark 12:38–44

Much can be learned about individuals and congregations from observing people as they come into services of worship. The patriarchs and matriarchs of the church may be afforded great honor, while newcomers nervously await a kind greeting. People enter with different expressions on their faces. Some come to worship with joy and expectancy. Others come with blank expressions, waiting passively for the "show" to start. Each person contributes in some measure to the recognition of God's presence and his grace toward all who come to worship.

One day Jesus sat down to watch people coming into the Temple for worship. Across the way stood the trumpet-shaped brass offering pots. Situated at the entrances to the outer court of the Temple, the offering pots confronted everyone who entered. What a spectacle it was! People from Palestine and lands beyond came in their finest clothes. Each brought some offering. Occasionally heads would snap in the direction of the offering pots as wealthy worshipers emptied their bags of coins into the offering pots with great pomp and clatter. What lavish gifts some gave!

A small, stooped woman came to worship. People brushed by her without paying her any attention as they hurried into the Temple. Poverty cases like her filled the streets. Jesus noticed her, though, and called the disciples to watch. With stiff fingers she struggled to untie the cloth that secured the two small coins. With a silent prayer and a nod of quiet assurance she placed the coins in the treasury. Jesus said to the disciples. "She gave more than all the rich people combined. They gave their leftovers; she gave her all."

I. Sometimes the loudest clatter does not identify the most faithful voices in worship. We are impressed by the spectacular. Our heads are turned by conspicuous displays of piety. Too often, however, we give out of unexpected surpluses of money and time, rather than through consistent, faithful commitment to God. Our giving may be done so that others can see and hear how much we have done. We may give "to the everlasting glory of ourselves and in loving memory of God."

II. Our offerings rightly are reflections of our hearts and lives, not ends in themselves. Unfortunately, we often approach our offerings to God from a "bottom line" perspective. How much do we give toward the church budget? What is the missions offering goal? How much (or how little) will we give for benevolence ministries? While the ministries of the church may require monetary support, the more important issue is the commitment of our lives to God. The tangible offerings we bring in worship should reflect how we love God with heart, mind, soul, and strength.

III. Like the faithful widow in the Temple, our prayer and commitment in worship should be, "Lord, all to thee!" Richard Baker's hymn "All to Thee" expresses for us the full response we can make to the call of God. May we give all we have through faith in Christ.—J. Edward Culpepper

SUNDAY: NOVEMBER SEVENTEENTH

SERVICE OF WORSHIP

Sermon: Are We Ready for Him?
TEXT: Matt. 25:1–13

I. *Preparedness* is a word with grim connotations. When we use it, we think of being prepared for the worst. Actually we need to be prepared for the best as well. Our Lord was keenly conscious of this fact and made it the basis of one of his best-known parables, that of the wise and foolish maidens.

The entire point of the parable is contained in the words "You must be ready, for the Son of man is coming at an hour you do not expect." This is a way of saying you must be ready for the best that could happen to you, for the all-important events in your life.

II. This parable helped the early church face and master two crushing disappointments and shattered hopes that might easily have put an end to their movement.

(a) The first was the hope that the Jews would accept Jesus as the long-awaited Messiah. But struggle as those early apostles, preachers, and missionaries might to achieve this objective, the hope was never fulfilled. While a precious minority of Jews did so accept him, the overwhelming majority did not. It was an answer to this, then, that the notion came into being that God had rejected Israel because Israel rejected Jesus Christ and that God was making of Christians a new Israel, a new people with a new covenant.

(b) The second frustration of the early church centered in whether, when, and how the risen Lord was going to return to save his people. For the early church, to a man, believed not only that he had risen from the dead and ascended into heaven but also that he would come again in power and glory to judge the earth, to reward evildoers and righteous ones alike. So far as our records go—and they are scanty enough—the overwhelming consensus of the first Christians seems to have expected an early return.

Heady hopes die slowly, but this one either had to die or be restated radically because the expected day of judgment simply did not come. Christ did not return as expected in the Book of Revelation. The early church was faced with the grim alternative of either admitting that the hope was wholly wrong or that it had been misstated.

A growing body of second-, third-, and fourth-generation Christians went over the entire matter again. They noted several important facts that somehow either had been lost to view or permitted to slip out of focus.

(1) First and all-important was the experience of each Christian that Christ had really come to him as a personal Savior, both saving him from sin and death and calling him to be one of his witnesses. In a sense, then, not understood and never to be wholly explained, Christ had already returned to each one of them, in spirit and in truth.

(2) Further, the early Christians felt his presence and power in and through their fellowship as Christians. He was present at their table; he was with them in the law courts; he was with them on their lonely voyages; he was at their side in the deadly arenas. He was not dwelling in or beyond the clouds awaiting the day of judgment—he was the beating pulse of their common life, their living Lord and leader.

(3) Thus within the church there was and has continued to be a real difference of opinion on whether he is to come again or has already returned. We feel some tension on this matter since a significant number seem to be unhappy unless it is affirmed that "he will come again." Ask them for evidence for this belief, and you discover that they have no more than that which led the early Christians to believe in it. You discover that it is an item of faith which you can neither disprove nor prove by any facts new or old.

But I most emphatically affirm both the reason for believing and the need to believe that he does stand at the door of every man's life and seeks entrance, that we need to be prepared for his coming to us, not once but time and time again as the Lord and leader of our life.

If, like the early Christians, we open the door of our life to his knock and invite him to sup with us, what sort of a person will we find him to be?

III. If we may rely on the experiences of those who knew him best and took the trouble to write down those experiences, we may say a number of things with confidence about "our guest."

(a) We will find a man at peace with God and with God's will for his life. He felt called by God to his work, and he had complete faith in God and in the work.

(b) We will find a man at peace with other men—friend, critic, and enemy alike. He neither looked down on sinners and outcasts nor up to the holders of property, prestige, privilege, and power. He heard the crying need for God which existed in all men, and he set himself to answering it. He went among them with the joyous news that he was offering them what they needed above all else: a new relationship with God and a place in the kingdom of God, which he was inaugurating.

(c) We will find a man at peace with himself. How could it be otherwise in one who had found peace with God and man? He was so much at peace with God that he never learned to hate his enemies; he never ceased loving all men.

(d) We will find a man who is not buying our ideas about what he ought to say and to do. We will find one whose purpose was his life as well as his message and we shall find one who expects his followers now as then to make their lives and their message one and the same thing. He knew that no man could hope to follow him without learning the bitter meaning of hard and dangerous living.

IV. I am certain that it would be a mistake for us to try to let him into our lives in any mystical sense unless we are prepared to follow him personally and socially in our day. For his instant and insistent call now as then is "Follow me." What may we expect if we try not only to believe in him as an item of faith but to follow him as the Lord of our life?

(a) As we follow, we will discover that religious faith is a vital, spontaneous, creative power. It was so with him and those most loyal to him. He was continually confronted by religious people like ourselves whose faith was no longer pliable and growing. Religion so easily settles into certain forms from which it no longer varies and which we no longer question. He ran into that situation repeatedly then, and his living Spirit encounters it now— among and within us.

To Jesus, religion must be spontaneous enough to relate God to the seemingly insignificant but actually poetic and beautiful elements in life. He seemed to find and to feel the presence of God throughout the whole range of Creation. Hence, he could speak of God's care for the sparrow, his consideration for the flowers of the field. He could see in the offering of a cup of cold water and in little children fitting symbols of the proper approach to God. Only one thoroughly alive to the beauty and meaning of commonplace things could see in these the building blocks of great faith. But he did, and he expects those of us who volunteer to follow him to learn to do likewise.

(b) A second emphasis which comes to us as we seek to follow him today is the sheer necessity of believing in God, of being loyal to God as the Lord of our life. God, for Jesus, was all-important. If he experienced normal doubts about the meaning of God, he had worked them through to an affirmative conclusion long before he began his preaching ministry. For, from the moment he steps on the stage of public life, every utterance attributed to him radiates faith in the reality of God and in the kingdom of God as the ultimate goal of the human quest. Hence his proclamation, "The kingdom of God is at hand; prepare ye for it," and his invitation, "If any man would come after me, let him deny himself and take up his cross and follow me."

(c) Still another thing needs to be kept in mind as we seek to be prepared for the one whom we want to hail as our Lord and our leader this day: Vital loyalty to him must concern itself with the needs of men, personal and social alike. Obviously, this emphasis landed him in serious trouble with the custodians of religion in his time.

Many of them seem to have been interested in the minute observance of the Law and temple rituals above all else. At least they had precious little concern over the ordinary needs of ordinary human beings. Jesus handled them with firm hands: "Woe to you, scribes and Pharisees, hypocrites! For you tithe mint and dill and cummin and have neglected the weightier matters of the law, justice and mercy and faith; these you ought to have done, without neglecting the others. You blind guides, straining out a gnat and swallowing a camel" (Matt. 23:23–24). That's plain enough, and it places the emphasis where prophetic religion has tried to keep it from that day to this: on the abiding ethical concerns of vital religious faith.

V. The invitation to be ready to receive him and to become a follower today is not an invitation to cease thinking and live some kind of lazy intellectual and spiritual life. It is no flight from reality, as some fear; rather it is a serious challenge to summon every energy we now have, to find others we do not now possess, to gird up our capacity for the mightiest endeavor possible to achieve not only a well-balanced personal life ourselves but to work unceasingly at the task of building a decent world order for all men.

If Christ is literally "the hope of the world" as we say in the easy parlance of church publications, then let us be clear on the fact that he must speak to and through people like us. There will be no "angel visitants," no voice thundering out of the dome of heaven calling instructions to men. Whatever utterance the will of God finds in our time will be articulated in and through people neither better nor wiser than we are.—Harold A. Bosley

Illustrations

CHALLENGE TO GROWTH.   At every stage throughout life, man is confronted in some manner by the living God, in the common crises of ordinary life. In each such confrontation, the human soul is challenged to growth and further maturity. And at every stage he can go forward in faith or shrink back in unbelief.—Lewis Joseph Sherrill

THE JOY OF BELIEVING.   He who is safe in eternity need no longer fear what time brings. He who has the peace that passes all understanding no longer needs to fear the specters of terrible future possibilities conjured up by his mind. He who knows that he is loved no longer kills himself in hating other men. He who serves the Prince of Life is no longer the slave of death. He who hears above him the song of angels, rejoicing because he has found his way home to the Father's joy, is no longer afraid of the war cries of the nations. He who knows him who overcame the world has escaped the specters. He who trusts the hand that rules the "ends of the earth" knows that even his poor, guilty life is being safely led through all the woes of dying, the grave, and the darkness of death to the Last Day and the Father's throne, where every tear will be dried and there shall be no mourning, no crying, and no more death, but only the song of the redeemed: Enter into the joy of your Lord!—Helmut Thielicke

Sermon Suggestions

WHEN GOD AT LAST HAS HIS WAY.   TEXT: Dan. 7:9–14. (1) A vision of God's power and judgment, verses 9–10. (2) A vision of the demise of earthly power, verses 11–12. (3) A vision of the universal and everlasting rule of Messiah granted by God, verses 13–14.

WHILE GOD'S PURPOSE AWAITS FULFILLMENT.   TEXT: Heb. 10:11–18. (1) We rely on Christ's once-for-all cleansing and redeeming sacrifice, verses 11–14. (2) We experience an inner consent to the will of God, verses 15–16. (3) We rejoice in our freedom from guilt, verses 17–18.

Worship Aids

CALL TO WORSHIP.   "I was glad when they said unto me, Let us go unto the house of the Lord" (Ps. 122:1).

INVOCATION.   Lord of the mighty Word, the abiding truth, and the still small voice; come to us in our need and fill us with thy power. As we worship, may we be blessed, and as we return to our homes, may we be fortified with the faith that informs life and outlasts it.—E. Lee Phillips

OFFERTORY SENTENCE. "He that is faithful in a very little is faithful also in much: and he that is unrighteous in a very little is unrighteous also in much" (Luke 16:10).

OFFERTORY PRAYER. The "earth is the Lord's" and "the cattle upon a thousand hills." We do not offer to your need, Lord, but because of our need—our need to worship you. This we do with our gifts.

PRAYER. O thou great Father of all! We draw near to thee as disobedient children, to confess our wrong and mourn over it and pray for deliverance from it. We beseech of thee that we may live worthy of our relationship to thee. We are thy sons. We are adopted into thy family. We are much loved and much forgiven. We are borne with and helped every day and on every side. Grant that every feeling of honor and gratitude and love may conspire to prevent our receiving all thy mercies, so many and so precious, and returning nothing but disobedience.

Forgive the past and inspire the future. Grant that we may never be discouraged. If there be any that have begun to walk the royal way of life and are perplexed and hindered and see little of growth in themselves, still let them go forward. Grant that none may look back and count themselves unworthy of eternal life. And we pray that thou wilt quicken the conscience of every one. Give a new and deeper sense of guiltiness. And grant that men who are named of thee may judge of their conduct and their character, not by human laws, but by the higher law of God. And so, by that spiritual and inward measure, may we measure their thoughts and their feelings and say, from day to day, "Against thee and thee only have I sinned and done this evil in thy sight." And so we beseech of thee that thou wilt raise up step by step above temptation, until at last we are prepared for that higher land where they sin no more and are tempted no more and rejoice together forever.

Bless the word that shall be spoken this day. Bless the servants of thy sanctuary here. May we take with us the spirit of Sunday into the week. May we be able to praise the Lord. While we are diligent in our business, may we know how still to be fervent in spirit. May we know how silently to teach men. And grant that so long as we live, we may be willing and abundant laborers in thy cause.

And when thou shalt have fulfilled thy will in us and our earthly career is over, may we then begin the glorious career in the heavenly land, where we will praise the Father, the Son, and the Holy Spirit.—Henry Ward Beecher

LECTIONARY MESSAGE

Topic: Yearning for the Future
TEXT: Mark 13:24–32

Everyone longs to see into the future. Fortunes could be made if one could only know how stocks and other investments would perform. If we knew in advance the sure course of our physical health, some might alter what we do to our bodies. Knowledge of the future might lead us to change our lives spiritually.

A rabbi was asked, "When is the very best time to repent?" The teacher thought carefully and replied, "The best time to repent is at the last possible moment." "But," protested the student, "you never know when the last moment will be!" "Exactly!" said the rabbi.

I. The future may be filled with judgment and suffering apart from Christ. The thirteenth chapter of Mark's Gospel perplexes, troubles, and fascinates us, all at once. Dark, ominous images abound in this "little apocalypse," a short peek into the travails of the world gone mad before the return of Christ. Deceit and destruction assuredly lie in the future for those who reject the true Word of Christ and salvation through faith in him.

II. In the midst of chaos and gloom, Jesus promises hope and life for those who will believe. Christian faith is eminently realistic. Believers are not exempt from natural disasters or from the blows of those who oppose our faith. Rather, God promises grace and strength for us to endure life's inevitable agonies. No matter how we are oppressed, we can never pass beyond God's gathering embrace. We can depend upon Jesus' parting promise: "I am with you always, even unto the end of the world" (Matt. 28:20)

III. The problem comes with our desire to know the future before we commit ourselves. God knows human nature. He knows that if we had precise knowledge of the future we doubtless would defer repentance and faith to "the last possible moment." We strain to look into the future; we are tempted to put our trust in our own predictions of what lies ahead. We may miss the blessings of life commitment to Christ while we wait for the time when we "really need" salvation.

IV. Jesus' words give us enough knowledge of the future to command our expectant faith. "Learn this lesson from the fig tree," Jesus says (v. 28). When we see fig trees and other plants greening and budding forth, we know that spring is near. We begin looking forward to warm days and to enjoyment of the good fruits of the earth. Frost and wintry blasts may yet appear, but we know for certain that spring is near. Anticipation of spring is one of the choicest joys of its coming. So it is with the coming fulfillment of God's grace. It is not ours to know the day or the hour; we may yet face difficult days. But Jesus has told us enough for us to look expectantly, joyfully, faithfully for the consummation of his love and grace.—J. Edward Culpepper

SUNDAY: NOVEMBER TWENTY-FOURTH

SERVICE OF WORSHIP

Sermon: Becoming an Authentic Christian

TEXT: Matt. 5:3

What does an authentic Christian look like? I am not referring to the type of dress or style of clothes, haircut, the externals, for obviously these vary from culture to culture. My reference is to the character, the principles and priorities that produce the behaviors so readily seen. What type of character does a believer possess? Are we different from nonbelievers? Should we be different, and if so, in what ways should we differ?

I. Contemporary Christianity has a major problem in that, as seen through surveys and through general observation, we have little or no impact upon the culture in which we live. Why? Because, as H. Richard Niebhur has so well taught us in his monograph *Christ and Culture*, the church has tended to mirror its culture rather than transform it. In our conforming pattern, we blindly accept the principles and priorities of our age without subjecting them to the radical call to discipleship that our Lord has issued.

(a) Our particular age is that of the

"quick fix." Whether it be liposuction or liquid-protein diets; cocaine, crack, or alcohol; casino gambling, racetracks, lotteries, or stock market manipulation; we live in an age that desires instant results.

(b) Yet there is no "quick fix" in Christianity. The quick fix is a result of cheap grace, which proclaims that because we are forgiven through the sacrifice of Jesus Christ it does not matter what we do or what we become, just so long as we trust in him. Cheap grace and the quick fix look for the big thrill for their motivation and view worship as entertainment in which they are spectators and the preacher and choir are the actors, rather than viewing worship as the corporate life of the body in which together it praises and worships God. The result is that worship becomes oriented to self rather than to God and our devotion to our church may last only as long as we are stimulated and motivated. Proper motivation is good and necessary, but ultimately it must come from the Lord Jesus Christ and our experience of his love and then our love to him.

II. So, what does it take to build an authentic Christian character? The answer is easy, though the process is not: submission to Christ and a resultant discipleship based upon the teachings of Christ and Holy Scripture. The Sermon on the Mount is the description by Jesus of what the character of a believer is to be. He ends this sermon with a warning in the form of the familiar parable of the two houses: one built on sand and the other on rock. Jesus is trying to alert us to the fact that we cannot ignore his teachings and the building of our character without great loss to our lives.

(a) The Beatitudes, as verses 3–12 are commonly called, contain the building blocks for an authentic Christian character. These verses are in ascending order, each builds upon the prior, so that without the preceding quality in place the latter ones will not develop properly.

Each verse begins with "blessed" *(makarios)*, which is sometimes translated as "happy." The connotation here is not one of deliriousness or superficial excitement but of a deep and resident joy and fulfillment, a peace of mind if you please. Each of these qualities leads to the full "joy in Christ" that becomes Paul's theme for the Christian life as he describes it in his letter to the Philippians.

(b) Jesus begins with a phrase commonly understood in his day but not so in ours: "poor in spirit." This phrase, recorded as "poor" by Luke in his Gospel, could be translated as "those who know their need for God." This particular word means more than just poor but carries the connotation of beggar. Just as a beggar cannot depend upon his self-sufficiency to meet the needs that he has for living, so each person, if he or she is to have an authentic expression of God in their lives, must acknowledge their poverty of spirit apart from the presence of God through the Holy Spirit. Entrance into the kingdom of heaven is not for the proud but for those who confess their unworthiness before God.

III. Until I am willing to admit spiritual bankruptcy, that the debt of my sin is far greater than I can ever pay, I will never come to Christ or become a part of his kingdom. The entrance requirements are simple: I must acknowledge my total unworthiness, accept his forgiveness, trust him as my Savior, receive him as my Lord, and follow him in discipleship.

(a) Why must I confess spiritual bankruptcy in order to be a disciple and an heir of the kingdom of God? First, because of the nature of human beings. Within each of us there is a hollow core that we are desperately trying to fill but which can only be filled by God. That's the way God created us, and that's the way we are. The Book of Ecclesiastes is the story of one who, with all at his disposal, tried everything to fill the void. This void was revealed when he said of God, "He has also set eternity in the heart of men" (Eccles. 3:11). Most of what is referred to as sin today is the manifestation of a people desperately trying to fill the hollow core with something other than God.

(b) A second reason for this confession of spiritual bankruptcy is that without the presence of the Holy Spirit of Christ in my life, a presence that comes only after my acceptance, one will never have the power to become the person he desires. Building an authentic Christian character is not something that one does alone, but it takes the power and guidance of the Holy Spirit to be an authentic replica of Christ. Without total dependence upon Christ, I cannot live the Christian life nor can I bear the fruit of the Spirit. That is why there are so many sand-castle Christians. They look so good and pretty but wash away when the first wave hits because there is no foundation in their life.

(c) This acknowledgment is the most difficult of all. No one likes to acknowledge bankruptcy—financial, spiritual, or otherwise. Why? Because we have too much pride. Pride is the "complete anti-God state of mind" according to C. S. Lewis, and right he is. Our Lord stated quite firmly and clearly, "Except you come as a little child, you shall not enter the kingdom of heaven." Little children do not worry about prestige or popular opinion but respond with their whole being to love. Pride is what keeps us from following Christ closer, is what keeps us moribund rather than active for God.

IV. What are the manifestations of pride? When we live in the kingdom of self rather than the kingdom of Christ; when we never look for self-interest in anything we do, say, or think but blithely assume that we are devoid of self-interest; when we assume that we know what's best for a situation rather than listening to others with an open mind; we are exhibiting pride. When we think that we are giving more than we are getting, we are living in the realm of pride. And it all leads to destruction. Why? Because "worldly men . . . cannot survive success, only godly men can survive victories and success."

The world says, "Blessed are the proud, the self-sufficient, the stoic, for they shall rule the earth." Jesus says, "Blessed are the poor in spirit, for theirs is the kingdom of heaven." Who do we believe was right?—Robert U. Ferguson

Illustrations

JESUS' SPECIAL APPEAL.   Only to one who can hear the Beatitudes and hear in them his own lack do they make sense: such a person knows very well that being poor necessarily means being "poor in spirit." By his amendment of the phrase, Matthew has made a most significant change—his version points out the danger of thinking that poverty is an honor. Poverty is not a virtue; it should no more be boasted about by the poor than despised (and upheld) by the rich. Matthew has been more insightful about what Jesus said than Luke, who merely translates Jesus' dictum literally into Greek. In Luke, the statement becomes simply the legalism that in heaven all conditions are reversed, so that the poor become rich and the rich poor. Matthew, by contrast, has retained the point that this saying becomes true only when the mystery takes place that the Old Testament calls an event of the "Spirit." A modern Jewish philosopher, Martin Buber, has said that the words of the Bible must never be isolated from the situation in which they were spoken; this applies with special force to the words of Jesus. Only in the emotional transaction occuring between Jesus and his hearers do his words become true. Matthew wished to derail the mere mechanical response to Jesus' words (the assumption of poverty as a ticket to heaven), so he added the phrase "in spirit" to emphasize the inner quality of Jesus' appeal.—Eduard Schweizer

HUMILITY.   When Albert Schweitzer one day began the building of a hospital, a native was asked to help. The native, however, refused, saying that he was an intellectual. "I thought I was an intellectual once," Schweitzer said as he returned to his work.—Charles L. Wallis

Sermon Suggestions

THE ULTIMATE RULER.   TEXT: Jer. 23:1–6. (1) The Messiah is not a ruler who divides and scatters his people. (2) He is not a ruler who causes fear and dismay. (3) He is righteous, wise, and just. (4) He blesses his people and gives them security.

THE GLORIOUS RULER FOREVER.   TEXT: Rev. 1:4b–8, especially verse 6, RSV. (1) How he feels toward us: he "loves us." (2) What he has done for us: he "has freed us from our sins." (3) The aim of his love and redemption: to make us "a kingdom, priests to his God and Father."

Worship Aids

CALL TO WORSHIP.   "Make a joyful noise unto the Lord, all ye lands. Serve the Lord with gladness; come before his presence with singing" (Ps. 100:1–2).

INVOCATION.   How can we appear before you, O God, except in praise and thanksgiving for all your goodness to us and to all peoples. We praise you for this opportunity to share this time and place as a family of faith in worship. We are grateful for your word of grace manifest in the history of the Hebrews and now fully made known in your only Son. May we come in such a spirit of praise and thanksgiving, "lost in wonder, love, and praise," as to experience a self-forgetfulness in which we discover our true self—the person you are calling us to be. Praise be to you—Father, Son, and Holy Spirit.—John M. Thompson

OFFERTORY SENTENCE. "Take ye from among you an offering unto the Lord; whosoever is of a willing heart, let him bring it, the Lord's offering: gold, and silver, and brass" (Exod. 35:5).

OFFERTORY PRAYER. In love, responding to your love, and thanksgiving, responding to your gracious gifts, we bring our offerings, Father. Use them as you will. Bless us with a sense of sharing in your purpose.

PRAYER. Eternal Spirit, not far from any one of us, in whom we live and move and have our being, we worship thee. In the world from which we come, we often forget thee, and things visible, tangible, sensual so obsess our thought, fill our eyes, and preoccupy our hearing that we lose sight and audience of thee. O God, make real to us in the sanctuary the things that are real. Here let small things seem small and great things great. Rearrange, we beseech thee, the perspective of our life. Round our little days throw such horizons that the seen and temporal may take their lower place and the unseen and eternal capture our imagination and our faith. We do not come to urge on thee our small requests but rather to put our lives at thy disposal that thou mayest do in and through and for us what thou dost wish. Thou art great and we are small; thou art eternal and our lives are bounded by a sleep; we are thy servants; thou, from everlasting to everlasting, art the God of all. Take us in thy keeping. Mold us to thy will. Make us the instruments and implements of thy purpose. Release thy power, O God, through us into the world, that because we have met here some great thing may be done on earth, not by us, but through us by thee. Dost thou not desire our inward peace? Therefore put us, we beseech thee, in such relationship with thee that peace may come. Let the anxieties and fearfulness of ordinary days grow dim. Let the great af-firmations of Christian conviction and faith be real in our hearts. Blow trumpets in our souls this day. Grant such margin of spiritual reserve around our need that the peace of God which passeth all understanding may be ours.

Dost thou not desire for us health of heart and mind and body? Therefore take from us those false anxieties, those needless tensions, which spoil our days, distract our lives, and make even our bodies ill. O God, the great and eternal God, who, when the doors are open, wilt come into a man and sup with him and he with thee, so enter into our lives today.

Dost thou not desire for us righteousness? Therefore grant us honesty with ourselves that we may not evade our sins but, sincerely facing them, be deeply penitent. Especially help us to remember before thee those things whereby our ill doing has hurt not only our own souls but the lives of others. Because we cannot keep within the narrow boundaries of our experience the consequences of our wrongdoing, because our sins always flow over to destroy other lives, make us penitent, that with hospitable hearts we may welcome thee like the sun to drive out our darkness with thy light.

Dost thou not desire our joy? Our goodness can commend itself to men only when it sings, when it is radiant, resilient, and joyful. Thou who hast taught us that the fruits of the spirit are love, joy, peace, we would be to thee like channels through which thy springs of joy can flow today. So help us to handle our benedictions, remembering them with gratitude, and our troubles, surmounting them with victory, that our lives, being strong, may be glad.

And as thus for ourselves we pray, we think of all thou dost desire to do for the world at large. Across the boundaries of race and nation, over the prejudices that sever folk from folk, thy purposes run, planetary, all-inclusive, for the brotherhood of man. This is thy purpose. As we pray for it, may we open up our lives to it, that through us it may come to pass.

We ask it in the Spirit of Christ.—Harry Emerson Fosdick

LECTIONARY MESSAGE

Topic: Christ the King
TEXT: John 18:33-37

What a confrontation! There was Pilate the governor—there was Jesus the king. There was Pilate the compromiser—there was Jesus true to his convictions. There was Pilate the cruel—there was Jesus the kindest. There was Pilate the judge—there was Jesus the defendant. Or was it the other way around?

I. *A troubled judge.* Pilate had not asked for custody. It had been inflicted upon him. Safely and comfortably settled in his palace-praetorium, he had been summoned forth by Jewish leaders whom he despised. Besides it was early in the morning. How quickly he would have disposed of the matter: You see to it!

Then he entered his palace again—the site of his power and prestige. It had become his refuge from the troubling Jews. He retreated into his praetorium. Such retreats are familiar to us all.

Questions of identity come first. "Are you the king of the Jews?" Herod the Great had made a similar inquiry more than thirty years earlier. Similarly troubled, he asked the wise men for help. Now Pilate, his successor, asked. Jesus parried the question—Who told you?

"Am I a Jew?" The meaning is clearly "I'm not a Jew, am I?" Perhaps he spoke it with a sneer. Filled with ancient and modern anti-Semitism the judge betrayed bias. Could either accusers or defendant secure justice from Pilate?

"What have you done?" His own nation and its religious leaders had accused him and brought him before a Roman authority. Why don't folks like you? Couldn't you get out of it? Why trouble me? Why me?

II. *A Calm Defendant.* Had it been a different defendant or different circumstances, the reply of Jesus might have been judged impertinent: Did you figure this out or did some one else tell you? It is probably further evidence of the independence that characterized his movement toward Jerusalem and the cross . . . "My time is not yet" . . . "My hour has not come."

I am a king! Not of this world, to be sure. You wouldn't understand (because you are not "of the truth"). The distinction is between the earthly and the heavenly, the physical and the spiritual. When Elisha was surrounded by the Syrian forces, his servant was terrified. Then his eyes were opened and he saw a tremendous force gathered for Elisha's defense. Jesus as king had hidden resources . . . armies of which Pilate did not know. He did not, nor does he, depend on palaces for refuge or soldiers for defense. What sort of kingdom is that? Pilate had struggled so long and so craftily to insure his strength. Now a defendant challenged his security.

He could not understand because he was not "of the truth."

III. *A true witness.* "You are a king, aren't you?" That's the way the question was asked. Clearly there are kings and there are kings. This suggests no great spiritual insight on the part of Pilate.

"I am a king"—you said it. It must be true if even Rome acknowledges it. And then, as if to deal fairly and honestly with the Roman judge, Jesus spoke patiently and clearly: "I was born a king." Go back to the manger with its shepherds, back to the place of the wise men's visit. Did Pilate know these stories? Probably not.

"I speak truth." This is my purpose, said Jesus. This had been his calling from the beginning of his ministry. When disciples pursued him for their own purposes, he replied, "For this cause I came forth" (Mark 1:38).

It is the nature of truth, the dynamic—he who is true understands. Only he is a subject of Christ's kingdom. "My kingdom is not of this world." Here is spiritual reality, spiritual power, spiritual sovereignty. This is the message of Pentecost. That which is not seen is more powerful than that which is seen!

In deep frustration Pilate asked the question, "What is truth?"—J. Estill Jones

SUNDAY: DECEMBER FIRST

SERVICE OF WORSHIP

Sermon: God's Great Nevertheless
TEXT: Luke 21:28

There you have the studied and settled effrontery of the whole New Testament. The gospel sets down its account of every situation with its eyes wide open. "There shall be signs in the sun and in the moon and in the stars"—only to throw all our careful deliberations to the winds: "When these things begin to come to pass, then look up." It takes a pencil and a piece of paper and reckons in every human resource, like a man getting ready for battle: lists the terrible odds over there on that side; piles them up high enough to suit anybody's taste; then blithely wrecks the whole business with something over here about lifting up your heads or something about being filled with all joy and peace in believing. Say it's nonsense, but don't say it isn't intentional nonsense. It is. If we really are what the Bible would have us know we are, then nothing else but a sort of nonsense could possible make God's kind of sense. For those who think the world is right side up, he has to talk upside down on purpose.

I. Take first the state of affairs in this excited, topsy-turvy panorama of monstrous evil. Everything seems to be just enough out of focus to keep us from bothering a great deal about it.

(a) Possibly, we say, Jesus was thinking about the destruction of Jerusalem, if that doesn't mean attributing even to him a little more foresight than he may have had! But, we add, the destruction of Jerusalem was a good long time ago. Why worry at this late date? Perhaps, with his Oriental, kaleidoscopic imagery, he was also looking beyond every one of these things to the end, which, we observe, promises to be a good long time off. Nothing there of any immediate concern. Suppose we change the subject.

(b) But these strangely urgent words have no intention of allowing you to do any such things. They don't let go so eas-ily. There is a certain stubbornness about them which keeps clamoring at the mind. Because, you see—if you will read the whole chapter you may be surprised to see—the core of all this was neither the wars nor the rumors of war; neither the destruction of Jerusalem nor what was going to happen when time had run out. Dig down to rock bottom, and it will begin to dawn on you that in everything Jesus said he was actually thinking all along of something else, on the other side of the words, in a still vaster context. Perversely enough, he simply didn't locate the real crisis of human existence anywhere in this "contaminated world." Not even at the end of it.

(c) It isn't any kind of trouble, here or hereafter, from which we may hope to be delivered by a bit of maneuvering, whether by means of our atomic stockpile or by way of adding a dash of religious education or group therapy here and there and going back to church again. Jesus was almost intolerably cavalier about all manner of trouble! Not that he was lacking in compassion. He was crucified for having too much. Simply that getting through was what mattered to him, not getting out. He talks in this particular passage about being accounted worthy to escape. What we fail to realize is that it was escape right down the middle, not around the edge; so that you could stand, not have to cringe or budge an inch, even before the Son of man: because by his grace you had succeeded in being bigger than things. And that was a larger order as Jesus put it, over against all this that was happening to the sun and the moon and the stars!

II. But now let's press beyond all these questions of the rough and the smooth. What is really upsetting is that life itself is the crisis we are up against. And that doesn't often occur to us. Life is the one precious thing we have in common. It is the rough and the smooth that matter; nothing's the matter with life.

(a) You'll come much closer to the truth

here in the twenty-first chapter of Luke if you'll stop long enough to let this strike home: that it's your very being alive and in the world that seems to close in on you as Jesus speaks. There is a NO EXIT sign over everything you thought was a door. They tell us that the only inborn fear we have is the fear of falling, of having all the supports withdrawn from under us, the props taken away. And that's exactly how it feels when all at once a lucid moment comes and we realize what it means to have things so comfortably as they are, without any assurance that any of them will be there tomorrow. Something, maybe it's death, something I don't want to face is trying to get into my world, waiting out there; and there's no security against it, none anywhere. Men say this and say that in order to cover up; or they take what others say. Too many of us are at odd times like some Charlie McCarthy sitting on our favorite ventriloquist's lap! When suddenly the powers of heaven are shaken and we feel again some nameless dread: our hearts failing us for fear and for looking after those things which are coming on the earth.

(b) "It's the instant when my throat seems to tighten," says Helmut Thielicke, "and I catch my breath at the unknown that has me surrounded." No use trying even to give it a name: it will come back when the name has worn off. You may call it the dashing of some hope or the loss of someone you love, and that's terrible. But it isn't the Terror underneath that's forever pressing in. You are the cat on the hot tin roof, and you'd like to jump off—but where? The whole world is like a wasteland, and you've already begun to suspect that the wasteland is inside. The morning and the afternoon narrow like a bottleneck, and you are forced on into the evening toward the twilight of all the gods you trusted, and the flood which they had conquered for a while sweeps on you again, the sea and the waves roaring.

III. If we can get at least that far with this strange chapter, it may not seem quite so much out of focus as we thought it was. But we have to go farther! It isn't only that we are up against life. That isn't all Jesus had in mind. We are up against God! And

you are not likely to find any "constructive solution" for that!

(a) You may want to object indignantly, maybe violently. "That's an outrage," you say. "God isn't a problem. He's the solution." I have heard so, more often than I sometimes care to remember! But come now, let me put it to you. When you find out from the Bible, and not from any popular opinion, who it is that's going to be there when you arrive and what he's like—incalculable, unmanageable, of whom men once said that he was a consuming fire, with the kind of compassion that's thoroughly capable of reversing everything you mean by the word and turning it upside down—when you find that out, does this business of taking off in his direction, so frequently recommended, seem to you like coming home to some dear shelter, or does it seem like setting foot on the shores of an undiscovered land, untamed, perilous, and wild?

(b) Ugly as we know ourselves to be—and we know it most painfully when we are at our best—which of us wants to be beset behind and before, as we are in the Bible, by a God who knows too much? Much better to say that he's good and mean by it what we mean by good; we are altogether in favor of the good. And the true and the beautiful—that's what God is! We have to decorate him somehow! And we can't. The God of the Bible is naked God. He watched in Gethsemane when Jesus prayed and did nothing about the cross when morning came. He left Stephen among the stones. He looked on and did nothing—so you would have said—as men and women and children sang their songs in the arena, with leopards leaping at them. And we can't stand it. So we set up in his place our little images, hoping they will run our errands for us and keep us safe. Certain it is you cannot prove we love God by the tricks we play to be quit of him. Waiting there at the end of the world, in the hour of death, waiting here now, not simply as we try to believe, with "comfort and kindness, but with holiness and judgment."

IV. And so at last, I think, we are plunged in where we've got to come, whether we like it or not. Now listen, as

Jesus turns all common sense everywhere upside down: "When these things begin to come to pass, then look up, lift up your heads!" You can never get Christ's measure until you chart the distance there from the edge of the abyss to this utter about-face. Never will you understand what sense it makes until you see what nonsense it is, not because of anything that can happen to us in time or when time itself is over, but because of what we are and what God is—with nothing now between him and us but the coming of a child in a manger and the death of a man on a hill.

(a) Jesus had to do more than merely to pronounce this vast *nevertheless* of God. He had to give it flesh and sinew and bone. When in the Temple he sketched for his disciples that cosmic upheaval and told them never to mind it, never to mind anything, do you think it would ever have been seared on their hearts, unforgetably, if Gethsemane hadn't followed it, and Calvary? Would Peter have gone telling of his glory "a many hundred miles to Rome," or Paul "to the sharp sword outside the city gates, glad beyond words to drink of his sweet cup?" Jesus lived out and died clean through God's *nevertheless*. And there's more in it now than a lad's hand in his father's, swinging away through the dark woods.

(b) "When these things begin to come to pass . . ." What things? It doesn't matter, says the New Testament, as long as you don't put off what Jesus said and think it meant some other time, not this time, not now. Beyond the smooth and the rough is life itself; but that isn't the crisis, God is. And he's trying the best he knows how—in us here—to invade this world of ours. From one of my classes comes a story of the day when the Allies landed on the beaches of Normandy. "Waiting in the stillness of dawn," ran the letter, "there was an oppressive silence. Eyes were straining at an angle above the water: the whine of landing craft pushing their burdens toward the shores of Europe, every man holding vigil at his station. Great expectancy was in the air. Here at last was the hour! We could look back at the blood and tears and the mighty planning which

had brought it." Back to Bethlehem in the gospel, and Calvary! "And we looked forward to victory. On this razor's edge of time, our hearts beat with joy."

Can't Christ get any of us to do as he says? "When these things begin to come to pass, lift up your heads!"—Paul Scherer

Illustrations

MIXED HAPPINESS. Shall one try to avoid those pleasures which connect one with the world's tragedy, and Thoreau-like, retire to one's own farm and live only with the pristine glory of the sun and the wind on a blue lake? But that same sun participates in droughts, and the wind can be a terrible hurricane, and the calm lake in which one enjoys swimming has drowned others who sought also to enjoy it. No pleasure is pure. No happiness runs only in one direction. Every enjoyment connects us with the tragedy and pain in someone else's life. Through all our happiness we hear the echo of that which is not happy; we learn "To look on nature, not as in the hour / Of thoughtless youth; but hearing oftentimes / The still, sad music of humanity" (Wadsworth.)—Rollo May

OUR VICTORY. There was a day in Martin Luther's life when the road grew suddenly dark and threatening and death seemed very near. "The pope's little finger," thundered the cardinal legate, "is stronger than all Germany. Do you expect your princes to take up arms to defend you—a wretched worm like you? I tell you, No! And where will you be then? Tell me that!—where will you be then?" "Then, as now," cried Luther, "in the hands of almighty God!"—James S. Stewart

Sermon Suggestions

THE DAYS ARE COMING. TEXT: Jer. 33: 14–16. (1) The promise, verse 14. (2) The protector, verse 15. (3) The purpose, verse 16.

THANKS AND PRAYERS. TEXT: 1 Thess. 3:9–13. (1) Reason for thanks to God: joy over the faith and affection of fellow believers. (2) Objects of prayers to God: increasing Christian love; hearts determined in faithful obedience to God, in view of the Lord's promised return.

Worship Aids

CALL TO WORSHIP. "Behold, how good and how pleasant it is for brethren to dwell together in unity!" (Ps. 133:1).

INVOCATION. Lord of life, as we deal with holy things today, purge from our hearts all that is unworthy and evil; open us by thy forgiveness and grace to the love that can change and shape us, through the revelation of Christ Jesus.—E. Lee Phillips

OFFERTORY SENTENCE. "Forget not to be kind and liberal; for with that sort of sacrifice God is well pleased" (Heb. 13:16—Montgomery).

OFFERTORY PRAYER. Teach us, O God, what is valuable in life not through what we are given but by what we are willing to give.—J. Scott Hickman

PRAYER. There are times, O God, when you seem so near, but there are other times when you seem *far away*. In our saner moments, we know that *you* have not moved. We are grateful that *your* presence does not vary with *our* vacillating moods. You are *always* here, in the greatest way you can be—in the fullness of your love in Christ. "O Love that wilt not let me go, / I rest my weary soul in Thee." Thank you, God!

Jesus, our Elder Brother, introduces you to us as "Our Father." But, you know, we have great difficulty in being "at home" with that relationship. Why is it? I guess it is easier to accept and understand your transcendence, that you are the "great God and the great King above all gods," that your immanence, that you are a down-to-earth God—that you have personally invaded this planet, and that you are present today and every day in Christ as your Word from the beginning and in your Holy Spirit dwelling in us. "To as many as receive you, *you do* give the power to become *your sons and daughters.*" In faith,

trusting; in love, reaching out; in hope, opening to infinite possibilities; may we receive you in the fullness of your creative power to make all things new. You are forgiving us our every yesterday, that this may be a bright new day. Increase our faith to receive it in all of its freshness. No person needs to stay the way he is, for your Word present in Christ *is* making *all* things *new*. This is of *your* ordaining, and it is marvelous in our eyes!

Our Father, we find ourselves mourning, but may we not mourn as those without hope, for in life *or* in death we *are yours*. For those ill, and for those loved ones and friends who keep prayerful vigil in their behalf, we pray. Grant us the wisdom—the faith—to pray for your mercy, whose death is a blessing releasing the Spirit from a diseased body. Bless those among us who are guests, that here they may experience the comradeship of your people, that together we may rejoice in the wonder of your love that so quickly removes any strangeness and baptizes into the communion of your Spirit.

O you who so lived the *world* that you have given yourself in its behalf, deliver us from the stupidity of those who persist in brandishing the sword when you are calling us to put up the sword and live in peace as one family caring for every person as brother and sister sharing the rich resources of this planet in life for all. The shalom you promised through the prophets is here present in the reconciliation effected in Christ. O God, may we not miss our day of your visitation.—John M. Thompson

LECTIONARY MESSAGE

Topic: Hope When Trouble Comes
TEXT: Luke 21:25–36

"Heaven and earth shall pass away, but my words will never pass away. . . . Pray . . . that you may be able to stand before the Son of man" (vv. 33, 36). In these words, Jesus gave comfort to the disciples in the midst of cataclysmic glimpses of the end of time. They had asked, as we long to ask, when the end will come. Imagine the pounding of their hearts and the tightening of their throats as they heard Jesus' description of suffering, deception, and cosmic chaos to come. Along with the picture of mayhem came a warning: "Be careful, or your hearts will be weighed down . . . and that day will close on you unexpectedly like a trap" (v. 34). The disciples needed some word of hope in an answer like that!

So do we. In the desperate hours of our lives, we need hope in order to stand the trouble. Anyone with the spiritual curiosity to read the Bible must wonder about the "end times." The three synoptic Gospels, the Book of Revelation, and several of Paul's letters present vignettes of the culmination of human history and the consummation of the kingdom of God. All of the visions of the end stress our need to be ready, to live faithfully toward Christ and his church. In the meantime, we are painfully aware of the trouble that comes throughout our days. We need hope rooted in the trustworthiness of Jesus' words when trouble comes day by day and in the end of the ages.

I. We naturally despair in times of trouble. Everyone of us is equipped with a "panic button." Threats and danger—real or perceived—call our faculties to attention. Sometimes we respond with all the reserves of mind and body, confident that we are fully capable in our own power to withstand the trouble. Sometimes we cringe and cower, sure that the threat is too great for us to endure. Often, when the trouble persists and neither response seems effective, we enter into depression.

Jesus cautioned the disciples about that reaction. Turning to a "fast-lane" lifestyle (dissipation), seeking comfort in substance abuse (drunkenness), or drowning in the anxieties of life can deepen depression and rob one of spiritual resources. Our hearts can be weighed down and faith can falter under the pressure of our problems.

II. Jesus gives us hope that can sustain us in our times of trouble. Prevention is the best cure. Jesus assures us that trouble will come into every person's life. Both the end of all time and to the end of our time are marked with travail. But "to be forewarned is to be forearmed." Jesus realistically points us to the signs that warn of trouble ahead. As the budding fig tree undeniably calls us to prepare for the coming of summer, so in life we may see early indications of rough times to come. The power that can sustain us in those days is not within ourselves but comes by cultivated faith in Jesus Christ.

When our worlds seem at an end, Jesus' words offer comfort and true strength: "I am with you always . . . I have prepared a place for you . . . I am the resurrection and the life." Jesus' call is to watch for the signs of trouble, to pray for strength, and in the power of his gift of faith, to live in this age and in the age to come with the victorious Son of man.—J. Edward Culpepper

SUNDAY: DECEMBER EIGHTH

SERVICE OF WORSHIP

Sermon: Refined and Purified
TEXTS: Mal. 3:1–4; Luke 3:1–6

I. Talk of "purity" is a trait at which we "with it" folks scoff. Purity, for us, is often associated with the backward, the uninitiated—especially the sexually uninitiated and the "holier-than-thou" types. Purity even makes us laugh, finds its way into our jokes and the barbs we cast at people behind their backs. Those of us who are "modern" in our reasoning may have

stopped desiring purity for ourselves.

(a) Now we're going to have to be certain what the Bible means when it speaks of purity, but we need to be clear about the fact that the Bible maintains a concern for purity as a trait of the people of God. It is of interest to us during the season of Advent, however, that we find reference to the purity that the presence of God brings to those who encounter it—prophetically seen as a "universal experience" at the end of time, but certainly an experience of the people of God upon all occasions of coming into the presence of the living God, our Creator and Sustainer.

(b) Purity—an effect of the presence of the living God, a goal, a fact; not funny, not optional, not corny, not out of step. Purity is a state of mind, a condition of our hearts, a kind of selflessness, a factor in our motives and actions that calls for faithfulness and fidelity, a reverence before what is sacred, like God and service in God's name and covenant relationship, which is any relationship based on mutual commitments. Purity is not naïveté or prudishness or separation from others or a perfect pattern of rule-keeping from which to condescend to the "less perfect."

II. Our Old Testament lesson is that gruff-sounding prophetic oracle in the last book of the Old Testament that Handel matched so well with music in the *Messiah.* "But who may abide the day of his coming? And who shall stand when he appeareth?" The implication of these questions is that no one can stand; no one can endure. As Elizabeth Achtemeier sees it: Unless God saves the people, even the people of God cannot endure God's coming (Elizabeth Achtemeier, *Interpretation: Nahum—Malachi,* p. 185).

(a) Actually, our Old Testament lesson is an excerpt from a longer response to a question posed more than once to God by the people of Judah (Mal. 2:17): "Where is the God of justice?" (See Christopher R. Seitz, *Advent/Christmas* [series C], proclamation 4, p. 19.) The question was not a sincere one but a cynical one or, at least, sarcastic. The people didn't see much evidence of a just God as they considered their world. But we must also say that the question was an ironic one. God certainly was looking at them—those who were supposedly in covenant relationship with God and thus obedient to God—and asking, "Where are the people of justice? Where are my people?"

(b) Through the prophet Malachi, God responds to the questions of the people of Judah. And our Old Testament lesson is a part of that response.

There are several parts to God's response here. This is the way it begins.

Look, I am sending my messenger who will clear a path before me (Mal. 3:1a).

God, Godself, is coming to the prodigal people, but God's messenger is coming in advance of that event to make the way for God; and that is taking place as the oracle is uttered. The messenger is coming. Not only does this messenger have work to do, but also by his very presence he is "foresignaling" the coming of God to the earth. Luke took John the Baptist to be just this kind of messenger who came before God when God came to earth in Jesus of Nazareth, and Luke recalled the vision of the prophet Isaiah of a messenger coaching the people on getting ready for the coming of God. Perhaps Malachi had no specific person in mind. Instead, could it be that his reference "is an illusion to the Oriental custom of sending messengers to the various towns and villages through which a king was to travel to notify the inhabitants of his approach, thereby enabling them to prepare a proper reception for him (T. Miles Bennett, "Malachi," *Broadman Bible Commentary,* vol. 7, p. 388). If so, it wasn't a banquet or high tea God would be expecting! God is not pleased about a disobedient people. The Lord says in a booming voice, confronting the apathy and sarcasm of the people, "The Lord whom you seek will suddenly come to his temple; the messenger of the covenant in whom you delight, behold he is coming, says the Lord of hosts" (Mal. 3:1b–d).

III. And it's strange, isn't it, that God's people had not done appropriately what God's people were supposed to do in their relationship with God, and somehow that was symbolized by the lack of effectiveness of their involvement with the Temple.

(a) God is not going to make this appearance to those who ignore God, who have never claimed any affiliation or relationship with God. God is going to come to the very center of religious life such as it is—where empty worship goes on, but where there has been true and proper worship; where persons now insult God with their childish charges, but where persons have called out to God in genuine, prayerful concern. If this is what goes on in a place dedicated to the worship of the living God, how bad are things outside the Temple? When conditions like that exist in the house of God, something drastic needs to happen.

(b) Malachi evidently believed that things could only be this bad when the end of all time had come. Consciously or not, he presents the end of time as an age so far gone that humanity is at its absolute worst; even the religion that professes to name the name of the Lord God has degenerated into virtual hatred of God, and an angry God it is who returns in judgment to make things right.

(c) I don't think I like the way Malachi lines this out. He envisioned the judgment of God falling first on the priests, the temple clergy. Surely the poor preachers can't be responsible for what the church members do or don't do! Nonetheless, Malachi said what he said, and the good ol' clergy people are going to be the first to feel the heat of the refiner's fire.

IV. Malachi used language and images that the people understood well. He sees God as working in ways similar to two well-known trades to do the refining and purifying that needs to be done; God's work of judgment is like the refining of precious metals and the cleansing of clothes.

(a) God comes to refine because the people of God are to be pure in their commitment to God and in their service and in their relationships with others, which are of necessity influenced by the basic commitment in life—commitment to God. Even in this context, which is shaded with references to God's anger and judgment and disobedience and failure, there is grace. The judgment of God is never an end in itself; rather, it is solely for correction and improvement.

(b) Malachi believed that it used to be done right, and that, no doubt, was part of the hope that it could be again. God or Malachi or somebody hadn't lost hope in humanity. And notice also Malachi's assumption that God's visitation at the end would turn things upside down in the world but was not an ending to the world; for him the new age would be a complete revision of this age but not a destruction of the old.

V. We're back to the Temple and the importance of our worship as the basis for right relationship with God and right relationships among ourselves and with others—all of which can be characterized as pure. The judgment takes place within the Temple—within the community of faith—and affects the clergy, first, and then the lay people, but finally gets around to all of us. And the judgment continues until it has done what must be done to bring the people of God back to a proper perspective with regard to God. It is like a refiner's fire; what is impure in the way we think and act and pray is exposed to what will burn away what creates the kind of arrogance and sinfulness that insults and angers and wearies God.

(a) I don't know what that is—that refiner's fire. I don't know how we're to know when we are being refined, but it certainly sounds extreme enough to make an impact. I do know that it will have something to do with corporate reform as the people of God, and I do know that it will have an impact on the way we live and serve our Lord as a result of such worship. I also know that any act of judgment is unnecessary if the people of God will heed the prophetic call to righteousness.

(b) So, if it gets to that, a refiner's fire; a scrubbing that feels like we got caught in the car wash—without a car. And another scrubbing and another one and another one—until we return ourselves to a right relationship with God. But why let it come to that?

Let's purify ourselves—in all dimensions of our faith and living—during this Advent worship. We can do so by pledging ourselves anew to the God who thinks that, whatever it takes, we're worth refining until we can, indeed, claim and enjoy relationship with God. Amen.—David Albert Farmer

Illustrations

WHY BE SORRY?   Sometimes our repentance is not real repentance at all; it is only remorse and fear. Sometimes we are sad and even in tears, not because we have done wrong, but because we have been found out or may yet be found out.

Here is a youth who comes to me in trouble. He has embezzled his employer's money, and his employer has found out. At any time the prosecution will begin.

So I go to the employer and plead with him to be merciful, tell him that there are ways in which the money can be restored and the youth can be saved, explain that this is breaking the heart of the boy's good parents, urge him to overlook the thing.

And he relents, accepts the money back, and calls the prosecution off.

When I have it all tidied up and tell the young man, to my amazement all his distress disappears in a moment. He smiles. He laughs. There's nothing left to worry about. All is well now. He seems to think it was a pity the money had to be paid back.

He isn't sorry for his sins at all. He is only sorry for the price he thought he had to pay.—W. E. Sangster

COSTLY REFINING.   A gentleman recently told me about a trip he had just made to California. Somewhere in that state, there is a silver mine out of which some six million dollars worth of unrefined silver has been dug. But as I understand it, the unrefined silver is simply left in piles outside the mine. Why? Because it would cost more than nine million dollars to refine it. God thinks we're worth refining even if it costs more than we can ever repay, so we must be careful not to associate God's anger with destruction—though not all the prophets presented it this way.—David Albert Farmer

Sermon Suggestions

WHEN GOD APPEARS.   TEXT: Mal. 3:1–4. It is a day of judgment that will touch all. (1) It will purify religious leaders. (2) It will renew the devotion of the people.

PARTNERSHIP IN THE GOSPEL.   TEXT: Phil. 1:3–11, RSV. (1) Occasion for thanksgiving. (2) Assurance of ultimate success. (3) Prayer for the qualities that are fitting for the Lord's return.

Worship Aids

CALL TO WORSHIP.   "O give thanks unto the Lord; for he is good; for his loving-kindness endureth for ever" (Ps. 136:1).

INVOCATION.   O Almighty God, who pourest out on all who desire it the spirit of grace and of supplication: Deliver us, when we draw near to thee, from coldness of heart and wanderings of mind, that with steadfast thoughts and kindled affections we may worship thee in spirit and in truth; through Jesus Christ our Lord.—*The Book of Common Prayer*

OFFERTORY SENTENCE.   "And they came, every one whose heart stirred him up and every one whom his spirit made willing, and brought the Lord's offering, for the work of the tent of meeting and for all the service thereof and for the holy garments" (Exod. 35:21).

OFFERTORY PRAYER.   "We givt Thee but Thine own, / Whate'er the gift may be: All that we have is Thine alone, / A trust, O Lord, from Thee."—William Walsham How (1823–1897)

PRAYER.   God of mercy, God of grace, show the brightness of thy face . . ." We gather in your presence. We worship in your name. You have brought us together from many places. You have called us from many backgrounds. We have come here in response to your call. We are at your service, Lord.

In our diversity, work understanding. Through our diversity, perfect love. Out of our diversity, bring unity. We thank you for your great variety in Creation. We thank you for your unity of purpose. Your love has drawn us to yourself. Your love has drawn us to one another.

And so we pray for one another. Where there is illness, grant your health. Where there is discouragement, grant fresh courage. Where there is anxiety, grant your calm. Where there is turmoil, grant your peace. Where there is loneliness, grant your presence. And we commit ourselves to one another, in understanding . . . in acceptance . . . in peace . . . in love.—J. Estill Jones

LECTIONARY MESSAGE

Topic: God Is Coming
TEXT: Luke 3:1–6

That is the message of Advent. "Crooked," "Captive," "Exile," "Fears," "Sins," "Strife," "Thorns,"—these are familiar words in a series of Christmas carols. It is from these circumstances that God's coming delivers us. How long the ancient world waited! A modern drama, *Waiting for Godot*, may symbolize in its frustration and disappointment, something of the spirit in the world before Jesus came.

God comes in the word and the word becomes flesh.

I. *The Word of God comes in a context.* The context is important for understanding. This is true for the written or the spoken word. The political context is significant. In our own day the Word of God concerning freedom will be understood differently in China and Russia and the United States. For the third time in this Gospel reference is made to political realities. The "fifteenth year" is more than a calendar crutch, though it does help to establish the year.

We know something about Tiberius Caesar and Pontius Pilate and Herod and Philip and Lysanius. We know of the tyranny and the suffering of those reigns.

The religious context is important. Annas was high priest by the grace of the emperor, and so was Caiaphas. Spiritual fitness was not necessary for the high priest—only money and position. Annas continued to exert influence during the

official rule of Caiaphas. Neither was noted for his holiness.

The social context is important. John is introduced as the son of Zacharias. Earlier Elizabeth had been prominent in the story. Here was a home, a priestly home, a wholesome home. There were many homes in the area. God's Word came in the context of homes and religions and political realities.

But God's Word came "upon" John, son of Zacharias.

II. *The Word of God is self-fulfilling.* There is evident fulfillment of the prophecies in the preaching of the early church. Luke wrote of this fulfillment. Isaiah had spoken and written to the exiles long ago. God had been coming all along.

God's fulfillment does not always come in Jerusalem nor even in Bethlehem. God's Word came in the wilderness where John was. Why had not John stayed with his family and properly exercised his inherited priestly office? What was he doing in the wilderness? Waiting for God to come.

It is a word of hope realized. For long years, God's people had endured exile, captivity, and loss of freedom. At this time John preached in occupied territory. Was there any hope? Was there any God? The prophet's word demonstrates that God had been working all along—consistent with his purpose. Now, get ready!

God's Word concerns God's salvation. Get ready. Proclaim it. Evoke a response. "And all flesh shall see the salvation of God." Note two simple truths: It is God's salvation. It is for all the world.

God comes in his word.—J. Estill Jones

SUNDAY: DECEMBER FIFTEENTH

SERVICE OF WORSHIP

Sermon: To Prepare the Way
TEXT: Mark 1:3

I. "Prepare ye the way of the Lord!" Those words have more than "a familiar ring"; they strike a resonant chord of hope and freedom. We hear these words proclaimed every Advent. In Isaiah, they

are a reminder that God is going to do a new thing. The Jews have been released in Babylon by Cyrus, and God is the ultimate cause of this renewal. In the New Testament, God is bringing in the day of salvation for all people in his beloved Son. John the Baptist proclaims this coming, calls for repentance, and ultimately points to the Lamb of God (Jesus) who takes away the sin of the world.

How do we hear those words? Many of us can't imagine going through the vicissitudes of life without the presence of the Lord in our lives. So we want for our children a vital growing faith, not "a form of religion denying the power thereof," not a socially acceptable routine but a life-changing relationship. We desire for our children, as they become youth, that they will "know the Lord." Our worst fear is that those we love will try to pack into the God-shaped vacuum in their lives experiences, relationships, self-made gods that will not fill the void. How then do we prepare the way of faith for our children?

II. First (and this step cannot be skipped over), we must hear the Word of the Lord: It is God who brings salvation, not we ourselves. The captives of Babylon, those caught in the quagmire of their sins at the time of Jesus' coming, were saved as they trusted in the Lord. Freedom came not through Cyrus or John but almighty God. Salvation is a gift; faith is a response. We cannot force faith on our children. Read Isaiah again: *God* lifts up the valleys of our lives, makes straight the pathways. You do not provide the way of the Lord for yourself or your children by pumping up the valley and bulldozing the rough places.

III. John the Baptist points to the Christ who is the love of God in the flesh, *and* yet John also tells of the need for repentance, warns of the rigors and demands of a new way of life. For John, preparing the way of the Lord includes both. This, indeed echoes our passage from Second Isaiah. For there the Lord is a shepherd, loving, tender, gathering his flock in his arms; but the shepherd is also one who leads, warns, admonishes those in his charge.

(a) How are we to prepare the way of the Lord? Will our children have faith? The answer again comes in the commitment that all of us make every time a child is baptized. As parents, friends, the church, we will bring these children up in the loving nurture and admonition of the Lord. We begin with love because this is where God begins with us. We point with our lives, not just our fingers, to the Lamb of God who took away the sin of the world. That is not superficial but sacrificial love.

The "King of Love Our Shepherd Is." Because we have learned the truth of the cross, God's costly acceptance of us enables us to love, accept our children before there is any hint of earning love. In this, we prepare the way.

It has been said that the best thing you can do for your children is to love your spouse. Likewise, if we prepare the way of the Lord for our children, *the* best thing we can do is love God with all our heart, mind, and body. Yes, our bodies are involved. You remember the bumper sticker that asked, "Have you hugged your kid today?" . . . not bad advice. There are all kinds of hugs: physical, verbal, spiritual. Without these hugs, something vital in us withers and dies. Let me push that thought a bit further: "Have you hugged someone else's kid today?"

I did not grow up in the perfect church (nor have I found it since then), yet there was a real sense in that church of being a family. Years later, when I drifted from the church, the one thing I could not deny was the genuine love that went beyond race and kin. This was the love that would not let me go. In that atmosphere, you knew you had more than one set of parents. Sunday school teachers had their faults, but they did not have to be coerced into teaching. Not one class lacked love. Church family came to my ball games, provided Christian books my family could not afford, stood by me when I was in trouble, and showed Christ's love in a hundred other ways.

(b) We are to prepare the way of the Lord not only in love but in admonition. *Admonition* is a word taken from the French: "to remind or warn." It means, "to reprove gently but seriously." It connotes for me such things as instructions, guidelines, discipline, and, when administered with a loving spirit, you have a powerful combination for good. A boy was sent to his room until his behavior improved. After a while, he emerged and told his mother he had thought it over and had prayed about it. "That's wonderful," said the mother. "If you ask God, he will help you be good." The boy replied, "Oh, I didn't ask God to help me be good. I asked him to help you put up with me."

It's very possible that the answer to prayer is both the courage to discipline and patience. One is not a substitute for the other.

As a matter of fact, if I was going to suggest another bumper sticker, it might be "Have you disciplined your child today?" The most loving thing we can do is to be clear about living life with "a frame." There are boundaries of responsible conduct, and it is an act of love to bring a child up in the "admonition of the Lord." Again, let me push past the comfortable zone. "Have you admonished someone else's child?" We have taken the "mind your own business" credo so far that children don't feel they are a part of a larger family. A few years ago, I received a letter from a man who had worked with me when I was in fifth grade and new to church. It was a warm, gracious letter, but he reminded me that when we first met, I was the most contrary young person when it came to the church. It's true, but he showed me tough love. He wouldn't give up. I remember on one Easter morning, I let it be known that I didn't want anything to do with church and said some things that broke my mother's heart. A woman in the church, a Sunday school teacher, took me aside and let me know in ways I will never forget that she loved me *and* I had better shape up. Love *and* admonition.

IV. Again, we cannot force faith, but *all of us* can prepare the way of the Lord. When I was a college chaplain, a lovely, bright Oriental student came to me and said, "How do I become a Christian?" I was only one small link in the chain. She told me of a fellow worker who loved Christ and a grandfather in China who prayed every day for her. They had prepared the way. If that's true in conversion, it's also true in Christian growth. Every person in this church who stands up and takes a vow at baptism has the responsibility to bring up a child in the love and admonition of the Lord. A juvenile court judge in this state said recently that the actual difference in children who do not run amuck is love, affection, respect, and discipline in the family. We are the larger family. It is a part of our responsibility as members of the Body of Christ.

Someone said that a real sign of maturity is being able to plant trees under who's shade we will never sit. A sign of Christian maturity is being a part of the Sunday school, the youth program, and ministry to children even when your child will not benefit. The vow at baptism is for more than parents.—Gary D. Stratman

Illustrations

RELIGION BY CONTAGION. In high school I hated mathematics and, like many another boy, looked forward with eagerness to the millennium when I should have passed my last examination in the abominable subject and would never have to look at it again. Then, going to college, I fell under the influence of one of the most inspiriting personalities I ever met. He was a professor of mathematics. I was always going to drop mathematics in college, but I never did—went straight through my course with it, elected everything he gave, did not so much learn it as absorb it. He performed the incredible miracle of making even mathematics contagious. If that can be done with mathematics, what shall we say about other more obviously personal, intimate, spiritual things, like poetry, for example. One can teach a child many things about poetry—meter, rhythm, scansion, and the rest—but if ever you find a youth who loves poetry, you may be sure that he caught that from somebody. The love of poetry is handed down by contagion.

So is religion. It is a fire that is passed from one life to another, not primarily by instruction, but by kindling.—Harry Emerson Fosdick

GOD'S INVASION. Someone has written that the Christian religion is a "storm in a golden frame." It occurs to me that the figure ought to be reversed. The storm is not at the center. The storm develops around the edges where God and his will come into contact with human life. The cross is the stormy reminder of what happens when God invades human life.

When a weather front of clear, cold, refreshing air moves down from Canada and hits a mass of hot, humid, stagnant air, storms develop along the edge of the cold front, often with lightning, thunder, and torrential rains. Even so does God's invasion of our world develop storms as it advances into the human scene. And insofar as you and I become in some measure agents or ambassadors of God in the world, we can expect a stormy time of it.—Edmund A. Steimle

Sermon Suggestions

WHEN THE LORD IS IN OUR MIDST.   TEXT: Zeph. 3:14–20. (1) We rejoice, verse 14. (2) We become confident once more, verses 15–18a. (3) We have new influence, verses 18b–20.

BECAUSE THE LORD IS NEAR.   TEXT: Phil. 4:4–9. (1) We rejoice, verse 4. (2) We are considerate of others, verse 5a. (3) We turn our cares over to God in prayer, verse 6. (4) We experience the unfathomable peace of God in Christ Jesus, verse 7. (Cf. Eduard Schweizer, *God's Inescapable Nearness.*)

Worship Aids

CALL TO WORSHIP.   "Praise ye the Lord. Sing unto the Lord a new song and his praise in the assembly of the saints" (Ps. 149:1).

INVOCATION.   Gracious Father, we are not here because we are perfect but because we are sinners. Grant that we may find your judging truth, your cleansing pardon, and your comforting promise.

OFFERTORY SENTENCE.   "For ye know the grace of our Lord Jesus Christ, that, though he was rich, yet for your sakes he became poor, that ye through his poverty might become rich" (2 Cor. 8:9).

OFFERTORY PRAYER.   Our gifts represent our personalities, our talents, our energies, Lord. As best we can, we commit ourselves afresh—our personalities, our talents, our energies—to you even as we bring our gifts.

PRAYER.   How strange it is, O Father, that we should have the privilege of knowing the gospel when there are so many who do not. We thank you for parents, for Sunday school teachers, for youth counselors, for ministers for friends who have lovingly and faithfully shared the good news of your coming with us. We praise you for congregations that have sounded your call, nurtured us, and set us forth. For guiding us to this faith where our hearts are strangely warmed with Christ's love, where our minds are challenged with fresh thoughts of all the newness that is in Christ, where we are called to mission that embraces all the world and all the worlds of people, we are grateful. We thank you, too, O Father, for those guardian angels who, when we have been threatened with shipwreck, have ridden out the storm with us, encouraging and supporting us, believing in us when we could not even believe in ourselves. With all your goodness and mercy in times past may we be confident of your providence today and for any future.

Having heard your Word, your call in Christ, may we respond with an eagerness to share your saving grace with all others. Pour out your Holy Spirit upon us, purifying our motives that we may seek only the good of the other, whoever the other may be, for only then do we serve to your glory.

For any brokenness among us—illness of body, infirmity of age, depression of spirit, loneliness of heart—we pray your health and wholeness. For our leaders who have the power to turn the tide from war to peace, we pray a change of mind to accept the new age of the coming of your kingdom in Christ, that all peoples may know life—not death.

And now, O God, grant us the courage to live as we have prayed through him in whom word and deed are one.—John M. Thompson

LECTIONARY MESSAGE

Topic: What Should We Do?
TEXT: Luke 3:7–18
"What should we do?" Everyone wants to know. John—plain-speaking, all-

natural, fresh-voiced herald of the Christ—tells them what to do. "Could he (John) be the Messiah?" they wonder. People who have answers for life's hard questions always look like the Messiah to some, perhaps to us. John's answers to the persistent questions are consistent and pragmatic: we are to live what we say we believe.

That may be the problem for most of us. We have a good idea of what we should do. The problem comes in actually putting into practice what we know and believe to be right. A current advertising campaign for athletic shoes advises us about various physical fitness programs: *just do it!* We know what we should do—but we ask the question, anyway, hoping some new voice will give us an easy way out. John will have none of such shortcuts to salvation. Neither will we. What should we do?

I. We will not get by with claiming special privilege for ourselves. Many Jews in John's day had wrapped themselves securely in the assumption that, as children of Abraham, they were recipients of God's special favor. John's message was different. The beginning of true relationship with God is the same for everyone, Jew or Gentile. God is "no respecter of persons," does not play favorites with any race or nation. We are not to begin claiming any special access to God. So, what should we do?

II. We should come to God in a spirit of genuine repentance. John does not mince words in his indictment of the people who came to hear him preach. Snakes! Rotten timber, ready for clear-cutting! Their lives did not square with the high ethical standards of the faith of Israel. Living in a "godly nation" did not avail them of salvation. John preached repentance for the forgiveness of sin as a necessity for everyone. But John also clearly directed his hearers to the true Messiah. John might be the answer man, but he was not the Messiah. True repentance and real salvation come from none other than the Christ to whom John testified.

III. We should live consistently with what we profess to believe. In John's words, we should "produce fruit in keeping with repentance" (v. 8). We already know the ethical standards of our system of beliefs, but conventional wisdom and our own desires get in the way of right conduct. "Cut corners, maximize profits, look out for Number One," go the standards of the day, and don't get too concerned about anybody else. So said the worldly wisdom of John's day, too. But people hungering for spiritual wholeness came to John to find better answers than those.

We who come with them in repentance before Christ ask, What should we do? The answer always returns, Share what you have; live honestly; care for all those whom God loves. As God has brought us salvation through our repentance and his forgiveness of our sin, so we are to offer salvation and grace to others by the way we live. We know what we should do—let us just do it!—J. Edward Culpepper

SUNDAY: DECEMBER TWENTY-SECOND

SERVICE OF WORSHIP

Sermon: The Glory of Christmas

TEXT: Luke 2:1–20

Is Christmas a holiday or holy day? How essential to your Christmas joy is the Christmas story? A mother went Christmas shopping with her young child. Feeling a drag on her arm, she saw that her child was stopping to look at a manger scene in a store window. Impatiently she snatched him away saying, "Will you come along—we don't have time for that."

The Bible takes us to the "that" which is the basic truth of Christmas. With a variety of passages it demonstrates the deep longing of the ages for a Savior who would come, the historical event of Christ's coming, the meaning of Christmas in God's plan for man, the personal understanding of Christmas through the experience of the transformed life.

Christmas is meant to be a joyous time—"Behold, I bring you good news of a great joy" (Luke 2:10). But it means joy about the Savior, not joy without the Savior. The Bible gives us the reason for Christmas joy—a Savior is born. As Bishop Lancelot Andrewes proclaimed in the court of King James I, "The reason for our mirth is Jesus' birth." This belief in the holy birth fills our hearts with joy. It is truly a merry Christmas only to those who know the meaning of the manger. Without the Babe of Bethlehem, the holiday becomes a hollow-day! As the carol expresses it, "Remember Christ our Savior was born on Christmas Day." When we are distracted by many things in the busy rush of the Christmas season, to remember this is the one thing needful—"To you is born this day in the city of David a Savior who is Christ the Lord" (Luke 2:11).

I. "The people who walked in darkness have seen a great light"—how our hearts leap with joy as we read these words in Isa. 9:2. In a rough and fear-filled world, suddenly there is hope! The plight of man is met by the power of God.

(a) The word of hope was given to Ahaz, a feeble king who lived in a world of fear. Isaiah gave his prophecy in a time of darkness, and it was a prophecy of light. Ahaz looked around for help; Isaiah looked up! Ahaz invited the Assyrians to help, with disastrous consequences. Isaiah looked up and found confidence in what he saw. Isaiah refused to be daunted by difficulties. He was not timorous in the presence of life's terrors. When the outlook was bad, he trusted the uplook. He knew that the light that comes from eternity is man's hope in this world of time: "For to us a child is born, / to us a son is given, / and the government will be / upon his shoulder" (Isa. 9:6). There should be one who would come, God's light in man's darkness, a child whose birth would bring a sure hope to men. This Prince of the Four Names will be a "Wonderful Counselor, mighty God, everlasting Father, Prince of Peace" (Isa. 9:6). As Counselor, he brings the light of God's eternal truth into the troubled affairs of men. As mighty God, he comes from eternity into time with the power to dispel the darkness and deal with the plight of men. As everlasting Father, he comes with divine compassion eager to save to the utmost, rescuing men from their desperate predicaments and giving new hope for time and eternity. As Prince of Peace, he brings a new kind of peace, not the uneasy truce that marks a temporary cessation of conflict, but the peace that comes from God's eternity based on a new spirit of truth and right and goodwill. On his shoulder will rest the government, and of the increase of his government and of peace there shall be no end. The choice is ours—to trust God's promise or stumble, like Ahaz, from disaster to disaster for lack of faith and heart and courage. Isaiah lifts a banner of hope of man. God will make clear his love and providence in the birth of his Son. We can trust his Word.

(b) Luke 2:1–20 tells the story of Christmas as a historical event. God's promise is fulfilled in fact—"a child is born, a son is given" as Isaiah had prophesied. To a world in darkness, God gave his Son to be the light of the world. For there was no Christmas then—until Christ was born. There was the iron world of might, filled with fear and dread. It was the world of Herod the Great, a ruler able, treacherous, and cruel, who murdered friends and family and attempted to murder the Christ child in the notorious massacre of the innocents.

(c) Yet there was hope. For to such a world, God gave Christmas. Here were good tidings of a great joy for all people. Ours is a God-visited planet. "Emmanuel" tells the story—"God with us." He really is! "The Word was made flesh, and dwelt among us" (John 1:14). God has done so much; how can we believe so feebly? Our Savior has come. He has taken the rainbow of hope and fastened it forever to the earth, linking earth to heaven. Here is our stairway to the stars. Here is our true hope, shining and splendid forever. In the presence of that hope, we are freed from our failures and our fears. Longing has become belonging. God's answer to man's need was given to the world in that first Christmas. The ages of longing have become the ages of belonging. Love came down at Christmas, and we rejoice in the

Savior who claims us for his own. To belong to him is to find our true life. When we know whose we are, we know who we are. And in that knowledge is our peace.

II. Only God can give a Christmas. And only as we turn to God can we really have a Christmas today. Will Christmas Day recur in you and me? God has done his deed. He has visited earth. He has given us Christmas. He has given us a Savior. Now the question is—what will be our response? Good tidings are here—will we believe them? A Redeemer is at hand—will we trust him? Light is shining in our darkness—will we look toward it?

(a) The shepherds made their response—and it is an inspiration to us. It was a "Let's go" response—"Let us go over to Bethlehem and see this thing that has happened, which the Lord has made known to us" (Luke 2:15). The shepherds had been afraid, but they trusted the angel's word, "Be not afraid . . . I bring you good news" (Luke 2:10). They adventured in faith, believing what God had made known to them. Because they followed the leading God gave, they found Christ the Savior. The men of faith are the great achievers. If we venture in faith, we find wonderful blessings God is eager for us to have. If we act upon our faith and trust his Word, every gloom will become a glory. We are not meant to be afraid. Good tidings are at hand. Arise and go to Bethlehem. Find the manger. Experience the love that is the heart of Christmas. Salvation is here! Is this too good to be true? No! It is too good not to be true. Christmas is the season when God calls us to cast out our fears about what the world is coming to and rejoice over what has come to the world! Without Christ, life is shadowed by fear. With Christ, it is lighted by the wonder of his love.

(b) St. Paul writes to the Galatians about the coming of Christ, "But when the time had fully come, God sent forth his Son" (Gal 4:4), and gives a succinct statement of the meaning of Christmas for Christian theology. Jesus was God incarnate, a child born of woman, come to give the glorious life of liberty, God's gift of salvation. God the heavenly Father has sent the Spirit of his Son into the hearts of the faithful to reveal the glad tidings that they are welcomed in love into God's family. No longer slaves under the Law but sons in the household of God and, if sons, then heirs. A world of blessing is at hand, and it is ours when we cry, "Abba, Father."

(c) In his letter to Titus, Paul looks at Christmas through the experience of the transformed life. Whereas former days were filled with wrong, "For we ourselves were once foolish, disobedient, led astray, slaves to various passions and pleasures, passing our days in malice and envy, hated by men and hating one another," now that he had experienced the glory of the transformed life, he rejoices in the coming of Christ—"But when the goodness and loving-kindness of God our Savior appeared, he saved us . . ." (Titus 3:3–5). So we look back upon that first Christmas when "the grace of God has appeared for the salvation of all men" (Titus 2:11), and our experience of God-given new life deepens our understanding of Christmas, and we rejoice in what God has done.

When St. Paul had difficult days in Macedonia, "afflicted at every turn, fighting without and fear within" (2 Cor. 7:5), God gave comfort by the coming of Titus. The good tidings of great joy had brought a glory into the life of Titus, and he was able to bring comfort and encouragement even to so sturdy a Christian warrior as St. Paul. Later, when Paul wrote to Titus giving guidance for the Christian work in Crete, he was moved to write some of his finest words of interpretation of the work of God in Christ. Martin Luther said of this letter, "It contains all that is needful for Christian knowledge and life." Paul's words speak home to our spirits because he experienced the "renewal in the Holy Spirit, which he poured out upon us richly through Jesus Christ our Savior, so that we might be justified by his grace and become heirs in hope of eternal life" (Titus 3:5–7). This is the glory of Christmas, the gift of new life through the coming of a Savior, born a babe in Bethlehem. The joy of the good tidings is ours to share. "The shepherds returned glorifying and praising God for all they had heard and seen." So did Paul. And so must we, for God's good news is for all the people!—Lowell M. Atkinson

Illustrations

THE USE OF TIME. In our hectic schedules, we are more likely to ask, "What time is it?" than the more basic question, "Whose time is it?" Time is, after all, one of God's gifts to us. The way in which we organize and use it reveals what we value. This is particularly true of the time we spend in worship. As James White has written, "The church shows what is most important to its life by the way it keeps time."—Paul A. Richardson

CHANGE OF FOCUS. To many of the people of his own time, Jesus of Nazareth appeared as the symbol of Israel's hope, the focus of their passionate anticipation. Probably no two of the persons whose lives he touched would have defined their expectations in exactly the same way. For some, he was to be a militant rebel, liberator of Israel from the yoke of Rome. For others, the herald to an end of history and the advent of rule by a celestial bureaucracy. For a few, a teacher of great wisdom, whose learning in the law and skill in debate would set straight the confused minds of men. And for many, the worker of mighty deeds of healing, one by whom the blind would be given sight and the lame made to walk.

Jesus was the symbol of widely diverse hopes, the focus of passionate expectations. But he was the fulfillment of none of these. His coming among men was a moment of truth, the point at which dream and fact had either to come together, like the two pictures in a stereopticon viewer, to show reality in new and deeper perspective or so blur the outlines of conflicting images that men would be confused and angered by the distortion of their visions. In Christ, the people of Israel had a chance to change the focus of imagination and see an old myth in a new dimension.— William Muehl

Sermon Suggestions

WHEN MESSIAH COMES. TEXT: Mic. 5:2–5a. (1) He comes from the small town of Bethlehem. (2) He comes from an ancient family line. (3) He is a unifying force for his people. (4) His authority is that of the Lord God. (5) He brings peace.

THE NEW SACRIFICE. TEXT: Heb. 10:5–10, TEV. (1) The passing of the old sacrificial system. (2) The obedience of Christ and the place of his once-for-all sacrifice. (3) Our consequent purification from sin "by the offering that he made of his own body."

Worship Aids

CALL TO WORSHIP. "Let everything that hath breath praise the Lord. Praise ye the Lord" (Ps. 150:6).

INVOCATION. We worship and adore you, O Father, that a common place like Bethlehem is the birthplace of a king— that every place is a Bethlehem, the house of God, the dwelling place of the Most High; that our common, everyday experiences are pregnant with the birthing of your kingdom. We rejoice that your coming is so firmly rooted in the terra firma of man's history—that we know that we are not alone but that we are kept by a love that will not let us go. Praise be to you: Father, Son, and Holy Spirit!—John M. Thompson

OFFERTORY SENTENCE. "And they came into the house and saw the young child with Mary his mother; and they fell down and worshiped him; and opening their treasures they offered unto him gifts, gold and frankincense and myrrh" (Matt. 2:11).

OFFERTORY PRAYER. Accept these gifts, Father, and use them to love your world, even as you loved your world supremely in the gift of your Son, Jesus, in whose name we pray.

PRAYER. We wait upon you, O God, as those who wait for the morning. We wait in faith, knowing that you are the God who comes. Your coming to this planet is such an advent that earth cannot contain the good news of it—but the heavens break forth with music and singing.

Something has happened that has never happened before, for almost every home has some symbol of your coming: a candle, a wreath, a tree, bright lights. We praise you for your coming in the meaning that enlightens us, in the mystery that fascinates us, in the beauty that inspires us, in the love that grasps us and does not let us go.

We praise you for your coming just now in the word, music, song, fellowship of this time and place. Our hearts have been strangely warmed; our minds have been challenged to grasp new heights and depths of the meaning of your coming; our imaginations have been dared to let go of "that-is" to perceive the "not-yet."

In the reveling of these days, may we not lose sight of our high calling to be stewards of your Word in the exigencies of the commonplace of our every day. Your Word comes with such promise of health, of wholeness, of life, but in this season we live in the presence of such brokenness: estrangement, sickness, death. We are conscious of persons in intensive care units in hospitals longing to be home with family but gasping for the next breath; there is the dear friend who lives all alone who fell and broke her hip who will be suffering her brokenness for weeks and months to come; there is the family who called off their Christmas party because the husband and wife—father and mother—are estranged, separated. There is the young man broken by the estrangement between him and his father when he was kicked out of his home. We are conscious, too, of the many walking through the valley of the shadow of death. But into the darkness has shined a light that no night can ever put out, and we are called to be bearers of this light into all the dark corners of our community and this world.

We pray for the peace of Bethlehem and Jerusalem, for we realize that we have ignored or neglected your call for justice for all peoples. May we commit ourselves to do that which we can do to influence our leaders to initiate and support a policy that both Jew and Arab may enjoy peace with justice.

Grant us courage born of the faith that there is a grace now present—in the Word becoming flesh and dwelling among us— that can reconcile all nations, peoples, and persons. May we faithfully pray and wisely work for that day when all Creation will echo back the angels' song of that first Christmas, when all peoples shall go out in joy and be led forth in peace, when the mountains and the hills shall break forth into singing, when all the trees shall clap their hands. Through him who is the "joy of man's desiring" we pray.—John M. Thompson

LECTIONARY MESSAGE

Topic: Mary, Our Companion in Hope
TEXT: Luke 1:39–55

This text divides neatly into two major sections, the narrative of Mary's visit to Elizabeth and the "Song of Praise" or Magnificat, which proclaims with great exultation the redemption of God. Verses 39–55 record Mary's prompt action after her encounter with the angel Gabriel. Her visit to Elizabeth is a part of the drama of preparing for the birth of the Messiah.

I. The New Testament does not idealize Mary.

(a) She is a poor and simple woman of Galilee, where her life is completely immersed in the social, political, and religious situation of her people. It is easy to imagine, in thinking about Mary, that all was easy and clear for her—that she knew that her son Jesus was the Son of the Most High or that she was the most highly blessed of all women. But the Gospels do not paint this idyllic picture. Instead, they present Mary as walking in the darkness of faith. Her cousin Elizabeth says it outright: "Blest is she who trusted . . ." (Luke 1:45). She does not understand everything that is happening (Luke 2:50). She is willing to accept God's mysterious ways. But she trusts, and her faith grows as she reflects and ponders things in her heart.

(b) She is a virgin, but she discovers that she is with child. She is disturbed and afraid; her virginity was an important part of the betrothal. What would Joseph think? What if Daddy did not want to take her back into her home? She comes to believe that it is by the action of the Holy Spirit that what is growing within her womb is somehow divine, and she welcomes the work of God. Elizabeth assists her in interpreting "what was spoken to her from the Lord."

(c) Mary accepts unseen realities and believes—because nothing is impossible for God. She realizes, however vaguely, that the salvation of all men and women depended upon her child. Then her life clarified what she had received by faith.

II. It is the part of faith to live in the twilight. Faith generates light as long as the individual accepts and surrenders to God's plan. This is our path, and it was Mary's narrow path. Faith is willing to live with perplexity and with the unseen. God's plan is not yet fully comprehended by any of us.

(a) Mary clearly expresses God's identification with the dispossessed and the disinherited. Maybe that is why we have not been very comfortable with Mary; she might stand in judgment against our comfortable ways of living. Her people, the *anawim,* were the faithful poor of the land. They knew their strength could only be found in utter reliance upon God; unlike the proud and self-sufficient, they knew their need of God.

(b) Mary proclaims that "God's mercy is upon those who fear the Lord from generations to generations." She was speaking of her people, a religious community who knew that in God's sight the ultimately blessed were not the mighty and the rich who tyrannized them. She knew wealth and power have no standing in God's sight; Mary's powerful testimony is that God has chosen to come in flesh through one who admitted that she was no more than a handmaid, a female slave. She is the symbol of freedom from the bondage of sexual and societal chains and a prophet of hope.

(c) Mary is willing to depend upon God. Such receptivity to God issues in bringing forth new life. This task involves pain that cannot be avoided. Mary—as well as all of those willing to trust God—recognizes the legitimacy and inescapability of suffering and blends it with hope. The travail necessary to give birth—whether it be to children, a tender congregation, a new identity—could not be undertaken without hope.

(d) Mary's hymn of praise reflects the good news of God's intervention through her child. It is God's purpose to effect a great reversal: to scatter the proud in the imaginations of their hearts; to put down the mighty from their thrones; to exalt those of low degree; to fill the hungry with good things, and to send the rich away empty.

The Magnificat has been called one of the most revolutionary documents in all of literature. It is a hymn from the Jewish-Christian community, full of Old Testament allusions—yet it is preeminently Mary's canticle, as Luke wisely knows.— Molly Marshall-Green

SUNDAY: DECEMBER TWENTY-NINTH

SERVICE OF WORSHIP

Sermon: God Wants You to Be Happy
TEXT: Deut. 16:9–12

The students who live in the house below here on Mousson Street once held a men's meeting to discuss the topic "The Christian's Duty to Enjoy Life."

I. That is a peculiar topic, isn't it? But it could very well be taken right out of our text. For God, indeed, tells us there this morning, "You shall rejoice." What a strange command! If God should say, "You shall not drink" or "You shall not smoke" if you want to be a true Christian, we could understand that command, and many of us would try hard to live up to it explicitly. But there it stands: "You shall rejoice."

And it is an excellent command. Could we, our family, all of those living with us, could this group taken as a whole find anything at all more necessary than this: rejoicing week in and week out? Perhaps the command means not only that we should have a joyful outlook or act joyfully but even that we should be joyful.

Who would want to utter such silly talk? You are joyful at heart or you are not. You have a reason to rejoice or a reason to complain. But God obviously does not think like that. He summons us to rejoice.

I am reminded of a doctor, a woman, who died last spring, with whom I was acquainted. The account of her life, written by her colleague, described the first phase of her life as very rich, "comparable to a bubbling spring," full of initiative, professional and social activity, and openness to science and art. Then came a second phase filled with the most serious illness, which confined her entirely to her room. She knew that her illness was incurable. She endured not only the present pain but the knowledge of the exact course her illness would take. On that, her colleague writes, "This second phase of her life was permeated by a joyousness, by a cheerfulness which was deeply rooted in quiet, unbounded trust in the fulfillment of divine leadings."

Rejoicing, then, does not depend entirely on our having everything that we usually regard as grounds for rejoicing. We must say more than that, of course. Rejoicing does not depend at all on our having a tendency toward joy or depression. There is a kind of rejoicing that can be very quiet and reserved. Perhaps it is hidden under depression and nervous breakdown. Yet it is true undaunted rejoicing. Such rejoicing can even lie dormant, as if covered by a sheet of ice.

II. We need now to give some thought as to whether we might have grounds for rejoicing. Sometimes it is good to read a text from back to front, like children who read the back of a menu first because the dessert is always listed last.

(a) "You shall rejoice," says God, ". . . at the place which the Lord your God will choose, to make his name dwell there." That is the dessert! God gives us a place in the world where his name dwells, where a person can find him, recognize him, and call him by name. In the

Old Testament this was the Temple. But God did not stop there. We have read that strange word of Jesus in which he said that his body, which would be crucified and resurrected, was the Temple of God (John 2:19–21).

God well knows that there are times when we do not pray, times when we cannot come to him. For that reason, he came to us and pursued us. Whether we can still believe it or not, God *was* in this world, and therefore this world is no longer without God.

But that is not all. We must also read that other word of Paul in which he says that we, the church, are the temple of God (1 Cor. 3:17; 6:19f.). God not only *was* in this world, he *is* in our world, actually present in all that makes up precisely our whole entangled world and our whole entangled life.

What is the church? A motley group of sympathetic and unsympathetic people, of brave and not-so-brave, of interesting and boring people. But it is at the same time the place where God's name dwells—the place where Jesus Christ is present, where the church hears his Word when it praises him in its songs and when it prays. Perhaps we cannot enter into these exercises as we should. Perhaps we do not understand the sermon and find it boring. Perhaps we let our mind wander during the prayers. But Jesus Christ is there, and brothers and sisters are there, too, who pray with me and for me and sing and praise God. That is the profoundest reason for rejoicing.

What possible help would some higher being called "God" be to us or some transcendent power which perchance stands back of everything? If God did not claim and sustain us, give us freedom to fall on our nose and then pick us up again when necessary, then he would be no cause for rejoicing at all. But God has also given us the place where he is *with us*, where he speaks with us again and again. He has given us the Temple, the church, Jesus Christ.

(b) In addition to this reason for rejoicing, there is a second sentence in our text: "You shall remember that you were a slave in Egypt; and you shall be careful to observe these statutes." Even to this day, the devout Israelite says to his child, "Remember that you were a slave in Egypt." In that way he says to him, "Remember what you were without God." So he eats unleavened bread at Easter (and our communion wafers are, of course, a reminder of it), never forgetting that time of need.

We should try to imagine sometime how it would be to live without God—without God on our deathbed and in our coffin; without God on the threshold of a new marriage; without God when our children come into the world; without God when they give us concern; without God when we are completely alone and have nothing to look forward to, when we would be left completely alone by everyone. By ourselves and no God there! Then, you may be sure, loneliness and death and pain and futility would be absolute lords. Then we would be only slaves. Then, considering the hardships and cruelties and distresses and insecurities in our world, I do not really know why we should still rejoice.

But we are not without God. There *is* a place where God's name dwells. We have Jesus Christ, and we have sisters and brothers who help us live with him. That is why we dare never forget what it means to live without God, without Christ.

(c) And God does still more for us— much, much more. He gives us a succession of very practical aids so that we cannot forget it. Nor can we forget that God is right here with his great gift in his arms, so that all we need to do is take it. He has forcibly demonstrated by the total life and death of Jesus that he is here for us and does not want to be without us. He has given us the people in the church with whom we can constantly share the testimony that God loves us. But more than this, God does what only he can, in order that we may give ourselves this gift correctly and not simply pass it by. He has done that with Israel for centuries. He wants to make it a practice with us also. That is precisely why he gave Israel the festival mentioned in the text.

(1) "You shall count seven weeks . . . from the time you first put the sickle to the standing grain. Then you shall keep the Feast of Weeks to the Lord your God."

God does not do everything for us! He wants *us* to count the days exactly until another feast day falls due. After all, he knows what we would do otherwise. We would, of course, never have time for a festival. We would keep on postponing it. Something would always keep interfering. We would be so preoccupied with making money and doing other things, that although we always intended to observe the feast, we would never get around to it. That is why God gives us Easter and Pentecost and Christmas every year. He well knows how much we need the festivals.

If the ages of your children are as close together as those of our children, then there is a long lapse of time between baptism and confirmation without special family feasts. When that is true, one is doubly convinced how wonderful it is to be able to celebrate a Sunday once in a while with friends. Then why is it that these Sundays or annual festivals more or less lack this distinctive quality of celebration? How much glamour can a mother give to Sunday—something a bit different for breakfast, a day without lessons, different clothes from weekday dress? (Even the old comfortable clothes which the English generally put on are better than simply wearing the same weekday clothes day in and day out.)

God wants us to celebrate, for he knows that we need the special touch, something extraordinary in everyday life.

(2) A second thing God asks us to do: "Then you shall keep the Feast of Weeks to the Lord your God, with the tribute of a freewill offering from your hand, which you shall give as the Lord your God blesses you." God helps us by expecting a gift from us. How comical it is that we Swiss put something into the collection box so bashfully. In England and America, the collection forms an important ingredient of worship. It is gathered, brought to the front, and presented to God with prayer.

But more important than the offering is the little postscript: "as the Lord your God blesses you." Here is why the gifts that God expects from us are so important to us: they help us to see what God has given to us to bless us. Every now and then we have to be nudged along. If my mother tells me, with a look of triumph, that she has been permitted to have four hours uninterupted sleep at night, then it occurs to me one day what a gift it is when God continually gives me eight hours sleep. Should we not take the opportunity to thank God once in a while for some particular gift? If we were sick and not able to sleep, we might pay hundreds of dollars for a remedy. Perhaps we ought to consider more carefully the gifts God gives us week by week. Then we would be aware that we are people upon whom gifts have been most lavishly bestowed.

(3) The third thing God asks us to do: "And you shall rejoice before the Lord your God, you and your son and your daughter, your manservant and your maidservant, the Levite who is within your towns, the sojourner, the fatherless and the widow who are among you." Church festivals are, indeed, a very great gift of God, because they enable us to get together occasionally with the persons whom God has given to us—with our children, who often go to school before we have had breakfast and return home in the evening after we have had to leave again for a meeting; but above all with the strangers, the widows, and orphans, that is to say, with all the lonely persons we know.

This means that we may have to change the pattern of our actions. Perhaps we may have to make a dozen telephone calls to invite one person to our festivals, the person nobody thinks of and everyone forgets. The single person, for instance. We have no idea what it means to many unmarried persons to be invited into a family occasionally. Many widows, even independent and strong women, suffer very painfully after the death of their husbands. A widow's social life comes to a sudden stop, and she no longer receives the invitations that they used to receive as a couple. If we stop to consider what our responsibilities may be to factory workers from foreign countries or others who are socially deprived, then we realize that the ones of whom God speaks in our text are still with us even today. And if we are successful in rejoicing with the strangers whom God has ready for us, we will be the beneficiaries.

The real basis of our rejoicing is in the fact that God chooses us, that he has told us so in the life and death and Resurrection of Jesus, and that he says it again and again in the church. Let us, therefore, be willing to take seriously the practical help which God gives us: the proper celebration of the festival, the offering by which we may always be reminded how much God has blessed us, and especially all the lonely people who await a call or a letter inviting them over for a snack or a cup of coffee or a Sunday outing.—Eduard Schweizer

Illustrations

GREAT LAUGHTER.   Part of the farce was that for the first time in my life that year in New York, I started going to church regularly, and what was farcical about it was not that I went but my reason for going, which was simply that on the same block where I lived there happened to be a church with a preacher I had heard of and that I had nothing all that much better to do with my lonely Sundays. The preacher was a man named George Buttrick, and Sunday after Sunday I went, and sermon after sermon I heard. It was not just his eloquence that kept me coming back, though he was wonderfully eloquent, literate, imaginative, never letting you guess what he was going to come out with next but twitching with surprises up there in the pulpit, his spectacles aglitter in the lectern light. What drew me more was whatever it was that his sermons came from and whatever it was in me that they touched so deeply. And then there came one particular sermon with one particular phrase in it that does not even appear in a transcript of his words that somebody sent me more than twenty-five years later, so I can only assume that he must have dreamed it up at the last minute and ad-libbed it—and on just such foolish, tenuous, holy threads as that, I suppose, hang the destinies of us all. Jesus Christ refused the crown that Satan offered him in the wilderness, Buttrick said, but he is king nonetheless because again and again he is crowned in the heart of the people who believe in him. And that inward coronation takes place, Buttrick said, "among confession, and tears, and great laughter."

It was the phrase *great laughter* that did it, did whatever it was that I believe must have been hiddenly in the doing all the years of my journey up till then. It was not so much that a door opened as that I suddenly found that a door had been open all along which I had only just then stumbled upon.—Frederick Buechner

Sermon Suggestions

GOALS OF SPIRITUAL GROWTH.   TEXT: 1 Sam. 2:18–20, 26. (1) Favor with the Lord. (2) Favor with the people.

WHAT IT MEANS TO BE THE PEOPLE OF GOD.   TEXT: Col. 3:12–17, TEV. (1) In terms of character, verse 12b. (2) In terms of deeds, verses 13–15. (3) In terms of Christian service and worship, verses 16–17.

Worship Aids

CALL TO WORSHIP.   "Praise ye the Lord. O give thanks unto the Lord; for he is good; for his loving-kindness endureth forever" (Ps. 106:1).

INVOCATION.   For the light of your coming in Christ—for the light of life—for the light of meaning—for the light of hope—for such a light that no darkness can ever overcome, we praise you, O God. We are grateful for your shining into our darkness and bringing the light of a new day. Praise be to you, Father of all light!—John M. Thompson

OFFERTORY SENTENCE.   "Thanks be to God for his unspeakable gift" (2 Cor. 9:15).

OFFERTORY PRAYER.   We are ministers of your good news, Lord, here and around your world, as we offer ourselves with our gifts. Accept them, bless them, and use them, we pray in the name of Jésus.

PRAYER.   Gracious God, we come here to find ourselves; it is so easy to get lost in the labyrinth of this world. We are your children by your grace—in Creation, in redemption, in sustenance day by day. When we are in good health and enjoying prosperity, hot grasping, possessive, and selfish we can be—forgetting the givenness of life. We do not acknowledge and confess that in you we live and move and have our being. Your daily providence we so often take for granted rather than receive with gratitude. How often, too, your grace has kept us from destroying ourselves. "If you should keep a record of our sins, Lord, who could stand?" We praise you, O God, that yours is a steadfast love and that with you there is plenteous pardon.

In Christ the fullness of your grace is present. In receiving your grace in him—the revolution begins—life is never the same again—a new day dawns. No longer do we seek laboriously to be worthy or to earn our redemption, but in faith we receive the new life that is here, to which before we have been blind. In your graciousness toward us, we discover a grace by which we can be gracious toward all others.

How we need your grace that there may be community among the nations that all people may live in peace and brotherhood and sisterhood, rather than in fear and hostility and the tragedy of war! How you have shed your grace upon us as a nation! May we not fail our calling to be gracious in bringing reconciliation and peace to the troubled areas where we have been partners in perpetrating and perpetuating hostilities and supplying implements of death. We pray for your church: for our church, "Grant us wisdom—grant us courage that we fail not man nor thee."

Wash us, O Father, and we shall be clean; heal us, and we shall be whole through him who is your word of grace.—John M. Thompson

LECTIONARY MESSAGE

Topic: Growing Up in Faith
TEXT: Luke 2:41–52

Jesus, too, was an adolescent! Like all growing youths, he struggled with parental boundaries, his own sense of identity, and the perplexing questions about the kind of world in which he was living. This is the simple story (recorded only by Luke) of a faithful family, committed to the religious nurture of their children; it is also a profound window into the character of the One whom we confess as both human and divine, God's own Son. This is the sole episode recorded in Jesus' life by Luke between the forty-day-old infant and the man of thirty years.

I. Jesus' parents were observant Jews; they went to Jerusalem every year at the Feast of the Passover. This festival, which commemorated God's deliverance out of Egypt, lasted approximately seven days. It played a unique role in the life of the Jewish people, serving to encourage and renew hope in God's faithfulness in the present, as in the past. It was also a family celebration and performed the significant function of unifying the bond from generation to generation. It is still considered the most important of the Jewish festivals.

II. Jesus fails to make connections with the caravan journeying together back home to Galilee. Another priority claims his attention. We do not know how long it was before Jesus' parents missed him; a twelve-year-old boy is on the boundary between childhood and manhood, so perhaps they simply trusted him to do what he was supposed to do. According to Luke, Jesus believed that he was doing exactly that.

When they did not find him among their company, Jesus' parents return to Jerusalem and inquire for him for three days before finding him in the Temple, engrossed in theological conversation with the teachers. He knows the Scriptures and is asking these sages of Israel who can offer deeper understanding for his inquiring mind. Ironically, later in his ministry, the majority of the religious authorities

will turn against him even though secretly marveling at the authority with which he taught. Even as a young lad, he has a strange sense of being at home in the Temple, which he calls "my Father's house."

III. Luke offers an enigmatic Jesus in this scene; Jesus cannot believe that Mary and Joseph would not know where to find him. Further, he speaks with remarkable detachment to them, stressing he had to be about God's business. Understandably, they did not comprehend the full significance of what he was saying; Mary, once again, was given more to keep in her heart and ponder.

Luke is very concerned to note the continuity Jesus has with the Old Testament and the institutions of Judaism. He wants his readers to understand clearly that rather than overturning these revered authorities, Jesus is the promised fulfillment of them. That he fully participated in the peity of Judaism is an important theme for Luke.

Jesus returned to Nazareth with his parents and was obedient to them, Luke carefully writes—lest someone interpret Jesus' responses in the Temple to his parents as impertinence. He had tested some of the limits of his emerging maturity and found a new degree of insight into his identify as one uniquely called and empowered by God. The role of his parents was not over, however. God continued to use them to enable Jesus "to grow in wisdom and stature, and in favor with God and humanity."

Like Jesus, our humanity is formed by the historical context and familial relations into which we are born as well as by the calling and impress of God on our lives. If and as we grow, we, too, attend to the claims of God and others on our lives.—Molly Marshall-Green

SECTION III.
Messages for Communion Services

SERMON SUGGESTIONS

Topic: You Can Go Home Again
TEXT: Luke 15:18

Several days ago a young couple in our church related the story of their young daughter's first night away from home. A friend had talked her into spending the night with her. Everything was all right as long as they were busy and having fun. However, when the night grew late and time came to go to bed, the little girl began sobbing. She cried so hard that her parents finally had to come in the middle of the night and take her home. Once in the father's arms the little girl said, "I wanted to come home, Daddy."

Oh! Here is a confession that has sobbed its way through the centuries. It is the cry of the prodigal. A young man was away from home, and he was having fun. Once the fun was over, sitting on the pig fence of life he cried, "I want to go home." This is the confession of one of the best-known personalities of the New Testament. It speaks to those who climb some hill of difficulty, perhaps in the valley of defeat. It speaks to those down and out, saying this can happen to you. You can go home again.

I have asked myself a hundred times, How did the young man get into the far country? Did he just wake up one morning and decide that he would ruin his life? No! We do not start the day with the idea of having some tragedy befall us. This young man was as normal as you and I. He wanted life, and he wanted to live it on the edge. He wanted to be happy! So he turned being sick of home into homesickness. He exchanged his father's home for a pigpen. He changed his dream into failure. Why and how? He wanted to be free, but more important than that, he wanted only to please himself. He set out on a life that would answer only to himself. He was his own man. He would do as he pleased whether it pleased anyone else or not.

Let us remember that it is the spring of selfishness from which all the streams of sin will flow. Selfishness is expensive. Ask Adam and Eve in the land near the Garden of Eden. Ask Samson as he pulls the pillars of that gigantic building down. Ask David as he looks at the long finger of Nathan, the prophet. You see, this young man wanted to be free, but selfishness is never freedom. In the end he was sent to the pigpen. He did not choose to go; he was sent. He lost his freedom because he sought to keep it.

I have heard the masters play the piano, and they were super. However, when I sit down at the piano I want freedom. I do not follow any music. Notes are not for me. Why, I just play what I want when I want, and no one wants to hear me play. You see, I am free, but I am a prisoner of my own freedom. I cannot express myself through music because I do not follow the rules of music. When you and I seek to hold onto our life, we are selfish, and we lose it. If we turn loose and give our life to God, then we truly find ourselves, and we are free.

You know, the real tragedy of the prodigal is that he was where he was needlessly. He made some bad choices that led him to the pigpen. Had he been put there, I would feel sorry for him. Had hard times struck, I could give him a little room, but he was there by choice. I am just glad the story does not end there. He got up and went home to the arms of a waiting, forgiving father. Perhaps you want to recall now those happy moments in your life when you went home to the Father. Maybe some readers will find time now to move away from that selfish life and learn that they, too, can still go home to the Father.—Jerry W. Mixon

Topic: Correcting a Misconception
TEXT: Mark 14:22–26

One of the tragedies in the life of Christ's church in our day centers around the general attitude toward the Lord's Supper. Unfortunately, many people feel that this experience is a departure from the normal in Christian worship. Pastors must share the responsibility for this gross error. Often, the supper is tacked onto the end of a service, is participated in hastily, and is not given the atmosphere of reverence that it deserves. Instead of occupying the center of the stage, it is pushed off to one side. Some congregations have received little explanation of the meal—its significance, its meaning, and correct participation by the Lord's people. Therefore, if church members are going to deliberately miss one worship period, many feel that they can be absent from the Lord's Supper. After all, it soon becomes "old hat." The participants listen to often-repeated and familiar scriptures. They go through the same motions: they chew on a little piece of dry cracker and drink a small amount of grape juice. The whole thing becomes an exercise in boredom, and many people find themselves hoping that it won't take too long. And so, what difference does it make if they miss this departure from the regular worship periods?

I contend that such an attitude is a tragedy because it deprives a person of what can be one of the most profoundly meaningful and effective worship experiences that he or she will know. Approached with reverence and expectation, and participated in prayerfully, the Lord's Supper can cause Christ's presence with his people to be felt as at few other times.

Ironically, one of the strange developments in the church has been the necessity of promoting the Lord's Supper. We are finding that we must urge people to come or to "stay for church" after Sunday school to participate in the Lord's meal. This would have been incredible to the early disciples. How could anyone not want to take part in this act given to the church by the church's Lord? If, somehow, they could observe our usual custom, they would be surprised that we do not eat together more as a fellowship. And they would be perplexed at our participation in Christ's meal once a quarter or once a month. Most likely, they ate and drank in remembrance of Christ each time they gathered; such an act was a vital part of their fellowship in worship. Glenn Hinson has suggested that one key to deeper fellowship in our churches may be a more frequent participation in the Lord's Supper. The early church joyfully anticipated this meal as an act of sincere worship.

As Christ's people, we should anticipate the master's meal *because the church never worships more genuinely than at this time.* Worship is the response of one's whole being to the God who is interested in the total person. It is opening life to One whose love can correct and strengthen. It is committing life anew to One who can nurture, develop, and use it in his high purpose. The supper was designed as an objective expression of just such an experience and expression.

All the elements of true worship are here: sincere thanksgiving for blessings received and anticipated; confession of wrongs committed and redemptive acts left undone; petition for creative forgiveness; dedication to service; witness to one's faithfulness to the fellowship. The supper can be a periodic experience of renewal in one's Christian living. It can become an avenue for repeated commitment.

The supper is a concrete expression of our identification with Christ and his church; it gives renewed awareness of his power to accomplish what he has promised and to do it through people; it serves as a reminder that we are engaged in his ministry.

Never are we more conscious of what God has done, is doing, and will do than when we are participating in Christ's meal. The meal provides a consciousness of God which we need desperately.

We should look forward to the Lord's Supper *because, by participating, we come as close as we will come to imitating an actual act of Christ.* He left two acts which he explicitly commanded that we keep: baptism and the Lord's Supper. The design for these two creative experiences came from the Savior's mind. We literally are following in his steps in at least two points.

We cannot go back to the upper room, to those crisis-laden hours. But we can recreate the moment in history. We are obeying Christ concretely, for all to see. Thus, our desire to participate should be an indication of our willingness to obey him at other points in our living.

Our willing absence, our take-it-or-leave-it attitude, our careless and casual participation all point to deeper disobedience and unconcern. These are surface indications of deeper difficulties in our relationship to Christ. These indicate an apathy eating away at our inner lives—a lethargy which threatens our usefulness and effectiveness.

You and I correct the misconception concerning the Lord's Supper by allowing it to have proper significance in our lives, by allowing it to be a renewing worship experience.—Eli Landrum, Jr.

Topic: Sharing

TEXT: 1 Cor. 11:17–34

The church at Corinth had a serious problem. What were intended to be Christ-honoring fellowship meals were turning into drunken revelries. Wealthier members arrived at the meals earlier than the slaves and poor people of the church. Rather than waiting for the poor and sharing with them, the more affluent members gorged themselves. As a result, some went hungry while others became drunk (v. 21). The poor were humiliated. The example of Christ was ignored.

Paul reminded the Corinthians of Christ's model of self-giving love reflected in the Lord's Supper. On the night that he was betrayed, Jesus took bread and gave thanks for it. He broke the bread and shared it with the apostles as a symbol of the way he shared his life with them. The sharing of the cup represented Christ's sacrificial death. For Christians to practice self-indulgence at the Lord's Supper was to eat and drink unworthily.

Paul further encouraged the Corinthians to wait for one another at the fellowship meal. If one can't wait, then one should eat at home rather than violate the spirit of fellowship.

I. *Examine the way we see others.* When the passage is preached, members are *not* to be challenged to examine themselves in order to see if they are worthy of participating in the Lord's Supper. The word *unworthily* in verse 27 is an adverb modifying the verbs *shall eat* and *drink.* It is *not* an adjective describing persons. No one is worthy to take the bread and the cup except by the grace of God. The purpose of examination is for each individual to test the attitudes he or she brings to the Lord's table. The manner in which the Corinthians observed the fellowship meal revealed an attitude of "our group" versus "their group" that was dividing the church into social factions. This passage gives the preacher an occasion to address problems such as the formation of elitist cliques that neglect the needs of church members outside their social circle.

II. *Examine the way we see Christ.* In contrast to the way some Corinthians behaved during the Lord's Supper, Jesus left the supreme example of sharing with others. As Christians approaching the observation of this ordinance, we must be mindful of the sacrifice Christ made so that we can share in his life.

III. *Examine the way we see ourselves.* Our motives for wanting to partake of God's grace and forgiveness cannot be self-centered and Christ-centered at the same time. Therefore, we examine our actions and attitudes toward others. We can't be cold, callous, and unconcerned when we remember the caring compassion poured out to us by the Son of God.—Joseph H. Coleman, Jr.

Topic: The Promise of Community

Text: John 15

The pain of social isolation can be met by the presence of community. This may seem rather simplistic. Am I saying anything more than "If you do not have relationships, then go make some?" I certainly am. I am well aware that it is no small feat for socially isolated persons to develop a pleasing balance of community and aloneness. Companionship and aloneness are essential components in a healthy community. The socially lonely long for a lifestyle through which they can keep in touch with other people and group events.

Jesus' words in John 15 may provide the best biblical model of how we are to face social isolation and alienation. This chapter is part of Jesus' last words to his disciples before his betrayal. In this chapter, Jesus described the relationships which characterize a believer's life. Jesus first described the relationships between him and his followers as like that of a grape vine and its branches. A first step in overcoming loneliness is to be a part of Christ.

Jesus was clear that we demonstrate our unity with him by prayer and obedience to his commandments. His commandment was to love one another (John 13:34; 15: 17). Our commitment to Jesus calls for us to love others. This is the second step in overcoming loneliness—to risk our own fears on behalf of others.

In John 15:18–27, Jesus instructed us in the third step for living a Christian social life. He warned us that the believer's relationship to others will sometimes bear the marks of misunderstanding and difficulty. Some persons in this world will not understand or accept us. This is true regardless of how well we learn to relate to others. I will use these three steps as a guide in discussing how social loneliness can be faced.

I. *Abiding in Christ.* Those who experience social loneliness will frequently believe that there is no one who cares about them or for them. Their sense of isolation may be overwhelming. It is important for Christians to remember first that we are never absolutely alone. Jesus knew that he was never alone: "Yet I am not alone, for the Father is with me" (John 16:32). Since the Holy Spirit, the Comforter, is always present with the Christian, we, too, can make the same claim: I am not alone, for God is with me.

This affirmation is not intended to trivialize a lonely person's pain. Nor is it intended to offer an easy answer to a very difficult problem. It is necessary, however, to set the appropriate context for relationships. Those who feel estranged, alienated, and lonely certainly need human companionship. They need someone to hear them. Wayne Oates has written to this point well.

> You will find at the core of countless numbers of individuals an estrangement, a loneliness, a feeling on their part that no one cares for their soul, and a querulous sense of strangeness that anyone would genuinely take the time to listen and understand them.

The lonely frequently need a listening human ear to remind them of God's compassion.

The truth must be maintained, however, that our human ears are but pale imitations of God's great compassion for us. Those who suffer from an absence of satisfying human relationships may also suffer from an absence of feeling God's presence. The socially deprived lonely may find benefit in increasing their times alone. These alone times can be used to allow communion with God. Solitude with God is not just idle time. It may involve activities such as enjoying God's Creation through walks in a forest or watching a sunset over the ocean. It may involve intensive study of Scripture. It may involve meditation and prayer in various forms.

The result of solitude with God can be dramatic. The importance placed on social deficiencies may be dramatically reduced. One's sense of living in a world of relationships and love may be increased. Sometimes the relational blocks which kept one from creative living are confronted in such times of solitude. These confrontations allow freedom to emerge as God brings healing. Communion with God is an essential backdrop for improving relational skills.

II. *Love one another.* The next arena of growth for the socially lonely is more direct. The question is usually asked something like, With whom and in what ways can I be a friend? How can I change my relationships so that I have friends?

The first step in friendship is to evaluate the friendships you already have. There are many levels of friendship. You may find it helpful to take pen and paper, write the categories which I will describe across the top of the page, and list persons under each category which fit that kind of friendship.

(a) *Convenience friends* are those with whom I routinely interact. They include people such as neighbors and work companions. We should not place too high expectations upon these friends for intimacy and closeness. We can hope for common courtesy and perhaps even occasional conversations about matters of mutual interest. We cannot build our worlds around these friends.

(b) *Special-interest friends* are those with whom we have a concern in common. These interests can include such things as sports, social and community-action programs, and certain work partners. These are members of our softball team or people who volunteer with us to teach a children's Sunday school class. At work, these would be the people with whom we extensively discuss common problems or projects. We can talk readily and deeply about the interests we share. We should not expect these friendships to go beyond this area. On occasion, a special-interest friendship can be broadened into a deeper relationship.

(c) *Historical friends* are those people from the past who were once close to us. We are likely to enjoy reminiscing with them. They are important because they add a sense of history to our daily lives. They help us remember where we have been, our goals and dreams, and our deeper emotional and cultural roots. They can help us keep a perspective on our current situation, especially if our life journey has meant large moves, either geographically or socially. High school or college class reunions may be times when we connect with these historical friends. The danger of these friends is that we can get trapped in nostalgia, the feeling of "the good old days." The days in which we did feel socially connected may lead to more pain than joy because of our present situation. Nevertheless, these friends offer potent resources for friendship.

(d) *Crossroads friends* are those who have shared a crucial intersection in our life. These intersections were usually a time of crisis or life change. These are people who were not very important to us prior to some crucial event and may not have been very close after the event. But at the moment of crisis they were there for us. For example, I recall a college friend who was very helpful to me during the time I was deciding to enter pastoral ministry. I have had very little contact with him since that time, but I will always recall his love with thankfulness.

(e) *Cross-generation friends* are those persons of different generations than our own with whom we have been mutually encouraging. We have learned from each other despite, or maybe even because of, our difference in age. I have watched my daughter enjoy such a friendship with one of my aunts. My daughter has learned several crafts from this aunt. She has also responded with warmth to my aunt's stories about her own childhood. On the other hand, I believe my aunt has found encouragement and energy through my daughter's curiosity and evident love.

(f) *Close friends* are those with whom we emotionally and physically maintain ongoing communication. It is these friends that the socially isolated have the most difficulty developing. Close friends are those we consider to be companions. We tend to plan activities and share dreams. We share a sense of empathy, of feeling the joy and pain of the other. Close friends can be called upon for the most important events and the most insignificant trivia of life. Friendship at this level does not demand constant, or even frequent, communication. But when close friends do communicate, they do so with much interest and investment.

Each of these levels of friendship is important. To "love one another" calls for a balanced network of friendship. We should not expect a person at one level of friendship to be closer and more intimate than is appropriate to the relationship. Friendships depend on a balance between togetherness and solitude in these relationships.

III. *Expect difficulty.* Jesus' message in John 15 also includes the message that we should expect difficulties in our relationships. Of course, the focus of Jesus' message was on the persecution that believers could expect from unbelievers. But the truth also applies to friendship patterns. One myth of marriage is "and they lived happily ever after." The truth is that marriages and friendships are full of disappointment and difficulty. Some who are socially lonely believe that since they cannot develop a perfectly satisfying relationship, they must not have any friendships. That is not true.

Even the best relationships will suffer through difficult times. In Acts we read of the Apostle Paul's first missionary journey. Barnabas was his trusted and close companion. Later, they came to a serious disagreement over another companion for the second journey. They had such a fight that Paul went one way and Barnabas another (Acts 15:36–41). There is no evidence that they ever reconciled their differences. However, later Paul did affirm Barnabas as an apostle of Christ (1 Cor. 9:6). No one has perfect friendships throughout life.

During difficult times in a friendship, specific steps should be taken to reconcile differences. The first step will usually be to overcome the fears which paralyze us from taking the risk of reaching out to others who have hurt us. Prayer and support from other friends may help overcome these fears.

The model for reconciliation found in Matt. 18:15–18 then offers clear steps to take. First, talk directly with the person with whom you have the difficulty. Be ready to clearly take responsibility for your part of the conflict. Expect them to take responsibility for their share. If that does not resolve the conflict, you may take

two or three trusted friends into your confidence. Express your concerns to them and go talk with your friend. Be ready to change your own thoughts and behavior where necessary. If these steps are unsuccessful, you may wish to talk with your pastor or spiritual leader. They may be able to provide guidance or act as a mediator in your conflict. If these steps do not resolve your difficulty, you and your friend may need to say good-bye to each other. This will certainly produce grief, but it will also give you freedom to begin new relationships.—Steven S. Ivy

Topic: Our Moral Obligation

TEXT: Rom. 15:22–33

A pastor from Virginia shared a penetrating story about a mission tour to the Far East. While in Hong Kong, he observed a hungry little girl outside a bakery window. She had fallen asleep with her face pressed against the window that separated her from the fresh bread inside. He photographed that touching scene. When sharing his slide presentation back home, the pastor always climaxed his sermon with that picture and an appeal for people to share Christ, the Living Bread, to a hungry world. Following one presentation, a perceptive worshiper asked him, "What did you do about it?" "About what?" the pastor replied. "About the little girl asleep at the bakery window, what did you do about that?"[1]

That is the question before us today as we consider world hunger. What will we do? What must we do? The facts are startling. In our world, one billion people live in a state of absolute poverty. Of that number, the best estimates indicate 700 million people live in a state of constant hunger in a world that, according to experts, has enough grain for everyone to have three thousand calories to consume each day.[2] To many Americans, hunger is

1. Drew Gunnells, "Resources for Special Occasions," *Proclaim* (October 1986):41.

2. *World Hunger: Helping Southern Baptists Respond to a Hungry World* (published by the Christian Life Commission of the Southern Baptist Convention, 1987), 10.

dinner a little late, causing a slight discomfort. For these hundreds of millions, hunger is a half-filled bowl once a day—the road to a slow death. Twenty million people die each year of starvation or hunger-related diseases—twelve million of those are children under the age of five.[3] If all of the world's hungry were lined up one yard apart, the line would circle the globe twenty-five times.[4]

In the United States, 15 percent of our population lives under the poverty level. An extensive study done by the Harvard School of Public Health found hunger in every state, every town, and every rural area examined. The researchers said, "We went into no region without finding hunger."[5]

But that is enough of the facts, for we can all be moved or bored by facts. The bottom line is, What will we *do* about world hunger? Christians have the ability and resources to relieve world hunger. If just the Christians in America would respond, world hunger could be tremendously decreased. The Bible speaks to us about our moral obligation and challenges us to become actively involved.

I. Feeding the world's hungry defines our moral obligation. The Apostle Paul was a tremendous preacher, a powerful missionary, and a dynamic witness for Christ. Often overlooked are Paul's social ethics. Economic sharing is an important theme in his writings. Growing out of that conviction was a general offering that Paul personally collected for the poor Christians at Jerusalem. He was eager to remember the poor and to assist the destitute in Jerusalem (Gal. 2:10).

In his letter to the Roman Christians, Paul postponed his mission trip to Spain to deliver hunger aid personally. He was pleased the Christians in Macedonia and Achaia had already made "some contribution for the poor among the saints at Jerusalem" (15:26, RSV). Not only were they pleased to do it, but the texts says they were obligated to do it. "Indeed they are in debt to them, for if the Gentiles have come to share in their spiritual blessings, they ought also to be of service to them in material blessings" (15:27, RSV).

The clear directives of Scripture leave no doubt as to our moral obligation for the poor and the hungry.

II. Feeding the world's hungry demands our personal involvement. The question with which we all struggle is, What can one person or one church do? The need is so overwhelming. A proverb of the Swahili tribe says, "Drop by drop the bucket fills." What one person or one church does often seems to be "just a drop in the bucket." But everyone adding "drops" can fill the bucket. Every one of us can become involved personally.

(a) Personal involvement must be *systematic*. In 1 Corinthians, Paul referred again to the Jerusalem collection and gave instructions to the Corinthian Christians to give systematically for those in material need. "On the first day of every week, each of you is to put something aside and store it up, as he may prosper, so that contributions need not be made when I come" (16:2, RSV). Systematic giving to special needs is the practical side of good stewardship.

(b) Personal involvement must also be *sacrificial.* Paul's strongest words to the Corinthians about this special collection came in his second letter to the church at Corinth. In 2 Corinthians 8–9, he again held up the example of the churches in Macedonia: "Their abundance of joy and their extreme poverty have overflowed in a wealth of liberality" (8:2, RSV). They gave according to their means and beyond their means. Their joyous, sacrificial, and unexpected gifts were used to challenge the Corinthians to demonstrate genuine love. Paul thus challenged the Corinthians to give sacrificially to this hunger offering. "I do not mean that others should be

---

3. *Louisiana Baptists' Gifts for Hungry People* (pamphlet published by the Louisiana Baptist Convention Hunger Committee).

4. Foy Valentine, "Hunger's Face and Hunger's Faces" (address at the Convocation for World Hunger, Pineville, La., September 30, 1983).

5. "Study Finds U.S. Hunger 'Epidemic,'" *Morning Advocate,* February 7, 1984.

eased and you burdened, but that as a matter of equality your abundance at the present time should supply their want" (8:13–14, RSV).

When we consider our gifts to world hunger, the hard reality is that our giving has been far from sacrificial.

However, personal sacrifice must involve more than just giving money. It is easy to give a dollar or a handful of change or even ten dollars and feel like we have done our part. Perhaps the real evidence of sacrifice can be demonstrated in our personal life-styles.

James Reston was a syndicated columnist for the *New York Times* for more than thirty years. In his final column for the newspaper, he wrote, "In America, we have learned something about how to deal with adversity since the Great Depression, but not much about how to deal with prosperity. We are very rich, but we are not having a very good time. We are producing so much food that we don't know what to do with the garbage, while half of the human race goes to bed hungry every night."[6]

Reston's words become more haunting when one considers that the United States wastes 20 percent of its food. An estimated $31 billion a year in food is thrown away or destroyed because of surplus.[7] A serious examination of our life-styles as well as our giving is needed, for we can make sacrificial adjustments in each area.

The issue of world hunger has eternal implications. Unless someone intervenes, the hungry ultimately will die. Our moral obligation is to do something about this problem. True Christians will be concerned. True Christians will become involved personally. After all, who's more important—you or an eight-year-old Indonesian boy? Does God say it is more important that you have food or that a young Korean mother have food? Is God more obligated to provide for your needs

or the needs of a migrant family in rural America? All of us know the answers to those questions.—Reggie R. Ogea

ILLUSTRATIONS

BY ROBERT C. SHANNON

THE REAL THING.   In the Kunsthistoriches Museum in Vienna, in a glass case protected by electronic alarms is a small piece of cloth. The card accompanying it says that it is a piece of the tablecloth from the upper room. Few people today would believe that, in fact, such a souvenir has survived. But what if it were true? What if we did have the very cloth from the upper room? Would that enhance our Communion? No! We do have something from the upper room. We have the living presence of Jesus Christ who said, "I drink it with you."

A TOAST TO GOD.   To drink a toast or to drink to someone's health may have had a very sinister beginning. The easiest way to poison someone was to slip the poison into his drink. To be sure that that didn't happen, a man would mix some wine from his cup with that of the man seated beside him, pouring from one cup into another. We have a remnant of that left today when we touch glasses. From thus drinking to one's health there has come the better custom of lifting a cup and drinking in someone's honor. In a sense we do that at Communion. We drink in honor of Christ. We lift the cup and drink a toast to him!

TAKING COMMUNION HOME WITH US. Table napkins are commonplace now. They were introduced by the Romans, but for a far different purpose than that for which we use them today. It was considered a compliment to the host for a guest to take some of the leftover food home with him. The host was disappointed if he did not. The guest used the napkin to wrap up the food he carried home. We need to carry something home with us

6. Quoted in "Global Glimpses," *The Commission* (October 1987):5.

7. *World Hunger* (Christian Life Commission), 10.

from the table of Communion. It's not the bread. It's not the wine. It's the sense of the presence of Jesus Christ.

THE EMPTY CHAIR.   In some churches it is the custom to serve Communion from a table behind which are two chairs. The one presiding sits in one chair. The other remains empty. It's a reminder of the Lord, present but unseen, who is really the host at that table. Such a custom recalls the empty chair at the Jewish Passover. It was reserved for Elijah who must come before the Messiah. We know that John the Baptist fulfilled that prophecy, but they leave a chair for Elijah. Elijah never comes! The empty chair at Communion symbolizes one who has already come and who is truly present.

EMPTY CEREMONIES.   In some parts of Austria, the first Sunday in Lent is marked by a strange ceremony. A witch made of straw is set on top of a blazing bonfire. Her head has been filled with gunpowder. It was once believed that the clouds of sparks would drive out the spirits of winter so that spring might come. Of course, the ceremony has long outlived the pagan faith that founded it. Now it is only an excuse to have a festival and break up the long winter. What about our ceremonies? Have they outlived the faith that formed them? What about Communion? Is it only a gesture to a nearly forgotten past, or is it a present communion with a real and living Lord?

SECTION IV.

Messages for Funeral Services

BY ALBERT J. D. WALSH

SERMON SUGGESTIONS

Topic: A Rock of Refuge

TEXT: Ps. 71:1–3

The trials and hardships of life are not new to those of us in the Christian community. Our ancestors struggled with life; with the pains inflicted by sickness and sorrow. There have been others, before us, who have known what it is to suffer, to feel anxiety and despair, to experience the waning of faith and hope. We can read the Psalms and hear reflected in certain words our own uncertainties and anxious questionings. The Psalms are all too human; we can find ourselves saying, "I, too, have felt just that way!"

Yet these words are more than reflections of human suffering and despair. They are songs of praise and thanksgiving; they are melodies filled with yearning and desire. The Psalms are an honest reflection of faith, as something more than wishful thinking or childish belief. They take us directly to the heart of faith, by revealing the very heart of the human struggle with God. The psalmists make no effort to clothe human anguish with the thin garment of religious convictions. For the psalmists, faith is nothing less than trust in God's purpose and plan for each individual and for Creation.

Not a blind trust, and not resignation. Faith, as expressed by the Psalms, is not an attitude of simply accepting one's fate, whatever that might be. Nor is it that form of optimism which seeks to convince the self or others that ultimately, it will all work out OK. Faith is a sense of being connected with God in a way that allows one to be honest about hardships and limitations. Faith is a way of envisioning the world and others, accepting them for who they are, and remaining present to/ for them as they grow and develop. Faith is that form of trust which frees one to allow others their own failures and folly, while caring enough to reach out in love when they falter and need a lift.

Faith is trusting that God will be God and that we can be human; faith acknowledges that we can't will God into existence and that no one can will God out of existence! Faith recognizes that human life is limited to a span of years while confessing that God is unlimited in the power to heal, restore, and renew our lives. Faith sees the presence of God in seemingly small and insignificant events: the smile of a child, the touch from a loved one, the word of encouragement from a friend. Faith is that powerful force in human life which will always have an effect in the lives of others.

Faith, then, is the one word that captures the essence of this person, whose memory we cherish. ———— was no blind optimist. He was, however, a man of quiet faith. He held faith in his heart; faith in God and faith in his family and faith in his Christian community. ———— was a builder and a mover. He knew that growth means change and that change can be difficult. ———— did not accept his sickness with resignation but only because he had a deep joy in and respect for life. He had faith in each member of his family; he

241

accepted each one, warts and all! And his faith was expressed in loving care and devotion and in his desire to see each of you become the best you could be. He recognized his own shortcomings, and that honesty made it possible for ——— to accept yours as well!

I think that ——— would not want us to speak of him in lofty terms, as though he were something more than each of us. And yet, I believe there was something very special about this man. I believe that he was a genuine person; an individual with character and integrity. Yes, he had his personal struggles and difficulties. But he lived that form of faith which is so very hard to find in our world today. He trusted God and loved his fellow human beings, and he never confused the two! ———'s faith was rooted in God, while his love was directed to others.

You will grieve, and your hearts will remain heavy for a time. That is as it should be. With time, I pray that the memory of this man, and his faith, will begin to touch you deep within. I pray that when it touches you, your inner eye of love will recognize how precious a gift he has given. And I hope that his gift to you will not be lost in silence and indifference. For the God who touched ———'s life, who sustained him throughout his time of trial, who strengthened him when weak and lifted him when in despair, is there for you and for me. And I believe ——— would desire us to see and embrace and find comfort in God's presence.

Topic: Keep Your Heart
Text: Prov. 4:23

For her daily prayer, ——— used the well-known devotional entitled *Our Daily Bread.* In her copy there are two pages marked out, each with a saying that reflects her faith character. One reads, "She pleases God best who trusts Christ most." And the other reads, "While the Christian must live in the world, she must not allow the world to live in her."

——— was a person of deep faith in Christ, our Lord. It wasn't the kind of faith that draws attention to the believer; rather, it was faith that always pointed away from the self to Christ. Her faith was like a quiet stream, running below the surface of her life, providing nurture and strength in times of trial and struggle. Her trust in Christ was evident throughout her life as she faced hardship and the loss of her husband; as she provided him with loving care and devotion. And she spoke of her faith with heartfelt conviction.

———'s faith was, like her character, soft and gentle. She expressed a deep and genuine concern for others. It wasn't so much that her heart was in her faith, as it was faith deep in her heart. This woman certainly lived in the world, with all its joys and sorrows. But I never felt that the world had taken a stranglehold on her heart. She held no bitterness or resentment. I was touched by this woman's sense of compassion and concern for others, and I was often inspired by her commitment to Christ and her witness to the power of faith. She had a personal relationship with our Lord. I had the impression that ——— talked with Christ, as one would a friend. Maybe that's why this chorus was her favorite: "He walks with me, and he talks with me, and he tells me I am his own. And the words we share as we tarry there, no other has ever known." Simple words, revealing a profound faith!

But where I really feel the presence of ———'s character is in the passage from Proverbs: "Keep your heart with all vigilance, for from it flow the springs of life." The heart is the center of all that a person will think, do, and say. The heart is the treasure chest, from which a person gives to others either "good" or "evil." ———'s heart, held open to friends and family, offered a treasure that was "good." She offered each one of you gathered here, a precious treasure of love, loyalty, and laughter. Her heart was filled with the "good things" of Christ, and she shared those gifts freely and graciously.

We tend, too often, to measure the quality of a person's life by the great contributions he or she has made to society or culture. But here was a woman whose life touched so many others with love and compassion. No great accomplishment in the eyes of the world! But what an accomplished life in the eyes of God: "She pleases God best who trusts Christ most!"

From the very center of ———'s heart, we each received some joy, some courage, some hope. She opened her heart, and the springs of life flowed freely to each one of us. That, I believe, is the true measure of this woman's greatness: Her willingness to share generously of herself, her faith, and her love.

I also believe that ———'s practice of daily devotion was an effort to keep her heart filled with the blessings of Christ. Not so as to hoard them and keep them for herself; rather, in the desire to remain filled with the grace of Christ and then to pour out that grace into the lives of family and friends. Her home and her heart were always open, inviting others to enter and be nurtured in faith. What more could anyone desire from a single human life, than to live out the grace of God with and for others. And that is exactly what ———'s life accomplished.

I will long remember her smile and her generosity in sharing love with me. My visits with ——— were always punctuated with laugher and a genuine joy in life. I would leave her home, refreshed and renewed. I knew that somehow, purely by grace, I had been in the presence of a person who knew and loved Christ our Lord. ——— will be missed. But the gifts she shared with us will never depart from our hearts. In the days and weeks ahead, those treasures of love and joy will begin to nurture and sustain you through your sorrow. And, with time, that love she shared with you and the inspiration she has imparted to each one of you will become the source of comfort and hope.

Topic: Unless the Lord Builds the House
TEXTS: Ps. 127:1; Matt. 7:24–25
Human life is fragile! Human life is susceptible to the rains, floods, and winds of turmoil and tribulation! Human life is, each and every day, vulnerable to sickness, deepening despair, loneliness, isolation, rejection, physical and emotional impairment! Human life appears subject to the "slings and arrows of outrageous fortune!"

Human life is also enduring! Human life is courageous, vibrant, colorful! Human life is, each and every day, triumphant over the forces of physical and emotional sickness, deepening despair, loneliness, isolation, and rejection! Human life is the object of God's benevolent grace, steadfast love, and providential care!

In this depiction of human life, I am referring to the person of faith and not to humanity in general. In fact, there is no such things as "humanity in general!" We are, all of us, creatures of the Creator, the living God; we are created by God, for God; and we are created by God for each other. Human life is less than it was created to be when it stands outside the boundaries of relationship to God and the neighbor. That is what our Christian faith teaches us, and that is what we believe!

But what, exactly, is this life of faith? What is it that distinguishes the person of faith from one who, consciously or unconsciously, stands outside this relationship to God and neighbor? So often we look to those who are "faithless" and say, "How the faithless prosper! Why is it that these 'faithless' ones appear unscathed by the 'slings and arrows of outrageous fortune?' How is it that they seem to suffer far less than those of us who confess to faith in God?" We are not the first to ask such questions, and we will not be the last! But, let me tell you something; let me tell you something that is rooted in the words of the psalmist and Jesus' teaching and my pastoral experience.

Appearances can be, and are too often, deceiving! Houses can, outwardly, have the appearance of beauty and stability, while just beneath the surface, they are weak, poorly constructed, and dangerously fragile! When the rains of trouble and the floods of tribulation and the winds of turmoil beat upon such houses, they begin to creak and groan; they are threatened with destruction. Like a "house of cards," they stand in constant peril of falling! I have ministered with those persons who lay no claim to faith, and in their hour of stormy existence, they sway to and fro, fearful that their lives will fall in total, irrevocable, destruction!

Such persons can, no doubt, give the outward appearance of security and wellbeing, while just below the surface their hearts are trembling with anxiety and apprehension; the very foundation of their existence begins to tremble as they face the inevitability of death! As long as skies are fair and the prospects of life are good, such persons appear strong and stable. But when the skies begin to darken, when the rains of trouble begin to fall, when the floods of physical and emotional distress begin to rise, when the winds of sickness and death begin to blow, then the inner structure of their lives can be seen for what it truly is: the feeble foundation of insecurity, uncertainty, and doubt!

The psalmist writes, "Unless the LORD builds the house, those who build it labor in vain!" Persons of faith know this to be true. The person of faith has given his or her human life into God's hands. The person of faith is a living, breathing, "temple of the Holy Spirit"; a house built upon the firm foundation of God's steadfast love and providential care; a house with its foundation and substructure built upon the "rock" of Jesus the Christ. And when the rains of trouble begin to fall and the floods of physical and emotional distress begin to rise and the winds of sickness and death begin to rage and "beat upon that house," it may tremble, but it will not fall into irrevocable destruction!

For, in the words of the Apostle Paul, "We [houses built upon the firm foundation of Jesus Christ, the apostles, martyrs and prophets]—we are afflicted in every way, but not crushed; perplexed, but not driven to despair; persecuted, but not forsaken; struck down, but not destroyed; always carrying in the body the death of Jesus, so that the life of Jesus may be manifested in our bodies"! (2 Cor. 4:8–10) This is the human life in faith, the house of faith built by God himself, that house founded on the "rock" of Jesus the Christ; and all the rains and floods and winds of hell itself shall not prevail against it!

—— was a builder; he knew that a firm foundation would insure that his home could sustain all the rains, floods, and winds of nature's fury! But more than that; he knew that human life needed a firm foundation in faith and that this faith must be founded and grounded in the Christ of God! ——'s life disclosed the truth of the psalmist's admonition: "Unless the

LORD builds the house, those who build it labor in vain!" And —— was not one to "labor in vain." He gave his life to Jesus the Christ; he built his life upon the firm foundation of faith in God; he placed his fragile, tender, vulnerable existence in the hands of Jesus—the Master Builder!

And when the rains of trouble began to fall heavy on his life; when the floods of physical and emotional distress began to rise, threatening his heart, mind, and soul; when the winds of turmoil and tribulation began to blow; he was not shaken to the core of his being. Rather, he stood firm and fast in the courage of faithful living; he revealed, for everyone with eyes to see, the depth of his commitment to Christ and the gospel! Both —— and ——, throughout this long and troublesome storm, gave witness to the firm foundation of their lives in Christ; for they were "afflicted in every way, but not crushed; perplexed, but not driven to despair . . . struck down, but not destroyed!"

Topic: The Love of Christ

TEXT: Rom. 8:35

The words of the Apostle Paul are familiar to most Christians. In this chapter of his letter to the Romans, Paul has one desire. He seeks to comfort those who are afflicted and to afflict those who are comfortable! I must admit, I've never before read these words in exactly that manner. But this week, as I thought about this precious woman and the struggles she endured over the past several years of her life, the words of Paul took on a new meaning. How so?

Well, to be frank about it, I'd always assumed that Paul meant to say that nothing could separate us from the love Christ holds for us. But now I find myself wondering if the apostle meant something more. Of course, he wants to assure us that Christ's love abides with us throughout the thick and thin of life! And yet, isn't it possible that Paul also meant this: Who can separate us from the kind of love Christ revealed? Think about that! What, in the name of God, does a Christian look like who fails to express the love of Christ? Can there be such a creature as a Christian, separated from the love of Christ? I have my doubts! Perhaps because I had the blessed opportunity to bask in the light of Christ's love radiating from the heart of ———!

It would have been much clearer if Paul had said, "What shall separate us from the love of Christ?" After all, that was his true intention! We all know that life can deal out some pretty lethal blows! One day we're high on life. The next day we're in the throes of turmoil! Today we can feel on top of the world. Tomorrow, we can feel as though the world is heavy on our shoulders. One day brings laughter and the next tears! On Sunday we can feel surrounded by friends and loved ones. Then Monday comes, and we can suddenly find ourselves isolated and lonely! And through it all, the real threat to our spiritual and emotional well-being is what?

Not that Christ withdraws his love from us. Rather, we withdraw from the love of Christ! It's so hard to express the love of Christ for others, when we feel crushed, abandoned, forsaken, and forgotten. The experience of sickness and pain can cause even the Christian to withhold the love of Christ from others. And then there are those other saints! They experience great hardship, and by some miracle of God's love, their hearts are enlarged! That was true of ———. Her heart was never separated from the love of Christ and, so, radiated the love of Christ!

Sometimes I wonder. Perhaps the greatest flaw in our Christian character isn't the failure to worship God or the desire to earn God's approval. Maybe our greatest flaw is in our unwillingness to follow the example of other saints who have come through their most difficult struggles still aglow with the love of Christ for others. Perhaps we are gifted with the presence of such persons as a reminder of what Christian life and love are really all about! Look at the life and love of ———. What do you see?

I see a woman who embodied the graceful presence of Christ and the power of his overwhelming love. I see a woman who knew more than her fair share of pain and sorrow, and yet, who never once withheld her love from her son, her family, or her church. I see a saint who taught us a profound and necessary lesson: If Christ will never withhold his love from us, then we, in turn, can never withhold his love from others. I believe that ———, like so many Christian saints, was God's gift to us. Looking to her life, touched by her love, remembering her courage, we can better understand the meaning of Paul's words!

"Who shall separate us from the love of Christ?" Quite frankly? Nothing! Certainly not from Christ's vantage point. But what about from our own? Will there be some person, some event, some trouble that will silence forever the love of Christ in our lives? There could be! The question is, Should there be? Well, not if we have been truly touched by the life of ———. Not as long as we have learned from her witness to faith, hope, and abiding love. And not so long as we see her life as a living, breathing testimonial to power of Christ-like love!

Personally, I will long treasure the memory of this woman. I thank our God for her life and her love! She certainly lived up to her name, Grace, didn't she? But above and beyond all else, I will remember her as a saint. As one who, time and again, throughout her struggles and sadness, radiated with Christ-like love! I will cherish her memory. Because ——— taught me so well, that if Christ will never withhold his love from us, then regardless of what life holds for us, we must never withhold his love from others!

ILLUSTRATIONS

BY ROBERT C. SHANNON

WON OR LOST? Francis Beaumont put in the mouth of Bellario this answer to the question, "Dost thou know what 'tis to die? It is but giving over of a game that must be lost." Is death really that: "the giving over of a game that must be lost"? Not to the believer. To the believer it is a game that must be won! In fact, it is a game that has already been won . . . and we are welcomed to share in the prizes of victory.

WE BELONG TO THE LORD. Black-bordered death notices are still commonly seen in Eastern Europe, posted in public places. Commonly one sees a star and knows that the deceased was a Communist or a cross and knows that the deceased was a believer. One such notice was posted for a Christian physician. He had suffered through a long battle with cancer and must have known that he was dying. Without doubt he chose the three verses of Scripture that were printed on his death notice. No star. No cross. But three verses from the Bible. One was 2 Tim. 4:7: "I have fought a good fight." Another was John 11:25: "I am the resurrection and the life." Most impressive was Rom. 14:8: "If we live, we live to the Lord, and if we die, we die to the Lord, so whether we live or we die, we belong to the Lord." What a philosophy for both death *and* life.

CONSTRUCTIVE GRIEF. Queen Milica had the horrible experience of losing both her husband and her two sons in the same day on the same battlefield. After the battle was over, she had someone bring to her the weapons her sons had carried. From them she made a lamp to hang inside the church in the convent where she spent the rest of her life. It was a new way of "beating swords into plowshares." We all re-spond to grief in different ways, but it's helpful to look for constructive ways to express our sorrow and constructive ways to perpetuate the memory of those we love.

JESUS TAKES OUR BURDENS. He was a young minister with four small children when the doctor told him he had leukemia. During the last days of his illness he was visited by another minister. This is what the young preacher said: "When the doctor told me that I must leave my wife and my children, I didn't think I could stand it. I've preached that Jesus takes your burdens, that he comforts, that he brings peace, and . . . I want you to know that it's absolutely true!"

TIME. They couldn't decide whether or not to tell the old man that he was terminally ill. Finally the family agreed that he should be told. So they gently explained to him that he was not expected to recover. They said, "It's only a matter of time." Wisely he answered, "That's what it's always been . . . only a matter of time." He spoke truly. From the moment we were born, it has been "only a matter of time." Some die sooner and some later, but this earth is not the permanent home of any of us, and it's always only a matter of time.

SECTION V.
Lenten and Easter Preaching

SERMON SUGGESTIONS

Topic: Beauty for Ashes
TEXT: Ps. 51:1–17

The phenomenon of nature that we sometimes experience here in southern California is to walk outdoors and be greeted by a fine mist of ashes filtering through the air. This can happen when there has been a devastating hillside fire that has raged out of control over acres of dry brush and chaparral. Homes and buildings also might be involved. The wind-driven flames consume everything in their path, and that same wind then carries particles of ash far over the surrounding area. When the winds die or the fires are conquered, the blackened hillsides present a sorry face, and from our cars or properties we brush the ashes away.

I. Not many of us would look upon this end result and pronounce it a thing of beauty. Ashes are the residue, the remains of something else, something that once may have been beautiful but now is no more. Ashes have other meanings for us, also somber. In our Judeo-Christian tradition, they have been used symbolically to remind us of our human mortality or to represent sadness and mourning for a lost life or a lost joy. Repentance also has been symbolized by the wearing of "sackcloth and ashes"—signs of humility and contrition. Long ago, outside of Jerusalem, there existed "the valley of the ashes," a solid mound larger than a football field, formed from the accumulated ashes of temple sacrifices. Visible from ancient until modern times, this dumping ground lacked any semblance of beauty or loveliness.

Yet Isaiah the prophet, fully aware of both the appearance and meaning of ashes, spoke dramatically about how God would exchange gladness for sorrow and encouragement for despair. Isaiah said that the Lord would grant "beauty for ashes" to those who grieved. Out of the bleakness of life could come a good and positive result. From the least likely source there could emerge a new brightness and hope. The Lord, taught Isaiah, is in the business of bestowing beauty for ashes. Transformation, we can call it, or the kind of change we all desire but feel powerless to accomplish.

Ash Wednesday is the time in the calendar of the Christian year when the pre-Easter or Lenten season begins. For forty days (plus the Sundays) Christians make their annual pilgrimage to the cross and then the empty tomb. Lent is a period designed to sharpen our spiritual sensitivities and lead us into a deeper personal relationship with the crucified and risen Lord. And it began with a day called Ash Wednesday.

II. On Ash Wednesday in liturgically oriented churches, Christians receive a smudge of ash on their foreheads vaguely resembling a cross. As this mark is made, the priest says, "Remember, friend, that thou art dust and unto dust thou shalt return." These are grim words intended to drive believers to their knees in confession and penitence; they thrust each person

247

upon the mercy of God and instill the reminder that all human beings are frail and mortal. The smudge of ash is a way of eliciting from humble hearts the response of Robert Browning's Count Guido. This man appealed before his judges first to his nobility, then to his ancestry, his influence, his friends, his good works, but ended at last by crying, "Sirs, my first true word, all truth and no lie is—save me notwithstanding."

"Save me notwithstanding." Is this not the yearning of our secret hearts whenever we reflect upon the passage of the years and recognize how short we have fallen of our own best intentions, to say nothing of God's? We want, perhaps more than anything else in all the world, to feel that we are worthy and valued, even so. We would like to know that our past need not be our future, at the point of prior failures and defeats. The transformation heralded by the prophet Isaiah seems so appropriate, the change we fervently desire but feel powerless to accomplish. So it is that we pray, "Grant to us, grant to us, O Lord, beauty for ashes." The mark of ashes upon us, real or symbolic, which attests to our frailty and prompts confession of our sins, thus becomes our badge of renewal—by the grace and mercy of God. "Save me notwithstanding": it is an honorable plea and the starting point for that pilgrimage through Lent that brings us to the glories of Easter.

III. "Ashes are a reminder of the way in which God creates." A former youth pastor of this church, Robert Wallace, made that statement. He elaborated by saying, "God formed men and women from the dust of the ground and breathed into them the breath of life. It is God who gives life, and that which is as lifeless as dust is the raw material for creation." When we in our weaknesses sense that the good has gone out of us and when we find words to admit it, then we are ready for the new creation. I refer to the type of confession offered by St. Paul when he said, "Even though the desire to do good is in me, I am not able to do it. I don't do the good I want to do; instead, I do the evil that I don't want to do." Out of ashes like that, God can bring beauty. When we acknowledge our darkness, God lets light shine.

Another way to say it is in the words of author Frederick Buechner. He has reminded us that just as there is buried in the lovely faces of our daughters the wrinkles and fears of an old woman, there is also in the old woman the promise of new life. God is in the business of bestowing beauty for ashes. He makes of our shabbiness, splendor.

But we have to want him to! We have to be ready and eager to pray, "Save me notwithstanding." That is the prayer, the plea, of hearts willing to be changed. Making no appeals to our status in the community or to the praises and opinions of others, we ask God simply to accept us as we are, that God might then make us new. And let us be clear in our understanding. Our personal need of God's transforming power is real, whether we are mired in sin (as the older explanations had it) or whether we are ordinary, good people capable of being ever more completely God's people. There are all sorts of things that keep us separated from fellowship with God. Evil and rebellious behaviors are not the only problems. There is indifference and pride and a lack of trust. These attributes also serve to keep us at a great distance from God. Acknowledgment of our need for a Savior in these ways becomes the starting point for turning life around. "Save me notwithstanding" is the cry that God will hear—and out of divine love, answer.

The promise of Lent is that the potential within us can be realized. The life latent in the ashes of our existence can spring forth as a thing of beauty and fulfillment. The strong words of the Fifty-first Psalm—a psalm of confession and penitence—describe the transformation of life that in our best moments we desire. Hear again these words of the psalmist's prayer: "Have mercy on me, O God, according to thy steadfast love; according to thy abundant mercy blot out my transgressions. Wash me thoroughly from my iniquity, and cleanse me from my sin! . . . Create in me a clean heart, O God, and put a new and right spirit within me. . . . Restore to me the joy of thy salvation, and uphold me with a willing spirit. . . ."

Reading or repeating these phrases from Psalm 51 on a daily basis throughout the Lenten season just might be the wisest thing we could do. The focus of this prayer is exactly right for most of us. It could well become the means of opening ourselves to the forgiveness, grace, and renewing power of God. Our temptation, of course, is to pray the prayer of procrastination: "Lord, make me good—but not yet." Psalm 51 speaks with the voice of immediacy and asks that we be not cast away from God's presence—cast away by our own tardiness or reluctance to respond. "Fill me with joy and gladness," the psalm-writer asked. And when that truly is our heart's desire, God is ready to grant it in abundance. Theologian Reinhold Niebuhr once remarked that the self "must be possessed if it is to escape the prison of self-possession." It is that about which I speak today: possession of our lives by the God who loves us and who asks us to give ourselves to him.

"Save me notwithstanding." As that becomes our plea, God becomes the intimate companion of our souls. To us, as to those addressed by Isaiah of old, the promise shall then be given. God will grant "beauty for ashes, the oil of gladness instead of mourning, the mantel of praise instead of a faint spirit: that they [that you and I!] may be called oaks of righteousness, the planting of the Lord, that the Lord may be glorified."—John H. Townsend

Topic: Dealing with Your Broken Dreams
TEXT: Luke 19:28–44
I. At heart, we are all dreamers. We dream that we shall succeed, that we shall be liked or loved, that we shall be happy. And the journey of life is strewn with the wreckage of dreams:

• The old darling in the retirement home, whose children never come to see her, though she gave them everything and expected they would care for her in her latter years.
• The couple who waited for years to have a child and then were given a

Downs baby and told they would have to alter their dreams.
• The concert pianist whose wrist was crushed in a car accident and who was told she would never play again, at least not professionally.
• The actor who got the big part he had waited for and discovered the next day that he had tested positive for the AIDS virus.

It is all *Death of a Salesman*, isn't it? The Willy Lomans of the world, always dreaming things will get better and then one day discovering that they don't, that you have to make peace with what there is, with what you have. Maybe this is why the audiences came out crying after seeing Arthur Miller's play; they knew this is the way life is.

What do you do when it happens to you, when the deal you had hoped for falls through, when the love of your life walks out and slams the door, when the house of your dreams burns down and you didn't have any insurance, when a policeman comes to your door and tells you your child is in jail for selling cocaine or, even worse, that she was killed in an accident on the freeway? What do you do when your dreams suddenly fall apart and you know there is no putting them together again?

II. Maybe it helps to see Jesus at the moment when he knew his dream had fallen apart. That's what's happening in our Scripture today, the story of his so-called triumphal entry into Jerusalem. It looks as if his dreams have all come true—the big crowds, the shouting, the royal reception with palm branches and clothing strewn in the road. But he knows better. He knows the politics of the time, the intrigue of his enemies, the fickleness of the crowds. He knows the demonstration is only a momentary celebration and that beneath it are the deceit and treachery that have kept his people in bondage for centuries. While the others are smiling and shouting and waving their palm branches, he is weeping and sees it all through tears.

"Would that even today," he says to the unheeding city, "you knew the things that make for peace! But now they are hid from your eyes. For the days shall come upon you when your enemies will cast up a bank about you and surround you and hem you in on every side and dash you to the ground, you and your children within you, and they will not leave one stone upon another in you; because you did not know the time of your visitation" (Luke 19:42–44).

He had seen it coming for a long time. It was not something that suddenly dawned on him. That is the way most dreams are broken, slowly, not abruptly. "O Jerusalem, Jerusalem," he had cried, "killing the prophets and stoning those who are sent to you! How often would I have gathered your children together as a hen gathers her brood under her wings, and you would not!" (Matt. 23:37). It is a sad and beautiful image: the mother hen, when the dreaded shadow of a hawk appears on the ground, summoning her little ones under the safety of her wings as she risks her own life to stand off the marauder. But the holy city was too steeped in evil to know it was in danger.

Clearly Jesus had hoped that his messiahship would come without bloodshed, that the people would realize God had sent his Son among them and would rally to him, heeding his teachings and reforming their private and public lives in keeping with God's ordinances. But it didn't work out that way. The wrong was too deeply entrenched. Rulers were jealous of their prerogatives. The Establishment was not about to turn over the keys to its inner offices. Jesus was on a collision course with the real powers of his time. His dream was not to be realized during his lifetime.

III. What did he do when he saw this? Maybe it would help us in dealing with our own broken dreams if we could only see what he did.

He did three things, as well as we can tell.

(a) *He held onto his faith in the sovereignty of God.* He continued to believe that God knew what he was doing and that God would work things out the way God wanted them worked out.

That is a big step to take, and it is not usually an easy one. Our first inclination, when things go wrong with our dreams, is to turn on God, to say that God must not

be there at all or God wouldn't permit things to go this way for us. The woman who loses her job, the man whose wife has just died in an operation, the young person who feels that he or she is not making any headway in life naturally become angry with God and say, "What good have all my prayers been? Why should I bother being religious if you don't help me when I need you?"

Maybe Jesus did this at first. We don't know. But we do know that he couldn't have done it for long. He went right on with his ministry, teaching and healing and trusting that God knew what God was doing, even if things didn't turn out the way he wanted them to.

And people ever since have found inspiration in Jesus' faith, in his holding onto belief in God's power even when God wasn't exercising it in his behalf.

(b) *Jesus held onto his faith in the sovereignty of God, and he prayed and submitted himself to the will of the Father.* That's what the whole business of Gethsemane was about—"Not my will, but thy will be done." Only it didn't begin in Gethsemane. It had been going on a long time before that. Luke says that when they went to Gethsemane that night to pray, it was their "custom." They prayed somewhere like that every night.

That's a wonderful lesson for us when things are going wrong, isn't it? Not to cavil at God for it, but to yield to God in humble submission, to say, "God, I don't understand this, but I will do whatever you want me to do in the situation."

What a difference it would make in our lives if we only lived this way!

(c) *Jesus kept his faith in God's sovereignty, he prayed and yielded himself to God, and he went on with his life with courage.*

Courage is part of it, too, isn't it? Courage. We don't make enough of courage today. The word comes from the Latin *cor,* for "heart" or "spirit." "You gotta have heart!" It isn't the property of the Rambos of the world; it's the quality of a lot of little people, a lot of quiet people who know how to suffer and keep going. People who are barely making it as teachers or nurses or social workers. People who are taking care of sick parents or retarded children.

People who are living with alcoholics or drug addicts. People whose dreams fell around their feet a long time ago, but they just keep slogging along, like good foot-soldiers in the army of the Lord.

Jesus knew what was coming for him. He knew that the fair day on Palm Sunday would give way to the stormy night before the cross. He knew his friends would desert him. He knew he would be hung out like the pelt of an animal, exposed to all the world and alone with his pain.

But he kept going. He didn't miss a step. He met the people all that week. He stood up to the Pharisees. He refused to back down from the truth God had given him to utter. And, in the end, he walked to Calvary with courage and died with a dignity the world had rarely seen. It made the Roman solder in charge of the Crucifixion pull on his beard and say, "Truly, this man was the Son of God!"

That's part of the way you deal with broken dreams.—John Killinger

Topic: Companionship with Christ—Failure

TEXT: Luke 9:51

In the Lenten readings, we have journeyed with Christ. We come now to a turn in the road, where the journey becomes less agreeable, less hospitable, and all too predictable. That "turn in the road" is indicated for us in the biblical narrative by the phrase found in all of the Gospels, which we have taken as our text in the version from St. Luke: "When the days drew near for him to be received up, he set his face to go to Jerusalem."

I. This was no ordinary journey to Jerusalem, and to go there meant almost certain death.

Time is short, frustrations are high, opportunities for the work of the gospel become fewer and fewer. These last days of the last journey become the days of testing and intensity, and no less so for those of us who "know" the story, as it were, as for those of his company, those beloved and bewildered disciples, for whom one day seemed as good as another and one story about as useful as another.

One such enigmatic story is the parable of the fig tree. The tree after three years bore no fruit, and the owner wished to chop it down as it was taking up valuable space. The owner, seeking his fruit and finding none, instructs the vinedresser to cut it down. It is the vinedresser who asks that the tree be spared, at least for one year. He will dig about it, dress it with manure, and otherwise encourage new growth and productivity, and, as he says, "If it bears fruit next year, well and good; but if not, you can cut it down." What stands at the center of the story is the failure of the tree to produce and in some sense the assumption of that failure on the part of the vinedresser. We do not know why the tree was barren, whose fault it is. We know only that it is barren and that the vinedresser is willing to make one last attempt to save it. We do not know if the effort will succeed, and neither does the vinedresser, for he allows for the ultimate failure when he says, "And if it bears fruit next year, well and good; but if not, you can cut it down." Time is short, things are not as they had been intended; what now can be done?

II. I suggest, without succumbing to some form of psychohistory or pretending to know more than we do, it is not only possible but desirable to see in these last tragic and heroic days of our Lord's earthly ministry a profound sense both of frustration and failure, a sense that he, like us, has not been able to do all that he set out to do. If we take the Passion of Christ and our sharing in it seriously, we must confess, to ourselves at least, that failure is at the heart of the entire human enterprise. It is the failure of God's love to work sufficiently for Adam and Eve in the Garden, their failure to trust in him and in themselves. The Bible is the record of our human failure to trust ourselves, our neighbors, and our God. And the failure of the Passion is both ours and Christ's. He can't promise that we will produce fruit; he can only ask for a little more time and hope that with a little more effort things might be better. And he goes to the cross, he sets his face toward that inevitable end, knowing that things are neither better nor worse; more's the pity, they are just the same as they have always been.

And what does it mean to fail? Is it

failure to miss somebody else's goals? The failure of the fig tree is that it failed to produce figs; that is, it failed to be what it was; it failed to do what it was supposed to do: it wasn't a failure because it wasn't a plum tree or a grape vine. The human failure is that we are not good at what we are supposed to be: human beings created in the image of God.

Failure, while fundamentally a human affair, is not exclusively so. For in some very real sense, God can be said to have failed when he made us in his own image but not well enough for us to survive fully without him. And, in the same measure, it can be said that Jesus failed to convince us of the truth of that condition and went to the cross as an ultimate witness to that failure. Salvation, the saving from the consequences of failure also is neither exclusively human nor divine but is, in fact, a cooperative necessity. God cannot "save" us without us, and we cannot be "saved" without God. God must give, in order for us to receive, and we must receive in order to enable God to give.

For the fig tree of our parable to function fully as a fig tree, it now requires the assistance of the gardener. Alone, the fig tree is seen to be capable of nothing. Alone, the gardener is of no use. Together, however, in the midst of the failure that is real, indeed, real on both parts, fig tree and gardener have an opportunity to *try again.*

When we fail at something, most of us think of it as the ultimate and irreversible tragedy of all time, from which there is no reprieve, no reversal. I see men and women suffering the aftereffects of marriages that have failed, failure in work, failure even in health. But, in the fashion of Robert Schuller, let me say this: Failure is opportunity, for out of failure emerges not only the opportunity but the necessity to *try again;* the glory of that opportunity is not in the achievement but in the effort. God in Christ allows us to *try again.* How easy it would be to give it all up as a bad job: God should retire from the business of humanity, and we should quit the business of divinity and leave it all to the devil, the only real success story we know of. But

the courage of the gospel, and the courage of Jesus as he faces his Passion, is that he does not quit in the face of failure. Our companionship with Christ, even in failure, makes the effort to *try again* worthwhile, and for that, we thank God.—Peter J. Gomes

Topic: Enthusiasm—Not Fanaticism
TEXT: Rom. 12:11, NEB

When Paul wrote to the Christian community, battling for their faith and risking their lives in Nero's Rome, he gave them eleven chapters of the most solid theology in the New Testament. He knew that to meet the demands of the hour they had to know what they believed. Then he swung into his conclusion with a call to action. Get going, run the race that is set before you, looking toward Jesus, and let his Spirit transform your life; "with unflagging energy, in ardour of spirit, meet the demands of the hour."

Now this word comes straight to us. This isn't the hour of the Roman Christians who met for worship knowing that their next meeting could be as victims in the Colosseum. This is not the hour when Jesus rode through cheering crowds in Jerusalem to a certain death. This hour of ours, if we are Christian believers trying to read the signs of our times, seems less dramatic. When we stop to think about it, we know that the challenge of our times—the worldwide tragedy of the hungry and the homeless, the threat to the planet God has committed to our care, with lurking in the shadows the "unthinkable" threat of nuclear annihilation—is even greater than was faced by our predecessors. What we need to put our credo to work is exactly what the apostle tells us—the infusion of new life, new enthusiasm, new confidence, and new hope. So: "With unflagging energy, in ardour of spirit, meet the demands of the hour."

I. I've used the word *enthusiasm.* Why do we not make more impact on the culture we live in and the serious ethical questions we face? We lack enthusiasm so we don't act "with unflagging energy, in ardour of spirit" to "meet the demands of the hour."

As an adolescent who was bored with the conventional church and tempted by the delights of a freewheeling agnosticism, I was brought back to the faith, not so much by a sermon or brilliant book of apologetics, as by the transparent enthusiasms of a few of my contemporaries for whom Christ was clearly a central factor in their lives. Their "unflagging zeal" and "ardour of spirit" were tempered by a genuine humility and sense of humor. They were not only sensitive and kind but actually seemed to get some fun out of their religion.

At the heart of any lively church is a core of real enthusiasts whose devotion to Christ and his church is evident—and expressed in a great variety of ways.

II. The enthusiasm I am talking about has little to do with temperament. It's the obvious delight that people of very different characters have in some cause, avocation, hobby, or sport. They talk about it, obviously enjoy it, and clearly would like you to share it.

There was enormous enthusiasm on display on that first Palm Sunday. The shouting of the disciples was the kind of demonstration we don't associate with religion—a football game, yes, but we don't express our religion that way.

There were fanatics around on that day, of course. I'm thinking now of the terrorists who lurked in that crowd hoping to spark a showdown with the Romans that would lead to bloodshed, and a very different set of fanatics, the ultrareligious, who were watching from the city wall. These were people so encrusted in their religious beliefs that they would go to any lengths to get rid of any enthusiast like Jesus who challenged their fanatical adherence to every jot and tittle of the laws of which they were the sole guardians and interpreters.

III. The kind of enthusiasm that lies at the heart of a true Christian and motivates the true disciple has nothing whatever to do with the fanaticism of the zealots with closed minds and closed fists who are ready to trample on the rights, the feelings, and even the loves of all who oppose them in the name of their God. That's the horror of *religious* fanaticism. A fanatic is the worst possible advocate of his or her faith.

The fanatic, in the name of his God, will stop at nothing to impose his will on others. The Christian enthusiast is one who has found another way to express his or her faith in God, the God whose true nature shines in the face of Jesus Christ. The enthusiast for Christ has come under his spell. When the young church broke upon the pagan world, the enthusiasm that swept them forward was not expressed in boastful words or violent actions but in a new and startling example of love in action. Would anything do more to reform the historic churches to "meet the demands of the hour" than a renewal of the true enthusiasm of those who joyfully find in him the Way, the Truth, and the Life?

Enthusiasm literally means "God in us." Christian enthusiasm means the living presence of the Holy Spirit at the center of our being. Perhaps the Holy Spirit is telling you and me to loosen up a bit in worship?

IV. Yet, Christian enthusiasm has, in the end, much more to do with the flourishing use of the daily, practical gifts of the Spirit. Paul once catalogued the kind of society in which he lived. These were his times—and they could be ours. "Anyone can see," he wrote, "the kind of behavior that belongs to the lower nature: fornication, impurity and indecency; idolatry and sorcery; quarrels, a contentious temper, envy, fits of rage, selfish ambitions, dissensions, party intrigues, and jealousies, drinking bouts, orgies. . . ." Then he draws for us the Christian contrast: "The harvest of the Spirit is love, joy, peace, patience, kindness, goodness, fidelity, gentleness, and self-control." Isn't that something to be enthusiastic about?—David H. C. Read

Topic: A Consuming Passion
TEXT: John 3:16

For the author of the Fourth Gospel, the answer to our overwhelming need to be loved and to love is found in this bold assertion: "For God *so loved* the world . . ." Unless there is One who loves us first, who sets the life-giving engine of love in motion, we are caught in a destructive cycle. We do not feel capable, worthy, acceptable, so we act out those convictions on others. Much of the abuse, neglect, and violence that presently plagues us comes from such a cycle. Love is the only power that can produce love. Or in biblical terms, we are able to love because he first loved us. We are *so loved* and, thereby, freed to love God, self, and others. But what kind of love is this?

To be *so loved* implies a height and depth and width of love almost beyond our imagining. How can we describe this love so that it cannot be confused with the counterfeits that claim so much and deliver so little? Fortunately, I ran across a single sentence of Ganse Little's that seemed a happy commentary on John 3:16: "God's love is the love that will not let us go, will not let us down, and will not let us off."

I. George Matheson was to pastor his first church in Inellan, Scotland, when he experienced a crisis of faith. He offered his resignation, but a wise presbytery refused. They prayed for him and believed in him until his faith returned, renewed and strengthened by the test. Out of that he wrote, "O Love that Wilt Not Let Me Go." This hymn sings the praises of a God who steadfastly pursues us and tenaciously holds onto us despite all that rages against us. What does it mean to say that we are *so loved?* First, it means that God is not one who sits back and waits to see how we handle our chores in life and then, as a disinterested judge, weighs the evidence, renders the verdict. God is more than benign spectator. He is Francis Thompson's "Hound of Heaven," relentlessly seeking us. God is the psalmist's Savior who plunges into the uttermost parts of the sea to rescue us. We make our bed in hell . . . he is pursuing us. He is the one who will not let us go.

In one of C. S. Lewis's children's stories, *The Horse and His Boy,* a boy named Shasta is riding along a treacherous mountain trail. He becomes aware of a mysterious presence keeping his horse from stumbling and him from falling into the abyss. The boy cries out, "Who are you?" The Great Lion Aslan answers, "One who has waited long for you to speak." Shasta learns that the Great Lion saved him as a baby and has been pursuing him, in love, to bring him new life. Are you caught up in good things but running from God, the One who has waited long for you to speak? God's love will not let us go. Compare this tenacious love to that of the father who told his small daughter, "I love you when you're good." It was the child who responded, "I love you all the time, Daddy." *God's love will not let us go.*

II. Even if we believe that, our greatest fear is a fear of being let down. We do not consciously admit that. But how many of our dreams have to do with our jumping and no one catching us, or someone and they leave or die? God's love promises not to leave us desolate, not to abandon you, not to desert me. When we let ourselves down, or others do, it is God's love that lifts us up again. I wish every Christian had a tape in his or her brain that would play, when needed, "Love lifted me, love lifted me, when nothing else could help, love lifted me."

This kind of love is the greatest gift we can give our children. Duke Ellington, the jazz great, once said in an interview, "When I was a little boy, I was loved so much and held so much I don't think my feet hit the ground until I was seven. . . ." Every child in this church, in this community, could be loved in that way. That's the meaning of our baptism: God's grace and love lifting us first. I was taught to put my name in this verse: For God so loved Gary—he gave his only begotten Son. My, that's personal . . . does God love us that way? Yes, and so we must believe personally.

But what about when it all gets too heavy? There is the sin I've committed, the doubts I've had, the shame I've experienced. It is then that we must hear . . . it's a matter of life and death . . . "nothing can separate us from the love of God." The love of God is greater than our guilt, our doubts, our shame. In the hour when you feel yourself sinking, stay before the cross. The love of God that gave all for you will not let you go.

When nothing else could help, love lifted me.

III. Finally, and this is the neglected one: God's love will not let us off. The faith of the church is not just expressed in hymns of a love that will not let us go and of a love that lifts us up. It is also expressed in "Christ to the World We Bring." For the promise is that God so loved the *world.* How will they know of God's redeeming love if we do not tell the world . . . show the world? This is love that pursued us when we weren't seeking, that lifts us up, keeps us from falling, *and* does not let us off easily. That may be the greatest sign of love yet; his consuming passion can become ours. Not consumed in the sense that we are burned up with feverish activity, but that we have within us a love that motivates our being in the world.

The old Scotswoman, bending but not broken, said, "We dunna always see, but God has a plan." And God so loved us that he made us a part of that plan. If God is to reach the world with love, it is through you and me. The world begins with the one God has given you. An embittered minister's son once told of his father taking him on his visits to parishioners' homes. The son always saw the kind, comforting actions of his father to the church members, but the busy minister was different when he returned to the car. He had nothing left for his son. That's a chilling story to me.

God so loved the world that he gave . . . If we are to reach the world with love, we, too, must give the love Christ has given us. How else can it be done? Where else can it begin?—Gary D. Stratman

Topic: The News of Easter
TEXT: Matt. 28:1–8

Every day the newspapers carry stories of newsworthy items. Some of the stories are heartwarming and encouraging, but the vast majority of the stories are not. All of the bad news in the papers can get depressing. With the coming of Easter, Christians have the opportunity to proclaim to the world that good news is still possible in a hectic and troubled world such as ours.

Historians tell us that the time for the breaking of the criminals' legs came at about three o'clock in the afternoon on that Good Friday. Because of the approaching sundown marking the beginning of the Sabbath, the executions of the three men needed to be completed soon. Heavy mallets were raised and lowered upon the hips of the two who flanked the sides of Jesus. Since he was already dead, there was no need to subject his body to such torture. The authorities allowed his body to be removed and buried. The tomb was sealed; but with dawn of the first day of the week, his followers found it empty.

The news of that Resurrection signifies at least three new possibilities for the world.

I. *A new promise.* God's power over death has never been more fully illustrated than when he raised his own Son from the grave. To those who place their faith in God through Christ, he promises that same victory over death. Paul asked of death, "Where is thy sting?" He and other early Christians knew that death was the final enemy to be destroyed by Christ.

Christians also are able to take advantage of God's promise of salvation through faith in Christ. Jesus himself said that if we believe in him we will have our sins forgiven.

Another promise of God through the Resurrection of Christ is that of eternal life. Jesus said that Christians will never experience spiritual death because of his conquest over death. When Communist party leader Mao Tse-tung died in China, thousands of his followers filed into the building housing his remains for a final view. When Jesus' followers came to mourn his death, they found no body. He had risen!

II. *A new presence.* Because of Christ's Resurrection, we also have the assurance of his presence in our lives. Jesus demonstrated his presence immediately after his victory over death to those gathered in the garden. His presence is available to all who will trust in him today. Paul referred to "Christ in you, the hope of glory."

It is the constant presence of Christ in us that enables us to resist temptation, overcome discouragement, and make proper choices regarding our future. We never need to ask for Christ's presence;

rather, we should simply acknowledge it.

III. *A new purpose.* Because of Christ's death and Resurrection, Christians have a new purpose in life. No longer are we destined to be aimless, wandering without a cause. Christ has called us to live for him as he empowers our lives (Gal. 2:20). We are also called to be his witnesses on this earth. Notice the reaction of the followers of Jesus after they are told of his conquest over death. The Bible says, "And they departed quickly from the tomb with fear and great joy and ran to report it to His disciples" (v. 8, NASB). We should have the same sort of excitement about telling others about his Resurrection today. Truly, the news of Easter makes the story worth telling and retelling time and again.—Calvin Kelly

ILLUSTRATIONS

BY ROBERT C. SHANNON

THE UNCLOUDED CROSS.   Prior to 1873, the Mountain of the Holy Cross in Colorado was the stuff of legends. The mountain has a vertical slash in its rock face, with a horizontal slash running across it. Snow accumulates there to form a perfect cross. Trappers had seen it from a distance, but then it seemed to vanish. Clouds moved in to obscure the view, and at times the mountain itself seemed to disappear. Finally, in 1873, pioneer photographer William Henry Jackson made a photograph that proved the tale was no legend but fact. Still today it's a challenge to photographers to catch the mountain at just the right moment and photograph the holy cross. Neither cloud nor mist can ever hide from view the cross of Christ! That cross is not legend but fact. That cross is the bold and public act of a self-sacrificing Christ for the sins of the whole world.

THE SHAPE OF THE CROSS.   We don't know the actual shape of the cross. It may have been shaped like the letter X or like the plus sign or, indeed, in the traditional shape with which we are familiar, a shape that has been called the Latin cross. Very

early, Christians began to stylize the cross and modify its design. The Jerusalem cross, sometimes called the crusader's cross, has four little crosses inside the arms of the larger main cross to symbolize the five wounds of Christ. The Greek cross has four arms of equal length, and it has been stylized to suggest the four corners of the earth to which the evangelists have gone. Another version of the Greek cross has an anchor at the end of each arm representing the four Gospel writers. Sometimes the cross is shown mounted on a three-step base, signifying faith, hope, and love. Whatever its shape or design, the cross always carried the same basic message: God reached down to earth, man reached up to God, Christ reached out to embrace the world.

CONTRADICTIONS OF THE CROSS.   The cross is the simplest thing in the world and the most profound in the world. It is the simplest thing that death should bring life. The seed dies that the plant may live. The mother goes to the gates of death that she may bring forth life. The soldier dies for the freedom of his family and his country. The cross is the simplest thing in the world. The cross is the most profound thing in the world. How did it give us life? How did it give us liberty? In what ways did it satisfy the claims of divine justice? "Jesus paid it all," but to whom did he pay it? To God? To the devil? The cross is the most profound thing in the world.

LIGHT IN THE TOMB.   Near Dublin, Ireland, there has been discovered a tomb 5,150 years old. It was carefully designed with a shaft so that sunlight could shine down a sixty-foot passageway *on one day of the year!* On December 21, the day of the winter solstice, and only on that day, a shaft of sunshine would bathe the entire burial chamber in light . . . for a few brief minutes. But the tomb of Jesus was opened for the sunlight to shine in all day long, every day. It was open for inspection. The sunlight shone in, and there radiated out from it a spiritual light that shines to this very day!

SAVIOR OF THE WORLD. When Lenin died in 1924, a public statement was issued that said, "His vision was colossal; his intelligence in organizing the masses was beyond belief . . . he was the lord of the new humanity and the savior of the world." People have gone to Moscow and joined the long lines to see inside the glass-topped coffin the lifeless body of this "savior of the world." But you cannot see the body of the true Savior of the world. He rose from the dead. No coffin could hold him. He is alive forevermore!

SECTION VI.
Advent and Christmas Preaching

SERMON SUGGESTIONS

Topic: The Strangeness of Christmas
TEXT: 1 Cor. 1:20–30

There is a strangeness about love—God coming in a little baby, born in a cattle stall in Bethlehem—and then the Babe of Bethlehem becoming the Man of Calvary? That is all very strange!

It seems to me that if we miss the strangeness of Christmas, we miss its meaning.

The Apostle Paul in one of his letters declares the strangeness of Christmas when he writes, "God has chosen the foolish things of the world to confound the wise and the weak things to confound the mighty." There is a sense in which "Jesus came revealing, not the familiarity of God, but his strangeness."

Lest we miss the meaning of Christmas, let us together explore its strangeness.

I. It seems to me the strangeness of Christmas is noted, first, in the humility of God. The Jews expected their Messiah to appear as a king in Jerusalem, ascending the throne of David, to wield his scepter over all the world. Therefore, they missed God's coming in a helpless baby born in "Bethlehem, the least of the cities of Judah." When Jesus ascended a cross rather than a throne, they were completely turned off. "This can't be the Messiah," they objected. They could not accept a Messiah who chose to rule from a cross rather than from a throne.

This is how humble God can be. "He took upon himself flesh like unto our flesh

and humbled himself, emptied himself, and became obedient unto death, even death on a cross. Here is the strangeness of Christmas—the humility of God—the Almighty in a baby, crowded out of an inn, the Eternal Spirit clothed in all the earthiness of our common life, the Immortal making his home in the mortal.

This strangeness of Christmas is that God makes his appearances incognito. He appears so quietly, so unobtrusively, with such meekness, God does not make himself known through the blatant. As the prophet of old discovered, "God is not in the earthquake, wind, or fire, but in the still, small voice." This same meaning is caught up in the words of one of the great hymns:

> . . . not with swords' loud clashing,
>   Nor roll of stirring drums,
>   . . . .
>   the heavenly Kingdom comes.

This strangeness of Christmas in God's coming incognito was expressed by Dr. George Buttrick when he wrote, "God came down as it were the back stairs at Bethlehem." Remember how Jesus expresses this fact: "Inasmuch as you have done it unto one of the least of these . . . you have done it unto me."

Since God was present in a babe in that Bethlehem manger, we can expect to find him in the seemingly most insignificant of persons and the most unlikely places. Is this not something of the meaning of the prophet when he proclaims, "A child shall lead them." Man in the pride of his own wisdom will miss God every time.

II. Christmas is strange in that God uses the foolish things to confound the wise; it is strange, too, in that he uses the weak things to confound the mighty.

How inconsequential to the vast affairs of the Roman Empire seemed the birth of a baby in obscure Bethlehem. Great events were afoot then. Yet, the Roman Empire has been long gone; the Roman legions have marched into oblivion; the caesars have turned to dust. All that had the headlines of the morning paper then has proven transient. But what occurred in seemingly insignificant Bethlehem, which did not even rate the back pages of the newspaper when it happened, has proven to be enduring. As the Apostle Paul had the insight to see, "God does use the weak things of the world to confound the mighty."

How weak Jesus appeared on the cross! Imagine what Jesus' ministerial report would have looked like on Good Friday afternoon! All his followers had deserted except John and two or three women. In his seeming helplessness, there were those who scoffed from the foot of the cross: "He saved others, himself he cannot save." What they were saying is the gospel truth, but they did not comprehend this fact. This is not weakness but the greatest strength—to so love as to save others.

When one thinks of the weak things of the world that confound the mighty, one is reminded of the circumstances that surrounded Handel in writing his outstanding oratorio, the *Messiah.* It is hard for one to imagine Christmas without this musical masterpiece! But it was out of much weakness that Handel's composition was born. His biographer writes of Handel, "His health and his fortunes had reached their lowest ebb. His right side had become paralyzed, and his money was all gone. His creditors seized him and threatened him with imprisonment. For a time he was tempted to give up . ., but then he rebounded to compose the greatest of his inspirations, the epic *Messiah.*"

Whether he could write the "Hallelujah Chorus" or not hung in the balance for weeks, teetering on the thin edge of doubt, until, in what looked like a hopeless situation, the Spirit entered into him and set him upon his feet again. In his weakness, Handel was caught up in the strength and glory of God.

Hallelujah: for the Lord God
  omnipotent reigneth.
The kingdom of this world is become
  the kingdom of our Lord and His
  Christ;
And he shall reign for ever and ever.
King of Kings, and Lord of Lords,
And He shall reign forever and ever.
Hallelujah! Hallelujah! Hallelujah!

III. The strangeness of Christmas, too, is in the fact that it is perennially new.

As I watched Christmas decorations going up this year, the thought struck me, how strange it is that, year after year, life is rejuvenated in this season. No matter how old and jaded the world may appear in November, there is that renewal of the spirit of peace and goodwill in December. Even after nearly twenty centuries, this celebration of God's coming in Christ seems as fresh and as new as ever. About some things, we say, "When you've seen one, you've seen them all," but I've never heard anyone say that of Christmas.

Christmas is perennially new. It is always new because love is ever new. The resources of love are inexhaustible, because love is of God and God loves to the uttermost: "God so loved the world that he gave his only Son . . ." Love is not something that we draw up out of our own vitals, but something that is mediated from the heart of God, the fountain of eternal love.

How do you share the good news of Christmas—the experience of Emmanuel, "God with us"—with those living in a seeming God-forsaken world? It is not easy. It cannot be done glibly. It can only have meaning as one identifies in love and enters into an understanding of the consternation of the other's loneliness.

Perhaps the appearance of the messengers on that first Christmas to the lonely shepherds, unlikely recipients of good news, is a parable to lonely people in every generation that they are not forgotten of

God but are loved with an everlasting love that does not let us go. This is the strangeness of Christmas—the unbelievable, the inexplicable, the presence of the Eternal in your time and mine—loving us into fulfillment, loving us to the end and beyond. There is a love that persists through the night of our loneliness with the light of a companionship that never forgets us or forsakes us. Love that is of God knows no limit to its endurance, no end to its trust, no fading of its hope; it can outlast anything, even a persistent, growing loneliness.

Do you see now why Christmas is an old, old story that never grows old? It is perennially new, with all the rejuvenating power of love—the Father's love. Life is renewed by love; and it is only love that will renew the world. Christmas is strange because we are such strangers to this love most of the year.

Not just that it happened in Bethlehem, as strange as that event is to the ways of men, but that it can happen to you and me, here and now, is the strangest thing of all. That God can dwell in you—in me—in all the aliveness of his eternal Spirit, in all the freshness of his love, in all the meanings of the Christ—this is indeed strange; it is the strangeness of God's amazing grace.—John M. Thompson

Topic: The Things That Are to Be

Texts: Hab. 2:3; Rev. 4:1

I. Advent reminds us that the future belongs to those who wait for God, who do not grow weary or impatient or fearful. The future belongs to those who are not beguiled by the charms of what appears to be permanent and who are not intimidated by what is unknown. Indeed, we are a people of history, and we look to see what God has done in history and how we have been brought to where we now are. The people of God are the people of memory. But Advent, more than any other season of the year, reminds us that we are people of the future as well, for it is in the future that God chooses finally and fully to reveal what now we can only see and hear in part. The future, indeed, is not what it used to be: it is no longer ours, it belongs to God. And the word at Advent is one of comfort: "Write down the vision, inscribe it on tablets, ready for a herald to carry it with speed; for there is still a vision for the appointed time. At the destined hour it will come in breathless haste; it will not fail. If it delays, wait for it; for when it comes will be no time to linger."

The prophecy of Habakkuk is like much of the prophecy of Israel, hope in the midst of unmitigated disaster, in this case, a colossal military defeat with the attendant fear, doubt, and despair. The future was mortgaged by the claims of the present, and history was irrelevant. The prophet had hoped for speedy recompense, quick revenge, and a stunning reversal of the defeat. But such vindication, instant gratification over the enemy, was not to be granted. He was then forced to consider the matter in a larger context, and he is described as "standing at his post and taking his position on the watchtower" to get a larger view. What is the word from the Lord? How do I reply when I am asked by friend and foe? And from his vantage point what does he see? A vision of God's future so urgent that it must be written down to be preserved, and with that vision of ultimate justice and hope is also given a healthy dose of patience. "Wait for it; it will not fail. If it delays, wait for it; for when it comes will be no time to linger."

II. But what does such a hope in the future, sure or unsure about it as we may be, say about our attitude toward the present in which most of us live? Does our attitude toward the future shape the way we live in the present? Or is our attitude in the present determinative of the future?

The church has always taught us that the future is in God's hands: it is not ours to possess; "when the kingdom comes, the kingdom comes." But the church has also taught that the present moments, weak and feeble as they may appear to be, do belong to us and that, because we have confidence in the future that is to be, we are encouraged and, indeed, made bold to witness to that future in the present. Thus, our posture is not simply standing on the watchtower waiting word of the battle of Armageddon. It is to be engaged here and now in the works of righteousness, waging the battle for light in the midst of darkness, serving as witnesses of the dawn against the night.

Thus it is, in my view, that the cause for social justice in our world is made neither by the requirements of the moment nor the tyranny of the past but rather by the cosmic demands of the future time in which God reigns in equity. We are encouraged, even required, to set about the business of human justice now because we believe in the divine justice that is to come. And if we fail in the bringing of the kingdom, here or in Latin America or in South Africa, it is only because the kingdom is not for us to bring in, at least not yet. The future does not belong to us, but we belong to the future, and to be in some remote sense responsible in that inheritance, we must now do the works of him who sends us. Where does the call for the just and humane society come from? Certainly not from any human or historical experience. I defy you to name a society of history whose example is of such worth and justice and humanity that we would return to it if we could. There is none. If you think it is the glory of Greece and Rome, ask their captive nations. If you think it is medieval Europe, ask the serfs and the Jews. If you think it is colonial America, ask the native Americans. If you think it is the glory of the British Empire, ask the Indians or the West Africans. Our models for justice and humanity come from places that never were and have not yet been: they come from the future, and for the Christian, they come from a future inhabited and ruled by God.

Thus, if we lost the future, if we are fearful and paralyzed by the things that are to be, we have lost everything, for there is nothing left at all. That is why Christian hope is the locomotion to Christian action, and Christian action a witness to our confident hope in the future, God's future. We cannot afford a spiritual nostalgia that suggests the work of God as accomplished in some past we must now recover. Indeed, if we are faithful to the past, we will discover that its heroic effort was always to recover the future, to prepare for it, wait for it, work for it, pray for it, and rejoice in it.

III. It is the vision for the appointed time that makes the time being worth living in, and, as we know, where there is no vision, the people perish. Advent reminds the faithful Christian people of God that we do not fear the future, for it is only in the future that God's kingdom can possibly be made real. The witness of the church is the witness of patience when others would tell us "give up" or "give in." It is the witness of Desmond Tutu, who believes that the things that are to be are the things of God and who is thereby not lulled into apathetic hope but whose patience in the hope causes him to energize the world.

At Advent, then, we do not simply wait for the coming of the Lord, sit on our hands and wait for God to do all the work. We embrace the coming day of the Lord as our own: we engage the future now! Not because it belongs to us, but because we belong to it. And we witness against fear and despair in the future by working with all that we have against fear and despair in our present. We work with and against the things that are in behalf of the glorious vision of the things that are to be. We light candles rather than curse the darkness; we pray for the kingdom of the coming and work as if it were already here. We await the coming of Christ, not as a harmless little baby, but as the master in whose behalf we have been hard at work, and we hope and pray he will have found us faithful, ready, and joyful.—Peter J. Gomes

Topic: Beginning Again with Christ

TEXT: "When in former times God spoke to our forefathers, he spoke in fragmentary and varied fashion through the prophets. But in this the final age he has spoken to us in the Son. . . ." Heb. 1:1, 2, NEB

READINGS: Deut. 18:15–19, RSV; Heb. 1:1–5, NEB; Mark 1:1–8

The apostle who wrote these words sets a good example to all preachers. He gets to the point right away. No elaborate introduction. No attempt to catch attention in oblique references to local politics or the latest scandal from Nero's court. (He's writing to a church in Rome.) And no funny stories.

The congregation he was addressing was probably composed of converted Jews, and they were having a hard time. Their enthusiasm for the Christian church was waning. They were threatened with a wave of persecution. Some were rethinking what they had been taught about Christ and were tempted to revert to the Judaism of the Law and the Prophets, accepting Jesus as nothing more than the latest in the long line of prophets who spoke for God or yet another messianic pretender. Others were avoiding trouble by deciding to let Christ appear as just another of the gods in the Graeco-Roman pantheon.

So the apostle takes his pen and, discarding all preliminary greetings and compliments, goes straight to the heart of the Christian claim: "When in former times God spoke to our forefathers, he spoke in fragmentary and varied fashion through the prophets. But in this the final age he has spoken to us in the Son. . . ." Christ, he says, is incomparable He is not just one in a long line of prophets or one among many divinities to be worshiped. He is asking those who were floundering in a sea of religious speculation, not sure any longer what they believed about Christ, to begin again by facing and confronting the One in whose name they had been baptized.

This is where we come in. We are not members of a tiny persecuted cult but of a universal church, claiming about a billion adherents around the world and with a two-thousand-year record of worship and charitable activity. But as this century comes to an end, we are faced with many of the questions with which this letter deals. The churches that claim the name of Christ are in disarray. There is a central group of believers in nearly every land who are willing to stand and confess, "Credo: I believe in Jesus Christ his only Son our Lord," but we are split into different denominations and different theologies, each drawing somewhat different conclusions from that confession. We are also faced with all kinds of fanatical new sects and movements brandishing the name of Christ but offering a religion we cannot recognize as ours. The most important factor we have to contend with if

we seek to be orthodox Christians today, however, is the triumph of religious pluralism in our culture. On the positive side this means that there has been a growth of tolerance and respect for other people's religious convictions. But on the negative side, pluralism often indicates an attitude of total indifference to any religion, based on the assumption that one's religious convictions are of no more significance than our passion for football or our taste in wines. It's not just that most citizens rightly object to the person who says, "I am in possession of the whole truth about God, human beings, and the destiny of the universe." Now it is fashionable to assert that there is no such thing as truth to be found and that when I say, "Credo: I believe," I am just making a meaningless noise, a conditioned reflex like the burp of a baby.

It is into this vacuum, I believe, that the church has still to proclaim Jesus Christ as not only the Way—giving meaning and direction to our lives, and as the Life-giver, providing spiritual vitality here and now and defying the grim boundary of death—but as the Truth that satisfies the mind. This letter to the Hebrews begins with a mind-blowing assertion of the dazzling supremacy of Christ as the revealer of God and goes on to stress that he is not just a symbol, an attractive Idea that once dawned on the human race, but a real flesh-and-blood personality who lived here, died here, and in between was tempted "in all points as we are." Like all the New Testament writers, this one tells the story of Jesus as "one of us," yet as being, as no one else ever was, "one with God."

When I speak about beginning again with Christ, I am not throwing the book at you and saying, "It's time you got back to the orthodox doctrines of the church that speak of the true divinity and true humanity of Jesus Christ." You could swallow the whole Athanasian Creed with one blind gulp of the mind—and be none the better for it as a Christian in New York this Christmas. I mean simply that it is Christ we have to begin again with—and not some theory about him. He makes his own impression, if we are willing to open the closed doors in our mind and the locked compartments of our heart. As I hear about him in the Gospels, as I see him at work in people I know, he seems to be always pleading for an individual response from each person he meets. He wants simplicity and sincerity. He detests hypocrisy. He is up against closed minds in high places and low places, as much in the notoriously religious as in the so-called pagan. And he makes it possible for all to begin again. I see him reaching out to Pontius Pilate as he turns away with the cynical question so common today: "What *is* truth?" I heard him plead with Nicodemus the devout and magnanimous scholar encrusted in the traditions of his ancestral faith, with his abrupt, "You must be born again." He tells Peter, the fisherman who was the first to recognize who he really was and yet denied him in the moment of his trial, "I have prayed for you that your faith may not fail; and when you have turned again [begun again with me], strengthen your brethren." Paul, apparently the dauntless apostle who never looked back, knew what it was in his moments of deepest depression to hear the voice saying, "My grace is sufficient for you," and to begin again with Christ.

It is this personal touch that makes Christ unique as the revealer of God. Our text this morning doesn't tell us that Christ is number one among the great prophets. Nor does it deny that God has spoken through others in what he calls "fragmentary and varied fashion." A Christian isn't asked to put down all the other great religions of the world as revealing no truth at all. What we are being told is that he reveals God in a unique and totally different way. "He has spoken to us in the Son." That means that this is a personal revelation. God, instead of sending another prophet, gave himself, came as a human child, born of a real human mother, in a human home, to live and die as we all do. That's what we celebrate at Christmas. If you listen to the words of the great carols whose music peals from stores and TV at this time of the year, you'll discover that this is the joyful song that has run through the centuries: "Veiled in flesh the Godhead see; hail the incarnate deity."

"In the bleak midwinter, a stable place sufficed, the Lord God almighty, Jesus Christ." "Word of the Father now in flesh appearing, O come let us adore him, Christ the Lord."

To begin again with Christ could mean for some recapturing the wonder and the mystery of the God who "came to visit us with great humility" so that we may be part of the great family that knows the personal touch of the Almighty. Nothing less than this has sustained the church for two thousand years and still speaks to the soul that longs for a God whose glory is infinitely beyond us but whose love comes infinitely near. "Closer is he than breathing and nearer than hands and feet." This is the Christ who is the answer to the first question of the Heidelberg catechism: "What is your only comfort, in life and in death?" "That I belong—body and soul, in life and in death, to my faithful Savior, Jesus Christ."

There are others for whom beginning again might mean something entirely different. I am thinking of those who have never questioned the orthodox teaching of the church about Christ and are vaguely disturbed by every book or movie that presents or offends the mental picture they have of their Lord. They are sure that he is their divine Lord but could begin again to think what it means that he was also truly human—with all our experiences of suffering, of temptation, of disappointment, and of days when the heavens seem empty. This was a real baby who was born in a real, dirty, smelly stable, not a prodigy who nestled in a glowing heavenly manger.

Everyone of us nourishes an image of Jesus that tends to become fixed over the years. Christmas is a good time to expand our vision. We need to ask not only the question, "Who was Jesus?" which is again agitating our secular world, but the believer's question, "Who is Jesus—for me?"—and be ready to let him speak. Might we not have to confess, for instance, that our image of Jesus has been colored by our times, our culture, even the color of our skin? If we were raised in this country, we probably absorbed printed pictures of Jesus in Bibles and books of prayers showing him to be very like the handsome boy next door: tall, blond, muscular, with the smile of a toothpaste commercial. I had to begin again more than once to realize, first, that Jesus was a Jew of his time and, then, that he transcends all limitations of race and culture. "The supreme miracle of Christ's character," writes C. F. Andrews, "lies in this: that he combines within himself, as no other figure in human history has ever done, the qualities of every race."

What better celebration for all of us at this season could there be than a common resolve to begin again with this Christ to whom we were introduced when infants and who has ever since been knocking at the door of our hearts and minds offering to reveal new truths to us, to enlarge our vision of his kingdom, our reception of his grace, and our understanding of his promise to be with us always even to the end of the world. Even so, come, Lord Jesus.—David H. C. Read

Topic: A Baby's Cry, a Soldier's Threat
TEXT: Matt. 2:13–18

There are those who say that it's very hard to get into the spirit of Christmas, what with all of the problems we're facing in the world.

It does seem like it is very hard to sing "Joy to the World" in times like these. But what we need to understand is that Christmas was not born into a world that was antiseptic and clean and free from problems.

Let us hear a soldier's threat and a baby's cry. The birth of Christ was not welcomed by everyone. Herod the king didn't want it. He was afraid of anyone that might grow up and become a threat to his rulership, so he sought to discover where the baby was. When he couldn't do that, he had every boy two years old or under in the area killed. Soldiers and their threats as they walked up to the door, the heart wrenching cry of the babies as they died—a horrible thought, but it is there in the midst of our Christmas story. What could that say to us?

I. *There is suffering in the world but also a God who comes to share it.*

The Bible is always realistic. It looks at

life as it really is, and the first Christmas story is no exception. Did the parents understand why little babies were killed? I'm sure they didn't. It was horrible, such innocent suffering!

But Jesus had to face danger, too. Mary and Joseph had to flee by night in order to keep him from being found by Herod's soldiers.

Yet that baby was a reminder of hope. That baby was God who had come into the world in the midst of all of its suffering.

This is what Christmas tries to remind us. It reminds us that there is a God who understands our struggles and our pain. He has come to share it with us. In our suffering we're not alone.

II. *There is uncertainty in the world but also a God who helps us face it.*

Mystery and uncertainty certainly surrounded the early Christmas story. Mary and Joseph did not have time to enjoy the birth of their baby. Instead, they had to snatch him up and run. What was going to happen to them? They didn't know. Egypt was a strange place to them.

Also, what would God do with them? They did not know. They lived on the edge of mystery and uncertainty, but they lived with God and that made the difference. For God had already gone before them to prepare for the birth. They had seen that. Therefore, they lived with the belief that God would go before them to prepare the way. Before them lay the unknown, but before them also lay God, and he was enough.

We do not know what is going to happen. Will we have to go to war? Will inflation get worse? Will I have enough money to retire on? Is the pain I feel serious? Will I ever get married? Will I ever get a job? Will I ever graduate? On the questions go, and we have no answers. We do not know. Tomorrow is a mystery and will always be.

However, Christmas tries to help us remember what we do know and that is this: God is in the tomorrow of our lives. It is an axiom of our faith that God will never ask us to do anything that we cannot do, but it is also true that God will never ask from us anything he will not help us to do.

III. *There is death in the world but also a God who overcomes it.*

How horrible it must have been to see the soldiers with their swords, to hear the cries of the babies as they died. But there is the paradox of Christmas. There is birth, and there is death. One baby is born; many babies die. The strange fact of the Christmas story is that this very baby who had to run for his life was the one who grew up to conquer death. He grew up to face it. He climbed the cross and suffered a terrible death, but he overcame it. He rose from the dead. This child had come to make sure that death was no longer to be feared. He would conquer death. Those who put their faith in him would discover that he is with them forever.

Death is a part of our lives, and we cannot overlook it, but Christmas sounded the death knell for death. Christmas reminds us that God has conquered death. Life with him is forever. Death is not the end but a passageway to that which is greater and better and more.

Those who have put their faith in the hands of God are always in the hands of God, and nothing in the world or beyond can ever, ever change it.

This Christmas, there will be horrible sounds to hear. It was the same with the world into which Christ was born. Suffering, uncertainty, and death—it was all there. Christ faced it all, but it was to such a world and for such a world that he came to help us struggle with these enemies and defeat them.

What God has done in Christ is forever. Therefore, despair can be swallowed up in hope; death can be swallowed up in life; and Christmas can be celebrated with joy and love because God has come, is come, and always will be here for us all.—Hugh Litchfield

Topic: You Also Must Be Ready
TEXT: Matt. 24:37–44
The Scripture for this first Sunday in Advent speaks about the ultimate Advent, or coming, of Jesus Christ. As Christians we believe that history is going somewhere. It's not like the child's pet hamster spinning on its circular treadmill, going nowhere. Nor is history like the winding down of a great cosmic timepiece. History is moving toward its God-designed, God-

timed completion when Christ shall reign forever and ever. As Frank Stagg commented, "The Christian must accept the necessity of living in the tension between knowing the certainty of Christ's coming and not knowing when."

What do we do with the tension? We let it stretch our awareness that we must watch and be ready (Matt. 24:42, 44). Maybe this is why the season of Advent, the four weeks before Christmas, emerged in the history of the church. Perhaps they knew centuries ago that it might take four weeks to prepare for true worship of the Bethlehem Babe. We have a yearly rehearsal to practice our watchfulness and readiness. These practices can not only convince but also condition us to be watchful and ready when the final day on God's calendar arrives.

The general, timeless teaching of our text, watching and being ready, will help us celebrate Christmas. Our celebrations of this turning point, the hinge act, in God's drama can prepare us for the final act. I have three cues which will become a sentence summary on how we might also be ready.

I. *Christ comes during the ordinary.* As Jesus spoke of "that day and hour no one knows" (v. 36, RSV), he reached back in holy history to remind us of the days of Noah. The neighbors of Noah were busy with the routines of life—eating and drinking, marrying and giving in marriage. They were not prepared, and they were swept away when the waters rose.

That's how it will be, Jesus continued, when he returns. He said, "Two men will be in the field; one is taken and one is left. Two women will be grinding at the mill; one is taken and one is left" (v. 40, RSV). Nothing could have been more commonplace than men working in the field or women grinding at the mill. Then and now the choice and the challenge is to find in such ordinariness the path to a meaningful life with Christ. Just as Jesus first came to us during the commonplace of a busy town crowded with taxpayers rendering unto Caesar, he still comes in our busy, workaday world.

Some notice him; others do not. One will receive him; another will not even be aware of his presence. One person may know fulfillment, joy, and eternal life, and another will be unblessed and unhonored. One will be taken into Christ's glory; another will be left in his fatal preoccupation with "what shall we do?"

I'm intrigued with the story of Nicholas Herman—Brother Lawrence, as he was called by those who served in a monastery in seventeenth-century Paris. Brother Lawrence was a layman who spent forty years working in the kitchen of this monastery. He was a quiet, gentle Christian who at the age of eighteen was found ready to receive Christ. His experience was nothing more than seeing a tree stripped of its leaves in wintertime. Brother Lawrence realized that in a brief time the bare branches would be filled with foliage and fruit. Yet because he was watchful, he was ready to hear God speaking to him through this ordinary, commonplace tree. Brother Lawrence received a high view of the power and providence of God. Through that experience he committed himself to serve Christ in the way he believed was best.

These days before Christmas we will busy ourselves with rather commonplace routines in comparison with the most uncommon event of Christ's birth. Let us be careful not to become so preoccupied with the seasonal preparations and so exhausted by them that we are not ready to enjoy the celebration. If we watch, we can find in the everydayness of these pre-Christmas days the little advents of Christ.

II. *Ordinarily we miss him.* Often we are so caught up in the ordinary that we fail to recognize his quiet, humble appearances or even his dramatic revelation. Some miss Christ because they don't bother to watch for him—or they don't look with eyes of expectation. The routine of life has lulled some to sleep or dulled their sense of wonder.

I remember a story about a rural mail carrier on his weekly trip through Hardin County, Kentucky. The time was February 1809. A local man met the mail carrier and asked what was happening in the outside world. The mail carrier told about trouble again between the United States and Great Britain, and he mentioned the talk about a national bank. Then the carrier returned the question: "What's happening in these parts?" The local man answered, "Shucks, Mister, nothin' ever happens back here. There was a baby born last night to Nancy Hanks and Tom Lincoln, but shucks, mister, nothin' ever happens back here." In the ordinariness of life, the miracle of birth—Abe Lincoln's birth—was missed.

Others miss Christ because they look too diligently for him. They look so hard, they get eyestrain and miss the subtle ways he comes. I remember seeing a Christmas play years ago about a humble village cobbler and his wife. It was revealed to the cobbler that Christ would be his guest on Christmas Eve. He and his wife made sure everything was just right. Soon there was a knock at the door. The guest! But it wasn't Jesus. It was just a poor beggar. Later came an orphan and then an old woman. Each uninvited guest was treated with dignity and cared for, but the old cobbler was disappointed that Jesus had not come. We in the audience remembered the words of our Lord, "As you did it to one of the least of these my brethren, you did it to me" (Matt. 25:40, RSV).

III. *Unless we watch.* He comes in the ordinary, during the routines of life, but ordinarily we miss him unless we watch. If we watch, there's much less chance that we'll miss him. Jesus illustrated the unexpectancy of his final advent by saying he would come like a thief in the night. Therefore, the householder must watch.

George A. Buttrick once said, "It is easy to miss God's writing on earth and sky. A man must 'Stop, Look, and Listen' for more than railroad trains!" Earlier I mentioned Brother Lawrence, who found God in the ordinary. He didn't quit looking. During those forty years in the monastery kitchen, Brother Lawrence did what he called "practicing the presence of God." Amid the pots and pans, vegetables and dough, Brother Lawrence stopped, looked, and listened for God's presence. He taught that all that was required to practice the presence of God is to live each moment with awareness of the love of God. Taking his own counsel had created within Brother Lawrence a sweet and calm disposition. He was described as one who was never impatient, frustrated, or hasty in the kitchen.

Christ comes in the ordinary—eating and drinking, marrying and giving in marriage, working in a field or an office, grinding at the mill or a factory, in the rush of a monk's kitchen, at the birth of a baby in rural Kentucky, or in the everydayness of your life and mine. Unless we watch we may miss him. We may lose brief moments to ponder his mercy and love.

Watch this Christmas! Be ready to experience the presence of Christ in the least obvious ways or in the most unexpected places. Look with the eyes of expectation. Listen with ears of hope. Let not the humdrumness of life or the negativism of another cheat us out of the wonder of our Lord's birth and the celebration of it. Watch! Be ready! For one day he will come again.—P. Randall Wright

ILLUSTRATIONS

BY ROBERT C. SHANNON

NO NEW DOOR. There is a small church in Zica, Serbia, that has seven doors, many more than are needed for such a small building. Over a period of two hundred years, seven Serbian kings were crowned in this little church. Each time, they built a new door so that the newly crowned king could emerge from a doorway that no one had ever used before. Christ came to earth through the same doorway we all used, the womb of a woman. Though he was King of kings, he came to earth as all humans do. It was meant to show us that he intended to fully share our humanity.

CHRISTMAS ISLAND. There are two islands called Christmas. One lies in the Pacific Ocean. It was discovered by Capt. James Cook on December 24, 1777. At that time it was uninhabited, but a few people now live there. In the Indian Ocean south of Singapore lies another and more populous island. It, too, is called Christmas Island. Christmas is always an island. It is a spiritual island in a secular world. It is an island of peace in a troubled world. It's an island of faith in a skeptical world. It's an island of hope in a pessimistic world. Come to Christmas Island!

THE GOD WHO BECAME A MAN. When *Time* magazine published an article about the death of Japanese emperor Hirohito in January 1989, they put under his picture these words: "The god who became a man." The reference is to the fact that the Japanese regarded the emperor as divine until their defeat in World War II. Everyone looked down when he passed. Children were told that if they saw his face they'd be struck blind. No one was allowed even to mention his name. The victorious Allies required him to disavow his deity and declare that he was only a personal symbol of his country. Thus *Time* magazine called him "the god who became a man." Once there really was a god who really did become a man. Jesus said, "Before Abraham was, I am," and, "He that has seen me has seen the Father," and, "I and the Father are one." Long ago brilliant men debated his nature and said at last that he was "perfect God and perfect man." No one has yet improved on that definition of the God who really did become a man.

WHEN TIME STOOD STILL. On the twenty-seventh of July, 1963, a devastating earthquake struck Skopje, Yugoslavia. The whole center of the city was destroyed and many, many lives were lost. The city has since been rebuilt, but if you stop by the railway station you will discover that the clock there doesn't give the correct time. Its hands still point to the hour and the minute of that devastating earthquake. When Jesus came "time stood still." Ever since his coming we mark all history as B.C. and A.D. It is as if history's clock stopped when Jesus was born and now forever points to that momentous time.

SECTION VII.
Evangelism and World Missions

SERMON SUGGESTIONS

Topic: Life in a Look

TEXT: Num. 21:4–9

A dynamic Christian told of his personal experience with Jesus: "I took one look at him, he took one look at me, and behold we were one forever." This truth of God's grace finds its roots deep in Old Testament history.

When Moses led the Israelites across the Red Sea, he was a hero. A few days later, however, the people were throwing brickbats instead of bouquets. "Would to God we had died . . . in the land of Egypt . . . you have brought us forth into this wilderness to kill this whole assembly with hunger (Exod. 16:3). Later in the journey, shortly after Edom had refused them passage and they were forced to skirt the borders, the people went on one of their worst temper tantrums.

"No bread! No water! We hate this vile manna!" Even the all-patient God could endure them no longer. He sent fiery serpents among the people, and they began to die. Someone described an immature person as one who "cusses when he gets mad and prays when he gets scared." The Israelites fit the pattern. Frightened because of something worse than being hungry and thirsty, they, in desperation, cried to God for help.

Following God's instructions, Moses made a brass serpent, placed it on a pole outside the camp, and said to the people, "Look on it and you will be healed!" Many did, and they were! Although the text does not tell us so, surely many did not and were not.

Centuries later, Jesus used this story to make simple a profound truth to Nicodemus. The Old Testament event was the shadow of a coming truth projected far before it and shows the figure rather than the substance. Yet our Lord saw in it an illustration of his own work on the cross which would be the universal remedy for man's sinful condition. He declared with authority, "And as Moses lifted up the serpent in the wilderness, even so must the Son of man be lifted up" (John 3:14). Four simple steps in the Old Testament narrative can be seen that find their parallel in the glorious gospel of God's grace in Jesus Christ.

I. *A defiant sin.* The Hebrews had three strong words to describe wrong conduct— *sin, transgression,* and *iniquity.* David used all three of them in his great Psalm of Confession (51). The root meaning of *sin* was "to miss the mark or fall short of a standard." *Iniquity* meant "moral perversity or crookedness." *Transgression* meant "rebellion."

When the people spoke against God and Moses, they were actually rebelling against authority. The root of all sin is at this point. God demands not only respect but obedience. The first step toward the various sins of the uncontrolled life is rebellion against God's absolute lordship.

Defiance comes because of a stubborn attitude. Jeremiah spoke of the heart as "deceitful above all things and desperately wicked" (Jer. 17:9). He then put his finger

268

on our greatest problem, that of recognizing or understanding our sinful ways, when he asked, "Who can know it?" People sin against God because they have rebelled against his authority and defied his claim upon their lives. We can try to account for the fact of sin by calling it theological fiction, an evolutionary legacy, the moral hangover from our alleged animal ancestry, or even the growing pains of the race. The one thing we cannot do, however, is to deny that it has made havoc of God's fair earth.

The old levitical law said that when man touched a dead animal he was unclean until evening, but when he touched a dead man he was unclean for seven days. A great truth is taught here. When man allows his animal nature to rule him, he is seven times more polluted than any beast of the field. The sin of Israel was the sin of us all. We have missed the mark, rebelled against authority, and become morally crooked.

II. *A deserved situation.* Sin is like that! Evil contains within it the seed of its own destruction. One of my professors in seminary used to say, "We're not punished so much *for* our sins as we are punished *by* our sin."

Israel's sin could not be tolerated. God must punish man when he goes astray, or else he ceases to be a God of holiness. The Scripture says, "And the Lord sent fiery serpents among the people, and they bit the people; and much people of Israel died" (Num. 21:6).

Sin enslaves, a fact directly contrary to the notion of most people. We hear often, "Why should I be fettered and confined by these antiquated restrictions of a conventional morality?" Laughing at Christian people who recognize the limitations under which God's Law has put them, they boast of their broad "emancipation from the narrow views of life." But reality is the other way. The man who lives by the sin principle is a slave and in the exact measure in which he does it. When we surrender too our own passions, we become slaves of them, and no one is free if he is hindered by his lower self from doing what his better self tells him he ought to do.

III. *A desperate supplication.* The Israelites

were dying! Their petition to God was no "polly-want-a-cracker" prayer. They meant it! They were in dead earnest. Perhaps they had already heard Moses say on another occasion what he said in his farewell speech on the plains of Moab and what Jeremiah was to say later, "And ye shall seek me, and find me, when ye shall search for me with all your heart" (Jer. 29:13). Prayer is indeed the "soul's sincere desire," "the upward glancing of an eye," and "the simplest form of speech that infant lips can try." But it is often even more! Prayer is the sinner's only hope for salvation. Whether a lost man can pray any other prayer to God or not, we will leave to the technical theologians. The realistic fact is that the one prayer he needs to pray above all others is, "God be merciful to me, a sinner."

IV. *A divine substitute.* If a man is drowning, we do not give him a lecture on how to swim. Rather, we throw him a life jacket. Likewise, when people are lost in sin, God does not give them a lecture on morality. He sends a Savior.

(a) Whatever else we understand about Jesus on Calvary, his death was, first of all, substitutionary. He died for me, in place of me—so that I might not have to die! The serpent on the pole symbolized, hundreds of years before the historical event at Calvary, the truth of God's redemptive love. Of course, the cross is too broad for human comprehension. If it were not, it would be too narrow to meet human need. If God's plan of salvation were not too deep for finite understanding, it would be too shallow to deal with the matter of sin. A lady once heard a minister speaking of Christ's call to the beautiful life. As he outlined the excellency of character that he wants us to attain, she spoke out audibly, "But what if we can't! Suppose we're too weak! Is there any hope?"

(b) The death of Christ says there is hope. Christ knew no sin but was made to become sin for us so that we might be God's righteousness through him. The Savior in eternity was rich, but he became poor so that we through his poverty might become rich. The death of Christ deals with the guilt of our sin. This is the first item on the agenda. Billy Graham said,

"Any man who accepts the Bible as the Word of God must come to the conclusion that Christianity is a religion of atonement. Its redemption feature distinguishes Christianity from any and all other religions . . . not merely a system of ethics, it is the story of redemption through Christ Jesus."

(c) But more than this, the cross deals with our guilt. Those who examined the ledger of a wealthy but generous medical doctor who died found written on many sheets, "Debt forgiven . . . too poor to pay." The widow insisted that he had rendered services and the estate should be paid. When the administrator asked her if the writing was her husband's and she replied affirmatively, he said, "Lady, there's not a court in the land that could or would make those people pay where the doctor wrote that the debt was forgiven." Likewise, sin is a debt, and divine forgiveness is God accepting the crimson coin of Christ's blood in payment for that debt.

(d) What do you see when you look at the cross? If we see only a pure and perfect man dying, we are as blind as the Roman legionnaires. If we see only an example of perfect innocence and patient suffering, we miss the truth as much as those who looked on that day without realizing what was happening. If we see Calvary with an unmoved heart, we are as blind as the rough soldiers. If we look at the event and our hearts fail to go out in thankfulness and we fail to lay ourselves at his feet in lifelong devotion, we are no better than the men who sat for hours, gambled over his garments, and, no doubt, swapped stories while the "awful thing" was happening. Another attitude, however, is possible. Nothing requires us to gaze at the cross without understanding. There is, indeed, "life in a look at the crucified One." That look, however, must be one which involves repentance to the utmost and faith to the utmost. We are, to be sure, not saved by our good works; but neither are we saved except by a faith that will produce good works.

When we are saved by the death of Jesus, a great event happens in our life. The power of the risen Christ enters our life and gives new meaning. We are redeemed completely. Our love is transformed. In fact, the cross of Calvary is the only place where our entire personality can be redeemed.

Past all of our fumbling efforts to solve the problem of sin, Calvary, plus the empty tomb three days later, is God's answer. The uplifted Christ is the highest revelation and most effective demonstration of God's love to us that has ever been made in history. More than a century ago, Tennyson, a great Christian poet, said in his poem "Guinevere," "We must needs love the highest when we see it." Calvary is God's highest and best. Let us see it through the eyes of faith and surrender to the person who died for our sins and is now alive forevermore.—Fred M. Wood

Topic: The Positive Power of Forgiveness

I. There are some people who have an obvious need for forgiveness. But the point Jesus makes again and again in the Gospels is that forgiveness is not only something needed by people who have committed very obvious sins but something needed by *everybody* all the time. It is not the special preserve of those who have dramatically erred with their lives—the crooks and prostitutes and murderers—but the daily requirement of average people, people like ourselves, who may not have any strong sense of wrongdoing.

(a) You will remember, of course, the story of the paraplegic who was carried to Jesus by four of his friends and let down through the roof because of the great crowd of people gathered in and about the house. The first thing Jesus did, after this surprising entry, was to *forgive* the man. Now, if you reflect on it, that is rather amazing. What great sins could this poor fellow have committed, being bedfast as he was? There are not many commandments he could have broken, for some of them require a fair amount of mobility. But Jesus forgave him, suggesting that there are always sins of the heart that do not demand any social interaction for fulfillment.

(b) And there is Jesus' famous parable of the Pharisee and the publican, about the two very different men who went up to the Temple to pray. The Pharisee, who worked hard at living righteously every day—Robert Burns might have called him one of the *unco guid,* or uncommonly good persons—stood before the holy altar and thanked God that his life was unsullied, which was more than he could say for the tax collector he saw kneeling and beating his breast nearby. The tax collector, a virtual outcast in the Jewish community, was publicly bewailing his degraded status and begged God to have mercy on his soul.

Jesus gave a twist to the story that ought to go straight to the heart of every one of us. This poor man, he said—the tax collector—went home with God's approval, while the Pharisee didn't, because the Pharisee was blind to his own need to be forgiven. The Pharisee was such a good man, in his own eyes and the eyes of the community, that it simply didn't enter his mind to ask for God's forgiveness.

That should make us think—especially those of us who haven't recently felt any guilt and haven't bothered to beseech God for our own forgiveness. Maybe we even said the Lord's Prayer—"forgive our debts as we forgive our debtors"—without a ripple of consciousness, thinking, "Of course, I don't really have any debts right now."

II. What it's all about, you see, is *being dynamically rejoined to God and the community of holiness through his active forgiveness at every moment of our consciousness.*

(a) It isn't that God is mad at us and is sulking because we are sinners. It is simply that there is what Kierkegaard once called "an infinite qualitative distance" between us and God—and we should bear this in mind at all times and, whenever we think of it, seek God's forgiveness for this distance and be spiritually rejoined to the Holy Spirit.

(b) But it is not only with God that we should desire forgiveness, said Jesus; it is with other human beings as well.

(1) Just as we are not whole when there is distance between us and God, we are not whole when there is distance between us and other persons. Therefore, said Jesus, "if you are offering your gift at the altar and there remember that your brother has something against you, leave your gift there before the altar and go; first be reconciled to your brother, and then come and offer your gift" (Matt. 5:23–24).

(2) If someone needs our forgiveness, by the same token, we should not make it difficult for that person to receive it. "For if you forgive men their trespasses," said Jesus, "your heavenly Father also will forgive you; but if you do not forgive men their trespasses, neither will your Father forgive your trespasses" (Matt. 6:14–15). In fact, said Jesus on another occasion, the kingdom of heaven itself is like a king who went to settle his accounts with his servants and found that one owed him a staggering debt. When the man could not pay it, the king forgave him. But when the man went out and tried to extract payment of a much smaller debt another man owed him and, when the sum was not forthcoming, had the man thrown into prison, the king called him in and had *him* imprisoned because he was not forgiving as the king had been (Matt. 18:23–35).

It is interesting that Jesus would say this is what the kingdom of heaven is like—it is a society of mutual forgiveness, of renewed fellowship and intimacy based on God's forgiving us and our forgiving one another.

III. As I suggested before, it all has to do with a kind of psychic *wholeness,* with our being part of the entire community of God in such a gentle and loving way that no enmity exists among us. The wholeness is so important that we should actively seek it at all times, first by praying regularly and sincerely for our own forgiveness and then by seeking it and giving it freely among our fellow human beings. God's wrath erupts against those who withhold their forgiveness, but his fellowship is also denied to those who do not seek it for themselves.

(a) The question is, Who can afford to live without this forgiveness daily?

I now realize that I need this every day—not just occasionally or in special seasons. This is why Jesus placed "Forgive us our debts" just after "Give us our daily bread" in the Lord's Prayer. There is a dailiness about the act of forgiveness, just as there is about receiving physical nourishment.

(b) One of the finest pictures of the working of forgiveness I have ever seen was in a sermon by W. E. Sangster, the great pastor of Westminster Central Hall in London. Sangster was talking to his congregation about experiencing forgiveness. He asked the people to imagine all the "undesirable things" in their minds being loaded on a "sludge vessel" and dropped at sea.

The conclusion is obvious: God's love is the Black Deep where our sins are dropped and buried for all eternity. What else could we do with our evil, our failure, our rebellion, our insincerity, our unfaith? There is only one thing that will get rid of it. God must bear it away. God who is holiness. God who is righteousness. God must bear away our sins and sink them in the depths of his love, where they will be purified and made sweet again.

IV. Do you see the power in forgiveness? It is the power to be renewed, to feel cleansed, to know we are restored to God's favor and to wholeness in the community God is building. It isn't a negative power at all but a positive power. In fact, it is the most positive power in the world. Nothing else can rebuild a life the way it can. Nothing else can so change the life of an individual or a nation. Forgiveness is a dynamo waiting to regenerate our lives.

But we have to see this. We have to see it and realize that the garbage need not pile up in our lives. Our psyches don't have to be full of refuse. God's sludge vessels are waiting to take away the irreducible filth and decay of our existence. All we have to do is realize this and say, "Here, Lord, I yield myself to you. Take away my sin through the mystery of your love and receive me into oneness with you and your divine community."

And lo and behold, it is done.

In the twinkling of an eye.—John Killinger

Topic: How to Survive Temptation

TEXT: 1 Cor. 10:11–13

It's a fact! Christians are going to face trials in the form of temptations. Yet good can always come out of even the most severe trials. Although Satan desires otherwise, God always desires that the very best

come from trials. Jesus made this clear in Luke 22:31–32 when he said, "Simon, behold, Satan hath desired to have you, that he may sift you as wheat. But I have prayed for thee, that they faith fail not." Just as it requires more cuts from the jeweler's chisel to bring out the inherent beauty in a precious stone, so are trials often necessary to bring out the hidden beauty of a Christian.

In our text, Paul deals with the subject of temptation. The King James translation of the Greek word *peirasmos* (temptation) also refers to trials or testings. How we react to these difficulties often determines our spiritual growth and maturity. "Knowing this, that the trying of your faith worketh patience. But let patience have her perfect work, that ye may be perfect and entire, wanting nothing" (James 1:3–4). After showing how our spiritual predecessors in the Old Testament dealt with temptation, the Christian is told how to deal effectively with the subject of temptation.

I. *How to prepare for temptation.* Since Jesus himself experienced temptations, we should expect them ourselves. But take hope. Just as the Master faced them and won, so can the Christian master temptation. Jesus "was in all points tempted like as we are, yet without sin. Let us, therefore, come boldly unto the throne of grace, that we may obtain mercy and find grace to help in time of need" (Heb. 4:15–16).

What helped Jesus deal with temptations? Prior preparation through mastering the Scriptures enabled him to ward off the tempter. In each temptation he quoted Scripture. To prepare for temptation, we *must* saturate our minds with Scripture to stand firm. Paul said that "all these things happened unto them for examples, and they are written for our admonition" (v. 11).

The Old Testament saints overcame difficult or impossible situations and turned defeat into victory. They merit our study, and the example they provide can often supply the answer to overcoming temptation. The psalmist wrote, "Thy word have I hid in mine heart, that I might not sin against thee" (Ps. 119:11).

II. *How to prevent falling to temptation.* An old adage applies perfectly to the problem of temptation: Prevention is the best cure. This is not to say that we can prevent temptation from coming; we cannot. But we can do something to prevent falling prey to the overwhelming power of temptation.

Paul gave some practical advice when he said, "Wherefore let him that thinketh he standeth take heed lest he fall" (v. 12). Paul was referring to our basic attitude toward temptation and the danger of becoming presumptuous. Presumption on the part of the Christian is a deadly weakness. Paul said that we should never allow ourselves to think that we are strong enough to stand alone. "For I say . . . to every man that is among you, not to think of himself more highly than he ought to think; but to think soberly, according as God hath dealt to every man the measure of faith" (Rom. 12:3).

III. *How to prevail against temptation.* To defeat an enemy one must first understand him. To overcome temptation we must also completely understand it. So that we can overcome the temptations that come our way, Paul described its nature (v. 13).

First, temptation is something that is not exceptional to anyone; we all have to face it.

Second, God both allows and limits it. He knows our limits and will not allow temptation to exceed our capacity to withstand it. In the Book of Job, the Lord allowed Satan to try Job; but in each case limits were set.

Third, God always provides a way of escape. The Greek word used is *ekbasin* and denotes the picture of an army, trapped in the mountains, which is able to escape from an impossible situation through a pass. God will provide a way of escape, even as he provided a solution to the problem of Abraham as he prepared to sacrifice Isaac.

If we can master these suggestions from Paul, then no matter what form temptations take, we can defeat them. So, whether the particular temptation we face is lust, compromise, or even the temptation of mediocrity, adhering to the words of Paul can be of tremendous importance

in warding off the "fiery darts" of Satan. We must also remember that Christ will strengthen us. "I can do all things through Christ which strengtheneth me" (Phil. 4:13).—Jack G. Wingate

Topic: The Wisdom of Faith in God

Text: The Book of Proverbs

Does it concern you that God knows everything about you? Prov. 15:3 suggests the eyes of the Lord are everywhere. This verse speaks of God's omniscience and God's omnipresence.

"The eyes of the Lord" (15:3) is an expression in the Hebrew language which refers to the omniscience of God. God is so wise it is as if his eyes are present in every place.

God knows what is going on everywhere (15:11), including the regions beyond the grave. No person, whether alive or dead, can hide any of his thoughts from God.

I. Faith in God begins with repentance that rejects evil (3:7; 14:12; 16:2). The Book of Proverbs makes it plain that wickedness must be recognized for what it is— rebellion against God. Because God knows all about us, we need to turn to him for salvation. We cannot come to him and cling to evil at the same time.

Some years ago in Memphis, Tennessee, I entered an airplane and sat down, only to have the flight attendant come to check my ticket. She informed me I was on the wrong airplane. If I stayed on it, I would go in the opposite direction from my desired destination. Of course, I got up, walked off the plane, and followed her directions to the right plane that would take me where I wanted to go. Repentance is like that. It involves a change of mind, a change of will, a change of direction, and a change of destiny!

One must not trust his conscience completely. A person's conscience must be informed by the Word of God. Prov. 14:12 declares there is a way which seems right to a person, but the end is the way of death. Prov. 16:2 declares there are ways that may seem clean to a person in his own eyes, but it is God who weighs or judges the person's spirit.

II. Faith in God expresses itself in commitment to God (3:5–6). The word for "trust" in the Hebrew language is a word for complete confidence in God. The Hebrew word expresses the idea of commitment—putting God first, remaining steadfast to God, recognizing God's righteousness and credibility. This kind of faith puts itself into God's care. One of the literal meanings of the word is to lean on God. The meaning expressed by this word is confidence to the end. Prov. 28:26 declares, "He who trusts in his own heart is a fool" (NASB). Prov. 29:25 affirms, "He who trusts in the Lord is safe" (RSV). Persons who come to God must approach him with total commitment. The phrase repeated throughout the Book of Proverbs and throughout the entire Bible is "with all your heart."

W. T. Conner used to say conversion is the end of salvation. He would explain that conversion is the front end! Faith is the beginning of an eternal pilgrimage. Heaven begins in this life and extends into the life beyond. The word for "trust" in the Hebrew language is similar to the New Testament idea of faith—complete commitment. This is a faith with all the being of the believer. He trusts with all his heart. He does not rely on himself or anything else. His faith is without qualification or mental reservation. It is a continuing faith. The faith that saves is the faith that keeps on believing.

Some missionaries were seeking to explain the concept of faith to some persons who didn't have the word for faith in their language. After many futile attempts, one day one of the missionaries sat down in a chair and expressed the idea of fatigue. He said, "I am so tired I just want to rest all of my weight on this chair." One of the natives understood the idea the missionary had been trying to convey for days. "Is that what you have been trying to get us to do for God," he asked, "to cast all our weight on him?"

Deut. 6:4–6 contains the ancient Hebrew Shema: "Israel, remember this! The Lord—and the Lord alone—is our God. Love the Lord your God with all your heart, with all your soul, and with all your strength. Never forget these commands that I am giving you today." The person who trusts in God will acknowledge him in all his ways. The Good News Bible includes the idea of remembering the Lord in everything you do. This focuses on the mental attitude of the believer.

This kind of faith in God not only makes its initial commitment to God, but it is demonstrated in self-control, industrious living, and in all the ethical relationships of life. This kind of faith is more than a theological concept. It is as practical as the Book of Proverbs!

III. Faith in God results in eternal security (2:21–22; 3:25–26; 10:25–30). The faith that saves is the faith that keeps eternally. The Hebrew idea of well-being was to have the promise of living in God's land forever. Although a theology of heaven was not fully developed at the time of Solomon, the idea of security in the Lord was well established. The main emphasis was on an eternal quality of life which resulted from faith in God. Security can be the present possession of the godly person. He need not fear present peril or future danger. He is privileged to rest confidently in the Lord.

There is as much difference between the person who trusts in God and the person who doesn't as there is between a fleeting whirlwind and a solid foundation stone. Security that results from faith in God is like a strong shield that protects the godly person. True religion is more than something worn temporarily on the arm. It is like the gigantic fortress which the man of God can hide behind, safe in his Father's protective arms.

The word for "upright" (2:21–22) means one who has right standing with God. This person is contrasted with the person who has fallen. The man who trusts in God stands straight. He is safe. He will live long in the land of promise. The word translated "perfect" in the King James Version refers to one who is mature. He is trustworthy. His standard of righteousness coincides with God's standard of righteousness. The Good News Bible gives the right idea of the word: "integrity." The promise of long life, in the Hebrew language, does not mean number of years as much as it means quality of life.

Verses 3:25–26 carry the promises of God for the safety of the person who trusts in him. The believer does not need to worry about sudden disasters. He has committed his life to God. Verse 26 pictures an animal walking through the forest in danger of stepping into a trap. God promises his faithful followers will not step into traps that will cause them to go down into hell.—Scott Tatum

ILLUSTRATIONS

BY ROBERT C. SHANNON

OUR LEGACY.   Tourists traveling along the Adriatic coast always visit three places: Dubrovnik, Split, and Mostar. In each place there is something distinctive that has been left for us by previous generations. In Dubrovnik it is a wall. In Split it is a ruin. In Mostar it is a bridge. What will we leave behind us when we are gone? A wall to divide people? A ruin to discourage them? A bridge to unite them? When we give support and encouragement to world missions we help to build the bridge that unites people to God and to one another. The building of that bridge is the most significant task ever undertaken!

THE UNSUNG HERO.   Nobody knows the name of the man who rescued the infant John Wesley from the burning parsonage at Epworth, but all succeeding generations of Christians are in his debt. No one knows the name of the man who saved the young Abraham Lincoln from drowning, but he blessed millions! No one knows the name of the person in Genesis 37 who told the young Joseph where he could find his brothers and their flocks, but he changed history. It may be that you will do a deed someday that will change history. You may do something of eternal significance and never know that you have done it. We know the names of our missionary heroes: Livingstone, Moffatt, Carey. We don't know the names of the people whose sacrificial giving made their work possible! God knows. Jesus said that he who gives so much as a cup of cold water will not go unnoticed by his Lord.

SERVING LEADS TO LOVE.   A young Hungarian Christian was describing his home life. He said that his father was not a believer and had divorced his mother. He said he had never liked his father. But then his father fell seriously ill. There was no one to care for him. So the son went to his father's house every day to do the difficult and unpleasant tasks that needed doing. The young man said, "I served him until he died, and in serving him I came to love him." Perhaps that is exactly what Jesus had in mind when he taught us to love our enemies and to do good to those who hate us (Luke 6:27). No doubt he understood that sometimes the deed must precede the emotion; that if we behave as if we loved people, we will discover that we do. What about our world? It's so easy to resent it, to dislike it, to hate it. But when we serve the world we will come to love it in the sense of John 3:16: "God so loved the world!"

MIRRORS OR WINDOWS.   Most all visitors to France go to Versailles to see the great palace of the sun king. The centerpiece of the palace of Versailles is the famed hall of mirrors. In that room, wherever one looks, he sees himself! Some people live in such a room. All they ever see is themselves. We need to move out of our hall of mirrors into a room with windows, windows through which we can see not ourselves but others who need the gospel, who need Jesus, who need the church, who need us!

WASTEFUL LIVING.   Many years ago a Turk living in what is now Skopje, Yugoslavia, figured out how much it was costing him to use tobacco. He decided to quit the habit and save the money. With the money he built a mosque, and it stands yet today. It is called the Tutun Sun Mosque, which simply means "without tobacco." In so many different ways we waste so much. And we could do so much good in the world if we only redirected the money we waste.

SECTION VIII.
Resources for Preaching on Stewardship

BY RICHARD B. CUNNINGHAM

When the average pastor announces an upcoming sermon series on stewardship, most church members immediatley think, "The pastor is going to preach on money again." The announcement itself predictably triggers resistance among a number of church members that is often matched by the preacher's dread. Not uncommonly, pastors think of stewardship sermons as a task to be done and congregations as a series to be endured. How tragic when that is the case. Some preachers themselves sometimes have a superficial, narrow, reductionistic understanding that stewardship primarily concerns giving to the church. Consequently, they preach on stewardship only at budget subscription time or in connection with special offerings or building fund campaigns. The comprehensiveness and centrality of biblical stewardship is lost in the process.

Stewardship preaching ought to be exciting, engaging, positive, and comprehensively related to many dimensions of everyday life. Stewardship is among the central themes of the Bible. Although the specific words translated as "stewardship" are not frequently used, the concept itself is prominent. The stewardship concept focuses basic themes of God's purposes in Creation and redemption, particularly in the interplay between God and humanity. Far from being an idea restricted to giving or the use of material wealth, stewardship is cosmic in scope and refers to the total management of life as a trust from God. In my book *Creative Stewardship*, I define stewardship as the human being's "responsibility before God to live all of life within God's world according to the will of God as revealed in Jesus Christ."[1] That gets at the heart of biblical teachings on stewardship. Stewardship responsibility applies to every sphere of human life, individual and corporate and to the way we manage the resources entrusted to us by God.

The Hebrew term translated as "steward" is *ashur-beth,* which literally means "one who is over a house." A similar meaning is found in the Greek term *oikonomos,* which most frequently was used for a slave entrusted with the management of the business affairs of a household, which often included managing money, property, goods, or other slaves. That root meaning of "trustee" is retained in biblical usage of the terms *oikonomia* (stewardship) and *oikonomos* (steward). Jesus himself uses specific stewardship vocabulary only in the two parables of the wise and foolish servants (Luke 12:42–48) and the unrighteous steward (Luke 16:1–18). But the theme runs through many other parables. It is also basic in the New Testament Epistles.

Rightly understood, stewardship can become an illuminating model for creative and responsible Christian living. The model's themes address the central issues of the Christian life. As absolute creator and redeemer of the universe, God is the

1. Richard B. Cunningham, *Creative Stewardship* (Nashville: Abingdon Press, 1979), 16.

276

sole owner of all the world's resources and wealth. Out of grace and love, God creates humans and makes them his representatives in the world. He mandates that humans manage his resources in responsible freedom and faithful obedience to God's will for the world, as he has revealed that in Jesus Christ. Thus, every person is trusted to manage the world's resources for the good of humanity and to the glory of God. God holds individuals and societies responsible for their stewardship trust. Those motifs apply to the individual's management of one's private resources within all spheres of life—one's physical, mental, and spiritual health; one's time, abilities, and material wealth; one's vocation and calling as a Christian; and one's social life. Stewardship responsibilities apply throughout society as well—to family, church, citizenship, business, industry, education, government, the arts, and social services.

The stewardship of material wealth and giving is basic to good stewardship. But financial stewardship can be only understood within the larger framework of the stewardship of life. Consequently, stewardship preaching should be developed within the larger model and preached on a regular pulse-beat throughout the year. When that is done, sermons on giving become only one, even if a critical, part of sermons on the stewardship of life. Rightly understood, stewardship becomes a model for creative living that can be applied to a wide range of human concerns and responsibilities.

In *Creative Stewardship,* I deal with a great number of texts related to many dimensions of Christian stewardship. Preachers might examine that book for a catalog of preaching ideas. But here let me suggest a number of sermon topics that are examples of a holistic approach to stewardship preaching.

Topic: The Responsible Steward
Text: Luke 12:42–48
Jesus tells a parable of an owner of a household who appoints a servant to be steward or manager of his household while he is on a journey. The steward is charged to provide for the household but

is given no specific instructions. During the owner's absence, he is free to care for or to abuse the other servants.

The master will return unannounced and hold the steward accountable for his management. If he cares for the household, the master will bless him and put him in charge of all the master's possessions. However, if he beats the servants and engages in a life of revelry, the master will judge him as unfaithful and punish him. He will be beaten for not doing the master's will. The greater the trust, the greater the punishment.

I. The master is the owner of the estate. God is the owner of everything within the universe, by right of creation and redemption. All that persons are and have are simply a gift from God. Humans and all created things come to be and pass away. But God continues to lay claim to the universe. The Psalms picture God as saying, "For the world and all that is in it is mine" (Ps. 50:12).

II. The steward's management of the household is a temporary trust from the master. The steward in the parable is to provide for the other servants' needs. Human's are privileged to be partner's with God in the process of creation and redemption. Gen. 1:26f. pictures humans made in the image of God and commanded by God to multiply, fill the earth and subdue it, and exercise dominion over all living things. That management responsibility covers the full range of human experience in the world—everything that enriches and fulfills human life, including nature itself, individual life, family life, society, government, economics, material wealth, the arts, and religious life.

III. The steward is to manage the estate in responsible freedom according to the will of the owner. Given little detailed direction, he is free to manage the estate as he chooses. He may provide for the servants or abuse them. Humans are responsible stewards within God's world, mandated to do God's will in accordance with his purposes in Creation and redemption. God gives general principles that apply in all major areas of life. But freedom is a mark of bearing the image of God—in modern terms, of being a person.

Personal life can only occur when freedom truly exists. God creates humans for fellowship with himself and to do his will in the world. Love cannot be coerced. It can only be freely given. Consequently, God generally respects even the misuse of human freedom. That is a risk he chooses to take in the human enterprise. In the full range of human experience, people are free to do good or evil, to glorify God or to reject God, to be good or bad stewards.

IV. The owner holds the steward accountable. Upon his return, he will reward or punish the steward for the way he manages the owner's estate. Two things are notable about the return.

(a) The master will return when the steward least expects him and judge the steward according to what he finds. The master is a severe taskmaster who allows no correcting of past mistakes or rectification of wrongs after he arrives. Jesus warns, "You also must be ready; for the Son of man is coming at an hour you do not expect" (Luke 12:40).

(b) The severity of judgment will depend upon the level of the individual steward's responsibility. Those who know the master's will and fail to do it will receive a severe beating. Those who do not know will receive a light beating. This is a stark admonition for those who have heard the full gospel and grasp God's expectations for Christian living. Those who do not live up to the high demands of Christian stewardship will be severely punished for their unfaithfulness. Here is a note of warning for the easy conscience of modern humans. Our historical choices carry eternal implications. There is no easy reprieve in the end time. We are eternally accountable for what we have done with our temporal lives. Jesus says, "Every one to whom much is given, of him will much be required; and of him to whom men commit much they will demand the more" (Luke 12:48). All life is a stewardship from God and is to be lived to his glory and for the good of the human family.

Topic: The Stewardship of Individual Resources

TEXT: Matt. 25:14–30

Jesus tells a parable about a rich man who was going on a journey. He called his servants and entrusted to them varying amounts of talents, units of money worth perhaps a thousand dollars. He gave five talents to one, two talents to another, and one talent to a third. Upon his return, the man with five talents and the one with two talents had doubled their holdings through wise trading. The master was pleased with their stewardship and rewarded them with responsibility over even more of his estate. The third man, knowing that the owner was a hard taskmaster, hid his money in the ground and had only one talent. The master rebuked him, charging that if he was unwilling to risk trading, he should have placed the money in a bank and drawn interest. So the master took the one talent from the poor steward and gave it to the servant who had ten talents. The worthless servant was then cast into outer darkness.

Although the parable is built upon the stewardship of money, it is actually a parable about the stewardship of life, of which money is only one part. Matthew sets the parable in the context of teachings about the kingdom of heaven and the coming of the Son of man in judgment. It is followed by the parable of the sheep and goat judgment in which the standard of measuring one's life is whether a person has ministered to the hungry, thirsty, stranger, naked, and imprisoned.

The parable underlines the responsibility of stewards for the resources that God places at our disposal upon this earth. We are to take God's gifts and multiply them through effective investment in the marketplace of life. All of our personal, financial, and temporal resources are pure gifts from God and are to be returned to God through aggressive service in the kingdom of God. All that we are and have are gifts of Creation and redemption that encompass the whole sphere of one's life. Individual stewardship involves one's use of time, abilities, and treasure as well as one's role in the various social relationships of family life, labor, and government. In this sermon, we will confine our thinking to one's individual possessions of time, abilities, and treasure. In the total scope of biblical stewardship teaching,

one has a responsibility both for proper management of all of life's resources and for proportionate giving of time, abilities, and treasure to the life and work of the church.

I. Stewardship involves the responsible management of one's treasure. This parable centers upon the steward's management of money in the estate owner's absence. Although stewardship encompasses far more than money, financial stewardship is a good barometer of the overall level of an individual's stewardship. Two key passages help inform an understanding of financial stewardship. In Matt. 6:21, Jesus says, "For where your treasure is, there will your heart be also." In Acts 20:35 it is remembered that Jesus had said, "It is more blessed to give than to receive."

Financial stewardship involves the total management of our material wealth, including how we acquire, use, and dispose of our possessions. Generous giving cannot offset the irresponsible management of the remainder of our wealth.

We are to *acquire* our money and possessions in ways consistent with God's purposes in Creation. Among other things, we are to earn wealth through hard work in tasks that enrich humanity. We are never to earn money to another person's detriment or as an end in itself. The Bible consistently condemns the rich who gain great wealth at the expense of labor of the poor (Lev. 25:35ff.; Exod. 22:25; Amos 2:6–7; Luke 16:19–31; et al.).

A good steward responsibly *uses* one's wealth. Money enables one to buy many of life's basic necessities, provide for the family, fund the larger welfare of society through taxes, and help the needy. God blesses one's money so long as it is subordinated to one's primary commitment to the kingdom of God and used for God's basic purposes in Creation and redemption. Then one can distinguish between needs and luxuries, trust God to supply basic needs, and be freed from anxiety about the future.

A good steward also responsibly *disposes* of one's wealth. One can be a good steward in acquiring and using wealth but irresponsible in not providing for the disposal of one's estate. A responsible steward will insure that an estate goes to causes and needs that glorify God. A person usually wants to provide for one's family. Many Christians with even modest estates often want to will money to the church or church institutions along with other causes that benefit the human family. In the American system, one may determine the distribution of an estate through a will, insurance, cash gifts, various types of trusts, and other means. Good stewardship requires long-term planning before death intrudes unannounced. In this way, one may multiply the talents of the parable long after one's death.

Proportionate giving is a major part of financial stewardship. Christians may give to various causes outside the church that enhance the quality of human life and meet human need. A substantial portion of one's giving will go to the church, in which God is creating a new humanity that becomes his saving instrument in the world.

II. Stewardship involves the responsible management of one's personal resources—our bodily life, relationships, and abilities. One has a responsibility to manage all aspects of one's bodily life in the world—the health of the body and mind (1 Cor. 16:19–20; 1 Cor. 9:25, 27; Phil. 2:5), behavior (Eph. 4:1), conversation (Matt. 12:36), and influence (Mark 9:42). All are to be used to the glory of God and in the service of humanity.

God also confers certain natural abilities and spiritual gifts that are to be developed and invested in the good of the human family and in the ministry and mission of the church. Paul suggests that the Holy Spirit distributes spiritual abilities to all members of the church, as he chooses (1 Cor. 12:4–6), to serve the common good of the church (1 Cor. 12:7). Paul urges that each Christian should discover and then use one's gifts (Rom. 12:6; Eph. 4:16.) Good stewardship requires a Christian to offer one's unique abilities to the church's ministry in the world.

III. Stewardship involves the responsible management of one's time. Individual stewardship occurs in a limited amount of time between the poles of birth and death.

The importance of time is heightened in this parable and other parables that emphasize the suddenness and finality of the estate's owner's return. To the rich man preoccupied with building barns, Jesus says, "Fool, this night your soul is required of you" (Luke 12:20).

The wise steward will make each minute count for eternity. All life is to be lived to God's glory as one embodies a redeemed style of life, contributes to the welfare of the human family, and pursues values that matter eternally. But a portion of one's time, like one's financial wealth, will be given to the life and work of the church. That principle originates in the sanctifying of the Sabbath among the Hebrews and continues in the Lord's Day within the church. If one does not have time for the church, one is irresponsible in the grace of giving back to God a portion of what God has given us.

Eph. 5:15–17 states the importance of time and the totality of our stewardship within the time that is ours: "Look carefully then how you walk, not as unwise men but as wise, making the most of the time, because the days are evil. Therefore do not be foolish, but understand what the will of the Lord is." The return of the estate owner symbolizes the end of history and the parousia of the Lord. In other teachings, death marks the end. Either in death or the parousia of the Lord, time will come to an end, and each person will face God's judgment over one's personal stewardship of God's great good gifts in life.

Topic: Keeping Life's Priorities in Perspective

TEXT: Matt. 6:19–24

"For where your treasure is, there will your heart be also" (Matt. 6:21). In that epigram, Jesus insists that humans must keep life's priorities straight. Many earthly values constantly compete with the ultimate value of the kingdom of God in human life. Jesus recognizes that human beings enjoy many good created things and experiences, including values within the world of material things. Many of these are created and willed by God for human welfare and enjoyment. They are blessed by God as long as they do not usurp the place of God at the center of a person's heart. The heart symbolizes the core of the self and the seat of ultimate allegiances. The clue to the heart's ultimate loyalty is disclosed by observing what one most treasures in life.

Jesus places a clear choice before us: "No one can serve two masters. . . . You cannot serve God and mammon." Mammon specifically symbolizes money, property, or wealth. In a larger sense, mammon is a primary symbol of earthly things and possessions or finite values and goods that compete with God for the central attachment of the human heart. This text provides helpful insight into keeping life's priorities in a proper perspective, particularly in our relationship to the world of material things.

I. Material things have a legitimate place in human life. Humans live in a material world and in our embodied lives have continuity with matter itself. Like all living creatures, we require food and water, shelter and physical protection, for our survival. When Jesus asks, "Is not life more than food and the body more than clothing?" he recognizes that life requires those material things even though it should not be reduced to living only for those things. In fact, Jesus promises that if one seeks first the kingdom of God, then God will provide all life's basic necessities.

The importance of the material world is underlined in Genesis 1 when God creates humans, appoints them as his managerial representatives in the world, and mandates work as a basic responsibility of humans. Work becomes the primary instrument through which God provides the basic necessities for human life. Within certain broad limits, God even blesses some of the material rewards that come through work. The Bible evaluates the accumulation of wealth in different ways. During much of Hebrew history, wealth was viewed as a blessing of God. In contrast, the New Testament generally condemns wealth, although in some passages it approves the responsible accumulation of money if it is then used for the right purposes.

II. Material things can become a rival

god to the God who created the world. Mammon is the name of the god of material things. When one worships mammon, the production and accumulation of wealth becomes the dominating value of an individual. The worship of mammon is not confined to the wealthy. Mammon does not symbolize the size of one's bank account but the material priorities for which one lives. Poor or middle-class people can be just as preoccupied as the rich with making money and accumulating the things money can buy.

III. Mammon cannot provide the sustaining foundation for human life. Jesus warns, "Do not lay up for yourselves treasures on earth, where moth and rust consume and where thieves break in and steal." Several things can be noted about the fragility of a material foundation. Like all finite and temporal things, wealth erodes, dwindles, and disintegrates during the relentless march of historical life. Given the way world economies work, various economic factors can nibble away at one's wealth. Jesus says that at any point thieves can break in and steal.

Material wealth is limited in its contributions to life. It cannot necessarily provide human happiness or fulfillment. It cannot purchase the gift of new life or the gifts of the Spirit (Acts 8:18–24). It often cannot buy good health for an aging body, a miracle cure for a life-threatening disease, or a reprieve from one's inevitable death. Money cannot buy a happy marriage or family. Above all, we cannot take wealth with us beyond our death. Wealthy or poor, we all depart this world just as we came in—with no money in our pockets. In Paul's words, "We brought nothing into the world, and we cannot take anything out of the world" (1 Tim. 6:7). Money has no eternal value. Since death is unpredictable, one may not be able to shift loyalties from mammon to God before one dies. Jesus warns the rich man, "Fool! This night your soul is required of you; and the things you have prepared, whose will they be?" (Luke 12:20).

IV. People should live for eternal values. Jesus says, "Lay up for yourselves treasures in heaven." Or to put it another way, "Seek first his kingdom and his righ-

teousness, and all these things shall be yours as well" (Matt. 6:33). To seek the kingdom is to live under the rule of God, committed primarily to doing his will in the world. With that unqualified commitment, one can then trust God to provide life's necessities for his kingdom people. Just as God cares for the birds of the air and the lilies of the field, God will provide for those who do his will. Such trust frees people from anxiety about tomorrow and enables them to live joyfully and thankfully in the world of material things. Then the material world and things within it can have a real transposed value, so long as they are subordinated to the rule and purposes of God in his world. C. S. Lewis put this unforgettably: "Aim at heaven and you will get Earth 'thrown' in; aim at Earth and you will get neither."[2] The key is in keeping life's priorities in perspective!

Topic: The Purpose of Giving
Text: 2 Cor. 9:13
Churches and preachers talk often about giving. Many church members are only vaguely knowledgeable about where the money goes. Why exactly should a Christian give money to the church? Perhaps the best summation of the purpose of Christian giving is found in 2 Cor. 9:13, where Paul writes to the Corinthians about their share in the offering for the church in Jerusalem. Although the text refers to a specialized offering, he specifically suggests three purposes and intimates a fourth that are applicable to the total sweep of Christian giving.

I. We give first and above all to glorify God. Paul writes, "Under the test of this service, you will glorify God...." The first intention of giving glory to God is at the heart of the whole Hebrew tithing and giving traditions. In the classic words of the confession, the chief purpose of life is "to glorify God and enjoy him forever." Giving is a primary way of glorifying God, because through giving we acknowledge allegiance to the kingdom of God and do what God commands.

2. C. S. Lewis, *Mere Christianity* (New York: Macmillan, 1953), 104.

The grace of giving glorifies God in a special way because it reflects the heart of God's own nature. As *agape* love, God lavishly gives life to a created order and redemption to fallen humanity. God creates human creatures who uniquely bear the image of God and are to embody something of his nature on earth. In imitating God's pattern of giving, we particularly reflect the essence of the divine nature. The act of giving signifies that we imagebearers are consciously living as God's representatives on earth and acting to his glory. Giving provides tangible evidence that humans acknowledge God as sovereign in the universe and the source of all of life's blessings.

II. We give as a way of disciplining the self in the continuing process of growth toward Christian maturity. The glorifying of God occurs, in Paul's words, "in your obedience in acknowledging the gospel of Christ." Giving is a measurable expression of our obedience to the gospel. By returning a portion of our income and accumulated wealth to God, we honor God as lord of our lives and the owner of all created things in the universe. Giving testifies that we have been touched by the Spirit of God and are patterning our lives after his own lavish giving. It is a visible indicator that we are not worshiping mammon through feverishly accumulating material wealth. It is a constant reminder that the kingdom is our first priority and that we are not to be bound by self-interest.

III. We give to serve the needs of human beings. Paul speaks of "the generosity of your contribution for them and for all others." The Jerusalem offering was designed specifically to relieve the suffering and famine of Christians within the Jerusalem church. Just as we express love to God through our love of human beings, so our gifts to God serve a wide variety of human needs through the church's ministries. This motif is deeply rooted in the Hebrew tithing and giving systems. The Hebrews gave part of their tithes and various other charity gifts to serve directly the needs of people (Deut. 14:28–29). In the Gospels, Jesus speaks more often about giving alms to the poor than he does of giving to the Temple. Christian giving should support a wide variety of human needs—the poor, widows, orphans, suffering, sick, imprisoned, broken, spiritually impoverished, and people with other needs. Every Christian has a responsibility to help insure that one's gifts through the church are substantially targeted for ministries to human need.

IV. We give to support the life, ministry, and mission of the church. This purpose is implied when Paul speaks of "obedience in acknowledging the gospel of Christ." That gospel is at the heart of all the church is and does. Ministry is both internal and external to the church. Worship, education, community life, and other ministries contribute to the development of Christian disciples for ministry in the world. Mission is a defining mark of the church. We are to bear witness to Christ and minister to human need throughout the world. When we are blessed by the ministry of the church through hearing and responding to the gospel and being baptized into the church, we assume a major responsibility to share personally and financially in the ministry and mission of the church. That involves the gifts of our time, abilities, and money.

Financial support is especially important. Through the gifts of money, Christians enlarge the scope of their own ministries by enabling the ministries of other Christians. One purpose of giving is to support the vocational ministers of the church. This is one aspect of what Paul refers to as a "partnership in the gospel" (Phil. 4:15). Such giving allows one indirectly to go, witness, and serve where otherwise one could never go. Our financial gifts support the ministers of the local congregation; the professional staff of denominational institutions, boards, and agencies; and ministers and missionaries on the frontiers of the Christian church in the world. This cooperative sharing of the good news throughout the world gives glory to the God who created and is redeeming the universe.

Topic: Giving—A Link to God and Humanity

TEXT: 2 Cor. 8 and 9

Giving is an act that links the individual

to God and humanity. It is a central expression of Christian discipleship that reflects one's redemption into a life of service. Proper giving demonstrates that one has been set free from self-interest to love God and to love others as ourselves. It is important *why* and *how* people give as well as *that* they give. The most comprehensive model for right motives and method in giving is found in 2 Corinthians 8 and 9, where Paul encourages the Corinthian Christians to participate in the Jerusalem offering for the impoverished and famine-stricken Jerusalem Christians. These chapters will serve as our guide for the next two sermons, "Giving—A Link to God and Humanity" and "A Guide to Christian Giving."

The value of Christian giving, from God's perspective, depends heavily upon one's motives in giving. People often give out of unworthy, sometimes self-serving, motives. One may give in order to get recognition, to be memorialized, to manipulate God into bestowing special favors or rewards, to alleviate a guilty conscience, or grudgingly in response to a manipulative stewardship campaign in a church. Modern financial stewardship appeals, in fact, are often made with the objective of raising money more than of the development of responsible Christian discipleship and proper funding of Christian ministries.

The Jerusalem offering provides a classic model for Christian giving as a way of glorifying God and meeting human need. The Jerusalem church was experiencing severe economic need. Its ministry of financial support to many poor and dependent widows had exhausted its meager funds. The problem was compounded by persecution and a famine in Palestine. This offering for the physical needs of fellow Christians becomes a model of how all giving links together the giver with God and humanity. Paul's teachings provide several critical principles for proper motives in giving.

I. *Give as a response to God's grace.* The ability to give roots in God's gracious redeeming activity within the Christian's life and finds its model in God's gift of Christ for our redemption. Paul writes, "For you

know the grace of our Lord Jesus Christ, that though he was rich, yet for your sake he became poor, so that by his poverty you might become rich" (2 Cor. 8:9). The natural response to the reception of God's grace within our lives is to give as an expression of gratitude. As Christ gave, so we are to give.

Paul calls giving "a gracious work" (2 Cor. 8:7). The act of giving itself is enabled by that same grace as it turns us inside out. In our alienation from God, we live rebellious, self-serving lives. We define the universe with ourselves at the center. The self-giving grace of God emancipates us from our preoccupation with the self and enables us to give as we freely have received from God. Paul climaxes his teaching on giving by praising God for grace: "Thanks be to God for his inexpressible gift!" (2 Cor. 9:15).

II. *Give the self to God before any material gift.* Paul says that the Macedonian Christians "first gave themselves to the Lord and to us" (2 Cor. 8:5). The right ordering of our gifts is critical. People are often tempted to substitute a material gift for a basic commitment to Christ as Lord. Some people contend that when God gets a person's pocketbook, the heart will follow. When that occurs, it may be the motivation is not the love of God but a thinly disguised act of self-interest—a protective and controlling attitude about the money one has given. Many churches occasionally receive large memorial gifts from members who rarely give on a systematic basis to support the routine work of the church and who exhibit few of the wider graces of Christian discipleship.

God's rule is clear: First give the self, then the material gift! When one gives the self to God and all of life to the service of God, financial gifts inevitably will follow. Giving is one useful, even if only a negative, test of genuine Christian commitment. Although generous giving is not conclusive proof that one *is* committed to God, a *lack* of responsible giving is good evidence that one *is not* committed to God. If one can live for a period of years without being willing to give, it is a sign that God has not yet received the gift of that person's inner self. Our first gift to God must be the self!

III. *Give as a proof of love.* Paul speaks of how he had boasted to the Macedonian church about the generosity of the Corinthians. So he urges them to give generously as a proof of their love and his boasting (2 Cor. 8:24). Christians speak a great deal about love for God and humanity. Love is an action word. Love is not simply warm emotions or good intentions. Love is something we do. It is acting out, speaking out, caring out. Giving is a concrete expression of the love Christians have for God and for the needs of the world. We need to put our money where our stated intentions are. Paul says that giving proves that our love is genuine (2 Cor. 8:8).

IV. *Give in response to human need.* If the first duty of the Christian is to love God, that love of God is best expressed in the love of human persons made in his image. Love links the individual with God and other persons. As a form of love, giving to God ties us to our neighbor in need.

In 2 Cor. 8:14, Paul makes a specific application of the principle of loving others when he contends that the Corinthian Christians' abundance should supply the want of the Jerusalem church. People who live in abundance, he argues, should share with those in need in order that all be equal. Paul proposes a principle of reciprocity in human relationships. There may be a time when the Jerusalem Christians will supply the needs of the Corinthians.

Giving should provide for the physical needs of people. Jesus spoke often of giving alms to the poor. The early Christian church allocated large portions of their giving to the care of the needy, widows, and orphans. Christians should meet human need both through giving to the church and in direct giving to needy people one encounters in the world. The Good Samaritan (Luke 10:29–37) remains the highest human example of giving to those in physical need.

People have many needs beyond the physical. In our complex modern world, those needs include family life, emotional problems, spiritual struggles, fractured re-

lationships, addictive patterns of life, vocational stresses, political rights, and many other areas that enhance or inhibit authentic living. Not least, all people have a need to hear and experience the transforming gospel of Jesus Christ. Within the life of the church, there are those who need to be evangelized and those who need edification. Financial giving to the church enables Christians to minister to the total needs of humanity—physical, mental, spiritual, and social. Giving helps the church to evangelize and edify, to serve God by serving humanity.

V. *Give as an expression of thanksgiving to God.* Paul comments that the Jerusalem offering overflows in many thanksgivings to God (2 Cor. 9:12). Giving is an integral part of worship. Thanksgiving was a central ingredient of the Hebrew system of tithes and offerings, with the prime example being the practice of the thank offering (Lev. 7:12–13). Every Sunday ought to be Thanksgiving for the Christian church. The offering ought to be a central component of most of our worship in the church.

Yet all giving to human need and ministries to human need, in whatever context, can be an offering of thanks to God. Paul, for example, interprets the Philippians gift to support his ministry as "a fragrant offering, a sacrifice acceptable and pleasing to God" (Phil. 4:18). The truest test of our love for God is whether we have turned from ourselves to love human beings. Our giving to meet human need becomes a song of thanksgiving to God for the rich spiritual, human, and material blessings he bestows on us.

Topic: A Guide to Christian Giving

Text: 2 Cor. 8 and 9

How does one determine the right method for Christian giving? How much should one give? And where? Many sincere Christians who love God and want to be obedient to God's expectations for giving would like to have specific guidance on how to give. Paul suggests some helpful principles in his correspondence to the Corinthian Christians about their participation in the Jerusalem offering. Even though this is a special need offering, the principles are applicable to the full range of Christian giving. One might explore other biblical teachings about giving, yet here Paul provides a useful, condensed "Guide to Christian Giving."

I. *Give systematically.* As chief administrator of the Jerusalem offering, Paul is concerned that things be done in an orderly way. Paul provides a systematic approach to both the Corinthians' giving and his own administration of the gift. He asserts that he is acting honorably in raising and administering the offering (2 Cor. 8:21) and that he has tested the earnestness of the brother who will represent him to the Corinthians (2 Cor. 8:22). Paul encourages the Corinthians to be systematic in bringing to completion what they originally intended to give to the offering. He informs them that he is sending his representatives ahead of him so that they can have the Jerusalem offering completed upon Paul's arrival in Corinth (2 Cor. 9:3–5).

Christians should be systematic in their own giving. Systematic giving was built into the original Hebrew tithing and giving systems, so that giving encompassed carefully prescribed gifts as well as spontaneous giving to specific human needs. That principle continues into the New Testament church. In 1 Cor. 16:2, Paul suggests a specific method for the contribution to the Jerusalem offering before his arrival in Corinth: "On the first day of every week, each of you is to put something aside and store it up, as he may prosper, so that contributions need not be made when I come." Systematic regular giving is far easier for most Christians than giving large amounts of money in major special fund-raising efforts.

Two aspects of biblical financial stewardship teachings encourage regular giving. Our worship each Lord's Day should normally involve a specific financial gift as a concrete expression of our love and praise to God. Also the biblical principle of giving God the first and the best always encourages systematic giving. The Old Testament tithing system required the Hebrews to give God the firstfruits of the harvest and the best of the animals (Exod. 22:29f.; Deut. 17:1; Mal.1:6f.). When the Christian offers God the first portion of

one's weekly income, the steward will give an acceptable amount and symbolize the dedication of the remainder of one's income to the service of God.

Responsible stewardship also requires the church systematically to receive the gifts of its members and to distribute the financial resources of the church to needs that are prioritized in relation to the kingdom of God. The best way of achieving a responsible allocation of funds is through systematic budgeting. The careful handling of funds inspires the confidence of church members and systematically expends received gifts for the church's most important ministries. Paul is concerned with both systematic giving and expending of financial gifts.

II. *Give proportionately, as God prospers one.* Many Christians wonder, "How much should I give?" Paul never mentions percentages. He does suggest guiding principles. The New Testament as a whole, in contrast to the Old Testament, never advocates a specific percentage of one's income to be given to God. The tithe likely remained as a broad model for giving. However, the Hebrew tithing and gift traditions were more complex and diverse than many people understand. They were basically agricultural tithes. In the time of Jesus at least three different tithes along with numerous offerings were advocated in the rabbinic interpretations. A pious Jew would have given far more than 10 percent.[3] The New Testament commends various sizes of gifts (see Mark 12:40; Matt. 19:21; Luke 12:33; Acts 2:44–45; 4:37; 5:1–11).

Proportionate giving is the New Testament standard. Paul here provides a specific basic principle for giving within the freedom of the Christian life: "It is acceptable according to what a man has, not according to what he has not" (2 Cor. 8:12). The real size of the gift is relative to the wealth of the giver. In God's evaluation of a gift's value, the lesser dollar value gift may be the larger gift. Jesus appraised the widow's mite to be a far more generous gift than most of the wealthy's gifts, be-

---

3. Cunningham, *Creative Stewardship*, 101–104.

cause she gave out of her want all that she had (Luke 21:3–4).

III. *Proportionate giving should be liberal and sacrificial.* Christian freedom is no excuse for a Christian to be irresponsible or stingy in giving. The principle of tithe continues as a powerful reminder that a sizable portion of one's income is to be given back to God. It is clear that the early Christians practiced liberal, generous, sacrificial giving. Their practice provides two measuring rods for determining the adequacy of a proportionate gift.

(a) Proportionate giving should be liberal and generous. For the Christian, the liberality of love supercedes the legal rules of the Old Testament tithing and giving systems. Paul describes how the Macedonians in their extreme poverty and affliction begged for the favor of contributing to the Jerusalem offering and then gave in an overflow of liberality beyond their means (2 Cor. 8:1–5). God holds us accountable by this standard. Paul writes, "He who sows sparingly will also reap sparingly, and he who sows bountifully will reap bountifully" (2 Cor. 9:6). The reward of giving—the sense of being obedient to God, the joy and satisfaction of helping others, the awareness of sharing in God's work in the world—is always relative to the level of generous giving.

(b) Proportionate giving should be sacrificial. How much is enough? One standard is that the amount should require a sacrifice in our standard of living in comparison to non-Christians with similar incomes. The church should be understanding of the quite varied economic situations of modern families, which sometimes involve family health, aging persons, or other problems that place severe financial demands upon some families. Sacrifice is relative to particular family situations.

IV. *Give voluntarily.* Paul insists that a gift should not be exacted from a reluctant giver. The only gift that matters to God is one freely given by a loving, grateful person. Financial stewardship preaching should only encourage and positively motivate. It must never be manipulative or coercive. Paul advises, "Each one must do as he has made up his mind, not reluctantly or under compulsion, for God loves a cheerful giver" (2 Cor. 9:7). This principle roots in the freedom of the Christian steward. Freedom is basic to the development of persons. For that reason, God is more concerned with the giver than with the gift. He will not exact obedience in any area of life. He is pleased when one has grown to the point of giving joyfully and freely. That style of giving is one expression of an individual steward's choosing to live by the highest Christian standards in accordance with God's will as revealed in Jesus Christ.

SECTION IX.
Preaching from 1 John

BY R. ALAN CULPEPPER

What stirs a preacher's blood? 1 John is addressed to a situation in which the church is divided. One group has departed from the community's historic beliefs. Both doctrine and ethics are at issue. A pastor's finest preaching is often called forth by crises. Here is a brief tractate that calls the community back to its doctrinal roots and its commandment to show love for one another. Where division or complacency threaten the church, 1 John still speaks with prophetic relevance.

Little imagination is needed in order to picture the situation to which 1 John is addressed. The three Johannine Epistles were probably written around the end of the first century by the same person, a leader of the community who calls himself an "elder" (2 John 1; 3 John 1). Some members of the community had withdrawn from the group that remained with the elder (1 John 2:19). Assuming that the teachings and influence of this group are the elder's primary concern, we may infer that they are the ones he calls "false prophets" (4:1). The error of their teaching concerns the nature and role of Christ. They denied that Jesus Christ came "in flesh" (4:2). Rather than a blanket denial of the Incarnation, the problem seems to be that this group taught that Jesus' role was simply to bring the Spirit, through which we have eternal life. They maintained that neither the real humanity nor the death of Jesus were important for salvation. Although the elder and the opponents shared the tradition of the Johannine community and agreed on

many points, the elder charged that those who had withdrawn from the community erroneously devalued the Incarnation and death of Jesus; held to a false view of the Spirit; erroneously believed that, because they already had eternal life, they were sinless and beyond judgment; and did not live by the new commandment, to love one another.

In the opponents we see a misappropriation of the Fourth Gospel's emphases on Jesus as revealer, the anointing of each believer with the Spirit, the present experience of eternal life, sin as essentially unbelief, and the present realization of traditional hopes for the future (realized eschatology).

The sentences that begin "If we say . . ." (1:6, 8, 10) and "He who says . . ." (2:4, 6, 9) probably echo the claims of the opponents that they walk in the light and that they have no sin.

In response, the elder returned to traditional, perhaps even primitive formulations of the community's teaching. He urged those who remained faithful to "abide" in what they had heard from the beginning (2:24). He reasserted the importance of Jesus' death, i.e., his work as redeemer as well as revealer (5:6). While not denying the importance of the Spirit's anointing (2:27), the elder reemphasized the need for obedience as well as belief. Although he, too, held to the ideal of perfection (3:6, 9), he recognized that Christians continue to sin and need to ask for forgiveness (1:9; 5:16–17). The parousia or coming of Jesus also has a place in his thought (3:2), probably as an antidote to the opponent's exaggerated emphasis on the present realization of hopes for the future. The new command is cited but only in the charge that the opponents have failed to show love for their brothers and sisters. Never does the elder admonish the faithful to show love for those who have gone out from them. Nevertheless, 1 John contains one of the New Testament's most profound treatments of the nature of love.

Once the historical context of the Epistle is understood, its cryptic but vigorous words take on a new force. We see the elder fighting for the integrity of the community. The issue was nothing short of whether the Christian faith will be perpetuated or perverted. Regardless of our particular circumstances, the issue is the same every time we rise to preach.

Topic: Partial Fellowship, Incomplete Joy
TEXT: 1 John 1:1–4

You don't want to have to lick the calf twice. When a mother cow cleans a newborn calf, she cleans it thoroughly. Have you ever had to get after a teenager who rushed through an unpleasant job? Have you ever done something halfway the first time and then spent twice as long redoing the job? I once had a car repaired. The body shop put such a light coat of paint on it that I later had to have it painted a second time. It's always more trouble when you have to lick the calf twice.

Some Johannine Christians apparently felt that their joy was already complete. They had "the Word of Life" (1:1). Jesus was the one who had been with God from the beginning and who had come in flesh. Through him we have life from the Father (1:2).

Christians proclaim their faith so that others, too, may live in fellowship with God through Jesus Christ. As long as there are those who have not received the Word of Life, how can our joy be complete? A gospel song exalts the triumphalism of a private faith: "Oh, that will be glory for me, glory for me, glory for me." The elder recognized that our joy can never be complete as long as others remain outside our fellowship. While others

are oppressed, can we celebrate our freedom with no tinge of sadness? While others are homeless, hungry, victimized by drugs, or consumed with bitterness, how can our joy be complete?

Partial joy is the Christian's perpetual burden. We celebrate the life in Christ that has dawned, but we reach out to bring the love of God to others as well. Apart from their well-being, our joy can never be complete. As long as there are still others who need to receive the Word of Life, our job is not done, our fellowship is unfulfilled, and joy will be incomplete.

Topic: The Dangers of Denying Sin
TEXT: 1 John 1:5–2:2

Learn from the plight of the alcoholic: Denial is a powerful instinct. When there is something wrong, our first impulse is to deny it. Denial protects us from the pain of having to deal with reality. It is a part of both dependency and grief. We don't want to hear bad news: "No! That can't be true!" We deny physical and emotional problems. We deny marital difficulties. We also deny the power of sin in our lives.

1 John was written to a group that was in danger of accepting the teaching that Christians are immune to sin. The false prophets had apparently seized on the concept that sin is above all unbelief (John 16:8). Believers, therefore, by definition, have no sin. Moreover, because they have the Spirit and because they are children of God, they can say they have no sin.

Everyone agrees on the first point: God is light (1:5). There is no darkness, no corruption or evil, in God. Those who deny their own sinfulness think they walk in light because they know God. In fact, as long as their lives show that they are still walking in darkness, their lives expose the lie of their confession (1:6). The consequence of hypocrisy is *deception*. Cleansing, on the other hand, makes fellowship possible.

It is always easier to see someone else's shortcomings. We see the splinter in their eye more clearly than the plank in our own. The second danger of denying sin is *self-delusion* (1:8). Our moral failure is apparent to everyone but us. On the other hand, if we confess our sin, God is faithful in forgiving us and cleansing us from wrongdoing.

The third consequence of thinking that we are now free from sin is *blasphemy* (1:10). God has called us to repentance, so when we deny our sinfulness, it is as though we were calling God a liar. We show thereby that his Word is not in us.

Jesus Christ is our righteous advocate. He is the means of our forgiveness and the salvation of the world. Before we can confess our sin, however, we must be honest with ourselves and recognize our need for forgiveness. Take a good look in the mirror.

Topic: Three Tests of Spiritual Health
TEXT: 1 John 2:3–11

If you could take a medical test that would analyze your genes and tell you whether you were likely to contract a fatal disease, would you take the test? We might not want to know our medical future even if that information were available to us. What about your spiritual condition? Would you take a diagnostic test that could tell you what your spiritual condition is?

Three times in these verses the elder quotes the claims of the opponents (2:4, 6, 9). Their words are not objectionable, but the elder denies their right to make such claims. Spiritual claims must be confirmed by committed living.

The test of knowing God is obedience to his commands (2:3–5). John 17:3 defines eternal life as knowing God. The phrase sums up the meaning and goal of the Christian life. Some may claim to know God by mystical union, a vision, or divine revelation. The question to be asked is, Who is living by God's commands? For John, those commands are, above all, the command to believe in Jesus Christ and to love one another (John 13:34; 14:1; 1 John 3:23). The love of God is perfected in those who live by these commands.

The test of abiding in God is the new command (2:6–8). "Just as" is an important phrase for the ethics of 1 John. The believer ought to live "just as" Jesus lived or "walked." The essence of Jesus' life is wrapped up in his command to love one

another "just as" he loved them. Jesus loved his own to the end, to the cross. This command is not really a new one; it is part of the core of the community's tradition.

Finally, the test of being in the light is that we love our brothers and sisters (2:9–11). This test is hardly different from the second test, but it underscores that it is ludicrous to say that we walk in light while we have hatred for a brother or sister. Our hatred shows that the darkness within us has blinded us.

These tests challenge us to measure our spiritual health by asking whether our relationships to others measure up to the standard of Christ's love. How about it?

Topic: A Challenge to the Family
TEXT: 1 John 2:12–17

I recently heard my teenage son using some language he had picked up at school. He did not know that I was nearby, so it startled him when I called his name and then said simply, "We don't talk that way." I hoped that this reminder would be enough to engender in him a pride in his family identity and thereby encourage a higher ethic (and vocabulary!) than that which evidently prevailed at school.

Verses 12–17 comprise two paragraphs: a paragraph of encouragement for the church, assuring victory; and a paragraph of admonition, warning that resistance to the world is required. Here is a family blessing and a word of admonition.

The first paragraph poses a number of problems for the interpreter. Who is meant by "children," "fathers," and "young men"? Evidently, these are references to different groups within the Johannine community. Moreover, there is the question of whether the elder writes to these groups *that* they have won the victory or *because* they have won. Either is possible, but *that* is preferable. The paragraph is, therefore, a word of encouragement that sin has been conquered; in Christ victory is assured.

The second paragraph assumes a tone of exhortation. Victory is assured, but the battle is not over yet. The most subtle compromise to which a Christian is vulnerable is the compromise of loving those things that are prized by the enemy. John's thought is sharply dualistic. There is no conflict between the words of the evangelist, "For God so loved the world . . ." (John 3:16), and the words of the elder, "Do not love the world . . ." (1 John 2:15). The elder explains what he means in the phrases that follow: lust, greed, and covetousness. The family is never safe when such self-centered desires are unchecked. "We don't live that way."

The family of God is blessed, but vigilance in keeping our eyes fixed on God's values—not those of the world—is required.

Topic: Living by a Counterfeit Faith

TEXT: 1 John 2:18–27

A counterfeit bill is a phony that is made to look like the real thing. It is not just play money. The danger is that someone will accept it when in reality it has no value at all. Those who make counterfeit money can be arrested and put in jail, but we don't have such protections from those who offer counterfeit religious teachings. Lawyers must pass the bar exam, and doctors must be licensed to practice, but any quack can offer religious teachings. How can you tell the real thing from a counterfeit?

The elder warned that the presence of those who preached doctrines contrary to the gospel of Jesus Christ are actually Antichrists, even if they call themselves Christians. This is harsh language, and we must be very careful how we apply it today. It requires, first, that we reaffirm those principles that are fundamental to the gospel: love, peace, justice, grace, and concern for the oppressed. Success, materialism, wealth, and power are not gospel values. They are counterfeits offered to the innocent by purveyors of a false gospel. The test of such counterfeit values is that they create division in the Christian community.

You have the confession of Christ, while others deny him (2:22–25). The test of any counterfeit is whether it actually confesses Christ or whether it is actually serving some other person or end. Only that which proceeds from the lordship of Christ can authentically bear the word that gives life.

Finally, you have the anointing of the Spirit (2:26–27). The Spirit should be our guide as it directs us to the call of Christ to serve him. We do not need the guidance of a counterfeit prophet. False leaders and false teachings inevitably lead to division in the community. Be sure you have got the real thing, not a counterfeit.

Topic: Children of a Righteous God

TEXT: 1 John 2:28–3:10

Russell Dilday, president of Southwestern Baptist Theological Seminary, tells of visiting an outlet store while on vacation in Maine. A sale table offered beautiful, hand-carved mallard duck decoys at half price. Each was slightly flawed or damaged, and they were marked seconds. After selecting one of these prizes, he walked to the back of the shop to meet the artists.

"What are you working on today?" he asked, expecting an answer of "mallards" or "wood ducks." But the answer came: "Well, today we're carving seconds. They're selling so well, we're busy making decoys for the bargain table."

Imagine, creating flawed merchandise on purpose! God does not create "seconds." We are not children of a "lesser God" but children of a righteous God. We may have confidence, therefore, in the righteousness of God. Moreover, the righteousness of Christians confirms that they have been born of God.

The hope of the righteous is that they shall see God. God has shown us love, that we might be called God's children. The world may not recognize God's children, but they have confidence that when God appears they shall be like God.

The mission of the righteous is to live righteously. God was made manifest in Christ in order that he might take away the sin of the world. Those who have seen God in Jesus Christ put away all unrighteousness. They cannot continue to live sinfully.

The children of God and the children of the devil are known by the way they live. One who has been born of God has been transformed. The love of a righteous God is born within them, and they will live righteously. The elder's ideal is no less than that stated by Jesus in the Sermon on the Mount: "Be ye therefore perfect, even as your Father which is in Heaven is perfect" (Matt. 5:48, KJV). We were not born of God to be "seconds." After all, we are children of no lesser God.

Topic: Worshiping East of Eden
TEXT: 1 John 3:11–24

Cain and Abel were brothers. Cain tilled the soil, while Abel kept the sheep. When they came to worship, Abel's offering was accepted, but Cain's was not. In fury, Cain killed his brother. It is the oldest story of sibling rivalry, a parable of our estrangement from one another.

First John 3:12 provides a simple answer to the perplexing question of why Cain's offering was not accepted: His works were evil, but those of his brother were righteous. Righteousness comes by keeping the commands of the covenant, and the new command is that we love one another. The reasoning of the elder moves in full circle, but it underscores the fundamental command of the community, the love command.

Jesus said that if you go to worship and remember that your brother has something against you, leave your offering and go seek reconciliation with your brother (Matt. 5:23–24). The abandoned offering can be a powerful symbol of the church's ministry of reconciliation.

Worshiping God east of Eden requires that we seek reconciliation with our estranged brothers and sisters. Those who have material goods are estranged from those who live in need (1 John 3:17). Loving others in word and deed requires, therefore, that we abandon our offerings until we have first established our relationship as brothers and sisters to those in need.

Topic: The Tests of Truth
TEXT: 1 John 4:1–6

Wolves in sheep's clothing can confuse the community. What are the faithful to do when respected religious leaders are shown to be imposters? Surely the sins of a few do not discredit the gospel of Jesus Christ. But with so many conflicting messages being preached, how can the people of God discern truth and falsehood?

The first test is the test of content (4:2–3). Those who confess Christ having come in the flesh, the historic teaching of the church, speak God's Word. Those who deny or distort the historic teaching of the church deceive the community. Regardless of how pious a preacher may seem, if the preacher's message is not grounded in Scripture, is not doctrinally sound, or serves self rather than Christ, that preacher is a false prophet. Integrity of word and deed under the direction of the Spirit of truth is the mark of the true prophet.

The second test is the test of reception (4:5–6). The people of God hear the words of a true prophet, while the world follows a false prophet. The ways of God are so radically opposed to the popular philosophies of the world that only those who live by faith will follow a true prophet. That's the way it has always been. How many stood with Elijah on Mount Carmel when he opposed the prophets of Baal? How many stood with Paul when he called for the reception of gentile believers? How many stood with Clarence Jordan when he sought to provide housing for blacks in Georgia in the fifties and sixties?

There are two spirits, the Spirit of truth and the spirit of deception. Who speaks truth, and who hears the truth? These are questions that have plagued the church from the beginning, but we have the assurance that the Spirit among the people of God is greater than the spirit that is in the world (4:4). Truth will be spoken, and the truth will be heard. Take care how you listen.

Topic: The Secret of Perfect Love
TEXT: 1 John 4:7–21

The suggested title for this sermon illustrates the problem. It smacks of schmaltz and soap operas. We can hardly talk of love anymore because we have so cheapened the word. We long to love and to be loved. We crave the love of one to whom we can give ourselves fully, and the very idea that we are loved by God is too much for us to take in.

Verses 7–10 proclaim that God is the source of perfect love. Echoing and perhaps commenting on John 3:16, the elder declares that God is love. We know love only as we have experienced God's love for us. It is not that we have loved him, but that he has loved us.

Verses 11–16a affirm that we experience God's love when we confess that Jesus Christ is his Son. Because God revealed his love in Jesus, we can receive that love only by placing our faith in Christ. Then God abides in us and we in him. Through this mutual indwelling in faith, that love of God is perfected.

Verses 16b–21 explain that the perfection or fulfillment of love occurs through the redemptive work of God's love in us. The experience of God's love gives us confidence and hope for the future. We have no fear of life or death because we know that God is and that God is love. Perfect love, God's love, therefore, casts out fear.

The perfect love, however, is seen not just in God's love within us but also in our love for one another. Love for God cannot be separated from love for others. Indeed, the latter is the proof of the former. God's love for us is the secret of our ability both to receive love and to pass it on.

Topic: The Evidences of Genuine Faith

TEXT: 1 John 5:1–12

What do you expect from your faith? Do you expect it to give you miracle-working power so that you can move mountains? Do you expect it to give you immunity from life's troubles? Do you expect it to give you material rewards? Some today hold each of these expectations. These verses guide us to three results of genuine faith: victory, testimony, and life.

The first evidence of genuine faith is victory over the world that is opposed to God (5:4). Faith itself is a victory because it is a denial of the forces of evil and an affirmation of the love of God. Faith here means faithfulness to the lordship of God in Christ and obedience to God's commands.

The second evidence of genuine faith is God's testimony to Jesus as his Son (5:9). The water, the blood, and Spirit all bear witness to the reality of the Incarnation. God was present among us in Jesus Christ, drawing us to faith. Those who believe in Christ, therefore, have been born of God.

The third evidence of genuine faith is life (5:12). Through faith we already begin to experience eternal life. The body of both the Gospel of John and 1 John end with a promise of life through faith. There is a higher dimension to life, the experience of living in response to the knowledge of God and the love of God as it has been revealed in Jesus. That life is self-authenticating. It is the evidence of the genuineness of faith.

Topic: The Certainties of Faith

TEXT: 1 John 5:13–21

Uncertainty, even despair, afflicts all of us from time to time. In an age of skepticism, relativity, and secularism, conviction and certainty are rare commodities. Take stock of your certainties. Of what are you sure? The closing words of 1 John resoundingly declare the certainties of faith. Some form of the verb *to know* occurs forty times in 1 John, and *we know* is the leit-motif of the letter's conclusion.

First, we know that we have eternal life (5:13). Eternal life is assured for those who believe in the Son of God. The Johannine writings emphasize that eternal life is that quality of life that comes from living in the knowledge and fellowship of God (John 17:3). It begins not after we die but now and continues without end (John 5:24; 3:14).

Second, we know that God hears our prayers (5:14–17). Because we are God's children, he hears us as loving parents hear their children. The elder admonishes the community to pray for those who sin but excludes prayer for mortal sin. In the context of this letter, the mortal sin is probably the sin of the opponents: denial that salvation comes through Jesus Christ, who came in flesh.

Third, we know that we can have confidence in God. Three assurances are given in verses 18, 19, and 20. We know that one who has been born of God does not sin but is kept by the Son of God (v. 18). We know that we belong to God while the whole world is controlled by evil (v. 19), and we know that the Son of God has come and has given us the gift of discernment (v. 20).

These are words of assurance for a broken and shaken community. Lift up your eyes. Strengthen your hands. These are the certainties that sustain us.

For further resources, see Raymond E. Brown, *The Epistles of John,* vol. 30 of the *Anchor Bible* (Garden City, NY: Doubleday, 1982); Stephen S. Smalley, *1, 2, 3 John,* Word Biblical Commentary (Waco, TX: Word Books, 1984). R. Alan Culpepper, *1 John, 2 John, 3 John,* Knox Preaching Guides (Atlanta: John Knox Press, 1985), provides the exegetical basis for the sermons sketched above.

SECTION X.
Children's Stories and Sermons

January 6. Happy New Year
TEXT: Matt. 6:31–34
Method: Question and answer.
This is the beginning of a new year! Does anyone know what year it is? [Allow children time to answer each question.] What is going to happen to you this year? How many of you are going to have a birthday this year? How many of you are going to get bigger this year? Is anything else going to happen?

What are you going to do for God this year? What do you think God will do for you this year? Let's remember that God has given us this new year. Let's spend this year doing good things for God.

Will you pray with me and thank God for this new year?—L. Michael Lanway

January 13. Who Does Jesus Love?
TEXT: Matt. 15:21–28
Method: Singing; question and answer.
How many people does Jesus love? Do you think he loves everybody? He does love everybody, and there is a song that tells us so, and I'll bet you know it. It's called "Jesus Loves the Little Children." Let's sing it together.

That song tells us that Jesus loves everybody, no matter who they are, no matter where they live, and no matter how old or how young they are. Jesus loves everybody! Jesus loves you and you and you . . . [touch each child as you say this].

There are some people who don't know that Jesus loves them, and that is sad. Let's make them happy by telling them about Jesus and his love for them. How can we do that?

Let's pray together and thank Jesus for loving us and ask him to help us to tell others that Jesus loves them, too.— L. Michael Lanway.

January 20. Who Lives in Your House?
TEXT: Psalm 127
Method: Question and answer.
Are you the only one who lives in your house? You're not?! Tell me who else lives in your house. [Allow several children to name their households.] Does anybody have any pets? Is that everybody who lives in your house?

How about God? Does he live in your house? The Bible tells us that God is with us wherever we are. That means he is in our house, too. He watches over our house, he protects us, and he gives us things so we can live in our house. What kinds of things does God give us?

Our God is good. He is always there with us in our houses. Let's thank him for being there.—L. Michael Lanway

January 27. Let's Clean Up
TEXT: Ezra 3 and 4
Method: Question and answer.
Do you ever have to clean up your room? Why do you have to clean up your room? Because our mommies and daddies tell us to, and because if we didn't clean it up at some time, it would get dirtier and dirtier and dirtier. Our rooms would be so messy that we wouldn't even want to go in them! It is important to clean up our rooms, even if we don't like to do it.

The Bible tells us that it's important to

clean up our church and to make it as nice as we can for God. Just imagine what our church would look like if we didn't clean it up. Do you know who helps keep our church clean? Our custodians. Do you know who they are? [Have the custodians stand.] They work very hard to keep our church clean, and we should say thank you to them every chance we can. We can help them keep our church clean by picking up pieces of paper when we see them on the floor, by putting garbage in the wastebasket, by having special work days to wash walls and to paint, and by even putting in new carpet when we need to do so.

Let's thank God for our church and for our custodians. [Have the custodians come and sit with the children as you pray.] Let's promise God we will help keep his church clean.—L. Michael Lanway

February 3. Are You Growing Up?

TEXT: Heb. 5:11–6:12

Method: Object lesson; question and answer.

Do you want to grow up and get big? How big are you going to be? Are you going to be bigger than your mommy? Are you going to be bigger than your daddy? You are already bigger than you once were. How big were you when you were just a baby? [Hold hands about three feet apart and progressively bring hands together until about eighteen inches apart.] You were once only this small, and now you are much bigger. Let's see how big you are now. [Use a tape measure to see how tall each child is.] See, you have already grown a lot! And you are probably going to grow a lot more.

Who is it that helps us grow? God does. God helps our bones get longer and our muscles get stronger so we can grow. Let's thank God for making us bigger and ask him to help us get as big as he wants us to be.—L. Michael Lanway

February 10. Your Place in Sunday School

TEXT: Matt. 28:16–20

Method: Question and answer.

How many of you come to Sunday school? Do you like to come to Sun-

day school? Do you know what I like best about Sunday school? They have a place just for me. I have a Sunday school room I go to; I have my own Sunday school teacher to learn from; I even have my own chair to sit in. All those things make me feel good. You have all those things, too! Do they make you feel good?

Whether you go to Sunday school or not, they have a special place for you in Sunday school, and they always will. I hope you come to Sunday school and will keep on coming. If you will, together we will learn to love God better and to love each other better, and to invite other people to come with us. That will make Sunday school really fun and make us feel really good.

Let's thank God for making sure that everyone has a place in Sunday school.—L. Michael Lanway

February 17. That's Not Fair

TEXT: Amos 5:7–27

Method: Storytelling.

I like to play games, do you? What kind of games do you like to play? Do you like to play kickball? I want to tell you a story about a little boy who wanted to play kickball. One day this little boy was with his friends, and they started to pick teams. When the picking was over, no one had picked this little boy to be on a team. All the other boys and girls began to play. The little boy said, "Hey! I want to play, too!" But his friends wouldn't let him play. How do you think this made the little boy feel? The little boy began to cry, and he said, "That's not fair!"

It wasn't fair, was it? The little boy got left out. Everybody else got to play except him. His friends weren't fair to him.

There are other people besides that little boy who feel left out, too, and they are sad. But it is for different reasons other than playing kickball. Some people are hungry and want to eat, but they have no food, and the people who have food won't give them any. Is that fair? There are other people who are cold and need coats, and the people who have extra coats won't give them any. Is that fair? There are people who have no homes and don't have any place to stay, and people who do have homes won't share them. Is that fair?

Let's ask God to help us to be fair with other people and to share the things that we have.—L. Michael Lanway

February 24. How Much Does God Love You?

TEXT: John 3:16

Method: Question and answer.

[Have children sing "Jesus Loves Me" during the worship service before the children's sermon.]

How much does God love you? Does he love you this much? [Hold your fingers barely apart.] How much, then? [Allow them to answer; one little girl said, "As big as the whole wide world!"] God loves us so much that he sent Jesus to show us his love. God loves us so much that he is building a big house for us to live in when we get to heaven. God loves us so much that he promises we will always be with him.

Let's thank God for loving us so much and tell him that we love him, too.—L. Michael Lanway

March 3. Listening to God's Word

TEXT: Amos 8:11–12

Method: Question and answer.

When someone has something for us to do, it is important for us to listen to them, isn't it? For instance, we better listen to our parents when they tell us to do something, because if we don't, what will happen to us? What will happen if we don't listen to our teacher? We probably won't learn what we need to learn.

We also need to listen to God, don't we? But how do we listen to God? We have to listen to God differently than we listen to other people. God speaks to us through the Bible. The words in this book are God's words, and that is how he talks to us. So when our teacher or our parents or our preacher reads the Bible to us, we are hearing words from God.

Let's pray and ask God to help us listen to him whenever the Bible is being read. Let's also thank him for his words and promise to read them or have them read to us every day.—L. Michael Lanway

March 10. How Did You Get Here?

TEXT: Matt. 1:1–17

Method: Question and answer.

I am glad you all are here today! How did you get here today? Did you fly here in an airplane? Did you walk? Did you drive? Well, whether you walked or whether you drove, no matter how you got here, God helped you get here today. Did you know that? God made sure that you were safe.

Do you know how you were born into your family? You were born into your family because God decided you would be. God decided that your mommy and daddy would be —— and —— ——. It is all a part of God's plan.

Let's thank God for bringing us here today and for putting us in our family. Let's thank God for his plan.—L. Michael Lanway

March 17. Holding onto the Rope

[Supporting missions]

I brought this long piece of rope with me today, and I want each of you to hold it tightly. [Start the rope on one end and let each child hold part of it. You keep the other end.] I need you to practice holding onto this rope because one of these days, I might take my end and go down into a well. If I did that, I would be in trouble if you didn't hold on, wouldn't I? I need to trust that each of you will keep on holding this rope, because if some of you forgot and let go, the others might not be able to hold me all by themselves. I have to hope that you like me and care about what happens to me. Otherwise, you might decide that holding onto me with this rope really isn't such a big deal. Then I would be in trouble.

Long ago a man named William Carey was going to be a missionary. Before he went, he told some gentlemen that he was going into a well and he needed them to hold the rope for him. He wasn't going into a real well, but he was going to a place where he would be alone and where things would be hard and maybe a little frightening. He needed to know that his friends were there, on the other side, remembering and supporting him in his work.

You and I should be doing the same thing for our missionaries. We have an important job to do. We have to hold the rope for them while they are doing their work. We need to be remembering them in our prayers. We need to be supporting them with our offerings, so they might continue their work. We even need to be willing to be missionaries ourselves, if that is what God wants us to do.

Whenever we talk about missionaries and the work they are doing all over the world, think about the work you can do to help them. Let's thank God for people who are willing to serve him—both the people who go far away and the people like you who support missionaries.—Brett Younger

March 24. Bringing People to Church

It is great seeing you up here for the children's sermon. I really look forward to this time of talking with you every Sunday. I love seeing your familiar faces week after week. You are such a terrific bunch of people that I think other people might like to join you. In fact, why don't we invite some new people to come up here with us right now? I want each of you to go into the congregation and pick out someone to invite to the children's sermon. When you've done that, just bring them right back here. [Give the children time to go and get their guests and be seated at the front again.]

This is fun, isn't it? Since this worked so well, why don't you and your friend go and get another friend and bring that person back with you for the children's sermon? [Allow time for them to do this.]

It wasn't really hard to find someone to come up here, was it? Some people have joined us that never have participated in our children's sermon. They came because you asked them. That's the way we should reach out as a church, too. Most of the time new people come to church because a friend invited them. Sometimes we say we don't talk to our friends about Jesus or about our church because we don't know what to say. We're afraid they might ask us something we don't know or they might think less of us. When Jesus invited the disciples to be part of his ministry, he didn't give them a lot of explanations, and he wasn't afraid of what they would think.

He just said, "Follow me." All of us need to do a better job of inviting people to follow Jesus. We may start with our friends. We might find that it isn't as hard as we thought. In fact, it might even bring us a lot of joy.—Brett Younger

March 31. Two Holidays in One

Objects: A Christmas ornament and an Easter egg.

I have a feeling everyone knows what this is. That's right, it's a Christmas ornament. Do you remember what it was used for, just a few months ago? Yes, to decorate the Christmas tree.

Here's another item that is used to celebrate a holiday, an Easter egg. Soon you'll be decorating some of these and maybe even have an Easter egg hunt.

But what do a Christmas ornament and an Easter egg have to do with each other?

Both of them are small parts of the way we celebrate a special day. Yet both Christmas and Easter mean much more than ornaments or eggs. At Christmas we celebrate the birth of Jesus, and on Easter we celebrate the fact that God raised him from the dead after he was crucified for our sins.

You see, Christmas and Easter go together. We couldn't have Easter if Jesus hadn't been born as a tiny baby in Bethlehem. Yet Christmas would not have any meaning for us without the great gift Jesus gave when he went to the cross, dying for you and for me. And just three days later, on that first Easter morning, God raised him from the dead!

We celebrate Easter because that same Jesus who was laid in a manger as a baby, who died on a rugged cross on Good Friday, who was raised from the dead on Easter—that same Jesus lives today and wants to live in us.

As you and I give our lives to him—asking him to direct our lives and help us serve him—we experience a special Easter celebration in our own hearts.

Ornaments and eggs are nice, but they are only reminders of a much greater truth: that God loves us and wants to live in us. That's what Christmas and Easter are all about.—J. Michael Duduit

Learning to Listen—A Series of Six Children's Sermons

Instructions: It would be ideal to make an audio tape for the series to record the sounds for each lesson, stopping the tape each Sunday at the conclusion of that Sunday's sound, thus leaving the tape ready for the following week. Nevertheless, the sounds are simple and from week to week can be made in the manner suggested below. An appropriate title for this series might be "Hearing the Voice of God by Hearing the Sounds of God's World."

April 7. The Wind (Spirit of God)

TEXT: John 3:8

Girls and boys, today we begin a new group of talks about hearing. What do you hear with? [Response from the children.]

That's right, your ears. Ears are very important. They pick up sounds, enlarge them, send them into our minds, and in this way we hear things. I want to make (play) a sound and see if you can tell me what it is. Close your eyes so you can't see. [This instruction if you are not using a tape.] Listen carefully. When you think you know what the sound is, put up your hand. Don't tell what the sound is, just listen. I want to see how many of you can guess. Then I'll call on one of you to tell me what you think the sound is. Then, when I call on one of you, each one of you will have a chance to know if you guessed what the sound was.

[Play the sound of wind. Or blow through a microphone. Or let out the air from a balloon you have prepared and kept hidden in a sack.]

Now, what was that? [When several have raised their hands, call on one until the right answer is given, or if you must identify the sound, do so.]

Yes, that was air. What do we call it when air blows? The wind. One time a very wise man came to Jesus. Although he was wise, he did not know what the word *spirit* meant. Sometimes even little and much-used words are hard to define or describe.

This man, whose name was Nicodemus, asked Jesus what spirit was. Jesus said that spirit is like the wind that blows freely. Even though you cannot see the wind, you

can see the results of it blowing. See this small strip of paper. Watch while I hold it in front of my lips and blow. Did you see it move? You did! Did you see my breath? No! But you knew I was blowing because you heard the sound and saw something happening. Jesus was very wise. He told Nicodemus that the Spirit of God is like the wind. You cannot see the Spirit, but you know God's Spirit is working with people and in people when you see them doing good things and kind things like Jesus did.

This story is a wonderful help from the Bible. It will remind you every time you hear the wind to remember the Spirit of God. And every time you see someone do a kind and good act, like Jesus, you will remember that this is the Spirit of God working through people.

Let me read a verse from the Bible about the Spirit of God being like wind. Let us pray; then you may return to your places.—William L. Hendricks

April 14. Water (Son of God)

TEXTS: John 4:13; Rev. 1:15

Boys and girls, remember last week we heard the sound of wind? What is the wind supposed to remind us of? That's right, the Spirit of God.

I want you to use your ears today to hear a different sound. Listen, then put up your hand when you know what it is.

[Play the portion of the tape on which running water is recorded, or take two jars, one half-filled with water and pour the water into the empty jar slowly—during which time the children will close their eyes.]

Yes, that was a very familiar sound. It was the sound of water being poured. When do you hear the sounds of water? [Responses from the children.]

Yes, when you want a drink, when you want to wash. Sometimes, when it has been very dry, you hear the sound of rain, as God pours water on the earth to make things grow.

Water is very important. Did you know that there is more surface of our planet earth covered by water than there is covered by land? That is true. Water is very important. Maybe you have been somewhere where you could not easily get a drink. Recall how glad you were when you came to a fountain that gave you a nice cool drink of water. All things must have water to live: plants, animals, and people.

One day Jesus went to a well and sat beside it, very thirsty. Just then a woman came with a bucket. Jesus asked her for a drink. She was surprised because he was a stranger. She gave him some water. Then Jesus promised her an inner, spiritual water that would satisfy her thirst. Remember the wind that reminded us last week of God's Spirit? In this story, the water reminds us of Jesus who is called the Water of Life. Just as God helps us with spiritual breath, so Jesus is like living water. Our ears have heard familiar sounds—wind and water. When you hear clear, cool water trickling, remember that just as we must have water to keep alive, so also we need Jesus to quench our spiritual thirst.

Let me read you a verse from the Bible. Let us pray about Jesus as the Water of Life.—William L. Hendricks

April 21. Bird (God's World)

TEXTS: Ps. 84:3; Luke 12:6–7

For the last two Sundays we have heard sounds that remind us of God. We heard wind, which reminds us of ———— [God's Spirit, children respond]. We heard water, which reminds us of ———— [God's Son, children respond]. This third Sunday I want you to hear something that will remind us of God's world and God's care for God's world.

[Play a recording of birds, or ask a young person in the congregation who can do bird whistles to do so, or buy an inexpensive bird-caller from a hardware store. When several have raised their hands, ask one to identify the sound.]

Yes, those were the sounds of birds. How many kinds of birds do you know? [Children name various kinds of birds.] Do you know who made the birds? [Children respond.] Yes, God made the birds. You know the birds are an important part of God's world. Before people could fly in airplanes, birds knew how to fly. There are large birds and small ones. In fact, there are hundreds of kinds of birds. The most

common bird we know is the sparrow. The sparrow is so small and so common. There are so many sparrows that they do not seem very important. But nothing is so small that it is unimportant to God. Let me read you what the Bible says about God's world and says about the sparrows. Long ago, when the children of Israel worshiped in the Temple, the altar of God was so important that only a few people could even come close to it. But the small birds were not afraid; they even built their nests on the altar of God. Let me read some verses from the Bible about the birds and about you.

[Read the texts.]

So you see, God cared about the birds, and God cares about you also. Every time you hear a bird sing remember that God made the birds and that God cares for the birds and God cares for you.

Let us thank God for the care we and all of God's creatures receive from God.—William L. Hendricks

April 28. Animals (God's World)

TEXTS: Gen. 2:19; 6:19

Girls and boys, we have been listening to sounds. There was the wind. The wind is like ———— [the Spirit of God, children respond]. We heard running water. Water is necessary to life. Water is like ———— [the Son of God, Jesus, children respond]. After we listened to sounds that reminded us of God, we heard a sound that reminded us of God's world. What sound did we hear last Sunday?

[Birds! children respond.] Yes, and the birds teach us about God's care.

Today there are other sounds from God's world. Listen! (Or close your eyes and listen!)

[Play a tape of various animal sounds, including a dog and cat, or make the sounds as best you can.]

Now, what were those sounds? [Let the children reply as to the various animals they have heard.] Yes, and what do we call all of these different things? Animals. Animals are living things.

All life and all living things come from God. Do you think that God likes animals? [Response.] It is true. God loves all of God's own Creation with a love that is appropriate to each special thing. This is true of trees, rocks, flowers, animals, and people like you and me. There are two stories I want to tell you about animals. One story teaches us that animals are not as important as people. God created Adam. God created animals also. Adam saw all of the animals. He was curious about them. He liked them. Do you suppose any of them was a good friend and companion to Adam? Was any of them really like Adam or as important as Adam was? [Children respond.]

No! Not one of the animals was really like Adam. Not one of them could really talk to Adam. Not one of them was able to be Adam's very best friend. God created Eve, who was as important to God as Adam was. She became Adam's best friend. This story helps us to see that people are more important than things and animals.

But a second story helps us to see that animals also are loved by God. Once, when there was going to be a great flood, God told a good man, Noah, to build an ark. And God told Noah to take animals into the ark, all kinds of animals, so they would be safe from the flood. This story shows us that God loves and helps the animals, too. If God loves and helps the animals, should we hurt good animals who help us and are our pets? [Response.] No! We should not hurt good animals because they, too, are loved by God in a way that is appropriate to love animals. Let today's sounds and stories remind you that God made all things and loves all things.

Let me read you the Bible verses. Then I have asked ———— to sing a song that reminds us that God made everything and that God loves what God made. [Arrange for someone to sing a verse of "All Things Bright and Beautiful"—after which the children return to their places.]

May 5. Sounds of Songs (The Worship of God)

TEXTS: Ps. 95:1; 149:1

This is the fifth week we have been listening to sounds to remind us about God and about God's world. I have a special treat today. You will not need to close your eyes. You will not need to guess. You

know the sounds I am going to play; they are the sounds of music.

[Play one or two brief church songs that are appropriate for children.]

Singing is a beautiful sound. We sing when we are happy, and we sing when we are sad. We can sing alone. We can sing with other people. When we sing in church, we are singing to God. Singing to God is one way to worship God. Helping people to worship God is one way to serve God. Today, as a special surprise, I want you to sing. I would like for us to sing a song to God. It would also be good to help other people worship God. So, we are going to put your song on tape; and someone will take your song this week to people who are ill and cannot come to church. Your singing will be a way of worshiping God. Your singing will also be an act of serving God by helping others to worship God.

[Lead or have someone lead in a hymn or song the children know. If you do not have access to an audio-recorder, have the children sing for the congregation as an act of worship.]

Now let's hear how you sound. [Play back the song for the children that they have recorded.]

There are many places in the Bible that speak of singing. Let me read two of them for you. [Read texts.] Remember when you hear the sounds of music that music is a way of worshiping God, just as prayer is a way of talking to God.

Let us pray.—William L. Hendricks

May 12. Sounds of a Book (The Word of God)

TEXTS: Ps. 119:11, 105

Boys and girls, this is the sixth week we have been using our ears to hear and learn about God.

————, let me see your hand. I want to borrow your fingers to count off the five things we have already learned by listening to sounds [Using a child's fingers, count off the five previous lessons.]: (1) We listened to the wind to remind us of God's Spirit; (2) we listened to water to remind us of God's Son; (3) we listened to birds; (4) we heard the sounds of animals; these remind us of God's world and God's care of God's world; (5) we listened to the sounds of music. Singing is a way of worshiping God and of serving God.

Today is the sixth sound. It is the last day of this series. I have a special sound for you. It will be hard to guess. Listen carefully.

[Play on tape the sound of turning pages or ruffling the leaves of the Bible. If you are not using prerecorded sounds, have the children close their eyes and turn the leaves of a Bible. Even if you are using recorded sounds, when the children have guessed the sounds, you should ruffle through the leaves of your Bible, so that the children will associate the sound with a Bible.]

This is a very important sound. Turning pages means that we are reading. Reading means that we are learning. When we are reading and learning from the Bible, we are hearing the Word of God. All of the stories I have told you and the good things we have learned have come from the Bible. The Bible is a very special book. I hope you will love the Bible and learn from the Bible all of your life. We should memorize verses from the Bible because these verses will help us to remember God when we are in difficulty. [At this point either hear Bible verses the children have learned or teach them a verse to repeat together.]

Now let me read you two verses from the Bible that remind us that God's Word is like a light and that it will help us when we remember it. [Read the texts. If you have timed these lessons to an appropriate time of presenting copies of the New Testament and Psalms to the individual children, do so at this time.]

In the Bible we have a prayer Jesus taught us to pray. I want to pray that prayer with you before you return to your seats. [Pray the Lord's Prayer.]—William L. Hendricks

May 19. Worship in Colonial America

What if you lived in America during the time when the first settlers came to this land? What was it like to go to church in those early days? The first colonists worshiped in homes or outdoors. Soon, however, they began to build church buildings. The Puritans who came to New England—Massachusetts, Connecticut, and New Hampshire—built meetinghouses for worship. Many of these buildings were simple in their design with a pulpit in the center, a communion table in front of the pulpit, and rough benches where the people sat. The service itself was also quite simple, including Scripture reading, prayers, and sermons. The people sang only the Psalms because they believed that those words were the only inspired songs that the church should sing. The sermon preached by the minister was often over an hour long. People would bring certain herbs or bark to chew on during church to keep them from getting sleepy or thirsty during the long service. People who went to sleep might be tapped on the head by a person who used a long stick to wake them up. Many of the churches were unheated and in winter the inside walls sometimes were covered with frost. Worshipers wore heavy coats all during the service and some people even brought iron pots full of hot coals to keep their feet warm. Many people came on foot or on horseback to the meetinghouse. It was a rough time, and life was very hard. Yet the Christian people found great strength together in their churches and in their worship together. Their faith has come down to us in our own churches and worship today.—Bill J. Leonard

May 26. Quakers Worship in Colonial America

Last week we talked about the way Puritans worshiped in the American colonies, long before America was an independent country. Today we want to talk about another group of Christians in colonial America. These are members of the Society of Friends, or as they were also called, the Quakers. The Quakers began in England around the year 1650 under the leadership of a man named George Fox. He traveled around the country calling people to follow the "Inner Light" of God in each person. He warned people that God lives in every heart, not in church buildings or in formal religious services. He called people to stop fighting wars and give attention to the needs of the poor, the imprisoned, and the hungry. Quakers tried to treat every person—rich or poor—the same, with love and kindness. Many Quakers were persecuted for their faith, and many came to America to escape imprisonment. Quakers also built meetinghouses but without pulpits or elaborate decorations. They believed that every person was a minister, so every person could preach, pray, or sing in worship if inspired by the Spirit of God. Quakers had what we call "silent worship" services. The people sat quietly in the meetinghouse with women and girls on one side and men and boys on the other. Sometimes no one said anything at all and the people worshiped God in the quietness of their own hearts. Sometimes a person would feel inspired to speak or pray, recite Scripture or sing a hymn. Men and women, boys and girls were all equal in God's sight, and anyone could speak up if they felt God was telling them to do so. The Quakers remind us of the need to be quiet sometimes and listen to God speaking to us in the quiet of our own hearts. Let us be quiet for a moment and think about God's love for each one of us.—Bill J. Leonard

June 2. Camp Meeting on the American Frontier

In the early 1800s, many Americans moved from the eastern coast to the frontier region, which covered the areas we now call the states of Ohio, Kentucky, and Indiana. They sometimes came down the Ohio and Mississippi rivers or traveled in wagons that traveled only about sixteen miles each day. Life on the frontier was very difficult. There were few towns and very few churches. One important way of worshiping on the frontier involved camp meetings held around the frontier. These gatherings brought people from miles around who set up tents or slept outside on the ground. The meetings lasted for several days and were held outside. People stood or sat on the ground. Preachers—Methodists, Baptists, and Presbyterians—preached dramatic sermons calling people to believe in Christ. Often the people would shout, sing, or dance as an expression of their joy and religious enthusiasm. Many people became Christians as a result

of the camp meetings and many new churches were formed on the frontier. The camp meetings helped to improve family life and community in frontier areas.—Bill J. Leonard

June 9. Worship among Blacks in Slavery Time

For a long time in American life, many black people were kept as slaves of white people. They were bought and sold like animals or property. It was a terrible, cruel time in American history. Sometimes slaves were allowed to go to white churches, and many became members of those churches. But many masters did not want their slaves to hold their own religious meetings. They were afraid that blacks would talk too much about freedom or would plan ways to escape if they worshiped by themselves. So slaves who wanted to worship together had to slip away to remote, secret places in the fields or the woods. These gatherings were sometimes called "hush arbors" because the slaves had to be very quiet so as not to be discovered by their masters. Sometimes they would use spiritual songs to tell each other when one of these secret worship services would occur. While working in the field they might sing, "Steal away, steal away, steal away to Jesus." This meant that people should slip away to a secret meeting. It was also a beautiful song of their love and devotion to God. Many songs that we call "spirituals" were written by black people during slavery time. At these meetings the slaves could pray, sing, and preach together. These meetings helped them endure the difficult days of slavery and pray for a time when they would be free. That day finally came, their prayers were answered, and freedom secured. Thank God.—Bill J. Leonard

June 16. Christian Worship: Many Ways to Praise God

We have talked the last few weeks about different ways in which Christians worship. This is a way of illustrating that there are many ways in which people give praise to God; each is very special and important. Most worship services involve music, prayer, readings from the Bible, a sermon, and a time for quiet thoughts. At the same time, worship services are very diverse. Some people sing songs using many musical instruments—organs, pianos, guitars, even large orchestras. Others sing with only their voices and without the help of musical instruments. Some worship in church buildings, some in homes, and some outdoors. Some have very elaborate worship services, while others have simple gatherings. Some churches use special books that guide their prayers, songs, and Scripture readings. Some churches emphasize the importance of silence and spontaneous prayer. Whatever form worship may take, it is an important time for singing God's praise, listening for God's presence in our lives, and seeking God's love with one another. What is your favorite part of the worship services in our church?—Bill J. Leonard

June 23. The Music of the Church

For several weeks we have talked about different kinds of worship in the history of the church. We said that one very important part of the church's worship involved the singing of hymns and the use of music. Through music we sing praise to God and we join our voices together in hymns of faith and encouragement. One of the first things that the church teaches boys and girls is how to sing together. During the next few weeks we want to talk about different kinds of music that people have used to express their love for God.

Singing the Psalms. The Psalms are ancient hymns through which religious people have expressed their faith for centuries. The ancient Hebrews wrote the Psalms over a long period of time as they experienced God's presence in special moments of history. The book in the Old Testament that we call the Psalms is really a hymnbook of 150 songs. Many of them were written by King David, one of the great leaders of Israel. He wrote the Twenty-third Psalm, perhaps the best known psalm of all. It is sometimes called the "shepherd psalm" because it begins, "The Lord is my shepherd, I shall not want," and describes God's care for us in the way a shepherd takes care of the sheep. The Psalms sing about every human emo-

tion and experience: fear and courage, faith and doubt, love and hate, friends and enemies, light and darkness. They also speak of God's guidance of Israel through difficult times. Yet many of the psalms also help us to sing God's praises. Psalm 100 says, "Make a joyful noise to the Lord, all the land! Serve the Lord with gladness! Come into his presence with singing!" We should all learn to sing the Psalms together and in our own hearts.—Bill J. Leonard

June 30. Early Christian Hymns

Today we want to talk about some of the hymns of the very earliest Christians. The first Christians met together for worship in homes, caves, and outdoors. They sang the Psalms, and they sang other hymns that told of their love for and belief in Jesus Christ. One of the earliest hymns of the church is found in Luke, chapter 1. It is a song sung by Mary the mother of Jesus as she rejoices that she has been chosen by God to be the mother of a child who "will be called holy, the Son of God" (Luke 1:35). In response to that good news, Mary sings a beautiful song that the early Christians also sang. It begins, "My soul magnifies the Lord, and my spirit rejoices in God my Savior." Mary sings about the greatness of God and God's protection of the poor and the lowly people of the earth. Sometimes we call this New Testament hymn by a Latin name, the Magnificat. The book of Luke also has another song, sung by Zechariah the father of John the Baptist. It sings about the life his son John will have in making known the good news of God's love in the world. It begins, "Blessed be the Lord God of Israel, for he has visited and redeemed his people" (Luke 1:68). The New Testament contains many hymns that the early Christians used to express their thankfulness to God and their love for Jesus Christ.—Bill J. Leonard

July 7. St. Francis: A Hymn to All Creatures

Throughout the church's history, many important people have written hymns that we continue to use. One of the most interesting hymns and hymn writers was a man named St. Francis of Assisi. Francis was a gentle, humble man who lived in the small Italian town of Assisi. He believed that God had called him to tell everyone of God's love and care for all Creation. He traveled around the countryside, singing and preaching about peace and love, calling people to be happy and to care for each other. He was particularly concerned for poor people who had little to eat and no one to help them. Francis was also concerned for all God's creatures. He showed love and care for wild animals, birds, and all living things. One of his most famous hymns is called the "Canticle of the Sun" (canticle means song or hymn). In it he praised God for earth, fire, wind, water, and all the beauties of Creation. Today we still sing that song in a hymn we call "All Creatures of Our God and King." Each verse ends with the word *alleluia*, which means praise to God. St. Francis still helps us to remember that we belong to God's world and that we should be thankful for Creation and seek to take care of it. Let's listen to the words of the hymn as we sing it together.—Bill J. Leonard

July 14. Martin Luther: Songs for the People

For the past few weeks we have been talking about the hymns of the church and how we got some of them. Today we want to talk about another hymn writer in church history. His name is Martin Luther, and he lived in Germany during the 1500s. Luther helped to begin a very important movement in the church, a time when many people renewed their faith and trust in God. We call this the Reformation. Among the many things that he did, Martin Luther was concerned that the common people of his day participate in worship with new energy and enthusiasm. He wrote many hymns as a way of encouraging people in the congregation to enjoy music and singing in the church. Some of the melodies to his songs were taken from the "pop" music that the people sang at folk gatherings. The tunes were catchy and easy to learn. He encouraged all the people to sing praises to God. One of the most famous songs that Martin Luther wrote is called in English "A Mighty For-

tress Is Our God." In Luther's day there were many castles or fortresses around Europe. In times of danger the people would go to these castles as the safest possible place to stay. Castles were strong sources of protection. Luther wrote a hymn that reminded people that God is a source of strength and protection for God's people. When they sang that song they knew that God would take care of them, even in difficult times. Listen as we sing the words to this great hymn.—Bill J. Leonard

July 21. The Hymnbook: A Songbook of Faith

Today I want to talk to you about the hymnbook that we use in our church. It is a collection of the great songs of the church. These hymns were written by a large number of men and women in many times and places. Some of the hymns are very old and have been sung for many hundreds of years by Christian people around the world. Some were written more recently, and their words have only been sung for a few years. Some of the hymns help us to praise God; many of them use the words of the Psalms, which we discussed a few weeks ago. Some of them use the words taken directly from the Bible. Some are poems written by one person and set to music by another. Some of the hymns are used at special seasons of the year such as Christmas and Easter. Some are sung loudly with enthusiasm while others are quiet prayers. All of the hymns help us to sing God's praises and say what we believe. They are all like prayers, sung and prayed by the people of God. Can you name some of your favorite hymns?—Bill J. Leonard

July 28. Disobedience

TEXT: Gen. 3:1–13

"You'd better listen to me and obey what I say!" When I was a child that's what my mother would say to me, especially if I had disobeyed her. In the beginning of the Bible there is a story about disobedience.

Now the serpent, the Bible says, was smarter than all the other animals God had made. And he said to the first woman,

"Did God say, 'You shouldn't eat of any tree in this garden?' " And she said to the serpent, "We're allowed to eat the fruit on all the trees in the garden except one. We're not supposed to eat from the tree in the middle of the garden. God said we shouldn't even touch that tree, or we will die." "Well," the serpent said, "you won't die. God doesn't want you to eat from that tree because it will make you as smart as he is. You will know all right from wrong."

The woman saw that the tree had tasty fruit on it. It was pretty to look at; its fruit would make a person smart. So she ate some. She also gave some of the fruit to her husband. He ate it, too. As soon as they ate it, they knew they had disobeyed God.

Then they heard God walking in the garden. They hid from God because they were afraid. And God said to them, "Why are you hiding? Did you do something wrong? Did you disobey me? Did you eat from the tree in the middle of the garden?" The man quickly said, "The woman that you brought to me tricked me into eating it!" And the woman replied, "The serpent fooled me, and I ate the fruit." And God was so disappointed because the man and the woman disobeyed him.

Whenever we disobey, we disappoint those who love us—our friends, our parents, and God. Let's pray that God will help us to be obedient to his words for our lives.—Craig A. Loscalzo

August 4. Do What You Can Do
TEXT: 1 Sam. 17:38–49

Can you imagine a young shepherd boy fighting a frightening giant? Sounds like a fairy tale, doesn't it? It's not! That's just what David the shepherd boy did. David was only a lad when he came to talk to King Saul. The king was sad because the giant Goliath and his army were going to beat King Saul and his army of Israelites. Every day Goliath would make fun of the king's men and God.

Well, one day David came to the king and said, "I'm going to fight that giant myself. I'm going to beat him!" The king looked at the little shepherd boy and said, "You can't do that! You're just a boy." David kept asking and asking. Finally the

king said, "Okay, but I don't want you to get hurt. So wear my armor when you fight Goliath." King Saul put his armor on David. That must have been a funny sight. The king was big and tall; David was short and small. The armor was way too big. The helmet pushed David's ears way down and covered his nose. He couldn't even breathe. David tried to walk around in the armor. He almost fell over. David came back to the king and said, "This armor fits you. You know how to fight with it. It doesn't fit me. Even if it did, I don't know how to use it. I have this here sling shot. It worked well on a bear and a lion, and I know how to use it!"

So David went down to a brook and picked out some stones. He then went out and said to Goliath, "Today you are going to die. Not because I'm strong. Not because I know how to use this sling shot. But because of the power of God working through me." And David beat Goliath.

David did what he could do. He didn't try to be like King Saul. He did what he knew how to do, he did it for God, and God blessed him.—Craig A. Loscalzo

August 11. The Story of the Potter
TEXT: Jer. 18:1–6

Have you ever played with play dough? I remember making a little green turtle with clay. You can make all kinds of things with clay. And the neat thing about clay is that if you don't like how you've made something, you can change it.

There's a story in the Bible about a man called a potter who made pots out of clay. One day God was talking to a man named Jeremiah. God told him, "Go down to the potter's house. I want to show you something." So Jeremiah went. When he got there, he saw the potter working with some clay. As the potter was working on a pot, he saw that it didn't look the way he wanted it to look. So the potter crumbled the clay in his hands. Then he rolled the clay. Then he started making the pot again. This time the potter was very happy with what he had made. And Jeremiah was delighted, too.

Then God spoke to Jeremiah again, "The potter was able to make something good with the clay. I can do the same thing with the people who love me. Just like the clay in the potter's hand, people can be like clay in my hand." And Jeremiah was very happy to hear this from God.

Have you been able to guess what the story of Jeremiah says to you, boys and girls? If we are like clay in God's hand, what does that mean? God loves us. God cares for us. Sometimes we hurt others by the words we say. Sometimes we do things we know we are not allowed to do. We can think about the story of the potter and the clay. And God can help us and change us. For example, God will help us be kind to others and obey our parents. God can make us the best we can be. Next time you play with clay, think about what God can make with you.—Craig A. Loscalzo

August 18. The Story of the Lost Son
TEXT: Luke 15:11–24

Jesus told this story. There was a man who had two sons. The younger son said to his father, "Give me the money you have saved for me." The father divided his money between his two sons. A couple of days later, the younger son got all of his things together. He took his clothes and everything he owned. Then he went on a long trip to a faraway country. He wasn't careful with his money when he got there. He spent more than he had, and he spent it very quickly. Then a big problem came up in the land. There was no food for anyone to eat.

The boy became very hungry. So he went and asked a farmer if he could have something to eat. The farmer gave him a job feeding the pigs. He would have been happy to eat some of the food he was giving to the pigs. No one gave him anything to eat.

Just then he got the idea: "How many of my father's servants have plenty to eat. They even have leftovers, but I am starving to death in this faraway country. I'll go home to my father. I'll say to him, 'Father, I've sinned. I shouldn't even be called your son anymore. Treat me as one of your servants.' " So he got up and headed for home.

While the lad was still at a distance, his father saw him coming home. His father felt bad for his son but was so happy to see him. The father ran as fast as he could, and he hugged him and kissed him. "I have sinned," said the son to his father, "I shouldn't even be called your son anymore." The father exclaimed to his servants, "Bring the best robe we have and put it on my son. Put a ring on his finger. And cook some of the best beef we own. Let's have a party! Because my son, who seemed to be dead, is alive again. He was lost, but now he is found." And they had a wonderful celebration together.—Craig A. Loscalzo

August 25. The Story of the Older Brother
TEXT: Luke 15:25–32

Last time we talked, I told you the story of the lost son. When the story ended, you'll remember, the father had just thrown a wonderful party for his son. He was so happy that his son had come home. Well, while they were celebrating, the older brother was in the field working. He walked toward the house and heard something unusual. "Is that music I hear?" he may have thought. "Yes, it is music and dancing," he exclaimed! The older son yelled to one of the servants, "What's going on?" And in an excited voice the servant shouted, "Your brother has come home! Your father has prepared a wonderful roast beef dinner for him because he is safe and sound!"

Well, the older son kicked the dirt. He was so mad. Sitting on the porch, he wouldn't even go into the house. He didn't want to have any part of that stupid party. His father came out and said, "Please, oh, please, come inside and celebrate with us." But in his anger he answered his father, "I have always helped you work around here. I have always been a good boy. I haven't ever disobeyed you. You never even barbecued hamburgers for me and my friends. But when he comes home, after he has foolishly spent all the money you gave him, you give him a big party."

After the older son spoke, the father answered, "Son, you are very special to me. You are always here when I need you. Everything I have is yours. But it was only right that we should celebrate because your brother has come home. Your brother seemed as though he was dead, but now he is alive. He was lost. Now he is found. That is why we are so happy."

The story ends there. I wonder what the older brother thought then. I wonder what you think.—Craig A. Loscalzo

September 1. Choosing What Is Better
TEXT: Luke 10:38–42

"Busy, busy, busy!" Have you ever heard an adult say that? "I'm so busy today. There's not enough time in the day. I can't play with you now, I'm too busy." We grown-ups sure spend a lot of time being busy. The Bible tells us about a grown-up who was too busy even to listen to Jesus.

Jesus and his friends were walking on their way. They came to a village where a woman named Martha lived. She welcomed Jesus and his friends into her home. Martha had a sister named Mary. As Jesus was talking with his friends and teaching them, Mary sat on the floor right in front of Jesus. She liked listening to him, too.

Now Martha was busy, busy, busy in the kitchen. She didn't have time to listen to Jesus. The biscuits had to be cut; the country ham had to be cooked; and the gravy had to be made. And nobody was helping her. Martha thought to herself, "Oh, that Mary! She never wants to help me in the kitchen. She makes me so mad, sitting out there while I'm in here sweating!" Well, Martha just couldn't stand it anymore. She stomped out of the kitchen. "Jesus!" she exclaimed. "Don't you care that my sister left me in the kitchen to do all the work by myself? Tell her to get up and help me!"

Jesus turned to her and spoke calmly, "Martha, Martha, you are worried and upset about many things. So busy, busy, busy. Only one thing is really necessary. Mary has chosen what is better. She has chosen to listen to me now rather than be busy. That cannot be taken away from her."

Sometimes we are so busy, busy, busy that we forget Jesus. We forget to pray. We forget to read the Bible. We choose to do a lot of things. Let's remember also to choose, like Mary did, what is better.—Craig A. Loscalzo

September 8. The Earth Is the Lord's

Today I'm going to give each of you a small ball of imaginary clay. [Hand each person "the clay."] I want you to take a few minutes to create something incredible with your clay. Use your imagination and make anything you'd like. While you do this, does anyone remember what kinds of things God made in the first chapter of the Bible, in Genesis? [Mention some of the things God created.]

I can see that you have been doing some amazing work here. Would anyone like to tell me what you made with your imaginary clay? [Take a minute for responses.] That was very good. Now I'd like you to put your masterpieces on the floor right in front of you so we may finish our children's sermon. [As the children place their creations on the floor, have someone walk on top of each one, as though they were mashing them up.]

That was awful, wasn't it? After all your hard work and after you made such nice creations with your clay, someone just came and messed them all up. Does that make you mad or hurt or sad?

Sometimes we don't take care of the wonderful world God created for us, do we? We pollute the air and litter the ground and use more of our natural resources than we really need. Some of the beauty that God made for us is destroyed. How do you think God feels about that? He has given us a wonderful gift when he created the world, and our job is to help him take care of it. It is easy to take his gift for granted. Let's ask him to help us remember what a great treasure his Creation is.

Dear God, we know how bad we feel when people mistreat the things we make. We're sorry when we don't treat your world the way that we should. Help us to do a better job of being thankful and taking care of your good gift. Amen.—Carol Younger

September 15. Solving Mysteries

Have you ever noticed how much people love to solve mysteries? You can usually find a detective show on television. Some of the most popular books are mysteries—like Nancy Drew or the Hardy Boys. The game "Clue" has been around a long time. People can even go on "mystery weekend" vacations and try to solve make-believe crimes. We like to figure things out, so we like mysteries.

If I told you we had a mystery to solve this morning about who turned on the lights in our building today, how would we solve it? The best way to solve a mystery is to start with the information we know. We might start with who usually comes to church first on Sundays. We might try to find out who actually did come to church first today. We would ask some questions and keep working on it until we had our answer. Do we know who turned on the lights today?

Our faith is filled with mysteries. Some of them we may never know or understand. Some of them make us so curious that we want to keep asking questions and working on them so we will know more. The best way to work on a mystery is to start with the information we know. When we have questions or doubts, we should decide what we do know. If we wonder what God is like, we begin with what we know about him through the Bible, through other people, and through praying to him. If we question whether he cares about us, we should think about the times that we knew he cared. We should talk to people who have known him a long time. Learning more about God can be the best adventure we will ever have. The exciting part is that he is our partner in all the discoveries. When we ask questions, he is with us then. When we are confused, he is there to help comfort us. When we get on the wrong track, he helps us get straightened out. Let's thank him for all the things he's taught us and for all the things he helps us learn—Carol Younger

September 22. The Lie That Grew Too Big

Once upon a time, Matt and his friend Mike were playing full-court Nerf basketball inside his house. In the middle of their court was the dining room table. On the table was Matt's mother's favorite crystal vase. Shortly into the second quarter, the vase went down. It broke into a million pieces. Matt and his friend agreed on the cover-up story. Some man with a ski mask, they would say, had chased Mike through the house. Mike had run into the table. Hearing the vase break, the man disappeared, sure that someone would be on his trail. This cover-up seemed easy enough. But when the boys told their mother, she called the police so they could describe this man to the officer. To keep the story going, the boys gave the man a foreign accent. In a few days the police called with news. The man had been identified as a spy. Top officials in both countries were negotiating what they would do about this situation. "But," said the police, "rest assured. The man will not be back to break anymore vases or hold anymore house chases."

Now this is a silly story. Breaking a vase will not usually lead to international conflict. However, it is true that all small lies have a tendency to get bigger. At first the lie seems manageable, but it may grow to the point that you can't seem to stop it. The hard part about a lie is that when you tell that first one, you usually have to keep it more to cover it up. Before too long you may be in over your head in lies, and you may not know what the truth is anymore.

When God gave us the commandment to tell the truth, he was giving us a good rule to live by. He was trying to keep us from that awful way we feel when we haven't been honest. He was trying to help us see that telling the truth is such an important thing to do.

When we start to say something that isn't true, let's remember where that first lie might lead us. Let's think about how much God wants us to tell the truth. In fact, let's say a prayer about that right now.—Carol Younger

September 29. The Best Gifts

How many of you have already told someone what you want for Christmas? Has anyone you know looked in a Christmas catalog and written down the page numbers of things he or she wants? Have you ever known anyone who wrote a letter to Santa? Have you ever heard anyone cry,

"I just have to have it. I'll be so sad if I don't get that present"? Choosing gifts is exciting and fun. But if we are not careful, Christmas will become just a time for toys and commercial presents, and we will miss the best gifts Christmas brings us.

Did you ever hear the story of King Midas and the golden touch? This old king loved gold so much that he could never get enough of it. He always wanted more. The only thing he loved as much as gold was his daughter, Marygold. So when a stranger visited the king one day and offered to grant him a wish, the king wanted to have the golden touch. He wanted everything he touched to turn to gold. It happened, and for a little while Midas loved it. He loved having gold clothes and gold roses and a gold bed. But then he realized something. He couldn't eat anything! The minute the food touched his lips, it turned to gold. How would he ever eat again? And the most horrible part of it was that when his daughter Marygold tried to hug him to make him feel better, she turned into a gold statue. King Midas realized that the best things he ever had were not made of gold. His best gifts were the simple things he took for granted, like food he could eat, water he could drink, and the daughter that he loved.

You and I won't be turning things to gold anytime soon. But just like King Midas, we can get so caught up in the things we want, and the things we want more of, that we miss the best gifts that we could have. It is possible to be so busy thinking about our presents that we miss the real fun of giving to someone else. You might spend so much time worrying about what you might get that you forget to celebrate what you've already gotten—good gifts like family and time together and special traditions and church. We might care so much about what's under our Christmas tree that we take for granted the best gift we were given—Jesus and his birth. If we are not careful, we might be just like old Midas and find ourselves feeling sad and empty because we didn't choose the best gifts—all those gifts that point to God's love. Jesus talks about that in Matt. 6:19–21. He says we should be careful what treasures we choose. He tells us not

to store up the kind of earthly treasures that break, rust, get stolen, or run out of batteries. We should choose the treasures that really count, the things that matter to God. Christmas is a good time to practice choosing the best gifts.—Carol Younger

October 6. Getting Stuck

Have you ever seen someone who was stuck in something? Have you ever seen someone whose head was too large to slip a sweater over, so she is stuck for a moment with a sweater on her face? Has your little brother or sister ever crawled into a box or a laundry basket and gotten stuck in there? Have you ever seen someone try to get a piece of gum off the bottom of his shoe? Sometimes we think it's funny when someone is stuck, until it happens to us.

Do you remember the story of Brer Rabbit and the tar baby. Brer Rabbit thought he was so clever to make that tar baby. He just knew that it would cause the wolf to get stuck and keep from catching him. But what happened? Brer Rabbit was the one who ended up stuck. The more he tried to get away from the tar baby, the more stuck he became.

Sooner or later everyone gets stuck in something. Sooner or later something will stop us from doing what we want to do and being who we should be. Sometimes what stops us is something simple that we can easily fix. Sometimes we get stuck by something that isn't easy to fix. A bad habit, like lying or stealing or cheating, slows us down. Staying angry with a friend keeps us from growing. Refusing to do something we know we should do keeps us stuck.

Once Jesus said that everyone who sins is a slave to sin (John 8:34–36). Everyone who does something wrong gets stuck in what they do. The good news is that he can help us when we get caught. He told us that we can get "unstuck" by following him. He will make us free from those things that want to keep us stuck so that we can't grow. The next time you are stuck because you made a mistake and did something wrong, think about Jesus. Ask him to help you fix the problem, so that you can start doing the things you know he wants you to do.—Carol Younger

October 13. World Hunger Day

You're sitting at the table with a large portion of brussels sprouts on your plate. You stare at them, but they don't get any smaller. Then Mom says, "Clean your plate. There are children starving in India." Have you ever heard that at your house? Have you ever responded to her with that old familiar line, "Well, let's just send it to them"? You may have said it with a smirk, because you knew that by the time your brussels sprouts reached India, they would be no good at all (even if they weren't that good to start with).

The "clean-your-plate" discussion that happens in many families may seem silly to you. But, if we think about it, it might not be so strange after all. It's so easy to take more than we really need and waste what we don't use. Maybe "clean your plate" could remind us to just use what we need, because other people have need of the same thing.

When we know that people are hungry and we have food left, is it really such a strange idea to send it to them? No one wants to get a package of spoiled food, but sometimes there are ways to share our food that we've never even thought of before. One church had so much food left-over after a banquet that they took it straight to a soup kitchen and supplied a meal there. One group of girls in elementary school saved part of their snack money for a week and gave it to world hunger. In Louisa May Alcott's novel *Little Women*, the March family, who did not have a lot themselves, took their special Christmas breakfast to a family who was having a hard time. After they did, they realized that they really celebrated Christmas.

All through the Bible we are taught to share what we have and give to hungry people. Jesus tells us to feed the least of these. Jesus feeds a hungry crowd with a little boy's lunch. Jesus tells us to give one coat away if we have two. Can you think of ways that we might share our food?— Carol Younger

October 20. A Thank-You Note to God

[Have a large piece of poster board set up to look like a piece of stationery. Print, "Dear God, Thank you for ——— because ———." Repeat the thank-you line several times.]

Have you ever had to write a thank-you note to someone? Sometimes, no matter how much we liked the gift and the person who gave it to us, writing thank-you notes just feels like a chore. It's something your mom or dad makes you do before you may do something more fun. Why do you think we don't like to write thank-you notes? Have you ever gotten a thank-you note that sounded like the person who wrote it didn't really want to send it? It might sound something like this: "Dear ———, Thank you for the gift." We don't know from that short sentence whether the person was really thankful or not, do we? Have you ever read a thank-you note that sounded like the person *was* thankful? "Dear ———, When I opened your gift I was so excited. I always wanted a pair of pajamas with the feet in them, just like my little boy wears. You pick out terrific presents."

Which of these thank-you notes would you rather read? I would choose the second one because it tells me more about the person writing it. It shows that he or she really wants me to know how he or she feels. That person took the time and the energy to tell me what he or she thought. It takes more effort to write the second kind of note, but it is worth it. It might even be fun to write that kind of thank-you.

At Thanksgiving and at other times, too, we usually tell God what we're thankful for. We make a list of all kinds of things, and we say thank-you to him. But if we're not careful, our prayers might just sound like the first kind of thank-you note. It might be something we say just because we're supposed to. It might not mean very much to us at all. When we thank God, we need to put more into it than that. We need to tell him why we're thankful.

On our giant piece of stationery, I want us to write a thank-you note to God. [You may choose to start the letter by listing a few of the things we are usually thankful for.] I'd like you to help me add to the letter by finishing the sentences. Thank you, God, for ——— because ———.

[Take a few moments to work on these.]

Every time we pray and thank God for something, let's remember our thank-you note to God. Let's take the time and thought that will tell him that we are truly thankful for the good gifts he has given us. [If you have written down the children's responses about why they are thankful, read the letter as your closing prayer.]— Carol Younger

October 27. Telling Baby Stories

Most people love to hear stories about what happened to them when they were little. Have your parents or your brothers and sisters told you things that you did or said when you were too young to remember what was going on? You may have heard the stories a hundred times, but they are so important to you that you always like hearing them. Sometimes you can learn something from them that you didn't know before. For instance, do you know what happened on the day you were born? Where were your parents and what were they doing just before they had to go to the hospital? Do you know who came to visit you during your first few weeks of life? Do you know how your parents felt when they saw you for the very first time? [At this point you may wish to tell a few baby stories of your own or about a child in the group.]

When our son Graham was born, my husband and I each kept a journal about everything that happened. We tried to describe just how we felt about that wonderful event. Someday when he is older, I hope Graham will love to hear all the stories as much as we love telling them.

This Christmas you will hear a wonderful baby story about Jesus. We will hear about what happened to Mary and Joseph just before he was born. We will read about where they were and who Jesus' first visitors were. We will try to understand what they must have felt at that special event.

You've probably heard the story many times. You probably know most of the details of the story, just like you know what happens in the stories you hear about yourself. Telling the story of Jesus as a baby is important for us. It tells us more about him. It helps us feel closer to him. We may learn something we didn't know before. Just as telling our baby stories is such a special part of family life, telling Jesus' story reminds us that we are a part of his family.—Carol Younger

November 3. A People Machine

[Line up all the boys and girls side by side, facing the congregation, or choose a few people to line up side by side, facing the children.]

If we could make a machine today, what kind of machine should we make? [Decide what you should make.] Let's get started on this book-making machine. The key to a good machine is for every part to have a job to do and to keep each part working with the other parts. [Go down the line and give each person a simple task to do that fits with the next person's task. For example, the first person picks up imaginary paper and hands it to the second person. The second person straightens it up and hands it to the third person. The third person staples it and gives it to the fourth person. The fourth person puts a cover on it, etc.] Now that we all know our jobs, let's run our machine. [Let the machine continuously run several times. Thank the machine and have it sit down.]

Did our machine work? When everyone did their part it went well. What would have happened if our cover-putter-on-er decided she didn't want to work in the machine anymore? What would have happened if our stapler decided he wasn't a very important part of the machine, and he just quit? For us to have made any books at all we needed every part working together, right?

First Corinthians 12:14–27 talks about how the church has many members who have different jobs to do. Paul says that we need all these different people with different gifts and talents to do the work of the church. It's like a body. We don't need five ears, four feet, and no eyes or hands. Our machine wouldn't make a good product if everyone wanted to staple and no one wanted to put the paper together. Every job in the church is important, and it takes all of us working together to be the church. Everyone has something they can do for God's church. You as children have jobs you can do. Some of you make it your job to invite your friends to church. Some of you help your teachers in your classes. Some of you love to sing, and you add joy to our worship. Some of you are good with younger children and older people, and you make them feel good. I'm glad that you have a part in our church, and I'm glad that we're all learning to work together. Let's thank God for that and ask him to help us continue.—Carol Younger

November 10. Living with an Eraser

Object: An eraser.

Over two hundred years ago, there lived a man by the name of Joseph Priestley. He was very interested in things of nature.

One day he came across some sap from a tree in South America. He discovered something special about this material. If you wrote on a piece of paper with a pencil and then rubbed this sticky sap over what you had written, it could remove the pencil marks. So he called the substance "rubber."

That name has also been given to other things that are hard yet spongy—like the tires on a car or the eraser on the end of this pencil.

Now, why would a person want to invent an eraser? One reason is that we all make mistakes and the eraser helps us to correct those mistakes.

Our faith in Jesus also gives us an eraser—the forgiveness of God. When God forgives our sins, he removes our past mistakes and allows us to start over.

The next time you pick up a pencil to write and notice the eraser on the end, let it remind you of how God's love and forgiveness can erase the sin in our lives and make us new in Christ.—Kenneth Mortonson

November 17. Little Donkey

Donkey, little donkey, you are acting like a mule!

Do not be so obstinate, and don't be such a fool!

No one wants to bother you and take your job away!

It's much more fun to work a bit than just to run and play.

Think of what the world would be if no one worked at all!

No houses and no radio, no doll or bat or ball,

For work is really making things, and making things is fun,

So let's pretend our work is play, and work will soon be done.

Of course, we cannot make all of our work into fun, but that does not matter. It is good for us to do some work that is hard just as it is good for us to learn to keep God's laws even if it is hard to do. It keeps us from being sissies, and it helps us to be strong. And besides, of course, it teaches us to do things and to make things. We really feel much better when we are doing things and making things than when we are just watching other people work. On days when we run about out-of-doors and think of nice games to play and help Dad mow the lawn or help Mother hang up her clothes, we are much happier than on days when we just sit still and look at the television for hours and hours. That is because God made us to be like him, and he does things and makes things all the time—he is a Creator. And after we have been doing things either in work or in play (and it is hard to tell the difference, because we sometimes work very hard in our play and we can learn to play very hard in our work), then we really feel good when we get through and sit down and rest. We have a lovely comfortable feeling because the little mind inside is pleased. And if we were to listen to God's voice, we would feel that he says, "That's good. I'm proud of you. Now you're keeping time with me."—Agnes Sanford

November 24. Thanksgiving in Bible Times

Preparation: Learn all you can about the Feast of Booths. Look through your picture sources and find a picture of a Jewish family celebrating the Feast of Booths.

Prepare the children: Say, "Next Thursday is a special day. What is that day? What happens on that day? Why is that day called Thanksgiving Day?" [Give the children time to respond to each question.]

If you had lived when Jesus lived, you would have celebrated Thanksgiving each year. However, that celebration would have been much different from the way you will celebrate next Thursday. Listen as I tell you about it.

The celebration was called the Feast of Booths or the Feast of Tabernacles. This feast was held in September or October after all the crops had been harvested. The celebration that lasted for eight days would not have taken place inside your house. Rather, your family would have gathered tree branches and palm leaves and would have made a hut or booth from them. You would have lived in the booth for an entire week. You would have probably strung garlands of grapes, olives, and other fruits and hung them in your booth.

Everywhere you looked you would have seen families living in booths. They would have been on the streets, on the flat rooftops of houses, in courtyards—everywhere.

But the week was full of celebration and fun. It was also a time for the family to remember. There had been a time when the people did not have houses to live in. They wandered about in a wilderness and lived in tents. The booths of tree branches and palm leaves helped the people to think of the tents their families of long ago used to live in. The garlands of fruit helped the families to remember how God provided food for the people as they wandered. Each day the family feasted on the food from the harvest and talked about God. [Show the picture of the Feast of Booths.]

It is very possible that your family may have traveled to the city of Jerusalem to celebrate the Feast of Booths. You would have made your booth there in the city. But each morning, you would have seen barefooted priests and Levites dressed in white linen robes come through a gate of the city called the Water Gate. One of the priests would have carried a gold pitcher filled with water from the Pool of Siloam that he would later put on an altar in the Temple. Had you been in the crowd, you would have waved a tree branch with your right hand and would have carried a lemon in your left hand. The branches and lemon would have helped you think about

the harvest. As you walked with the priests, you would have sung psalms of praise and thanksgiving.

At night, the Temple area would have been aglow from the lights of four huge candelabra. People at the Temple would have carried lighted torches and would have danced while Levites chanted psalms to the music of flutes.

Of all the feasts and celebrations, the thanksgiving feast, or Feast of Booths, was the most enjoyable one of all.—Leon W. Castle

December 1. Be a Model for Jesus
TEXT: (1 Tim. 1:12–17).
Object: A picture of a person modeling clothing from a catalog or magazine.

Good morning, boys and girls! This morning I have something that most of you have looked at many times before. [Show the catalog.] What do you turn to when you look at a catalog? Probably the toy section, right? Well, this morning I want us to turn to a section which your mother and father turn to when they need new clothes.

It is the section in the catalog where persons who are called models show off the clothing that is for sale in the catalog. You will notice that these persons are good-looking persons and that they do their best to make the clothing they are showing look good, too. Right? [Get their agreement.] So if you want to know what is in fashion and what might look good on you, what do you do? That's right, turn to the models in the catalog and imagine how it might look on you.

Now, let me ask you this. If you wanted to know what it is like to be a Christian—how a Christian acts and what a Christian says—what might you do? [Let them answer.] Yes, you might look in the Bible. But another thing you could do would be to find a person who says she or he is a Christian and watch that person for a while. Such a person would be a model Christian like the models in the catalog are models for the clothing there. In our Bible lesson today, St. Paul says that he is an example or model of who a Christian is. Any person who shows us what it is like to live Jesus' way is such a model. But that also makes you and me models, too, doesn't it? We believe in Jesus, and we try to be loving and forgiving toward others as Jesus would have us do. That means that Jesus wants to help us to be loving and helping toward others so that people who are watching us as models will really know what he is like.

Ask Jesus to help you be a good model for him this week.—*Children's Sermon Service Plus*

December 8. You Can Do Something Special

TEXT: Matt. 9:35–38

Method: Demonstration; question and answer.

I can do something that not many other people can do! Do you want to see it? I can whistle like a bird; listen! [Substitute for the whistle anything special you would like to do.] You can do something special, too. [See if anyone would like to show you something they can do; one girl in my church snorted like a pig.]

I know some special things you can do that no one else can do. You can smile like nobody else can. You can hug like nobody else can. You can make other people feel good like nobody else can. And it is all because you are special.

There are some people who need to see your smile to make them feel better. There are other people who need a hug from you to feel better. Jesus wants you to help other people with your smile, with your hugs, with your specialness.

Let's thank God for all the special things you can do and ask him to help you share those special things with others.—L. Michael Lanway

December 15. Wants or Needs?

TEXT: "And my God will supply every need of yours according to his riches in glory in Christ Jesus" (Phil. 4:19).

Visual introduction: A long list of items scrawled on a piece of adding tape.

Sentence summary: There is a difference between wants and needs.

Here is a long list of items some child wrote down while preparing for Christmas. This is something we have all done. We want a new bicycle, a tape player, bas-

ketball, doll, wagon, "Monopoly" game, telephone, television, air rifle, jump rope, boxing gloves, roller skates, and teddy bear. And that's not all. Every time we see something else, we want it. So the list just goes on and on.

But do we always get everything we want? Not at all. We never get everything we want. But so what? We may be disappointed, but we can get along quite well without most of these items. They are not necessary for us to live. Call them *wants.* We want them, but we will not die if we do not get them.

On the other hand, some things we really do need, like food, a pair of shoes, a house or apartment where we can live, a table and a few chairs, bed, blanket, stove, plates and glasses to eat from—these are all items of genuine need. So we call these *needs.*

So there is a big difference between wants and needs. We can get along without the wants. The things that we need to stay alive are the most important.

The Bible teaches that if we have faith in God, he will provide those basic things that we need in life. God gives us warm sunshine, hands to work, food to eat, and air to breathe. Those are genuine needs provided by God. Listen to this Scripture verse: "My God will supply every need of yours according to his riches in glory in Christ Jesus."

Notice that we are not promised every want. God promises us that he will supply every need. There is a big difference between those two words.

And remember that God gives to us from his riches. He is not poor. He has enough to give and give and yet never be poor. Every need (not want) will be supplied to us according to his riches in glory in Christ.—C. W. Bess

December 22. Christmas: God With Us

TEXT: " 'Behold a virgin shall conceive and bear a son, and his name shall be called Emmanuel' (which means, God with us)" (Matt. 1:23).

Main truth: Through Jesus we see God's love clearly.

Object: Plain card with the words *I love you* printed too small to be read from more than a few inches away. One magnifying glass.

Memory maker: A magnifying glass for each child. Inexpensive ones are available from vending suppliers or even retail.

I have a message for you this morning. I want you to be sure and get it, so I wrote it on this card. Here it is [hold up card]. What? You can't read the message? Well, it's important, and I sure do want you to get it.

Here's a magnifying glass. It makes small things look bigger. Let me hold it up to this important message. Can you read it now? That's right! It says, "I love you!"

That's the message I wanted you to get. I love you. I wrote it small, but you can read it when it's magnified.

God's message to us is, and always has been, "I love you." But how could he best get this message to people? Well, the answer is found in the meaning of Christmas. Jesus came to earth as a person to give all people God's message, "I love you."

When Jesus was born, God became flesh and dwelt among us. God poured himself and all his love into the person of Jesus. God sent Jesus to magnify his message, "I love you."

Through Jesus we see God's love clearly. Everything Jesus did and said from the cradle to the cross, from birth to Resurrection, shows us God's love. That's what Jesus came to do. That's the meaning of Christmas.

Before Jesus was born, an angel came to Joseph in a dream and told him, " 'Behold, a virgin shall conceive and bear a son, and his name shall be called Emmanuel' (which means God with us).''

Jesus was God with us. He magnified God's love. Through him we see God's love clearly. And that's why we celebrate Christmas!

I have a magnifying glass for each of you to help you remember that through Jesus we see God's love clearly.—Roy E. DeBrand

December 29. Why Do We Come to Church?

TEXT: Luke 14:15–24

Method: Question and answer.

Do you like coming to church? What do you like best about church? Church can be a lot of fun because you get to sing and pray and do things and learn about Jesus.

Why do you think we do all those things in church? Is it just because we are supposed to be busy for three hours on Sunday morning? Is it because someone told us we *have* to do all those things? We do all these things because the more we learn about Jesus and about God, the more we know that God loves us, that Jesus loves us, and that we love Jesus and God, too. Then we can do the things that God wants us to do, like bring people with us to church and let them hear about God's love, too.

Let's thank God for all the things we do at church and ask God to help us get ready to do the things he wants us to do.— L. Michael Lanway

SECTION XI.
A Little Treasury of Sermon Illustrations

BY ROBERT C. SHANNON

ATTITUDES. It was F. M. Cornford who wrote, "Every public action which is not customary is either wrong, or, if it is right, is a dangerous precedent. It follows that nothing should ever be done for the first time." Many will testify that they know folk who never heard of F. M. Cornford but who nonetheless follow that philosophy that "nothing should ever be done for the first time."

ATTITUDES. "We are like dwarfs on the shoulders of giants, so that we can see more than they and things at a greater distance, not by virtue of any sharpness of sight on our part or any physical distinction, but because we are carried high and raised up by their giant size."—Bernard of Chartres

BIBLE. They used to say in China that one word of Chairman Mao was worth 50,000 of any other! Time will prove that that was more than a gross exaggeration. It was far, far from the truth. But time will continue to show as it has in the past that the words of Scripture are truly more valuable than any other. They answer the questions others cannot answer, the deepest questions of life. They solve the problems others cannot solve, the deepest problems of life. Truly the words of the Bible are worth more than the words of any other book.

BIBLE. This story is true. It came out of Iran. A lady living there came into the possession of a Bible. She began to read it. Family members reported her to the po-

lice. They beat her until the blood came. Then they threw her into prison. When she was released she said, "What kind of book is this, that they don't want me to read it?" So she began to read it again. Again she was thrown into prison. Upon her release she escaped to Turkey, thence to Yugoslavia, and finally to Canada, where she is now free to read the Bible as much as she chooses! Never take your freedom lightly! Never take the Bible lightly!

BIBLE. When David Livingstone went into the unexplored heart of Africa, he took with him a mirror. Once they knew what it was, natives would come to his tent and ask to see it. "Is that me?" they would ask in wonder. "I didn't think I looked like that. What a big mouth I have!" Until Livingstone came, they had never seen themselves! He also introduced them to the mirror of the Word of God (James 1:23–25). Until then, they had not seen themselves as they really were. In fact, none of us has really seen himself until he has seen himself in the mirror of Scripture.

BLESSING. The motto of the State of Arizona is *Ditat Deus,* which means "God enriches." With copper, lead, zinc, silver, and gold beneath its surface, Arizona has certainly enriched people. But we make a mistake if we expect that God enriches materially those who follow him. He may, of course, and he may not. For whatever we have, we thank God. But we would still be poor if God did not enrich us in ways that are spiritual, not material. . . . Faith in God makes us richer in ways that are abstract but certainly real. Those who follow God have more and better friends, fewer regrets and a happier life. They may take Arizona's motto as their very own: *Ditat Deus.* God enriches!

BLOOD.   Often traditional Serbian garments will feature a very special flower called the Kosovo peony. A legend says these red flowers sprang up on the plains of Kosovo after the great battle of 1389 between the Serbs and the Turks. Much blood was shed there, and these red flowers seemed a kind of living memorial to the men who died there. The greatest battlefield was Golgotha. One man did battle there with the combined forces of sin, death, and the grave . . . and won! His sacrifice is not commemorated by a red flower, or a red flag, but by the blood red wine of Communion and by the living sacrifices of his followers.

CERTAINTY.   Before the great battle of Blenheim, one soldier was said to have prayed, "O God, if there be a God, save my soul, if I have a soul!" Paul did not write with such uncertainty. John did not write with such uncertainty. Jesus did not speak with such uncertainty. "We know," wrote Paul. "We know," wrote John. "We know," said Jesus.

CHANCE.   It was Albert Einstein who said, "God does not play dice." Certainly we live in a world of chance, where accidents do occur and where senseless things happen. But God in wisdom and providence is looking over this world, and "God does not play dice!" He has plans and purposes, and God's plans always work out, and God's purposes are always realized.

CHANGE.   One reason change is so hard to effect is that custom becomes such a binding thing. Charles Davenant called it "that unwritten law, by which the people keep even kings in awe." Because it's an unwritten law, it's hard to repeal. Still, we cannot allow mere custom to stand in the way of needed and helpful change.

CHILDREN.   Two names common in Yugoslavia are Zeljkos (for a boy) and Zeljkas (for a girl). The names mean "the wished-for ones." One cannot help thinking how nice it would be if every child were desired and welcomed into the world with joy; if every child were a "wished-for one."

CHILDREN OF GOD.   He was an authority on gypsy culture and history, and he could speak their Romany language. He wrote the first definitive book on the gypsies. When he visited Russian gypsies, they earnestly asked him to tell them what kind of people they were and from whence they had come! They had no traditions about their past and knew nothing of their background. They were a people without a past. We all want to know what kind of people we are and from whence we came. We want to know it in a sense that runs deeper than ethnic background. What kind of people are we human beings? From whence did we come? The Bible quickly answers that we were made in the image of God; that we were made by the hands of God; and that those who believe become the children of God.

CHRIST.   The greatness of Christ our king and his superiority over others is well put in these lines written by John Chandler:

Conquering kings their titles take
From the foes they captive make:
Jesu, by a nobler deed,
From the thousands he hath freed.

CHRIST'S BIRTH.   There are several accounts of the birth of the goddess Athena. The best-known says that she sprang full grown and in full armor from the head of Zeus when it had been split open by an axe. Another says that Zeus split open a cloud, and she came forth. A third says that she was the daughter of the river god, Triton. How dramatically different is the account of the birth of Jesus: born as all of us are born, yet conceived as none of us was conceived.

CHRISTIAN.   Many cities have changed names through the years as there were political or social changes in the country. What was once Fiume in Italy is now Rijeka in Yugoslavia. The city that was Pressburg in the Austro-Hungarian empire is today Bratislava in Czechoslovakia. The Russian city of Leningrad once was called Petrograd and before that St. Petersburg. It is not only cities that change their names. So do people. In many missionary lands, people wear names associated with pagan deities. When they become Christians they like to change their names, often taking the names of Bible characters. In a sense, we all were given a new name upon our conversion. "And the disciples were called Christians." In heaven, we'll be given another new name (Rev. 2:17 and 3:12).

CHRISTIANITY. Benjamin Disraeli said of one, "His Christianity was muscular." Christianity has not always seemed muscular, though it has always been muscular. We have represented it so poorly that it has seemed to some weak and ineffectual. It isn't. Read church history. Read the Book of Revelation. True Christianity is always strong, vital, viable, muscular.

CHURCH. It is said that Oliver Cromwell asked that his picture be painted as a true likeness and not touched up to flatter him. He asked that all the "roughness, pimples, warts" be included. He said that if it were otherwise, he wouldn't pay for it. Sometimes we are so concerned about ideals that we seem to picture only the warts and blemishes of the church. At other times, anxious to show God's perfect design, we cover them up. A true picture of the church must show both. Thoughtful people will understand that it is Christ for whom we claim perfection, not the church. Underneath the warts and blemishes they will see the Body of Christ as God intended it to be.

CHURCH. We will likely not find ourselves in complete agreement with Cyprian when he said, "He cannot love God for his father who has not the church for his mother." On the other hand, we dare not dismiss the church as being of little or no importance. Christ died for the church.

The church is the bride of Christ. We cannot welcome the bridegroom and despise the bride. We must regard them both with the same love and affection.

CLEANSING. Just inside the gates of the old walled city of Dubrovnik there is a fountain. Once it served the needs of peasants coming into the city from the countryside. They were required to wash their hands and feet upon entering the city. How that reminds us of the ritual washings of the Jewish priests in Old Testament times and the ritual washings of Muslims in our own time. How it symbolizes baptism. How it echoes an old gospel song: "Are you washed in the blood of the Lamb?"

COMPROMISE. There is an old story of a man who wanted a fur coat, so he went bear hunting. He met a bear who was also hunting . . . for meat. The bear said, "Let's just sit down and talk this over. I suggest that you throw away your gun, and I'll throw away my teeth." The hunter agreed. He threw away his gun. The bear threw away his teeth. Then the bear hugged the man. The man got his fur coat, and the bear got his meat.

CONSISTENCY. Dr. John Armstrong, who lived in the eighteenth century, wrote of a certain man,

Of right and wrong he taught
Truths as refin'd as ever Athens heard
And (strange to tell) he practis'd what
  he preach'd.

It's grand to know that he practiced what he preached, but sad to know that Armstrong labeled it as something most unusual, something "strange to tell."

CONVICTIONS. The Bogomil heretics claimed to be Christians but rejected the Old Testament, the Incarnation, the cross, and the sacraments. They lived a harsh ascetic life. When the Turks took over, they struck a deal. They would become Muslims if they were allowed to continue their strange, harsh life. It was agreed, and they switched allegiance in order to keep their customs! Do we sometimes have trouble distinguishing custom from doctrine? Do we sometimes value custom more than doctrine?

CREATION.   A certain lily grows in only one place on earth: a tiny Adriatic island called Svete Nikola. There are 1,040 other Adriatic islands, but the lily does not grow on any of them. Nor does it grow on the mainland. It grows only in this one tiny spot. Such is the richness of God's varied Creation. There are other lessons to be drawn from it. There are some virtues, some distinctive qualities of life and character, that will only grow in the climate of faith . . . and the Tree of Life only grows in the climate of heaven.

CREATION.   In Nordic mythology, dwarfs carved two trees, an ash and an elm, into what we know today as human shapes. Three gods found them. One god gave them life. Another gave them reason. The third gave them blood and color. They became the first man and the first woman. How different, how much nobler, is the biblical story of Creation in which God made man and woman "in his own likeness, after his own image."

CREATION.   The movement of the heavenly bodies is so precise that it may be accurately calculated both backward and forward. We know, for example, that the next total eclipse of the sun visible in the United States will be in the year 2017! Is such accuracy only an accident? How it strains one's credulity to believe that! Surely a wise Designer put it all in place in such a way that we are able to discover the precise details of that design.

CROSS.   On the day he died, Jesus fulfilled thirty-three prophecies: sixteen from the Psalms, five from Zechariah, eight from Isaiah, and one each from Genesis, Exodus, Daniel, and Amos. Truly, he died "according to the Scriptures" (1 Cor. 15:3).

CROSS.   There is a legend that when Barabbas stirred up his revolt in Jerusalem, several people were killed, including the only son of a carpenter in that city. Bent on revenge, the bereaved father bribed the Roman soldiers to let him make the three crosses. He made the one for Barabbas much heavier than the other two so that he would suffer all the more. But Barabbas was set free, and Jesus had to carry that cross. It was so heavy the soldiers forced a passerby, Simon of Cyrene, to help carry it. That heavier cross made Jesus' suffering worse than the others. It's only a legend, but Jesus did bear a heavier load than the two thieves. He not only carried a cross; he carried the sins of the whole world.

CROSS.   In an odd but instructive coincidence, the Chinese character for the world *come* is a cross with two men below it and one man on it! It's only a coincidence, of course, but it illustrates the fact that the cross says, "Come!" in a way that is more convincing, more appealing, than any other invitation.

DEATH.   What conflicting emotions must have been in Emily Dickinson's heart when she wrote,

Because I could not stop for Death
He kindly stopped for me—
The Carriage held but just
    Ourselves—
And Immortality.

Many of us think we're too busy to stop for death, but death will certainly oblige us and stop for us. Beyond death lies eternity. The word *immortality* does not really express the Christian view of life after death. We see it, not as something that is our right by nature, but rather as something that is a gift from God, made possible by the Resurrection of Jesus and made real to us by his grace.

DEATH.   There is no greater challenge to death, outside of the Bible itself, than the words of John Donne, who wrote,

Death be not proud, though some
    have called thee
Mighty and dreadful, for thou art not
    so.

For those whom thou think'st thou
dost overthrow
Die not, poor death; nor yet canst
thou kill me.

DEATH.   They wrote a little song about
that verse in the Bible, "O death, where is
thy sting!" It was sung by soldiers in the
British army during the First World War,
and it went like this:

O death where is thy
sting-a-ling-a-ling?
O grave, thy victoree?
The bells of Hell go tin-a-ling-a-ling
For you but not for me.

The mighty challenge of 1 Corinthians
chapter 15 deserves something more dig-
nified than that little jingle. It is the greatest challenge ever flung across the
universe. It is a challenge first raised by
the prophet Hosea, but it becomes convincing only in the light of the Resurrection of Jesus, and it becomes believable
only in the gospel.

END OF THE WORLD.   Buddha taught
that the world is going to exist forever. "It
will never come to an end," he said, "and
since it has no end, it has no beginning."
Such a view does not satisfy the human
mind. Such a view runs counter to all that
we know about the universe. What will
happen when we have depleted the last
acre of soil and pumped the last barrel of
oil? What will happen when the sun burns
itself out? The view of Buddha runs
counter to science, and it most certainly
runs counter to Scripture. "All these
things shall be dissolved," says the Bible.

ETERNITY.   Joseph Addison called eternity a "pleasing, dreadful thought." The
contradiction fits our own feelings. When
as a child we first thought of eternity, it
was truly dreadful. As the years passed, it
became more comforting than frightening. Of course, eternity is beyond our
imagining, and we need not worry about
trying to picture it. We do need to concern
ourselves that we are prepared for it.
Whether it is a pleasing or dreadful pros-

pect depends entirely upon where it will
be spent.

ETERNITY.   The Scots had a saying, "Be
happy while you're living, for you're a
long time dead." Within reason, the motto
is a good one. We are foolish to postpone
happiness and to allow life to become a
drudgery. We are equally foolish if we
allow some transient pleasure to rob us of
the eternal joys of our Lord.

EVIL.   In the March 6, 1989, issue of
Time magazine there is an interview with
novelist E. L. Doctorow, who remarks that
"we conduct our ordinary lives in meta-
phors of violence and death. In business
we make a killing; in sports we beat or
clobber the opponent." He explains it by
saying, "Most of us are not contemptuous
of law and mortality. But we have a weakness for the idea of a person who makes
his own rules and lives free of ethical con-
straints . . . a longing for criminal license
may be basic to all our activities and relationships." Those words are frightening.
Is there really that much evil deep within
us? If there is, then we need all the more
the grace of God, the power of the Holy
Spirit, the defense of prayer, and the protection of Scripture.

FAILURE.   The name of John James
Audubon is forever associated with the
magnificent paintings he made of the birds
of North America. No one else has so accurately painted the birds and the natural
environment in which they were found. It
might not have happened had he not gone
bankrupt in business! In 1808, he opened
a store in Louisville, Kentucky. It was after
he went bankrupt in 1819 that he began
traveling and painting birds. We are all
richer because of his business failure. Who
knows but that your failures, or mine, may
turn out to be disguised blessing to us or
to others.

FAITH.   At last we've developed electro-
optic systems that give humans a night vision that not only equals but excels that of
cats . . . and radar that not only equals but
excels that of bats. But the cats and the
bats had it first. God created the cats, the

bats, and the brains of the scientists and engineers that made it possible for man to finally catch up.

FAME. Appomatox Court House is only a small town in Virginia. Historic events made it famous. There on April 9, 1865, the American Civil War ended with the surrender of General Robert E. Lee to General Ulysses S. Grant. It is not the first or the last time that a small and insignificant place gained fame through some history-making event. The prophets spoke of little Bethlehem. It remains little to this day. It is the same with Nazareth and Capernaum and Jericho. Their fame far outshines their size and economic importance. If the birth of Jesus could transform Bethlehem and the life of Jesus could transform Nazareth, think what the grace of Jesus can do to your little life and mine.

FAME. Jane Austen is still regarded as one of the greatest authors in the English language. Her novels *Pride and Prejudice* and *Sense and Sensibility* are always regarded as among the very best. Yet her name never appeared on a novel during her lifetime, though she did see many of them published. Perhaps it was by design that she kept away from fame. If so, it's quite surprising when so many will give up character, health, and family for a little fame. They make a very poor bargain.

FORGETTING. It was Matthew Arnold who said that we forget "because we must, not because we will." Everybody complains about not being able to remember, but if the truth were told, many have the opposite problem. They are unable to forget. Matthew Arnold is right. We *must* forget. If we don't learn how to forget, then life will become intolerable. We must forget our past failures. We must forget the past injuries and insults we've received. We must forget our forgiven sins.

FORGIVENESS. Queen Elizabeth once said to the countess of Nottingham, "God may pardon you, but I never can." Perhaps we also sometimes harbor such an unforgiving spirit. The Bible assures us that it is only those who forgive their debtors who will have their debts forgiven. Jesus said that those who do not forgive the trespasses of others cannot expect God to forgive their trespasses.

FORGIVENESS. "Even God," said Agathon, "cannot change the past." Perhaps that's true, but God can forgive the past . . . and he does! After all, old Agathon wrote about 400 B.C. and thus lived and died before Christ. The gospel teaches us that the past *can* be forgiven *and* forgotten.

FRIENDSHIP. It was Ralph Waldo Emerson who wrote "the only way to have a friend is to be one." So many complain that they are friendless but never go out of their way to be friendly. So many complain that they are lonely but never go out of their way to be a companion to someone else who might be lonely. So many complain that no one helps them, yet they never think of helping another.

GIVING. Andrew Carnegie is famous for his philanthropy. He built libraries all over the world. It is estimated that he gave away 300 million dollars. He said, "The man who dies rich . . . dies disgraced."

GOD. In his book *City Temple Sermons,* R. J. Campbell quoted the French writer who said, "In the beginning, God created man in his own image, and ever since then man has been returning the compliment by making God in his!"

GRACE. Catherine the Great once said, "I shall be an autocrat; that's my trade. And the good Lord will forgive me; that's his." We can hardly take grace so lightly as that. It cost something for the good Lord to forgive us. It cost the cross. It costs us something to be forgiven. It costs repentance. A true understanding of forgiveness will cause us all to cry out with hymn writer Robert Robinson, "O to grace how great a debtor, daily I'm constrained to be!"

GRATITUDE. In Greek mythology, Atalanta agreed to marry the man who could outrun her in a foot race but declared that any who tried and lost must die. Hippomenes got three golden apples from Aphrodite, and one by one he dropped them in front of Atalanta during the race. She couldn't resist the temptation to stop and pick them up. Hippomenes won both the race and Atalanta. However, the couple forgot to thank Aphrodite, so she had the goddess Cybele turn them into lions! We experience no immediate penalty for our ingratitude and so conclude that there is none. In fact, the penalty for a thankless heart is there, built-in in the heart and in the life.

GREED.   J. K. Galbraith wrote, "In the affluent society no useful distinction can be made between luxuries and necessaries." It may be true that we often confuse the two, but the distinction *must* be made. God has promised to supply all we need, not all we want. One man thought of that when he experienced hunger and concluded that maybe what he needed was to experience hunger!

GRIEF.   He was a pilot in the U.S. Air Force. He'd been through advanced training and through survival training. When his closest friend died in a plane crash, he remarked that he had not been prepared to face that. He had had *survival* training, but he had never had *survivor's* training. Churches must provide some help for the survivors of death, for the people who are left with grief and loneliness and guilt and regret.

HEAVEN.   Ignoring the dangers of World War II, a missionary couple were returning to their post aboard a freighter crossing the Atlantic. Because of the threat of air attacks, the crew always brought their mattresses up on deck and slept there. The missionary couple slept as usual in their cabin. "Aren't you afraid?" the crew asked. "What if the ship goes down?" "If the ship goes down," said the missionary, "we go up!"

HEAVEN.   Emily Dickinson wrote that "parting is all we know of heaven and all we need of hell." Certainly the worst part of life is the parting that comes at death. Certainly the best thing we know about heaven is that there is no parting there.

HEAVEN.   The name of the old city of Babylon meant "gate of god." Today the city does not even exist! Our God builds no city on this earth, and his followers are always only visitors here. They call themselves strangers and pilgrims (Heb. 11:13–16). They confess that they have *here* no permanent city, but they look for a city that is to come and are confident that "God has prepared for them a city."

HEAVEN.   On the Yugoslavian island of Brac, two distinct dialects are spoken, depending upon the place on the mainland from which one's ancestors came. Christians don't speak the language of the land from which they came, but they do speak the language of the land to which they're going—the new Jerusalem.

HISTORY.   With the fall of Rome in the fifth century there was a loss of all interest in the past. Ancient languages were forgotten. Ancient literature was lost. Ancient monuments were pulled down so that the materials could be reused. It was not until the Renaissance in the fourteenth century that interest in the past was revived. We cannot ignore the past. We are part of the past. It has helped to make us what we are, and it has made our world what it is. To study the plant without the root is foolish. Some will share the pessimism of Hegel who said, "What experience and history teach is that people and governments never have learned anything from history or acted on principles deduced from it." Most of us will disagree with that and argue that we cannot ignore what has gone before.

HOLY LIVING.   There are 1,040 Yugoslavian islands along the Adriatic coast. All of them are formed from rock, but one. Only the island of Susak is made of sand. There are no stones, no trees. It is absolutely unique. So the Christian stands as a unique person in the world. He is different from his environment. He is not the same as his neighbors. He has been transformed by the grace of God and he is different!

HOLY SPIRIT. There are so many distinctive winds in the world. There is the *fohn,* that wind from the south that warms Europe even in the dead of winter. There is the *bura,* a northeasterly wind, harsh and bitter, that threatens shipping on the Adriatic Sea. There is the *chinook,* which warms the Canadian provinces of Alberta and British Columbia, and the *Santa Ana,* which brings intense heat to southern California but at the same time drives the smog away. There are the trade winds that made possible early shipping routes across the Atlantic to the New World. There is the Christmas wind in the Caribbean, when the prevailing westerlies are suddenly replaced by wind from the opposite direction. Is it surprising that our Lord should say that the Spirit is like the wind?

HONESTY. Arthur Hugh Clough made some shrewd comments on our twisting of the Ten Commandments when he wrote,

Thou shalt not steal; an empty feat,
When it's so lucrative to cheat.
Thou shalt not covet; but tradition
Approves all forms of competition.

We do tend to work our way around the real intent of the Ten Commandments and end up proclaiming that we follow them while, in fact, we tread them under our feet.

HONESTY. Margot Asquith said of Lady Desborough, "Ettie has told enough white lies to ice a cake." The same thing could be said of a great many people. Of course, one could raise the question, "Is any lie ever white?" And if it is, how can we distinguish the little white ones from the big black ones? For some of us, it's easy. The ones I tell are the little white ones. The ones you tell are the big black ones.

HYPOCRISY. The capital of Yugoslavia is Belgrade. The name means White City. The city is anything but white. The smoke of industry and the exhaust of automobiles have turned it into a Gray City. But the city was named for the white rocks along the river . . . and they remain. Often we are not all together what we claim to be and not all together what people expect us to be. We need to be careful that no legitimate charge of hypocrisy can ever be leveled against us. We may never be able to live up to the expectations of others, but we must certainly live up to the claims we make for ourselves.

INVOLVEMENT. John Donne, the British poet, described well our inevitable involvement in humanity when he wrote, "Any man's death diminishes me." That's especially hard for us in the modern world, where television and radio report to us instantly the suffering of the world. But it's still true. "Any man's death diminishes me." Donne went on to reflect on the British custom of ringing bells in the village church whenever there was a death in the community. Naturally, when folks heard the bell they would ask, "Who died?" Reflecting this custom Donne wrote, "Ask not for whom the bell tolls. It tolls for thee."

KINDNESS. A young man had just been elected a don at Cambridge. Dr. F. J. Foakes Jackson said to him, "It's no use trying to be *clever*—we are all clever here; just try to be *kind*—a little kind." In the movie *Harvey,* the lovable leading character says his mother once told him that to get on one had to be very clever or very kind. He said he'd tried the first but opted for the second.

KINDNESS. Isaac Bickerstaff wrote a little poem in 1761 that goes like this:

There was a jolly miller once,
Lived on the river Dee;
He worked and sang from morn till
   night
No lark more blithe than he.

And this the burden of his song,
For ever us'd to be,
I care for nobody, not I,
If no one cares for me.

But to "care for nobody" is not the road to a happy and jolly life. It is the road to sadness and pessimism and discontent. The road to happiness is found by those who care for those who do not at all care for them, those who love their enemies and do good to them that despitefully use them.

LAUGHTER.   "If we may believe our logicians," said T. Joseph Addison, "man is distinguished from all other creatures by the faculty of laughter." Certainly there are many other differences, but this one is significant. A sense of humor has saved many a situation. One man lists it as the first qualification for a missionary! Another lists it as the first qualification for a minister! He who has no sense of humor does not see life whole. Someone said that God gave us a conscience to convict us of what we are not; laughter to console us for what we are!

LIFE.   Before he became the Enlightened One, Buddha lived 530 lives, according to the holy books of Buddhism. Forty-two times he was a god. Eighty-five times he was a king. Twenty-four times he was a prince. Twenty-two times he was a learned man. Twice he was a thief. Once he was a slave. Once he was a gambler. Many times he was a lion, a deer, a horse, an eagle, a bull, a snake, and once he was even a frog. But in all 530 lives he was very wise, wiser than the other animals, wiser than the other slaves, wiser than the other kinds. Christ lived one brief life of thirty-three years, and yet has more adherents than Buddha. We ourselves will live only one life.

Only one life
'Twill soon be past
Only what's done for Christ
Will last.

LOVE.   We've all heard the saying, "Absence makes the heart grow fonder." But someone asks how that can be reconciled with that other saying, "Out of sight, out of mind." The answer is given by the French writer Comte de Bussy-Rabutin who wrote, "Absence is to love what wind is to fire; it extinguishes the small, it enkindles the great."

MAN.   Benjamin Disraeli asked, "Is man an ape or an angel?" Then he answered his own question. "I am on the side of the angels." While many may sometimes act like an ape, the Bible says that we, like Christ, were made "a little lower than the angels." Created in the image of God, we are distinct and separate from all living things, certainly much more than apes and yet not quite angels.

MARRIAGE.   Perhaps many have become as cynical about marriage as Sir John Davies who wrote,

Wedlock, indeed, hath often
    compared been
To public feasts, where meet a public
    rout,
Where they that are without would
    fain go in
And they that are within would fain
    go out.

It really isn't true that everyone who is married wants out. Nor is it true that all those who are unmarried want in. But there is enough truth in it to make us think.

MEEKNESS.   F. E. Smith, who was the earl of Birkenhead in England, once said, "We have the highest authority for believing that the meek shall inherit the earth; though I have never found any particular corroboration of this aphorism in the records of Somerset House." The meek *do* inherit the earth, even though you, like Smith, will never find a record of it among the deeds of the county courthouse. But if you will look around you—at the wife who patiently loves a difficult husband, at the child who honors an undeserving parent, at the employee who adapts to the unreasonable employer—you will eventually see that Jesus was right. The meek do inherit the earth. In the short run the go-getter, the intimidator, the pusher may seem to win, but in the long run it is still true that the meek inherit the earth.

MEMORIALS.   A winding road leads up from the bay of Kotor to the Yugoslavian mountain town of Cetinje. If you stop to look back, you'll see hairpin turns below that spell out the letter *M.* But the ground is not very steep at that point, and the turns seem unnecessary. The story is that the road was designed by a young Austrian engineer who was madly in love with the Montenegrin queen Milena. Of course, he did not dare to show his feelings, but he built her initials into the road as a permanent memorial to his unrequited love.

MEMORIALS.   It is said that the son of the great British architect Sir Christopher Wren once said, "If you seek for a monument, gaze around." And it's true that any direction you look in London you'll see the work of that great architect. We may say the same thing of Christ. "If you seek a monument, gaze around." For the memorials to Jesus Christ are everywhere: in the date on the calendar, in the art of the museums, in music, in literature, in architecture . . . and in the lives of men and women!

MISSIONS.   We always think of Japan and the Philippines as mission fields, and they are. But Christians in both lands recognize that one must give as well as receive. Currently there are 180 Filipino missionaries serving abroad and 291 Japanese missionaries serving abroad. What a wonderful way to show their appreciation for the missionaries who have come to them!

MISUNDERSTANDINGS.   Ralph Waldo Emerson wrote, "Is it so bad to be misunderstood? Pythagoras was misunderstood and Socrates and Jesus and Luther and Copernicus and Galileo and Newton and every pure and wise spirit that ever took flesh. To be great is to be misunderstood."

MODERN MAN.   T. S. Eliot wrote those cutting words about modern humanity:

We are the hollow men
We are the stuffed men
Leaning together
Headpiece filled with straw.

There is truly an emptiness to many people today. There is a hollowness that can only be filled by God.

NAMES.   The different Bechuana tribes of Africa wear names of animals they fear: *Bakatla* means "they of the monkey"; *Bakuena,* "they of the alligator"; and *Batlapi,* "they of the fish." It is thought that they may once have worshiped these animals, but when Europeans first discovered them these tribes lived in dread of the very animals for which they were named! Christians wear a name born, not out of fear, but out of love . . . Christ's love for us and our love for Christ.

NOSTALGIA.   A hundred years ago someone wrote a letter to the editor of *Punch,* the British humor magazine, complaining that the magazine was not as funny as it used to be. Francis Burnand, the editor, commented, "It never was!" When someone says the church is not what it used to be one might answer, "It never was." We often see the "good old days" through a very smoky lens that filters out the bad and leaves only the good. That may be beneficial, but it does make for unfair comparisons.

PARDON.   Agesilaus was a rich Roman patrician who fell out of favor with Septimus Severus and was sent into exile. But then the emperor Caracalla read a poem by Agesilaus's son and pardoned the whole family!

PEACE OF MIND.   "The sense of being well dressed," wrote Miss C. F. Forbes, "gives a feeling of inward tranquility which religion is powerless to bestow." No doubt she said it tongue-in-cheek and didn't intend to be taken literally. The peace that comes from Christ is so great the Bible calls it "the peace that passes understanding."

PERSEVERANCE.   The town of Ulcinj, Yugoslavia, is bounded on one side by the Adriatic Sea and on the other by the border of Albania. There are three towns here. The first fell into the sea in 1444. The second, built higher up, was destroyed by an earthquake. The third, a modern town, survives. Every time, the people rebuild. What an example of perseverance! We may need such perseverance in our personal lives. Kipling in his famous poem "If" asked "if you can see the things you gave your life to broken and stoop and build them up with worn-out tools." There is also here a reflection of the collective perseverance of faith. Again and again believers have had to rebuild the church by spiritual renewal.

POWER.   When Matthew Boulton was showing his engineering works to Boswell, he commented, "I sell here, sir, what all the world desires to have—*power.*" It's certainly true that power is what all the world desires. Even Christians fall into the trap. Yet Jesus proved that spiritual power is best expressed through those who are powerless by the world's standards. Paul said that God had chosen the weak things to confound the mighty. You can see the lust for power in nations, in communities, in churches, even in families. It is a temptation we must guard against every day.

PRAISE.   Samuel Butler wrote that "the advantage of doing one's praising for oneself is that one can lay it on so thick and in exactly the right places." Solomon's advice was better: "Let another praise you and not your own mouth" (Prov. 27:2).

PRAYER.   How sad was the comment of Edward FitzGerald (1809–83), who wrote,

And that inverted Bowl we call the Sky
Whereunder crawling coop't we live and die
Lift not thy hands to *It* for help for it
Rolls impotently on as Thou or I.

We've all had the experience of being disappointed in prayer. But the more we pray, the more we experience answered prayer. The people who pray the least are the ones with the least confidence in it. The people who pray the most are the ones with the most confidence in it. God answers prayer.

PRAYER.   Before the Battle of Edgehill, Sir Jacob Astley prayed, "O Lord! thou knowest how busy I must be this day; if I forget thee, do not thou forget me."

PRAYER.   A little boy once wanted very much to have a little brother or sister to play with. So he prayed that God would send him a little brother. He continued for several weeks but saw no sign that his request was being granted. So he quit praying about it. Some months later his mother gave birth to twins. His comment was, "I'm sure glad I quit praying when I did."

RESPONSIBILITY.   Lord Mahavira was a reformer of Hinduism who lived at the same time as Buddha. He deserted his family. For twelve years he traveled as a beggar, never speaking a word. During this time he gained the wisdom he sought, and after twelve years he went all over the country spreading his ideas, but he never returned to his family. He taught that all of a man's life was suffering; birth, illness, death, all were suffering. Without doubt his family would have agreed. Christianity teaches that life is good and beautiful and that it is to be lived responsibly. Mahavira said, "The suffering of the world comes from desire," but Paul said that God has given us richly all things to enjoy!

RESURRECTION.   In Greek mythology, Adonis was killed by a boar while hunting. Aphrodite so grieved for him that she persuaded Zeus to allow Adonis to spend part of each year on earth. His death and annual resurrection represent winter and spring. Similar myths of a dying god can be found in Babylonia, Egypt, Mesopotamia, and Syria. The death of the god brought about the decay of natural life. His resurrection and return brought a revival of nature and of vegetation. How different is the biblical account of death and resurrection! How straightforward! It is written as history not myth. It is not tied to some explanation for the cycle of the seasons. It is not a part of intrigues among the gods and goddesses. It is a wholly different pattern, a wholly different story. It is a story that can be confidently believed.

RESURRECTION. It was John Donne who called death "one short sleep," echoing the description that both Jesus and Paul gave of death, for they both called it sleep. And in the same verse, Donne suddenly addresses, not the reader, but death itself and hurls this threat: "Death thou shalt die!" Many have called the Resurrection of Jesus "the day death died."

SALVATION. The February 16, 1989, issue of the *International Herald Tribune* reported a major festival that was then occurring in Allahabad, India. Between February 6 and March 6, thirty million people were expected to come and bathe in the chilly waters where the Ganges and Yamuna rivers come together. The most auspicious day was February 7 when the sun, the moon, and the planet Jupiter and the constellations Capricorn and Aries were in a special configuration. Hindus are convinced that a dip in the waters at this time will fulfill wishes, grant salvation, and cleanse away sin, although one participant admitted to some doubts. "You could say that a mixture of reasons is responsible for such a large assembly," he said. "It's a mixture of faith, curiosity, and the force of tradition." Upon reading about such an event, one seems to hear the echoes of an old gospel song: "What can wash away my sin? Nothing but the blood of Jesus!"

SATAN. Richard Bancroft, who was born in the sixteenth century and died in the seventeenth, once said, "Where Christ erecteth his Church, the devil in the same churchyard will have his chapel."

SECURITY. Maria Edgeworth wrote that "some people talk of morality and some of religion, but give me a little snug prop-

erty." But no amount of property will really give us security or peace of mind. The more property we have, the less peace of mind we have. The penniless man never worries about thieves! We all know about inflation. We all know that property values can change suddenly, dramatically, and not always in our favor. Possessions will never make you secure. Security is born of faith and trust.

SERVICE. The ancient city state of Budva had a charter of human rights written in 1371. It provided a place of refuge. If a fugitive serf got to Budva, he was allowed to live there and was required to serve no person and no state except to be loyal to Budva itself. We have freedom in Christ. We are now obliged to serve no one, except, of course, Christ himself.

SERVICE. In a humorous twist, Joseph Addison wrote in *The Spectator,* "We are always doing something for Posterity, but I would fain see Posterity do something for us." Posterity does do something for us. It gives us a sense of perspective. It tells us that our investments in serving God and others can outlast us. It tells us that we may cast a helpful shadow that is longer than our lives.

SIN. Don Marquis wrote an imaginary conversation between a rat and a moth in which the rat asks the moth why moths risk their lives flying into lights and flames. The moth replies that they "get bored with the routine and crave beauty and excitement . . . we know that if we get too close it will kill us but what does that matter. It is better to be happy for a moment and be burned up with beauty than to live a long time and be bored all the while." He adds that we "are like human beings used to be before they became too civilized to enjoy themselves." There *is* a distinct similarity between the moth's relationship to fire and our relationship to sin. We get bored. We crave excitement. We know that if we get too close it will destroy us, but we do it anyway. How foolish!

SIN.   Roger Ascham, who lived in the sixteenth century, wrote that Englishmen traveling in Italy remained "men in shape and fashion" but became "devils in life and condition." It is true that sin distorts the human personality and marks the image of the Maker.

SIN.   There is a serpent in Africa so poisonous that even after it has been killed it will continue to secrete poison from its fangs, sometimes for hours after its head has been cut off. We are not surprised that in the Bible the serpent should be the symbol of evil.

SIN.   Many ancient writers told of fruit growing along the Dead Sea that appeared very beautiful but had nothing but ashes inside. Called "apples of Sodom," they were probably gallnuts that had been stung by an insect. There is also a small tomatolike fruit that is called "apples of Sodom." The botanical reference is not important. The symbolic reference is vital. We often give ourselves to things that appear beautiful on the outside but that are filled with ashes on the inside. The apples of Sodom have destroyed many souls.

SIN AND RIGHTEOUSNESS.   Charles Dickens said of Mrs. Squeers that "she frequently remarked when she had made any such mistake, it would be all the same a hundred years hence." And it's often true of the things we worry about that it will make no difference a hundred years from now. On the other hand, there are deeds we do that *will* make a difference a hundred years from now or a thousand. There are deeds we do that will make a difference to all eternity. Our unforgiven sins will make a difference in eternity. Our deeds of righteousness will make a difference in eternity.

SINGING.   It is said that Edward Bok imported nightingales to his beloved gardens, which he gave to the public in Lake Wales, Florida. They couldn't adjust to the climate, and soon they all died. But still today one can hear the nightingale's song in those gardens. It's neither magic nor miracle. The mocking birds learned the nightingale's song before the nightingales died, and they now repeat it every day! In some sense, our poor worship on earth really echoes the purer and better worship of heaven.

SONGS.   Andrew Fletcher once wrote that he knew a very wise man who said that, "if a man were permitted to make all the ballads, he need not care who should make the laws of a nation." Have you listened to our contemporary popular music? If that man is right, we're in trouble.

SINCERITY.   T. S. Eliot said, "The last temptation is the greatest treason: To do the right deed for the wrong reason." God is not just concerned with what we do. He's also concerned with why we do it. The deeds of our lives are important to him. The motives of our hearts are even more important.

SINCERITY.   The great composer Beethoven often stayed in Baden, near Vienna, Austria. In one place he would jot down spontaneous musical ideas on the shutters at the window. Eventually, he left that house but came back to resume his residence in the same rented quarters. The landlord made him buy new shutters because he had ruined the old ones. The landlord didn't tell Beethoven that he had, in fact, sold those shutters to admirers of Beethoven! It's a good thing that Jesus wrote only in the sand! Otherwise, someone would have tried to profiteer from the things he wrote. Even so, Paul called some "peddlers of God's word" (2 Cor. 2:17). He contrasted them with those who sincerely believed and preached the Word of God.

SPEECHES.   In Alice's *Adventures in Wonderland,* Lewis Carroll wrote this bit of conversation: "Where shall I begin, please, your Majesty?" he asked. "Begin at the beginning," the king said gravely, "and go on till you come to the end; then stop." That's good advice for all public speakers.

SYMBOLS.   Everyone is familiar with the staff and serpent that have become the symbol of healing used today by the medical profession. Few will know that the symbol comes from the Greek god Asclepius (from whose name we get the word *hospital*). It was his symbol because he is alleged to have received a medicinal herb from a serpent's mouth. Snakes were dedicated to him and those who were healed sacrificed cocks to him. Of course, no physician today believes such nonsense . . . but the symbol remains, all that is left of a legend from long ago. Not all symbols are like that. Some symbols retain their original significance through the years and continue to have meaning. The cross is one example, and bread and wine. They still symbolize what they symbolized in the days of our Lord: his love, his sacrifice, our communion with him, our forgiveness by his grace.

TIME.   Dion Boucicault wrote, "Men talk of killing time, while time quietly kills them." But time will never kill the believer. "Death hath no more dominion." "Death is swallowed up in victory." "He that liveth and believeth in me shall never die." Time may threaten all human beings, but time is powerless before the eternal Christ who shares his immortality with all his followers.

TIME.   An anonymous French writer left us this little gem that translates to "Everything passes, everything perishes, everything palls." But it's not completely true. Everything passes, but not everything perishes. And while in time most things pall, some things always retain their interest and value, such as love and faith, goodness and grace.

TIME.   In North America, a clock is a common enough gift, and a watch an even more common one. But in the People's Republic of China, one must never give another a clock. It's a symbol of bad luck. Of course, there is no such thing as an object that can bring bad luck or good luck. But the clock is a powerful symbol in any culture; a symbol of the passing of

time; a symbol of the certainty of death. Remember the grandfather clock in the song that "stopped short, never to run again, when the old man died." For us it may stand as a symbol of passing opportunities that may be seized or ignored but that will never come again.

TIME.   When a new pope is consecrated, flax is burned to symbolize the transient nature of earthly glory, and while the flax burns these words are spoken: *Sic transit gloria mundi* (Thus passes the glory of the world). We all do well to remember that, whether we are powerful or powerless, famous or unknown. The glory of the world fades. When Peter wrote his first letter, he quoted the prophet Isaiah. "All men are like grass, and all their glory is like the flowers of the field; the grass withers, and the flowers fall, but the word of the Lord stands forever."

TRUTH.   Alcuin wrote to Charlemagne, "And those people should not be listened to who keep saying the voice of the people is the voice of God." We long to see the day when the opposite is true; when people echo what God has said so that the voice of God is heard in the voices of the people.

TRUTH.   Aristotle was the devoted student of Plato. He once said, "Plato is dear to me, but dearer still is truth." We must all prize truth above all other things. No person must be dearer to us than the truth. No goal must be greater than to know the truth and no objective greater than to tell the truth.

TRUTH.   Some anonymous writer combined Prov. 12:22 and Ps. 46:1 to come up with this statement: "A lie is an abomination unto the Lord, but a very present help in time of trouble." Many people actually do believe both. They would not lie in ordinary circumstances, but in "time of trouble" they do not hesitate to do it. Lies, however, only get us into more and more trouble. We must take Jesus as our model. "He did not sin, neither was guile found in his mouth."

UNITY.   It is a sad commentary on Christian unity that the Church of the Holy Sepulchre in Jerusalem must be shared by Catholic, Orthodox, Armenian, and that the key, therefore, must be kept by a Muslim. But there is a positive side to it all. You would see it if you were there on Good Friday. You could hear the chant, "We adore Thee, O Christ. Thou hast redeemed the *world.*" You would hear it in Latin chanted by Franciscan monks as they walked through the Arab markets, stopping at each station of the cross; at the Polish chapel that marks the spot where the Lord staggered; at the Armenian church that marks the spot where he encountered his mother; at the Greek chapel that honors Veronica, who is said to have wiped his forehead; at the Coptic church where where he fell again. The worldwide significance of Christianity is vividly dramatized in that short walk.

UNITY.   Charles de Gaulle once said, "The French can only be united under the threat of danger. Nobody can simply bring together a country that has 265 kinds of cheese." We have a similar difficulty in bringing the divided church together, but we need to try, for we face very real dangers.

VICTORY.   When victorious Roman generals came home to Rome, there was always a great procession of triumph. In front were the members of the Roman senate. Then came wagons loaded with the spoils of war. Behind the wagons were led the defeated generals and other captives. Then came the victor himself, in a chariot drawn by four horses, and behind him the soldiers that had won the victory. They marched up the Via Sacra, the holy way, to the temple of Jupiter, where worship was offered. That is the background for Paul's intriguing text in 2 Cor. 2:14:

"God . . . always leads us in triumphant procession in Christ."

VICTORY.   Several Muslim princes bore the surname Al-Mansur, which means "victorious." Some actually *were* victorious, some were not. While we don't wear the name, every Christian *could* add to his or her name *victorious.* In a sense, it's our family name. God has given us the victory through our Lord Jesus Christ.

WAR AND PEACE.   The railings around the Vlaska church in Cetinje, Yugoslavia, were made from the barrels of Turkish muskets, taken in battle, and the gun sights can still be seen. They used two thousand of them to make the railings around the church. It was a unique way to beat swords into plowshares.

WORDS.   The mountainous region of Montenegro never fell to the Turks, though the rest of eastern Europe did. But they had many clashes with the Turks. During one siege, they were so short of ammunition that they melted down the metal type of the Cetinje printing press to make bullets . . . adding a new meaning to "the power of the press."

WORSHIP.   Worship is a subject coming into the audience room of the king. One must come quietly and submissively. Worship is a priest coming into the holiest place of all. One must come reverently and humbly. Worship is a child coming home to the Father. One may come joyfully and with a sense of intimacy. There are contradictory elements here: the intimate and the ultimate. Sometimes we seem to take only the priest in the temple as our model with solemnity and detachment. Ideally, our worship provides a mix of both.

ACKNOWLEDGMENTS

Acknowledgment and gratitude are hereby expressed to the following for kind permission to reprint material from the books and periodicals listed below:

HARPER & ROW PUBLISHERS, INC.: Excerpts from Arnold J. Lowe, *Power for Life's Living,* Harper & Bros., © 1954, pp. 124–29; Excerpts from Robert J. McCracken, *Putting Faith to Work,* Harper & Bros., © 1960, pp. 26–33; Excerpts from Harry Emerson Fosdick, *A Book of Public Prayers,* Harper & Bros., © 1959, pp. 22–23, 36–37, 50–51, 52–53, 58–59, 78, 92–93, 106–7, 118; Excerpts from Robert E. Luccock, *If God Be For Us,* Harper & Bros., © 1954, pp. 53–63; Excerpts from George M. Docherty, *One Way of Living,* Harper & Bros., © 1958, pp. 88–101; Excerpts from Karl Barth, *Deliverance to the Captives,* Harper & Bros., © 1961, pp. 36–41; Nels F. S. Ferre, *God's New Age,* Harper & Bros., © 1956, 1958, 1960, 1962, pp. 31–41; Excerpts from Halford Luccock, *Marching Off the Map,* Harper & Bros., © 1952, pp. 144–57; Excerpts from Helmut Thielicke, *Christ and the Meaning of Life,* Harper & Bros., © 1962, pp. 56–58; Excerpts from Charles R. Brown, *Being Made Over,* Harper & Bros., © 1939, pp. 125–37; Excerpts from Edgar DeWitt Jones, *Sermons I Love to Preach,* Harper & Bros., © 1953, pp. 92–104; Excerpts from William Sloane Coffin, *The Courage to Love,* Harper & Row, © 1982, 1984, pp. 23–29; Excerpts from David H. C. Read, *Unfinished Easter,* Harper & Row, © 1978, pp. 52–58; Excerpts from Frederick W. Robertson, *Sermons,* Harper & Bros., © pp. 487–95; Excerpts from Harry Emerson Fosdick, *What is Vital in Religion,* Harper & Bros., © 1955, pp. 118–21; Excerpts from Gerald Kennedy, *Fresh Every Morning,* Harper & Row, © 1966, pp. 41–50; Excerpts from Clovis G. Chappell, *Sermons on Old and New Testament Characters,* Harper & Bros., © 1925, pp. 29–38; Excerpts from Harold A. Bosley, *He Spoke to Them in Parables,* Harper & Row, © 1963, pp. 174–82; Excerpts from Paul Scherer, *The Word God Sent,* Harper & Row, © 1965, pp. 153–59; Excerpts from Agnes Sanford, *Let's Believe,* Harper & Bros., © 1954, pp. 105–11.

SUNDAY SCHOOL BOARD OF THE SOUTHERN BAPTIST CONVENTION: Excerpts from: Jerry W. Mixon, *Along the Way Home,* (Nashville: Broadman Press, 1989), pp. 115, 117. © Copyright 1989 by Broadman Press. Excerpt from Eli Landrum, Jr., *More Than Symbol,* (Nashville: Broadman Press, 1983), pp. 55–57. © Copyright 1983 by Broadman Press. Excerpt from Joseph H. Coleman, Jr., *Hearing the Same Message,* (Nashville: Broadman Press, 1990), pp. 114–115. © Copyright 1990 by Broadman Press. Excerpt from Stephen S. Ivy, *The Promise and Pain of Loneliness,* (Nashville: Broadman Press, 1989), pp. 99–105. © Copyright 1989 by Broadman Press. Excerpt from Reggie R. Ogea, "Our Moral Obligation," from *Proclaim,* October–December 1989, pp. 49–50. © Copyright 1989 by The Sunday School Board of the Southern Baptist Convention. Excerpt from Calvin Kelly, "The News of Easter," from *Proclaim,* April 1982, pp. 20–30. © Copyright 1982 by The Sunday School Board of the Southern Baptist Convention. Excerpt from Hugh Litchfield, *Preaching the Christmas Story,* (Nashville: Broadman Press, 1984), pp. 99–104. © Copyright 1984 by Broadman Press. Excerpt from P. Randall Wright, "You Also Must Be Ready," from *Proclaim,* October–December 1988, pp. 6–8. © Copyright 1988 by The Sunday School Board of the Southern Baptist Convention. Excerpt from Fred M. Wood, "Life in a Look," from *Award Winning Sermons,* vol. 4, ed. by James C. Barry, (Nashville: Broadman Press, 1980), pp. 98–105. © Copyright 1980. Excerpt from Jack J. Wingate, "How to Survive Temptation," from *Proclaim*, April–June 1989, pp. 28–29. © Copyright 1989 by The Sunday School Board of the Southern Baptist Convention. Excerpt from Scott Tatum, "The Wisdom of Faith in God," from *Proclaim*, July–September 1989, pp. 7–8. © Copyright 1989 by The Sunday School Board of the Southern Baptist Convention. Excerpt from Larry Payne, "Our Lives, His Witness," from *Award Winning Sermons*, vol. 2, ed. by James C. Barry (Nashville: Broadman Press, 1978), pp. 137–42. Excerpt from a devotional by W. Clyde Tilley from *Open Windows*, July–September, 1989, for August 30. © Copyright 1989 by The Sunday School Board of the Southern Baptist Convention. Excerpt from Raymond Bryan Brown, *The Fire of Truth*, (Nashville: Broadman Press, 1982), pp. 69–72. Excerpt from Daniel C. Whitaker, "The Energy of Love," from *Award Winning Sermons*, vol. 1, ed. by James C. Barry (Nashville: Broadman Press, 1977), pp. 83–88. Excerpt from Leon W. Castle, *52 Children's Sermons*, (Nashville: Broadman Press, 1988), pp. 92–93. Excerpt from C. W. Bess, *Children's Sermons for Special Times*, (Nashville: Broadman Press, 1988), pp. 40–41. Excerpt from Roy E. DeBrand, *Children's Sermons for Special Occasions*, (Nashville: Broadman Press, 1983), pp. 27–28. For each of the above publications: All rights reserved. Used by permission.

WORD, INC.: Excerpts from sermon by Eduard Schweizer from *God's Inescapable Nearness*, ed. and trans. by James W. Cox, © 1971; used by permission of Word, Inc., Waco, TX, pp. 111–17.

INDEX OF CONTRIBUTORS

SERMON TITLE INDEX

(Children's stories and sermons are identified as **cs***; sermon suggestions as* **ss***)*

SCRIPTURAL INDEX

INDEX OF PRAYERS

INDEX OF MATERIALS USEFUL AS CHILDREN'S STORIES AND SERMONS NOT INCLUDED IN SECTION X

INDEX OF MATERIALS USEFUL FOR SMALL GROUPS

TOPICAL INDEX